CORRECTIONAL
INSTITUTIONS

WITHDRAWN

WITHDRAWN

CORRECTIONAL INSTITUTIONS

SECOND EDITION

EDITED BY

ROBERT M. CARTER
UNIVERSITY OF SOUTHERN CALIFORNIA

DANIEL GLASER
UNIVERSITY OF SOUTHERN CALIFORNIA

LESLIE T. WILKINS
STATE UNIVERSITY OF NEW YORK, ALBANY

J. B. LIPPINCOTT COMPANY
PHILADELPHIA
NEW YORK / SAN JOSE / TORONTO

Second Edition

Copyright 1977, 1972 by J. B. Lippincott Company

ISBN 0-397-47356-7

Library of Congress Catalog Card Number 76-44347

Printed in the United States of America

35798642

Library of Congress Cataloging in Publication Data

Carter, Robert Melvin, 1929-   comp.
  Correctional institutions.

  Bibliography; p.
  Includes index.
  1. Correctional institutions—United States—Addresses, essays, lectures. 2. Corrections—United States—Addresses, essays, lectures. I. Glaser, Daniel. II. Wilkins, Leslie T. III. Title.
HV9471.C29 1977   365'.973   76-44347
ISBN 0-397-47356-7

CONTENTS

V

SECTION II
THE CORRECTIONAL INSTITUTION AS A COMMUNITY

SECTION III
SPECIFIC PROGRAMS IN CORRECTIONAL INSTITUTIONS

SECTION IV
FUSION OF INSTITUTIONAL AND COMMUNITY PROGRAMS

INTRODUCTION

FOREWORD

This second edition of readings on correctional and penal institutions answers admirably the present need of the campus community for a general, all-purpose text, and that of the correctional practitioner and administrator for an up-to-date review of the literature of the field. For the nonprofessional, interested citizen the anthology provides a general portrait of these institutions, seen in both theoretical and practical perspectives.

The complexity of correctional institutions, in terms of their closely interwoven historical, traditional, operational, and legal aspects, is illuminated by this broad range of readings. The contributors of these theoretical, empirical, and descriptive articles are administrators, practitioners, scholars, and researchers from within and from outside the field of corrections. Such a cross section assures a varied array of views—some conflicting—of institutions as seen by some of the people who have made major contributions to the theory and practice of corrections.

The editors themselves represent different disciplines—criminology, sociology and methodology—and have had intense and diverse experiences in corrections in the areas of administration, practice and research. Their incisive judgment and informed perception are clearly revealed in the selections made.

Not only does this edition present an historical review of correctional and penal institutions and examine the current state of achievement, but it serves a particular need in pointing to the requirements of the future. A sense of urgent concern for meeting needs as yet only dimly foreshadowed is clearly communicated by this volume. The accomplishments of yesterday and of today are valued for what they teach about tomorrow. The increasingly complex challenge of crime to those responsible for corrections demands insight and knowledge derived from both past and present so that the future may be more intelligently faced.

E. K. Nelson, *Professor*
School of Public Administration
University of Southern California
Los Angeles

PREFACE

The ways in which organized society has dealt with criminal offenders constitute a long and painful chapter in the history of man. In primitive societies, each individual dealt with wrongs done him or his family in his own way. The victim was motivated chiefly by ideas of revenge, retaliation, or compensation for loss of property.

Even as modern societies developed, the basic concept behind the intervention of government continued to be that of retribution—a balancing of the scales of justice.

In the beginning, the scales tended to be balanced on the side of the superior power of the state. The death penalty was the most common response to ordinary crime. It is recorded that in London, in January 1801, a seventeen-year-old boy was hanged for stealing a silver spoon. With a relatively small population there were eight hundred executions in a year in England alone toward the end of the sixteenth century. Then, even more than now, the recipients of these harsh punishments were mainly the poor and the underprivileged.

The Quakers provided the keystone around which modern penal reform developed in America, while concurrent reforms were taking place in England and on the Continent. Becarria[1] published his great Essay on *Crime and Punishments* in 1764. John Howard, High Sheriff of Bedfordshire, the famous English philanthropist and prison reformer, was a central figure in the movement.

Following the uprising of the common people and the advent of modern democracy in France and in America, the Quakers developed strong allies in their drive for the humane treatment of offenders and for the substitution of imprisonment for corporal and capital punishment.

These penal reforms were logical corollaries to the concepts set forth in the Declaration of Independence, to the effect that all men are created equal and are endowed with certain inalienable rights and that these include life, liberty, and the pursuit of happiness. These concepts came into even sharper focus with the adoption of the Bill of Rights, contained in the first ten Amendments to the American Constitution.

The translation of the rights expressed in the Constitution into statutes and practices has been a slow and tortuous process. It is, perhaps, relevant to point out that from their adoption in 1791 until 1865, our country still tolerated slavery, and that it has taken a long succession of controversial Supreme Court decisions, continuing up to this very day, to implement forcefully the concepts set forth so clearly and so simply nearly 200 years ago.

The slowness with which we have moved is related to many factors, some economic, some philosophical, some political and administrative.

Fundamental Dichotomies in Basic Principles

The idea of retributive punishment is deeply rooted in the minds and emotions of man. This attitude—this simple atavistic impulse to punish and to overpunish offenders—remains the central trunk of the administration of criminal justice throughout the world. Welded onto this central trunk, sometimes very insecurely, are ideas of human compassion, of deterrence of potential wrongdoers , of the rehabilitation of offenders who must be reabsorbed into society after imprisonment, and of the broader concept of the need for protection of the public from personal, economic, or social injury.

That all of these concepts are not completely compatible should be clear to any thoughtful person. To overpunish makes rehabilitation more difficult and at times impossible. To underpunish, or not to punish at all, belies the purposes of deterrence and fails, at least partially, in the broad objective of public protection.

While the social sciences have made long strides in understanding social phenomena, there is still no central, widely accepted, and scientifically supported theory of crime-causation.

The practice of retributive punishment is rooted in the belief that each man possesses a free will and by his own decisions and actions determines his course. At the other end of the continuum, there is the idea that man's behavior is mainly the result of his environment and inheritance, as well as of the social and economic opportunities which are available to him in a complex society. We therefore continue to administer criminal justice on a basis of fundamental concepts which are confusing and often incompatible, particularly when applied to the factual circumstances of individual cases.

Administrative Fragmentation

Another basic problem which criminal justice systems have faced from the beginning and continue to face, especially in America, is the fragmentation of the administrative entities which comprise the justice systems. First, we have the constitutional separation of powers into the judicial, legislative, and executive. Legislators are particularly prone to try to solve the crime problem by passing punitive laws, but, conversely, they fail to appropriate adequate funds to implement the administration of the criminal law, whether it be excessively punitive or not.

The police, because of their particular position in the game of maintaining peace and order, have difficulty in understanding the roots of delinquent and criminal behavior, and tend to respond more vigorously than any other segment of the system with demands for strong, punitive methods.

The courts, being in the province of the legal profession, are generally not only skilled but dedicated to assuring fair and equitable procedures in the process of determining guilt or innocence. On the other hand, when guilt has been established, the decision concerning what disposition should be made of each individual case—in terms of public protection, deterrence, retributive punishment, or rehabilitation—leaves most judges in a deep quandary. They face each case at the point of sentence with varying combinations of compassion, anger, puzzlement, personal bias, and political anxiety, but almost never with the armamentarium of scientific knowledge that would help them to decide what disposition might best serve the total society within the limits of the law and public tolerance.

It is small wonder that the disposition and management of public offenders remains the most controversial phase of the administration of justice.

Intergovernmental Difficulties and Economic Problems

The American faith in local government has also contributed to vast difficulties in the administration of justice. The development of state prisons and correctional institutions for both adults and juveniles came about gradually because local jails and workhouses found it difficult to handle small numbers of the more serious offenders, classified as felons and serving relatively long sentences.

An important economic factor is also present in the shifting of this part of the penal and criminal load to the states because the long-term confinement of offenders in secure institutions is relatively expensive even if very little rehabilitative and retraining effort is made. Shifts in our economy have affected the taxing capacity of local government in a negative way. This makes it necessary that some of the tax revenues collected by the federal government and by the states be redistributed to local government or that some of the services normally rendered by local government be transferred upward to the state or federal level.

In the handling of offenders, lack of revenue has on occasion tempted local governments to commit cases to state or federal institutions where the law permits, not because this is necessarily the best solution to either society's or the offender's problems, but rather because the cost of the care and management of the case is shifted from one unit of government to another.

Measures have been taken at both federal and state levels of government to insure equitable treatment of public school pupils, welfare recipients, and the like, but no similar efforts of any consequence are in effect in this country with respect to the management, control, and corrective treatment of public offenders.

This phenomenon is most visible in the disparities in institutional facilities, but it also affects the administration of the so-called community-based programs. Local jails and probation services vary widely in effectiveness, leadership, and financial support from one community to another.

SHIFTS IN CORRECTIONAL STRATEGIES

The acceptance of the use of imprisonment as the keystone in the treatment of public offenders was, as we have noted, an important change made more than a century and a half ago. It soon became apparent, however, that imprisonment alone did little to insure long-range public protection because less than five percent, even of those sent to state and federal institutions for the most serious crimes, die in prison, and an even smaller percentage of those committed for shorter periods of time to jails and juvenile institutions are not eventually released. Thus we found ourselves paying substantial sums of money to maintain residential establishments—an expenditure often out of proportion to the short periods of incapacitation actually served.

The logic of the situation leads inevitably to the conclusion that there should be alternatives to incarceration wherever the public welfare can be equally well served. To those accustomed to the need to *punish* and *deter*, rather than to *control, treat,* and *rehabilitate,* the alternatives to imprisonment seem not only mild and lenient but emotionally unsatisfying both to victims and average citizens. Furthermore, the limited number of empirical studies of the relative effectiveness of available alternatives, such as fines, weekend sentences, probation supervision, and halfway houses, have not been dramatically convincing one way or the other.

The factor differentiating imprisonment and contemporary alternatives which is most apparent and easily demonstrated is that of financial cost. In terms of dollars expended per case the ratio runs at about $10 for incarceration to $1.00 for probation or other "community-based programs." If the current trend toward reducing the proportion of persons convicted to those imprisoned is to continue, we must begin to spend more of the 90 percent saving on improving the quality and effectiveness of the nonprison alternatives.

Probation

The essential weakness of probation, as with many other aspects of the correctional process, is the lack of adequate numbers of qualified probation officers to supervise the caseload of the jurisdiction. Caseloads of individual officers may vary from one jurisdication to another from as few as twenty-five to as many as three hundred. It is generally agreed by students in this field that adequate service for those who require supervision demands average caseloads of not more than thirty-five or forty per probation officer.

Probation officers are essentially caseworkers and belong to the people-helping services. They also have peace officer functions and therefore often find themselves faced with philosophical conflicts. However, as the use of probation has grown, in the last quarter-century in particular, it is gradually being recognized that the role of the probation officer is a specialized one, requiring specific training and skills, different in many respects from those required of the social agency caseworker and the public welfare worker.

It should be noted also that each caseload is made up of a diversity of offenders with widely disparate needs calling for new and highly sophisticated treatment approaches. Most overburdened probation personnel in the system today are ill-equipped either by training or opportunity to deal differentially with the kind of clientele they must serve.

Prisons

The conditions most characteristic of American prisons between World Wars I and II were enforced idleness, inadequate and untrained personnel, and gross overcrowding; they indeed constituted an almost complete negation of the high-sounding principles enunciated at the first convention of prison executives at Cincinnati in 1870.

The failure of the prisons to rehabilitate, and the maintenance of conditions of idleness, overcrowding, and lack of programs generally made many of them crucibles of crime and degradation rather than instruments of reformation and resocialization. It should come as no surprise, then, that the courts are rebelling against sending offenders to these institutions unless they feel it to be absolutely necessary as a measure of public protection. This movement away from imprisonment unfortunately has not been matched by well supported and effective alternatives.

The Indeterminate Sentence and Parole

During the last fifty years the earlier ideas of the indeterminate sentence began to come into wider use. The concept of the indeterminate sentence was advanced for two widely different reasons: first, because individual judges had such dissimilar ideas about the appropriate length of a sentence, there was great need for a system of sentencing which could insure some degree of consistency. Disparity in sentencing is still a major problem in most jurisdictions. The second justification for the indeterminate sentence was that, if rehabilitation and retraining were, in fact, to be supported by the law, the people who administer the system, rather than the courts, should determine, within some broad limits, the appropriate time to release an offender from an institution, dependent upon his readiness to assume a law-abiding role in free society. The first idea, it can be seen, is based upon the concept of equal justice, and the second, upon the unequal needs of individual offenders for training and treatment.

In a few states, wide discretion has been delegated to parole boards or parole authorities to fix the time limits of sentences for adult felons within statutory limits set by law for each offense and to grant release on parole (conditional release under supervision) within the terms so fixed. However, the second concept behind the indeterminate sentence has been relegated to a minor consideration in most of the states because the parole boards have been kept organizationally independent of the administrative and treatment personnel of the correctional establishment.

The practical consequence of this arrangement almost invariably has been that these independent lay parole boards have proven to be so vulnerable to unreasoned attacks, and to the resultant concern for the protection of the political figure who appoints and reappoints them, that they tend to err on the side of extreme conservatism, at tremendous public cost, without demonstrable evidence that their actions really support the totality of the public interest.

The statutes of every state are different, but where they provide for discretionary release "on parole", there are usually minimum terms provided for in the law. It is rare that any substantial number of offenders are released at the expiration of the minimum term. On balance, the net result of the adoption of greater indeterminancy in the sentencing and parole statutes in a state has been longer rather than shorter time served before release.

The popular notion which equates parole with leniency is 180 degrees wrong. Here we encounter the common phenomenon of public opinion being formed on the basis of a few well publicized "bad" cases without regard for the total parole picture.

The decade of the seventies has seen a revival of interest in the problems of sentencing. U.S. District Court Judge Marvin E. Frankel has explored the subject in his book *Criminal Sentences: Law Without Order*. There seems to be widespread agreement that the various forms of the indeterminate sentence are not working well. The debate relates chiefly to the many proposed alternatives. A consensus appears to be evolving around the following concepts:

(a) The law should provide a normative or presumptive sentence for each offense, permitting limited discretion to increase or decrease the sentence when factors in aggravation or mitigation of the crime can be demonstrated.

(b) There should be some oversight of trial court practice by a higher court by such methods as issuance of guidelines, sentence review through an appellate process, and maintenance of a statewide information system on sentencing practices.

(c) The role of the executive branch should be limited chiefly to the administration of good conduct credits and executive clemency.

(d) If parole boards are to be retained, it is argued by some that they should be restricted to advising the governor on pardon and executive clemency. And if discretionary parole is to be retained at all, it should be limited to cases of offenders serving very long terms and to other case decisions involving parole violations.

POSTWAR INNOVATIONS IN CORRECTIONAL THEORY AND PRACTICE

Correctional institutions and programs received little nourishment during the Depression years of the 1930s and little public attention during World War II. But the ten years following the war saw the effects of fifteen years of neglect. Prison riots, parole scandals, and evidences of correctional maladministration became so common throughout the land that the public and responsible political leaders, for the first time in many years, began giving the correctional problem new attention.

Demands for the abandonment of the conventional prison for all except the few dangerous and irredeemable offenders have become commonplace.

A reappraisal of the decision-making process, both in the courts and in the parole boards, has been urged.

Responses to dissatisfactions with old programs have resulted not only in demands for improvements in them, but also in active attention to new alternatives. Innovation is the magic word in applications for experimental and demonstration funds.

The Ford Foundation, through the American Justice Institute, funded a survey of modern correctional practice in the Western world in 1959.[2]

The Congress in 1964 recognized the deplorable state of the correctional field by appropriating over two million dollars to conduct a three-year study of correctional manpower and training.[3]

President Johnson established a Commission on Law Enforcement and Administration of Justice (National Crime Commission) on July 23, 1963. Twenty of the Commission's recommendations published in 1967 deal directly with correctional matters.[4]

In 1968 the Congress passed the so-called Safe Streets Act which established the Law Enforcement Assistance Administration in the U.S. Department of Justice. Besides providing many millions of dollars in aid to the States and local governments it has issued a series of volumes on "Standards and Goals" including one on all aspects of corrections.

The basic thrust behind these and numerous other studies in the last decade lies in a deep dissatisfaction with the organization, the methods, and the results of correctional effort in all of its dimensions.

Upon the recommendation of Chief Justice Warren Burger, the American Bar Association in 1970 formed a high level *Commission on Correctional Facilities and Services,* intended to focus the attention of the country upon the needs for reform in our correctional systems.

A new revolution in correctional theory and practice is in the making now, at the beginning of the second century after the first statement of correctional principles in 1870.[5]

THE FUTURE OF CORRECTIONS

Predictions of things to come are, of necessity, a combination of hardheaded logic and hopeful expectation. Those which follow are no exception.

(1) Fewer offenders, and especially the younger ones, will be confined for long periods in custodial institutions. The emphasis on incarceration versus community supervision will continue to fluctuate on a cyclical pattern but the long-term trend will continue in favor of less institutional confinement.

(2) The programs of these institutions will place greater emphasis on preparation for release and reintegration into normal society and less on the prevention of escapes and on economic production, unless it contributes to occupational competence.

(3) The new correctional institutions for both youths and adults will be much smaller, perhaps with less than a hundred residents each, and will be located in cities, not on farms as has been our tradition.

(4) There will be less and less of the sharp dichotomy between incarceration and parole- or probation-supervision. Offenders will move in and out among varying degrees of restraint. Work and training furloughs, weekend sentences, halfway houses, and similar community-based programs will become more common and more varied.

(5) Probation services will expand, but they will be better supported and will include a much wider variety of programs: hostels, group homes, training programs, job placements, sheltered workshops, psychiatric services, and special counseling.

(6) Post-institutional supervision (parole) will also exhibit changes in variety and character similar to those in the community programs for probationers.

(7) The character, composition, and function of parole boards will change. These boards, made up largely of lay persons appointed by state governors, are seldom well qualified for their decision-making tasks, and, to compound the problem, they are peculiarly vulnerable to the most reactionary influences in the society.

(8) New forms of sentencing and of the term-fixing function will be developed.

(9) Community-based programs must make more and more use of related community resources, both public and private. To do this, the organization and management of the correctional services must be consolidated and coordinated in each community. It is now the rule rather than the exception in major cities, in an area say, ten miles square, to find from five to ten separate governmental agencies

(federal, state, county and city), supervising several thousand probationers and parolees of all ages and both sexes. There is no valid excuse for the cost, confusion, and inefficiency of this arrangement.

(10) More and more attention will be given to the development of information systems making use of modern computer technology so that decision-makers throughout the justice system can operate on a basis of facts instead of opinion and guesswork.

(11) Empirical research methods will be employed more and more as the means of defining and refining the problems of crime and delinquency and of evaluating and testing the effectiveness of programs.

(12) From the standpoint of the offender who would seek to escape the consequences of his behavior, the "New Corrections" will be far more difficult to evade than is the case under our present system; conversely, for those who need help, professionally competent assistance will be provided. And the long-term needs for public protection will be better served.

RICHARD A. MCGEE, *President*
American Justice Institute
Sacramento

1. Cesare Bonesana; Marchese di Beccaria, Italian jurist and reformer, 1738-1794.
2. John Conrad, *Crime and Its Correction: An International Survey of Attitudes and Practices* (Berkeley & Los Angeles: University of California Press, 1965).
3. The Joint Commission on Correctional Manpower and Training, which completed its studies under this grant in the Spring of 1969.
4. U.S. President's Commission on Law Enforcement and Administration of Justice, National Crime Commission, *The Challenge of Crime in a Free Society* (the General Report) (Washington, D.C.: U.S. Government Printing Office, 1967), Chap. VI.
5. "Declaration of Principles of 1870," as Revised and Reaffirmed at the Sixtieth Annual Congress of the American Prison Association, held at Louisville, Kentucky, October 10-16, 1930.

I

HISTORY AND CURRENT STATUS

INTRODUCTION

To understand correctional institutions today one must know their history. In "The Human Cage," Norman Johnston, a specialist in this subject, traces the fascinating architectural evolution of prisons in many parts of the world, from dungeons in the sewers of ancient Rome to fortresses in modern cities. Occasionally more imaginative construction has eased the pressures of involuntary group confinement. One notable change is abandonment of the notion that "bigger is better." Innovations usually begin in facilities for juveniles or women, then gradually spread to prisons for adult males. As Johnston implies, however, it takes more than a physical edifice to make corrections effective in attaining any of its several goals.

The history of correctional programs, as well as of architecture, is elaborated further in "Major Institutions," from the National Advisory Commission on Criminal Justice Standards and Goals. This study relates trends in American prison development to the social and cultural aspects of the environment. Its statistics and illustrations also highlight the inertia in correctional institutions, that is, the tendency for their least adequate facilities and programs to survive long after their deficiencies are evident.

The third chapter summarizes findings from the nation's first systematic census of state correctional facilities, in 1974. About 600 separate establishments housing nearly 200,000 people were found to vary immensely in size, staff, inmates, programs, services and other features.

Criminologists Waller and Chan present a unique comparison of the extent to which governments of several other countries use prisons. This immediately raises questions about what is to be called "prison" and even who is to be called "prisoner." The dilemmas of definition, when comparing countries, include distinctions between "sentenced" and "unsentenced," between "adults" and "juveniles," and between "correctional" and "mental" institutions. No matter how these dilemmas are resolved, great diversity among nations is evident in rates of imprisonment, with the United States midway between the extremes. Much variation is also demonstrated among the states and provinces within the United States, Canada and Australia.

Prospects of change in prison use are examined by social work professor John Flanagan. He forecasts a "crisis in prison population," starting in the late 1970s, because the birth rate in the United States peaked around 1950, the median age of prisoners is around 30, and there seem to be limits to the use of probation or parole. Changes in these limits, as well as the growing decriminalization of some so-called victimless offenses such as drug use, public drunkenness, prostitution and voluntary private homosexual acts among adults, could alleviate this crisis, especially in jails.

Although incarceration in jail is the main form of involuntary confinement experienced in the United States, the jails have generally been neglected by governments and by researchers. The deficiencies of these places, as well as approaches to their improvement or replacement, are outlined in "Local Adult Institutions," by the National Advisory Commission on Criminal Justice Standards and Goals.

Further information on jails is provided by extracts from the Survey of Inmates of Local Jails conducted by the U.S. Bureau of the Census during 1972. This report reveals much regional variation in the use of jails, and in their staffing, services and architectural design.

Concluding this overview of the history and current status of correctional institutions is the chapter on "Organization and Administration" from the National Advisory Commission on Criminal Justice Standards and Goals. Responsibility for correctional operations in the United States is shown to be highly fragmented, resulting in serious deficiencies of coordination, fiscal resources and flexibility. Directions for change, including new methods of management and planning, are indicated in detail.

1

THE HUMAN CAGE

NORMAN JOHNSTON

EARLY PRISONS

If we think of a prison as a place where persons are kept involuntarily by some constituted authority, and realize that occasions when this would be temporarily if not routinely expedient must have existed all through history, then it is understandable that we cannot date meaningfully or accurately the earliest use of prisons.[1]

It is sometimes assumed that prisons in early times were exclusively for detention prior to trial rather than for punishment or improvement of the criminal. This seems to be an oversimplification. Apparently imprisonment was usually a prelude to execution, banishment or other various forms of punishment. But it was also used in lieu of these penalties for some political prisoners of high rank, and it was used to coerce payments of debts owed the government or individuals. It seems also to have been used as punishment for some minor offenses as early as the 14th century.[2] There is also considerable evidence that forced labor on public works, which would have required detention of workers, has a long history at least dating back to Roman times.[3]

Early places of confinement were crude structures, seldom built for the use to which they were finally put. They were likely to be strong cages within a fortress or castle enclosure or subterranean portions of public buildings. Although both classical Greece and Rome are reported to have used stone quarries as prisons, and a number of large public prisons existed in Rome for different kinds of offenders,[4] the only place of confinement about which much is known is the Mamertine Prison. Begun about 640 B.C. by Ancus Martius, and later

Source: From *The Human Cage: A Brief History of Prison Architecture* (New York: Walker and Company, Inc., 1973), pp. 5–54 (editorial adaptations). Copyright 1973 by the American Foundation, Inc. Reprinted by permission of the author and publisher.

enlarged, it appears to have been a "vast system of dungeons" constructed, for the most part, under the *Cloaca Maxima,* the main sewer of Rome.[5] The construction existing in the late 19th century consisted of two chambers, one below the other. The upper room measured 30 x 22 feet and received light from a hole in the ceiling 16 feet above the floor. The lower chamber, which was reached by means of an aperture in the floor of the room above, was cone shaped with a diameter of 20 feet and was completely dark.

With the coming of gunpowder, the military and strategic value of the fortified dwelling began to decline and eventually castles were often used only as dwelling places or as local jails. Such structures with thick, solid walls and partitions, largely windowless for previous defensive purposes and always located in the center of the town, were well suited as stopgap prisons as long as the numbers of inmates continued to be small and their stay relatively brief.

RELIGIOUS IMPRISONMENT

In searching for the antecedents of both the philosophy of imprisonment as well as the architecture which came to be associated with it, it is necessary to consider briefly the use of imprisonment by the Christian church, especially during the late medieval period. The concept of imprisonment as a substitute for death or mutilation of the body was derived in part from a custom of the early church of granting asylum or sanctuary to fugitives and criminals. Begun largely during the reign of Constantine, this ancient right existed earlier among Assyrians, Hebrews and others. The church at that time had under its aegis a large number of clergy, clerks, functionaries, monks and serfs, and, except the latter, most of these fell under the jurisdiction of the church courts. Traditionally forbidden to shed blood and drawing on the Christian theme of purification through suffering, these canon courts came to subject the wrongdoer to reclusion and even solitary cellular confinement, not as punishment alone, but as a way of providing conditions under which penitence would most likely occur.

Confinement in one's own monastic room, cubicle or little house was mildest of the possible punishments available to the abbot, though little evidence exists as to how extensively it was used. Some of the monastic quarters provided totally separate facilities for each monk,[6] so that it was a simple matter to lock up an errant brother for brief periods.

As "mother houses" of monastic orders had satellite houses often located in less desirable places, it was also the practice to transfer monks for varying periods of time to such locations. There is some evidence that some of these satellites came to be regarded as punitive facilities.

For more serious offenses, as early as 500 or 600 A.D., inmates or serfs were placed in prison rooms specifically designated for that purpose. Some orders were more severe than others. Statutes of the order of Cluny specified that the prison must be without door or window, the only entrance being in the middle of the vaulted ceiling, through which a ladder could be lowered. Sometimes prisoners were in irons and seldom was light, heat or wine provided. Although such quarters were on occasion underground, not much is actually known about the appearance of these church prisons. It is not likely that there were ever very many persons confined in them, even in the largest abbeys, and probably only one or two rooms were provided specifically for imprisonment. More than one prisoner must have been confined in some rooms. The 12th century prison in Durham Abbey was a 10 x 20 foot vaulted room with an adjoining chamber containing a latrine and a sort of hatch for passing food to the occupants.[7] In Eastern Europe, especially Austria and Russia, monastic prisons with a larger number of underground cells continued to be used well into the 20th century.

Aside from monastery prisons, every seat of church government, episcopal palace and the like, contained prisons. One of the most famous structures in France is Mont St. Michel, which has served successively as an ecclesiastical, civil and military prison. The citadel was built between the 11th and 14th centuries, and although it was subjected to extensive mutilation and restoration, two small cells known as the "Twins" still exist on the lower level of the Abbey. Directly above them was the ecclesiastical court in the abbot's residence. The jailer's job was made relatively simple as circular trapdoors in the floor gave access to the two cells below. These cells are about 10 x 15 feet and remain nearly dark, light and air coming from a narrow slit piercing the thick exterior walls. Each cell has a small niche in the wall with a hole in the floor as a latrine.

A third type of ecclesiastical prison was exemplified by the prisons built during the Inquisition. Some were newly built, others adapted from already existing structures. Almost no reliable information is available on these structures. Quarters for those imprisoned for life were usually in single rooms underground.[8] Sometimes they were completely dark. The church prison at Goa, Portuguese India, built in the 1600s, consisted of a complex of building each two stories high, containing a total of about 200 separate cells. A corridor ran the length of the buildings with seven or eight cells on each side. On one side, cells were about 10 x 10 feet, some with a small, barred, window in the vaulted ceiling. The cells on the other side ..rk, somewhat smaller and lower. Walls 5 feet thick separated rooms, each of which was entered through a set of double ....rs with space between so that one could be locked before the other was unlocked. The inner door was heavily reinforced with iron latticework and had an opening for food and clothing to be passed into the cell.

The influence of these various types of ecclesiastical prisons upon latter-day penology is difficult to assess. Frequently the philosophy must have been misunderstood or ignored by prison keepers. However, there can be no question as to the Christian religious influence upon the later workhouse movement. All in all, the church dogma of reformation of prisoners left upon later thought and social theory a strong imprint that would be hard to deny.

PRISONS AND THE WORKHOUSE MOVEMENT PRIOR TO 1780

The breakup of feudalism, coupled with the enclosure movement, resulted in growing social disorder and unrest in Europe during the centuries following the medieval period. This was accompanied by a large increase in the number of vagrants, prostitutes and petty criminals of all sorts. The new humanitarian spirit of the times demanded less sanguinary treatment for these minor offenders than had heretofore been in force. The answer of the 16th century was the workhouse or house of correction, an institution built around the idea of the rehabilitative value of regular work and the formation of "habits of industry." In 1557 the famous London Bridewell was opened, and its motley collection of prisoners was housed in a converted royal palace. Other English towns followed suit and in 1576 Parliament passed an act calling for each county to erect its own "bridewell."

In 1596 a house of correction was set up in Amsterdam for petty offenders. Within a few years other such establishments were opened in other cities in Holland and Germany. The Dutch houses of correction, rather than the earlier English institutions, were to exert a pervasive influence in Belgium and Scandinavia, and possibly also in Spain and Italy.[9]

Through descriptions of the English reformer John Howard, these "bettering houses" of Holland became models for some of the legislation and reform in both Britain and the colony of Pennsylvania.

Although the principles of these houses of correction represented a significant departure from older methods of treatment, the architecture revealed no break from the past. Workhouses were frequently in the form of a hollow square, much as the hospitals and convents of the time. In fact, many were located in buildings once used for such purposes. Prisoners worked and slept in common rooms, although the youthful recalcitrants committed by their well-to-do parents might be lodged in private rooms.

PRISON REFORM FROM 1780 TO THE AMERICAN INFLUENCES

The workhouses, local prisons and houses of correction built in Britain and on the Continent during the 17th and 18th centuries with such sanguine expectations had badly deteriorated by the last half of the 18th century. The public awareness of the shocking conditions in these institutions started a reform movement in England in the 1780s that spread to the Continent and the Americas. To a remarkable extent it was set in motion by the labors of one unassuming man, John Howard. Howard traveled extensively, visiting all the jails and prisons of Britain and the more important ones all over Europe, some as far away as Russia and the south of Italy. His detailed observations appeared in successive editions of his *State of the Prisons,* first published in 1777.

The operation of jails and prisons at that time was often a sinecure, a moneymaking operation for a particular official who had no government funds to run his institution. As a consequence, buildings were in disrepair, living quarters were incredibly crowded and unsanitary, prisoners were rarely provided with food and had little means of keeping clean. Howard was struck by the almost complete lack of supervision and control over prisoners. Shakedowns and assaults were common and the more sophisticated inmates freely corrupted the younger and more naive.

In Britain especially, public attention and debate about prison matters following these disclosures led, if not yet to a coherent penal philosophy, certainly to a more detailed consideration of prison construction than had ever occurred before. As the prisons were beginning to accommodate large numbers of prisoners, while only a decade earlier similar offenders were being sent to the gallows, imprisonment was, of course, expected to punish. But it was abundantly clear from Howard's writings and subsequent parliamentary committee testimony that prisoners influenced one another in ways that made reformation unlikely. As individual celling was seldom tried during this period because of the cost and inconvenience, the alternative was great reliance upon careful and continual surveillance by the guards and governor over the prisoners in their yards, workrooms, and in some cases, living quarters. This was strengthened by an often elaborate system of classification which separated the inmates into various classes within the prison. Constant, unseen inspection became the *sine qua non* of a good jail design and administration, the mechanism whereby the prison setting could be freed of its old abuses and the prisoners protected from corruption and disruptive behavior. The other great concern of the reformers was the health of the prisoners. Within the limits of the medical knowledge of the times and the general standards in the civilian population, there was a great concern for proper toilet facilities, baths, a piped supply of clean water, covered sewers and an infirmary. Because epidemics were thought to stem from impure air or "miasmas" rather than contagion, proper ventilation of buildings and their location were given much attention.

SYSTEMS DEVELOP AND COMPETE IN THE 19TH CENTURY

In tracing innovations in prison architecture thus far, attention has been focused exclusively on Europe, and, in the decades between 1780 and 1820, particularly on Great Britain. But at this juncture the development both of coherent philosophies of imprisonment and characteristic related architecture was taking place in North America, especially in Pennsylvania. It was no accident that prison reforms blossomed so soon and so well in this colony. Beginning with William Penn's revolutionary penal code of 1682, Pennsylvania Quakers continuously pressed for penal reform. The first prison of any consequence to come from their efforts was the Walnut Street Jail, opened the year the Revolution broke out. Although a model in its early days, its architecture was quite ordinary. While a small "penitentiary house" was built in the yard of the prison for solitary confinement as regular treatment, it was apparently used mostly for disciplinary purposes. The remainder of the prisoners lived in congregate cells, which very soon became greatly overcrowded.

Wrestling with the same obvious flaws in their prisons which Howard and other reformers had identified in Britain, the Pennsylvania Quakers gradually forged their philosophy of total isolation of each prisoner night and day. Solitude would serve several purposes: it would be punishment *par excellence,* but more importantly, it would give a man time for reflection and contrition and protect the naive from contamination by the more sophisticated, preventing also plots, escapes and attacks on keepers, which were at the time most prevalent. Religious instruction, work in the cell and visits by philanthropically inclined individuals would complete the job.

The Pennsylvania System of solitary confinement upon which

the foregoing examples were based was soon in trouble. Not only did it have an adverse effect on the mental and physical health of prisoners, but the cost of both buildings and maintenance was very high. Although the system was somewhat softened and modified, prisons continued to be built with separate exercise yards and stalls in chapels, and generally prisoners worked and exercised in silence through most of the 19th century in Europe. Well into the present century vestiges have remained of this system, and in many countries prisoners still eat in their cells and spend the initial months of their sentence in their cells.

Moving to relieve overcrowding in the old state prison on Greenwich Street in New York City, the state began constructing a new prison at Auburn in 1816. The original wing was arranged according to the congregate system with rooms holding from two to ten prisoners. Following its opening there was considerable disorder and rioting, and consequently in the subsequent construction of a new cellblock a brief experiment with the Pennsylvania System was tried. Cells were 7½ feet x 3 feet 8 inches x 7 feet high, arranged back to back on five tiers in the center of a long cell building. Cell doors opened onto balconies facing a 9-foot-wide space open from ground level to ceiling. The wing was heated by stoves placed in the corridors and ventilated with ducts through which the prisoners communicated easily.

The experiment in solitary confinement lasted three years but was abandoned because of the effect on the physical and mental health of the prisoners. The tiny cells were inadequate for work, there were no exercise yards and no outside visitors were permitted. A new warden, Elam Lynds, subsequently worked out what came to be called the Auburn System—congregate work in silence in the daytime in workshops, coupled with solitary confinement in sleeping cells at night. The Auburn System prevailed over the Pennsylvania System because the prison shops in the former had a higher level of inmate productivity than cell labor when the prisoner was isolated. The latter system was also more expensive to operate as it lacked inmate labor for housekeeping duties and the buildings were more expensive to construct. America, with its tradition of hard work and its chronic labor shortages, could not really tolerate the degree of relative idleness which Europeans would permit running their prison systems under the Pennsylvania regimen.

In 1825 prisoners arrived in leg shackles from Auburn at a site on the Hudson River, later to be known as Sing Sing, to construct a new prison. The plan was similar; tiny cells back to back on five tiers, with stairways on either end and in the center of the very long range.

Cell doors were iron with grillework in the upper portion, and they fastened with gang locks. Cells received small amounts of light coming through a tiny window located 9 feet away in the outer wall opposite the cell door. These cells were extremely damp, dark and poorly ventilated and, like those at Auburn, contained no toilet facilities except buckets. The East House, which alone contained 1,000 cells and continued in use until 1943, was to become the prototype for most American prison cellhouse construction, rather than the earlier Auburn prison from which the system took its name.

For the remainder of the 19th century in this country, the characteristic layout for nearly all prisons was to consist of a central building housing offices, mess hall and chapel, usually flanked and joined on each side by a multitiered cellblock. In the prison enclosure formed by the wall would be shops, hospital and power plant.

20TH CENTURY DEVELOPMENTS

The great rash of prison construction in the last half of the 19th century was followed by 30 years of relative inactivity. Two standard architectural solutions had been developed for handling large numbers of men in high security—the radial plan developed by Blackburn, Haviland and Jebb and common in most countries, and the system of flanking cell wings with inside cells which evolved in the Auburn System prisons in the United States. A third important plan developed which came to be called the "telephone-pole" or "telegraph-pole"—a series of parallel cellblocks, service facilities and shops flanking a long central corridor. It should be noted in passing that the third type of architecture was only that. The era of "systems" of penal treatment was past. The United States and European countries were henceforth to experiment with particular kinds of treatment strategies, none of which would ever come close to being regarded as an all-embracing panacea with an associated architecture as in the 19th century.

The evolution of the telephone-pole layout must be considered to have been inevitable. With the eclipse of the "systems," a moderate relaxation of the older discipline and an added use of vocational training, education and professional services resulted in increased movement of prisoners within the confines of the prison.

One of the most useful modifications of the telephone-pole plan has been the use of corridor zones or completely separate areas set off according to type of facilities or degree of custody of the living quarters. This cuts down on supervisory problems, makes possible the closing of some areas in the evening hours and the separation of different offender groups within one institution. In the federal prison at Marion, Illinois, opened in 1963, all facilities are off four corridors which join at a central control area at a level midway between the two-story wings in order to facilitate observation and traffic flow.

Brief mention should be made of another type of plan which enjoyed some brief though limited popularity in the 1930s and 1940s. Public buildings in the past have often been constructed in the form of a hollow, self-enclosed square. One of John Howard's model jail plans of the 1770s consisted of a rectangular array of six squares with open courts. But such a plan offered little appeal until the prison wall was dispensed with. Then the self-enclosing plan seemed like a secure substitute for the expensive wall. The state prison opened at Attica, New York, in 1931 had a wall but the cells were arranged in four blocks facing each other to form a very large square. The federal government built medium security institutions without walls at Milan, Michigan (o.1933), Danbury, Connecticut (o.1940), and Englewood, Colorado (o.1940), which were self-enclosed. Although not completely self-enclosed, the Michigan State Prison at Jackson (1924–1929) contains huge cellblocks on three sides with two walls joining the ends and enclosing 57 acres. There are over 5,700 individual cells.

On the 19th century penal treatment systems were grafted in makeshift fashion various "reforms" of a humanitarian nature which tended to mitigate but not fundamentally alter the nature of the prison structure or the prison experience. Education, vocational training, classification, and various kinds of casework and evaluation by behavior specialists became part of most North American prisons in the 20th century. Concurrently, the rigors of 19th century prison life were considerably ameliorated. It was even discovered, partly it must be admitted due to increasing construction costs, that high security facilities were not necessary for the majority of prisoners.

But following World War II, some of the old optimism and self-confidence which had characterized American penology began to erode, accompanied by a slow but fundamental change in orientation. The reasons for this are not hard to find: with increasing systematic study by penologists and behavior scientists, some disconcerting things were being uncovered about the "new penology." The prison, with all its 20th century improvements, seemed to be still essentially the same ineffective, hit-and-miss instrument of social policy it had been from the beginning. The new techniques, when rigorously tested, turned out not to work very well, and one of the main causes was the existence of a homemade social system among the prisoners. This of course had always existed in varying degrees, but it turned out that its influence on the careers of inmates was much greater than the formal measures of rehabilitation.

With the increasingly demonstrated failure of classification, vocational and academic training, and limited psychological contacts to live up to expectations, coupled with the rediscovery of the importance of associations among prisoners, a new breed of career-oriented and educated correctional administrator began a determined search for new solutions. For the first time since the Pennsylvania and New York reformers of the early 19th century, planners and architects began to focus on the *inmate,* his contacts with fellow inmates, and now, how these contacts might be properly structured—rather than cut off—through new architectural devices.

Out of all this came new kinds of correctional institutions for adults with layouts similar to those used heretofore only with juveniles or women. Freed from the preoccupation with security, architects have devised an architecture which must be regarded as much more significant than the telephone-pole structures or self-enclosed institutions already described. In such an arrangement, cottages or dormitories along with school, dining and other service facilities might be grouped formally along a central mall. Rectangular-shaped cottages or cell buildings were most commonly used.

CONCLUSION

Within the limits of space we have tried to trace the development of prison architecture from its antecedents in castle, dungeon and fortress, through the early little houses of correction and local prisons especially in Britain, to the rise of the Pennslvania and Auburn systems with their very large, highly secure institutions, down to the 20th century telephone-pole prisons and the new breed of open, dispersed, minimum security facilities. The architects of prisons for adults up until very recent times had rather unambiguous demands made of them: to build a prison which was above all secure, which met minimum standards for sanitation and which would provide facilities for prisoners to work.

In the 19th century prison, a regimen so far removed from normal living was carried out that a series of complicated and unusual architectural arrangements were required. Even if workshops and work were available, prisoners remained in their cells for long periods of time and it was these little bedroom-dayrooms which, in large numbers, became the central core of the prison. The judicious and secure arrangement of those cells was the primary task of the architect. For the Pennsylvania System surveillance of cells where inmates spent most if not all of their time made the radial plan useful; for the Auburn System a series of living units near a number of workshops was typical. But as the size of prisons grew and the activities of prisoners aside from work and confinement in their cell increased, emphasis shifted away from the cell and its surveillance. It became necessary to provide plans to cope with the complicated and increased movements of prisoners about the prison. The telephone-pole plan appeared and possessed a particular kind of utility for large, secure institutions. During this time the earlier preoccupation with visual surveillance over everything all the time gave way partially to a new preoccupation with mechanical equipment and hardware as a way of containing and restraining the inmates. This proliferation of gadgetry is certainly predictable, given American technical competence, our long-standing love affair with things mechanical, and careful salesmanship campaigns mounted by manufacturers.

But by the 1940s, especially in the United States, a rather different sort of trend was becoming evident, evident but not overpowering yet. For a variety of reasons too complex to go into here, really new kinds of demands were being made on the architect. After a century of penological handwringing about the evils of size, there was now an increasing insistence that institutions be smaller. There was an unmistakable veering away from the idea of maximum security for everybody towards the idea that most prisons need much less security. Only two walled prisons were built in North America after 1940.

This "new permissiveness" in penology has had rather dramatic if not entirely successful consequences for the architecture of penal institutions. During the exuberant period of prison reform in the late 18th and early 19th centuries, there existed a lively interest in prison architecture, a sanguine and sometimes naive faith in what it could achieve, and a participation by the best architects of the day in these experimental building ventures. But the period of vitality was followed by one of somnolence when a series of mediocre and inexperienced architects copied one another and the models of the past. Now, after generations of unimaginative duplication of first the radial, then the Auburn and finally the telephone-pole plans—at this point by unimaginative and entrenched architectural firms rather than individuals—correctional architecture seems to be once more entering into a period of innovation, vitality and creativity. This is demonstrated not only by some of the new institutions going up from Canada to Argentina, but by the fact that again first-rate architects are being drawn into competitions and planning, and that once more architects and penologists are sitting down and listening to each other.

The continual trend towards amelioration of the harshness of past prison life and the stress on normal living in groups, the use of much smaller institutions, and the increasing use of therapeutic techniques, have all resulted in the elimination of some of the prisonlike qualities of prisons.[10] But how far this trend will continue will depend on the community's willingness to support nonvindictive treatment programs and the eventual discovery of successful treatment techniques. But it also depends, in the immediate future at least, on some rather substantial contributions from the architect. If there is anything to be learned from this review of past prison building, it must certainly include the following points:

1. Prisons must be designed with a realistic understanding of the pressures and consequences of group living in institutions. This may mean consultations with not only the policy makers in administration but also guards and prisoners.

2. The large size of institutions may not be the main reason for their failure. But it is safe to assume that while a small prison is not certain to be successful, a large one *is* sure to be unsuccessful.

3. The dismal pattern presented on the preceding pages of stereotyped imitations and repetitions of fashionable plans must not continue. If anything is certain about correctional techniques over the next 20 years it is that they will change. This means that maximum flexibility must be provided for in every new design.

4. Undue reliance on ingenious plans, mechanical contrivances or structural innovations to effect rehabilitation, insure security or guarantee a smooth-running institution will only continue the long series of errors of the past. Human efforts can at best be aided, not supplanted, by such devices. The prison structure cannot be considered as the *deus ex machina* which will extricate us miraculously from the quicksand of prison practices.

5. Finally, the history of prison architecture stands as a discouraging testament of our sometimes intentional, sometimes accidental degradation of our fellow man. Prison structures have continued to be built in a way which manages by one means or another to brutalize their occupants and to deprive them of their privacy, dignity, and self-esteem, while at the same time strengthening their criminality. The 19th century allowed vast and dreary buildings and physical cruelty to grind down the prisoner. The contemporary prison seems to allow mechanical contrivances to dominate the prisoner. Architects in the future must share some responsibility for the unintended indignities made possible by their works.

2

MAJOR INSTITUTIONS

NATIONAL ADVISORY COMMISSION ON
CRIMINAL JUSTICE STANDARDS AND GOALS

The term "major institutions" as used in this chapter does not refer to size but to State-operated penal and correctional institutions for juveniles, youths, and adults (as distinguished from detention centers, jails, work farms, and other types of facilities which in almost all States are operated by local governments). Names used for major institutions differ from State to State. Institutions for juveniles carry such names as youth development centers, training schools, industrial schools, and State homes. Institutions for adults variously are called prisons, penitentiaries, classification and reception centers, correctional institutions, reformatories, treatment centers, State farms, and others. Altogether there are about 200 major juvenile and 350 major adult correctional institutions in the United States.

This chapter also discusses maximum, medium, and minimum security institutions. It is difficult to make clear-cut distinctions, however, in view of the enormous diversity. Generally the terms refer to relative degrees in the use of security trappings and procedures. All three security classifications may be used, and usually are, in the same institution. Moreover, what may be considered maximum security in one State may be considered only medium security in another. Some so-called minimum security institutions might actually be considered medium security by some authorities. The terminology—maximum, medium, minimum—is as imprecise as the wide variety of names that may be used formally to designate individual institutions. The terms indicate the rough classifications traditionally used.

Source: From *Corrections*(Washington, D.C.: U.S. Government Printing Office, 1973), pp. 341–349.

HISTORICAL PERSPECTIVE

Institutionalization as the primary means of enforcing the customs, mores, or laws of a people is a relatively modern practice. In earlier times, restitution, exile, and a variety of methods of corporal and capital punishment, many of them unspeakably barbarous, were used. Confinement was used for detention only.

The colonists who came to North America brought with them the harsh penal codes and practices of their homelands. It was in Pennsylvania, founded by William Penn, that initial attempts were made to find alternatives to the brutality of British penal practice. Penn knew well the nature of confinement because he had spent six months in Newgate Prison, London, for his religious convictions.

In the Great Law of Pennsylvania, enacted in 1682, Penn made provisions to eliminate to a large extent the stocks, pillories, branding iron, and gallows. The Great Law directed: ". . . that every county within the province of Pennsylvania and territories thereunto belonging shall . . . build or cause to be built in the most convenient place in each respective county a sufficient house for restraint, labor, and punishment of all such persons as shall be thereunto commited by laws."

In time William Penn's jails, like those in other parts of the New World up to and including the present, became places where the untried, the mentally ill, the promiscuous, the debtor, and myriad petty offenders were confined indiscriminately.

In 1787, when the Constitutional Convention was meeting in Philadelphia and men were thinking of institutions based on the concept of the dignity of man, the Philadelphia Society for Alleviating the Miseries of Public Prisons was organized. The society believed that the sole end of punishment is to prevent crime and that punishment should not destroy the offender. The society, many of whose members were influential citizens, worked hard to create a new penology in Pennsylvania, a penology which to a large degree eliminated capital and corporal punishment as the principal sanctions for major crimes. The penitentiary was invented as a substitute for these punishments.

In the first three decades of the 19th century, citizens of New York, Pennsylvania, New Jersey, Massachusetts, and Connecticut were busy planning and building monumental penitentiaries. These were not cheap installations built from the crumbs of the public treasury. In fact, the Eastern State Penitentiary in Philadelphia was the most expensive public building constructed in the New World to that time. States were extremely proud of these physical plants. Moreover,

they saw in them an almost utopian ideal. They were to become sta-
bilizers of society. They were to become laboratories committed to
the improvement of all mankind.[11]

When these new penitentiaries were being planned and constructed, practitioners and theorists held three factors to be the primary contributors to criminal behavior. The first was environment.
Report after report on offenders pointed out the harmful effects of
family, home, and other aspects of environment on the offender's behavior. The second factor usually cited was the offender's lack of
aptitude and work skills. This quality led to indolence and a life of
crime. The third cause was seen as the felon's ignorance of right and
wrong because he had not been taught the Scriptures.

The social planners of the first quarter of the 19th century designed prison architecture and programs to create an experience for
the offender in which (1) there would be no injurious influences, (2)
the offender would learn the value of labor and work skills, and (3) he
would have the opportunity to learn about the Scriptures and accept
from them the principles of right and wrong that would then guide
his life.

Various States pursued this triad of purposes in one of two basic
methods. The Pennsylvania system was based on solitary confinement, accompanied by bench labor within one's cell. There the offender was denied all contact with the outside world except that
provided by the Scriptures, religious tracts, and visits from specially
selected, exemplary citizens. The prison was designed painstakingly
to make this kind of solitary experience possible. The walls between
cells were thick, and the cells themselves were large, each equipped
with plumbing and running water. In the cell were a work bench and
tools. In addition, each cell had its own small walled area for solitary
exercise. The institution was designed magnificently for its three purposes: elimination of external influences; provision of work; and
opportunity for penitence, introspection, and acquisition of religious
knowledge.[12]

New York's Auburn system pursued the same three goals by a
different method. Like the Pennsylvania system, it isolated the offender from the world outside and permitted him virtually no external contact. However, it provided small cells in which the convicts
were confined only on the Sabbath and during nonworking hours.
During working hours inmates labored in factory-like shops. The con-
taminating effect of the congregate work situation was eliminated by
a rule of silence. Inmates were prohibited from communicating in any
way with other inmates or the jailers.

The relative merits of these two systems were debated vigorously for half a century. The Auburn system ultimately prevailed in the United States, because it was less expensive and because it lent itself more easily to production methods of the industrial revolution.

But both systems were disappointments almost from the beginning. The awful solitude of the Pennsylvania system drove men to insanity. The rule of silence of the Auburn system became increasingly unenforceable despite regular use of the lash and a variety of other harsh and brutal punishments.

Imprisonment as an instrument of reform was an early failure. This invention did, however, have some notable advantages. It rendered obsolete a myriad of sanguinary punishments, and its ability to separate and hold offenders gave the public a sense of security. It also was thought to deter people from crime by fear of imprisonment.

Imprisonment had many disadvantages, too. Principal among them was the phenomenon that so many of its "graduates" came back. The prison experience often further atrophied the offender's capacity to live successfully in the free world. The prison nevertheless has persisted, partly because a civilized nation could neither turn back to the barbarism of an earlier time nor find a satisfactory alternative. For nearly two centuries, American penologists have been seeking a way out of this dilemma.

TYPES OF INSTITUTIONS

Maximum Security Prisons

For the first century after invention of the penitentiary most prisons were built to be internally and externally secure. The early zealots who had dreamed of institutions that not only would reform the offender but also would cleanse society itself were replaced by a disillusioned and pragmatic leadership that saw confinement as a valid end in itself. Moreover, the new felons were seen as outsiders—Irishmen, Germans, Italians, and Negroes. They did not talk or act like "Americans." The prison became a dumping ground where foreigners and blacks who were not adjusting could be held outside the mainstream of society's concern. The new prisons, built in the most remote areas of the States, became asylums, not only for the hardened criminal but also for the inept and unskilled "un-American." Although the rhetoric of reformation persisted, the be-all and end-all of the prison was to hold.

From 1830 to 1900 most prisons built in the United States reflected that ultimate value—security. Their principal features were high walls, rigid internal security, cage-like cells, sweat shops, a bare minimum of recreation space, and practically nothing else. They kept the prisoners in and the public out, and that was all that was expected or attempted.

Many of these prisons were constructed well and have lasted long. Together they form the backbone of our present-day correctional system. As Table 1 shows, 56 of them, remodeled and expanded, still are in use. They currently house approximately 75,000 of the 110,000 felons in maximum security facilities. Today 56 percent of all State prisoners in America are in structures built to serve maximum security functions. (See Table 2.)

Any attempt to describe the "typical" maximum security prison is hazardous. One was constructed almost two centuries ago. Another was opened in 1972. The largest confines more than 4,000 inmates, another less than 60.[13] Some contain massive undifferentiated cell blocks, each caging as many as 500 men or more. Others are built in small modules housing less than 16. The industries in some are archaic sweat shops, in others large modern factories. Many provide absolute-

TABLE 1
Date of Opening, State Maximum Security Prisons Still in Operation

Date of Opening	Number of Prisons
Prior to 1830	6
1831 to 1870	17
1871 to 1900	33
1901 to 1930	21
1931 to 1960	15
1961 to date	21
Total	113

Source: American Correctional Association, *1971 Directory of Correctional Institutions and Agencies of America, Canada and Great Britain* (College Park, Md.: ACA, 1971).

TABLE 2
Population of State Correctional Facilities for Adults,
By Security Classification of Inmates

Classification	Inmates	Percent of Total Population
Maximum	109,920	56
Medium	57,505	30
Minimum	28,485	15
Total	195,910	100

Source: ACA, *1971 Directory* and poll taken by the American Foundation's Institute of Corrections, which contacted the head of every State department of corrections.

ly no inside recreation space and only a minimum outside, while others have superlative gymnasiums, recreation yards, and auditoriums. Some are dark, dingy, depressing dungeons, while others are well glazed and sunny. In one the early warning system consists of cow bells strung along chicken wire atop the masonry wall, while in others closed circuit television and sensitive electronic sensors monitor the corridors and fences.

Maximum security institutions are geared to the fullest possible supervision, control, and surveillance of inmates. Design and program choices optimize security. Buildings and policies restrict the inmate's movement and minimize his control over his environment. Other considerations, such as the inmate's individual or social needs, are responded to only in conformity with security requirements. Trustworthiness on the inmate's part is not anticipated: the opposite is assumed.

Technology has brought much to the design and construction of these institutions, and development of custodial artifacts has far outpaced skill in reaching inmates and in using rapport with them to maintain security or control. A modern maximum security institution represents the victory of external control over internal reform.

The prison invariably is surrounded by a masonry wall or double fence with manned towers. Electronic sensing devices and lights impose an unremitting surveillance and control. Inside the institution, the need for security has dictated that men live in windowless cells, not rooms. Doors, which would afford privacy, are replaced by grilles of tool-resistant steel. Toilets are unscreened. Showers are taken under supervision.

Control, so diligently sought in these facilities, is not limited to structural considerations. All activity is weighed in terms of its relationship to custody. Dining is no exception. Men often sit on fixed backless stools and eat without forks and knives at tables devoid of condiments.

Lest security be compromised by intrusions from outside, special devices are built to prevent physical contact with visitors. Relatives often communicate with inmates by telephone and see them through double layers of glass. Any contacts allowed are under the guard's watchful eyes. Body searches precede and follow such visits.

Internal movement is limited by strategic placement of bars and grilles defining precisely where an inmate may go. Areas of inmate concentration or possible illegal activity are monitored by correctional officers or by closed circuit television. "Blind spots"—those not capable of supervision—are avoided in the design of the secure institution. Places for privacy or small group activity are structurally, if not operationally, precluded.

Maximum security institutions, then, may be viewed as those facilities characterized by high perimeter security, high internal security, and operating regulations that curtail movement and maximize control.

In his masterful description of penitentiaries in the United States, Tocqueville wrote in 1833 that, aside from common interests, the several States "preserve their individual independence, and each of them is sovereign master to rule itself according to its own pleasure. . . . By the side of one State, the penitentiaries of which might serve as a model, we find another whose prisons present the example of everything which ought to be avoided."[14]

He was right in 1833. His words still ring true. . . .

Medium Security Correctional Centers

Since the early 20th century, means of housing the offender in other than maximum security prisons have been explored. Developments in the behavioral sciences, increasing importance of education, dominance of the work ethic, and changes in technology have led to modified treatment methods.

Simultaneously, field service—parole and probation—increased. Institutions were set up to handle special inmate populations, men and women, youths and adults. Classification was introduced by employing psychological and sociological knowledge and skill. Pretrial holding centers, or jails, were separated from those receiving convicted felons. Different levels of security were provided: maximum, medium, minimum, and open. Much of the major correctional construction in the last 50 years has been medium security. In fact, 51 of the existing 110 medium security correctional institutions were built after 1950. Today, over 57,000 offenders, 30 percent of all State inmates, are housed in such facilities. (See Table 2.)

Today medium security institutions probably embody most of the ideals and characteristics of the early attempts to reform offenders. It is in these facilities that the most intensive correctional or rehabilitation efforts are conducted. Here inmates are exposed to a variety of programs intended to help them become useful members of society. But the predominant consideration still is security.

These institutions are designed to confine individuals where they can be observed and controlled. All have perimeter security, either in the form of masonry walls or double cyclone fences. In some cases electronic detecting devices are installed. Towers located on the perimeter are manned by armed guards and equipped with spotlights.

Internal security usually is maintained by: locks, bars, and concrete walls; clear separation of activities; highly defined movement paths both indoors and outdoors; schedules and head counts; sight-line supervision; and electronic devices.

Housing areas, medical and dental treatment rooms, schoolrooms, recreation and entertainment facilities, counseling offices, vocational training and industrial shops, administration offices, and maintenance facilities usually are clearly separated. Occasionally they are located in individual compounds complete with their own fences and sally ports. A complex series of barred gates and guard posts controls the flow of traffic from one area to another. Central control stations keep track of movement at all times. Circulation is restricted to specified corridors or outdoor walks, with certain spaces and movement paths out of bounds. Closed circuit television and alarm networks are used extensively. Locked steel doors predominate. Bars or concrete substitutes line corridors, surround control points, and cross all external windows and some internal ones.

Housing units in medium security institutions vary from crowded dormitories to private rooms with furniture. Dormitories may house as many as 80 persons or as few as 16. Some individual cells have grilled fronts and doors.

The variations found in maximum security institutions also are seen in medium security correctional facilities, but they are not so extreme, possibly because the latter were developed in a much shorter period.

Several heartening developments have occurred recently in the medium security field. Campus-type plants have been designed that largely eliminate the cramped oppressiveness of most confinement. Widely separated buildings are connected by meandering pathways, and modulated ground surfaces break monotony. Attractive residences house small groups of inmates in single rooms.

Schools, vocational education buildings, gymnasiums, and athletic fields compare favorably with those of the best community colleges. Yet external security provided by double cyclone fences and internal security enforced by excellent staff and unobtrusive building design protect the public from the inmates and the inmates from each other.

If confinement to institutions is to remain the principal sanction of our codes of criminal justice, medium security plants and programs such as these, not the traditional "minimum security" prison farms, should be the cornerstone of the system.

Minimum Security Correctional Centers

The facilities in this group are diverse but generally have one feature in common. They are relatively open, and consequently custody is a function of classification rather than of prison hardware. The principal exceptions are huge prison plantations on which entire penal populations serve time. Minimum security institutions range from large drug rehabilitation centers to small farm, road, and forestry camps located throughout rural America.

Most, but not all, minimum security facilities have been created to serve the economic needs of society and only incidentally the correctional needs of the offenders. Cotton is picked, lumber is cut, livestock is raised, roads are built, forest fires are fought, and parks and State buildings are maintained. These are all legitimate tasks for prisoners, especially while our system still (1) receives large numbers of offenders who are a minimal threat to themselves and to the general public, and (2) holds men long after they are ready for freedom. Moreover, open facilities do serve therapeutic purposes by removing men from the stifling prison environment, separating the young and unsophisticated from the predators, and substituting controls based upon trust rather than bars. All these aspects are laudable.

However, these remote facilities have important deficiencies. They seldom provide educational or service resources other than work. Moreover, the predominantly rural labor bears no relationship to the work skills required for urban life. Separation of the prisoner from his real world is almost as complete as it would have been in the penitentiary.

One remarkable minimum security correctional center was opened in 1972 at Vienna, Ill., as a branch of the Illinois State Penitentiary. Although a large facility, it approaches the quality of the nonpenal institution. Buildings resembling garden apartments are built around a "town square" complete with churches, schools, shops, and library. Paths lead off to "neighborhoods" where "homes" provide private rooms in small clusters. Extensive provision has been made for both indoor and outdoor recreation. Academic, commercial, and vocational education facilities equal or surpass those of many technical high schools.

This correctional center has been designed for 800 adult felons. Unfortunately, most of them will come from the State's major population centers many miles away. Today this open institution is enjoying the euphoria that often accompanies distinctive newness. One may speculate about the future, however, when community correctional programs siphon from the State's prison system many of its more stable and less dangerous offenders. Fortunately, this facility will not be rendered obsolete by such a development. The nonprisonlike design permits it to be adapted for a variety of educational, mental health, or other human service functions.

One generalization about the future of minimum security facilities seems warranted. As society finds still more noninstitutional and community-based solutions to its problems, the rural open institutions will become harder and harder to populate. Already they are operating farther below their rated capacities than any other type of correctional facility.

Institutions for Women

The new role of women may influence profoundly the future requirements of corrections. For whatever reasons, the treatment given to women by the criminal justice system has been different from that given men. Perhaps fewer commit crimes. Certainly six men are arrested for every woman. The ratio is still higher for indictments and convictions, and 30 times more men than women are confined in State correctional institutions. Montana in 1971 incarcerated only eight women; West Virginia, 28; Nebraska, 44; Minnesota, 55. Even populous Pennsylvania incarcerated only 127 women.[15]

Tomorrow may be different. As women increasingly assume more roles previously seen as male, their involvement in crime may increase and their treatment at the hands of the agencies of justice change. A possible, if unfortunate, result could be an increase in the use of imprisonment for women.

Correctional institutions for women present a microcosm of American penal practice. In this miniature model, the absurdities and irrationalities of the entire system appear in all their ludicrousness. In one State, the few women offenders are seen to be so dangerous as to require confinement in a separate wing of the men's penitentiary. There they are shut up in cells and cell corridors without recreation, services, or meaningful activity.

In other places, new but separate facilities for women have been built that perpetuate the philosophy, the operational methods, the hardware, and the repression of the State penitentiary. These facilities are surrounded by concertina fences, and the women's movements are monitored by closed circuit television. Inmates sit endlessly playing cards, sewing, or just vegetating.

A woman superintendent has observed that these institutions should release exclusively to San Francisco or Las Vegas because the inmates have been prepared for homosexuality or card dealing. Everything about such places—their sally ports, control centers, narrow corridors, small cells, restrictive visiting rooms—spells PRISON in capital letters. Yet these institutions were not built in the 19th century. They are new.

Compared to women's institutions in other States, the prisons just described demonstrate the inconsistency of our thinking about criminals in general and women prisoners specifically. One center— the Women's Treatment Center at Purdy, Wash.—vividly demonstrates that offenders can be viewed as civilized human beings. Built around multilevel and beautifully landscaped courtyards, the attractive buildings provide security without fences. Small housing units with pleasant living rooms provide space for normal interaction between presumably normal women. The expectation that the women will behave like human beings pervades the place. Education, recreation, and training areas are uncramped and well glazed. Opportunity for interaction between staff and inmate is present everywhere.

About 200 yards away from the other buildings are attractive apartments, each containing a living room, dining space, kitchen, two bedrooms, and a bath. Women approaching release live in them while working or attending school in the city. These apartments normally are out of bounds to staff except on invitation.

The contrasts among women's institutions demonstrate our confusion about what criminals are like and what correctional responses are appropriate. In six States maximum security prisons are the correctional solution to the female offenders. At least 15 other States use open institutions exclusively.

This contrast raises questions about the nature of correctional planning. What is it really based upon? The propensities of the offender? The meanness or enlightenment of the general population? The niggardliness of the public? The broadness or narrowness of the administrator's vision? Whatever the reason, the architecture of these correctional institutions tells us either that women in State A are profoundly different from those in State B or that the correctional leadership holds vastly differing human values.

Youth Correction Centers

The reformatory movement started about a century ago. With the advent of the penitentiary, imprisonment had replaced corporal punishment. The reformatory concept was designed to replace punishment through incarceration with rehabilitation. This new movement was aimed at the young offender, aged 16 to 30. Its keystone was education and vocational training to make the offender more capable of living in the outside world. New concepts—parole and indeterminate sentences—were introduced. An inmate who progressed could reduce the length of his sentence. Hope was a new treatment dynamic.

The physical plant in the early reformatory era was highly secure. One explanation given is that the first one, at Elmira, N.Y., was designed as a maximum security prison and then converted into a reformatory. Other States that adopted the reformatory concept also copied the physical plant. Huge masonry walls, multi-tiered cell blocks, mass movements, "big house" mess halls, and dimly lit shops were all part of the model. Several of these places are still in operation. Later, in the 1920's, youth institutions adopted the telephone-pole construction design developed for adults; housing and service units crisscross an elongated inner corridor. More recently campus-type plants, fenced and unfenced, have been constructed. Some of these resemble the new colleges.

Most recently built reformatories, now called youth "correction" or "training" centers, are built to provide only medium or minimum security. (However, the newest—Western Correctional Center, Morganton, N.C.—is a very secure 17-story facility.) These centers usually emphasize academic and vocational education and recreation. Some supplement these with counseling and therapy, including operant conditioning and behavior modification. The buildings themselves are central to the program in providing incentives. At the Morganton center, for example, as a youth's behavior modifies he is moved from the 17th floor to the more desirable 16th, or from on open ward to a single room, etc.

Overall plant, security, and housing, as well as education, vocational training, and recreation space, are similar in youth centers to those provided in adult centers of comparable custody classification. The only major difference is that some youth institutions provide more programs. The amount of space, therefore, often exceeds that of adult centers. Some youth centers have highly screened populations, and the center provides only one function—to increase educational levels and vocational skills. The effectiveness of such centers is highly dependent on inmate selection, placing a heavy responsibility on the classification process.

Facilities and programs in the youth correction centers vary widely from institution to institution and from State to State. While some provide a variety of positive programs, others emphasize the mere holding of the inmate. In the latter, few rehabilitative efforts are made; facilities are sparse and recreational space is inadequate. The general atmosphere is repressive, and the physical plant prohibits program improvement.

Youth institutions include at least two types of minimum security facilities, work camps and training centers, which present a series of dilemmas. In work camps, outdoor labors burn up youthful energies. But these camps are limited severely in their capacity to provide other important needs of youthful offenders. Moreover, they are located in rural America, which is usually white, while youthful offenders frequently are not. The other type of minimum security youth center has complete training facilities, fine buildings, attractively landscaped surroundings, and extensive programs. These, too, usually are remote from population centers. Though they probably represent our most enlightened form of imprisonment, quite possibly they soon will be obsolete.

Even today the various States are finding it difficult to select from their youthful inmate populations persons who are stable enough for such open facilities. Many are operating, therefore, far below normal capacity. Walkaways present such serious problems that insidious internal controls, more irksome than the visible wire fence, have been developed.

These open centers serve three important functions:

1. They bring the individual every day face to face with his impulse to escape life's frustrations by running away.
2. They remove youths temporarily from community pressures that have overwhelmed them.
3. They provide sophisticated program opportunities usually not available otherwise.

In the near future, it is to be hoped, these three purposes will be assumed by small and infinitely less expensive community correctional programs.

Institutions for Juveniles

Almost all human services in America have followed a similar course of development. When faced with a social problem we seek institutional solutions first. The problems presented by children have been no exception. Early in our national development we had to face the phenomenon of child dependency, and we built orphanages. Children would not stay put, and we established the "Home for Little Wanderers." When children stole we put them in jails, filthy places where the sight of them incensed pioneer prison reformers. They turned to a model already common in Europe where congregate facilities, often under the auspices of religious groups, cared for both dependent and delinquent children.

The first such facility in America was established in New York in 1825. Reflecting its purpose, it was called the "House of Refuse." Others followed, coinciding almost exactly with the first penitentiaries. The pioneering juvenile institutions were just about as oppressive and forbidding, emphasizing security and austerity. By today's standards they were basically punitive. In time they tended more toward benign custodial care along with providing the essentials of housing and food. They became characterized by large populations, with consequent regimentation, and by oversized buildings.

In the latter decades of the 19th century, attempts to minimize the massive institutional characteristics led to the adoption of the "cottage concept." Housing was provided in smaller building. "House parents" aimed at simulating home-like atmospheres. This model has remained and today continues as a common, perhaps the predominant, type of institution for juvenile delinquents.

Institutions for the delinquent child usually have vastly different characteristics than those holding adults. Often they are located on a campus spreading over many acres. The housing units provide quarters for smaller groups, invariably less than 60 and frequently less than 20. Often they also provide apartments for cottage staff. Dining frequently is a function of cottage life, eliminating the need for the large central dining rooms. Grilles seldom are found on the cottage doors and windows, although sometimes they are covered by detention screens. Security is not the staff's major preoccupation.

Play fields dot the usually ample acreage. Other resources for athletics, such as gymnasiums and swimming pools, are common. Additional recreational activity often is undertaken in nearby towns, parks, streams, and resorts. Teams from youth institutions usually play in public school leagues and in community competition. The principal program emphasis at these children's centers quite naturally has been education, and many have fine, diversified school buildings, both academic and vocational.

Exterior security varies, but most juvenile centers have no artificial barriers separating them from the community at large. Space frequently provides such a barrier, however, as many juvenile centers are in rural settings. Fences do exist, especially where the institution borders a populated area. Usually they do not have towers. Walkaways are quite frequent and cause considerable annoyance to neighbors, who sometimes hold public subscriptions to raise money for fences.

At the risk of oversimplification this section describes two predominant but conflicting philosophies about the care of delinquent children. This is done because they suggest profoundly different directions for the future.

One has its roots in the earliest precepts of both the penitentiary and reformatory system. It holds that the primary cause of delinquent behavior is the child's environment, and the secondary cause is his inability to cope with that environment. The response is to provide institutions in the most remote areas, where the child is protected from adverse environmental influences and exposed to a wholesome

lifestyle predicated on traditional middle-class values. Compensatory education, often better than that available in the community, equips the child with tools necessary to face the world again, some day. This kind of correctional treatment requires expensive and extensive plants capable of providing for the total needs of children over prolonged periods.

The second philosophy similarly assumes that the child's problems are related to the environment, but it differs from the first model by holding that the youngster must learn to deal with those problems where they are—in the community. Institutions, if required at all, should be in or close to the city. They should not duplicate anything—school, recreation, entertainment, clinical services—that is available in the community. The child's entire experience should be one of testing himself in the very setting where he will one day live. The process demands that each child constantly examine the reality of his adjustment with his peers.

The first model clings to the traditional solution. Yet institutions that serve society's misfits have never experience notable success. One by one, institutions have been abandoned by most of the other human services and replaced by community programs. The second model, still largely untested, moves corrections toward more adventurous and hopeful days.

Reception and Classification Centers

Reception and classification centers are relatively recent additions to the correctional scene. In earlier times there were no State systems, no central departments of corrections. Each prison was a separate entity, usually manged by its own board, which reported directly to the governor. If the State had more than one institution, either geography or the judge determined the appropriate one for the offender. As the number and variety of institutions increased, classification systems and agencies for central control evolved. Still later, the need for reception and classification centers seemed apparent.

Not all such centers operating today are distinct and separate facilities. Quite the contrary. In most States, the reception and classification function is performed in a section of one of its institutions—usually a maximum security facility. Most new prisoners, therefore, start their correctional experience in the most confining, most severe, and most depressing part of the State's system. After a period of observation, testing, and interviewing, an assignment is made, supposedly reflecting the best marriage between the inmate's needs and the system's resources.

Today 13 separate reception centers for adult felons (most of which are new) are in operation. Their designers have assigned priority to security on the premise that "a new fish is an unknown fish." Generally these institutions are the most depressing and regressive of all recently constructed correctional facilities in the United States, with the possible exception of county jails. Nowhere on the current correctional scene are there more bars, more barbed wire, more electronic surveillance devices, more clanging iron doors, and less activity and personal space. All this is justified on the grounds that the residents are still unknown and therefore untrustworthy. Moreover, their stay will be short.

A notable exception is worthy of brief description. Opened in 1967, the Reception and Medical Center at Lake Butler serves the State of Florida. The plant is campus style with several widely separated buildings occupying 52 acres enclosed with a double cyclone fence with towers. There is a great deal of movement as inmates circulate between the classification building, gymnasium, dining room, clinic, canteen, craft shops, visiting area, and dormitories.

Housing is of two varieties. Three quarters of the men are assigned to medium security units scattered around the campus. One maximum security building accommodates the rest.

Men not specifically occupied by the demands of the classification process are encouraged to take part in a variety of recreational and self-betterment activities conducted all over the campus. An open-air visiting patio supplements the indoor visiting facility that ordinarily is used only in inclement weather. Relationship between staff and inmates appears casual. Movement is not regimented. Morale appears high, and escapes are rare.

The contrast between this reception center and one in an adjacent State is vivid. In the Medical and Diagnostic Center at Montgomery, Ala., the inmate spends the entire reception period in confinement except when he is being tested or interviewed. Closed circuit television replaces contact with correctional personnel—a contact especially needed during reception. In that center escapes and escape attempts are almost as common as suicide efforts. A visitor, observing the contrast between these two neighboring facilities, might speculate on the relative merits of the new correctional artifact vis-a-vis the responding human being and be heartened that man is not yet obsolete in this technological age.

As physical plants contrast, so does the sophistication of the reception and classification process. Diagnostic processes in reception centers range from a medical examination and a single inmate-caseworker interview without privacy to a full battery of tests, interviews, and psychiatric and medical examinations, supplemented by an orientation program. The process takes from 3 to 6 weeks, but one competent warden feels that 4 or 5 days should be sufficient. It seems unlikely, considering the limitations of contemporary behavioral science, that the process warrants more than a week.

3

CENSUS OF STATE CORRECTIONAL FACILITIES

LAW ENFORCEMENT ASSISTANCE ADMINISTRATION, U.S. DEPARTMENT OF JUSTICE

This ... report presents selected findings from the Census of State Correctional Facilities, conducted in January 1974 for the Law Enforcement Assistance Administration (LEAA) by the U.S. Bureau of the Census. The census, the first attempt to collect data on these facilities, obtained information on the types of institutions and the number of inmates housed therein, the age of physical plants, institutional payroll and operating expenses, staff personnel, and programs and services provided.

State correctional facilities were counted only if they were administratively separate institutions, i.e., administratively capable of providing a unique inmate count and information on their own staffing pattern, payroll, and budget. Data on facilities that were unable to provide these figures were subsumed with those of a parent institution even though a particular entity or entities may have been geographically apart and functionally distinct from the larger facility. As a result, information on some institutions, particularly those classified as closed prisons, encompasses figures for the parent entity and one or more administratively related facilities; data for the latter are not given separately. Although an administratively separate institution may have served several correctional functions, it was counted only once and was self-classified as to type of institution by what it considered its primary function.

The Census of State Correctional Facilities was undertaken as part of the National Prisoner Statistics (NPS) program. Based on a voluntary reporting system, the NPS program was instituted to col-

Source: From *Census of State Correctional Facilities, 1974, Advance Report:* National Prisoner Statistics, Special Report Number SD–NPS–SR–1 (Washington, D.C.: U.S. Government Printing Office, July 1975), pp. iii–14 (editorial adaptations).

lect and interpret data on State and Federal correctional institutions and their inmates. The program was initiated by the Bureau of the Census in 1926 and was transferred to the Bureau of Prisons in 1950 and to LEAA in 1971. Since 1972, the Bureau of the Census, acting as collecting agent for LEAA, has had responsibility for compiling the statistical data required.

GENERAL FINDINGS

As of January 1974, there were about 600 administratively separate correctional facilities in the United States operated or funded by State governments. These facilities, which housed almost 190,000 prisoners, ranged from small community centers, or halfway houses, whose inmates often held jobs in the community, to closed prisons containing upwards of several thousand securely confined inmates. Staff varied in size from a few persons to as many as 500, and annual expenditures ranged from a few thousand dollars to several million dollars.

Conditions were found to vary greatly from institution to institution, even among facilities of the same type. In many cases this appeared to result not from the specific requirements of the clientele but from disparities in available resources. Some institutions were relatively new and benefited from the latest innovations in prison design; others were characterized by physical facilities built years ago. Some suffered from overcrowding and others, even if underutilized in terms of physical capacity, were handicapped by inadequate staff, budget, and programs. In many institutions, a variety of rehabilitative programs and services was available.

Type of Institution and Location

The January 1974 census recorded, compiled, and processed data on 592 facilities, or approximately 97 percent of all the facilities that had been identified as administratively separate State correctional institutions.[16] By type and number, these institutions were divided into 401 prisons, 158 community centers, and 33 classification or medical centers.[17] Facilities classified as prisons were further subdivided into 172 closed prisons, 80 road camps, 41 prison farms, 41 forest camps, and 67 institutions that were designated as "other prisons" and comprised certain vocational training centers, reformatories, honor camps, youthful offender facilities, and State-operated community correctional centers, i.e., jails, in Alaska and Connecticut. All together, the various types of prisons accounted for 9 out of every 10 of the 187,982 inmates reported as being held by State correctional institutions on January 31, 1974.

About half of all State correctional facilities in the United States were located in the South, with the remaining institutions about equally distributed among the other three regions of the country. North Carolina had the largest number of facilities (76), followed by Florida (46), Virginia (38), and California (35).

Every State, except Mississippi, had at least one institution classified as a closed prison, the type of facility conforming most closely to the popular image of a prison, and these institutions accommodated 63 percent of all inmates in State correctional facilities. In Idaho, Montana, Nevada, Rhode Island, and South Dakota, a closed prison was the only administratively distinct correctional facility operated by the State, and consequently housed all inmates in each of these jurisdictions.[18] In 33 other States, a majority, usually a substantial majority, of the State's inmate population was confined in a closed prison, and in still others the largest single number of inmates was so held. North Carolina had the most closed prisons (20), followed by California (11) and New York (10). However, North Carolina's closed prisons typically were much smaller than those in either California or New York.

Prison farms housed 14 percent of all inmates in State correctional facilities. All of Mississippi's inmate population were accommodated in a single institution classified as a prison farm, and a majority of inmates in Arkansas, Louisiana, and Texas was held in one or more such farms. All together, 28 of the 41 prison farms in the Nation were in the South; Texas, with 10, had the largest number. Prison farms in the South accounted for about 94 percent of all inmates held in such institutions. Among non-Southern States, only Indiana and North Dakota confined more than 10 percent of their inmate populations on prison farms; there were no administratively separate institutions classified as prison farms in any of the jurisdictions in the Northeast.

Nine percent of the Nation's inmate population was accommodated in facilities classified as "other prisons." Most were housed in institutions in 10 States—California, Connecticut, Florida, Georgia, Maryland, Missouri, New Jersey, New York, Oklahoma, and Texas—each of which had 800 or more inmates in such facilities. Relative to the total inmate population in each State, Alaska and Connecticut had the largest number of inmates in "other prisons," principally in State-operated community correctional centers. The proportion in Alaska was 85 percent; it was 38 percent in Connecticut. Missouri also held 38 percent of its inmates in "other prisons."

Most of the States had no administratively separate classification or medical centers, and only two States had more than two—North Carolina, with five, and New York, with four. These facilities, where inmates are tested and evaluated to determine the correctional setting most conducive to rehabilitation, held 5 percent of all inmates in State correctional institutions.

Community centers also accommodated 5 percent of the inmates in State correctional facilities. These centers, known variously as halfway houses, service camps, prerelease homes, etc., normally receive inmates nearing the end of their sentences and provide work-release programs designed to facilitate reintegration into society at large. North Carolina had the largest number of such centers (29) and the largest number of inmates accommodated therein. Florida was next. Vermont had the highest proportion of inmates (65 percent) housed in community centers. Other States with at least 10 percent of their inmate populations in community centers were North Carolina (25 percent), Main (21 percent), Hawaii (15 percent), Arizona and Maryland (12 percent), South Carolina (11 percent), and Tennessee (10 percent). Thirteen States, including Ohio and Texas, had no administratively separate State-operated community centers.

Road camps, housing 3 percent of the inmate population in State correctional institutions, were an entirely southern phenomenon, except for one facility in California. Virginia, with 27, had the most, followed by North Carolina, with 15, and Florida and Georgia, each with 13. Virginia also had the highest proportion of its inmate population (37 percent) in road camps; North Carolina had 16 percent and Georgia had 13 percent. Only Alabama and Maryland, in addition to the jurisdictions mentioned above, operated road camps.

Accommodating 1 percent of all inmates in State correctional institutions, forest camps were operated in 12 States. California, with 15, and Michigan, with 10, accounted for about three out of every five forest camps in the Nation. No State housed as many as 10 percent of its inmates in forest camps; Michigan held 9 percent.

Security Confinement Status

All types of institutions, except forest camps, held at least some prisoners in each of the three security classifications: minimum, medium, and maximum. Of the total number of inmates in the 592 facilities, 39 percent were held under maximum security, 34 percent under medium security, and 27 percent under minimum security. Prisoners in maximum-security status constituted a majority of inmates on prison farms and in classification or medical centers. By contrast, all inmates of forest camps and 98 percent of those in community centers were held under minimum security. In closed prisons, 44 percent of the inmates were held in maximum-security status, compared with 18 percent under minimum security.

Authorized Staff Positions

Over 40 percent of all State correctional institutions had fewer than 20 authorized full-time payroll staff positions; by contrast, only 4 percent had 500 or more (Table 3).

As would have been expected, the number of authorized full-time payroll staff positions varied by type of institution. Closed prisons had the largest number of such positions, followed by prison farms. Of 153 institutions reporting 100 or more authorized staff positions, 106 were closed prisons and 21 were prison farms; of 22 institutions with 500 or more authorized positions, 19 were closed prisons and 2 were prison farms. By contrast, none of the road or forest camps reporting on staff had as many as 50 authorized positions; only 2 of the community centers had 50 or more. Most community centers had between 10 and 19 staff positions. The majority of road camps had fewer than 20 positions; the majority of forest camps had fewer than 10.

In most institutions, the full-time payroll staff consisted largely of custodial personnel. As shown in Table 4, the average number of

TABLE 3
Number and Percent of Institutions, by Number of Authorized Full-Time Payroll Staff Positions

Number of Authorized Full-Time Payroll Staff Positions	Number of Institutions	Percent of Total
Total	592	100
Less than 5	18	3
5–9	80	14
10–19	152	26
20–29	47	8
30–39	38	6
40–49	13	2
50–99	38	6
100–199	54	9
200–299	32	5
300–399	30	5
400–499	15	3
500 or more	22	4
Not available	53	9

TABLE 4
Number of Custodial Personnel, by Type of Institution

Type of Institution	Number of Institutions	Number of Custodial Personnel	Average Number of Custodial Personnel Per Institution
All institutions	592	37,929	64
Classification or medical centers	33	2,253	68
Community centers	158	1,131	7
All prisons	401	34,545	86
Prison farms	41	3,247	79
Road camps	80	1,277	16
Forest camps	41	329	8
Closed prisons	172	26,357	153
Other prisons	67	3,335	50

such personnel varied widely by type of institution, from a low of 7 in community centers to a high of 153 in closed prisons.

Monthly Payroll

For the 579 State correctional institutions providing the relevant information, the aggregate monthly payroll exceeded $50 million. It ranged from less than $4,000 in 22 institutions to $300,000 or more in 51 facilities. A majority of all institutions had monthly payrolls of less than $20,000; only 16 percent had payrolls of $200,000 or more.

Operating Expenses

Operating expenses for the latest fiscal year, reported by 547 institutions, ranged from less than $50,000 to more than $3 million. Expenditures made by each institution were a function not only of its type and size, but also of such factors as the proportion of inmates in each security confinement status, the amount of labor contributed by inmates toward operating and maintaining the facility, the existence of prison industry, the scope of rehabilitative programs, and the extent to which volunteers performed certain functions.

Not surprisingly, closed prisons accounted for two-thirds of all State correctional facilities with annual operating expenditures of $1 million or more. One hundred and sixteen out of 161 closed prisons reporting on expenditures spent sums of that magnitude; 75 reported expenditures of $3 million or more. Twenty-two prison farms and 13 classification or medical centers also had annual operating expenses of $1 million or more. No road or forest camp and only one community center spent that much. A majority of road or forest camps had annual operating expenses of between \$150,000 and \$299,999; for community centers, the figure was between \$75,000 and \$199,000.

Physical Plant and Quarters

At the time of the January 1974 census, 6 percent of the 577 facilities reporting the date when construction was first begun on the site had been built after 1969, 41 percent dated from the 1949–69 period, 32 percent from 1924–48, 11 percent from 1899–1923, and 6 percent from 1874–98. Twenty-four facilities, 19 of them closed prisons, had been built before 1874. Facilities occupied by closed prisons were older than those of any other type of institution. About 7 of every 10 closed prisons occupied facilities on which initial construction had begun before 1949; only 8 closed prisons had been built after 1969. In contrast, a majority of facilities occupied by road camps, forest camps, "other prisons," and classification or medical centers had been built after 1948.

All together, State correctional facilities in the United States contained 116,708 cells and 2,055 other inmate quarters, including dormitories. Of the total number of cells, about 86 percent were designed for one inmate, 13 percent were for two inmates, and 1 percent was for three or four inmates. Accommodations for inmates varied by type of institution. Although 45 closed prisons had no one-inmate cells, cells of that size predominated in the closed facilities, as well as in classification or medical centers. Quarters other than cells were found in a majority of institutions of all types except the classification or medical centers; they were the only type of accommodation for housing inmates in forest camps and the principal type in road camps and community centers. A reported 503 of the 592 State correctional institutions had at least one type of inmate accommodation other than cells; the median number in these 503 institutions was 3; median capacity was 50.

Amenities in inmate quarters varied widely by the size of the accommodation, with "other" quarters being somewhat better equipped than cells. Toilets and sinks typically were available in cells in at least 83 percent of all institutions with such accommodations, but other cell amenities were seldom found in more than half the total number of facilities. There was some relationship between certain amenities and the size of the cell. Thus, one-inmate cells normally were more likely to have had reading lamps than cells accommodating two inmates, and the latter, in turn, were equipped with reading lamps relatively more often than three- or four-inmate cells. On the other hand, the three- or four-inmate quarters were most apt to have been equipped with a fan, and the one-inmate cell was least likely to have had such an amenity.

A majority of all institutions with "other" quarters equipped these accommodations with toilets, sinks, drinking fountains, desks and chairs, and fans, and most also had window ventilation. About 45 percent of the institutions with "other" quarters supplied these accommodations with reading lamps and 38 percent provided for ventilation other than that from windows or fans. The availability of amenities differed by type or institution. Irrespective of type, toilets and sinks were usually available within the accommodation; desks, chairs, and reading lamps were less commonly supplied. Forest camps and community centers with "other" quarters were most likely to have equipped them with desks, chairs, and reading lamps. Such amenities were infrequently encountered in road camp accommodations.

Medical Facilities

A majority of all State correctional institutions had a dispensary in which medicines were kept for distribution to inmates upon a physician's order. More than half also had quarters where sick or injured inmates were isolated from the general institutional population. Some institutions had both a dispensary and a sick bay.

Closed prisons were the most likely of all State correctional institutions to have had a medical facility. In fact, only 1 of the 172 closed prisons lacked a dispensary and only 13 were without a sick bay. At the other extreme, dispensaries were found in little more an half of all community centers, and sick bays were provided in fewer than one-fourth of all forest camps. Sick bays also were relatively uncommon in community centers.

Recreational and Other Facilities

Almost all State correctional institutions, irrespective of type, had a general purpose room or rooms either purposely set aside for recreational pursuits or usable for such activity. A majority also had libraries, athletic fields, and barber shops, but only slightly more than one-third had gymnasiums.

Rehabilitative Programs and Services

Most State correctional facilities offered a number of rehabilitative programs and services, but the types of programs and services offered varied markedly by type of institution. For example, fewer than half of all road camps offered drug treatment, vocational assessment, or college degree programs. On the other hand, approximately three-fourths of the closed prisons and community centers provided all 11 of the specific programs and services measured by the canvass.

Religious worship was the most commonly provided service. Ninety-six percent of all State correctional institutions provided for religious services. Individual counseling was available in 91 percent of the institutions; remedial education, in 89 percent. Least likely to have been offered were drug treatment and college education programs. Nonetheless, drug treatment programs were carried on in 74 percent of all institutions and in 84 percent of all closed prisons; corresponding proportions for college education programs were 65 percent and 77 percent.

In addition to rehabilitative programs offered within the institution, some facilities provided work- or study-release programs that allowed selected inmates to spend part of their time in the community. Some 61 percent of all State correctional facilities had work-release programs; 35 percent had study-release programs. As would have been expected, a far larger proportion of community centers offered such programs than any other type of institution. However, more than half the closed prisons had work-release programs and slightly more than one-third provided for study-release programs.

Prison Industry

Prison industries were operated in 164 of the 592 State correctional facilities. Such industries grow, process, or manufacture products for use within the correctional system or for sale to other government agencies or on the open market. Prison industries were found most usually in closed prisons and on prison farms. They were operated in only 2 percent of the community centers.

4

PRISON USE: AN INTERNATIONAL COMPARISON

IRVIN WALLER AND JANET CHAN

Authors' Note: The research for this study was sponsored by a contract from the Solicitor General of Canada. The views of the authors do not necessarily represent the view of the Solicitor General of Canada.

Canada has a larger proportion of its population in prison on an average day than most European democracies of a similar size or level of industrialization and urbanization. It has a rate, however, of less than half the lowest estimates for the U.S.A. which does not even have a reliable estimate of the maximum number of persons in prison on any single day of a year. . . . Scandinavian countries and Holland have proportionately many fewer people in prison. Perhaps equally importantly the proportions in prison in each province in Canada vary widely as in the States of Australia or U.S.A.

We will not try to decide between the explanations of why some countries appear to use prison more than others except to comment on the statistical and definitional problems that arise. We will, however, try to present a list of the more cogent explanations, to aid any person interested.

We were led to write this article out of surprise as to the misleading nature of many of the earlier discussions of comparative imprisonment rates. Hogarth (1971, p. 41), in what may otherwise be respected as a classic on sentencing produced clearly erroneous statistics to suggest that Canada used prisons at a rate of 20 per cent above that for the U.S.A. Blumstein and Cohen (1973) suggested that punishment remains at stable levels by examining only those imprisoned in State or Federal institutions thus ignoring nearly 160,000 persons held in local jails. In the same article they examined total imprison-

Source: From "Prison Use: A Canadian and International Comparison", *Criminal Law Quarterly*, Vol. 17 (1974-75), published by Canada Law Book Limited, 80 Cowdray Court, Agincourt, Ontario, Canada M1S 1S5. Pp. 47-71 (editorial adaptations). Reprinted by permission of the authors and publisher.

ment rates for Norway, thus implying a much smaller disparity than really exists between the two countries and found a stability that we will also question. We have been amazed by the number of respected researchers who have quoted these figures and conclusions without question and also by a number of other errors in the compilation of such statistics made by other authors.

Many of these errors arose because the researcher—let alone his readers—were not clear on their definitions. As the dictum of *caveat emptor* must apply, we have set out below some definitions to look for, when discussing imprisonment rates. This semantic detour will also make the reader aware of the limits of our own assumptions.

PRISON[19]

A prison is usually thought to be a place "where persons are deprived of liberty on the grounds that they are believed to have commited a criminal offence". Importantly this means that a penitentiary (Canada), a borstal or detention centre (England), a correctional institution (Ontario) are all prisons. However, Blumstein and Cohen (1973) cut the prison population of the U.S.A. in half by using a definition of prison which omitted local jails—generally believed to be the most inhumane and antiquated part (National Jail Census 1970; Sparks 1971) of the criminal justice system and incidentally the one through which most people pass. A similar interpretation in Canada would result by considering only the penitentiary population, which would reduce our rate by one-third.

Our definition of prison would apply to the substance if not the form of mental hospitals. Indeed, Holland used until very recently legislation whereby criminals who were thought to be insane were sentenced by a court to a mental hospital for a fixed period after they had been "punished" for a fixed period in a prison. Should one include mental hospitals? If so does one distinguish involuntary admission and those detained "voluntarily" under the threat of involuntary certification? Such semantics are central to our discussion as there may be more persons involuntarily held in mental hospitals in Canada than in prison as is the case in many other countries. Also, several authors have pointed to an inverse relationship between the number of people in prison and in mental hospitals (Biles, Penrose, Brenner).

Should one include juvenile institutions or special schools; how does one distinguish between a training school, an approved school or a residential treatment centre administered by a welfare agency, but receiving children originally found delinquent under the Juvenile

Delinquents Act? From 1968 to 1970 the number of juveniles involuntarily incarcerated in Canada dropped by 30.9 per cent. One of the principal reasons was the change in name and philosophy of schools in B.C. and Alberta. Some juveniles were moved to group homes and some to minimum security camps, but the major change was in administrative responsibility. While it is generally agreed that those are more humane and less bureaucratic, the juveniles are still detained.

Should one include those adults detained for a crime in a prison before trial? Approximately one-third in Denmark and one-half in Holland of persons held in prison are awaiting trial (Great Britain Expenditure Committee Report 1971). In several European countries periods of two or three years on pre-trial, or so-called preventive, detention are quite common. This in itself can be misleading as they may have been convicted in the court of first instance, but are awaiting courts of second instance. Apparently the court of second instance rarely changes the earlier decision so that the difference may be due at least partially to differences in the case with which appeals can and are made.

Another factor is the number of persons in prison for civil debt and the non-payment of fines.[20] It is not always clear whether these two categories are included and they can account for a large proportion of the prison population.

In many States of the U.S.A. no statistics are kept routinely for local lock-ups where persons may be detained before trial or sentenced to terms of up to 30 days. However, recently (National Jail Census 1970, p. 1) it was found that 52 per cent of the "jail" population or 25 per cent of the total "prison" population in the U.S.A. were pre-trial detainees.

Most countries do not include police cells in their statistics as persons are thought to spend only 24 to 48 hours there. However, practice in some countries, and legislation in others, allows persons to be held for periods of often more than a week. The National Jail Census (1970) in the U.S.A. did not include drunk tanks. Again considering the number of persons arrested each day, these may make a significant difference to the total. Undoubtedly there is a need to carry out a census that includes police cells.

PERSON

A rate must reflect the number of persons in prison relative to the total number of persons within that jurisdiction or country but what is a person? Half the population is female, yet women are only infrequently arrested for "serious" offences, and therefore unlikely to be imprisoned. Of males many are children or outside the crime-prone age groups of say 15 to 40, thus unlikely to be arrested for crime. Taking into account only the most readily available demographic variables—age, sex and race, the population at risk can be markedly reduced. As Greenberg (1973) has suggested in addition, "including socio-economic factors, previously incarcerated offenders are only marginally more likely to be reincarcerated than 'others not previously convicted from the same walk of life.'" It is thus crucial to define what is meant by a person or a person at risk.

Another measure used is that of the number of beds or cells available. Unfortunately the definition of a bed is unclear. In a prison in the Ivory Coast, prisoners sleep on the ground as they would in their own home. In England, placing three men in a cell is a normal or at least not an abnormal practice. In Canada there is considerable flexibility in the number of places available for similar reasons, though most inmates live in single cells.

A person has the unique characteristic of being easily defined and therefore counted. In addition, he is the person who undergoes the prison experience, which is usually why we ask the questions in the first place. Specifically:

    (i) is person restricted to adults, if so at what age does a person become adult and does it include persons of both sexes? Just in Canada there are five provinces with the age for juvenile delinquency at under 16, there is one at 17 and three at 18. In 1972 the number of juveniles known to be incarcerated in training schools on one day was 1,877 or nearly 10 per cent of what we will later estimate as the total prison population of Canada.

    (ii) does person mean both males and females?

    (iii) does person mean all ages? Eighteen per cent of the Canadian population is under 10, effectively ineligible to go to a "prison". Generally this proportion does not vary between developed countries. However, developing countries tend to have much larger proportions of their population in younger age groups.

At the most basic level, the arguments against imprisonment in official documents have emphasized the need to use alternatives such as probation, fines or absolute discharge for first offenders. England has recently extended its legislation for those under 21 to all first offenders so that they can only be sent to prison after all alternatives have been exhausted.

Prison is thus seen as a measure of last resort. Should a comparative study take this into account? Should we be comparing the proportion of persons in prison with previous convictions? A recent study (Waller 1974) not only confirmed that four out of five penitentiary inmates had previously been sentenced to imprisonment, but the majority of the other one in five had been previously arrested, some as juveniles. Once again the difficulty lies in the question as to what information is available.

LENGTH OF SENTENCE

It is generally believed that the major decisions on the use of imprisonment are taken in the courts.

Let us assume now that we have decided on "persons", "prisons" and "population." How would we measure length of sentence to reflect on the use of prison? In jurisdictions within a definite sentencing structure, the problems are complicated enough.

(1) Does one take the average of sentences given in court? If so, does one take aggregate sentence *per* person ignoring concurrent sentences but adding consecutive sentences?

(2) What does one do about "dead" time or the period of time spent in "prison" before sentence?

(3) What does one do about remission, which, whether legally defined as statutory or earned is acknowledged by most to be automatic and results in substantial reductions in time served?

(4) What does one do about full and temporary parole?

The best way to manage this problem would be to compute the length of time served in prison. Most jurisdictions are hybrid between definite and indeterminate or indefinite. Typically there is some form of conditional release, ticket of leave or parole. In some jurisdictions, the sentence is largely statutorily determined and the parole authority decides the release date. It is grossly misleading in indeterminate jurisdictions to talk about the mean sentence as the average of the maximum terms, when with few or no exceptions, the parole authority releases men before even a third of this maximum sentence is served.

On the other hand the mean time served before release may be confusing, as a large proportion of the offenders may be reincarcerated during their period of conditional release without incurring a new sentence. In many jurisdictions including Canada, there is a provision for a period of living under conditions similar to those for parole. However, the mandatory parole starts after the normal release date from the institution. In these cases a "technical violation" can lead to an additional period of time in the institution. In Canada, the provisions for mandatory supervision result in an additional period of 25 per cent of the original time served before the start of mandatory supervision (Waller 1974).

In the case of both parole by application and mandatory parole, a new "criminal" offence may result in addition to the period for violation of the condition to a new sentence. Return to finish term (TFT) and with new term (WNT) have been shown to depend more on administrative characterization than on the characteristics of the offence or the offender (Takagi and Robison 1969). These authors have also pointed out the growing porportion of offenders in California, who are held as a result of the Adult Authority rather than decisions taken in a court as it would be known in Canada or England.

However, the criminal justice system is normally activated by a member of the public and only a small proportion of public crime reports ever reach the court. Also, as we will see, many persons are spending time in prison before the courts have ruled on a sentence, as a result of suspicion of a crime. Length of sentence and time served are thus unsatisfactory measures of the use of prison.

CRIME

If we are considering the relative use of imprisonment, it might be better to allow for the rate of crime in each country. Indeed, some of the earlier comparisons in imprisonment rates used a measurement of crime. Unfortunately, despite the use of apparently similar legal terms, crime is notoriously difficult to define and so to measure.

It has been assumed that legal terms like indictable offence (Evans, 1973, Hogarth 1971), felony or *crime* mean the same in different jurisdictions. For instance, in England as in Canada, indictable refers to a definite group of supposedly more serious offences and some offences can be proceeded with either by indictment or summarily. Where the option lies with the prosecution, it is more than likely that the more serious offences, where a prison term is sought, are proceeded with by indictment.

It is now well recognized (for instance Biderman 1967, National Crime Panel 1974), that only a proportion of occurrences that fulfil the legal definitions of serious (such as FBI crime index) crimes are reported to the police and further that by no means all of these are recorded as crime by the police. In addition only a small proportion of serious crimes recorded by police result in convictions of persons. There is every reason to suppose that these proportions will vary considerably from one jurisdiction to another and so negate inter-jurisdictional comparisons using "crime."

RATE OF IMPRISONMENT

Assuming we know what we mean by "prison" and "persons" but are unable to use length of sentence or crime, we still have not decided what rate to use. Christie (1963) was one of the first to calculate such rates. He used the number of persons in prison on a given day per 100,000 population. He was correctly quoted by Wilkins (1964). Hogarth (1967 and 1971) did not follow the same definitions and has continued an illusion of higher Canadian imprisonment rates than the facts warrant. Hogarth's rate is difficult to derive, but presumably is the number of persons admitted during a year, though he may have used the wrong denominator—population age 16 and over instead of total population.

Logically a rate includes a number of persons relative to another count of persons. Either of these counts may be (i) static, or (ii) flow. By static is meant the count on one day of persons in prison or persons in the population. By flow is meant the number of persons passing through—admitted or released. In Canada in 1971, there were approximately 36,000 persons sentenced in an adult court to prison (C.l.). This estimate may include some persons sentenced twice. Whereas, on any one day there were approximately 20,000 in prison.

We have discussed the semantic problems surrounding ideal comparisons. The next question is pragmatic. What is available? What is reliable? What is valid in the light of our discussion?

Most countries have information on prisoners in total including males and females, adults and juveniles, sentenced and those awaiting trial. Most countries have statistics on the total population. For both these items definitions can be applied uniformly across different jurisdictions. Unfortunately any further subdivision would require new research in individual countries. We have therefore had to abandon the ideal comparison even at the level of providing rates for males and females broken down by age group, degree of urbanization and by socioeconomic status—factors well known to be related to the rate of police-recorded crime. We have adopted a comparison using the total number of persons in prisons on an average day compared to the total population of the same country.

We feel that prison can be adequately defined in most countries as a place, where persons are deprived of liberty on the grounds they have committed a specified offence. We have excluded mental hospitals and police lock-ups, but have included juvenile institutions and particularly jails. Our person is a human being in a developed country of any age, sex or race. Our rate is static as it looks at numbers in prison on one day or an average day, although we will make some comparisons over time. It does not define crime except to include all behaviour bringing a person into a prison rather than to a psychiatrist. Pretrial detention, length of the courts' sentence and parole decisions, affect the numbers in prison on one day and so are partially and implicitly taken into account.

Finally this information is usually, if not easily, available for several countries.

Indeed, in several instances figures were taken initially from a U.N. Study, but verified with the country itself. The Crime Prevention and Criminal Justice Section of the United Nations Secretariat initiated in 1972, a project to establish an annual census of prison population. The survey consisted of a simple summation of numbers in prison according to sex and whether the prisoner was convicted or awaiting trial. The data were collected on the basis of responses to a questionnaire which was sent to the national correspondents.

COMPARATIVE RATES

Based on the statistics in Table 5, Canada has approximately half the rate for U.S.A. of the number of persons in prison *per* head of the population on an average day. However Canada has a rate four times that of Holland. Although in 1965 this rate for the U.S.A. was 208.0 (President's Commission), its rate in 1970 was 200.0 slightly above that of Poland.

The Commonwealth countries of Australia, New Zealand, Canada and England and Wales have rates relatively close to each other, as do the Latin countries of France, Italy and Spain. However, the Scandinavian countries vary widely.

While we have provided a nominal remand rate in parentheses this should be treated with extreme caution, as it is not possible to derive a unique definition of remand, which is applicable to all jurisdictions. The statistics are included as they are meaningful in comparisons between certain jurisdictions, say, in the Commonwealth and within jurisdictions over time.

In Table 6, the various countries, provinces and States have been grouped into four arbitrary categories. Quebec is usually believed to be a heavy user of prison. This comes from examining proportions of persons convicted who are sent to prison. However, by our definition, it has one of the lowest imprisonment rates in Canada—nearly 15 points below Ontario and 40 points below British Columbia. New Brunswick however, has a rate as high as Alberta and Saskatchewan. There are four States, including California, which have rates over two and one-half times that of Canada. There are also five States, three of which are close to Canada's South Eastern border, that have rates close to that of Quebec and nearly half that of Canada. There is thus a huge disparity within the U.S.A., that is almost as large as that within Canada or indeed Australia.

In Figure 1, the States in the U.S.A. have been plotted on a map.

TABLE 5

Selected Countries Ranked in Order of the Number of Persons in Prison per 100,000 persons in the Population for the most Recent Year Information was available

Rank	Country	Year	Imprisonment Rate Per 100,000 Population	(Remand Rate Per 100,000 Pop.)
1	U.S.A.[3]	1970	406,531/203,200,000 = 200.0	
2	Poland[1]	1972	62,748/ 33,070,000 = 189.7	(88.8)
3	Australia[1]	1972	16,615/ 12,960,000 = 128.2	(9.2)
4	Finland[1]	1972	4,947/ 4,630,000 = 106.8	(11.0)
5	New Zealand[6]	1972	2,643/ 2,850,000 = 92.7	—
6	Canada[1]	1972	19,668/ 21,850,000 = 90.0	(11.0)
7	England & Wales[5]	1971	39,708/ 48,900,000 = 81.3	(6.1)
8	Denmark[2]	1971	3,350/ 4,800,000 = 69.8	(22.0)
9	Sweden[2]	1971	4,977/ 8,090,000 = 61.4	(6.9)
10	France[1]	1972	31,573/ 51,700,000 = 61.1	(21.8)
11	Italy[1]	1972	27,812/ 54,350,000 = 51.2	(27.8)
12	Japan[1]	1972	49,241/105,990,000 = 46.5	(7.9)
13	Spain[1]	1972	13,826/ 34,680,000 = 39.9	(16.6)
14	Norway[4]	1971	1,432/ 3,870,000 = 37.1	(13.7)
15	Netherlands[2]	1971	2,919/ 13,120,000 = 22.4	(10.4)

Sources:

1. UN Census of Prison Population (1972) Population as of December 1, 1972.
2. Great Britain Expenditure Committee Report (1971) Population as of January 1, 1971.
3. Estimated from total of State & Federal Institution, local jails and juvenile institutions. Sources: *National Prisoners Statistics Bulletin*, US Bureau of Prison #47 (1972); *National Jail Census* (1970) US Department of Justice; *Children in Custody* (1971) US Department of Justice. In 1965, the equivalent statistics were 404,049/194,240,000 = 208.0 (US Task Force Report 1967).
4. Report of the Department of Justice, New Zealand (1973). Average daily population.
5. Home Office. Report on the work of the Prison Department (1971). Average daily population.
6. Remand rate is not restricted to those awaiting arraignment or their first trial. In some European jurisdictions such as Italy, this includes those awaiting a hearing in a court of second instance.

It is interesting to note the cluster of North Eastern States that have rates close to those of Quebec and Newfoundland. Given the sparsity of population in the territories any conclusion from similarities between them and the Southern States are tempting, but tenuous.

TRENDS IN COMPARISONS

One cannot use statistics for one year without realizing that there are substantial fluctuations in rates over time. Some countries are surprisingly stable as Christie has shown for Norway; others vary irregu-

TABLE 6
Countries and Jurisdictions Grouped as to High, Medium or Low Rates of Persons in Prison Per Head of Population

Ranges	Countries	Canadian Provinces	Australian States	U.S.A.
Extra High Over 250/100,000	—	Yukon and West Territories	—	California, Florida, Georgia, Nevada
High 150-249/100,000	Poland, U.S.A.	—	—	19 States mainly in South and West, but including Texas, New York and Michigan
Medium 75-149/100,000	Australia, Canada, England & Wales, Finalnd, New Zealand	Nova Scotia, New Brunswick, P.E.I., Ontario, Saskatchewan, Alberta, B.C., Manitoba	N.S.W., Tasmania, South Australia, West, Australia	20 States mainly in North and East, including Illinois, New Jersey, Ohio, Pennsylvania
Low 0-74/100,000	Denmark, France, Italy, Japan, Netherlands, Norway, Spain, Sweden	Quebec, Newfoundland	Queensland, Victoria	Connecticut, Hawaii, Massachusetts, North Dakota, Vermont

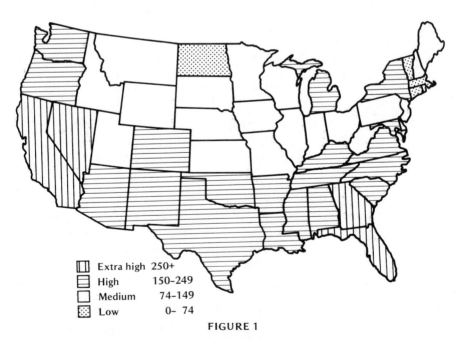

Extra high 250+
High 150–249
Medium 74–149
Low 0– 74

FIGURE 1

Imprisonment rates in the United States 1970. (Number of persons in prison per 100,000 population) (See Appendix A and Bibliography for sources.)

larly as Finland. Several writers have used data on these rates over a number of years. Regrettably they do not all use the same definitions and so our comparison for Canada has had to be restricted to England and Wales, Norway, Finland and Canada. Similar trends but gross approximations are available for France and the U.S.A., but always omitting a crucial group such as juveniles or persons in local jails.

In Figure 2, we have compared trends over time for Canada, England and Wales, Finland and Norway. Norway follows a similar pattern to Sweden, which was therefore not included. The figure illustrates the lack of consistent pattern with major changes usually associated with societal dislocations such as the depression or wars. We will not attempt an interpretation ourselves. However, we should point out that these data appear to refute the hypothesis that the use of imprisonment remains constant over time.

In Figure 3, we have tried to provide the information in more detail for Canada. This table does not show the recent upsurge in the penitentiary population, which would have taken the Canadian rate over 100/100,000, but it does illustrate the substantial drop in the use of prisons at the provincial level in the last ten years. A downswing similar to the early 1930's and 1940's.

EXPLANATIONS

Some take delight in drawing macro-sociological conclusions from data such as these. We would caution against an over theoretical stance, as some of the explanations appear simple. There are certain important constraints on trends in imprisonment rates. All the countries which we have chosen for the comparison have some sort of relatively identifiable institutions called prisons. They also have some sort of Criminal Code and probably other statutes more numerous than the Criminal Code which contain similar penal provisions. All these countries have been influenced by industrialization, money economies and bureaucratization. There is usually a limit to the number of persons who can be placed in the institution at one paraticular time although the point at which that limit is reached is relative and varies from one country to another. Institutions technically require a number of years to build, let alone be planned, so that leaps downwards are much easier than sudden leaps upwards unless it is to return to a previous level of imprisonment.

We have had an opportunity to hear the views of some people from these countries on the rank order of imprisonment rates. The following are some of the factors which seem to be associated with the variations. Based on the information we have been able to col-

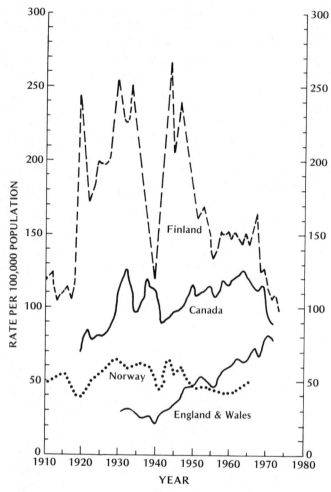

FIGURE 2.

Number of persons in prison per 100,000 population in Canada, England and Wales, Finland and Norway (1920 to present).

lect or would have been able to collect within a short period of time, we would not be justified in going beyond our data to try and identify which of these are the more important explanations.

1. Level of Violence in the Country

The work of Sellin and Wolfgang (1964) has emphasized in the United States that personal injury is considered to be very much more serious than property loss in the way that the public assesses

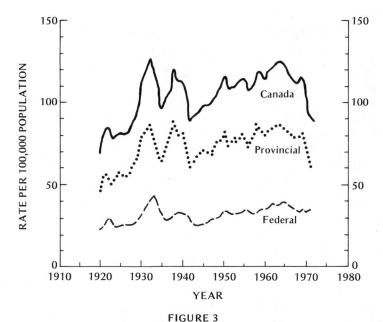

FIGURE 3

Number of persons in prison per 100,000 population in Canada. (1920 to present) Trends in Provincial and Federal Institutions.

the seriousness of a crime. In most jurisdictions offences involving violence have not only higher maximums but the sentences given in court tend to be longer. It is therefore no surprise that those countries with higher murder rates (U.S.A. and Finland)[21] and, therefore, presumably more violence tend to have more people in prison. The international comparisons carried out for the President's Commission on violence *per* 100,000, in the United States pointed out that the United States had more homicides per 100,000 of the population than Finland which had more than Canada which had more than England and Wales. This ranking is similar to the relative ranking on the use of imprisonment.

2. Status of Alcohol and Drugs in the Jurisdiction

The President's Commission on Law Enforcement and Criminal Justice pointed to the large number of prisoners who were in U.S. prisons for public drunkenness and similar offences related to alcohol. In the low imprisonment rate countries, however, the way a country responds to drunken drivers is another factor that could be important.

3. Attitudes to Crime and Criminal Justice

Attitudes to crime and the criminal justice system are also important determinants. These include the attitudes of the public in determining whether they will report an offence and push for severe penalties. These must be contrasted with the quantitatively less important action of the police in deciding to arrest a person, the action of prosecutors and finally to the views of judges and parole boards. It is possible that the extent to which the country has been urbanized and therefore its levels of literacy and advanced education, may effect the level of imprisonment, through their effect on both crime and attitudes to crime.

4. Alternatives to Prison

Undoubtedly the alternatives to imprisonment, particularly availability of probation, have a significant impact on the number of people in prison. Another factor that must not be overlooked is preventive detention and bail provisions. Another group of explanations relates to the use of mental hospitals.

5. War and Amnesty

War may have an effect in two directions, (i) in increasing the prison population if a country is invaded by an outsider, or (ii) decreasing the prison population if the men are required in the army. Amnesty is a more general way of controlling the prison population in certain countries. In Italy, from 1969 to 1970, there was a drop in the prison population from 34,509 to 22,117. This resulted from an amnesty. There are similar examples to this in France and Finland.

CONCLUSION

We have discussed some of the key elements in deciding what definitions to use to compare countries' or States' use of prison. We have compared static rates for recent years and examined some trends over time. We have found Canada with a rate of 93.3 persons in prison *per* 100,000 persons in the population to have a rate similar to that of other Commonwealth countries and northern rural U.S. States, but much higher than southern European or Scandinavian countries and much lower than Finland or the more populous U.S. States. We have listed a few of the more important explanations and challenged the reader and hopefully other researchers to think about these reasons.

The question still remains as to whether these variations are justified. The variations in number hide huge variations in conditions and costs. Given the little that systematic analysis has shown us about criminal justice dispositions, it is unlikely that these variations are associated with any extra protection, reduction in crime or indeed retributive relief for the public. It is also unlikely that these disparities are the result of equal consideration before the law. While the discretion to place a person in prison is human, it is not necessarily just or humane.

APPENDIX A
Comparative Rates for Candadian, Australian and U.S. Jurisdictions

(i) Comparative Rates for Provinces in Canada

Country/State	Year	Prison Population	Total Population	Rate Per 100,000 Population
Canada	1971	20,127	21,568,310	93.3
Newfoundland	1971	230	522,104	44.1
Nova Scotia	1971	604	788,960	76.5
New Brunswick	1971	704	634,557	110.9
Prince Edward Island	1971	110	111,641	98.2
Quebec	1971	4,520	6,027,764	75.0
Ontario	1971	6,933	7,703,106	90.0
Manitoba	1971	953	988,247	96.5
Saskatchewan	1971	1,007	926,242	108.7
Alberta	1971	1,739	1,627,874	106.8
British Columbia	1971	2,507	2,184,621	114.8
Yukon	1971	59	18,388	327.8
North West Territories	1971	158	34,807	454.0

(ii) Comparative Rates for Australian States*

State	Year	Prison Population	Total Population	Rate Per 100,000 Population
Western Australia	1970	1,440	1,001,000	143.9
South Australia	1970	921	1,178,000	78.2
Tasmania	1970	386	396,000	97.5
New South Wales	1970	3,953	4,764,000	83.0
Victoria	1970	2,389	3,481,000	68.6
Queensland	1970	1,243	1,820,000	68.3

*All juvenile institutions are excluded.
Source: Personal correspondence with David Biles.

(iii) Comparative Rates for States in the U.S. (1970)

	Rank	State	Prison* Population	State Population	Imprisonment Rate/100,000 Population
Extra	1	Nevada	1,445	488,738	295.5
High	2	Florida	18,599	6,789,443	274.0

(continued)

(iii) Comparative Rates for States in the U.S. (1970)

	Rank	State	Prison* Population	State Population	Imprisonment Rate/100,000 Population
Extra	3	California	52,705	19,953,134	264.2
High	4	Georgia	11,839	4,589,575	258.0
	5	S. Carolina	6,007	2,590,516	231.9
	6	Oklahoma	5,854	2,559,253	228.8
	7	Louisiana	8,235	3,643,180	226.0
	8	Texas	25,051	11,196,730	223.7
	9	Arizona	3,603	1,772,482	203.3
	10	Maryland	7,944	3,922,399	202.5
	11	Alabama	6,808	3,444,165	197.9
	12	Tennessee	6,890	3,924,164	175.6
	13	Virginia	8,064	4,648,494	173.5
High	14	Kentucky	5,542	3,219,311	172.2
	15	N. Carolina	8,549	5,082,059	168.2
	16	New Mexico	1,703	1,016,000	167.6
	17	Michigan	14,868	8,875,083	167.5
	18	New York	29,458	18,190,740	161.9 .
	19	Colorado	3,547	2,207,259	160.7
	20	Arkansas	3,044 (est.)	1,923,295	158.5 (est.)
	21	Oregon	3,287	2,091,385	157.2
	22	Mississippi	3,366	2,216,912	151.8
	23	Washington	5,141	3,409,169	150.8
	24	Ohio	15,105	10,652,017	141.8
	25	New Jersey	10,140	7,168,164	141.5
	26	Missouri	6,371	4,677,399	136.2
	27	Kansas	3,002	2,249,071	133.5
	28	Indiana	6,822	5,193,669	131.4
	29	Nebraska	1,824	1,483,791	122.9
	30	Wyoming	404	332,416	121.7
	31	Idaho	847	713,008	118.8
Medium	32	W. Virginia	2,032	1,744,237	116.5
	33	Wisconsin	4,951	4,417,933	112.1
	34	Pennsylvania	13,189	11,793,909	111.8
	35	Delaware	596	548,104	108.7
	36	Illinois	11,705	11,113,976	105.3
	37	S. Dakota	698	666,257	104.8
	38	Utah	1,013	1,059,273	95.7
	39	Montana	627	694,409	90.3
	40	Iowa	2,438	2,825,041	86.3
	41	Minnesota	3,061	3,805,069	80.4
	42	New Hampshire	577	737,681	78.2
	43	Maine	758 .	993,663	76.3
	44	Massachusetts	4,179	5,689,170	73.5
	45	Connecticut	1,568	3,032,217	51.7
Low	46	N. Dakota	305	617,761	49.3
	47	Hawaii	325	768,913	42.2
	48	Vermont	184	444,732	41.3

Rhode Island, Alaska, D.C. NOT INCLUDED
*Total of State and Federal Institutions and Local Jails, excluding juveniles
Sources: *National Prisoners Statistics Bulletin*, U.S. Bureau of Prison #47 (1972)
National Jail Census (1970) U.S. Department of Justice

APPENDIX B
Figure 2. Sources:

Canada	Prison Statistics:		
	1920–1956	"Statistics of Criminal & Other Offences" Dominion Bureau of Statistics	
	1957–1971	"Correctional Institution Statistics" Statistics Canada	
	1972	Census of Prison Population 1972, A project initiated by the Crime Prevention and Criminal Justice Section of the UN Secretariat.	
	Population Statistics:		
	1920–1961	"Historical Statistics of Canada" Editor: M. C. Urquhart, Macmillian 1965.	
	1962–1972	UN Demographic Year Book	
England and Wales	"Annual Abstract of Statistics", 1950–1973 Central Statistical Office.		
Finland, Norway	Christie, N. (1963).		

Figure 3. Sources:

Same as Figure 1 on Canada.

BIBLIOGRAPHY

Biderman, Albert D.
 1967 "Surveys of Population Samples for Estimating Crime Incidence." The Annals of the American Academy of Political and Social Science, Philadelphia, 374(November):16–33.
Biles, D. and G. Mulligan
 1973 "Mad or Bad?—The Enduring Dilemma." British Journal of Criminology 13, No.3.
Blumstein, A. and J. Cohen
 1973 "A Theory of The Stability of Punishment." The Journal of Criminal Law & Criminology.
Brenner, Harvey M.
 1973 Mental Illness and the Economy. Cambridge, Mass.: Harvard University Press.
Christie, N.
 1963 "Changes in Penal Values." Scandinavian Studies in Criminology, Vol. 2. London: Tavistock Publications.
Courtis, Malcolm C.
 1970 Attitudes to Crime and the Police in Toronto: A report on some survey findings. Toronto, Centre of Criminology.
Cousineau, D. F. and J. E. Veevers
 1972 "Incarceration as a Response to Crime: The Utilization of Canadian Prisons." Canadian Journal of Criminology and Corrections 14, No. 1(January):10–31.

Evans, R., Jr.
    1973   Developing Policies for Public Security and Criminal Justice. Pre-
            pared for the Economic Council of Canada.
Greenberg, D.
    1973   Incidence of Serious Recidivism in Offender Population and Con-
            tribution of Offender Population to Serious Offenses, unpublished.
            Washington, D.C.: Committee for the Study of Incarceration,
            quoted in Robison, 1974.
Harries, Keith D.
    1974   The Geography of Crime and Justice. Toronto: McGraw-Hill Book
            Co.
Hogarth, J.
    1971   Sentencing as a Human Process. Toronto: University of Toronto
            Press.
Hogarth, J.
    1967   "Towards the Improvement of Sentencing in Canada." Canadian
            Journal of Corrections 9, No. 1.
Penrose, L. S.
    1939   "Mental Disease and Crime: Outline of a Comparative Study of
            European Statistics." Medical Psychology XVIII.
Robison, J., et al.
    1974   Alternative Parole Models, unpublished. Berkeley: Criminological
            Research Associates.
Sellin, T. and M. E. Wolfgang
    1964   The Measurement of Delinquency. New York: John Wiley & Sons
            Inc.
Sparks, R. F.
    1971   Local Prisons: The Crisis in the English Penal System. London:
            Heinemann.
Takagi, P. T. and J. Robison.
    1969   "The Parole Violator: An Organizational Reject." Journal of Re-
            search in Crime and Delinquency 6, No. 1:78–86.
Waller, Irvin,
    1974   Men Released from Prison. Toronto: University of Toronto Press.
Wilkins, L. T.
    1964   Social Deviance. London: Tavistock Publications, pp. 82–85.
Wolf, Preben
    1971   "Crime and Development: An International Comparison of Crime
            Rates." Scandinavian Studies in Criminology 3:107–120.

GOVERNMENT PUBLICATIONS

Australia:
Tasmania. Gaols Department. *Report of the Controller of Prisons 1969/70.*
Western Australia. *Prisons Department Annual Report 1968/69.*

Queensland. Prisons Department. *Report of the Comptroller-General of Prisons 1969/70.*
South Australia. *Prisons Department Report 1969/70.*

Canada:
Statistics of Criminal and Other Offences, 1971, Statistics Canada.
Correctional Institution Statistics 1971, Statistics Canada.
Ontario Department of Correctional Services. *Report of the Minister 1971/72.*
Historical Statistics of Canada, edited by M. C. Urquhart, Macmillan, 1965.

Denmark:
Beretning om Faengselsvaesenet I Danmark 1967. Afgivet af Direktoren For Faengselsvaesenet Statsfaengslets Trykkeri I Nyborg 1970.

England and Wales:
Great Britain Home Department, *People in Prison 1969.*
Great Britain Home Department, *Report on the Work of the Prison Department 1971, 1972.*
Great Britain Annual Abstract of Statistics, Central Statistical Office.
House of Commons, First Report from the Expenditure Committee; together with evidence taken before the Environment & Home Office Sub-Committee. Appendix: Probation and After-care (H.C.47). (SBN 10-204772-3) 1971.

Finland:
Criminal Cases Tried by the Courts 1969, Official Statistics of Finland, Helsinki.

Japan:
Summary of the White Paper on Crime 1971. Research and Training Institute of the Ministry of Justice.
Correctional Institutions in Japan 1970. Correction Bureau, Ministry of Justice.
Criminal Justice in Japan 1970. Correction Bureau, Ministry of Justice.

New Zealand:
Report of the Department of Justice for year ended March 31, 1973.

Norway:
Criminal Statistics. Prisoners 1971. Central Bureau of Statistics of Norway, Oslo 1973.

Spain:
Direccion general de instituciones penitenciarias Memoria. Madrid 1972.

Sweden:
The Correctional System 1972. Official Statistics of Sweden. Published by the National Correctional Administration 1973.

United Nations:
UN Demographic Year Book 1971, 1972.

U.S.A.:
Task Force Report: Corrections. Task Force on Corrections.
The President's Commission on Law Enforcement and Administration of Justice, 1967.
U.S. Bureau of Census. *Historical Statistics of the U.S. Colonial Times to 1957.*
U.S. Department of Commerce 1960.
U.S. Bureau of Census. *Statistical Abstract of the U.S. 1971.*
U.S. Bureau of Prisons. *National Prisoner Statistic Bulletin 1971.*
The California Prison, Parole & Probation System. Technical Supplement No. 2.
A special report to the Assembly by James Robison.
National Prisoner Statistics: State Prisoners: Admissions and Releases 1964. U.S. Department of Justice.
National Jail Census 1970, U.S. Department of Justice, Law Enforcement Assistance Administration. National Criminal Justice Information and Statistics Service.
California Bureau of Criminal Statistics. *Crime in California, 1964.*
Children in Custody 1971. A Report on the Juvenile Detention and Correctional Facility Census of 1971. U.S. Department of Justice, Law Enforcement Assistance Administration, National Criminal Justice Information and Statistics Service.

5

CRISIS IN PRISON POPULATIONS

JOHN FLANAGAN

True or False:	T	F
Prison populations are declining in most states.	( )	( )
The increasing use of probation, pre-trial intervention and other diversionary programs is causing prison populations in most states to drop.	( )	( )
In the near future we will be able to close many prison facilities.	( )	( )

In 1973, most professionals would have agreed that the correct answers to the above questions were true. However, in 1975, the correct answers are false, false and false. Despite popular thinking and despite the contrary predictions of the National Advisory Commission on Criminal Justice Standards and Goals, prison populations are rising. They will continue to rise and most states will find it necessary to build new facilities or renovate old buildings they had hoped to close, or both.

There are a number of reasons for this. The major two are that the population at risk is increasing and there is an empirical limit to the proportion of convicted people who can be diverted. In addition, "get tough" policies (mandatory sentences, tough narcotics laws, three times loser laws, etc.) and high unemployment will further contribute to this inevitable increase in prison populations.

Where states are not prepared to accommodate these increases, where no building or renovation has been done for several years, overcrowding will occur. Overcrowding may spark riots and other inmate demonstrations such as were frequent in the early seventies.

Higher prison populations, of course, mean increased costs. As costs skyrocket, correctional administrators may experience a backlash of public criticism. Those who are convinced that prisons should be abolished may see a conspiracy behind the increasing prison

Source: From *American Journal of Corrections*, (November-December 1975): 20–21, 36. Reprinted by permission of the author and publisher.

population. In fact, in one state the parole board has already been accused of conspiring to keep people incarcerated in order to protect the jobs of the correctional officers!

It is important, therefore, that we recognize now that prison populations are increasing all over the country; that we understand why this is happening; that we make the public aware of the impact of "get tough" policies in terms of both social and fiscal costs; and that we take immediate steps to alleviate the bad effects of overcrowded prisons.

WHY PRISON POPULATION WILL RISE

The population at risk is increasing. The peak of the post World War II "baby boom" is now (1975) in the ages of 15–19 and is about to enter the prison age bracket (about 20–30).

The census indicates the distribution of the young population by age in the total U.S. in 1970 was: 0-4 years, 17.2 million; 5-9 years, 20.0 million; 10-14 years, 20.8 million; 15–19 years, 19.1 million; 20-24 years, 16.4 million; and 25-29 years, 13.5 million. The general population at risk (20-30) will reach its peak about 1985, when it will be about 50 percent higher than it was in the late sixties. It will return to the 1975 level about 1995. However, the birth rates in the urban lower class neighborhoods which produce a disproportionately high share of prison populations have not been conforming to the "zero population growth" policy. Because they are just now beginning to experience a reduction in birth rate the population at risk in these neighborhoods will remain high through the rest of the century.

There is an empirical limit to the percentage of convicted people who can be diverted from prison. In the late Sixties, increased use of probation and other new diversionary programs led to a decrease in prison populations. Obviously there were a number of people being incarcerated who were not a threat to society and could be handled as well, or better, by other methods. In California, 51 percent of felony convictions resulted in probation in 1965. When the state agreed to subsidize the cost of good probation services, the percentage of probations began to rise while the prison population dropped. By 1971, 70 percent of felony convictions resulted in probation. Many other states began to emphasize probation.

The success of many states in reducing their prison populations in this way lulled everyone into feeling that many prisons could be closed. However, common sense tells us that the courts will draw the line somewhere. Every conviction cannot result in probation.

The California experience indicated that courts draw the line in the area of 70 percent probations. In California, the probation rate has remained at about 70 percent since 1971. After a probation ceiling is reached, increases in convictions result in increases in *both* probation and prison populations. In other words, an increasing probation population no longer means a decreasing prison population.

For those states that began emphasizing probation much later than California, there may be a time lag before the prison population rises. Increased use of probation may temporarily decrease the prison population, or at least slow its increase, but this decrease will be temporary. An increase in the near future is inevitable.

That prison populations will rise is not only a theoretical model projected from statistics. It is a fact which is already being experienced by many states. A survey of 10 prison systems from all parts of the country, including seven of the largest, shows that after a decade of decreasing prison populations, intake rates reached their lowest points about 1972. By 1974 prison populations were all on the rise (see Table 7). Clearly, increasing prison populations is a national phenomenon.

There is theoretical reason to expect prison population to climb at this time. Durkheim theory predicts that prison rates per 100,000 population will remain relatively constant. Blumstein and Cohen offer some empirical support to the position. Since prison rates in the late Sixties were as low as they were during World War II, this would lead one to expect the prison rate per 100,000 population to increase ("get tough" policy). Although the prison population in absolute numbers has started to increase, it is not yet clear whether the rate is increasing.

However, there are indications that public attitudes are moving toward a "get tough" policy. President Ford is only one of the many people calling for mandatory and longer sentences. Whether or not one agrees with this philosophy, the implications, in terms of its effects on prison population, are clear. Not only will more people enter prison, but they will also spend more time there. There will be more inmates and even more inmate-days. Total inmate-days, of course, are as important in budget and building space considerations as total inmates.

Add the facts that high unemployment tends to increase crime, that the "baby boom" is also going to keep unemployment high for some time, that inflation escalates petty thefts into grand larcenies, and that inflation puts further stresses on the unemployed.

In summary, every indicator—economy, policy, public attitudes, crime rates, prison rates, exhaustion of alternatives and population

TABLE 7
Prison Population Trends

Year	Calif. (2) YEP/CY (1)	Federal (3) YEP/FY (1)	Ill. (4) ADP/CY (1)	Mich. (5) YEP/CY (1)	Minn. (6) YEP/FY (1)	New York (7) YEP/CY (1)	Ohio (8) YEP/FY (1)	Penn. (9) YEP/CY (1)	Texas (10) YEP/CY (1)	Wis. (11) ADP/CY (1)
1962		24,600	10,041		1,602			6,977	12,203	2,978
1963		24,200	10,095		1,448			6,861	12,084	2,885
1964	24,524	23,000	9,824	8,028	1,391	19,439		6,535	12,278	2,892
1965	24,498	22,400	9,397	7,345	1,411	19,073	11,829	6,210	12,845	2,855
1966	25,383	21,000	8,660	6,754	1,268	16,417	11,150	5,843	12,392	2,842
1967	25,388	19,800	8,203	7,037	1,244	14,670	10,393	5,349	12,313	2,706
1968	25,606	20,200	8,030		1,181	13,380	10,403	4,830	12,215	2,652
1969	24,403	20,200	8,262	8,049	1,243	12,998	10,056	5,049	12,622	2,782
1970	22,399	20,700	7,268	9,079	1,294	12,597	9,610	5,458	14,331	2,870
1971	18,391	21,200	6,475	9,547	1,230	12,525	9,369	5,492	15,989	2,755
1972	17,758	21,300	6,196	8,471	1,049	12,444	8,920	4,968	15,719	2,218
1973	20,589	22,800	6,005	7,874	1,008	13,437	7,944	5,378	17,073	2,108
1974	22,711	22,300	6,137	8,639	1,284	14,387	8,516	5,564	16,833	2,380
	June 75 22,688	Oct. 75 24,376	Oct. 75 over 7,400	Oct. 75 10,655	Oct. 75 1,686	Oct. 75 15,800	May 75 10,318	May 75 over 6,000	May 75 17,652	Oct. 75 over 2,959

Notes: (1) ADP = Average Daily Population; YEP = Year End Population; FY = Fiscal Year; CY = Calendar Year. (2) California data by courtesy of Vida Ryan. Excludes Civil Narcotics cases. New parole board has recently been granting relatively many paroles following a couple of years when relatively few paroles were granted. (3) Federal (Bureau of Prisons) data by courtesy of Jerry Collins. Figures are taken from graph and are approximate. Has been at about 23,000 plus or minus a few hundred since May 1973. Expect to increase about 400 or 500 a year in near future. (4) Illinois data by courtesy of Dennis Levandowski. (5) Michigan data by courtesy of Don Matthews and Bill Kine. The decrease of about 1,000 from 1971 to 1972 was in large part a function of changes in drug laws. (6) Minnesota data by courtesy of Jan Schwarz. Minnesota has been encouraging community programs and probation and some sentenced felons are held in county facilities. (7) New York data by courtesy of Henry Donnelly. The decrease of about 2,500 from 1965 to 1966 was in large part a function of removing the criminally insane from corrections. (8) Ohio data by courtesy of Bob Baker. All institutions above capacity in May 1975. (9) Pennsylvania data by courtesy of John Mease. Persons serving sentences of less than five years can be held in local facilities. (10) Texas data by courtesy of Bob Waldron. (11) Wisconsin data by courtesy of Perry Baker.

at risk—points to higher prison populations, greater budget and building needs. If some indicators pointed up, while others pointed down, the prediction might be somewhat cloudy. The various influences might cancel one another out, but where all indicators simultaneously point up, it seems clear that prison populations will go up drastically.

PRISON SPACE NOT AVAILABLE

That institutional space is not available to meet this increase is also clear. Many states followed the advice of the National Advisory Commission on Criminal Justice Standards and Goals which, in 1973, said: " . . . we already have more prison space than we need . . . there is no need to build additional major institutions . . . for at least 10 years." The states that followed this advice exactly are going to have serious trouble in meeting the increase. Others did some building with the idea of phasing out some of the older facilities. For example, the federal system has added about 3,000 beds in recent years. Ohio has done some replacement building and plans a $75 million building project. Michigan has added about 1,700 beds. As the increasing population materializes, they will be less overcrowded than they might have been. But clearly this won't be enough, everyone is going to have problems.

Most prison systems are at capacity and any increase will mean overcrowding. Large increases will be mean excessive overcrowding, which is likely to lead to repeats of the prison riots of the early Seventies. Correctional administrators may be blamed for the population increase, for the lack of adequate facilities, for the increased costs, for the prisoner disturbances and for the court actions resulting from the living conditions produced by the overcrowding. This phenomenon of blaming the victim is well documented in social science literature.

Corrections personnel must revise some goals, make building plans to meet anticipated needs, alert legislators and taxpayers to the expected cost increases, and caution people about the fiscal implications of "get tough" policy decisions. LEAA, which sets national priorities and directs much state spending with the carrot of federal matching funds, must also change some of its priorities to match the needs of the Seventies and Eighties. Catch up building and renovations after years of neglect will be expensive.

All efforts must be made to hold the prison population increase down to a minimum. States that have not made maximum use of probation should do so. Where there are policy choices, such as whether to use mandatory sentences, the policy makers must be told the cost implications of their choices, and correctional professionals must actively and aggressively educate the public. They can talk to civic groups, write letters to the editor of local papers, hold press conferences. The public should be taken out of its complacency.

Most important, LEAA must begin to direct some of its funds into institutional programs.

REFERENCES

Blumstein, A. and J. Cohen
   1973   "A Theory of the Stability of Punishment." Journal of Criminal Law and Criminology 64:198–207.
National Advisory Commission on Criminal Justice Standards and Goals
   1973   Corrections. Washington, D.C.: U.S. Government Printing Office.
President's Commission of Law Enforcement and the Administration of Justice
   1967   The Challenge of Crime in a Free Society. Washington, D.C.: U.S. Government Printing Office.
U.S. Bureau of Census. General Population Characteristics 1970.
   1972   Washington, D.C.: U.S. Government Printing Office.

6

LOCAL
ADULT INSTITUTIONS

NATIONAL ADVISORY COMMISSION ON
CRIMINAL JUSTICE STANDARDS AND GOALS

Remote from public view and concern, the jail has evolved more by default than by plan. Perpetuated without major change from the days of Alfred the Great, it has been a disgrace to every generation.

Colonists brought to the new world the concept of the jail as an instrument of confinement, coercion, and correction of those who broke the law or were merely nuisances. In the early 19th century, the American innovation of the State penitentiary made punitive confinement the principal response to criminal acts and removed the serious offender from the local jail. Gradually, with the building of insane asylums, orphanages, and hospitals, the jail ceased to be the repository of some social casualties. But it[22] continued to house the town's minor offenders along with the poor and the vagrant, all crowded together without regard to sex, age, and history, typically in squalor and misery.

Many European visitors came to examine and admire the new American penitentiaries. Two observers—Beaumont and Tocqueville—also saw, side by side with the new penitentiaries, jails in the old familiar form: ". . .nothing has been changed: disorder, confusion, mixture of different ages and moral characters, all the vices of the old system still exist." In an observation that should have served as a warning, they said:

There is evidently a deficiency in a prison system which offers anomalies of this kind. These shocking contradictions proceed chiefly from the want of unison in the various parts of government in the United States.[23]

By and large, the deficiencies the two travellers found remain today, the intervening decades having brought only the deterioration

Source: From *Corrections* (Washington, D.C.: U.S. Government Printing Office, 1973), pp. 273-288.

of jail facilities from use and age. Changes have been limited to minor variations in the clientele. Jails became residual organizations into which were shunted the more vexing and unpalatable social problems of each locality. Thus, "the poor, the sick, the morally deviant, and the merely unaesthetic, in addition to the truly criminal—all end in jail."[24]

Although larger urban areas have built some facilities for special groups of offenders, in most part of the country a single local institution today retains the dual purposes of custodial confinement and misdemeanant punishment. The most conspicuous additions to the jail's function have been the homeless and the drunks. Thus jails are the catchall for social and law enforcement problems.

Jails are the intake point for our entire criminal justice system. There are more jails than any other type of "correctional" institution. Indeed, the current trend toward the decreased use of confinement in major State institutions promises to increase the size and scope of the burden jails must bear. Perhaps this is a short-term expedient that will not become permanent. There are some faint stirrings of hope that it will not be so. For the first time since the colonial era, attention is being given to the place where social problems originate—the community—as the logical location for solving these problems.

MAJOR CHARACTERISTICS OF THE JAIL

A jail census conducted in 1970 by the U.S. Bureau of the Census under an agreement with the Law Enforcement Assistance Administration found 4,037 jails meeting the definition of "any facility operated by a unit of local government for the detention or correction of adults suspected or convicted of a crime and which has authority to detain longer than 48 hours."[25] These institutions ranged from New York City's festering "Tombs" to the infrequently utilized small municipal lockup.

With more than 4,000 jails, implementing recommendations and standards delineated in this chapter will require localities to make precise specification of their needs and resources. The prescriptive content of this chapter will consist of elements that may be combined into a suitable solution for any given situation. There is no single answer to the problems of jails.

Local control, multiple functions, and a transient, heterogeneous population have shaped the major organizational characteristics of jails. Typically, they are under the jurisdiction of the country government. In most instances, the local area has neither the necessary tax base from which to finance a jail adequately nor sufficient size to justify even the most rudimentary correctional programs. Local control inevitably has meant involvement with local politics. Jails are left in a paradoxical situation: localities cling tenaciously to them but are unwilling or unable to meet even minimal standards. "The problem of American jails, put most concisely, is the problem of local control."[26]

Beyond their formally acknowledged tasks of correction and detention, jails have been adapted to perform a variety of "social welfare" tasks and provide easy answers to law enforcement problems. For example, Stuart Queen, a jail critic of 50 years ago, noted the "floater custom" in California counties by which transients were arrested, brought to the jail, and from there "ordered to disappear."[27] Similarly, Sutherland and Cressey observed the "Golden Rule disposition" of misdemeanant arrest in which the individual is held with no intention of bringing him to trial but only until his condition changes (as with drunkenness, disorderliness, etc.).[28] Such uses, as well as detention of suspects and witnesses, are understandable responses to difficulties encountered by law enforcement personnel. They are, however, short-term expedients that rarely solve anything.

Because of their multiple uses, jails house a population more diverse than any other correctional institutions. The 1970 jail census found that, of 160,863 persons held on the census date, 27,460 had not been arraigned, 8,688 were awaiting some postconviction legal action, 69,096 were serving sentences (10,496 for more than a year), and 7,800 were juveniles.[29] Thus accused felons and misdemeanants and juveniles all are found in American jails, often unsegregated from each other.

However, jail populations do share common socioeconomic characteristics. Inmates are typically poor, undereducated, and unemployed. Minority groups are greatly overrepresented. Fifty-two percent (83,079) of the inmates in the 1970 census were unconvicted, awaiting arraignment or trial.

It is crucial to note that the population of a jail bears no necessary or logical relationship to the size of the general population it serves. A study of Nebraska's county jails found that counties with the largest populations do not necessarily have the largest number of jail inmates.[30] The National Council on Crime and Delinquency recently advised that area population growth is not a suitable basis for projecting future jail population. "Jail populations are controlled more by statute and court practices than they are by population growth."[31] Variations in law enforcement practices, availability of alternatives (detoxification centers, State misdemeanant institutions, etc.), and attitudes of the local citizenry also affect jail admissions. It is doubtful that variations in crime rates cause the large disparities in jail population among localities. These facts require considerable flexibility in planning for the future.

For the most part, jails are not places of final deposition. In Illinois, an estimated 169,192 jail confinements occurred during 1967.[32] Extrapolating from these and other States' figures, an estimated 1.5 to 5.5 million jail commitments occur in this country annually.[33] The obvious result is a highly transient jail population. Yet the Illinois survey found that pretrial detention can stretch into years through legal maneuvering by both prosecution and defense. In general, the processing rate of any given jail depends on local practices and on availability of alternative placements for certain population groups.

In many of the jail riots in recent years, a trial has been a major, if not the only, demand by inmates. Nor is this demand surprising. The great number of men who spend months and even years in jail awaiting trial exacerbates miserable jail conditions. In the District of Columbia Jail in the spring of 1971, 80 percent of the inmates were there awaiting trial. At the same time, the jail was housing 1,100 inmates in a facility designed to hold 550.[34]

JAIL CONDITIONS TODAY

In addition to the problem of local control, the principal problems facing the Nation's jails today are condition of physical facilities, inadequate personnel, poor administration, and of alternative programs and dispositions.

A study of conditions in the District of Columbia Jail which was undertaken for the American Civil Liberties Union by volunteer lawyers and law students documents the results:

> The District of Columbia Jail is a filthy example of man's inhumanity to man. It is a case study in cruel and unusual punishment, in the denial of due process, in the failure of justice.
>
> The Jail is a century old and crumbling. It is overcrowded. It offers inferior medical attention to its inmates, when it offers any at all. It chains sick men to beds. It allows—forces—men to live in crowded cells with rodents and roaches, vomit and excreta. It is the scene of arbitrary and capricious punishment and discipline. While there is little evidence of racial discrimination (the Jail "serves" the male population of the District of Columbia and is, therefore, virtually an all-black institution), there are some categories of prisoners who receive better treatment than others.

The eating and living conditions would not be tolerated anywhere else. The staff seems, at best, indifferent to the horror over which it presides. This, they say, is the job society wants them to do. The facilities and amounts of time available for recreation and exercise are limited, sometimes by a guard's whim. Except for a few privileged prisoners on various details, there is no means by which an inmate may combat idleness—certainly nothing that could be called education, counselling or self-help.[35]

The sad fact is that conditions in the D.C. Jail are by no means unique.

Physical Facilities

The most striking inadequacy of jails is their abominable physical condition. The National Jail Census found that 25 percent of the cells in use in 1970 were built before 1920.[36] And the chronological age of the facility is aggravated by the manner in which it is used. Jails that hold few persons tend to be neglected, and those that are overcrowded repeatedly push their equipment and fixtures beyond the breaking point. Given the fact that most jails are either over-utilized, and hence overcrowded, or are using only a portion of their capacity, it is not surprising that most of the physical facilities are in crisis condition.

The National Jail Census found 5 percent of jails included in their survey overcrowded, with the propensity to be overcrowded increasing with design capacity.[37] On the other hand, on four census dates, a survey found 35 percent to 45 percent of Idaho's jails unoccupied.[38] Neither the situation of the overcrowded urban jail nor that of the underutilized rural facility will be ameliorated merely by constructing new buildings. The means of delivering detention and correctional services must be reexamined. Otherwise, the new will merely repeat and perpetuate mistakes of the old.

In nearly all jails, the available space is divided into inflexible cells or cage-like day rooms. Rows of cells compose self-contained cellblocks that face a large cage or "bullpen." The arrangement is designed "so that a relatively small number of staff can insure the secure confinement of a comparatively large number of inmates."[39] Items are passed into the bullpens through slotted doors, largely preventing contact between staff and inmates.

Many jail cells have neither toilets nor wash basins. The majority of inmates have access to shower facilities less than once a day. These inadequacies, combined with the short supply or complete lack of such items as soap, towels, toothbrushes, safety razors, clean bedding, and toilet paper, create a clear public health problem, not to mention the depressing psychological effects on inmates. Mattick declares that, "If cleanliness is next to godliness, most jails lie securely in the province of hell." He points out further disheartening physical conditions in jails:

> Considering that sanitary fixtures are a necessity, yet are often absent, it is not too surprising to find that other facilities for handling and treating prisoners, some of which are not as indispensable, are also lacking. Only the largest jails have such luxuries as classrooms, an adequate infirmary, a laundry, a separate dining area, recreation space, and a chapel.[40]

Lack of Adequate Staff

The neglect of local jails is as apparent in staff as in dismal physical facilities. Jail employees almost invariably are untrained, too few in number, and underpaid. They are second-level victims of the societal arrangements that perpetuate the jail.[41]

A 1970 jail survey in California found 25 percent of the deputies and 41 percent of the nonsworn personnel in 58 county sheriff's offices engaged in custodial activities.[42] Although these are full-time employees, assignment to the jail frequently is only one of several roles they must perform. Moreover, "the law enforcement psychology of a policeman is to arrest offenders and see to it that they get *into* jail; the rehabilitative psychology of a correctional worker should be to prepare an inmate to get *out* of jail and take his place in the free community as a law-abiding citizen."[43] When law enforcement officers are not used, the solution has been to hire low-paid custodians who are even less qualified than those they replace.

While staff-inmates ratios often appear satisfactory, the need to operate three shifts and the erratic nature of many employees' duties must be considered in interpreting such figures. Nationally, there were 5.6 inmates per full-time equivalent employee in 1970. State ratios ranged from 1.3 to 11.4[44] Interpreting these ratios on the basis of a 24-hour, 7-day operation gives an average of 1 2/3 full-time workers per shift with an average of 40 inmates.[45] Given the nature of jail architecture and the numerous duties the employees must perform both inside and outside the facility, these staffing levels are simply too low to permit regular supervision of inmates. In Nebraska, staff members were able to see all prisoners from their station in only five of the 90 county jails.[46] During the night, lack of supervision becomes more acute. In Idaho, for example, only 32 percent of the jails had a full-time staff member present at night.[47]

Professional workers, too often missing from jail staffs, are necessary for the initiation and operation of any reintegration or referral program and for training other staff members. A 1965 survey by the National Council on Crime and Delinquency ferreted out only 501 professional jail employees in the Nation. These employees were primarily social workers and vocational and academic instructors, with a scattering of psychologists and psychiatrists.[48] All of these professionals were working in the larger urban jails.

This should not be construed as an argument for jails staffed by psychologists and social workers. The skills involved in relating to another human being are inexact, and professionals do not monopolize them, although training provided by the professional staff to fellow jail employees can be helpful. The need is to break the now-ancient pattern of uninterested and reluctant jail employees who lack the minimal training needed for the efficient performance of an extraordinarily difficult task.

Administration by "Custodial Convenience"

The fundamental principle underlying the relationship between jailers and inmates is that of "custodial convenience," in which "everyone who can, takes the easy way out and makes only the minimal effort."[49] Because of insufficient staffing and funding and the lack of effective screening for incoming inmates, the population is separated into several large groups and placed in specific cell blocks. Each division represents an attempt to replace continuous, or even frequent, staff supervision with a maximum security setting. With such an arrangement, jailers effectively abandon their control and concentrate solely on any untoward occurrences.

Thus the inmates are left to work out their own internal order. For this reason, "control over inmate behavior usually can be achieved by other inmates more immediately, directly, and completely in jails than in other types of confinement institutions, such as penitentiaries or State hospitals."[50] In past eras, kangaroo courts flourished in many jails and still do in some.

While most such "judicial" trappings have gone the way of many traditions, the basic features remain in force. Jail inmates face many uncertainties arising from a threatening environment and an ambiguous relationship to the machinery of the criminal justice system. Under these conditions, individuals experienced in crime and accustomed to life in State penitentiaries assume positions of leadership and control.

The "custodial convenience" philosophy is marked by an almost fanatic concern with security, but one practice totally contradictory to security is found in many jails. To operate and maintain the jail, selected inmates are granted the rank of trusty. They have free access throughout the jail and frequently to the outside as well. All too often, the result is a jail run by its inmates. In most instances, trusties, or at least their "barn boss" or foreman, are well schooled in prison life, and jailers must offer them privileges in return for cooperation.

"Custodial convenience" also dictates a solution for the multitude of social and medical problems entering the jail. Here too, inmates are left to solve their mutual problems, with the elderly, sick, intoxicated, suicide-prone, and addicted all thrown together. The assumption is that they somehow will arrange to take care of each other.

Jail inmates do not have the opportunity for even the momentary or limited privacy available to most prison inmates. Participation and conformity to the prevailing expectations of the jailhouse subculture are mandatory for all.[51] The daily routine generally is one of unrelieved idleness. Card playing, conversations, meditation, and occasionally television viewing are the only options available. In the Nation as a whole, 86 percent of all jails counted in 1970 had no recreational facilities, and 89 percent had no educational facilities.[52]

Even acknowledging the resource limitations, such solutions produce reprehensible results. When the police department and the district attorney's office studied sexual assaults in the Philadelphia jail system during 1968, they found that such assaults were epidemic. "As Superintendent Hendrick and three of the wardens admitted, virtually every slightly built young man committed by the courts is sexually approached within a day or two after his admission to prison. Many of these young men are repeatedly raped by gangs of inmates."[53]

Daniel Glaser has captured the overall effect of current jail conditions as follows:

> The major costs to society from jail conditions probably stem not from the clear violations of moral norms that the inmates suffer there, but rather, from the prolonged idleness of the inmates in highly diverse groups cut off from much communication with outsiders. In this inactivity and crowdedness day after day, those inmates most committed to crime "brainwash" the inexperienced to convert initial feelings of guilt or shame into smug rationalizations for crime. Also, jail prisoners become extremely habituated to "killing time," especially during pretrial confinement. Thus, deficiencies of ability to support themselves in legitimate employment, which may have contributed to their criminality, are enhanced at their

release. While reformatories and prisons are often called "schools for crime," it is a far more fitting label for the typical urban jail.[54]

SHORTCOMINGS OF STATE SUPERVISION

In addressing the needs presented by current jail conditions, the trend toward seeking change through State-set standards and inspections of local jails is open to question. *The Passing of the County Jail,* published 50 years ago, was no isolated utopian exercise but the product of an era of jail reform, written by an experienced and tough-minded practitioner. The book assessed the growing State involvement in local correctional efforts that had occurred in the preceding two decades. State boards of charities and corrections had been established in several States and charged with inspection of jails. Results of inspection surveys were published in California and Illinois. In Alabama, a State prison inspector was granted broad powers by statute to oversee jail activities, including the right to set standards. By and large, however, these measures did not meet expectations.

In the fall of 1971, the National Clearinghouse for Criminal Justice Planning and Architecture attempted to assess the status of current State inspection efforts. Letters sent to the 50 State agencies responsible for corrections requested them to send a copy of any jail standards in use or to notify the clearinghouse if no standards existed. Twenty States replied that they had no responsibility for local jails and no statewide standards were in force. Three States provided standards governing planning and construction but not operation. Two States replied that, while minimal standards existed, they were old and, in one instance, were about to be replaced by pending legislation. (See Figure 4.)

Twenty-four States replied with copies of their current standards. One State answered that the need for standards had been eliminated through State operation of all county jails.

Standards now in use vary considerably—from minimal statutory requirements to detailed instructions, from mimeographed sheet to printed book. But such standards neglect the myriad connections jails have with other components of the criminal justice system. Many standards are vague and thus difficult to enforce. Several State agencies theoretically responsible for such enforcement complained of insufficient funds to carry out the inspection function. The all too frequent difficulty in identifying the specific department of State government responsible for supervision is probably indicative of the quality of the inspection services.[55]

FIGURE 4
Existing State Jail Standards*

	Operational Standards		Facility Planning and Construction	
	Yes	No	Yes	No
Alabama				
Alaska				
Arizona		•		•
Arkansas		•		•
California	•		•	
Colorado		•		•
Connecticut		•		•
Delaware		•		•
Dist. of Columbia		•		•
Florida	•		•	
Georgia		•		•
Hawaii		•		•
Idaho	•			•
Illinois	•		•	
Indiana	•			•
Iowa	•		•	
Kansas		•		•
Kentucky				
Louisiana		•		•
Maine	•		•	
Maryland	•		•	
Massachusetts	•			•
Michigan	•		•	
Minnesota	•		•	
Mississippi				
Missouri	•			•
Montana		•		•
Nebraska		•		•
Nevada				
New Hampshire				
New Jersey				
New Mexico		•		•
New York	•		•	
North Carolina	•		•	
North Dakota	•			•
Ohio		•		•
Oklahoma	•			•
Oregon		•	•	
Pennsylvania	•		•	
Rhode Island				•
South Carolina	•		•	
South Dakota	•			•
Tennessee		•		•
Texas	•		•	
Utah	•			•
Vermont	•		•	
Virginia	•		•	
Washington	•		•	
West Virginia				
Wisconsin	•		•	
Wyoming				•

*Survey conducted by National Clearinghouse for Criminal Justice Planning and Architecture, Fall 1971.

Existing State standards and inspection procedures may have alleviated some of the most glaring physical defects in local jails. However, they do not constitute a program of action; they fail to cover the large complex of processes and agencies to which the jail is related. Furthermore, they inevitably involve political considerations. Standards and inspections aimed at institutional procedures are only two necessary components of the process by which jails may be dramatically reformed. Minimal standards that include only a small portion of the problem's components inevitably will perpetuate a haphazard approach to jail reform.

For individuals seeking reform of local adult corrections, precautions must be taken not to set off in the wrong direction. Hans Mattick has articulated well what must be avoided.

At least two kinds of investment should be *postponed* in any statewide jail reform program based on a phased-stage implementation of State standards: the building of new jails and the hiring of more personnel. Investment in new jails, or the major refurbishing of old ones, would merely cement-in the old problems under somewhat more decent conditions . . . . Increasing the number of personnel in existing jails would only have the effect of giving more persons a vested interest in maintaining the status quo and contribute to greater resistance to future change. By and large, new buildings and more staff should come only after the potential effects of criminal law reform and diversion alternatives have been fully considered. Such collateral reforms, combined with an increasing tendency toward regionalization of jails, would require fewer jails and fewer, but better qualified and trained, jail personnel.[56]

This position may be difficult for some to accept because at first blush the answer to poor jails seems to be to build better ones; the response to inadequate personnel, to hire more. It must be remembered, however, that this is not the first generation to confront the plight of American jails. Concerned individuals have been speaking out for at least a hundred years. But, for the most part, the situation has not improved. New jails have been built, but they now present the same problems as those they were built to replace. History shows clearly that only a different attack on the problem holds real promise. The new approach must involve all components of the criminal justice system.

TOTAL SYSTEM PLANNING

As indicated earlier, the composition of jail populations varies widely, depending on law enforcement practices and community values. If, as this report recommends, confinement is an alternative of last resort and is limited to offenders representing a threat to others, the dangers of a piecemeal approach to problem solving are obvious.

Nature of the Process

In this discussion, "system" is defined as a group of related and interdependent activities, actions, or events organized to achieve a common purpose. The range of these items necessary to explain phenomena under examination determine the system's "scope." For some purposes, the scope may be limited to a State *corrections* system; for others, to the State *criminal justice* system. Throughout this discussion, corrections will be considered a subsystem of the criminal justice system. "Component" will be used as a generic term to refer to activities, actions, events, and subsystems.

"Total system planning" is a process that defines, analyzes, and develops responses to problems of a specific service area. The process is open ended. That is, it describes the interactions between activites or components of one system and those of another. Changes in any single component of an open system or a related system will affect all other components. For example, arraignment scheduling directly affects the number of persons awaiting trial and consequently the detention capacity required. Similarly, jail population may be reduced by diverting alcoholics from the criminal justice system to a detoxification center that is a component of a health services system. The system resulting from the planning process must be open to link offenders' needs with definitive solutions.

Results from one step in the planning process may be affected subsequently by feedback from those of another step. In the above example, creating detoxification programs may change judicial practices that previously were considered a constraint on reducing jail populations. Feedback emphasizes that planning is a process, not a discrete event.

Functional integration, at least within a geographic area, is required to implement the results of the planning process. Part of solving a *corrections* problem (e.g., overcrowding) may involve changing a *court* procedure (e.g., rescheduling arraignments). A crime prevention program operated by a criminal justice system component may involve certain activities of the education, housing, and employment systems. Different systems and subsystems often must work together to attain a solution to a common problem. Thus their functions will overlap or be complementary.

Coordination for Planning

When the total system is not limited to a political subdivision, interjurisdictional cooperation in planning (for example, city-county, multicounty, State-local) is required. The term "coordination" is used intentionally to reflect a somewhat less structured working relationship than that implied by "integration."

Open-endedness implies that the planning process should account for interactions between systems and their components in different political jurisdictions. Related practices in different jurisdictions should be examined for their effects on the flow of offenders through a system. For example, one jurisdiction decides to defer prosecution of narcotics-related offenses and supply treatment programs, but a contiguous jurisdiction continues to prosecute them aggressively. To decrease the likelihood of getting caught, the addict has only to move to the jurisdiction that does not prosecute, and drug treatment programs there quickly become overloaded.

The planning process should consider the consistency of related practices between jurisdictions, even though changing them may be unlikely. This aspect of an open system adds an intergovernmental complication to an intragovernmental operation.

The service area concept is basic to total system planning. Service areas are demarcated by the scope of a particular problem that frequently crosses jurisdictions. Underlying the concept is the realization that social problems and their solutions do not confine themselves to geopolitical boundaries. Each service area may have distinct problems and resources, but there is sufficient commonality to warrant subsystem coordination.

In the simplest case, an agricultural economy and low population density may be conducive to regionalized correctional services. The multistate Standard Metropolitan Statistical Area (SMSA) represents the other extreme. The SMSA is an integrated economic and social unit containing several distinct but interdependent communities or cities. Total system planning for an SMSA is indeed possible. "Local" criminal justice problems can be related conceptually and operational coordination developed. But the difficulty of interjurisdictional planning is added to the difficulty of functional integration (police, courts, corrections, health, welfare).

Steps in Planning

The process of total system planning for a corrections service area is summarized in Figure 9.5. There are six phases:

Problem definition.

Survey.

Analysis.

Program linkage.

System concept.

Physical translation.

Each phase involves a definition of the context (for example, the service area), an end product (statement of the problem), and a course of action (how to allocate planning funds). Each end product and course of action determines what is to be done in the next phase. Subsequent phases may affect prior ones through the feedback mechanism; for example, an initial service area demarcation (Phase 1) may be modified by an analysis (Phase 3) of survey data (Phase 2).

Identifying the service area to be covered is the initial step of the planning process. This step will determine the scope of the overall effort and result in a preliminary statement of the correctional problem being addressed.

Given the diversity, quantity, and quality of data, the survey and structured analysis of its results are critical steps, on which subsequent decisions regarding planning, program development, and construction are dependent. Lack of objectives and use of obsolete planning standards will perpetuate ineffective programs and inflexible facilities. There are always information deficiencies (unreliability, lack of coverage, inconsistency) that force "best guesses" based on professional judgments. Tables, graphs, charts, and diagrams should be used to organize survey data for the decisionmaker and to highlight information gaps.

These products should result from Phases 2 and 3:

• An inventory of existing correctional programs in the service area.

• An assessment of current law enforcement, judicial, and detention practices as represented by types of offenders flowing through the system.

• An inventory of programs and resources not part of the criminal justice system.

• A project of criminal justice system population.

These four items are used to assess the community's ability to meet specific program needs.

The "program linkage" phase (Phase 4) should include examination of alternative correctional service networks. For example, the population of local institutions can be reduced by diverting certain classes of offenders from the criminal justice system. An alternative flow for alcohol-related offenses would emphasize aftercare and social service programs not available in a jail. For offenders not diverted, the potential for community alternatives to incarceration should be examined, including summons in lieu of arrest, release on recognizance, and release to a third-party volunteer.

The underlying objective is to divert, either from the criminal justice system entirely or from incarceration, as many offenders as possible. Representatives of public and private social service agencies, community groups, and professional organizations should be involved in developing these alternatives. Public interest and support is an important element in a planning process that contemplates extensive use of community-based programs.

A VISION OF THE FUTURE

Following an analysis of program relationships, there are two further steps in the planning process: system concept (development of definitive programs) and physical translation. When a community is working to achieve social change, development of a vision of what the future could look like is undoubtedly more effective than continuing to present facts that contradict the old way. Thus, while the details of programs or "delivery systems" developed will vary depending on the service area's requirements, the Commission envisions emergence of community correctional centers as a basic component of local adult corrections. A community correctional center is more a concept than a place. To illustrate, the community correctional center concept may be structured on either a regional or network approach.

The Regional Approach

Where resources and offenders are not sufficient to justify separate rehabilitation programs, localities may pool on a regional basis. Regionalization consolidates existing facilities through cooperative interjurisdictional planning and, in some cases, operation of a new institutional complex. *A Regional Approach to Jail Improvement in South Mississippi: A Plan—Maybe a Dream* describes one regional arrangement for five contiguous counties.[57] The report recommends building a new facility in one of the service area's five counties. The host county maintains jurisdictional control, and the other counties contract with it for their correctional services. The Liberty County, Georgia, Regional Detention Center is another example of planning a regional facility under difficult conditions. This center will provide correctional and staff training services to 14 primarily rural counties.[58] In numerous States, a statutory authority for multijurisdictional jails currently is in force. In North Carolina, for example, authority has been available since 1933 but has never been used.[59]

To encompass the planning required in such an approach and to provide the resources it requires, governmental responsibilities for local corrections must be redistributed. At the two extremes, the underutilized rural facility and the crowded urban facility clearly are incapable of furnishing the services required. However, regionalization is not without complications.

In some respects, a regional community correctional center is a contradiction in terms. In regions comprised of scattered medium-sized cities, it will be difficult to keep individuals involved in their home community. To facilitate reintegration, the inmate must interact continually with his community and must be allowed furloughs to find postrelease employment and housing. The distribution of jobs over a large territory makes work-release programs difficult, though not impossible.

A frequent objection to regionalization is the time and cost involved in moving people to and from facilities. A systematic analysis of cost factors should be part of the planning process and be included in the overall cost projections for any delivery system—regional or network.

The Network Approach

In major metropolitan areas, the corrections program can be developed on the basis of a *network* of dispersed facilities and services geographically located to perform their functions best. The traditional correctional institution, with its inclusion of all functions in a single facility, creates an unnatural physical and psychological environment. For example, in the free community, boarding schools are not used for adult education, and individuals rarely work in the same building in which they live. Correctional institution arrangements may be convenient for management, but they are unrealistic for the inmate.

It is inconsistent with the intent of community corrections to provide all rehabilitation services in one building. The range of facilities within a network provides for offenders' special needs, including the potential for some total institutionalization. An additional variable is provided by the progression of an offender from one program or facility to another. Within the service area, a network is established, with the community correctional center serving as the coordinating point.

Following survey of program needs, inventory of diverse area resources, and development of detailed program linkages, the planning process must translate this information into physical resource requirements (Phase 6, shown in Figure 5). The facilities planning process will not be discussed in detail, but the essential components are summarized in Figure 5. For details, reference is made to the University of Illinois publication, *Guidelines for the Planning and Design of Regional and Community Correctional Centers for Adults.*[60]

FIGURE 5

Phase	1 Problem Definition	2 Survey	3 Analysis	4 Program Linkage
Context	Service Area • administrative • political • physical Need • jurisdictional coordination • systems integration • program analysis • master planning • other	Criminal Justice System • law enforcement • courts • corrections practices and trends Community • social services • community agencies • resources Socio-Cultural • demographic composition • demographic distribution • jurisdictional Physical • urbanization pattern • transportation • geographic • system component proximities • facilities	Judicial Practices • courts • corrections • law enforcement Population Projection • arrest • offender categories Community Resource Potential • agencies • programs Physical Features (Service Area) • limitations • potentials	Diversion • social • medical Nonfacility • pretrial release • nonresidential treatment • probation • conditional release Facility-Based • pretrial • postadjudication Community Interface • functions • agencies • volunteers

Process Flow ⟶ ◄— Feedback —⟶

Output	Preliminary Problem Statement • background • goals • scope	Data Tabulation • tables • charts • graphs • maps • diagrams	Planning Parameters • restrictions • limitations • alternatives	Program Alternatives • relationships • design implications • operational implications
Action	Strategy Formulation • planning coordination • allocation of planning funds	Data Analysis • public participation • interagency participation	Data Synthesis • program definition	Assessment of Alternatives • public response • agency response

Total Systems Planning Process

Phase	5 System Concept	6 Physical Translation	7 Program Interpretation	8 Program Analysis

Context	Program
	• facility
	• nonfacility
	Systems Components
	• facilities
	  type
	  scale
	  location
	System Configuration
	• network
	• regional
	• composite
		System Development
		• programs
		• facilities
		• administration
		• funding
		• operational
		• implementation
			Interpretation
			• system plan
			• facility descriptions
			• operational system
			• treatment programs/ alternatives
				Research
				• staff/manpower needs
				• operational relationships
				  interfacility
				  intrafacility
				• alternatives to detention
				• facility alternatives
				  new
				  existing (remodel)
				• shared use agencies
				• client needs characteristics
				  types
				  numbers
				• budget sources limits
				  facilities
				  operations

(continued)

FIGURE 5 (continued)

Phase	5 System Concept	6 Physical Translation	7 Program Interpretation	8 Program Analysis
Process Flow				
Output	Correctional System Concept Plan • definition of components	System Description • definite design of components	Develop Design (Objectives) • goals • facility • location	Develop Design (Physical Parameters) • definition • interpretation • evaluation
Action	Public Review • legislative action • funding	Physical Implementation • facility construction • staffing • operation • research	Compare With Total System • goals and configuration	Design Determinants (Definition) • priorities • alternatives • public participation • agency participation

Total Systems Planning Process		Facility Planning Process		
9 Program Synthesis	10 Design Development •Preliminary•	11 Design Development •Definitive•	12 Physical Implementation

Design Determinants Site
• location-site selection
• site development
• resource proximities
Facility
• space requirements
• functional relationships
• scale
• image
  character
  compatibility
• accessibility
• combined use
• economics
  site
  facility
	Preliminary Design
	• spatial activity design
	• functional optimization
	• security/detention (secondary priority)
	• community interaction
	• normative environment
	• range of security provisions (zone control)
	• residential clusters
	• individual occupancy
	• flexibility
	  internal change
	  external change
	• budget analysis
	• environmental impact
		Definitive Design
		• input analysis
		  public review
		  agency review
		  budget review
		• alternative selection
		• final design
		  development
		  structural
		• engineering
		  development
		  H.V.A.C.
		  electricity
		  plumbing
		  transportation
		  fire
		  security
			Final Development
			• production
			  working drawings
			  specifications
			  final cost estimates
			• bidding documents
			• construction
			  scheduling
			  demolition
			  remodeling
			  renovation

Feedback			

Develop Design (Concepts)
• functional relationships
• spatial relationships
• structure
• site development
	Develop Design (Solutions)
	• alternatives
	• schematics
	• recommendations
	• costs
	• phasing
		Develop Design (Translation)
		• budget analysis
		• presentation
		  documents
		  models
		  graphics
			Final Construction Documents
			• plan
			• specifications
			• scheduling

Evaluation • feasibility Approval (Concepts) Site Acquisition	Review • public review • agency review • evaluation • approval • modification • funding applications	Review • evaluation • feasibility analysis • budget analysis • approval	Bidding-Award • construction • occupancy

FUNCTIONS OF COMMUNITY
CORRECTIONAL CENTERS

Whether an area develops a regional or network service delivery system, a number of functions need to be served. It should be stressed again that the center concept is not suggested as a rigid formula for all communities but rather as an approach to meeting existing and projected needs, a way to structure the diverse activities now operating there.

Court Intake Services

Where at all possible, court intake personnel should be located in a community correctional center. Such an arrangement will facilitate communication between court and corrections staff by virtue of proximity and functional relationships that must be developed to attain an integrated local adult corrections system.

Screening is the initial phase of intake services. Both diversion from the criminal justice system and referral to appropriate community resources are predicated on an effective screening process. An increasing body of experience shows that in many instances it is neither desirable nor necessary to process certain types of persons through the criminal justice system. Alternative dispositions must be developed at the local level so that as many offenders as possible may be diverted. Chapter 3, Diversion from the Criminal Justice Process, discussed programs that avoid criminal processing at the community and police levels as well as court-based diversion programs. The latter involve suspensions or holding of criminal charges while an individual participates in a specified program such as job training. If the individual completes the program successfully, a recommendation is made to the court that charges be dismissed. New York City's Court Employment Project[61] and similar programs elsewhere demonstrate the feasibility of increasing alternatives to confinement without a concomitant increase in danger to the community.

In other cases, an individual may be referred to non-criminal justice agencies when it appears that their services would be more appropriate. For example, alcoholics, addicts, and the mentally ill should be referred to health or social service agencies.

Both referral and more formalized diversion programs offer the opportunity for utilizing resources that appear more likely to be successful in meeting an individual's need than the resources of the criminal justice system. Such programs help him to avoid the interruption of life patterns and the stigmatization associated with criminal proceedings and conviction.

Intake personnel also serve an important function in providing services to the courts for cases in which there will be criminal proceedings. After the decision has been made to press criminal charges, intake staff perform social investigations to aid the court in making pretrial release decisions. The role of intake staff and procedures used to increase use of release on recognizance, police summons release, supervised release, bail, and other pretrial release programs are discussed in Chapter 4, Pretrial Release and Detention.

After arranging for the pretrial release of all persons possible, intake staff must provide services to those for whom pretrial detention has been deemed necessary. At this point, the desirability of locating intake services within a community correctional center becomes obvious, since the moment the decision to detain is made, intake staff should begin to work with other personnel at the community correctional center. Typically, those brought to local correctional facilities bring with them unresolved problems that demand immediate attention. The very fact of their arrest may have created problems. The staff of the community correctional center must deal with them. Beginning with intake staff, the community correctional center should serve as a crisis intervention resource. While such services should be available to anyone reaching court intake, persons being detained are particularly likely to need assistance.

Court intake personnel also provide presentence investigation reports to the courts as discussed in Chapter 5, Sentencing, and should be involved in community classification teams for the State correctional system, as discussed in Chapter 6, Offender Classification. Again, these functions require cooperation and assistance from other personnel of the community correctional center.

Residential Care

Community correctional centers will provide four types of residential care: services to persons awaiting trial; services to persons serving sentences; prerelease services to persons moving from major institutions; and services to short-term returnees. While many of the services offered and conditions required will apply to all residential services, there are certain distinctions.

Persons Awaiting Trial

Adequate screening, referral, diversion and pretrial release procedures should greatly reduce the number of persons detained pending trial. For that part of the accused population that is denied pretrial release, the best way to keep populations low and jail stays short is speedy trial. (See Chapter 4, Pretrial Release and Detention, and the Commission's Report on Courts.)

Those detained should be housed separately from convicted offenders. Females and juveniles should be separated in housing from adult males. Anyone received for detention who is mentally or physically ill or is an alcoholic or drug addict should be routed to more appropriate facilities.

Every effort must be made to insure that nothing in the treatment of pretrial detainees implies guilt and that the exercise of their rights is maximized to the extent possible. (See Chapter 2, Rights of Offenders).

Sentenced Offenders

Elsewhere in this report, the need is stressed to reserve confinement for the fewest number of convicted offenders possible. Chapter 5, Sentencing, presents the numerous dispositional alternatives available to the courts that are preferable to incarceration. Traditionally misdemeanants have been sent to local jails, while felons were sent to State institutions. With increasing use of dispositional alternatives, local correctional facilities may be able to serve both types of offenders. Eventually, the community correctional center may replace the prison as the place of incarceration for felons who cannot be released immediately to the community.

At present, however, local correctional facilities can be expected to house mostly misdemeanant offenders with relatively short sentences. Given the fact that very few of these individuals are perceived as "dangerous" to others, it is astonishing how little use has been made of work release, study release, "weekender" sentences, and similar programs that take advantage of community resources.

States should adopt work-release statutes such as Wisconsin's pioneer Huber Law, which authorizes daytime release for work, with return to jail in the evening. Earnings are used to finance the program and to meet the cost of the inmate's room and board and support of his dependents, with any remainder being deposited in the inmate's account. Such statutes should also extend to school or training programs, medical treatment, job hunting, and family visits.

"Weekender" programs, which enable offenders to remain in the community during the work week while returning to jail over the weekend for punishment, should also be used much more extensively. Judging from current practice, "weekender" sentences need not be authorized by statute, although States may wish to formally recognize the practice by law.

In addition, early release opportunities, such as parole or release to a small halfway house, which are generally available for felons in State institutions should be offered to community correctional center inmates. Such programs are less costly than incarceration, can serve as incentives for inmates, and avoid the dangers of protracted unnecessary confinement.

For too long the local jail has been used as a place of total confinement for all who were sent there. Much more imagination and variety need to be employed to assure that sentenced offenders are not worse off when leaving than upon arrival.

Prerelease from State Institutions

As jails evolve into community correctional centers, serving as a coordinating point for community correctional services, their desirability as a prerelease resource will increase accordingly. Individuals originally assigned to State institutions should be transferred to the community correctional center in their own community to facilitate the reintegration process. All of the partial release programs described above should be available to such offenders.

Short-Term Returnees

The remaining type of person for whom the community correctional center should be a residential option is an offender in the community who needs a short period of support, structure, or supervision. Parole boards should view a short return to a community correctional center as a desirable alternative to recommitment to a State institution in many cases of parole violation. Ideally, this option should be available to offenders in community programs on a voluntary basis as well. A model for such an arrangement exists in the community mental health field, where it has been found that major problems or recommitment can be avoided by opening up facilities to those who feel a temporary need for them. Such an option is also fully consistent with the move to alleviate the abrupt transition from total confinement to freedom in the community.

COMMUNITY CORRECTIONAL
CENTER PROGRAMS

The community correctional center not only should be located in a community but also should be part of it. The center would not duplicate services already available from government or private sources. Psychotherapy, education, and skills training can be brought to the center, or residents can participate in programs being operated at other locations. Increased community participation would improve the potential for reintegrating inmates.

Confined individuals also can receive services from community organizations—Alcoholics Anonymous, family service organizations, legal aid, neighborhood centers, vocational rehabilitation agencies, and others. Such groups can work with the individual while he is in confinement and after release.

The center would also coordinate the various correctional services now based in the community. A classification committee would include center staff, parole and probation officers, and representatives of volunteer groups and relevant government agencies. In this way, the various organizations working with the inmate could meet as a group and make joint decisions. This type of classification committee is used in the Vermont community correctional centers[62] and is recommended in the California jail standards.[63]

The overall goal of the community correctional center is to furnish physical and social environments conducive to the individual's social reintegration. Central to this goal is the provision of a safe, positive environment in which the individuals have a chance to express and develop their innate abilities. The emphasis is not on traditional training, instruction, or adjustment to institutional requirements but rather on:

- Accurate observation of the individual.
- Intensive staff-client interaction.
- Opportunities for reality confrontation and reality testing.
- Discussions.
- Choice.
- Positive leisure-time options.
- Optimal living and constructive learning situations.
- Community and group interaction.

There is one additional function that community correctional centers should perform. Numerous observers have commented that—more often than not—time, rather than need, is the factor which signals the end of correctional service. Thus, many individuals may be released from correctional custody or supervision with no provisions being made to help them in any way after their sentence has expired. While it is true that the vast majority of offenders today are only too glad to be free from correctional control, some offenders may want or need additional services. Community correctional centers should be authorized to offer services to ex-offenders for at least one year after the expiration of their sentences. Employment assistance, family counseling, aid in finding housing, or help in overcoming or removing legal or other restrictions placed on ex-offenders are examples of the kinds of services that should be available through the community correctional center.

Facility Design Suited to Program Goals

Facility design that separates residential from program areas would not achieve program goals, and design based mainly on security controls and surveillance functions is inappropriate and counterproductive. The physical setting supportive of contemporary program activities will not be found by examining past models. Replicating such models has only produced failure and will continue to do so.

The physical environment is of profound significance to the support and encouragement of program goals. Only by provision of adequate and appropriate space can a broad array of human activities essential to correctional programming be realized.

More details on facility design are offered in Standard 9.10.

7

THE NATION'S JAILS

LAW ENFORCEMENT ASSISTANCE ADMINISTRATION, U.S. DEPARTMENT OF JUSTICE

PREFACE

As defined for this study, a jail is a locally administered institution that has authority to retain adults for 48 hours or longer. The "intake point for the entire criminal justice system," the local jail is used both as a detention center for persons facing criminal charges and, along with prisons, as a correctional facility for those serving sentences.

GENERAL FINDINGS

Local units of government throughout the United States operated 3,921 jails at midyear 1972. These jails housed 141,588 inmates, an average of about 36 per facility. Of the total number of jails in operation in 1972, 2,901, or roughly three out of every four, were small institutions, accommodating 20 or fewer inmates. Medium-sized facilities, i.e., those with inmate populations between 21 and 249, numbered 907. The remaining 113 jails, accounting for 3 percent of the total, were large facilities, holding 250 or more inmates.

Location And Size

The largest number of jails was in the South, the smallest number in the Northeast. In fact, jails in the 16 southern States and the District of Columbia, which at midyear 1972 collectively held 39 percent of the Nation's jail population, constituted 48 percent of all jails in the United States. Jails in the Northeast, while accommodating 19 percent of all jail inmates, accounted for only 6 percent of

Source: From *The Nation's Jails* (Washington, D.C.: U.S. Government Printing Office, May 1975), pp. iii–16 (Editorial Adaptations).

the total. The North Central Region held 17 percent of the Nation's jail inmate population in 29 percent of the country's jails; the corresponding proportions for the West were 25 percent and 17 percent.

These region-to-region contrasts in the number of jails and in the size of the inmate population result in large measure from . . . the differential patterns in historical development of State political subdivisions, variation in State laws, and disparate practices in the sentencing of convicted offenders. It is apparent, however, that the region-to-region differences correlate to a considerable degree with the size of jail predominant in a given region. Thus, in the Northeast, where the total number of jails was relatively small compared with the total jail population, the majority of all jails were medium-sized, whereas in all other regions the vast majority were small facilities. In the West, where, as in the Northeast, the proportion of the total number of the Nation's jails was smaller than the percentage share of the total jail population, the number of large jails was greater than in any other region. Proportionate to the total number of jails in each region, however, the Northeast had the most institutions accommodating 250 or more inmates.

On a jail-by-jail basis, the Northeast averaged 118 inmates per local facility, compared with 52 in the West, 30 in the South, and 20 in the North Central Region.

Jails in New York had an average of 200 inmates per facility, the highest figure in the Nation except for the District of Columbia (703). Other States in which the average number of inmates per local jail exceeded 100 were California (167), Massachusetts (115), New Jersey (107), and Maryland (101). In contrast, Vermont had four inmates in four jails, an average of one per institution. Jails in North Dakota housed an average of three inmates each; those in Montana held an average of four.

Physical Facilities

About three-fifths of all local jails occupied buildings that also served as the county courthouse, the sheriff's office, or the local police station. Another one-third were located in separate structures, and the remainder were housed in a variety of other types of quarters or failed to report on the location of their facilities. As would have been expected, the larger the size of the facility, the more likely it was to have been housed in a separate structure. Approximately 58 percent of all large jails had their own separate building or buildings, compared with 39 percent of medium-sized jails and 31 percent of small jails.

Local jails confined their inmates in a variety of accommodations: one-inmate cells, two-inmate cells, three- or four-inmate cells, and dormitories.[64] Of the 3,683 jails that reported on accommodations, 47 percent had at least some one-inmate cells, 57 percent had some two-inmate cells, 50 percent had some three- or four-inmate cells, and 52 percent had at least one dormitory. As is obvious, a sizable number of jails had more than one type of accommodation; some undoubtedly provided all four types. The larger the jail, the more likely it contained at least some one-inmate cells. Thus, 73 percent of the larger jails had such accommodations, compared with 58 percent of the medium-sized facilities and 42 percent of the small institutions. Large jails were also most apt to have at least one dormitory; medium-sized facilities were more likely than small jails to have a dormitory. Relatively fewer large institutions had three- and four-inmate cells than either small or medium-sized jails.

Roughly 44 percent of all jails in the United States had at least one drunk tank, that is, a dormitory-like accommodation in which inebriated persons are confined, often for their own protection, to sober up. The proportion for small jails was 42 percent; it was 52 percent for medium-sized institutions and 27 percent for large jails. The relatively small proportion of large jails with drunk tanks probably reflects the fact that the large facilities generally are located in the more populous communities, where other types of facilities, such as detoxification centers, are used to confine drunk persons. Although a majority of all jails with drunk tanks equipped these accommodations with such amenities as heat, light, ventilation, beds or mattresses, toilets, and drinking fountains or water taps, these amenities were not universal. In fact, none of these amenities was available in drunk tanks in 19 jails. Drunk tanks were heated and lighted in 93 percent of the 1,711 jails with such accommodations. They had toilets in 86 percent, drinking fountains or water taps in 80 percent, windows or a fan in 74 percent, beds or mattresses in 60 percent, a seating space in 50 percent, showers in 38 percent, and air conditioning in 26 percent. Drunk tanks in small jails were more likely to have had beds or mattresses than those in either medium-sized jails or large jails; drunk tanks in medium-sized facilities were most apt to have had seating space. Otherwise, the likelihood of drunk tanks having been equipped with amenities increased with the size of the jail.

Separation of Inmates

Local jails followed diverse practices in separating specific types of inmates from the general jail population. Irrespective of size, almost all jails that held juveniles usually confined them separately from adults. Only 79 customarily mixed their juvenile and adult inmates; four-fifths of these were small jails, but included among the number were three large institutions—one each in Missouri, Ohio, and Pennsylvania.

About 9 out of every 10 jails that accepted mental patients awaiting commitment normally segregated them from other inmates. This practice was common among jails of all sizes. Among the 240 jails that did not separate mental patients from the general jail population were 6 large facilities—2 in Texas and 1 each in Arizona, California, Florida, and Missouri.

Jails in the United States were about equally divided between those that customarily separated drunks and traffic offenders from the general inmate population and those that did not. Medium-sized facilities were more likely to follow a practice of separation than either small or large jails.

Of 3,408 jails that reported whether or not they separated pre-trial inmates from sentenced prisoners, 41 percent usually followed a policy of segregation. The proportion was 37 percent in small jails, 51 percent in medium-sized institutions, and 66 percent in large facilities. About 26 percent of all jails also normally separated first offenders from repeat offenders; the proportion was roughly identical in jails of all sizes.

Only a minority of jails operated work-release programs. Of those that did, approximately 55 percent of these confined participants apart from other inmates. The proportion was 47 percent for small jails, 71 percent for medium-sized institutions, and 76 percent for large jails.

Meal Services

In 2,753 jails, representing approximately 70 percent of all jails, meals served to inmates were prepared in the jail, whereas in 1,135 other jails the meals were prepared elsewhere and brought in. Only in small jails was it fairly common practice for the sheriff or chief jailer to have arranged for meals to be brought in, 37 percent of the small facilities having used this arrangement.

Excluding the 2 jails in which no meals were served, 3,876 institutions reported on the frequency with which their inmates were fed. Of these, 2,628, or slightly more than two-thirds, served meals three or more times daily, whereas 1,241 fed their inmates twice a day. In the remaining seven jails, only one meal a day was provided; these seven were all small facilities. With but two exceptions, large jails served at least three meals a day; 86 percent of the medium-sized institutions and 61 percent of the small jails also followed this practice.

Of 3,885 jails that reported on the type of meal served to inmates, all but 45 (38 small jails and 7 medium-sized facilities) indicated that a hot meal was served at least once a day. In the 45, no hot meals were served.

Meals were served exclusively in dining halls in 12 percent of the Nation's jails and solely in cells in another 59 percent. About 17 percent of the jails used both dining halls and cells; 10 percent had other arrangements. Information on the remaining 2 percent was not reported. Meals were served exclusively in cells in two-thirds of the small jails and in slightly more than two-fifths of the medium-sized jails. In contrast, only 17 percent of the large jails followed this practice. Large institutions were more apt to have a dining hall than either small or medium-sized jails.

Medical and Recreational Facilities

One out of every eight jails had some sort of in-house medical facility, although in relative terms such facilities were commonplace only in large institutions. Fewer than 5 percent of the small jails and about 30 percent of medium-sized jails possessed in-house medical facilities. About 86 percent of the large jails had infirmaries, compared with 27 percent of the medium-sized jails and 2 percent of the small jails. Three out of every five large jails had infirmaries with beds.

Slightly more than three-fifths of all jails provided their inmates with some form of recreational opportunity or entertainment, but such diversion was quite restricted except in large institutions and was totally lacking in 1,308 small jails and 187 medium-sized jails. It was also lacking in three large jails, one each in Georgia, Indiana, and Ohio.

Almost three-fourths of all large jails had an exercise yard. The proportions for small and medium-sized jails were 10 percent and 30 percent, respectively. Sports equipment was available in 70 percent of the large jails, but in only 26 percent of the medium-sized institutions and in but 3 percent of the small jails. The percent of jails with radios, television sets, and record players is shown in Table 8.

TABLE 8
Percent of Jails With Radios, Television Sets,
and Record Players, by Size of Jail

Item	All Jails	Jails with Fewer Than 21 Inmates	Jails with 21–249 Inmates	Jails with 250 or More Inmates
Radio	50	44	66	79
Television set	25	15	51	88
Record player	7	4	13	19

Facilities for showing motion pictures were available in half of all large jails, in one-tenth of medium-sized institutions, and in less than 1 percent of all small jails.

Employees

Locally operated jails in the United States employed 44,298 persons at midyear 1972. Of these, 39,627, or 89 percent, were full-time employees and the remainder worked part time. For all jails, the average number of employees, both full-time and part-time, was 11. It was 4 in small jails, 17 in medium-sized facilities, and 145 in large institutions. Small jails were more likely to have employed part-time workers than either medium-sized or large facilities. At midyear 1972, about 21 percent of all employees of small jails worked part time only; proportions for medium-sized and large jails were 10 percent and 3 percent, respectively.

As would have been expected, the South, with the most jails, also had the largest number of persons employed in local jails. It was followed, in order, by the Northeast, the North Central Region, and the West (Table 9). The average number of employees per jail, however, was lower in the South than in each of the other regions.

TABLE 9
Number of Jail Employees, by Geographic Region

Region	Number of Employees	Percent of Total Employees	Number of Inmates Per Employee
Northeast	10,948	25	2.5
North Central	9,853	22	2.4
South	14,916	34	3.7
West	8,581	19	4.1

Nationally, the ratio of inmates to jail employees, both full-time and part-time, was 3.2 to 1. There were 2.4 inmates per employee in jails in the North Central Region, 2.5 in the Northeast, 3.7 in the South, and 4.1 in the West. Among the States, the ratio of inmates to employees fluctuated widely. In both North Dakota and Vermont, the number of local jail employees at midyear 1972 exceeded the number of inmates in local jails. On the other hand, the ratio of inmates to employees was at least 5 to 1 in Arizona and California jails.

Of the total number of persons employed by local jails throughout the United States, 46 percent were custodial personnel, i.e., guards and jailers; 27 percent were administrative staff; and 17 percent were engaged in clerical or maintenance functions. The remainder were mainly specialized personnel, such as medical doctors. Only 7 percent of the custodial, administrative, and clerical or maintenance employees, considered as a group, were part-time workers, whereas 40 percent of the specialized staff worked less than full time.

Local jails followed diverse practices with regard to whether or not their custodial personnel were sworn police officers. Of 3,383 jails that supplied information concerning sworn personnel on their custodial staff, 46 percent had no sworn officers, and 11 percent had some. In the remaining jails, all custodial personnel were sworn law enforcement officials. Jails with fewer than 5 full-time employees and those with 80 or more were about equally divided between those with at least some sworn personnel and those with none. Jails with between 5 and 79 full-time staff members were more likely to have had some sworn personnel among their custodial staff than to have had none.[65]

Relatively few jails employed such specialized staff members as medical doctors, nurses, psychiatrists, psychologists, social workers, and teachers. As would have been expected, the size of the jail, measured by the number of confined inmates, was a significant factor in whether or not such personnel were employed. For example, 84 percent of all large jails employed a medical doctor, full-time or part-time, compared with 38 percent of all medium-sized jails and 10 percent of all small jails.

Medical doctors were the most commonly employed of the specialized personnel. Nonetheless, only 744 of the Nation's 3,921 jails, or 19 percent of the total, had a medical doctor on their staff. Furthermore, of the 1,063 physicians so employed by these jails, only 34 percent served on a full-time basis. Even in large jails, medical doctors were likely to be part-time personnel. New York had the

largest number of medical doctors working in local jails (178), followed by California (74).

Although a majority of the 747 nurses employed by local jails
in the United States worked full time, only 229 jails, or about 6
percent of the total, employed such personnel. The proportion was
2 percent for small jails, 11 percent for medium-sized institutions,
and 68 percent for large facilities. Jails in California employed a
total of 177 nurses; those in New York, 145. None of the jails in
Alaska, Arkansas, Maine, West Virginia, or Wyoming employed
nurses.

Other than medical doctors and nurses there was no other type
of specialized professional person employed in as many as 5 percent
of the country's jails. Even the large jails were much less likely than
not to have psychiatrists, psychologists, social workers, or teachers
on their staff.

Psychiatrists served as staff members in 114 jails, or in approximately 3 percent of all jails in the United States. They were employed, either full time or part time, in 1 of every 90 small jails, in
1 of every 17 medium-sized institutions, and in 1 of every 4 large
facilities. The 114 jails employed a total of 166 psychiatrists, of
whom about three-fourths worked on a part-time basis only. New
York jails employed 45 of the 166; New Jersey jails, 20. Jails in
no other State accounted for as many as 10, and there were no
psychiatrists on the staff of any jail in Alaska, Indiana, Louisiana,
Mississippi, Nevada, New Hampshire, North Dakota, South Carolina,
South Dakota, Vermont, and Wyoming.

A total of 95 jails had a psychologist on their staff. All together,
these jails employed 137 psychologists, of whom roughly one-half
worked full time. Although only 30 of the 113 large jails included
psychologists on their staff, these 30 collectively employed 64 of
the 137. In contrast, the 21 small jails having a psychologist employed 22, and the 43 medium-sized facilities employed 51. Taken
as a whole, jails in New York had the largest single number of psychologists (27), followed by those in the District of Columbia (15)
and Illinois (11). None of the jails in 16 States employed
psychologists.

Social workers were found in 56 small jails, 79 medium-sized
institutions, and 47 large facilities. Together, these 182 jails employed a total of 487 social workers, about two-thirds of whom
were full-time employees. Almost half of all social workers employed
by U.S. jails (and more than half of the full-time employees) worked
in those jails accommodating 250 or more inmates. Collectively,
jails in the District of Columbia employed more social workers (47)

than those in any other jurisdiction. Jails in New York employed a total of 43, as did those in Pennsylvania; those in Missouri employed 41. No social workers were reported among employees of jails in Alaska, Idaho, Louisiana, Nevada, New Mexico, Oklahoma, South Carolina, South Dakota, and Vermont.

One hundred thirty-six local jails employed academic teachers. This number represented 3 percent of all jails. The proportion was 35 percent for large jails, 9 percent for medium-sized facilities, and less than 1 percent for small jails. Collectively, the 136 jails employed a total of 367 academic teachers, of whom 48 percent were full-time employees. Pennsylvania's jails reported a total of 73 academic teachers; New York's, a total of 50. There were no academic teachers employed in any jail in 21 States. Vocational teachers were reported in but 78 jails throughout the country. All these 78 jails employed 209 vocational teachers, of whom about 7 out of every 10 worked full time. California had the largest number (21) of vocational teachers working in local jails. It was followed by Mississippi and New Jersey, each with 17. In 22 States, not a single jail reported vocational teachers on their staff.

Social and Rehabilitative Programs

Social and rehabilitative programs or services, some funded by the Federal Government and some sponsored by a variety of other entities, were provided in various combinations in the Nation's jails. However, such programs and services, except for religious worship, were offered in only a small proportion of jails. Consequently, only a fraction of the total jail population had access to them.

All together, 16 specific activities, and other activities of a miscellaneous nature, were identified as funded by the Federal Government; most were in the field of manpower training and support. A total of 475 jails, or 12 percent of the total, offered one or more of these activities, with the likelihood of jails providing them rising as the size of the institution increased. Thus, 51 percent of the Nation's large jails conducted at least one program funded by the Federal Government, compared with 26 percent of the medium-sized facilities and 6 percent of the small institutions. Of the 16 specific programs, adult basic education was the most commonly offered, although provided in only 215 jails, or 5 percent of the total. Vocational training, conducted in 135, was the second most commonly provided of the federally financed programs.

A total of 635 jails, presumably including many of those that offered federally funded programs for inmates, at release referred their previously incarcerated prisoners to comparable federally financed programs outside the jail setting. Again, the larger the jail, the more likely it was to follow a practice of referral.

Programs or services sponsored by entities other than the Federal Government were offered in 2,646 jails, or approximately two-thirds of the total. Religious services were provided in almost three-fifths of all jails, but no other single type of program was found in as many as half of all jails, and many were conducted in only a relative handful. Except in the field of vocational training, the Nation's jails relied heavily on extramural local entities, such as churches, civic groups, schools, and service organizations, to operate these programs or services.

Religious services were conducted in 49 percent of all small jails, in 85 percent of the medium-sized facilities, and in 89 percent of all large institutions. In about one-fourth of the jails providing for religious worship, the service was sponsored by the jails themselves; in the remainder it was supplied by a group or groups outside the institution. Small jails depended most heavily on this outside support for their religious services, only 13 percent sponsoring their own worship observances. In contrast, roughly three of every five large institutions provided for their own religious services.

Alcoholic treatment programs were found in 35 percent of all jails. The proportion in small jails was 30 percent; it was 49 percent in medium-sized facilities and 66 percent in large institutions. Thirteen percent of the jails with an alcoholic treatment program conducted their own programs; in the remainder it was operated by entities outside the jail. Even among large institutions, a majority relied on outside sponsorship or assistance.

Slightly more than one-fourth of all jails operated some sort of drug addiction program. Such programs were provided in 20 percent of the small jails, 40 percent of the medium-sized facilities, and 68 percent of the large institutions. The pattern of sponsorship for drug addiction treatment programs essentially was the same as that for alcoholic treatment programs.

A total of 678 jails offered group counseling programs, 542 provided vocational training, 491 supplied job development and placement services, 419 furnished remedial education programs, 348 offered assessments of vocational potentials, and 226 provided pre-vocational training. None of these programs or services was found in as many as one-fifth of the Nation's jails. Except for programs of group counseling and remedial education, they were not provided even in a majority of the large jails.

Community volunteers were the mainstays of social and rehabilitative programs or services, predominating in jails of all sizes.

Nearly two-thirds of the jails that reported on the types of persons used in conducting these programs or services indicated that they relied solely on volunteers. About 4 percent reported that ex-offenders were used exclusively in such activities; in the remainder, both community volunteers and ex-offenders were utilized. However, about one-fourth of all jails providing social and rehabilitative programs or services failed to report on the type of person used in conducting these programs or services.

As indicated earlier, 542 jails provided some sort of a vocational training program. Ten percent of the small jails offered such training, compared with 23 percent of the medium-sized facilities and 43 percent of the large institutions. Slightly more than one-half of all jails conducting vocational training operated their own programs. Irrespective of the size of the jail, the most commonly offered vocational training was that preparing inmates for jobs as craftsmen.

In addition to conducting institution-based social and rehabilitative programs, some jails allowed selected sentenced inmates to spend part of their time working in the community. Slightly more than two-fifths of all jails sponsored such work-release programs, which are designed to enable sentenced inmates to hold outside jobs while spending nonworking hours in confinement. The practice serves not only as a means of facilitating the inmates' eventual reintegration into the community, but also enables family breadwinners to continue to provide support for their dependents. Size of jail was not an especially significant factor in whether or not a particular facility operated a work-release program.

A related practice, namely allowing some sentenced inmates to serve their time on weekends, was permitted by 46 percent of the Nation's jails. Medium-sized and large jails were more likely than small institutions to follow this practice. In relative terms, more jails in the West and the Northeast had work-release programs than those in the South. Jails in the West were the most likely of all to have adopted a weekend sentence program.

All jails in Alaska and New Hampshire had work-release programs; such programs also were operated in at least four out of every five jails in Arizona, Maine, Minnesota, and Wisconsin. At the other extreme, only 19 percent of South Carolina's jails had work-release programs, and the proportion in New York was 22 percent. Allowing selected sentenced inmates to serve their time on weekends was a practice followed in all of Alaska's jails and in four out of every five jails in Idaho, New Hampshire, and Washington. Jails in the District of Columbia and Vermont did not follow this practice; only 18 percent of those in Mississippi did.

8

ORGANIZATION AND ADMINISTRATION

NATIONAL ADVISORY COMMISSION ON CRIMINAL JUSTICE STANDARDS AND GOALS

American corrections is a diffuse and variegated system. Its organization and management processes reflect those conditions. The range includes huge, centralized departmental complexes and autonomous one-man probation offices; separation of corrections from other governmental functions and combination of corrections with law enforcement, mental health, and social welfare; highly professionalized management methods and strikingly primitive ones.

In spite of these differences, there are commonalities. Of special interest are the stubborn problems and dilemmas which run through the whole fabric of correctional organization. These focal problems and concerns will be discussed in the following pages.

BASIC PROBLEMS OF CORRECTIONAL ORGANIZATIONS

What is the nature of correctional organizations in the United States? What are the attendant problems facing correctional agencies, and how, if at all, are these problems being addressed?

The answer to the first question is made clear by a series of statistical reports recently prepared by the Law Enforcement Assistance Administration.[66] The reports, which provide data on justice services at State and local levels, reveal that we have an almost incomprehensible maze of departments, divisions, commissions, and boards functioning at city, county, and State levels, developed and maintained without the benefit of inter- or intra-governmental coordination. Contributing also to this diversity are the Federal institutions

Source: From *Corrections* (Washington, D.C.: U.S. Government Printing Office, 1973), pp. 439–449.

dealing with both adult and juvenile offenders that operate independently from the functions of the State and local governments.

The national summary of the LEAA reports indicates that there were 5,312 corrections facilities in the United States in 1971 (4,503 for adults and 809 for juveniles) and 2,444 probation and parole agencies.[64] While a cursory examination of these figures may not be startling, more detailed evaluation reveals the fact that only 16 percent of the adult and juvenile correctional facilities are operated at the State level, with the remaining 84 percent, consisting predominantly of county and local jails and lockups, dividing among the 3,047 counties in the Nation and an even greater number of cities, townships, and villages.

Dividing correctional activities into the two major divisions, institutions on the one hand and probation and parole activities on the other, provides a clearer understanding of the national corrections picture. For example, LEAA statistics show that approximately 12 percent of adult correctional facilities in the Nation are provided at the State level, while the remaining 88 percent are provided by city and county governments. Juvenile correctional facilities are distributed more equally. Approximately 45 percent of them are provided at the State level, with the remaining 55 percent supported almost exclusively by county governments. With regard to probation and parole agencies, approximately 30 percent are administered by State governments, with the remaining 70 percent at the local level. As in the case of juvenile correctional facilities, the county governments perform the majority of the local functions.

While the statistical description of correctional services confirms claims of fragmentation, isolation, and multiple levels of delivery of services, further insights into the scope of the problem can be gained through an examination of a 1971 report by the Advisory Commission on Intergovernmental Relations, *State-Local Relations in the Criminal Justice System.* The information provided by this report details the broad spectrum of organizational arrangements that presently characterizes our correctional agencies and reinforces the image of corrections established by the national statistics cited earlier. (See Appendix.)

Major Issues in Organization

The summary of the Advisory Commission's major findings indicates that in the area of organizational and jurisdictional problems, the following major issues have been identified.

All but four States have highly fragmented correctional systems, vesting various correctional responsibilities in either independent boards or noncorrectional agencies. In 41 States, an assortment of health, welfare, and youth agencies exercise certain correctional responsibilities, though their primary function is not corrections.

In over 40 States, neither State nor local governments have full-scale responsibility for comprehensive correctional services. Some corrections services, particularly parole and adult and juvenile institutions, are administered by State agencies, while others, such as probation, local institutions and jails, and juvenile detention, are county or city responsibilities.

More than half of the States provide no standard-setting or inspection services to local jails and local adult correctional institutions.[68]

The States that exercise control over all correctional activities within their systems have become five in number since the report was written. They are: Alaska, Connecticut, Delaware, Rhode Island, and Vermont.

Three basic problems emerge from this analysis of correctional organization in the United States:

- The problem of unifying and coordinating a highly fragmented array of services and programs.

- The problem of shifting fiscal resources from Federal and State levels to local governments, while guiding and assisting localities to improve the quality of their services.

- The problem of changing correctional organizations from closed, hierarchical systems oriented to retribution and restraint into open and flexible systems capable of rehabilitating and resocializing the offenders committed to them.

Coordination is needed not only among correctional agencies, but between them and the other components of the criminal justice system. Moreover, the interrelationships between correctional agencies and other organizations concerned with human problems (e.g., mental health, social welfare, poverty reduction) are of vital importance. Linkages must be established with the private as well as the public sector. Paradoxically, intimate relationships between corrections and law enforcement may impede the ability of corrections to develop reciprocities with the health, education, and welfare complex. Thus, coordination and unification are delicate functions, requiring finesse as well as firm use of available sanctions.

The problem of financing correctional improvements is of critical importance. Ironically, the greatest fiscal capability has existed within large and senior government units, while the services most needed are at the level of local government, whose fiscal impotence is known to everyone.

As to the problem of rigid, stratified, and encapsulated forms of correctional organization, it must be remembered that these organizations were in many cases established in the late 18th or early 19th century. Consequently their structures follow the traditional authoritarian model—one that was appropriate to achieve the then-held goals of revenge and restraint. However, correctional organizations have superimposed additional goals since that time—rehabilitation and, more recently, reintegration of offenders into the community. It is probably impossible to achieve these goals in a traditional organizational milieu. The incompatibility of these more recent trends with the traditional physical plant and organizational structures of corrections represents a profound problem in the renovation of correctional systems.

Some Directions for Change

How can the organization of correctional services be redesigned to meet the problems described above? What can be done to overcome fragmentation and duplication of scarce resources? How can existing finances be reallocated and new funds generated? Are there ways of changing closed and hierarchical systems? There are no easy answers, but there are directions that can be taken with the assurance of significant improvement over the present inadequate scheme.

To begin with, there can be a more rational and coordinated distribution of tasks and missions among the various governmental jurisdictions involved. The Federal Government should relinquish most direct correctional services for offenders, retaining only those which cost-benefit analyses indicate are inappropriate for State and local governments.[69]

At the same time, the Federal level should greatly increase its role in providing financing, standard setting, technical assistance, and manpower development to the correctional services carried on locally. Leadership, stimulation, knowledge discovery, information, coordination, and catalytic influence should be key features of the new Federal role. There are encouraging indications that the Law Enforcement Assistance Administration is moving in this direction. It is less apparent that the Federal Bureau of Prisons and Federal probation services are prepared to divest themselves of major elements of operating responsibility.

The major arena for reintegrative programs is the local community. Administrative power and sanction must be placed there if such efforts are to be strong, well articulated with local resources, and suitably responsive to local needs and problems.

The key to such a redistribution of authority and responsibility lies in the development of new methods of financing correctional services. The probation subsidy program in California is one illustration of a strong effort to strengthen county services and reduce reliance on State institutions. Experimentation with varied subventions, grants, and other forms of intergovernmental assistance will be required. A combination of assistance and regulation—carrot and stick—will be necessary to bring about the needed changes.

There is, moreover, a major opportunity for regional solutions to problems which no single jurisdiction can meet unilaterally. It is essential to have intergovernmental agreements and flexible administrative arrangements which bring offenders to the optimal location for supervision and rehabilitation.

The solution to the traditional reliance of corrections upon hierarchical, authoritarian forms of organization lies in breaking that mold in favor of more creative systems. Instead of large, isolated, custodial institutions operating as self-sufficient baronies, there is a need for small, community-oriented facilities, linked in myriad ways with the resources required for successful reentry to legitimate life.

Instead of jails which operate as appendages of law enforcement and *at best* merely "warehouse" the misdemeanants sentenced to them, the need is for jails which are a part of integrated correctional services, tied closely to probation and parole, and providing such obvious services as medical aid, educational and employment assistance, and attention to the gross, statistically overwhelming problems of alcoholism, drug abuse, and social alienation.

It should be noted that, while the accomplishment of these organizational changes is a formidable task, certain trends and innovations already are taking place. Examples of such activities are provided in the following statement from a previously quoted report of the Commission on Intergovernmental Relations:

> Nine States have established regional juvenile detention facilities while regional jails and correctional institutions have been established in at least seven others.
>
> Over ten States provide inspection services for juvenile detention facilities, jails, and local correctional institutions, and a comparable number of States have stipulated minimum standards for jails, local institutions, and juvenile and misdemeanant probation services.
>
> In four States, a single State department administers all juvenile activities; in three States, the same agency is responsible for administering both juvenile and adult correctional services.[70]

The Commission believes that unification of all correctional programs within a State will allow it to coordinate programs that are essentially interdependent, better utilize scarce human and fiscal resources, and develop more effective programs across the spectrum of corrections. This concept is elaborated in Chapter 16, The Statutory

Framework of Corrections, particularly in Standard 16.4, Unifying Correctional Programs.

In this section an effort has been made to examine the organizational arrangements that characterize corrections today. Some general perspectives and directions for change have been noted.

The following sections approach the development and improvement of correctional administration in a broader context. Several recent theories of how to secure organizational growth and change are applied to the problems of the correctional field.

CORRECTIONAL ORGANIZATIONS

Corrections is a "human resource" organization: that is, its material is people, its product, behavior. The unique features of this type of organization complicate its structural design and management and make both a central part of implementing programs discussed in other chapters of this report.

Unlike a manufacturing operation, the "production process" consists of trained specialists operating on intangibles, and so organizational design must consider the added interpersonal dimension of employee-client relationships. Behavioral and attitudinal effects of specialists on the client are interdependent, and the degree to which various functional specialists are integrated into a "team" determines organizational effectiveness. The relation of functional integration to the effectiveness of human resource organizations places a premium on clearly defined and mutually agreed-to objectives whose identification must precede structural design. Too frequently, organization analysis begins with a set of diagrams rather than a detailed analysis of the problem as a description of alternative functional groupings in relation to previously specified objectives.

Managing a human resource organization is probably even more difficult than managing other public agencies because many traditional management tools are not directly applicable. Data describing effects of the correctional process relate to behavior or attitudes and are subject to subjective, frequently conflicting interpretations. The feedback loops necessary for judging the consequences of policies are difficult to create and suffer from incomplete and inaccurate information. There has not been in corrections an organized and consistent relation between evaluative research and management action.

The management of corrections as a human resource organization must be viewed broadly in terms of how offenders, employees, and various organization processes (communications, decisionmaking, and others) are combined into what is called "the corrections process."

ORGANIZATION DEVELOPMENT

Management by objectives (MBO), planning and organization analysis are elements of a relatively new concept called organization development (OD). Bennis defines it as "a response to change, a complex educational strategy intended to change beliefs, attitudes, values, and structure of organizations so that they can better adapt to new technologies, markets and challenges and the dizzying rate of change itself."[71] Demands for innovation, the trend toward integrated services, and disagreement over objectives suggest that OD programs are applicable to the correction field. To specify how this could be done would require a separate book. Hence the discussion here will outline only the interrelations between basic elements of OD and will concentrate on three areas considered to be of top priority in corrections today: organization analysis, management by objectives, and planning. However, ideally and for completeness, any contemplated activity in these areas should not be considered apart from the broader concept of OD.

Organization development is based on two sets of ideas: one relating to groups and organizations, and the other to individuals.[72] Organizational development views organizations as many interrelated subsystems mutually affecting each other. Problem solving, therefore, is interdependent. In corrections, a simple example would be a change in the industrial production schedule that limited the time offenders could spend in counseling programs.

A distinction is made between tasks or functions and the processes used to perform them. A planning function, for example, can be performed by a task force or a planning office, and it may begin at the operating level or the executive level. OD emphasizes *how* things are done, on the assumption that *what* is done will be determined in large part by the process. In turn, the work climate (e.g., the leadership styles discussed later) is a determinant of which processes are selected.

Reflecting OD's social science origins, anonymous questionnaires and interviews are used to collect data on work group interrelationships, employees' attitudes, etc. Findings then are discussed with employee groups to improve their insights into such organizational processes as line-staff and executive-staff communications, location of decisionmaking, and perceived roles.

Within the organization, individuals are encouraged to develop mutual trust, be candid, openly discuss conflict, and take risks. A premium is placed on the individual's self-actualization fulfillment of his needs within the organization's overall goals and objectives.

A variety of specific interventions are used to implement these ideas and are limited only by the creativity of the change agent. Team building, intergroup problem solving, surveys, reorganization, training in decisionmaking and problem solving, modifying work flows, and job enrichment are examples of the types of techniques frequently employed.[73] An OD program usually involves an outside consultant to begin with, but it is essential to have (or develop) a capability for continuing the program within the organization. Generally, these techniques and processes are used in the work situation —the functions to be performed—to integrate the factors necessary for employee effectiveness (interpersonal skills, individual performance objectives, etc.) with the goals of the organization. OD practitioners feel that this complex process is necessary to relate organization design, planning, objectives, and employee performance.

ORGANIZATION ANALYSIS

Organization analysis and design is a specialty that should not be left to whim, the pressures and forces of the moment, or the experience of individuals whose direct personal knowledge of the organization is limited. On the other hand, the analyst should realize that reorganization may have salutory political effects by giving the appearance of change while everything remains the same.

The historical correctional proclivity for fads should be avoided in organization design. Calling for simple unification of institutions, parole, and probation into a State department of corrections has become a frequent suggestion. While in some situations this will improve correctional services, it is a delusion to believe that tinkering can, by itself, effect the functional integration desired. Frequently, sub-units of large-scale organizations carve out a functional territory and vigorously guard it against intrusion and change. Organization, although important, is not the panacea for all operational problems; formally redefining roles does not automatically change actual operations.

There are many types of organizational structures and many ways to analyze them. Depending on the assumptions, an organization may be divided on the basis of region, line-staff relationships, functions, or missions. These divisions rarely appear in pure form; for example a regional organization may be subdivided on the basis of functional groupings. In corrections, it is not unusual to base organizations on the sex, age, and offense of the clientele. Regardless of the type chosen, the correctional manager should recognize that the specific structure should be evaluated in terms of its relation to decision-making, the objectives of the organization, and the environment in which it operates.

As one organization analyst states, "Among the first things to consider in the organization of work are basic, underlying assumptions. All too frequently work is organized in terms of solutions, practices, even theories; yet basic beliefs about individuals who make up the organization are either ignored, or are merely implied."[74]

Principles of organization analysis are as numerous as the structures they produce. How phenomena are interpreted depends on the way they are analyzed. In one view, the organization is conceived as an "organism," the critical features of which are its ability to (1) test reality, (2) interpret the test, and (3) adapt to changes.[75] Another model focuses on the psychology of the individuals who make up the organization (motivations, desires, gratification, etc.).[76] A sociological view would identify the various groups comprising the organization, the norms governing their interaction, and the prevailing value systems.[77] A more mechanical interpretation of organizations sees subunits as carefully integrated contributors to the production process which perform their assigned duties routinely without regard for the work of other units.

Any reorganization problem should be viewed from all these perspectives to draw out the possible implications or effects of the particular structure being proposed as a solution. The exigencies of the time may require a compromise of specific "principles" of organization. For example, two basic principles frequently violated by correctional organizations are "unity of direction" and "equality of authority and responsibility." Interposing a policy board between the State's chief executive and the correctional agency limits the governor's authority over an organization for which he is responsible to the public. Policy authority is divorced from operational authority, even though there may originally have been sound reasons for this departure from "principles."

Similarly, overlapping responsibilities are not, per se, undesirable. In some situations, in fact, they may positively contribute to a stated organizational objective. For example, the Air Force does not have sole responsibility for military air operations. The Marine Corps and the Army also have organizational units providing air services because the prime objective for the Marines is troop mobility and for the Army, air support of ground maneuvers. When visibility is an objective, a program-based organizational unit (e.g., narcotics treatment) may be superimposed on a functional categorization (e.g., education, counseling).

Failure to recommend a specific solution will not satisfy the manager who wants a meal and not a recipe. But there is no single or simple answer. Rather the most appropriate organizational arrangements must be decided after the problem is analyzed from a variety of perspectives and in relation to what the particular structure is ultimately to accomplish.

The important features in a reorganization are the *actual* changes in employee interrelations and the policies communicated to them, not the arrangement of boxes in an organization chart. Effective work groups and interpersonal relations are not formed and dissolved by policy statements. A reorganization cannot be accomplished solely by pronouncement. It must include a specification of what processes (meetings, group discussions, timing, etc.) will be used to implement it. Management disenchantment with reorganization usually arises because these processes are ignored.

An organization's objectives partially determine its most effective structure. Although offenders are affected, corrections' retribution objective relates primarily to serving society. A rehabilitation or reintegration objective focuses direction on the individual, and consequently organizational arrangements must be different from those focusing on retribution.

The emphasis on opening institutions to the community increases the number of employees whose primary frame of reference is external to the organization.[78] Such "boundary persons" typically have attitudes more congruent with persons outside the organization, a fact which may increase the difficulties of resolving internal conflicts.

The emphasis on offenders' rights implies more than a new office or changed procedures; it will require a more independent organizational subunit and an attitude of negotiation rather than confrontation. The present stress on innovation and the prospects of a continuing demand for change in corrections require flexible organizational arrangements where work groups are viewed as fluid and temporary.

Analysis of Correctional Organization

For many years it has been an almost universal practice in the corrections field to refer to "systems" when considering the corrections process. Earlier, the reference was to "penal systems" or "prison systems." Currently, the phrases "correction systems" or even "criminal justice systems" are favored. This long-term and widespread use of the word "systems" has tended to obscure the fact that most correction jurisdictions are neither designed nor managed as organizational systems.

Correctional services can be described only as nonorganized. Virtually all larger correction agencies have organization charts that presume to depict the flow of authority and accountability among the diverse elements that comprise each specific correction organization. Many such organizations also have policy manuals, job descriptions or position profiles for staff, job specifications, other organizational and personnel documents, and standard operating procedures that reinforce the notion of organization. But the salient characteristic of virtually all correction organizations today is their high degree of inter- and intra-organizational separatism for legal, political, and bureaucratic reasons.

In substantial part this organizational fragmentation is the heritage of the legal background from which all contemporary correction organizations have evolved. This legal heritage limited the operational boundaries of "correctional" responsibility to the time span between sentencing to institutional custody and release from institutional custody. What may occur earlier is perceived as the responsibility of legislative bodies, police, courts, and probation. Whatever may occur subsequent to conditional release from institutional custody is perceived as the responsibility of parole.

Among the negative consequences occurring directly or indirectly from the acceptance by most correction managers of the legal frame of reference are these:

- Managerial thinking has tended to become constricted and reactive to the emergence of problems, rather than innovative and anticipatory.

- The boundaries of the corrections field largely have been accepted as statutorily and bureaucratically defined, rather than creatively probed and, where appropriate, professionally challenged. For example, definition and prevention of crime tend to be seen as the responsibility of others. Relatively few correctional administrators have been concerned professionally with the existence of wide disparities in the law and court practice regarding sentences.

- Input of offenders into correction organization tends to be accepted without demur, the attitude of correctional managers too often being "we take what they send us and do the best we can." This acquiescence frequently has resulted in the sentencing of juveniles to adult institutions, imprisonment of offenders who need psychiatric or other mental health care in institutions that lack competent staff and adequate facilities, and acceptance from the criminal justice process of inordinately large numbers of the black and the poor.

- The focus of correction organizations tends to be institutional, reflecting the emphasis in the criminal justice process on whatever facility is perceived as the "appropriate" extension of the court of jurisdiction: the training school for the juvenile offender, the prison for the convicted adult violator.

Traditionally, the institutional focus has been custodial, whatever may be the philosophic rhetoric of the correction jurisdiction. This orientation too stems from an historic perception of the institution as the "holding" extension of the courts.

The nonorganization of corrections also results from political arrangements. The Federal Government, through the Department of Justice and the judiciary, operates three distinct correctional agencies: the Bureau of Prisons, the Board of Parole, and the Probation Service. As noted earlier in this chapter, each of the 50 States operates a corrections "agency." And, through bureaucratic subdivision, many operate several separate agencies; for example, juvenile corrections, adult corrections, probation, and parole. Local governments present varied organizational patterns, ranging from a relatively complex correctional organization in New York City to simple detention facilities in small city police stations or rural courthouses.

Further separatism is the product of bureaucracy. Even within those States with administratively grouped correctional responsibility, there nonetheless is the tendency to establish bureaucratic subjurisdictions. Administratively these may be divided into probation and parole, juvenile corrections, and adult corrections.

These major categories sometimes are further subdivided on the basis of the individual's offense, age, and sex. Hence, the "organization" of corrections in each political jurisdiction tends to emphasize separate institutions for the adult offender, subdivided in turn into minimum, medium, and maximum security facilities for men and women. Until recently, State correction agencies and local facilities segregated each category of offender on the basis of race, often in separate institutions for each offender category.

Within correctional agencies and specific institutions of such agencies, there is often a philosophic and operational separation of staff members whose duties are principally custodial from those whose responsibilities concern offender programs. Also, like all large-scale organizations, corrections has informal or social organization of staff and of inmates, frequently working at cross-purposes to the formal goals of the organization.

Fragmentation hampers the ability of an organization or a group of organizations to respond to new environmental forces and stress. An organization's ability to achieve specified objectives is contingent on its detection of and responsiveness to changing environmental factors. It first must recognize and accurately assess changes that affect its operations (e.g., public attitudes toward alcoholism) and then develop a response consistent with overall objectives (e.g., treat alcoholism as a medical problem). Similarly, as the general population's education level increased, correctional agencies were required to provide college-level programs for offenders.

The corrections field already is being substantially affected by dramatic changes occurring in American society. The incidence of crime nationwide has risen at an alarming rate, and younger persons comprise a disproportionate amount of this increase. Therefore, it reasonably can be expected that the number of offenders requiring services will rise substantially in the immediate future. Because of the national pattern of high birth rates from the end of World War II into the mid-1960's, the average age of offenders probably will decline somewhat, at least in the immediate future.

There have been perceptible shifts in public opinion regarding correctional operations and their effects on offenders. This has been reflected in growing legislative criticism and demands for reform. The judiciary has extended the application of civil and constitutional rights to almost all aspects of corrections. Professional groups such as the American Bar Association have assumed an active role in advocating reform and direct services to offenders.

The field of corrections faces a period of rapid and dramatic change with a highly fragmented organization and a substantially inappropriate management orientation. Considerable evidence exists to suggest that the organizational arrangements and managerial approaches that largely characterize the corrections field today did not serve well the relatively stable situation of the past. There is every reason to believe that they will serve even less well in the dynamic and fluid environment of tomorrow.

MANAGEMENT BY OBJECTIVES

Management by objectives (MBO) emphasizes a goal-oriented philosophy and attitude. Goal-oriented management focuses on results with less concern for method, as long as it is within acceptable legal and moral limits. Traditional management, on the other hand, tends to be task-oriented, with emphasis on task performance without adequate regard for results.

The purpose of management by objectives is to: (1) develop a mutually understood statement regarding the organization's direction and (2) provide criteria for measuring organization and individual performance. The statement is a hierarchical set of interrelated and measurable goals, objectives, and subobjectives. If properly conducted, the process may be as important as the objectives themselves because it improves vertical and horizontal communication and emphasizes interdepartmental integration.

For an MBO system to be implemented successfully, it must be based on a participative management philosophy and fulfill several specific conditions.[79]

First, the full support of top management is essential. Indeed at each level of management the superior's degree of acceptance of his managerial approach will determine substantially whether or not subordinates accept the system and try to make it work.

A second necessary condition is a goal oriented management philosophy. The motivational value of an MBO approach depends in great part upon giving each manager and employee responsibility to carry out a job without constant supervision and then assessing him on his degree of accomplishment.

Third, each superior-subordinate relationship should be characterized by the highest degree of cooperation and mutual respect possible.

Fourth, managerial focus should be on any deviations from agreed-upon levels of goal attainment, not on personalities; and the evaluation system should report any such deviations to the manager or employee establishing the goal, not to his superior.

The fifth condition is feedback. If managers are to be evaluated on the results they obtain, they require timely and accurate readings of their progress to take corrective action when necessary. Further they need substantially accurate projections and interpretations of demographic, technical, social, legal, and other developments likely to affect their progress and performance.

Finally, to be successful, an intensive training program must precede organizational implementation. A followup consultative service should be available to organizational members of units requiring assistance in implementing this system.

Implementing MBO

Designing and implementing management by objectives requires the achievement of the following sequential steps:

1. An ongoing system capable of accurately identifying and predicting changes in the environment in which the organization functions.
2. Administrative capability through a management information system to provide data quickly to appropriate organizational members, work groups, or organizational units for their consideration and possible utilization.

3. Clearly established and articulated organizational and individual goals, mutually accepted through a process of continuous interaction between management and workers and between various levels of management. Unilateral imposition of organizational goals on lower echelon participants will not result in an MBO system but another bureaucracy.

4. An ongoing evaluation of the organizational and individual goals in the light of feedback from the system. Such feedback and evaluation may result in the resetting of goals.

5. A properly designed and functioning organizational system for effective and efficient service delivery. In such a system, goal-oriented collaboration and cooperation are organizationally facilitated, and administrative services fully support efforts at goal accomplishment.

6. A managerial and work climate highly conducive to employee motivation and self-actualization toward organizational goal accomplishments. Such a climate should be developed and nurtured through the application of a participative style of management, to be discussed shortly.

7. A properly functioning system for appraising organizational, work group, and individual progress toward goal attainment.

CORRECTIONAL MANAGEMENT'S PLANNING RESPONSIBILITY

It is an unfortunate reality that most correction agencies do not engage in planning in the fullest sense. While many have a general notion of where they are going and some engage in specific aspects of planning such as facilities construction, few are engaged in the full planning process. This process involves development of integrated long-range, intermediate-range, and short-range plans for the complete spectrum of their administrative and operational functions.

Several rationalizations are offered to account for the lack of comprehensive planning. Perhaps the most common is "We can't tell what the legislature is going to do." This "explanation" ignores the fact that what the legislature does (or does not do) often comes about precisely because no practical, planned, and documented alternative has been proposed by corrections management. Also commonly heard is the rationalization, "There is simply not enough time—our organization is already overworked and understaffed." But corrections management always finds the time and staff resources to deal with crises rising in the system.

Planning, contrary to the opinion of many, is not something new and difficult. To paraphrase the historian Arnold Toynbee, "One of the characteristics of being human is that one makes plans." While the efficiency experts of World War II and the PPB (Planning, Programming, Budgeting) experts of the mid-1960's may lay claim to a large share of the limelight and insight, planning is something that all men engage in to varying degrees. One need only recall the past 50 years to recognize the continuum of changing planning styles that has taken place in the United States:

- Long-range corporate planning from the 1920's to the present.
- New Deal economic planning.
- World War II military operations and production planning.
- Fair Deal, New Frontier, and Great Society full employment and social welfare planning.
- Surburban growth and urban renewal planning.
- Systems planning (PPB and PMS) and application to human resources programs.

Too frequently, planning has been left to an isolated office staffed with technicians, and the organization has received their product with reluctance. Failure to differentiate types of planning (e.g., strategic and tactical) has led to two extremes: either the planning function is considered the total purview of top management, or it is seen as the aggregation of individual plans from many organizational subunits. In fact, it is neither. The planning process should involve input (information, objectives, progress, etc.) from all organizational units, but the major decisions regarding goals and resource allocations are the responsibility of top management.

Role of the Planner

The effective planner is not an ivory tower technician, but some unique features of his role should be recognized and supported. His effectiveness depends in part on a sensitivity to the changing conditions under which the organization must operate. Therefore, he is frequently seen as an "outsider" by the rest of the organization because he continually raises questions not immediately impinging on daily operations. The planner is a "devil's advocate" and questions the basic assumptions and operating practices of the organization. In examining alternatives to the status quo for their possible application to the organization, he is placed in the role of an unwanted change agent.

The planner sometimes contributes to his own alienation by not recognizing that large organizations always contain conflicting opinions that must be reconciled by the chief executive. There are pragmatic restrictions on what ideally should be a rational process. Even though management decisions may be at odds with the "compelling evidence," the planning function should at least make the reasons for the decisions explicit.

The planner should be a participant-observer in the short-term decisionmaking of top management. Only in this way can he be in a position to point out the relationships between daily action and long-range intentions. Planning can be called a manager's technique to invent the future. It can also be thought of as a systematic examination of future opportunities and risks and the strategies to exploit the opportunities and avoid the risks. It would appear, however, that planning more clearly is the rational process of directing today's decisions toward the accomplishment of a set of predetermined short- and long-range goals. This process depends upon how problems are identified, broken down into manageable dimensions, related to one another, and resolved through the choice of a number of alternatives.

Planning and Budgeting Systems

The budget expresses in financial terms the correctional manager's plans or goals. Budgeting is an administrative mechanism for making choices among alternative and competitive resource uses, presumably balancing public needs and organizational requirements against available and requested funds. When the choices are coordinated with the correctional organization's goals, the budget becomes a plan.

Like planning, budgeting is something that everyone does including the wealthy. We budget our time, money, food, entertainment, and other requirements with a general view to meeting our personal and family goals. The correctional manager is charged with budgeting his resources to meet organizational, staff, and offender goals.

Operating, annual, capital, or facilities budgets are common differentiations in types of budget. The distinction largely is related to differences in timing (annual vs. long-range), degree of uniqueness (ongoing requirements vs. one-time expenditures), and differentiated financing arrangements (annual tax collection vs. bonded indebtedness).

The distinction between line-item and program budgets is of substantial managerial significance. The line-item budget is input-oriented, focusing on specific, discrete items of expenditure required to perform a service and categorized by organizational units. A program budget is output-oriented, focusing on the function or service performed.

The line-item budget tends to focus the attention of decisionmakers, including legislators, on specifics such as food, supplies, clothing, and books. The program approach tends to elevate the decisionmaking focus to the level of programmatic concern and consideration of alternative courses of action.

The Program Planning and Budgeting System (PPBS), popular in the 1960's, is a system-oriented effort to link planning, budgeting, and management by objective processes through programs. Under this system an agency or organization first would ask itself: "What is our purpose, and what goals are we attempting to realize?"

Once our purposes or objectives have been determined, action programs to achieve these objectives would be identified or, if nonexistent, designed.

Next, each such program would be analyzed. In existing programs, the analysis would be in terms of the extent to which they were oriented to achievement of the organization's objectives. Reference would be made to the level of effectiveness at which they were functioning toward such attainment. In the case of newly formulated, objective-oriented programs, the analysis would be in terms of their anticipated costs and expected contribution to accomplishment of organizational objectives.

Finally, in terms of the decisionmaking process, existing and new alternative programs would be analytically compared as to their respective costs and anticipated benefits. Should an alternative, on the basis of such a cost-benefit analysis, be deemed preferable to an existing program, the latter would be discarded and the alternative adopted.

Implicit in this management system is a longer-range programming perspective coupled with a continuous process of reevaluation of objectives, programs, and budgetary amounts as circumstances change.

Regardless of how organized and formal an organization's planning, there are six criteria by which managers may judge the comprehensiveness and adequacy of the planning process. These criteria are stated in terms of questions that should be asked repeatedly with reference to any specific planning approach:

- Has the system's planning process adequately identified the key influences in development and trends of American society, the region, and the State, and properly evaluated the impact of each such influence on the field of corrections, its functional components, and on the specific correction system itself?
- Have the strengths and weaknesses of the system been assessed accurately?
- Have the capacities and capabilities of different system functions to support the plan been projected far enough ahead?
- Have alternatives been considered and evaluated adequately?
- Is there a realistic timetable or schedule for implementation?
- What provisions have been made for possible future reverses?

The basis of correctional planning must shift from individuals to a group framework, as the concerns of the correctional manager and planner quickly become more universal.

"One of the great challenges facing . . . [the planner] is the necessity of coordinating knowledge, influence, and resources on a scale commensurate with the human problems he is addressing. . . . [These] problems are interrelated, complex and resistant to piecemeal efforts."[80] Clearly, a logical, systematic planning approach is needed that recognizes problem complexity, changing concepts, and changing priorities, and provides a means for developing more effective programs.

The objective of community corrections, for example, is to maximize offenders' access to local resources, not as an alternative to incarceration but as a solution itself. This goal requires more integration of criminal justice components (statewide and within each local area) and coordination with other social service delivery systems. (See Chapter 9.)

Planning for the Future of Corrections

The rate of change in corrections has not reached a pace that makes planning impossible. Many of today's problems are related directly to the failure to anticipate the operational impact of general social and environmental changes. The extension of the range of offenders' rights, for example, was a natural outgrowth of a similar movement involving racial minorities and students.

The need for a more coherent approach to correctional programs long has been recognized. Historically, correctional reform has been limited to minor variations on a discordant theme. Reform can and should be a continuing process, not a reaction to periodic public criticism. The planner's role as a skeptic or devil's advocate regarding underlying concepts and basic assumptions can keep the corrections field from a state of complacency.

Even the best plan, however, is of little value if the organization's climate, structure and employee resistance obstruct its implementation. Employees react negatively to changes imposed from above. So access to decisionmaking is important, even though the chief executive's leadership responsibilities require that innovations cannot always be vetoed by subordinates.

As human resource agencies, corrections must make a special effort to integrate various functional specialties into an organization team that holds mutual objectives vis-a-vis the client not only among its members but also between members and the organization. Accomplishing this organization climate will require a participatory and nonthreatening leadership style in which employee, offender, and the organization needs are met in a compatible way.

THE CORRECTIONAL INSTITUTION AS A COMMUNITY

INTRODUCTION

The basic experience of living together in a group probably determines the effects of confinement on prisoners to a greater extent than all the institutional purposes, guidelines, procedures or programs a government can ordain. Locking up large numbers of people for months or years, thus greatly restricting their choice of companions, activities and schedules, may affect their behavior even after release in ways that are not anticipated if one looks only at the formal aspects of correctional management.

The readings in this section describe and explain some variations of institutional life. Theoretical guidance for identifying and interpreting these variations is provided by Clarence Schrag, a distinguished sociologist at the University of Washington, who has also been employed in several positions, including that of state director, in the Washington prisons. His outline of "foundations for a theory of correction" examines the communication channels, the shared expectations, and the reciprocal, complementary or symbiotic relationships among prison staff and inmates. These interactions generate an unofficial system of authority and obligation somewhat independent of the official administrative hierarchy. Four major patterns of inmate adaptation to these circumstances are delineated, and are attributed to the sociocultural experiences of inmates both in and out of prison.

The "social context of jails" is distinctively reported by sociologists David B. Rottman and John R. Kimberly. Their description and analysis indicate that the close acquaintance of staff with most inmates in these usually small institutions, as well as the preoccupation of unsentenced prisoners with their plea bargaining in court, makes the informal organization different from that of large prisons.

An intimate view of prison experience from the convict's perspective is presented by sociologist John Irwin. It is based on the author's past experience as a prisoner, and on his unusually extensive contacts with inmates and ex-inmates of California prisons. Irwin describes the inside affiliations and outside identifications maintained during confinement;

the differences among inmates in motivation toward various types of endeavor; the segmentation of their social groups by prison programs; and as a result of all these features, a great diversity of adaptations to imprisonment.

During the 1970s new features in the unofficial social organization of many prisons reflected changes in the slum street life of our largest cities. Prominent among the urban developments were rapid spread of drug abuse, resurgence of fighting gangs in communities where minority groups predominate and widespread possession of handguns by delinquent and criminal youth. In the same period, the granting of probation to nonviolent and nonaddicted offenders increased, so that among those sentenced to prison a larger proportion were confirmed addicts or were prone to assaultive conduct than in other eras. Sociologist James Jacobs shows that in Illinois these trends resulted in the importation into prison of the hierarchies, rivalries and ideologies of Chicago's four leading minority group street gangs. The author thus clearly contradicts some older claims that the inmate subculture is primarily a product of prison life. Anthropologist John Davidson not only describes vividly the long-traditional traffic in contraband among prisoners, but claims that by 1970, when well-organized Chicano inmate groups attained dominance in California penitentiaries, this unofficial economy reached new heights in dollar volume, corruption of staff and fomenting of violence.

Some differences from men's prisons, but many similarities to them, were found by sociologist Esther Heffernan in her exceptional study of the District of Columbia's prison for women. She observes that inmates there distinguish three styles of adaptation to imprisonment—the square, the cool and the life—that pervade all aspects of their institutional activity. She also found parallel behavior patterns among staff.

A perspective on "the social meaning of prison homosexuality" is provided by sociologists John H. Gagnon and William Simon, who have carried forward the famous research on sexual conduct initiated at Indiana University by the late Alfred C. Kinsey. They point out that prisons will always foster sexual nonconformity as long as they are sex-segregated, but that the extent and nature of sexual maladjustment there depend on the age, gender and prior sexual and social history of the inmates. These researchers view homosexual activity in prisons as an effort to offset the social deprivations of confinement rather than as simply a striving for sexual release.

During the four-day disturbance at New York State's Attica prison in 1971, 43 died and almost twice that number were wounded. Thirty-nine were killed by state police in their 15-minute gunblazing assault on September 13th, the single bloodiest day of conflict between American groups since the 19th century Indian and Civil wars. Sociologist Robert Martinson argues provocatively that riots in early American prisons were mass escape attempts, that most late 19th and 20th century riots were struggles to improve conditions within prisons, but that Attica represents a third development, expressive mutinies. These he ascribes to decline of faith in the psychological treatment programs that placated prisoners for two decades following a wave of riots in the early 1950s. Viewing Attica in the light of his own experience as an imprisoned northern white Freedom Rider in Mississippi during the civil rights controversy of the previous decade, the author discusses four features of collective behavior in prison: militant leadership, ecstatic solidarity, magical thinking and social bluff.

The report of a Task Force to Study Violence in California prisons during the early 1970s describes a marked increase in the number of inmates stabbed and employees assaulted. Officials reacted to these events mainly by locking up prisoners to a greater extent than before, thus sharply reducing work, education, recreation and other inmate group activities. Among measures designed to reduce violence the Task Force recommends first of all, improvement of custodial controls, but it also urges pay increases for work done by prisoners, improved communication between inmates and staff, reduction in the drabness of institutional life and expansion of California's innovative program of conjugal visits for prisoners, as well as facilitation of other types of visits by outsiders. At this writing there has been some decrease in the amount of violence in California prisons, but it is difficult to determine whether the decline is due to these measures or to other policies, such as informing the inmate sooner of the probable date of his parole.

9

SOME FOUNDATIONS FOR A THEORY OF CORRECTION

CLARENCE SCHRAG

THE CORRECTIONAL COMMUNITY

Cultural Determinants of Correctional Policy

Problems of criminality and activities of criminals have attained such prominence in contemporary social life that nearly all persons have some conception of the methods or techniques of crime, the supposed causes of crime, and tactics of crime control. Common conceptions of criminality exert an important influence on the activities of correctional administrators because administrators regard themselves as representatives of the broader community in their dealings with criminals. Moreover, they are so regarded by the members of the broader community. Correctional officials, in other words, carry a public trust, and their duties and responsibilities are defined for them in terms of conventional beliefs concerning criminal behavior. Thus, the objectives and policies of correctional institutions are largely reflections of beliefs and values that are indigenous to the broader community.

If their objectives deviate very far from those of the broader community, correctional officials encounter various forms of public opposition. Consequently, the assessment of changes or trends in public expectations is an inevitable and important task for the correctional official. To the extent that social conventions are supportive of confused or contradictory correctional objectives, it may be expected that prison policies will reflect these confusions and contradictions.

Source: From *The Prison: Studies in Institutional Organization and Change,* edited by Donald R. Cressey. Copyright 1961 by Holt, Rinehart and Winston, Inc. Reprinted by permission of the author and publisher.

According to available evidence, the foremost responsibilities assigned to prison officials are maintenance of custodial security and protection of society against convicted offenders. Therapy comes next. "You can't treat the prisoners if you can't keep them," and similar mottoes indicate the relative values ordinarily attached to treatment and custody. Among the goals that receive weaker public endorsements, although they are strongly invoked in special cases and in times of crisis, are deterrence of potential offenders and reinforcement of cultural norms and values.

While the relative importance attached to different correctional objectives may vary somewhat in different segments of the community, the protective functions of correctional institutions are usually given the highest rankings, followed by the therapeutic or restorative functions, and finally the integrative functions. Moreover, staff members of correctional institutions, in general, follow the same order of rankings, the primary exception being that top-level administrative officials who have been indoctrinated in modern treatment philosophy tend to place a higher premium on therapy.

Like the goals and objectives of correctional institutions, the policies of such organizations are greatly influenced by conventional assumptions concerning criminal behavior. Correctional programs are founded on a public conception of the criminal as a person who habitually engages in deliberative misconduct. In fact, the conception of malicious intent is an essential ingredient of criminal conduct as defined by statute. Furthermore, persons who are regarded as being incapable of willful wrongdoing, namely, children and the insane, do not ordinarily come under the purview of criminal law or under the correctional policies that are presumably designed for deliberative offenders.

Although the above conception of criminal behavior may be gradually changing under the impact of contemporary explanations of human conduct, it seems clear that the bulk of opinion and the weight of official and legal doctrine are still largely in support of the traditional notion that the criminal knows the difference between right and wrong, that he makes a rational and considered decision against the moral order, and that his choice is subject to voluntary control. Criminals and prisoners, in other words, are believed to be capable of conformity but disposed to playing the role of the rebel. Prisoners consequently are expected to exhibit antisocial attitudes and to be resistive and unruly in their contacts with correctional authorities. To the degree that prisoner roles are conditioned by the traditional assumptions mentioned, these assumptions may be expected to strengthen the staff-inmate conflicts and the negativistic attitudes of prisoners that have been so frequently noted in correctional research.

The role of the prison official, as perceived in the broader community, also reflects the influence of the assumptions mentioned above. In effect, inmates are absolved of any responsibility for prison programs and policies; and officials are held fully accountable for the attainment of correctional objectives, the maintenance of plant and equipment, the protection of inmate health and welfare, and the enforcement of inmate conformity and obedience.

The focus of traditional prison policies is the enforcement of compliance and obedience despite the expected opposition of the inmates. Strict surveillance and punitive actions are deemed necessary to show the prisoner that society is stronger than he is. Force and restraints, according to the view that seems dominant in the broader community, should only be used when necessary to maintain control; but they should always be available in sufficient degree to insure the maintenance of control. Thus, correctional institutions are frequently viewed as autonomous societies having police powers sufficient for the prompt detection of any rule violations and for rigorous enforcement of official rules and regulations.

The prison world, as seen from a conventional perspective, is a world of conflict between forces of good and of evil. Prisoners are expected to exercise their antisocial propensities if they can get away with it. Officers are, or are expected to be, the sentinels of the good society who carry the full authority of the official community in their relations with the inmate caste. Their first objective is to obtain by means of external constraints the compliance that prisoners are disinclined to display voluntarily.

Significantly, the traditional view of the prison is also the view of most staff members and inmates. Striking similarities can be noted in the previously mentioned assumptions and in the way staff members and inmates perceive their own social roles and the roles of each other.

To illustrate, staff members and inmates were questioned concerning various possible solutions to problematic situations that frequently arise in correctional institutions. In addition to stating their own preferred solutions to the problems, officers and inmates indicated the solutions that they thought would be adopted by most officers and by most inmates. Then the observed preferences of the two groups were compared with their anticipated preferences.

Responses to the questionnaires clearly show that the role of the inmate is quite uniformly perceived as an "antisocial" role, whereas the role of the officer is just as consistently perceived as an "authoritarian" role. That is, both staff members and inmates regularly overestimate the number of antisocial solutions to prison problems that are actually chosen by the inmates. Likewise, both staff members and inmates, in attempting to anticipate the solutions that are chosen with greatest frequency by staff members, consistently assign to prison officials a higher degree of authoritarianism than is warranted by their actual choices. Moreover, differences in the role of the inmate as perceived by officers and by the inmates themselves are relatively minor. The same thing holds for the role of the officer.

The conclusion suggested is that staff members and inmates share perceptual distortions in such a manner that they see the differences in their assigned roles as being greatly exaggerated. These distortions tend to reinforce the traditions of conflict between the two groups. Furthermore, the distortions are in complete accord with the conventional view of the prison as a world of conflict. It may consequently be assumed that the distortions reflect the influence of cultural factors upon the cognitive behavior of staff members and inmates. The cultural expectation of staff-inmate conflict impregnates the perceptions of the members of the prison community, and in this way it may function as a self-fulfilling prophecy.

The strategies for "reforming," "rehabilitating," "treating," or "correcting" criminals in institutions also are greatly influenced by the assumptions of persons in the broader society, and these assumptions have been importantly revised during the course of correctional history. Early efforts were to be aimed at "breaking the will" of the offender. Current conceptions of treatment place greater emphasis upon the inculcation of useful habits, such as thriftiness and industriousness, and the acquisition of social and occupational skills. Thus, the treatment function of the prison is to make available to inmates a variety of facilities, including programs of academic and vocational training, medical care, religious instruction, counseling, and parole planning, to mention only the standard treatment devices.

But the assumption that it is entirely up to the inmate to take advantage of treatment opportunities if he is so inclined is still an important feature of treatment philosophy. Behavior is still regarded as primarily a matter of personal volition. Reorganization of attitudes and modification of affective attachments to objects and persons in the social environment are generally viewed as personal issues over which prison policies have little control. The possibility of redefining the roles and changing the social positions of inmates by means of administrative procedures receives relatively little consideration, although some efforts along these lines are being initiated through various forms of group therapy. . . .

Administrative Organization of the Prison

The structure of prison administration is organized around conventional definitions of correctional objectives and conventional assumptions concerning criminal behavior. More specifically, the administrative structure of the prison is comprised of a hierarchy of offices or staff positions, each of which implies certain duties and responsibilities, and a chain of command linking the various offices in a rationally predetermined manner. The immediate objective of this structure is the attainment of uniform compliance to a set of official rules and regulations that designates the behavior expected of staff members and inmates.

The articulation of authority patterns and staff positions provides a powerful and intricately balanced mechanism for manufacturing policy decisions. Everyday observations of inmate behavior are reported from the lower levels of command up the ladder to higher levels, where the numerous reports are collated and official decisions are made. Then directives and supportive information, sanctioned by top-level administrators, flow back down the ladder in a unilateral sequence, from division chief to supervisor to officer and, in turn, to the inmates. Hence, the typical communication pattern in the close-custody prison is for reports of a first-hand factual nature to move upward in the chain of command and for policies, directives, and interpretations of factual materials to move down the ranks of employees.

Despite the clear logic of its structure, there may be significant defects in the system of unilateral authority relations. First, the system assumes that officers are fully committed to the objectives and policies announced by the chief administrator. Secondly, it assumes that the administrative machinery of the prison embodies the power and authority of the broader community in dealing with the inmates. Thirdly, it assumes that inmates occupy a caste-like status that deprives them of any influence in the determination of policy. None of these assumptions is very realistic if judged in terms of social activities that are normally observed in the prison community. Let us briefly examine these assumptions in the order mentioned.

Alienation of the Officer

Instead of insuring agreement between rank-and-file officers and top-level administrators, the unilateral flow of authority and communication may tend to produce a considerable barrier between the low-ranking officer's world of everyday experience and the picture of that world as it is viewed from the top levels of command.

Frequently persons in highest authority are far removed from the scene of contact between staff members and inmates where the relative worthiness of alternative policies is most clearly revealed. Administrative decisions regarding specific situations are based chiefly on facts reported by subordinates. Therefore, administrative judgments are sometimes jeopardized by the distortions of fact that tend to occur when reports are repeatedly reviewed, digested, and passed upward through the ranks of the administrative hierarchy. In addition, the highest authorities may be among the last persons to learn about the impact of their decisions upon the relations between staff members and inmates. Generally, the higher the rank of the administrative officer, the greater his dependence on reports of the observations of others and the less direct the sources of his information.

Again, the officers who are most immediately affected by correctional policies are the ones who play the least part in policy formation. The task of low-ranking officers is to carry out orders, not to evaluate them. Feedback, such as criticism of directives received, is minimized, and in some institutions no official procedure for such reverse flow of communication is available. When reverse flow of critical comment is tolerated, it is often restricted to informal relations among trusted associates and is not treated as a matter of policy. Failure of unilateral communication to exploit the possibilities of feedback encourages the development of unofficial channels for the diffusion of messages. This may seriously interfere with the operation of the formal machinery of administration.

Official communication, based on the unilateral design, seems to be at a distinct disadvantage when competing with the mutual give-and-take that characterizes unofficial relations among officers or between officers and inmates. Two factors are of special significance in this connection. First, official directives generally assume the form of unqualified and universal imperatives. This results from the tendency for rationalizations, justifications, and elaborations to get lost or misinterpreted as the directives filter down the ranks of the administrative hierarchy. Secondly, for every official directive that is issued there is likely to be an unofficial interpretation which results from comments and discussions occurring outside the official channels of communication. For subordinate officials, it is perhaps the unofficial version that has the more comprehensible meaning and fits the directive into the over-all plan of prison administration. If this is the case, the unilateral system of communication, instead of eliminating the influence of hearsay and rumor, may tend to make unofficial messages an essential part of the officer's conception of prison policy.

Allegiance to the official administration may be less important to the subordinate officer than are his many involvements in the unofficial conventions of the prison community. His knowledge of the official program is sometimes limited to the specific rules and regulations that are his immediate concern. His information about prison affairs comes primarily from sources other than those that are officially prescribed. For example, over half of the subordinate officers in a state prison were unaware of the existence of a certain group therapy program that had been in operation for more than nine months. And the majority of those officers who knew about the program stated that they had learned of it from inmates or fellow officers rather than from their superiors.

In many institutions, the status of subordinate officers is essentially connected with their lack of official information, their limited influence, and their minimal participation in matters of administrative policy. Attitudes of detachment and feelings of powerlessness or meaninglessness with respect to the official program are also commonly noted. Objective factors related to the status of subordinate officers tend to reinforce their feelings of powerlessness, and vice versa. The result is that officers of the lower ranks frequently are alienated from the official program. This is reflected, for example, in the negative correlation that is observed between the length of service of low-ranking officers and the degree of their confidence in prison treatment programs.

The Illusion of Unlimited Authority

Because of the primacy of custodial functions, the greatest concern of prison administrators is the constant threat of prisoner escapes and uprisings. Major techniques for the control of inmate rebellions are, first, the show of force and, secondly, appeals to the inmates based on the notion that the prison's administration embodies the power and authority of the political state.

However, neither technique seems to be nearly as effective in organizing the routine activities of the prison community as are the unofficial alliances between staff members and inmates. Routine activities of the prison are largely governed by a system of symbiotic social relations that is designed to eliminate the necessity of force except in emergencies. This symbiotic system is based on certain fundamental weaknesses in the official structure of prison administration.

First of all, the repeated use of force is often self-defeating. Its cost is excessive in terms of manpower and material resources. It is detrimental to inmate morale and interest in staff-inmate harmony. Force begets force in the sense that officers who are employed in the continued use of force are thereby deprived of the major social means for obtaining voluntary inmate cooperation. This is largely the reason for the traditional separation of custodial and therapeutic functions in the close-custody prison.

A more crucial reason for restraint in the employment of force is that public opinion generally denies the necessity of its continued use in correctional institutions. Withdrawal of public support from correctional administrations that are founded on repetitious displays of official violence has occurred with increasing frequency during the course of our penal history. For example, the use of force in the recent wave of prison riots almost always resulted in public inquiries into the complaints of the rioting prisoners. These inquiries clearly revealed that public opinion was by no means unanimous in its support of prison policies, a situation that was apparently anticipated by the riot leaders and may have contributed to their rebellions.

While social conventions hold administrators responsible for the conduct of prison inmates, they also assume that strict surveillance and rigorous enforcement of appropriate penalties should make major displays of violence a rare occurrence. Consequently, most prison administrators, in order to maintain their official positions, must utilize devices other than violence in gaining inmate conformity and obedience. Force, then, is increasingly regarded as a device to be used as a last resort in case of emergency. Its public justification is sometimes threatened by the conventional belief that efficient prison administration should make its use unnecessary.

For the above reasons, the appeal to authority is a far more prevalent mechanism of official control. However, the functions of authority in the prison community are also subject to common misunderstanding. Authority is based on the assumption that persons in subordinate positions will voluntarily submit to the dictates of their superiors. But authority is effective only if subordinates share the social perspectives of their superiors. Our discussion of alienation has already suggested that officers occupying different ranks in the administrative hierarchy do not necessarily share similar views of the official program.

It is sometimes naively assumed that an officer's instruction to an inmate carries the full sanction of the prison's administration and that the officer's failure to enforce his order is evidence of the "corruption" of his authority. This is not necessarily the case. It would be far more realistic frankly to admit that the officer's control over an inmate depends primarily on his skills of persuasion and leadership.

Consider, for example, the alternative procedures that are available to an officer in the event that an inmate refuses to obey his command. First, he might resort to physical force. Generally, there are official regulations that restrict the use of force except in cases of attempted escape or threatened bodily injury. These regulations are designed to prevent unnecessary use of force. Therefore, if the officer uses force, he must justify his actions to his superiors in the same way that his superiors need to justify violence in the face of public opinion. His superiors are likely to hold the common opinion that effective leadership and preventative methods should make force unnecessary. Repeated involvement in violence against inmates is consequently likely to result in termination of the officer's employment by the institution.

Again, the officer may use the more common procedure of reporting inmate misconduct to his superiors. Penalties against the inmate may then be determined by a disciplinary committee. However, should the committee receive an extraordinary number of complaints or reports from a given officer, this too may be interpreted as evidence of incompetence on the part of the officer. Inmates, of course, are fully aware of the role they play in the official evaluation of an officer's services. Thus continued employment of a given officer depends largely upon the degree of voluntary cooperation that he can win from the inmates. Skill in interpersonal relations is more important in this situation than is the "corruption" of highly restricted authority, and the idea that officials have unlimited authority is simply not consistent with the essential evidence.

The Fiction of Official Autonomy

Another defect of the unilateral system of communication and authority is the assumption that prison policies are autonomous and uninfluenced by inmate pressures. Official policy views the prisoner as being habitually antisocial and inclined to violate regulations if he can get away with it. Further, policy holds that the only defensible role for the officer to play is to enforce all rules to the letter and "let the chips fall where they may." Since the inmates are not involved in the formulation of policy, their only opportunity for influencing the administration of the institution is in the area of policy enforcement. Therefore, if the rules are enforced without deviation, complete domination over the inmates presumably can be gained.

For instance, rules aimed at curbing food pilferage may define as contraband all items of prison fare that are found in any place other than the mess-hall. As a consequence, any inmate found in possession of unauthorized food is officially presumed to be guilty of theft or somehow involved in the food racket. Excuses don't count.

Similar presumptions of guilt operate with respect to other rules and regulations. The apparent purpose of the presumptions is to base the decision of guilt upon objective factors and to eliminate problems of judgment concerning extenuating circumstances. In this way it is belived that the possibility of inmate influence in the dispensation of prison justice will be minimized.

However, undeviating enforcement of all rules can involve an officer in the repeated employment of force and/or the issuance of innumerable rule-infraction reports. The practical effect, in either case, may be to create official doubts concerning the officer's competence, as has already been mentioned. Furthermore, the officer may have full knowledge of extenuating circumstances in certain cases and may therefore disagree with the official presumption of guilt. If the officer takes into consideration the alleviating conditions and gives the inmate a "break," he is in danger of official reprimand. In addition, toleration of rule infractions in the face of a policy of complete enforcement makes the officer vulnerable to charges of collusion with the inmates. This is precisely the point at which conniving inmates seek to "get something on" the officer, to be held against him later in more important situations and progressively to bring him under inmate domination.

The traditional policy of complete rule enforcement breaks down because it does not allow room for individual judgment concerning the circumstances related to rule violations. It places the officer in a fine dilemma. As a practical matter the officer can neither enforce all rules to the letter nor can he admit that he tolerates certain rule violations. This is why many correctional institutions, including some close-custody prisons, are developing mechanisms for taking into account the circumstances related to rule violations. However, all of these mechanisms, so far as can be ascertained, involve distinctive modifications of the unilateral system of communication; they either give the officer considerable discretion in reporting violations, a procedure that is euphemistically called "counseling," or they provide for the inmate an official opportunity to defend his actions.

Nevertheless, insistence upon unilateral relations among staff members and between staff members and inmates, rather than paucity of treatment facilities, is the feature most characteristic of the traditional close-custody prison. Restrictions against feedback and participation in policy formation, of course, are extended to the inmate population. However, such restrictions apparently run counter to some of the assumptions underlying modern therapeutic techniques. Modern methods of group therapy and guided participation in programming activities, for example, encourage the inmate to evaluate and perhaps initially to criticize the behavior standards that he is expected eventually to adopt as his own. Frank expression of skepticism and freedom of discussion, instead of insuring rejection of social norms, are believed to improve the inmate's understanding of social controls and to further the development of self-imposed discipline.

If the above analysis of defects in traditional prison policies is valid, then it seems clear that the unilateral organization of the close-custody prison may place severe limitations upon the treatment potential of our prisons and may provide a greater barrier against the resocialization of the offender than do the bars and walls that attract such adverse comment. How to modify traditional policy so as to integrate the roles of inmates and officers within a more efficient official organization continues to be one of the most difficult problems of prison administration.

Some Aspects of Prisoner Society

Juxtaposed with the official organization of the prison is an unofficial social system originating within the institution and regulating inmate conduct with respect to focal issues, such as length of sentence, relations among prisoners, contacts with staff members and other civilians, food, sex, and health, among others. The unofficial system, contrary to administrative rules and regulations, does not demand uniformity of behavior. Rather, it recognizes alternative roles that inmates may play with respect to each of the focal issues.

In various subtle ways the unofficial social system encourages reciprocal, complementary, or symbiotic relationships among inmates and between inmates and officers. Behavior prescriptions are based on interlocking role alternatives that are organized around the focal issues. Alternative roles are allocated among the inmates so as to maintain a fairly stable social equilibrium within the society of prisoners. To illustrate, consider some of the alternative roles that are organized around the procurement of illicit foods. Codes of conduct pertaining to food pilferage differ for "scores" (spontaneous or unplanned thefts) and "routes" (highly organized thefts). An inmate who "scores for food" may consume it or share it with friends, perhaps for past or expected favors, but he is not expected to sell it. Food obtained through organized theft is ordinarily sold in the illicit food racket.

Sale of pilfered food is regulated by an intricate division of labor and responsibility based on a network of symbiotic roles. Designated inmates are assigned the job of obtaining the food and delivering it to distributors. Distributors, in turn, may sell on credit to trusted inmate customers. Or the food may be sold on a cash basis to inmates from whom knowledge of procurement techniques is carefully concealed. Roles affiliated with the food racket are further delineated in terms of the kinds and quantities of foods stolen; in terms of the food sources, such as the officer's mess or the inmate's mess, for example; and finally, in terms of the methods of distribution and exchange.

Only those inmates who are involved in the food racket, of course, need to know the details of the system. Designation of role incumbents is handled informally, chiefly by mutual agreement among the persons concerned. But once a role has been assumed, it places upon the incumbent fairly precise requirements regarding his relations with others who participate in the racket, and with non-participating inmates and staff members as well. Furthermore, the amount of knowledge and skill required of an inmate depends upon the degree of his involvement in the racket. The food racket may be so well organized, however, that if all persons involved in it know and fulfill their assignments, the pilferage system can operate with an efficiency that is alarming and costly to the prison's administration.

Maintenance of a *sub rosa* organization such as the food racket requires that inmates be capable of assessing the probable behavior and the loyalty attachments of their fellows. Roles and statuses must generally be appropriate to the skills and interests of the persons involved. Errors made by the inmates in the assignment of roles ordinarily work to the advantage of the prison's administration and its officials. In order to minimize such errors, a fairly elaborate system of role allocations is set into operation not only with respect to food pilferage but in all areas of behavior related to the focal issues.

Allocation of roles is based on evidence regarding the affective orientations of the inmates, the accuracy and consistency of their perceptions of role requirements, and the degree of agreement between their perceived role requirements and their performance. Role allocations not only reflect the assessments and expectations of fellow inmates relative to the person in question, but they also in a large measure determine this person's opportunities for future social contacts and his access to information and to other social resources.

Evidence relevant to role assignments is obtained from observations made during initiation ceremonies and from a variety of contrived testing situations that accompany the introduction of an inmate into the prisoner community. The process of role allocation commonly proceeds in a standardized sequence of events. First, a degree of consensus is attained regarding the inmate's relative loyalties to the administration and to his fellow prisoners. Attempts are made to determine whether a given inmate generally evaluates situations according to the codes of prisoner society or according to the dictates of the officials. Then, the inmate's knowledge of prisoner roles and his skill in dealing with problematic situations are carefully examined. Knowledge of prisoner society indicates a given inmate's potential for aiding or obstructing the goals and strategies of his fellow prisoners. Finally, the consistency, reliability, and integrity of the inmate's behavior are investigated in a variety of contrived situations. Within six months, or so, after the inmate's admission into the institution, his major roles in the prisoner community seem to have been pretty well established. Role assignments, of course, are sometimes modified through a continuous re-evaluation of the inmate's performance, but the frequency of such modifications is usually not great enough to disturb the social equilibrium.

In addition to exercising great care in the allocation of roles, especially in areas involving high risk of detection by the officials, inmate society sets up expectations of mutual care and protection among the prisoners. These expectations, of course, conflict with the official suggestion to "do your own time," and they provide a basis for strong inmate morale in the face of persistent staff opposition. Roles played by prisoners with respect to forbidden activities create sets of mutual obligations that define conceptions of loyalty and protect organized rackets from interference by nonparticipating inmates or staff members. The rule that an inmate should not do anything to interfere with another's participation in forbidden activities is apparently the strongest commandment in the prisoner's code of conduct.

For example, inmates engaged in the food racket, in order to maintain a climate favorable to the continuation of this enterprise, may be expected to support and protect various other forbidden activities. Inmates who profit from such support or nonintervention are required to reciprocate in like manner. A system of largely unspoken but finely graded reciprocities of this kind tends to integrate prisoner society in its opposition to the prison's official administration.

But the system of inmate reciprocities, like the official system of unilateral communications, is vulnerable in crucial ways to outside interference. Deviations from the system, although they may be largely concealed from many of the inmates, are as much the rule as the exception. One problem is competition among inmates who are striving for higher status and authority within the society of prisoners. Again, the system is far less autonomous than the inmates would like to believe, and whenever it is disrupted by official intervention, there is great difficulty in determining exactly what went wrong. Finally, many of the inmates refrain from full involvement in the system; they may feel an allegiance to the official codes or they may be greatly influenced by official rewards and punishments. All of this lessens the effectiveness of the social controls that are primarily accessible to the prisoners.

The result is that neither the official system nor the society of prisoners can long retain dominance in the prison community. Symbiotic relationships tend to develop in such a way that, although the integrity of the two systems may be retained on the surface, the behavior of an inmate or a staff member in almost any given case is determined by intersecting influences that cannot be realistically accredited solely to either system. It is to this topic that we now turn our attention.

PATTERNS OF INMATE ADAPTATION

Sets of role alternatives, as previously indicated, reflect the organization of inmate behavior with regard to given focal issues. The conception of a social system, however, signifies a higher level of organization than that dealing with specific issues. Society, as an abstract concept, implies that the role alternatives assumed by given individuals with respect to various issues are interrelated in a more or less systematic manner. Thus, the pragmatic problem related to the concept of the social system is for research to determine the empirical regularities, if any, among sets of role alternatives. We call such regularities role configurations.

Major Role Configurations

Role configuration implies that a particular alternative regarding a given focal issue will be empirically connected with a certain alternative related to a second issue. A straightforward empirical procedure for identifying configurations of role alternatives would be to list all logically possible combinations of alternatives and then determine the frequencies with which the combinations occur. This procedure is unrealistic, of course, because the combinations rapidly reach staggering proportions and the relevant observational data are not available. An alternative procedure is to focus attention on the role configurations that are implied in the prison's symbolic system, including its argot, proverbs, legends and beliefs.

Prison argot makes many sharp distinctions between alternatives, which define the separate roles organized around a given issue, and configurations, which specify sets of alternatives that are perceived as being interrelated. "Merchant" for example, denotes the salesman role in a variety of situations, whereas "food peddler" identifies a single role alternative. The "merchant" configuration cuts across a number of focal issues. It is involved in a variety of *sub rosa* organizations and consequently arouses stronger inmate support or opposition. The term, as it seems to be used in prison, does not merely label a given role alternative, but implies that several alternatives are empirically connected.

It is immediately apparent, however, that inmates may erroneously perceive a particular set of role alternatives as being interrelated. Therefore, a distinction should be made between perceived relationships and confirmed or empirically verified relationships among role alternatives. Likewise, it is necessary to distinguish between normative statements, or behavior *pre*scriptions, and statements about overt performance, or behavior *de*scriptions. Since these distinctions are not ordinarily made in the use of prison language, great caution must be observed in relying upon the prison's symbolic system as a guide in the identification of role configurations.

Keeping in mind the perceived-confirmed and the prescribed-performed dichotomies mentioned above, a number of cross-tabulations were made of roles that are supposed to be interrelated according to prison argot, proverbs and legends. Several configurations were found that cut across a number of issues within the prison community. Most important, in our opinion, is a set of configurations that deals primarily with issues involving social relations among inmates, contacts with staff members, and access to the civilian world. The set includes four major configurations, to which are attached the prison labels "square John," "right guy," "con politician," and "outlaw."

Briefly, inmates who fall within the "square John" configuration consistently define role requirements in terms of the prison's official social system. By contrast, "right guys" just as regularly perceive requirements according to the norms of prisoner society. "Con politicians" shift their frame of reference from staff norms to inmate norms with great alacrity. "Outlaws," deficient in aptitude for identification, are in a perpetual anarchistic rebellion against both normative systems and against affective involvements in general.

Whereas the above argot labels refer to specific sets of interconnected role alternatives, our interest is in developing a typological system relating these role configurations to other social or cultural aspects of the prison community. In order to emphasize this distinction, a shift from argot labels to a more neutral terminology seems advisable. Consequently, the terms *prosocial, antisocial, pseudosocial,* and *asocial,* will hereafter be used in lieu of the argot labels in the respective order in which they have appeared. These role configurations, in the interest of brevity, will be called, collectively, social types.

Career Variables

To investigate the assumption that there are distinctive variations in the careers of the various social types, groups of inmates belonging to different types were interviewed and their case-histories were carefully examined. Clear distinctions were noted in the criminal records of the social types, their family and community experiences, and their attitudes towards crime and society. Major findings are summarized below.

Prosocial inmates are most frequently convicted of violent crimes against the person, such as homicide and assault, or naive property offenses, chiefly forgery. Few have prior arrests, and their criminal careers are initiated relatively late in life. Their offenses are situational. That is, the offenses reflect extraordinary social pressures frequently involving real or imagined misbehavior on the part of a spouse or of close friends.

While in prison, prosocial inmates maintain strong ties with family and civilian associates, and they are sympathetic and cooperative toward prison officials. Generally supportive of established authority, they believe in the efficacy of punishment, show strong guilt for their offenses, and expect to pay for their crimes in order to renew civilian life with a clean slate. Naïve about illegal techniques and strategies, they have little knowledge of, or contact with, organized crime.

Antisocial inmates are highly recidivistic, their careers frequently progressing through stages of truancy, expressive theft with other gang members, instrumental theft involving contacts with "fences" and other organized criminals, and culminating in patterns of unsophisticated crimes, such as robbery, assault, and burglary.

Coming chiefly from families having other delinquent members and living in underprivileged urban areas, antisocial inmates frequently earn a livelihood via contacts with organized crime, but do not often rise to positions of power in this field. Rebellion against conventional norms has continuity in their careers and is noted in their educational, occupational, and marital adjustments. Close ties with the parental family were commonly seen, however.

In prison, the antisocial offenders continue their close association with criminalistic elements and their rebellion against civil authorities. Their philosophy of life, as reflected in the slogans "only suckers work," "all politicians are crooks," and "big shots and real criminals never get caught," alleviates their sense of guilt and solidifies inmate opposition against the prison's administration.

Pseudosocial inmates are involved primarily in subtle, sophisticated, profit-motivated offenses, such as embezzlement, fraud, and forgery. Relatively few have juvenile records, and onset of criminality often occurs after a position of respectability has already been attained in the civilian community.

Family and community backgrounds are frequently middle-class, but evidence of inconsistent parental discipline and other family disharmony is the most striking feature of their preinstitutional careers. Apparently, pseudosocial offenders acquire their facility in role-playing at an early age, and they are frequently described as having a pleasant, ingratiating manner. Educational and occupational records are far superior to those of antisocial offenders.

In prison, pseudosocial inmates display chameleonic skill in shifting their allegiances from staff members to inmates, and vice versa, according to the exigencies of the moment. Pragmatic and instrumentally oriented, they exploit to their own advantage the conflicts and inconsistencies inherent in the prison's social structures. Although they are recognized to be unreliable, their strategic position between the two social systems makes them the mediators in staff-inmate conflicts and results in rewards, such as relatively short sentences, desirable prison assignments, and reduced custody, among others.

Asocial inmates commit a variety of offenses against persons and property, frequently using bizarre methods without clear motive or reason. Recidivism is extremely high, and there is early evidence of severe behavior disorders, although age at first arrest varies considerably.

Paramount among findings regarding social backgrounds is the seemingly universal evidence of early rejection. Asocial offenders are frequently reared in institutions, shifted around various foster homes, or are otherwise lacking reasonable care and attention from their parents. Social abilities and skills in the use of social symbols are greatly retarded. The careers of asocial offenders are marked by high egocentrism and an inability to profit from past mistakes or to plan for the future. These persons often exhibit an apparent distrust and fear of personal ties of any kind. Their problems are solved by direct and immediate aggression.

In prison, asocial inmates are the undisciplined troublemakers who are chiefly involved in riots, escape plots, and assaults on both inmates and officers. Nevertheless, their lack of capacity for cooperative enterprise means that most of their rebellions are destined for failure.

Several tentative conclusions can be drawn from the above findings. Generally, antisocial offenders are reared in an environment consistently oriented toward illegitimate social norms. Asocial and pseudosocial offenders exhibit defective normative perceptions growing out of early parental rejection and patterns of inconsistent discipline, respectively. They suffer severe personal frustrations at an early age and acquire distinctive adaptation techniques. Prosocial offenders, although utilizing legitimate normative standards, seem unable to cope with intense social pressures or unique personal problems. That persons with such varied problems of adjustment should play distinctively different roles in the prison community does not seem surprising.

Cognitive and Affective Orientations

It will be remembered that staff members and inmates uniformly perceive sharp and consistent distinctions between role requirements that are defined conventionally and those defined in terms of the prisoner social system. The concept of criminal subculture, at least so far as staff and inmate perceptions are concerned, does have specifiable pragmatic meaning as a set of behavior prescriptions. Consequently, criminal subculture, as a deviant or an illegitimate normative system, may be useful in revealing additional distinguishing characteristics among our social types.

Speculation concerning the life organizations of individual offenders and their knowledge of, and attachments to, cultural standards leads to the expectation of systematic variations in the frames of reference employed by the various social types. That is, some types are expected to utilize legitimate norms and others illegitimate norms as frames of reference. Moreover, variations in cognitive and affective orientations toward the two normative systems, unless our speculations lead us astray, should be highly associated with the patterns of personal and social traits that were noted previously.

More specifically, prosocial offenders appear to evaluate problematic situations with reference to legitimate norms, to have greater cognitive understanding of legitimate role requirements than of illegitimate requirements, and generally to apply legitimate norms in specific situations regardless of the personal discomfiture that might result. Conversely, it is expected that antisocial offenders will consistently employ deviant or illegitimate norms as standards of reference, to exhibit detailed cognitive knowledge of illegitimate role requirements, and likewise to display their allegiance to these norms irrespective of the impact on personal goals or objectives. Their general opposition to legitimate means of achievement is expressed figuratively in the motto, "only suckers work." The two types, then, are alike in emphasizing collective values, such as loyalty, mutual aid, and group solidarity, but they differ in the normative systems used as standards of judgment.

Pseudosocial offenders, by contrast, are capable of shifting their normative perspectives according to the availability of instrumental rewards. They stress personal achievements rather than collective goals, exploitative strategies rather than conventional procedures, and affective neutrality rather than strong identifications with persons or social conventions. Their cognitive knowledge and role-playing skills extend to the deviant realm as well as to the conventional one. Above all, to be bound by social conventions or moral commitments is for them a sign of weakness.

Asocial offenders are similarly detached from social conventions and moral commitments. However, in their case, detachment reflects ignorance of role requirements and deficiency in role-playing ability rather than emancipation. Moreover, their conceptions of the illegitimate system appear to be as much distorted as their conceptions of legitimate norms. They are greatly incapable of developing affective ties either with prisoners or with officials. Thus, their behavior is ordinarily impulsive and motivated by expressive functions; only rarely does it reveal the deliberative and instrumental characteristics so commonly noted among the pseudosocial inmates.

Information obtained by presenting to staff members and inmates alternative solutions to common prison problems has already been mentioned. The solutions chosen by members of the different social types seem to agree with the above arguments. For example, staff members and prosocial inmates tend to choose the same solutions, while pseudosocial offenders choose solutions representative of both conventional and deviant prescriptions. Antisocial offenders are fairly consistent in following the choice-pattern dictated by the illegitimate normative system. Asocial offenders make the greatest number of irregular choices.

Evidence regarding cognitive knowledge possessed by the social types has been difficult to obtain. However, tests of argot vocabularies suggest that, at the time of admission to the institution, antisocial offenders have the best knowledge of prison lingo. Pseudosocial offenders, though, appear to learn more rapidly and they may eventually attain a higher degree of proficiency. Asocial inmates, perhaps surprisingly, have a less adequate vocabulary, so far as labels for prisoner roles are concerned, than do the prosocial inmates; and both of these groups, of course, have vocabularies inferior to those of the antisocial or pseudosocial inmates. Further empirical investigation is needed, however, to demonstrate important anticipated differences in cognitive knowledge among the social types.

In summary, the social types reveal systematic differences in their cognitive and affective orientations toward the legitimate and illegitimate normative systems that are found in the close-custody prison, especially with respect to their attitudes regarding expressive (group-integrating) and instrumental (goal-achievement) norms. Some of the observed differences are indicated in Table 10, where (X) represents high knowledge or affective support for the norm, and (−) represents limited knowledge or affective rejection.

Social Contact and Participation

Normative orientations of prison inmates are importantly related to their patterns of social participation. In general, inmates are selectively responsive to those segments of their society that reinforce their own standards of judgment and provide continuity of experience. Persons having similar beliefs and values are sought out and their friendships are cultivated. Encounters with shocking or markedly dissimilar points of view are avoided, if possible. The same factors operate in contacts with staff members. Consequently, members of the various social types, since they are characterized by

TABLE 10
Cognitive and Affective Attachments of Social Types

Social Type	Legitimate Norms		Illegitimate Norms	
	Cognitive Knowledge	Affective Attachment	Cognitive Knowledge	Affective Attachment
Prosocial	X	X	−	−
Antisocial	−	−	X	X
Pseudosocial	X	−	X	−
Asocial	−	−	−	−

distinctly different normative orientations, may be expected to exhibit distinctive variations in their patterns of contact and participation within the prison community.

A reasonable expectation, for example, is that prosocial offenders will have extensive contacts with staff members, while their contacts with inmates are restricted largely to other members of the prosocial type. Conversely, antisocial offenders may be expected to have extensive contacts among the inmates, but minimal relations with the staff. Prosocial offenders may have a wider range of contacts involving both staff and inmates, while the asocial inmates may be restricted to fewer relations in either category. The expected patterns are listed in Table 11, assuming that contacts are dichotomized in terms of high and low frequencies, and that the relatively highest frequency of contact for a given social type is marked (X).

Direct evidence regarding inmate participation patterns is not yet available. Indirect evidence was obtained, however, by asking a sample of inmates to report the relative amount of their contacts with staff members and other inmates as compared with the contacts of the average inmate. The reported patterns are consistent with those hypothesized, except for the prosocial inmates who reported a somewhat higher amount of inmate contacts than was expected.

Amount of contact, however, may have less social significance than the quality of the relationships, such as friendship, animosity, or leader-follower patterns. Evidence pertinent to the quality of interaction comes from a sociometric study in which inmates reported the names of their closest prisoner friends. Friendship choices were classified according to the social type of the respondent and of the person chosen. Major findings are that members of every social type except one select their friends most frequently from their own type. The single exception is again the prosocial offender, who expresses a slight preference for pseudosocial friends over his choice

TABLE 11
Participation Pattern of Social Types

Social Type	Contact Patterns			
	High Staff/ High Inmate	High Staff/ Low Inmate	Low Staff/ High Inmate	Low Staff/ Low Inmate
Prosocial	—	X	—	—
Antisocial	—	—	X	—
Pseudosocial	X	—	—	—
Asocial	—	—	—	X

of prosocial friends. In addition, both prosocial and pseudosocial inmates receive fewer choices than would be expected if friendship were independent of social type; whereas antisocial inmates and, to a lesser extent, asocial inmates receive more than their proportionate numbers of choices.

The same study obtained the names of inmates designated as leaders. Most striking among the findings is the high frequency with which asocial inmates are identified as leaders. Even the prosocial and pseudosocial types, despite their sharp cognitive and affective differences as compared with asocial inmates, frequently select asocial inmates as leaders.

The rationale behind such choices may be revealed in a comment made by one of the respondents to the effect that, "One thing clear is that the outlaws aren't going to make any deals with anybody." Evidently the fears and suspicions aroused by members of the other social types result in leadership status for inmates who are incapable of any high degree of mutual effort. Presumably, then, the higher the tensions and anxieties within the prisoner community, the greater the leadership potential of the asocial type.

Thus it appears that while pseudosocial and perhaps prosocial inmates may have a wider range of contacts, the social climate of the close-custody prison provides for the antisocial and asocial inmates a higher social status and involves them more frequently in patterns of friendship and positions of leadership.

Degrees of participation in staff-sponsored activities and treatment programs likewise show consistent variations among the social types. Greatest participation in such organized activities, as expected, involves the prosocial offenders, followed in order by the pseudosocial, antisocial, and asocial types. Also, prosocial inmates, to a far greater extent than the others, engage in programs aimed specifically at therapy, while the pseudosocial and antisocial offenders display primary interest in recreation and other expressive functions. The relatively staff-centered orientation of the prosocial inmates is clearly revealed in the data.

Communication patterns mediate the intrapersonal processes of the inmates and their resulting self-conceptions. For example, various dimensions of self-conception are shown to vary according to the inmate's duration of confinement, his pre-institutional criminal record, his normative orientation, and his social position within the prison community. Included among the self-concept dimensions that show the above relationships are the inmate's perception of his own status in prisoner society, perception of the degree of his sophistication regarding criminal activities, and the amount of support he perceives as coming from persons in the civilian environment. These relationships, when measured by brief questionnaires, are not very strong, but they are consistently in the expected direction.

Even among juvenile delinquents, there is evidence, derived from responses to an adjective check-list, that the prosocial delinquent defines the correctional institution and the broader community as supportive agencies. In addition, he conceives of himself as a person who, although generally conventional in his conduct, has made a mistake that requires official attention. By contrast, antisocial delinquents perceive correctional institutions and civilian society as restrictive and antagonistic organizations. They conceive of themselves, in a sense, as leaders of the loyal opposition. Here, then, is another area in which further research is strongly indicated.

Patterns of contact and participation, as has been noted, are good indicators of inmate goals and interests. But they also regulate access to the means of goal achievement. They serve as integrative or divisive social forces that mold the individual according to the group's image of him or contrive his expulsion from the group. In consequence, the prosocial offender, for example, has a relatively clear path to conventional or legitimate behavior. He is divested of loyalty obligations toward the inmates, is ill advised concerning the illicit machinations of prisoner society, and in many other subtle ways is deprived of access to the means of goal achievement within the illegitimate social system. However, the ubiquitous pressures of the illegitimate system and the inevitable frustrations produced by his prisoner status make it increasingly difficult for him to maintain his prosocial orientation with the passage of time. Perhaps these are some of the main reasons for the positive correlation that has been observed between the parole violation rates of prosocial offenders and the duration of their confinement.

Participation patterns, then, by regulating access to social means and resources, apparently achieve some modification of inmate normative orientations and behavior standards. The reverse is also true. That is, inmates can sometimes produce changes in prison culture. Generally, prosocial offenders are cultural conservators for whom the stability of even a somewhat oppressive order is preferable to the uncertainties of social revision or experimentation. Pseudo-social inmates, in contrast, are the great innovators. Their exploitative interests, varied resources, and affective neutrality make them the natural catalysts of social invention and change. Antisocial prisoners are rebels who have a cause, namely, the subversion of established authority. Again, the nihilist role is played by asocial inmates, whose language is force, and who are frequently assigned the role of leader in riots, escapes, and similar rebellious activities.

The combined impact of the major role configurations and their related normative systems and participation patterns is to produce the social equilibrium that is commonly observed in the prison community, a fluid and moving equilibrium that enables the society of prisoners to make fairly easy adaptations to the many shocks and strains occasioned by changes in correctional personnel or policies or by other factors over which the inmates exercise relatively little direct control. Equilibrium implies some balance in the way the social types are interrelated, and the evidence outlined above suggests that among the more important balancing mechanisms are factors in the preinstitutional careers of the inmates, their normative orientations, and their patterns of social participation within the prison community.

10

THE SOCIAL CONTEXT OF JAILS*

DAVID B. ROTTMAN
AND JOHN R. KIMBERLY

According to a recent estimate (LEAA, 1971), there are more than 4,000 jails in the United States, jails which in 1973 confined for varying lengths of time between two and four million individuals. Despite the magnitude of their presence and the number of lives upon which they touch, jails have received scant attention from researchers and remain relatively invisible actors in our criminal justice system. This paper is written with the hope of making some progress toward removing this veil of obscurity.

Broadly defined, a jail is any facility utilized by a local criminal justice system for detention, and possibly for punishment, of those brought before it. Jails are mandated to hold in confinement all those felt to require such safekeeping to ensure their presence at some judicial or administrative proceeding. They are also charged with "correcting" those sentenced as misdemeanants by holding them in confinement for the periods specified by a judge.

Forbidding and remote in appearance, jails are readily conceptualized as stagnant, isolated structures. To date, this aspect has informed most research and writing on them. Glaser (1970:242) labeled American jails "storage bins for humans," while numerous commentators, among them DeTocqueville and Beaumont (1964:49–50), noted the wretched conditions and idleness of the jail regime.

These perceptions are accurate. Focus on formal properties, however, perforce overlooks the dynamics of social interaction involved in the internal operation of jails and in their relation to the variety of

Source: From *Sociology and Social Research* 59, 4 (July 1975), pp. 344–361. Reprinted by permission of the authors and publisher.

*Revision of a paper presented at the 1974 Annual Meeting of the American Sociological Association in Montreal. We are indebted to Hans W. Mattick and John Irwin for their comments on an earlier draft.

other organizations in a community that constitute the local criminal justice system. In large measure, the traditional approach to jails and the dearth of interest in them as research sites stem from the brevity of the average jail confinement, a brevity seen as precluding the emergence of an inmate social system and a set of understandings between the jailed and their jailers that can persist over time.

Exploratory field research in a moderate-size Midwestern county jail suggests that such an assumption is incorrect; both jail inmates and jailers are able to develop cultures responsive to their situation which merge into a set of tacit agreements unique to each jail. The purpose here is to present a perspective on jails that seeks to explain how this is possible. To an extent not paralleled in prisons and mental hospitals, jails are embedded in a web of inter-organizational and other involvements to a specific locality. It can be anticipated, therefore, that Mathiesen's finding (1971) that the nature of a prison's external communications profoundly affect its internal processes will prove even more applicable to jails. By focusing on what is termed here the "social context" of jails, it is hoped that these dynamic qualities can be described and elucidated.

Further, while attention in the media thus far has centered around large urban jails such as New York City's infamous "Tombs," there exists a substantial number of smaller jails which pose different though equally vexing social dilemmas and potential for research. While the usual disclaimers accompanying "case studies" are necessary, the social and sociological issues discussed here may have applicability well beyond the particular context observed.

The findings reported here resulted from five separate sessions, each of ten hours duration, in a Midwestern county jail. Both observational and interviewing activities were carried out primarily in the central area that corresponds to the sum of jail space not occupied by cells. This area encompasses a broad range of behavior within the jail. At any given time, a number of inmates, primarily the jail's trusties and those awaiting escort to a courtroom, will be present in the central area, as will be the jailer on duty. Representatives of various law enforcement agencies would also frequently be present. It was not, however, possible to directly follow the activity in the cell blocks from this vantage point.

The bulk of the interviewing was carried out informally through conversations with the various individuals present in the central area. In keeping with the exploratory intent underlying the research, both pre-determined and emergent themes were pursued in conversations with members of all categories of actor in the jail setting. These activities were augmented by a set of more formal interviews with inmates not generally having access to the central area. In addition, records were kept of the content of interchanges between the actors themselves. The setting and the explanation given for the researchers' presence were such that this could be done without intruding on what transpired.

THE RESEARCH SETTING

Physically, the jail studied is comprised of four wing sections, each totally sealed off from the remainder of the jail. Every wing is divided into a row of four-man cells and a large dayroom called the bullpen. Between the wings is a central area which serves as a multipurpose office and a waiting, conference and receiving room. Most of the interaction among inmates occurs in the wings, in the context of a highly routined set of activities defined by the formal rules and procedures set down by the jailers. While an inmate is in the wings, there is little occasion for contact with the jailer. The formal rules basically define a sequence of events or schedule for the movement of prisoners between their cells and that wing's bullpen, the arrival of meals, and the entertainment of visitors. The majority of the day is spent in the bullpen where the inmates eat, get their mail, and talk. They may take showers nearby without supervision. This set of rules, along with the physical constraints, form the "storage bins." As such, they are basic and limiting conditions within which the jail's social system develops.

The two largest wings, each with nine cells, confine the majority of the inmate population, one being officially reserved for felons, the other for misdemeanants. The remaining sections are used to confine those felt to require or deserve additional segregation, with women and "trouble-makers" sharing one wing, and the other serving as the miscellaneous bin. The jail is designed to hold up to 110 prisoners at any time, but this capacity is usually only half utilized; the average daily prisoner population is 55 inmates.

To date, research on jails, such as it is, has largely focused on this highly routinized context (for exceptions, see Queen, 1920; Spardley, 1970; Spardley, (1972); however, a variety of unscheduled activities also occurs. Taking place primarily in the central area, these activities may involve the movement of prisoners for administrative reasons such as transfer to the courtroom for trial or for conferences with their lawyers. They may also stem from a request made by an inmate, or from the discretion the jailers have in using inmates in tasks associated with running the jail and in trying to help certain prisoners. While such activities take place frequently, each occurrence is singular in that it is not encompassed by general rules or procedures, and deals with a specific individual. These non-routinized situations do not occur at predictable intervals, and several may be taking place simultaneously. Any attempt to understand the social context of these organizations that does not recognize the importance of these non-routinized situations will be incomplete.

In the jail studied, there is generally only one jailer on duty at any given time, and he must be concerned with maintaining order in all the wings as well as in the central area. Clearly, activities in the central area pose greater problems of uncertainty for the jailer, as they are non-routine and potentially greater threats to security. Observations suggest that social control in both situations is achieved by the development of a sophisticated, non-formal pool of information about the inmates which can be used in arriving at judgments about how to treat specific persons in particular contexts, and a shared group of norms governing conduct that has developed into a series of tacit understandings among inmates and between inmates and jailers.

Over time, each jail tends to develop a unique set of accommodations between jailers and the jailed which, in normal circumstances, largely manage events within the jail. The basis for cooperation between these two supposedly antagonistic groups is the desire of each to achieve certain ends that could not be reached without the aid of the other. To facilitate this exchange, a familiarity develops that probably is in many ways forced. While such agreements are inherently unstable, their basic form tends to be maintained despite the transient nature of the relationship between the inmates and the jail.

INFORMATION PROCESSES

Such accommodations and agreements are possible only insofar as a pool of information on the inmates has been cultivated and maintained over time. Through this information, the jailers can assess the probable response an inmate will make to a given situation. The nature of the jail environment is such that it is essential for the jailers to be able to trust, in varying degrees, several inmates simultaneously in situations where, if they so chose, they could easily be a serious threat to the security of the entire jail. Thus, the jailers must continually make decisions on how to treat individual inmates in a wide variety of situations.

The primary basis for these decisions appeared to be prior familiarity with the inmate. This familiarity derives primarily from non-formal, as opposed to official, sources of information and contact. In instances where the jailer lacked personal knowledge of a newly admitted inmate, he would generally initiate some non-official procedure for obtaining the information he desired, one based on personal contact, and a monitoring of the inmate's subsequent behavior through secondary sources—the other inmates in his section.

An inmate who is an unknown quantity is sized up, at times through an interview. The Chief Jailer stated that through this procedure he sought to weed out "tough customers" and "queers," and to spot possible trusties. In these face-to-face encounters the jailer and the new prisoner test each other. More frequently, others already in the jail will be asked to supply information on the new inmate, and some jailers prefer to leave the cell choice in such instances up to the other inmates in the wing selected. In this way, the jailer connects into the store of information in the jail, and will use the feedback received through this information system to guide his decisions in non-routinized situations.

The decisions made by the jailers often appeared to be relatively independent of the past criminal history or current charge facing an inmate. The jailers appeared far more willing to trust inmates who were awaiting transfer to a state penitentiary to begin serving a long sentence for a violent crime and who had lengthy criminal records than they were to trust inmates brought in for minor offenses such as traffic violations. The conclusions reached by the jailers in evaluating a prisoner are based on a set of data and evaluative criteria different from those an outsider to the jail would be likely to employ. Instead, they are likely to conform quite closely to the conclusions that might be reached about an individual by his fellow inmates. It is those inmates about whom the jailers can obtain little information that will generally be treated as posing the greatest security risks. What basically needs to be learned by the jailers is the degree to which the unknown inmates are attuned to the culture that prevails in guiding interaction among inmates and between inmates and jailers, as well as any individual idiosyncrasies such an inmate might possess that might upset the balance present.

The inmates are differentiated by the jailers into a number of "types" on the basis of these criteria. Because these distinctions have important implications for what goes on inside the jail, the way in which information is gathered by the jailers and the kind of data that are sought are of considerable importance to anyone interested in understanding jails. In tracing this flow of information, the extent to which the internal social structure of a jail is related to social structure on the outside becomes acutely apparent.

THE INMATE SOCIAL SYSTEM

As the jail is the only major facility for detaining those who have been arrested within the county its population includes individuals accused of every conceivable criminal offense. The variation in charges is, however, far greater than the variation in the social characteristics of those confined in the jail. Blacks and other minority groups are represented in proportions well beyond that in the general population, and even among these groups, membership in the population of the local jail is highly exclusive. People rarely go from being and "ordinary citizen" one day to being a jail inmate the next. A deviant career pattern is generally involved. As the jailers are very much aware, the charge currently facing a prisoner is relatively meaningless as an indicator of the person's criminality or character. While other people may commit and even be caught for an offense such as driving while intoxicated, those found in jail for this reason tend to come from a special group. Therefore, it appears to be a serious error to label jails as misdemeanant institutions and to assume that they confine a less crime-oriented population than do penitentiaries.

The population in jail for any single day, as compared with those placed in the jail over several months, will overrepresent those confined for more serious charges, as they are given higher bails and longer sentences and often must await transfer to the penitentiary system. A large proportion of those confined will also owe their presence to having violated the conditions of their parole or probation, possibly indicating a certain commitment to criminal activities. The daily population will also be more non-representative of the general population of the county in terms of its members' social characteristics, being more non-white, younger, and poorer. A "hard core" thus tends to accumulate in the jail, composed mostly of those awaiting trial for a serious charge, and then waiting for some administrative action after they have been found guilty, or, more frequently, plead guilty. It is these individuals whom the jailers get to know best, and who are the most significant in the jail's "social" life.

To a large extent, the inmates knew one another from confinement in not only this and other jails, but in other isolating institutions as well. Contact among them had often occurred on the outside also, and they appear to share a set of norms, values, beliefs, and other components of "culture" independent of whether they were in jail or not. The generality of this observation is untested, but Claude Brown's account of his experiences growing up in Harlem in the 1950's indicates it may be equally prevalent in a metropolitan setting. One of Brown's friends (1965:425) asserts:

The time I did in Woodburn, the times I did on the Rock, that was college man . . . Every time I went there, I learned a little more. When I go to
jail now, Sonny, I live, man. I'm right at home. That's the good part about
it . . . Now when I go back to the joint, anywhere I go, I know some people. If I go to any of the jails in New York, or if I do a slam in Jersey even,
I still run into a lot of cats I know. It's almost like a family.

Most of the jail inmates, and nearly all of those in the hard core,
are involved in career patterns that involve a series of confinements
in isolating institutions. Tied to many of the deviant careers identified
by Howard Becker (1963:25–39) and others there may be a concomitant career of confinements in reformatories, jails, prisons, and mental
hospitals. Our observations lead us to believe that these confinements
play a vital role in many deviant subcultures, and that these subcultures themselves have a major impact on the organization of the jail
and probably on many other institutions for housing "deviants."

The most obvious of these subcultures is that of young men who
have already spent considerable time in juvenile correctional facilities
and are now ready to graduate to the state penitentiaries. Other identifiable groups include drug addicts, alcoholics, and street gang members. As the most ubiquitous of all those organizations for confining
those committing deviant behavior, the jail encompasses the greatest
possible combination of career patterns. These various deviant subcultures, in the catchment area of the jail, combine into a general
subculture that develops around the jail. In the course of the confinements in isolating institutions that are part of many deviant careers,
one learns to live in the total institutional environment. Erving Goffman (1961:65–66) provides supportive evidence when he writes:

> Some lower-class mental hospital patients who have lived all their previous
> lives in orphanages, reformatories, and jails tend to see the hospitals just
> another total institution, to whom they can apply the adaptive techniques
> learned and perfected in similar institutions.

For the individuals involved in these deviant careers, the jail stay
can be very "useful" experience. For many inmates, being in jail increases their status in outside groups. What is more important, jail is
a place where various individuals involved in deviant behavior interact and learn from each other. While in jail they make contacts that
may help in future pursuit of activities that led to confinement in the
first place. Unfortunately, the stay itself labels the individual as a
deviant and narrows his opportunities for pursuing a normal career.
By the time he leaves the jail, he may have become more knowledgeable about a variety of criminal activities. In general, however, what
basically occurs is that the individual learns how to survive in the jail;
it becomes part of a person's repertoire.

The vacuum created by a lack of scheduled activities is filled by informal activities related to the various deviant subcultures represented in the jail, which serve as communication mechanisms for them and for the more general subculture. The inmate's day is spent in almost constant conversation, often over cards. In the course of these talkathons, they learn a great deal about each other, and this becomes part of the pool of knowledge held by the general subculture. From the county jail, this subculture feeds into various other local and state-run facilities. This familiarity among inmates seems to contribute greatly to the dynamics of the jail social life.

Everyone in jail has his own hard luck story and personal complaints about the "raw deal" he received. This common feeling of victimization and similarity of treatment received from the legal process is another factor contributing to the development of the inmate culture (Tannenbaum, 1938:71). The staples of jail conversations, even when the jailers are involved, are celebrities in the local criminal justice system: judges, lawyers, and prominent felons. In addition, the state penitentiaries and assorted ways of committing crimes are among the frequent topics of conversations.

An inmate's status among his fellow prisoners is largely dependent on the extent of his prior confinements in isolating institutions, particularly if these include the state penitentiaries. Eventually, one's status in the jail and in the general subculture can become identical, the status being independent of the particular facility one is in.

By virtue of their repeated and long experience in a variety of isolating institutions and resultant knowledge of the informal workings of the legal system, certain inmates are able to assume leadership roles in the cell blocks. Power in jails might be usefully understood in terms of the knowledge and experience that the various participants have. Leaders emerge through their ability to offer assistance and reduce the uncertainties that other inmates face in their dealings with law enforcement agencies, in adapting to the jail environment, and in activities they participate in on the outside. It is useful to look at jails as basically pools of knowledge and experience that persons confined gain access to during their stay. They serve to bring together a widely disparate group in an environment conducive to their interaction. This interaction is the content of the inmate social system in the jail.

The relations among the inmates are a product of the setting in which they occur, a setting that forces certain patterns of behavior on the individual if he is to survive. As he accumulates experience in jail, the inmate learns not only how to survive but how to behave toward certain individuals and groups outside the immediate confines of the cell block and day room. Knowledge of what judges, parole boards and probation officers, for example, want to hear is an important addition to his repertoire, as it increases his capacity to adapt his behavior effectively to a wide variety of situations.

While interviewing the inmates, one concern was to identify what they considered to be their basic grievances. Most complaints were directed not at the conditions of confinement, but at the local courts, prosecutors, and public defenders. The ongoing legal process provides the focus for the inmate social system. Though the jail was located at a considerable distance from any major metropolitan center, the inmates showed a political consciousness that was in many ways remarkable. Large urban jails have served as fruitful recruiting places for the Black Muslims and similar groups, and it appears that this phenomenon is spreading to medium-sized county jails. In this case, the influence derives primarily from the state penitentiaries, where local members of the general subculture have contact with these groups and then return to county jails where they had been previously confined. The influx of such individuals into the county jail and the consequent addition of new systems of beliefs about, and adaptations to, their situation are currently straining the tacit understandings by which the jail's social system has traditionally been governed.

JAILER-INMATE ACCOMMODATIONS

The jailers, all of whom are sheriff's deputies, had much the same socio-economic backgrounds as the inmates. The results appeared to be a benign attitude toward certain prisoners and a rich informal social system based on jailer-prisoner interaction. In fact, relations between the jail staff and some of the inmates often appeared to be quite friendly, though this was highly erratic and the nature of the friendship often changed without warning. This is important to the jailers from the point of view of social control. The jailers, for example, were confident that they would be notified of any planned escape attempt before it could materialize, and were able to cite several recent instances in which this occurred. In part, these relations reflect the jail's system of exchange in which the basic commodities sought by both the jailers and the most experienced inmates were certain kinds of information and the ability to make one's environment more livable. There were, however, times when real concern appeared to be present.

The attitudes of the jailers toward the prisoners and the nature of the inmate population were both clearly reflected in the pattern of cell assignments. The "types" into which the jailers differentiated the inmates appeared to be based not only on a concern for social control, but also on beliefs about the nature of the individual confined. Two inmates with identical prior criminal records and facing the equivalent current charge, often were treated completely differently. One would be trusted in a variety of situations, given special privileges, and assigned to a wing and cell intended to give him a break, while another received no special consideration at all.

By using the excess cell capacity available to them, the jailers are able to divide the jail into several groupings. The mix of inmates in each wing and cell must establish a balance, allowing for leaders to provide internal control as well as the separation of individuals whose interaction might prove volatile. This balance can generally be achieved, given the jailers' prior familiarity with the inmates and their access to the information maintained in the cell blocks.

On any given day, the felon wing confines about one-half of the jail population. Here prisoners are kept on charges ranging from petty theft to murder, the section's formal designation not necessarily being the basis for choice of occupants. Rather, they are placed together because of probable length of stay and a desire not to affect the others adversely. Such individuals tend to remain in jail for longer periods, regardless of the formal reasons for confinement. Security is not a factor in this division, as the misdemeanant wing is kept as securely locked as the felon wing.

The number of inmates in each cell varies, with most cells kept to capacity, four to a cell, to permit flexibility for separating certain individuals. Those kept in this wing are usually in their early twenties or are middle aged, and are the two basic groups of prisoners. It is they whom the jailers know best.

In many ways, the inmates in the felon wing appeared to be more dependable and easier to deal with than those in the misdemeanant side. One of the trusties responsible for feeding the other inmates commented on how much easier it was to care for the felon side. Those in the misdemeanant section have little at stake due to the brevity of their stay, and are not sufficiently schooled in how to get along in this type of environment.

The misdemeanant wing, while having the same capacity as the felon side, is generally more sparsely populated. Some inmates are given their own cell, generally when the jailers want to give them a "break" and to protect them from the other inmates. Individuals facing felony charges are also kept here when the jailers feel they deserve to be separated from the more hardened felons, or when an outside agency requests that partners in a crime be kept apart so they cannot communicate. In this section, the inmates tend to be either extremely young or rather old, and the turnover rate is high, though a few prisoners facing more serious charges or serving long jail sentences provide a certain degree of stability.

The occasional middle class youth who ends up in jail on a first offense will usually be placed in the miscellaneous wing, as will drunks and those brought to the jail because of behavior considered to border on mental illness. The trusties also have their cells in this section, and known homosexuals are segregated here. The bullpen in this section is not utilized.

The women's wing is less often used; it also contains the solitary confinement cell often used to cool off "trouble makers," and a padded cell for violent and suicidal individuals.

Traditionally, the rationale for the extreme emphasis on security in jails has been that the rapid turnover makes individual judgments on inmates impossible, and thus the worst must be assumed. In this study, the knowledge the jailers displayed indicates that this assumption may not be valid.

Connecting each wing to activities in other sections of the jail are the trusties. The physical layout and the fact that there is only one jailer at a time dictate that much of the daily work involved in maintaining the jail be carried out by these carefully selected prisoners. In the course of their duties, which include getting food to the inmates, acting as messengers, and distributing mail and supplies, the trusties have continual access to all parts of the jail and interact with everyone there. They are not locked in their cells and spend most of their spare time in the central area. Aside from their general duties, each trusty has a specific job; sometimes then even work outside the jail proper in one of the offices in the county building. In this case, they serve as a direct contact with the outside.

The position of trusty is one of considerable power. As a group they effectively run the jail within broad guidelines set by the jail administration and retain this control as long as everything runs smoothly. Their power derives from the information they possess, their monopoly on communication channels, and their access to valued objects. They are generally the only medium for communication between the guards and inmates in the wings, and they control not only the flow of most goods and services supplied by the jail, but also, the distribution of illicit items. They are abreast of what is going on in each wing, and the jailers rely on them for much information, and for help in keeping the prisoners subdued.

Since both the jailers and the prisoners must depend so heavily on the trusties, the process by which the latter are selected is extremely important. While it was anticipated that trusties would tend to be inmates in their first jail visit, charged with minor crimes, this was rarely the case. For the most part, trusties appear to be selected for their ability to control other inmates and the extent to which the jail staff know them. Therefore, they tend to be those with considerable prior experience in prisons and jails, but whose current conviction is for a relatively minor charge to be served out in the jail, for example, grand theft, disorderly conduct, assault, or deceptive practices. Selection of trusties reflects a sophisticated typing on the part of the jailers and is intended both to give certain prisoners a break and to make running the jail easier.

The trusties tie the jail into a single dynamic social system. The penal philosophy on which the jail's architectural plans were predicated may well have been based on a "warehousing" assumption. What is being stored, however, is people, and they are able to adapt the setting to their own purposes. Through these adaptations the jail is intimately connected and contributing to social systems and "deviant subcultures" on the outside, a curious reversal of the role the jail was intended to play. It is possible that such adaptations will persist regardless of many reforms that have been advocated.

A further dimension in the dynamics of the jail environment can be seen in the non-routinized activities that take place in the central area. Such situations arise when any activity involving an inmate is requested or required that is not contained within the jail routine. Such activities are an intimate part of the jail social system.

That frequently such activities are initiated by an inmate demonstrates the general nature of jailer-inmate relations in the jail. The jailers are often willing to accommodate those with whom they are well acquainted and feel they can trust. This can involve permission to use the jail's only phone (which is in the central area), permission to receive a visitor at other than the specified times, or simply a bull session with the jailers.

INTER-ORGANIZATIONAL LINKAGES

It is in this use of the central area that the inter-organizational involvements of jails intrude most concretely into the internal workings of the jail. The bulk of such situations observed in this study occurred upon entry of representatives of criminal justice agencies. These people are another important set of actors in the jail social system. The interaction that involves them reveals adaptations that reflect the informal role that jails play in the local criminal justice system. These actors enter either directly or by proxy, with the proxy generally being a message to one of the jailers. Such messages are based not on the formal role the sender has in the system, but on contact and familiarity between various local officials. Those who enter the jail directly use their formal roles to gain contact with the jail in order to develop informal procedures. In both cases, the results are instrumental to the performance of their law enforcement tasks as they define them.

The overriding concern in these formal and informal activities was the process by which negotiated pleas of guilty are obtained. Generally, presence of a defendant in jail while awaiting trial, as opposed to being released through cash or recognizance bond, serves as an inducement to plead guilty. If a defendant is out on bail, delaying disposition of his case works in his favor; if he is incarcerated, the opposite is likely to hold (similarly, see Blumberg; 1969; Landes, 1971; Katz, 1972; 204–205). Jail conditions are such that for many inmates a transfer to the state penitentiaries is a welcome event.

The jail has a larger role in the plea bargaining process than merely serving as a conducive physical setting. More important are the advice and the support for using plea bargaining that comes from the other inmates and from the jailers. Frequently, it is fellow inmates in the jail who first provide the suggestion that the neophyte defendant plead guilty "for consideration," a finding also reported by Blumberg (1969:235). Current plea bargaining maneuverings are a constant topic of conversations in the cell blocks. This is reinforced in that, given the socio-economic backgrounds of the bulk of the inmate population, nearly all the inmates had as their lawyer one of the two public defenders provided by the county.

The period before trial can be profitably used by the inmate. Over time, witnesses disappear, memories fade, the public indignation dies down. In the course of their maneuvering, the entire jail can become involved, particularly if the case is prominent. Other inmates provide advice, as do the jailers. Some of the more experienced inmates showed a remarkable ability to predict the outcome of court cases accurately, as to both the sentences given and the length of time that would ultimately be served.

Thus, the jail appears to be a vital element in the plea bargaining process, a process that has become a central mechanism through which the American criminal justice system functions. It provides leverage for the prosecutors and puts the inmate in the center of ongoing maneuverings. It is a testable hypothesis that if the pressures facing the prosecutors in a jurisdiction were known (e.g., caseloads, court backlogs), then the average pre-trial stay and the proportion of inmates released on bail could be predicted. Bail setting practices tend to gravitate so as to provide the degree of pressure on defendants necessary to induce them to plead guilty.

The jail stay can also be manipulated to effect unofficial punishment. Faced with a weak case, yet convinced of a defendant's guilt, a prosecutor can merely delay trial for the length of time he feels constitutes adequate punishment. Parole and probation officers are able to make similar use of the jail. When the transgression that caused an individual to violate the conditions of release is deemed serious enough to merit some punishment, but not sufficient to cause him to be sent to the penitentiary to finish his sentence, he may be held in jail under the pretext of awaiting administrative action for whatever length of time the officer desires.

Being placed in jail can serve as pressure to give evidence to the police, or agree to appear as a witness. It is a conducive environment in which to interrogate suspects, whether or not formal charges are intended. The local police can use the jail as an aid in a number of situations that can be resolved by a jail confinement that is not to be followed by a trial (see Sutherland and Cressey, 1960:357).

A local criminal justice system is tightly knit. It is based on informal cooperation, and this is magnified in the situation studied by the fact that nearly all of the agencies involved, including the jail, are located in a single building. The jail itself is the scene for much of the intimidation, negotiation, communication, and consultation by which the system operates. It was toward these informal adaptations that most of the inmates' bitterness was directed. The officials in the local criminal justice system comprise a third "culture" that influences what occurs within the jail. The presence of this group is most evident when its members gather for lunch in the jail kitchen. Like the other groups, this group tends on the surface to minimize the numerous conflicts inherent in its members' separate tasks so that each component can meet its own objectives.

The unique store of information possessed by the jailers on the inmates and the nature of their social relations with them plays an interesting role in the operations of the system. The jailers often serve as mediators between the official agencies and the prisoners. At times, they intervene on behalf of inmates, even with judges. They often advise prisoners, and serve as information gatherers for both inmates and outsiders. The jailers also conduct informal counseling sessions with certain inmates, trying to help them solve their problems.

The value of the jailers' knowledge is attested by the frequent requests for information on current and former jail inmates that they receive from parole and probation officers, law enforcement personnel on the local, state, and even Federal levels, and other criminal justice agency members. Furthermore, on the basis of these discussions, the jailers have information to transmit to the inmates. Their type of knowledge can be obtained only from personal contact, not from the official records available to judges and prosecutors.

In these interventions on behalf of inmates in assigning cells, choosing trusties, and distributing privileges the jailers have established the rudiments of a rehabilitation system. Treatment in these contexts is distributed very differentially by the jailers within the inmate population. The inmates most often selected are in the "hard core," those who, by an outsider's stereotypes, would be least deserving and least likely to respond positively to such efforts. Whatever the faults in such arrangements, they emerge because they fulfill vital needs which society thus far has been unable to deal with effectively and systematically.

Other organizations are also able to use the local jail, particularly other isolating institutions. Local orphanages, reform schools and similar institutions use it as a place to punish recalcitrant youths, as do some parents. A county jail like the one studied also assumes many of the functions other isolating institutions have officially been given. Jails are used to dry out drunks, to house people suspected of mental illness, and to shelter those who have no home. At times this is due to the absence of the organizations which might better care for these problems; in other cases it is because, though the organizations exist, they do not want the particular individual in them. The jail can thus become a repository for persons excluded from other isolating organizations for a variety of reasons, basically because the local jail is least able to resist demands for accommodations directed to it.

There appears to be a close working relationship between the staffs of these isolating organizations and that of the jail. In the course of their operations, formal contact occurs between their officials. This most frequently involves staff of the jail with officials of the various state correctional facilities or other county jails that are nearby. Much of the contact comes during the transfer of inmates from one to the other, an activity the jail participates in with juvenile facilities, mental hospitals, and even regular hospitals.

The jail staff can provide their counterparts in prisons with useful information about the new recruit they are about to receive. At times, the jailers will intervene on behalf of an inmate who is about to be transferred to a state penitentiary, obtaining a favored role for the inmate, such as participation in the work release program.

There are three basic sets of actors in the social system of the jail; the inmates, the jailers, and officials from outside agencies. Through the interaction among the members of each set, and between them and the other actors, informal workings emerge. The accommodations they develop constitute latent functions, possibility not all of them negative, of jails. Supporting these unofficial arrangements are public indifference and neglect, the parochial political situations in the localities, and the lack of alternative methods for dealing with social problems.

CONCLUSION

This summary of our observations is presented in the hope of stimulating both an interest in future research on the issues discussed and action toward social change. Both are desperately needed. In doing so, attention has focused on the dynamics of the situation; the horrors of American jails have been well documented by others. It is, however, these dynamics that account for the conditions in American jails and their resistance to change.

In attempting to step back and view jails in the context of these preliminary observations, what emerges most clearly is the need to view jails as "open systems." What occurs within a jail is closely related to events taking place on the outside. This interaction between a jail and other cultures and groups is more immediate and more intense than is the case for penitentiaries, mental hospitals or reformatories.

Three overlapping social systems can be seen to converge inside the jail. One is formed of the various individuals and groups involved in "deviant" enterprises within the locality. Jail inmates are characterized by repetitive confinements of short duration, and what occurs on the streets is brought into the jail with each new inmate, and what transpires within the jail exits with that individual upon release. The "street" and the jail are often two action spaces for a single way of life.

A second social system entering the jail can be found in the inmate subculture centered in the state's penitentiaries. There is a continual process of movement of individuals between the penitentiaries and the jail. In this way, the jail is a part of the larger subculture formed of individuals whose careers involve a series of confinements in total institutions. Attachments, beliefs, and events from one such setting are readily transferred to another.

The third social system entering the jail is that of the local courts. The plea bargaining practices in a locality appear to be the linchpin which shapes and holds together the various elements of the jail social order. Knowledge of the behaviors needed to manipulate various court officials is a primary basis for an inmate's status in the cell blocks. Jailers serve as middlemen between the inmates and the prosecutors, judges, and probation and parole officers. It is through this ability to intervene in the negotiating process that jailers are able to reach an accommodation with the inmates, obtaining the information contained in the other two social systems—that of the "streets" and of the penitentiary subculture—that they need to perform their job.

By virtue of the intersection within the jail of these three social systems, the continuity, information, and leverage needed for a stable social order to emerge are present. However, changes in these social systems cannot but have implications for the jail that may act to break down the prevailing social order and ultimately lead to the emergence of a new one.

The focus for research and for action toward social change must be on these connections between the jail and the larger society. Reforming the manifest functions jails are charged with has not in the past, and will not in the future, create meaningful change if the latent adaptations are not addressed. As students of American jails such as Hans W. Mattick (1974:821–823) have noted, all these attempts have accomplished is to establish a cycle of visibility, where periodic episodes of violence or scandal bring a jail into the glare of publicity. Frantic efforts toward placing blame quickly follow, but soon public concern fades and the system returns to a state of relative invisibility, the basic problems untouched. Over time, the discontent bubbling beneath the surface will again emerge in an overt demonstration, and the cycle will begin anew.

REFERENCES

Beaumont, Gustave de and Alexis de Tocqueville
    1964   On the Penitentiary System in the United States and its Applications in France. Carbondale: Southern Illinois University Press.

Becker, Howard S.
    1963   Outsiders: Studies in the Sociology of Deviance. New York: Free Press.

Blumberg, Abraham S.
    1969   "The criminal court as organization and communication system." Pp. 267–291 in Richard Quinney (ed.), Crime and Justice in Society. Boston: Little, Brown.

Brown, Claude
    1965   Manchild in the Promised Land. New York: New American Library.

Glaser, Daniel
    1970   "Some notes on urban jails." Pp. 236–244 in D. Glaser (ed.), Crime in the City. New York: Harper and Row.

Goffman, Erving
    1961   Asylums. Garden City, New York: Anchor Books.

Katz, Louis
    1972   Justice is the Crime: Pretrial Delay in Felony Cases. Cleveland: Case
            Western Reserve University Press.
Landes, W.
    1971   "An economic analysis of the courts." Journal for Law and Econom-
            ics 14 (April):61–108.
Law Enforcement Assistance Administration
    1971   National Jail Census: 1970. Washington, D.C.: U.S. Government
            Printing Office.
Mathiesen, Thomas
    1971   Across the Boundaries of Organizations: An Exploratory Study of
            Communication Patterns in Two Penal Institutions. Berkeley: Glen-
            dessary Press.
Mattick, Hans W.
    1974   "The contemporary jails of the United States: an unknown and ne-
            glected area of justice." Pp. 777–848 in D. Glaser (ed.), Handbook
            of Criminology. Chicago: Rand McNally.
Queen, Stuart A.
    1920   The Passing of the County Jail. Menasha, Wisconsin: Collegiate Press.
Spradley, James P.
    1970   You Owe Yourself a Drunk: An Ethnography of Urban Nomads.
            Boston: Little, Brown.
    1972   "An ethnographic approach to the study of organizations: the city
            jail." Pp. 94–105 in M. Brinkerhoff and P. Kunz (eds.), Organiza-
            tions and Their Environments. Dubuque: Wm. C. Brown.
Sutherland, Edwin and Donald Cressey
    1960   Principles of Criminology: Sixth Edition. Chicago: J. B. Lippincott.
Tannenbaum, Frank
    1938   Crime and the Community. Boston: Ginn and Company.

11

THE PRISON EXPERIENCE: THE CONVICT WORLD

JOHN IRWIN

PRISON-ADAPTIVE MODES

Many studies of prison behavior have approached the task of explaining the convict social organization by posing the hypothetical question—how do convicts adapt to prison? It was felt that this was a relevant question because the prison is a situation of deprivation and degradation, and, therefore, presents extraordinary adaptive problems. Two adaptive styles were recognized: (1) an individual style—withdrawal and/or isolation, and (2) a collective style—participation in a convict social system which, through its solidarity, regulation of activities, distribution of goods and prestige, and apparent opposition to the world of the administration, helps the individual withstand the "pains of imprisonment."

I would like to suggest that these studies have overlooked important alternate styles. First let us return to the question that theoretically every convict must ask himself: How shall I do my time? or, What shall I do in prison? First, we assume by this question that the convict is able to cope with the situation. This is not always true; some fail to cope with prison and commit suicide or sink into psychosis. Those who do cope can be divided into those who identify with and therefore adapt to a broader world than that of the prison, and those who orient themselves primarily to the prison world. This difference in orientation is often quite subtle but always important. In some instances, it is the basis for forming very important choices, choices which may have important consequences for the felon's long term career. For example, Piri Thomas, a convict, was forced to make up his mind whether to participate in a riot or refrain:

I stood there watching and weighing, trying to decide whether or not I was a con first and an outsider second. I had been doing time inside yet living every mental minute I could outside; now I had to choose one or the other. I stood there in the middle of the yard. Cons passed me by, some going west to join the boppers, others going east to neutral ground. The call of rep tore within me, while the feeling of being a punk washed over me like a yellow banner. I had to make a decision. *I am a con. These damn cons are my people . . . What do you mean, your people? Your people are outside the cells, home, in the streets. No! That ain't so . . . Look at them go toward the west wall. Why in hell am I taking so long in making up my mind? Man, there goes Papo and Zu-Zu, and Mick the Boxer; even Ruben is there.*[1]

This identification also influences the criteria for assigning and earning prestige—criteria relative to things in the outside world or things which tend to exist only in the prison world, such as status in a prison social system or success with prison homosexuals. Furthermore, it will influence the long term strategies he forms and attempts to follow during his prison sentence.

It is useful to further divide those who maintain their basic orientation to the outside into (1) those who for the most part wish to maintain their life patterns and their identities—even if they intend to refrain from most law breaking activities—and (2) those who desire to make significant changes in life patterns and identities and see prison as a chance to do this.

The mode of adaptation of those convicts who tend to make a world out of prison will be called "jailing." To "jail" is to cut yourself off from the outside world and to attempt to construct a life within prison. The adaptation of those who still keep their commitment to the outside life and see prison as a suspension of that life but who do not want to make any significant changes in their life patterns will be called "doing time." One "does time" by trying to maximize his comfort and luxuries and minimize his discomfort and conflict and to get out as soon as possible. The adaptation made by those who, looking to their future life on the outside, try to effect changes in their life patterns and identities will be called "gleaning."[2] In "gleaning," one sets out to "better himself" or "improve himself " and takes advantage of the resources that exist in prison to do this.

Not all convicts can be classified neatly by these three adaptive styles. Some vacillate from one to another, and others appear to be following two or three of them simultaneously. Still others, for instance the non-copers mentioned above, cannot be characterized by any of the three. However, many prison careers fit very closely into one of these patterns, and the great majority can be classified roughly by one of the styles.

Doing Time

When you go in, now your trial is over, you got your time and everything and now you head for the joint. They furnish your clothing, your toothbrush, your toothpaste, they give you a package of tobacco, they put you up in the morning to get breakfast. In other words, everything is furnished. Now you stay in there two years, five years, ten years, whatever you stay in there, what difference does it make? After a year or so you've been . . . after six months, you've become accustomed to the general routine. Everything is furnished. If you get a stomachache, you go to the doctor; if you can't see out of your cheaters, you go to the optician. It don't cost you nothing.[3]

As the above statement by a thief indicates, many convicts conceive of the prison experience as a temporary break in their outside career, one which they take in their stride. They come to prison and "do their time." They attempt to pass through this experience with the least amount of suffering and the greatest amount of comfort. They (1) avoid trouble, (2) find activities which occupy their time, (3) secure a few luxuries, (4) with the exception of a few complete isolates, form friendships with small groups of other convicts, and(5) do what they think is necessary to get out as soon as possible.[4]

To avoid trouble the convict adheres to the convict code—especially the maxims of "do your own time" and "don't snitch," and stays away from "lowriders"—those convicts engaged in hijacking and violent disputes. In some prisons which have a high incidence of violence—knifings, assaults, and murders—this can appear to be very difficult even to the convicts themselves. One convict reported his first impression of Soledad:

The first day I got to Soledad I was walking from the fish tank to the mess hall and this guy comes running down the hall past me, yelling, with a knife sticking out of his back. Man, I was petrified. I thought, what the fuck kind of place is this? (Interview, Soledad Prison, June 1966)

Piri Thomas decided to avoid trouble for a while, but commented on the difficulty in doing this:

The decision to cool myself made the next two years the hardest I had done because it meant being a smoothie and staying out of trouble, which in prison is difficult, for any of a thousand cons might start trouble with you for any real or fancied reason, and if you didn't face up to the trouble, you ran the risk of being branded as having no heart. And heart was all I had left.[5]

However, except for rare, "abnormal" incidents, convicts tend not to bother others who are "doing their own number." One convict made the following comments on avoiding trouble in prison:

If a new guy comes here and just settles down and minds his business, nobody'll fuck with him, unless he runs into some nut. Everyone sees a guy is trying to do his own time and they leave him alone. Those guys that get messed over are usually asking for it. If you stay away from the lowriders and the punks and don't get into debt or snitch on somebody you won't have no trouble here. (Interview, San Quentin, July 1966)

To occupy their time, "time-doers" work, read, work on hobbies, play cards, chess, and dominoes, engage in sports, go to movies, watch TV, participate in some group activities, such as drama groups, gavel clubs, and slot car clubs, and while away hours "tripping" with friends. They seek extra luxuries through their job. Certain jobs in prison, such as jobs in the kitchen, in the officers' and guards' dining room, in the boiler room, the officers' and guards' barber shop, and the fire house, offer various luxuries—extra things to eat, a radio, privacy, additional shows, and more freedom. Or time-doers purchase luxuries legally or illegally available in the prison market. If they have money on the books, if they have a job which pays a small salary, or if they earn money at a hobby, they can draw up to twenty dollars a month which may be spent for foodstuffs, coffee, cocoa, stationery, toiletries, tobacco, and cigarettes. Or using cigarettes as currency they may purchase food from the kitchen, drugs, books, cell furnishings, clothes, hot plates, stingers, and other contraband items. If they do not have legal access to funds, they may "scuffle"; that is, sell some commodity which they produce—such as belt buckles or other handicraft items—or some commodity which is accessible to them through their job—such as food items from the kitchen. "Scuffling," however, necessitates becoming enmeshed in the convict social system and increases the chances of "trouble," such as conflicts over unpaid debts, hijacking by others, and "beefs" —disciplinary actions for rule infractions. Getting into trouble is contrary to the basic tenets of "doing time," so time-doers usually avoid scuffling.

The friendships formed by time-doers vary from casual acquaintanceships with persons who accidentally cell nearby or work together, to close friendship groups who "go all the way" for each other—share material goods, defend each other against others, and maintain silence about each other's activities. These varying friendship patterns are related closely to their criminal identities.

Finally, time-doers try to get out as soon as possible. First they do this by staying out of trouble, "cleaning up their hands." They avoid activities and persons that would put them in danger of receiving disciplinary actions, or "beefs." And in recent years with the increasing emphasis on treatment, they "program." To program is to follow, at least tokenly, a treatment plan which has been outlined by the treatment staff, recommended by the board, or devised by the convict himself. It is generally believed that to be released on parole as early as possible one must "get a program." A program involves attending school, vocational training, group counseling, church, Alcoholics Anonymous, or any other special program that is introduced under the treatment policy of the prison.

All convicts are more apt to choose "doing time," but some approach this style in a slightly different manner. For instance, doing time is characteristic of the thief in prison. He shapes this mode of adaptation and establishes it as a major mode of adaptation in prison. The convict code, which is fashioned from the criminal code, is the foundation for this style. The thief has learned how to do his time long before he comes to prison. Prison, he learns when he takes on the dimensions of the criminal subculture, is part of criminal life, a calculated risk, and when it comes he is ready for it.

Long before the thief has come to prison, his subculture has defined proper prison conduct as behavior rationally calculated to "do time" in the easiest possible way. This means that he wants a prison life containing the best possible combination of a maximum amount of leisure time and maximum number of privileges. Accordingly, the privileges sought by the thief are different from the privileges sought by the man oriented to prison itself. The thief wants things that will make prison life a little easier—extra food, a maximum amount of recreation time, a good radio, a little peace.[6]

The thief knows how to avoid trouble; he keeps away from "dingbats," "lowriders," "hoosiers," "square johns," and "stool pigeons," and obeys the convict code. He also knows not to buck the authorities; he keeps his record clean and does what is necessary to get out— even programs.

He occasionally forms friendships with other criminals, such as dope fiends, heads, and possibly disorganized criminals, but less often with square johns. Formerly he confined his friendship to other thieves with whom he formed very tight-knit groups. For example Jack Black, a thief in the last century, describes his assimilation into the "Johnson family" in prison:

Shorty was one of the patricians of the prison, a "box man," doing time for bank burglary. "I'll put you in with the right people, kid. You're folks yourself or you wouldn't have been with Smiler."

I had no friends in the place. But the fact that I had been with Smiler, that I had kept my mouth shut, and that Shorty had come forward to help me, gave me a certain fixed status in the prison that nothing could shake but some act of my own. I was naturally pleased to find myself taken up by the "best people," as Shorty and his friends called themselves, and accepted as one of them.

Shorty now took me into the prison where we found the head trusty who was one of the "best people" himself, a thoroughgoing bum from the road. The term "bum" is not used here in any cheap or disparaging sense. In those days it meant any kind of a traveling thief. It has long since fallen into disuse. The yegg of today was the bum of twenty years ago.

"This party," said Shorty, "is one of the 'Johnson' family." (The bums called themselves "Johnsons" probably because they were so numerous.) "He's good people and I want to get him fixed up for a cell with the right folks."[7]

Clemmer described two *primary* groups out of the fourteen groups he located, and both of these were groups of thieves.[8]

Presently in California prisons thieves' numbers have diminished. This and the general loosening of the convict solidarity have tended to drive the thief into the background of prison life. He generally confines his friendships to one or two others, usually other thieves or criminals who are "all right"; otherwise he withdraws from participation with others. He often feels out of place amid the changes that have come about. One thief looking back upon fifteen years in California prisons states:

As far as I'm concerned their main purpose has been in taking the convict code away from him. But what they fail to do is when they strip him from these rules is replace it with something. They turn these guys into a bunch of snivelers and they write letters on each other and they don't have any rules to live by. (Interview, Folsom Prison, July 1966)

Another thief interviewed also indicated his dislocation in the present prison social world:

The new kinds in prison are wild. They have no respect for rules or other persons. I just want to get out of here and give it all up. I can't take coming back to prison again, not with the kind of convicts they are getting now. (Interview, Soledad Prison, June 1966)

Like the majority of convicts, the dope fiend and the head usually just "do time." When they do, they don't vary greatly from the thief, except that they tend to associate with other dope fiends or heads, although they too will associate with other criminals. They tend to form very close bonds with one, two, or three other dope fiends or heads and maintain a casual friendship with a large circle of dope fiends, heads, and other criminals. Like the thief, the dope fiend and the head tend not to establish ties with squares.

The hustler in doing time differs from the other criminals in that he does not show a propensity to form very tight-knit groups. Hustling values, which emphasize manipulation and invidiousness, seem to prevent this. The hustler maintains a very large group of casual friends. Though this group does not show strong bonds of loyalty and mutual aid, they share many activities such as cards, sports, dominoes, and "jiving"—casual talk.

Square johns do their time quite differently than the criminals. The square john finds life in prison repugnant and tries to isolate himself as much as possible from the convict world. He does not believe in the convict code, but he usually learns to display a token commitment to it for his own safety. A square john indicated his forced obedience to the convict code.

Several times I saw things going on that I didn't like. One time a couple of guys were working over another guy and I wanted to step in, but I couldn't. Had to just keep moving as if I didn't see it. (Interview, Soledad Prison, June 1966)

He usually keeps busy with some job assignment, a hobby, cards, chess, or various forms of group programs, such as drama groups. He forms friendships with one or two other squares and avoids the criminals. But even with other squares there is resistance to forming *close* ties. Square johns are very often sensitive about their "problems," and they are apt to feel repugnance toward themselves and other persons with problems. Besides, the square usually wants to be accepted by conventional people and not by other "stigmatized" outcasts like himself. So, many square johns do their time isolated from other inmates. Malcolm Braly in his novel *On the Yard* has captured the ideal-typical square john in prison:

Watson had finally spoken. Formerly a mild-mannered and mother-smothered high school teacher, he had killed his two small sons, attempted to kill his wife, cut his own throat, then poisoned himself, all because his wife had refused a reconciliation with the remark, "John, the truth is you bore me."

Watson stood with culture, the Republic, and motherhood, and at least once each meeting he made a point of reaffirming his position before launching into his chronic criticism of the manner in which his own case had been, was and would be handled. " . . . and I've been confined almost two years now and I see no point in further imprisonment, further therapy, no point whatsoever since there's absolutely no possibility I'll do the same thing again . . ."

"That's right," Red said softly. "He's run out of kids."

And Zeke whispered, "I just wish he'd taken the poison *before* he cut his throat."

Watson ignored the whispering, if he heard it at all, and went on, clearly speaking only to Erlenmeyer. "Surely, Doctor, as a college man yourself you must realize that the opportunities for a meaningful cultural exchange are sorely limited in an institution of this nature. Of course, I attend the General Semantics Club and I'm taking the course Oral McKeon is giving in Oriental religions, but these are such tiny oases in this desert of sweatsuits

and domino games, and I can't understand why everyone is just thrown together without reference to their backgrounds, or the nature of their offense. Thieves, dope addicts, even sex maniacs—"

Zeke threw his hands up in mock alarm. "Where'd you see a sex
maniac?"

"I don't think it cause for facetiousness," Watson said coldly. "Just
yesterday I found occasion to step into the toilet off the big yard and one
of the sweepers was standing there masturbating into the urinal."

"That's horrible," Zeke said. "What'd you do?"

"I left, of course."

"Naturally. It violates the basic ideals of Scouting."[9]

The lower-class man, though he doesn't share the square john's
repugnance towards criminals or the convict code, usually does not
wish to associate closely with thieves, dope fiends, heads, and disorganized criminals. In his life outside he has encountered and
avoided these persons for many years and usually keeps on avoiding
them inside. He usually seeks a job to occupy himself. His actual stay
in prison is typically very short, since he is either released very early
and/or he is classified at minimum custody and sent to a forestry
camp or one of the minimum-custody institutions, where he has increased freedom and privileges.

Jailing

Some convicts who do not retain or who never acquired any
commitment to outside social worlds, tend to make a world out of
prison.[10] These are the men who

> seek positions of power, influence and sources of information, whether
> these men are called "shots," "politicians," "merchants," "hoods,"
> "toughs," "gorillas," or something else. A job as secretary to the Captain
> or Warden, for example, gives an aspiring prisoner information and conse-
> quent power, and enables him to influence the assignment or regulation of
> other inmates. In the same way, a job which allows the incumbent to par-
> ticipate in a racket, such as clerk in the kitchen storeroom where he can
> steal and sell food, is highly desirable to a man oriented to the convict sub-
> culture. With a steady income of cigarettes, ordinarily the prisoner's medi-
> um of exchange, he may assert a great deal of influence and purchase those
> things which are symbols of status among persons oriented to the convict
> subculture. Even if there is not a well-developed medium of exchange, he
> can barter goods acquired in his position for equally-desirable goods pos-
> sessed by other convicts. These include information and such things as
> specially-starched, pressed, and tailored prison clothing, fancy belts, belt
> buckles or billfolds, special shoes, or any other type of dress which will set
> him apart and will indicate that he has both the influence to get the goods
> and the influence necessary to keep them and display them despite prison

rules which outlaw doing so. In California, special items of clothing, and clothing that is neatly laundered, are called "bonaroos" (a corruption of *bonnet rouge*, by means of which French prison trusties were once distinguished from the common run of prisoners), and to a lesser degree even the persons who wear such clothing are called "bonaroos."[11]

Just as doing time is the characteristic style of the thief, so "jailing" is the characteristic style of the state-raised youth. This identity terminates on the first or second prison term, or certainly by the time the youth reaches thirty. The state-raised youth must assume a new identity, and the one he most often chooses, the one which his experience has prepared him for, is that of the "convict." The prison world is the only world with which he is familiar. He was raised in a world where "punks" and "queens" have replaced women, "bonaroos" are the only fashionable clothing, and cigarettes are money. This is a world where disputes are settled with a pipe or a knife, and the individual must form tight cliques for protection. His senses are attuned to iron doors banging, locks turning, shakedowns, and long lines of blue-clad convicts. He knows how to survive, in fact prosper, in this world, how to get a cell change and a good work assignment, how to score for nutmeg, cough syrup, or other narcotics. More important, he knows hundreds of youths like himself who grew up in the youth prisons and are now in the adult prisons. For example, Claude Brown describes a friend who fell into the patterns of jailing:

"Yeah, Sonny. The time I did in Woodburn, the times I did on the Rock, that was college, man. Believe me, it was college. I did four years in Woodburn. And I guess I've done a total of about two years on the Rock in about the last six years. Every time I went there, I learned a little more. When I go to jail now, Sonny, I live, man. I'm right at home. That's the good part about it. If you look at it, Sonny, a cat like me is just cut out to be in jail.

"It could never hurt me, 'cause I never had what the good folks call a home and all that kind of shit to begin with. So when I went to jail, the first time I went away, when I went to Warwick, I made my own home. It was all right. Shit, I learned how to live. Now when I go back to the joint, anywhere I go, I know some people. If I go to any of the jails in New York, or if I go to a slam in Jersey, even, I still run into a lot of cats I know. It's almost like a family."

I said, "Yeah, Reno, it's good that a cat can be so happy in jail. I guess all it takes to be happy in anything is knowin' how to walk with your lot, whatever it is, in life."[12]

The state-raised youth often assumes a role in the prison social system, the system of roles, values, and norms described by Schrag, Sykes, and others. This does not mean that he immediately rises to power in the prison system. Some of the convicts have occupied their positions for many years and cannot tolerate the threat of every new bunch of reform-school graduates. The state-raised youth who has just graduated to adult prison must start at the bottom; but he knows the routine, and in a year or so he occupies a key position himself. One reason he can readily rise is that in youth prison he very often develops skills, such as clerical and maintenance skills, that are valuable to the prison administration.

Many state-raised youths, however, do not tolerate the slow ascent in the prison social system and become "lowriders." They form small cliques and rob cells, hijack other convicts, carry on feuds with other cliques, and engage in various rackets. Though these "outlaws" are feared and hated by all other convicts, their orientation is to the convict world, and they are definitely part of the convict social system.

Dope fiends and hustlers slip into jailing more often than thieves, due mainly to the congruities between their old activities and some of the patterns of jailing. For instance, a central activity of jailing is "wheeling and dealing," the major economic activity of prison. All prison resources—dope, food, books, money, sexual favors, bonaroos, cell changes, jobs, dental and hospital care, hot plates, stingers, cell furnishings, rings, and buckles—are always available for purchase with cigarettes. It is possible to live in varying degrees of luxury, and luxury has a double reward in prison as it does in the outside society: first, there is the reward of consumption itself, and second there is the reward of increased prestige in the prison social system because of the display of opulence.

This prison life style requires more cigarettes than can be obtained legally; consequently, one wheels and deals. There are three main forms of wheeling and dealing for cigarettes: (1) gambling (cards, dice and betting on sporting events); (2) selling some commodity or service, which is usually made possible by a particular job assignment; and (3) lending cigarettes for interest—two for three. These activities have a familiar ring to both the hustler and the dope fiend, who have hustled money or dope on the outside. They very often become intricately involved in the prison economic life and in this way necessarily involved in the prison social system. The hustler does this because he feels at home in this routine, because he wants to keep in practice, or because he must present a good front—even in prison. To present a good front one must be a success at wheeling and dealing.

The dope fiend, in addition to having an affinity for wheeling and dealing, may become involved in the prison economic life in securing drugs. There are a variety of drugs available for purchase with cigarettes or money (and money can be purchased with cigarettes). Drugs are expensive, however, and to purchase them with any regularity one either has money smuggled in from the outside or he wheels and deals. And to wheel and deal one must maintain connections for securing drugs, for earning money, and for protection. This enmeshes the individual in the system of prison roles, values, and norms. Though he maintains a basic commitment to his drug subculture which supersedes his commitment to the prison culture and though he tends to form close ties only with other dope fiends, through his wheeling and dealing for drugs he becomes an intricate part of the prison social system.

The head jails more often than the thief. One reason for this is that the head, especially the "weed head" tends to worship luxuries and comforts and is fastidious in his dress. Obtaining small luxuries, comforts, and "bonaroo" clothing usually necessitates enmeshing himself in the "convict" system. Furthermore, the head is often vulnerable to the dynamics of narrow, cliquish, and invidious social systems, such as the "convict" system, because many of the outside head social systems are of this type.

The thief, or any identity for that matter, *may* slowly lose his orientation to the outside community, take on the convict categories, and thereby fall into jailing. This occurs when the individual has spent a great deal of time in prison and/or returned to the outside community and discovered that he no longer fits in the outside world. It is difficult to maintain a real commitment to a social world without firsthand experience with it for long periods of time.

The square john and the lower-class man find the activities of the "convicts" petty, repugnant, or dangerous, and virtually never jail.

Gleaning

With the rapidly growing educational, vocational training, and treatment opportunities, and with the erosion of convict solidarity, an increasing number of convicts choose to radically change their life styles and follow a sometimes carefully devised plan to "better themselves," "improve their mind," or "find themselves" while in prison.[13] One convict describes his motives and plans for changing his life style:

I got tired of losing. I had been losing all my life. I decided that I wanted to win for a while. So I got on a different kick. I knew that I had to learn something so I went to school, got my high school diploma. I cut myself off from my old YA buddies and started hanging around with some intelligent guys who minded their own business. We read a lot, a couple of us paint. We play a little bridge and talk, a lot of time about what we are going to do when we get out. (Interview, Soledad Prison, June 1966)

Gleaning may start on a small scale, perhaps as an attempt to overcome educational or intellectual inferiorities. For instance, Malcolm X, feeling inadequate in talking to certain convicts, starts to read:

> It had really begun back in the Charlestown Prison, when Bimbi first made me feel envy of his stock of knowledge. Bimbi had always taken charge of any conversation he was in, and I had tried to emulate him. But every book I picked up had few sentences which didn't contain anywhere from one to nearly all of the words that might as well have been in Chinese. When I just skipped those words, of course, I really ended up with little idea of what the book said. So I have come to the Norfolk Prison Colony still going through only book-reading motions. Pretty soon, I would have quit even these motions, unless I had received the motivation that I did.[14]

The initial, perfunctory steps into gleaning often spring the trap. Gleaning activities have an intrinsic attraction and often instill motivation which was originally lacking. Malcolm X reports how once he began to read, the world of knowledge opened up to him:

> No university would ask any student to devour literature as I did when this new world opened to me, of being able to read and *understand*.[15]

In trying to "improve himself," "improve his mind," or "find himself," the convict gleans from every source available in prison. The chief source is books: he reads philosophy, history, art, science, and fiction. Often after getting started he devours a sizable portion of world literature. Malcolm X describes his voracious reading habits:

> I read more in my room than in the library itself. An inmate who was known to read a lot could check out more than the permitted maximum number of books. I preferred reading in the total isolation of my own room.
>
> When I had progressed to really serious reading, every night at about ten P.M. I would be outraged with the "lights out." It always seemed to catch me right in the middle of something engrossing.
>
> Fortunately, right outside my door was a corridor light that cast a glow into my room. The glow was enough to read by, once my eyes adjusted to it. So when "lights out" came, I would sit on the floor where I could continue reading in that glow.[16]

Besides this informal education, he often pursues formal education. The convict may complete grammar school and high school in the prison educational facilities. He may enroll in college courses through the University of California (which will be paid for by the Department of Corrections), or through other correspondence schools (which he must pay for himself). More recently, he may take courses in various prison college programs.

He learns trades through the vocational training programs or prison job assignments. Sometimes he augments these by studying trade books, correspondence courses, or journals. He studies painting, writing, music, acting, and other creative arts. There are some facilities for these pursuits sponsored by the prison administration, but these are limited. This type of gleaning is done mostly through correspondence, through reading, or through individual efforts in the cell.

He tries to improve himself in other ways. He works on his social skills and his physical appearance—has his tattoos removed, has surgery on physical defects, has dental work done, and builds up his body, "pushing iron."

He shys away from former friends or persons with his criminal identity who are not gleaners and forms new associations with other gleaners. These are usually gleaners who have chosen a similar style of gleaning, and with whom he shares many interests and activities, but they may also be those who are generally trying to improve themselves, although they are doing so in different ways.

Gleaning is a style more characteristic of the hustler, the dope fiend, and the state-raised youth than of the thief. When the former glean, though they tend to associate less with their deviant friends who are doing time or jailing, they are not out of the influence of these groups, or free from the influence of their old subculture values. The style of gleaning they choose and the future life for which they prepare themselves must be acceptable to the old reference group and somewhat congruent with their deviant values. The life they prepare for should be prestigious in the eyes of their old associates. It must be "doing good" and cannot be "a slave's life."

The state-raised youth who gleans probably has the greatest difficulty cutting himself off from his former group because the state-raised values emphasize loyalty to one's buddies:

I don't spend much time with my old YA [Youth Authority] partners and when I do we don't get along. They want me to do something that I won't do or they start getting on my back about my plans. One time they were riding me pretty bad and I had to pull them up. (Interview, Soledad Prison, June 1966)

He also has the greatest difficulty in making any realistic plans for the future. He has limited experience with the outside, and his models of "making it" usually come from the mass media—magazines, books, movies, and TV.

The dope fiend and the head, when they glean, tend to avoid practical fields and choose styles which promise glamor, excitement, or color. Most conventional paths with which they are familiar seem especially dull and repugnant. In exploring ways of making it they must find some way to avoid the humdrum life which they rejected long ago. Many turn to legitimate deviant identities such as "intellectual outsiders," "bohemians," or "mystics." Often they study one of the creative arts, the social sciences, or philosophy with no particular career in mind.

The hustler, who values skills of articulation and maintained a good "front" in his deviant life, often prepares for a field where these skills will serve him, such as preaching or political activism.

The square john and the lower-class man, since they seldom seek to radically change their identity, do not glean in the true sense, but they do often seek to improve themselves. The square john usually does this by attacking his problem. He is satisfied with his reference world—the conventional society—but he recognizes that to return to it successfully he must cope with that flaw in his makeup which led to his incarceration. There are three common ways he attacks this problem: (1) he joins self help groups such as Alcoholics Anonymous, (2) he seeks the help of experts (psychiatrists, psychologists or sociologists) and attends the therapy programs, or (3) he turns to religion.

The lower-class man is usually an older person who does not desire or deem it possible to carve out a radically new style of life. He may, however, see the prison experience as a chance to improve himself by increasing his education and his vocational skills.

The thief tends to be older and his commitment to his identity is usually strong, so it is not likely that he will explore other life styles or identities. This does not mean that he is committed for all time to a life of crime. Certain alternate conclusions to a criminal career are included in the definitions of a proper thief's life. For instance, a thief may retire when he becomes older, has served a great deal of time, or has made a "nice score." When he retires he may work at some well-paying trade or run a small business, and in prison he may prepare himself for either of these acceptable conclusions to a criminal career.

DISORGANIZED CRIMINAL

In the preceding discussion of prison adaptive modes, the "disorganized criminal" was purposely omitted. It is felt that his prison adaptation must be considered separately from the other identities.

The disorganized criminal is human putty in the prison social world. He may be shaped to fit any category. He has weaker commitments to values or conceptions of self that would prevent him from organizing any course of action in prison. He is the most responsive to prison programs, to differential association, and to other forces which are out of his control. He may become part of the prison social system, do his time, or glean. If they will tolerate him, he may associate with thieves, dope fiends, convicts, squares, heads, or other disorganized criminals. To some extent these associations are formed in a random fashion. He befriends persons with whom he works, cells next to, and encounters regularly through the prison routine. He tends not to seek out particular categories, as is the case with the other identities. He does not feel any restraints in initiating associations, however, as do the square john and the lower-class man.

The friendships he forms are very important to any changes that occur in this person. Since he tends to have a cleaner slate in terms of identity, he is more susceptible to differential association. He often takes on the identity and the prison adaptive mode of the group with which he comes into contact. If he does acquire a new identity, however, such as one of the deviant identities that exist in prison, his commitment to it is still tentative at most. The deviant identities, except for that of the convict, exist in the context of an exterior world, and the more subtle cues, the responses, the meanings which are essential parts of this world cannot be experienced in prison. It is doubtful, therefore, that any durable commitment could be acquired in prison. In the meantime, he may be shaken from this identity, and he may continue to vacillate from social world to social world, or to wander bewildered in a maze of conflicting world views as he has done in the past.

RACE AND ETHNICITY

Another variable which is becoming increasingly important in the formation of cleavages and identity changes in the convict world is that of race and ethnicity. For quite some time in California prisons, hostility and distance between three segments of the populations—whites, Negroes and Mexicans—have increased. For several years the Negroes have assumed a more militant and ethnocentric posture, and recently the Mexicans—already ethnocentric and aggressive—have followed with a more organized, militant stance. Correspondingly, there is a growing trend among these two segments to establish, reestablish or enhance racial-ethnic pride and identity. Many "Blacks" and "Chicanos" are supplanting their criminal identity with a racial-ethnic one. This movement started with the Blacks.[17] A black California convict gives his recently acquired views toward whites:

All these years, man, I been stealing and coming to the joint. I never stopped to think why I was doing it. I thought that all I wanted was money and stuff. Ya know, man, now I can see why I thought the way I did. I been getting fucked all my life and never realized it. The white man has been telling me that I should want his stuff. But he didn't give me no way to get it. Now I ain't going for his shit anymore. I'm a Black man. I'm going to get out of here and see what I can do for my people. I'm going to do what I have to do to get those white motherfuckers off my people's back. (Interview, San Quentin, March 1968)

Chicanos in prison have maintained considerable insulation from both whites and Blacks—especially Blacks—towards whom they have harbored considerable hostility. They possess a strong ethnic-racial identity which underpins their more specialized felonious one—which has usually been that of a dope fiend or lower-class man. This subcultural identity and actual group unity in prison has been based on their Mexican culture—especially two important dimensions of Mexican culture. The first is their strong commitment to the concept of "machismo"—which is roughly translated manhood. The second is their use of Spanish and Calo (Spanish slang) which has separated them from other segments. Besides these two traits there are many other ethnic subcultural characteristics which promote unity among Chicanos. For instance, they tend to be stoic and intolerant of "snitches" and "snivelers" and feel that Anglos and Blacks are more often snitches and snivelers. Furthermore they respect friendship to the extreme, in fact to the extreme of killing or dying for friendship.

Until recently this has meant that Chicanos constituted the most cohesive segment in California prisons. In prison, where they intermingle with whites and Negroes, they have felt considerable distance from these segments and have maintained their identification with Mexican culture. However, there have been and still are some divisions in this broad category. For instance, various neighborhood cliques of Chicanos often carry on violent disputes with each other which last for years. Furthermore, Los Angeles or California cliques wage disputes with El Paso or Texas cliques. Many stabbings and killings have resulted from confrontations between different Chicano groups. Nevertheless, underpinning these different group affiliations and the various criminal identities there has been a strong identification with Mexican culture.

Recently the Chicanos, following the footsteps of the Negroes in prison and the footsteps of certain militant Mexican-American groups outside (e.g., MAPA and the Delano strikers) have started organizing cultural-activist groups in prison (such as Empleo) and shaping a new identity built upon their Mexican ancestry and their position of disadvantage in the white society. As they move in this direction they are cultivating some friendship with the Negroes, towards whom they now feel more affinity.

This racial-ethnic militance and identification will more than likely become increasingly important in the prison social world. There is already some indication that the identity of the Black National and that of the Chicano is becoming superordinate to the criminal identities of many Negroes and Mexican-Americans or at least is having an impact on their criminal identities.

A dude don't necessarily have to become a Muslim or a Black National now to get with Black Power. He may still be laying to get out there and do some pimping or shoot some dope. But he knows he's a brother and when the shit is down we can count on him. And maybe he is going to carry himself a little differently, you know, like now you see more and more dudes—oh, they're still pimps, but they got naturals now. (Interview, San Quentin, April 1968)

The reassertion or discovery of the racial-ethnic identity is sometimes related to gleaning in prison. Frequently, the leaders of Blacks or Chicanos, for example, Malcolm X and Eldrige Cleaver, have arrived at their subcultural activism and militant stance through gleaning. Often, becoming identified with this movement will precipitate a gleaning course. However, this is not necessarily the case. These two phenomena are not completely overlapping among the Negro and Chicano.

The nationalistic movement is beginning to have a general impact on the total prison world—especially at San Quentin. The Blacks and Chicanos, as they focus on the whites as their oppressors, seem to be excluding white prisoners from this category and are, in fact, developing some sympathy for them as a minority group which itself is being oppressed by the white establishment and the white police. As an indication of this recent change, one convict comments on the present food-serving practices of Muslim convicts:

It used to be that whenever a Muslim was serving something (and this was a lot of the time man, because there's a lot of those dudes in the kitchen), well, you know, you wouldn't expect to get much of a serving. Now, the cats just pile it on to whites and blacks. Like he is giving all the state's stuff away to show his contempt. So I think it is getting better between the suedes and us. (Interview, San Quentin, April 1968)

THE CONVICT IDENTITY

Over and beyond the particular criminal identity or the racial-ethnic identity he acquires or maintains in prison and over and beyond the changes in his direction which are produced by his prison strategy, to some degree the felon acquires the perspective of the "convict."

There are several gradations and levels of this perspective and attendant identity. First is the taken-for-granted perspective, which he acquires in spite of any conscious efforts to avoid it. This perspective is acquired simply by being in prison and engaging in prison routines for months or years. Even square johns who consciously attempt to pass through the prison experience without acquiring any of the beliefs and values of the criminals, do to some extent acquire certain meanings, certain taken-for-granted interpretations and responses which will shape, influence, or distort reality for them after release.

Beyond the taken-for-granted perspective which all convicts acquire, most convicts are influenced by a pervasive but rather uncohesive convict "code." To some extent most of them, especially those who identify with a criminal system, are consciously committed to the major dictum of this code—"do your own time." As was pointed out earlier, the basic meaning of this precept is the obligation to tolerate the behavior of others unless it is directly affecting your physical self or your possessions. If another's behavior surpasses these limits, then the problem must be solved by the person himself; that is, *not* by calling for help from the officials.

> The convict code isn't any different than stuff we all learned as kids. You know, nobody likes a stool pigeon. Well, here in the joint you got all kinds of guys living jammed together, two to a cell. You got nuts walking the yard, you got every kind of dingbat in the world here. Well, we got to have some rules among ourselves. The rule is "do your own number." In other words, keep off your neighbors' toes. Like if a guy next to me is making brew in his cell, well, this is none of my business. I got no business running to the man and telling him that Joe Blow is making brew in his cell. Unless Joe Blow is fucking over me, then I can't say nothing. And when he is fucking over me, then I got to stop him myself. If I can't then I deserve to get fucked over. (Interview, San Quentin, May 1968)

Commitment to the convict code or the identity of the convict is to a high degree a lifetime commitment to do your own time; that is, to live and let live, and when you feel that someone is not letting you live, to either take it, leave, or stop him yourself, but never call for help from official agencies of control.

At another level, the convict perspective consists of a more cohesive and sophisticated value and belief system. This is the perspective of the elite of the convict world—the "regular." A "regular" (or, as he has been variously called, "people," "folks," "solid," a "right guy," or "all right") possesses many of the traits of the thief's culture. He can be counted on when needed by other regulars. He is also a "hoosier"; that is, he has some finesse, is capable, is levelheaded, has "guts" and "timing." The following description of a simple bungled transaction exemplifies this trait:

> Man, you should have seen the hoosier when the play came down. I thought that the motherfucker was all right. He surprised me. He had the stuff and was about to hand it to me when a sergeant and another bull came through the door from the outside. Well, there wasn't nothing to worry about. Is all he had to do was go on like there was nothin' unusual and hand me the stuff and they would have never suspected nothing. But he got so fucking nervous and started fumbling around. You know, he handed me the sack and then pulled it back until they got hip that some

play was taking place. Well you know what happened. The play was ranked and we both ended up in the slammer. (Field notes, San Quentin, February 1968)

The final level of the perspective of the convict is that of the "old con." This is a degree of identification reached after serving a great deal of time, so much time that all outside-based identities have dissipated and the only meaningful world is that of the prison. The old con has become totally immersed in the prison world. This identification is often the result of years of jailing, but it can result from merely serving too much time. It was mentioned previously that even thieves after spending many years may fall into jailing, even though time-doing is their usual pattern. After serving a very long sentence or several long sentences with no extended period between, any criminal will tend to take on the identity of the "old con."

The old con tends to carve out a narrow but orderly existence in prison. He has learned to secure many luxuries and learned to be satisfied with the prison forms of pleasure—e.g., homosexual activities, cards, dominoes, handball, hobbies, and reading. He usually obtains jobs which afford him considerable privileges and leisure time. He often knows many of the prison administrators—the warden, the associate wardens, the captain, and the lieutenants, whom he has known since they were officers and lesser officials.

Often he becomes less active in the prison social world. He retires and becomes relatively docile or apthetic. At times he grows petty and treacherous. There is some feeling that old cons can't be trusted because their "head has become soft" or they have "lost their guts," and are potential "stool pigeons."

The convict identity is very important to the future career of the felon. In the first instance, the acquiring of the taken-for-granted perspective will at least obstruct the releasee's attempts to reorient himself on the outside. More important, the other levels of the identity, if they have been acquired, will continue to influence choices for years afterward. The convict perspective, though it may become submerged after extended outside experiences, will remain operative in its latency state and will often obtrude into civilian life contexts.

The identity of the old con—the perspective, the values and beliefs, and other personality attributes which are acquired after the years of doing time, such as advanced age, adjustment to prison routines, and complete loss of skills required to carry on the normal activities of civilians—will usually make living on the outside impossible. The old con is very often suited for nothing except dereliction on the outside or death in prison.

12

STREET GANGS BEHIND BARS *

JAMES B. JACOBS

SOCIAL ORGANIZATION OF THE PRISON

The social organization of the prison has attracted the attention of sociologists since Clemmer (1958) published *The Prison Community* in 1940. In that work he emphasized the isolation of the "fish" arriving at prison and the gradual socialization into the inmate subculture through association with primary groups. Later students confirmed the identity stripping impact of the total institution upon the convicted individual and pointed to the functional importance of participation in primary groups as a solution to crucial situational problems, material and psychological (Garabedian, 1963; Goffman, 1961; McCorkle and Korn, 1954; Sykes, 1966).

Sykes and Messinger (1960) account for the structure and character of the inmate organization by reference to the special problems of adjustment found behind the walls. Three crucial problems are noted: social rejection, material deprivation, and sexual frustration. In response to these institutional pressures there emerges an inmate organization characterized by a code which embraces a deviant perspective in "solidary opposition" to conventional values and institutional goals. This code allows the individual to maintain a favorable image of self and to avoid identity collapse by providing a rationale which enables him to reject his rejectors (McCorkle and Korn, 1954). The inmate social system is also described as a system of interrelated roles and functions which enables the inmate to order and to classify experience within the walls in terms which deal specifically with the problems of prison life (Sykes, 1966).

In recent years, however, several students have shown that the solidary opposition theorists have paid too little attention to the im-

Source: From *Social Problems*, 21,3(Spring 1974):395-409. Copyright 1974 by the Society for the Study of Social Problems. Reprinted by permission of the author and publisher.

*The research was carried out under a Ford Foundation grant. Grateful acknowledgement is made to Norval Morris and Barry Schwartz for their enthusiasm and guidance in this research.

portance of organizational goals in accounting for the uncooperative and oppositional character of the inmate code (Grusky, 1959; Berk, 1966; Street, Vintner, and Perrow, 1968). They have demonstrated that where organizational goals have shifted from custody to treatment, the inmate normative system would also shift to a perspective favorable to staff and organizational goals. Rather than being socialized within the prison to reject the formal organization, those inmates committed to smaller treatment institutions would become socialized into an increasingly favorable orientation.

While this suggestion of "solidary cooperation" contradicted the solidary opposition theory, it was easily subsumed under the more general theory of "indigenous influence." The proponents of solidary cooperation, like those of solidary opposition, accepted the fact that socialization through primary groups into inmate perspective based upon situational variables was the standing explanation for inmate attitudes, values, and behavior.

An alternative to the indigenous influence theory itself was offered by Irwin and Cressey (1964), who found some support in Clemmer and Schrag for the proposition that criminal dispositions and behavioral patterns before prison have strong explanatory power in accounting for inmate behavior. These authors urge us to focus greater attention upon pre-institutional behavior patterns.

Like thieves, legitimate people are not necessarily stripped of outside statuses and they do not play the prison game. They bring a set of values to prison and don't leave them at the gate ... it seems a worthy hypothesis that thieves, convicts and do-rights all bring certain values and behavior patterns to prison with them, and that total "inmate culture" represents an adjustment or accommodation of these three systems within the official administrative system of deprivation and control. (Irwin and Cressey, 1964:241)

This exploration of inmate norms and behavior in terms of extra-prison variables has been termed a theory of "cultural drift" (Schwartz, 1971). Further force has been lent to this theory by the work of Giallombardo (1966), who explains sexual adjustment in a woman's prison by the sex roles prevalent in the wider society. Both Irwin and Cressey and Giallombardo make use of the Becker-Geer (1960) distinction between manifest and latent culture. Those authors argue that latent culture develops in anticipation of a social system in which the individual is not currently participating. An individual may therefore orient his behavior inside prison according to norms internalized while on the street.

The indigenous influence theory of inmate culture informs the rehabilitative model of the prison in much the same way as Merton's anomie theory provides a theoretical rational for "welfare state" programs of crime prevention through expansion of economic opportunity (Gouldner, 1970). If the behavior of the prisoner can be entirely explained in terms of the institutional environment in which he is placed, then the right mix of institutional policies and programs would produce a rehabilitated individual whose favorable disposition toward formal organizational goals would augur well for his later return to the community.

The policy implications flowing from the theory of cultural drift are far more pessimistic. The cultural drift theory casts doubt upon the potential of penal institutions for converting their clients. General acceptance of this theory would force the society to support its prison system with a rationale other than that of rehabilitation. The study reported here lends further support to the cultural drift theory. It suggests that in Illinois prisons the inmate organization is best understood as an extension of an identical organization imported from the streets of Chicago.

THE STUDY

This study was undertaken at Stateville Penitentiary between June and October, 1972. Located 30 miles from Chicago, Stateville is a typical walled-in maximum security penitentiary holding approximately two thousand inmates. The writer operated as a known observer for the entire period of the study. Contact was established with many gang leaders as well as with independents or "off brands." Formal interviews were conducted with key members of prison staff and of the Illinois Department of Corrections. Most of the time was spent interacting informally with inmates on their jobs, in their cells, and in the prison yard.[18] The most basic division of the inmate population is by race. Blacks account for 70 percent of the population; Latins contribute 10 percent; and whites 20 percent. From the outset of the fieldwork, special focus was placed upon the most salient aspect of the informal organization—the existence of four Chicago street gangs as viable organizations behind the walls.

Three of the gangs are black; one is Latin. Among the black gangs, the Black P. Stone Nation is undoubtedly the best known to the public due to the extensive publicity given to the trials of the leadership for extortion of federal anti-poverty funds. The Stones are extremely well organized and of the four gangs comes closest to constituting a professional criminal syndicate. On the streets of Chicago's South Side, as well as within the prison, the Disciples are the chief rivals of the Stones. At Stateville both groups claim some 400 adherents. The Disciples are far more loosely organized than the Stones, having fewer members in their late 20's and 30's, and account for more disciplinary infractions than any of the other gangs. The conservative Vicelords is an old gang associated with Chicago's West Side and especially with the Lawndale area (Keiser, 1969). In the late 1960's the Vicelords earned national attention for their efforts to clean up their community and to pioneer various small business ventures. Within Stateville there are between 150 and 200 Vicelords. Their organization is well disciplined; authority has remained firmly in the hands of several of the older original members. Rarely are Vicelords involved in serious disciplinary violations. The latter finding also holds true for the Latin Kings, which despite small numbers within the prison (30), is one of the largest gang federations in Chicago. At Stateville the Kings are extremely closely knit and at times also serve as spokesmen for all Latin inmates.

THE GANGS

The four gangs active at Stateville are parts of the largest street gangs in Chicago. All of them can be characterized as lower class gangs, territorially associated with Chicago's most dilapidated slum areas. Consistent with Thrasher's (1926) observations of one-half century ago, we find that on the streets these gangs are simultaneously involved in a wide variety of activities, including gang fighting, mugging, armed robbery, extortion, drug trafficking and, more recently, various legitimate business ventures and involvement in anti-poverty programs.

There can be no doubt that the existence of the gangs in the prison is inextricably tied to their continued viability on the street. Informants repeatedly emphasized that, were the gangs to dissolve on the streets, they would immediately disappear from the prison. It was recalled that various other gangs, having small followings at Stateville, evaporated when the parent gang became absorbed by a different group.

Gang fights on the streets are immediately felt behind the walls. A news report of a killing involving Disciples and Stones on Chicago's South Side at once raises the tensions of members at Stateville. Visits from ranking gang members, often under disguise, are frequent. Even more frequently, families carry information about the gang to and from the prison. In the last five years the influx of gang members has been so great that a communication link between street and prison has been established merely through the steady commitment of members.

Within the prison the visibility of the gangs is extremely high. Each gang vigorously affirms its own identity through symbolic representation. Members "represent" to one another by esoteric salutes and verbal greetings. Gang colors and insignias are worn on sweat shirts, t-shirts, and as tattoos.

Under the rubric of "political prisoners," "revolution," and "white racism," the four gangs demonstrate a rudimentary solidarity opposed to white society, white administration, and white inmates. While the young gang members have for the first time placed the older cons in fear of physical security, they have also brought into the prison a rebellious attitude toward all authority. Little distinction is made between various control agents. In fact, within the prison the security staff is referred to as the "police." Black (and Latin) consciousness and the political implications of incarceration have become salient issues. In contributing to the transformation of a group of inmates "in itself" to a group " for itself," the gangs can be said to have begun to politicize the prison.

SOCIALIZATION AND RECRUITMENT

The "gang thing" is the most significant reality behind the walls. The unaffiliated convict enters prison fearing that his life may be in danger from the gangs. Even if he is not immediately concerned with survival, he will face the prospect of being shaken down for commissary and sex. The security staff can be of little help in protecting him. In one way or another, a strategy must be carved out for dealing with the gang situation. Often the young white inmate may become a "punk" for one of the gangs. Some whites, the "crazy motherfuckers," have been able to maintain physical security because of demonstrated fighting ability; others because of supposed connections with organized crime.

The Latin Kings and Vicelords, skeptical of penitentiary members, do not recruit in the prison, but the Stones and Disciples recruit vigorously (as they do on the streets). Frequently solicitation will be forceful; it is often highly sophisticated. The fish will be confronted by both a "hard" and a "soft" sell.

In contrast to the recruitment pressures experienced by the unaffiliated convict, the gang member from the street has no trouble whatever in adjusting to the new environment. As the warden of Pontiac Penitentiary told me: "When a new guy comes up here it's almost a homecoming—undoubtedly there are people from his neighborhood and people who know him."[19] The chief of the Disciples claims to have known 75 Disciples upon arrival at Stateville. A young leader of the Latin Kings explained that because of his position in the Kings he knew all but two of the Kings upon arrival. The first afternoon he received a letter from the ranking chief welcoming him into the family.

B.P., chief of the Vicelords, explains that when a young Vicelord is spotted coming into the prison, he will see to it that the man is set up immediately with coffee, tea, deodorant, and soap. Visitors and correspondents will be arranged for those Vicelords deserted by their families. Normally the gang member will have the situation run down for him by his cell house chief. This orientation can be quite elaborate. Evidence the following written rules circulated by the Disciples:

I.   Degradation ot another Disciple will not be tolerated at any time.
II. Disrespect for any Governing body of said cell house will not be permitted.
III. There will not at any time be any unnecessary commotion while entering the cell house.
IV. Homosexual confrontation toward another Disciple will definitely not be tolerated.
V.   Dues will be paid up on time at any designated schedule.
VI. Fighting another Disciple, without consulting a Governing chief will result in strict disciplining.
VII. Upon greeting another Disciple, proper representation will be ascertained.
VIII. There will never be an act of cowardice displayed by any Disciple, for a Disciple is always strong and brave.
IX. There will not be any cigarettes upon entering the hole for those who relentlessly obstruct the rules and regulations of the organization, or the institution.
X.   Anyone caught perpetrating the above rules and regulations with disorder and dishonesty, will be brought before the committee and dealt with accordingly.

The parallel between these rules and an "inmate code," often described as prescribing solidarity among cons and opposition to staff, is striking. That the inmate code can be accounted for by reference to the norms of certain criminal subcultures is precisely the thesis advanced by Irwin and Cressey (1964).

SERVICES PERFORMED BY THE GANG FOR ITS MEMBERS

Besides physical security, the gang in prison, as on the street, serves important material and psychological functions for its members. To some degree the organizations function as buffers against poverty within the institution. Each gang has a poor box. Cell house chiefs in each of the gangs collect cigarettes from the members and store them for those who have legitimate need. When a member makes a particularly good "score" or deal, he is expected to share the bounty with the leaders and to donate to the poor box. While skeptical independents claim that these boxes are often depleted and that many benefits do not filter down to the soldiers, this observer has often seen the leaders giving away cigarettes. Furthermore, when a gang member is placed in isolation, he can always expect cigarettes and food to be passed to him.

The organizations function as a communication network. If McCleery (1960) is correct in asserting that a crucial concern of the convicted man is the lack of information about institutional decisions, then the organizations do function to keep their members informed and to place a coherent definition of the situation on all events within the institution. By having their soldiers assigned to jobs in the administration building, as runners, as yard gang workers, and as house help, the gangs insure that information can flow from front to back with great precision.

The gangs provide a convenient distributional network for contraband goods. One Latin King informant explained that where an independent might hesitate to attempt a score fearing that he might be unable to secrete the stolen items, a gang member knows that within a number of minutes he can divest himself of the major share of the contraband.

The role of the gangs in organizing illicit activities is unclear. What is clear is that no illicit activities operate within the prison without the tacit approval of the gang leaders. Gang affiliation enables the young inmate to establish connections in the illegal trafficking and to muscle in on any independents not already paying off to one of the other gangs.

By far the most important function which these four organizations play at Stateville is the psychological support they provide for their members. Whether one subscribes to the theories of Cohen (1955) or Miller (1958) in accounting for the origin of delinquent gangs, the important point here is, as Thrasher (1963) noted, that the gang serves as a membership and reference group providing the delinquent with status and a positive view of self. G.B., leader of the Disciples, explained:

> These guys in my branch [of the Disciple federation] are closer to me than my own family. Anything I do around them is accepted—for stuff that my parents would put me down for, these guys elevate me to a pedestal.

Over and over again inmate informants, gang members and off brands, expressed the opinion that the gangs provide a source of identification, a feeling of belonging and an air of importance.

> It's just like a religion. Once a Lord, always a Lord. Our people would die for it. Perhaps this comes from lack of a father figure or lack of guidance or from having seen your father beaten up and cowering from the police. We never had anything with which to identify. Even the old cons like me—

they are looking for me to give them something they have been looking for
for a long time.

Gang members consistently explained that on the street and within
the prison, it is the same—the gang allows you to feel like a man; it is
a family with which you can identify. Several informants soberly
stated that the organization is something, the only thing, worth dying for.

The organizations, with their insignias, colors, salutes, titles, and
legendary histories provide the only meaningful reference group for
their members. Within the organizational framework the soldiers are
allocated definite roles and can aspire to successive levels of status.

SOLDIERS AND INDIANS

For soldier, or "Indian," incarceration is not a career break. To the
contrary, role requirements are more stringent in the prison than
they were on the street, since in the prison the Indians are under the
24 hour scrutiny of their leaders. Indeed, they are in some cases presented with their first opportunity for associating with the revered
chiefs. This highly open or visible situation transforms the prison setting into an especially fateful field of action, where status can be
more easily won and lost. The Indian who represents well and "takes
care of business" can earn a title or promotion in rank (to cell house
chief's assistant, for example). He is also rewarded by access to the
inner circles, where he will be close to the chiefs, privy to inside information, and even come to be recognized as a kind of chief himself
by his peers. B.P. explained to me:

Last week one of our chiefs was caught with a knife in his cell. Since we
needed him out in the population one of the young Vicelords volunteered
to take the weight for it. He went before the Disciplinary Court and was
given 15 days isolation time, a Blue Shingle, and recommended to staff for
loss of good time. Because of the Blue Shingle he cannot go to the commissary to buy the stuff he needs, but all he's got to do is ask because
we're going to see to it that he gets anything he wants.

An Indian may be rewarded for carrying out such tasks as providing
starched clothes for the chief or being reliable in conveying messages.
Much depends upon the particular organization. The Vicelords would
not accord status to the senseless use of violence against inmates or
staff but would reward a member who was helping his brothers learn
to read. In the Disciples, status might be otherwise allocated.

Indians do not and are not expected to relate to the staff. Extensive interaction with security or professional personnel would be suspect for an Indian, although expected behavior for a chief. The
rank-and-file members are simply not responding to the administra-

tion. Instead, the prison experience is more likened to a game where status is accorded to the individual who continues to act in prison the part he was playing on the streets.

"Gang banging" is a popular activity for gang members on the street as well as in the prison. This activity, as defined by whites and off brands, refers to "rip offs," extortion, bullying, and general harassment by groups of gang members.

While the leadership does not necessarily approve of gang banging and often discourages it, they do not like to be placed in the position of policing their followers. To do so places the leader in an uneasy position. On the one hand, the administration questions their sincerity with respect to advancing prison reforms when their followers are involved in gang banging activities. On the other hand, the Indians are doubtful about their leaders' efforts to bridge the gap with the administration and are restless with the politics of negotiation. To be sure, the leaders cannot altogether afford to disregard the attitudes of their followers. The latter must be indulged or the chief may find his own influence waning at the expense of an ambitious rival.

LEADERS AND CHIEFS

Leadership is of crucial importance for the gangs. The leaders form the nucleus without which the group would cease to exist. They provide role models for the Indians and serve as the most significant others, both inside and outside the prison. In practical matters too, the leaders play an important part in the day-to-day life of the average member.

In contrast with the indigenous influence theory, which explains prison leadership as arising within the context of situational contingencies, Irwin and Cressey (1964) argue that each of the inmate subcultures, do-rights, convicts, and thieves, generate their own leadership. The thief leader has the most influence on the behavior patterns of the institution because the norms and values which he brings into the prison from the criminal subculture are respected by convicts and thieves alike. When it comes to exerting influence with respect to institutional concerns, however, the convict leader runs things. The important point is that this view shows leadership being imported into the prison.

At Stateville no clearcut division of the informal organization into do-rights, thieves, and convicts was observed. Yet it is clear that the leaders among the inmates are the same individuals who held high positions within the gangs on the street. There is no example at

Stateville of an inmate leader who is not also a gang leader. It is also true that when a higher ranking chief is committed to the institution, he must immediately assume command. There is no doubt in the mind of any informant, for example, that if Jeff Fort, supreme leader of the Black P. Stone Nation, were to be transferred to Stateville, the other chiefs of the Stones would step aside.

The chiefs of the four organizations tend to be older than the rank-and-file member. B.P. of the Vicelords, for example, is 37. He was one of the founders of the organization and an almost legendary figure in the eyes of the younger Vicelords. Several of the chiefs have chosen to remain in the shadows and to assert their authority only during private conversations with their inner council. This strategy is thought necessary in order to prevent harassment from the prison officials. Of course, in the case of celebrities like Jeff Fort, rank in the gang is already well known.

Berk (1966) has found that inmate leaders within the maximum security prison tend to be more aggressive individuals. Schrag (1954: 139) noted that the "institutional adjustments of leaders are marked by significantly greater numbers of rule infractions, including escapes, fights and assaults." At Stateville neither of these propositions is supported. The chiefs are distinguished by their reliance upon wits rather than fists. For visible and invisible leaders alike, involvement in serious disciplinary infractions is rare. Indeed, their disciplinary records are in many case exemplary. This underscores the sophistication of their leadership and their lack of concern for such prison luxuries as can be illicitly procured.

The gang leaders evince little interest in those rewards, legal or illegal, which can be gained in prison.[20] Many times the leaders have explained that there is nothing within the penitentiary which they want. Extra commissary, pressed clothes, and movies are not taken seriously. As one old con remarked: "From the administration's point of view, what's wrong with these young gang bangers is that they do not program."

In summary, the patterns of leadership exhibited behind the walls have been directly imported from the streets. The leadership among the inmates at Stateville is in no way dependent upon accommodation with staff or upon a good job within the formal organization. Nor, as Clemmer found, is the influence of leadership merely restricted to small primary or friendship groups.[21] On the contrary, the most salient characteristics of inmate leadership at Stateville is its autonomy from situational variables and its influence over large secondary groups.

INTER-GANG RELATIONS

Unaffiliated inmate observers have found it remarkable that gangs which have been killing one another for years on the Chicago streets have been able to cooperate under the extraordinarily demanding prison conditions. G.B., leader of the Disciples, has told me that the murderer of his mother is reputed to be among the inmates at Stateville but that he has taken no action to learn the individual's identity. For him to pursue a personal vendetta against a member of a rival gang could only result in the most disastrous consequences under the present circumstances of total confinement. There is an absolute consensus among the leadership that "international war" must be avoided at all costs. The victors of such a confrontation could only be the custodial staff, thought to be anxiously awaiting the day on which they can drag out their heaviest artillery. Quarrels among inmates or between inmates and staff have been repeatedly quelled by the gang leaders in an attempt to forestall what is foreseen as another Attica. Even those off brand observers hostile to the gangs have attributed the absence of a major riot at Stateville to the coolness of the gang leadership.

Any fight between two or more members of rival gangs can have explosive repercussions. Thus, the leaders have developed a list of international rules to which all of the gangs have pledged to abide. The rules include the following:

    I.   There will be no rip-offs between organization members.

    II. Each organization must stay out of the other organization's affairs. In a dispute between members of two organizations, members of a third are to stand clear and to attract no attention.

    III. No organization will muscle in on a dealer already paying off to another organization.

    IV. Organizations will discipline their own members in the offended party's presence.

    V. Organizations cannot extend their protection to non-members.

At the time of this study (a long hot summer), the Disciples did not feel that the international rules had been equally supported. In two cases Disciple chiefs disciplined (by administering beatings) their own members who were wrongfully involved in disputes with members of other organizations. But when the situation was reversed and the Disciples were the offended party, the Stones did not discipline their members. Consequently the rules held only ambiguous authority.

Most of the disputes within the prison occur between the Stones and the Disciples, the rival street gangs on Chicago's South Side.

When such conflicts do occur, the leaders have been extremely effective in forging solutions, often by agreeing to give up their members for a head-to-head fight. During the negotiations, the chief of the Vicelords often plays an important mediating role, acting as go-between for the two sides. To both sides is stressed the need to prevent the indians from jumping off and initiating a major riot.

IMPACT OF THE GANGS UPON INFORMAL AND FORMAL ORGANIZATIONS

While the basis for the gang leader's authority is his position on the street, neither he nor his lieutenants and followers remain aloof from institutional concerns. The chiefs attempt to control or to receive recognition from every area of the prison society. Actually the gang leaders have no coherent program and no real objectives which they seek to achieve within the prison. A clinical counselor at Stateville explained:

What the gang leaders want is a moderately comfortable existence for their people within the prison and an opportunity to maintain their ties with the gang on the street as well as to promote their gang identity within the prison

No area of prison life has remained unaffected by the mass influx of gang members. In contrast to the rational control exercised by the gangs and their leaders in preventing the outbreak of a gang war is the displacement of the old informal organization dominated by Stateville's old politicians and merchants. Given the prospect of cutting the gang members in or going out of business, many of the old cons active in the prison rackets chose to retire. To date the gangs themselves have not stepped in to organize these rackets. Dealers explain that this is due to a lack of finesse in gang members who do not know how to maneuver inside the prison. They further claim that there has been an absolute decline in the quantity of contraband trafficking since the gangs have taken over.

Moreover, the smooth running accommodation system formerly existent at Stateville, as elsewhere (Sykes, 1966), has broken down. Since influence within the informal organization is no longer dependent upon formal organizational support, the staff's leverage has deteriorated. That one of the most powerful gang leaders cannot get into the T.V. college program is evidence of the demise of the accommodation system. Furthermore, in attempting to understand this situation, it should be emphasized that the values of the white rural staff and the black urban gang member may also contribute to breakdown in communication and accommodation.

Life for the off brands has also been considerably altered by the presence of the gangs. A young, tough, and aggressive black inmate noted:

> You must respect what the hierarchy says. If they ask for a work stoppage, for example, you'd have to stop work or be badly beaten.

A 50 year old con-wise black inmate echoed the same opinion:

> The gang leaders have absolute control. T could just have told his men to tear it [Stateville] down and they would—a lot of these guys would die for their gang—dying doesn't mean anything to them. They'd rather die than let it be said that they wouldn't go all the way.

The rising importance of the gangs in the late 1960's was not lost upon several old cons who chose to join them as the best means of adaptation. The gangs accepted these men for their knowledge of prison ways and their readiness to be "fronted off." That is to say that these individuals were willing to serve as spokesmen for the gangs and to mediate with staff. The exchange provided the gangs with visible fall guys in case of an administrative crackdown and provided the old cons security, some degree of status, and an opportunity to continue exploiting the prison situation. However much importance these members appear to have in the prison, they have no regular rank within the organizations and could claim no place within the organization on the street.

Where the chiefs feel that their organizations and members will be benefitted by prison policies, they have not hesitated to support and work with the administration. B.P., Vicelord chief, points out that many of his people are deficient in reading and arithmetic skills. Remedial programs in that direction have been strongly supported by the organizations. The Stones have been particularly active in encouraging their members to get into the high school program. ALAS, a bilingual program for Spanish inmates, is the most advanced and successful program at Stateville today. The federal monies and academic talent assembled for this program were originally obtained through the efforts of a leading Latin King. Only the vigorous support of the Kings' leadership accounts for the success of ALAS.

As has been traditional at maximum security institutions, Stateville inmates are assigned to jobs in such areas as prison industry, yard maintenance, barber shop, laundry, and hospital. The smooth functioning of these work assignments is dependent upon the support and approval of the gang leadership. Each gang assigns one member on each job assignment the responsibility for reporting on all inmate and staff developments. The Disciples require these reports to be in writing and utilize a code to refer to Disciples, rival gang members, and staff. Where voluntary rehabilitation programs in such areas as drug abuse, vocational training, and education are evaluated negatively, they will not be patronized. One professor from a nearby junior college, who brought an automotive training program into the prison, reports that in the first few months he was approached by various gang members who candidly told him that they were checking out his program. The much touted group therapy program at Stateville had not attracted a single gang member at the time this study was carried out. This is not surprising. To the extent that the individual turns his attention inward, his commitment to the group is undermined. Group therapy shores up the definitions of the prison as an experience of *individual* adjustment, adaptation, introspection, and rehabilitation. Contrariwise, the gang promotes the definition of prison experience as a group response and group adaptation.

The dominance of the gangs at Stateville has posed grave challenges for the administration and especially for the security officers. The authority of the line officer has been sharply undermined. Today it requires a lieutenant to carrv out responsibilities which a line officer could have handled five years ago. When, for example, an officer decides to "walk" an inmate to isolation for a disciplinary infraction, it is not uncommon for the inmate gang member to refuse to go.

The inmate will say "fuck you, Jack, I'm not going." Then several members of his gang will gather around him. I'll have to call a lieutenant. Often one of the gang leaders will just come over and tell the man to go ahead.

The custodial staff sees their influence eroding in inverse proportion to the increasing influence of the gang leaders. This is a cause for low staff morale and increased tension.

To date the administration has not formally recognized the existence of the gangs (for example, by assigning them a role within the formal organizational structure), although informally it has been essential to take them into consideration. One key administrator of the reform administration stated:

I tried to deal with the gangs when I was superintendent. The gangs are here and they must be recognized. The leaders have tremendous power. No doubt they could inflict terrible damage upon the place if they wanted to. They have not done it so far because there is nothing to get out of that kind of thing.

Custodial and administrative personnel, as individuals, have also had to deal with the gangs. In numerous cases the chief guard has called the leaders to his office to discuss problems with one of their soldiers. In one situation he called to his office one of the Latin King chiefs to discuss the difficulties which a Spanish inmate (not a King) in the commissary was having with inmates pressuring him to steal for them. The chief was able to speak with several other leaders, and the problem was resolved in a couple of days. In another case a Disciple refused to go to isolation and locked himself in his cell. The chief guard called the Disciple leader to his office and discussed the potentially explosive consequences of the situation. Subsequently the leader went to the cell of the irate soldier and talked to him about the pros and cons of provoking a violent confrontation with staff: "If you think it's important enough, then we won't let them take you." The next morning the gang member went peaceably to isolation.

The point is that the gangs have been able to force their definition of the situation onto the lower levels of the staff. What the gangs are demanding is recognition of the legitimacy of their organizations and leadership hierarchies. The chiefs want it to be formally recognized that they have the right and the responsibility to intercede and speak in the name of their followers. When for several months a rudimentary inmate council, Project ABLE, was operating, the gang leaders agreed that the most important aspect of Project ABLE was that it allowed them the mobility to circulate through the prison, collecting information from their people which could be brought to the attention of the staff. The functioning of Project ABLE, thoroughly dominated by the gang leaders, certainly marked the high water point of the gangs' efforts to force their definition of the situation onto the formal organization of the prison.

The full ramifications of the mass jailing of Chicago street gang members and leaders have still not been felt on the streets of Chicago. Within the prison bitter enemies with long histories of warfare have learned to cooperate with one another. Certain leaders speculate about the development of a grand alliance and the rise of a Black Mafia to challenge the syndicate for control of Chicago vice. Other leaders have become increasingly convinced of the need to channel the energy of the gangs into political action. From behind Stateville's walls, the Latin Kings hammered out a treaty which produced six months of peace among all Latin gangs in Chicago in 1971. The details of that treaty were many months in the drafting, and the final execution of the agreement involved the coordinated visits of numerous gang leaders to Stateville. Such episodes underscore the need for further research on the relationships between prison and community.

CONCLUSION

Mathiessen (1966) has criticized the sociological literature of the prison for its inordinate concentration upon the similarities of all total institutions and for its inattention to the interrelationship between total institution and wider society. This exploratory report has highlighted an unusual development within Illinois prisons. It suggests that the inmate organization cannot be understood in terms of "indigenous prerequisites." By emphasizing the *importation* of organization, roles, and norms from the streets of Chicago, support has been offered for the Irwin-Cressey theory of cultural drift.

Within Stateville Penitentiary, gang members remain oriented toward the same membership group and leadership hierarchy as they did before having been committed to prison. Rather than experiencing a collapse upon passing through the gates, they have maintained the same self-identity conception as they held upon the streets. To the extent that adjustment needs to be made to the contingencies of incarceration, the adjustment is a group rather than an individual phenomenon.

No conclusion should be drawn from the above description of Stateville's social organization that similar developments have occurred in other states with different social, economic, and ethnographic patterns. Indeed, it is a central argument of this paper that the relationship between the social organization of the total institution and the surrounding society needs to be much more deeply explored. Comparative research on the prisons of states in other regions remains to be done.

REFERENCES

American Friends Service Committee
      Struggle for Justice. New York: Hill and Wang.
Becker, Howard S and Blanche Geer
    1960   "Latent culture: a note on the theory of latent social roles." Administrative Science Quarterly 5 (September): 304-13.
Berk, Bernard
    1966   "Organizational goals and inmate organization." American Journal of Sociology 71(March): 522-24.
Bettleheim, Bruno
    1947   "Individual and mass behavior in extreme situations." In Readings in Social Psychology. Edited by Eleanor Maccoby, et. al. New York: Holt, Rinehart and Winston.
Clemmer, Donald
    1958   The Prison Community. New York: Rinehart and Co.
Cohen, Albert K.
    1955   Delinquent Boys: The Culture of the Gang. Free Press.
Erickson, Gladys
    1957   Warden Ragen of Joliet. New York: E. P. Dutton and Co.
Galtung, Johan
    1961   "Prison: the organization of dilemma." In the Prison. Edited by Donald R. Cressey. New York: Holt, Rinehart, and Winston.

Garabedian, Peter G.
  1962   "Social roles and processes of socialization in the prison commu-
          nity." Social Problems, 11 (Fall): 139-152.
Garrity, Donald L.
  1961   "The prison as a rehabilitating agency." In The Prison. Edited by
          Donald R. Cressey. New York: Holt, Rinehart and Winston.
Giallombardo, Rose
  1966   Society of Women: A Study of a Women's Prison. New York: Wiley.
Goffman, Erving
  1961   Asylums. Garden City, New Jersey: Anchor.
Grossner, George P.
  1958   "The role of informal inmate groups in change of values." Children
          5(January-February): 25-29.
Grusky, Oscar
  1959   "Organizational goals and the behavior of informal leaders." Ameri-
          can Journal of Sociology 65(July): 59-67.
Irwin, John and Donald Cressey
  1964   "Thieves, convicts, and the inmate culture." In The Other Side.
          Edited by Howard S. Becker. New York: The Free Press.
Keiser, Lincoln
  1969   The Vice Lords: Warriors of the Streets. New York: Holt, Rinehart
          and Winston.
Mathiessen, Thomas
  1966   "The sociology of prisons: problems for future research." British
          Journal of Sociology 17(December): 360-379.
McCleery, Richard
  1960   "Communication patterns as bases of systems of authority and
          power." In Theoretical Studies in Social Organization of the Prison.
          New York: Social Science Research Council.
McCorkle, Lloyd and Richard Korn
  1954   "Resocialization within the walls." The Annals of the American
          Academy of Political and Social Sciences 293(May): 88-98.
Miller, Walter B.
  1958   "Lower class culture as a generating milieu of gang violence." Jour-
          nal of Social Issues 14(Summer): 5-19.
Morris, Norval and Gordon Hawkins
  forthcoming   "Attica Revisited." University of Chicago Law Review.
Reckless, Walter
  1956   "The impact of correctional programs on inmates." British Journal
          of Delinquency 6: 138-147.
Roebuck, Julian
  1963   "A critique of 'Thieves, Convicts and the Inmate Culture.'" Social
          Problems 11(Fall): 193-200.
Royko, Mike
  1971   Boss. New York: The New American Library.

Schrag, Clarence
    1960   "Leadership among prison inmates." American Sociological Review
             3(Fall): 11–16.
    1961   "Some foundations for a theory of corrections." In The Prison.
             Edited by Donald R. Cressey. New York: Holt, Rinehart and
             Winston.
Schwartz, Barry
    1971   "Pre-institutional vs. situational influence in a correctional commu-
             nity." Journal of Criminal Law, Criminology and Policy Science
             61: 532–543.
Short, James
    1963   "Introduction." In The Gang. By Frederick M. Thrasher. Chicago:
             The University of Chicago Press.
Short, James, Ray Tennyson and Kenneth Howard
    1963   "Behavioral dimensions of gang delinquency." American Sociologi-
             cal Review 28(June): 411–428.
    1972   South Carolina Department of Corrections. Emerging Rights of the
             Confined.
Street, David, Robert Vinter and Charles Perrow
    1969   Organization For Treatment. New York: The Free Press.
Sykes, Gresham
    1966   The Society of Captives. New York: Atheneum.
Sykes, Gresham and Sheldon Messinger
    1960   "The inmate social system." Theoretical Studies in Social Organiza-
             tion of the Prison. New York: Social Science Research Council.
Tittle, Charles R.
    1969   "Inmate organization: sex differentiations and the influence of
             criminal subcultures." American Sociological Review 34(August):
             492–505.
Thrasher, Frederick M.
    1963   The Gang. Chicago: The University of Chicago Press.
Wheeler, Stanton H.
    1961   "Social organization in a correctional community." American Socio-
             logical Review 26(October): 697–712.
Wilson, Thomas P.
    1968   "Patterns of management and adaptions to organizational roles: a
             study of prison inmates." American Journal of Sociology 74(Sep-
             tember): 146–157.
Yablonsky, Lewis
    1970   The Violent Gang. Baltimore: Penguin Books.

13

THE PRISONER ECONOMY

R. THEODORE DAVIDSON

CONVICTS AND INMATES

Many prisoners make a definite distinction between two types of
prisoners—convicts and inmates. However, the majority of inmates
(who also are the majority of prisoners) merely have a general awareness of the differences. . . .

Years ago, before the present emphasis on rehabilitation . . . much
of the prisoners' most meaningful activity was either against the law
or against the prison rules. . . . Because of these activities, the prisoners were in an almost continual state of warfare against the staff.

This fierce opposition . . . promoted . . . unity among the prisoners. . . . This opposition . . . was a key element that contributed to
the existence of convicts. . . . A convict did not want to be caught
interacting with the enemy on a friendly or excessive basis. . . .

An integral part of the new rehabilitation programs was the effective interaction between prisoners and staff. . . . Prisoners now were
serving sentences under the indeterminate sentence laws; and if a
prisoner was to be released before his maximum sentence, he first
had to be rehabilitated. Under this system, prisoners did almost anything to prove to the staff that they were rehabilitated, regardless of
how it would affect other prisoners. Since unity no longer existed
among most prisoners, each inmate was a single individual, trying to
get out as soon as possible . . . telling staff about the illegal and rule-
breaking activities of other prisoners. . . . The relatively few remaining convicts . . . were forced into even more covertness than before.
For convicts, the staff was not the only enemy now. Inmates were a
new enemy who could not be privy to convict activities. . . .

Today, even though they are only 8 to 10 percent of the prisoner

Source: From *Chicano Prisoners: The Key to San Quentin*(New York: Holt, Rinehart and
Winston, 1974), pp. 45-47, 55-56, 101-147(editorial adaptations). Copyright © 1974 by
Holt, Rinehart and Winston, Inc. Reprinted by permission of the author and Holt, Rine-
hart and Winston.

population, convicts are a significant, powerful type of prisoner. They have been able to mitigate the harshness of the present system through their illegal and rule-breaking activities. Most of these activities are economic in nature. . . .

It was noted . . . that a very small percentage of prisoners . . . do not fit into either the convict or the inmate types. . . . Gunsels (also called low riders) are . . . the younger, immature hoodlum element among the prisoners. Gunsels are the rip-off artists who take unfair advantage of other prisoners. They will burn or cheat others. . . . Even when caught doing illegal things . . . , the punishment is something to brag about among fellow gunsels. . . . They are not snitches; so they can be trusted by convicts—even though they really cannot be controlled. . . . gunsels serve a very important economic role—as both a link and a buffer between convicts and inmates. . . .

At an extremely covert level is hidden this third level of the prisoner culture—the Family. . . . If one does not comprehend the Family level, one will never fully understand the real prisoner culture. And, since almost all of the prisoners on the third level are Chicanos, such insight can be achieved only by fully comprehending Chicano prisoners. . . . Family and the Family level exist in all major California prisons.

FOUR TYPES OF ECONOMIC ACTIVITIES

The full details of production, distribution and consumption or use of all prisoner economic goods and services can be attained only from the Family level.

For comparative purposes, legal prisoner economic activities can be described as follows. They are formal and official, being subject to the laws of the streets and to the prison rules. In many respects they are important, but they are only the superficial, obvious part of the economy. Comprising only a small part of the total prisoner economy, they are known to all members of the staff and all prisoners. However, as will be shown later, they can be used for, or tied into, illegal aspects of the economy. In some instances, certain of these legal activities become an integral part of the illegal economic activities. The major example of this legal type of activity is the use of the canteen.

Turning to the illegal types, inmate economic activities are informal, usually being against the prison rules or sometimes unlawful. If unlawful, they usually do not involve serious crimes and are not considered consequential by staff. As with legal activities, they are important in many respects, often being the most important part of the economy to many inmates. These activities comprise a larger part of the economy than legal activities do; however, they are still a relatively small, yet evident, part of the entire prisoner economy. All prisoners engage in some of these inmate activities, but convicts and Family members do so to a lesser degree. These inmate activities are well known to staff members and prisoners, even though they are done on a covert basis. Normally they are hidden from staff; but little effort is made to conceal them from most other prisoners. An obvious exception would be the well-known snitches. Some staff members may understand the larger aspects of the prison setting and tolerate this activity as being reasonable. This "tolerated" illegal activity would include things such as small-scale, petty stealing of state materials, like food or clothing from their jobs; construction of shelves or cabinets for their cells; having a *very* small store; and fronting a store for a convict.

Convict economic activities are informal, but more serious. They may involve the breach of major prison rules; however, more frequently they involve unlawful acts, ranging through various misdemeanors to serious felonies. These activities comprise a much greater portion of the prisoner economy than either the legal or inmate types do. In general, convicts are the primary producers of these goods and services, with gunsels acting as the primary distributors to inmates. Inmates are the primary consumers or users of convict-produced goods or services, with one major exception—convicts and Family members are the principal users of drugs. Convicts may engage in these activities on an individual basis; however, they usually form a partnership or join a clique. The cliques range from three members to five or six members. At times, for a big deal, three or four cliques may join together temporarily. Convicts always conduct this activity with great efforts to conceal it from inmates and staff. Examples of this type of activity would include wholesale production of home brew, wholesale production of sandwiches in the evening in the cell block, bringing in dope for sale to others, production of hot plates for sale to others, and wholesale supplying goods for inmate retail stores.

Most staff members and inmates are generally aware of convict activities. However, they normally have a partial or confused view, for they are usually ignorant of most individuals and details. At best, some may know of, or suspect, a few details of one or a few convict operations; but since this would represent only a minute fraction of the almost numberless convict operations being conducted simultaneously, their information is not very full or useful. Some staff members become personally involved in these activities when they bring contraband into the prison for convicts; however, their awareness of details usually extends no further than the particular deal and the one or two convict contacts. Inmates become involved as purchasers of convict goods or services, but they usually know little more than the gunsel distributor from whom they purchase the goods or services. Accordingly, gunsels function both as a buffer and a link between convicts and inmates.

Gunsels and convicts usually have been personally involved in a number of these convict enterprises—the convicts as the producers and the gunsels as the distributors. They may have intimate knowledge of many past and present operations; however, they do not know the details of most convict activities, for such activities are too vast in number. No one individual could legitimately be involved with so many convicts. And it would be foolish to dig for additional detailed information of this type without good reason for personal involvement. To do so would be putting oneself in a vulnerable position—of having knowledge of an operation which could lead to suspicion—if someone should snitch on it. In other words, a convict or a gunsel does not want to know the particulars of an operation unless it is necessary for him to know.

At the very depth of the economy, below convict activities, is Family. Collectively, Family members generally know most convicts and some details of their activities. Family often provides the financial backing necessary for certain operations. Except for this financial involvement, Family, as an organized group, does not engage in convict economic activities. However, since Family members are all convicts, too, a member may act as an individual convict—he may engage in these convict activities; but such activity would *not* be Family activity. If a single convict enterprise should become too big and directly interfere with Family activities, Family will buy the convict out and take over the operation; or, if necessary, Family will force the convict out of business. In either case, the operation is turned into Family activity.

Family economic activities are informal in some superficial respects. However, there is a great degree of organization and formality behind them that is not evident to non-Family individuals, for Family business is *big* business. Usually involving a major felony, these activities account for the majority of serious prisoner economic activity. All such activities are financed and directed by Family.

Technically, in an economic sense, a man requires no money inside prison, for all of his indispensable needs are taken care of by the state. Essential goods and services such as food, clothing, certain toilet articles, religious services, personal counseling, and medical care are produced and distributed by the State. . . . However, . . .

the prisoners have many needs that are not indispensable in a technical sense, but which are quite real to them. These facts are recognized by both prisoners and staff, and both groups have taken steps to alleviate these undesirable conditions.

Staff attempts to reduce these inadequacies have been . . . limited to the area of consumer goods. They have long operated a canteen that is open to "qualified" prisoners during certain daytime hours, and offers such items as food, candy, cigarettes, toilet articles, magazines, and a few paperback books. However, the operation of the canteen has created inequities, for in effect it is partial to those prisoners with a legal source of money, and not all prisoners have such sources.

Legally, in order to qualify to purchase items from the canteen, a prisoner must have a privilege card and money "on the books"—in his inmate account. If his balance is sufficient, he is allowed to "draw" up to $45 each month, only on a specified day. If he fails to make his draw on the specified date, he loses the opportunity for that month and must wait until his date the next month. But, at that time, he is allowed to draw only the $45 maximum. Consequently, there is no way to make up for a missed draw, unless he normally draws less than the maximum and can make larger draws during the following months.

To make canteen purchases, a prisoner must obtain funds for his inmate account. These funds can come from any of several potential sources. One origin is money from outside. This can be from savings a man had prior to his incarceration, but the economic status of most prisoners precludes this from being a source. Money also can be sent in by approved correspondents; but, like the prisoner, their economic status usually prevents this from being a significant or reliable source. Consequently, money from outside is not usually available to most prisoners.

Another source of legal funds for a prisoner's account may be his job inside prison. However, the jobs which pay prisoners are few, so this source is not available to the vast majority of prisoners. Most jobs or assignments are nonpay, or "slave labor" as referred to by many prisoners. . . .

A final source of legal funds for a prisoner's account may involve his art and craft activities. Some have jokingly called this "criminal art" when discussing it with outsiders. However there is validity behind that statement—not because it has been produced by criminals, but because the price is usually criminally low.

Briefly treating prisoner production from the three levels, it should be noted that there is no economic leadership at the inmate level; for inmate activity is individualistic in nature. The meager productive resources are owned by the individual. The inmate producer normally uses his own products—like an individual's home consumption of homemade products on the streets. Inmate production has little impact on the larger prisoner economy. At the convict level of production, there may be some relatively minor manifestations of organization and leadership; however, convict ownership of resources and production of goods and services still are on an individual, a partnership, or at most a clique basis. Products from the convict level are for sale to other prisoners, but small amounts may be set aside for personal use. In addition, convicts depend upon profits from their productive activities to enable them to satisfy their own consumer needs. The considerable volume of convict production is similar to that of small businesses on the streets. In contrast, the high degree of Family organization and leadership is comparable to that of large businesses, corporations, and financial institutions on the streets. . . .

All Family resources are held through corporate ownership, not individual ownership. There is a corporate responsibility for liabilities as well as assets. True, an individual member may have control or possession of Family resources, or he may personally obligate Family to an economic commitment; however, Family, as a corporate body, assumes the ultimate responsibility in such matters. A considerable portion of Family resources are normally held in the form of cash. Family's capital cash account is maintained at a minimum level or above at all times. This cash serves as a reserve to insure Family against diverse economic contingencies. The money in the capital cash account is actually held in a wide variety of places, both inside and on the streets.

Whether in prison or on the streets, Family members may draw upon the capital cash account for Family investment purposes. Such investment is always on a short-term basis; upon completion of the business transaction, the members bring back the cash borrowed—plus the profit made. These business transactions normally yield considerable profit. For example, it is understood that if a profit of 150 percent cannot be made on a narcotics deal, it should not be attempted. At times, the business transactions made inside tend to be of a smaller scale than those made on the streets; however, members are active in both places.

THREE TYPES OF MONEY

There are three types of prisoner money: ducats, cigarettes, and cash. Ducats are the only legal type of money inside. Legally, they are used only for the purchase of goods from the canteen. Ducats are the pressed paper token money that is issued to a prisoner when he makes a draw from his inmate account. But not all prisoners have funds from which to make such a draw. Consequently, not all prisoners are able to use this type of money, nor are they legally able to buy goods which the canteen offers. In addition, since staff carefully control the use of ducats by the prisoner who actually makes the draw, ducats normally can be used only by that prisoner. The exception to this rule would be when a prisoner—through debt or some sort of obligation—gives all or most of his draw to a convict. Often he would be obliged to make numerous purchases of particular canteen items for the convict each month. Rather than be bothered with this, the prisoner might ask the convict if he could arrange to use his (the prisoner's) ducats. The convict will arrange to have a false privilege card made for himself, with the prisoner's number on it, to enable illegal use of the prisoner's ducats. Obviously, the debt or obligation has to be a major, long-term one to warrant this effort. Except for this single illegal use of ducats, it can be seen that ducats are useless as a medium of exchange for the purchase of prisoner-produced goods and services.

Inside, except for ducats, all forms of money are illegal and subject to confiscation upon discovery by staff. This is done to discourage all prisoner economic activity other than the legal use of the canteen by qualified prisoners. The prisoners are left without a legal medium of exchange to use as payment for goods and services that are produced by other prisoners. However, this has not discouraged or stopped prisoners, for they have had two types of illegal money to serve their purposes for a long time: cigarettes and cash. In general, cigarettes are used for small-scale economic transactions, and cash is used for large-scale ones.

Packs of cigarettes are used by prisoners as coins and dollars are used on the streets. Cartons are used much like 5, 10, 20, and 50 dollar bills. Although the denominations of cigarette monetary units do not directly accord with those of United States legal tender, the conversion is easily accomplished by prisoners. Normally, as the size of the transaction reaches about $100 or so, cigarettes are less likely to be used. For example, the sheer bulk of 20 to 25 cartons would make a transaction for that amount unnecessarily risky. Such transactions can be handled on a cash basis with much less chance of being detected by staff.

Possession of cash (legal tender) is illegal inside. Staff have tried to stop or discourage its use. However, they have failed, for cash is brought in through a variety of channels. The majority of it filters in through visitors in small amounts of $50 or $100. This source is quite extensive. For example, if a prisoner has bills to pay, what can he do if he has already used his monthly draw? Instead of letting interest pile up and in order to avoid getting into potential trouble over it, he has someone bring money in to him—assuming he has a friend who can and will do it. A 50 or 100 dollar bill can be folded very small and tied inside a finger stall (the finger tip portion of a rubber glove). It can be passed inconspicuously; and if need be, the prisoner can put it in his mouth, or even swallow it, to get it back in from the visiting room.

Another less frequently used way cash is brought in is by the bulls. When this method is used, the amount tends to be much larger though, ranging up to several thousand dollars. Any bull who is "running" (bringing contraband goods in) for convicts or Family also will bring cash in. Usually, the bull will pick up the money on the streets, from any of the various sources specified to him by the prisoners. He will bring it in; and when he turns the money over, he gets $50 for every $500 that he brings in. Some bulls don't like to make the actual pickup and want the money sent to them. However, there are negative aspects to having the money sent, for it must be sent by registered mail to protect the interests of those involved. Consequently, a receipt exists after the operation has been completed. There are other methods to get cash in; but, from the examples given, it can be seen that getting cash into prison is not very difficult. If an inmate has money on the outside, but no way to get it in, there are those who will gladly do it for him—for a percentage.

Normally, on an average weekend day, there is a great amount of cash money available in the yard. As an illustration, assume that Family, as a group, through great pressure, is pushed to come up with $100,000 cash. On an average Saturday morning, in the yard, Family could probably come up with almost that amount from its own stashes and creditors. If Family happened to be $10,000 or $15,000 short, it could easily borrow the rest at a three-for-two interest rate.

The ability of convicts to get cash is quite limited in comparison. However, a convict with a good credit rating could probably *borrow* $10,000 on a 90-day loan at three for two. To get a loan of this size would probably necessitate some questions being asked by Family and the personal backing of the convict's partner. Without questions and involvement of a convict partner, the convict could probably borrow $6,000 on similar repayment terms. A few convicts have excellent business connections, fine credit ratings, and many business activities going for themselves. On an average Saturday morning, if necessary, one of these convicts could easily pick up from $900 to $1,800 of his own funds from creditors and stashes. If he was really pushed hard, he might be able to get $2,500.

In striking contrast, inmates have *very* little—both in cash and ability to borrow. The average inmate is living on his draw. He might be able to borrow a sum equivalent to his draw. However, any amount above that would have to be insured by some other source of income —such as access to materials at his job. Even in such cases, it would be doubtful that he could ever borrow much over what he would get in two or three draws. These rather strict limitations are based on the fact that inmates are unable to hustle for any significant amount above what they draw. In contrast, convicts (owing to their ability to hustle) are often given credit above their actual resources.

A typical connection to bring in a shipment of narcotics might involve a number of people and tasks. An individual on the streets develops a source for purchasing narcotics. Another individual visits a Family member, relating details which will be further developed at a later visit. A Family member is the link to funds that will be used to purchase the narcotics. He also is the link to a convict. This convict is the individual who deals directly with the runner, giving him instructions as to when, where, and how the goods are to be picked up. He also gives the runner Family's cash to buy the goods. The individual on the streets delivers the goods to the runner at a certain place. The runner picks up and pays for the goods. Later the runner brings the goods in, inside his lunch pail. He gives the narcotics to the convict with whom he deals. The convict pays the runner for performing his task and delivers the goods to the Family member with whom he deals. There may be a greater or lesser number of tasks and individuals involved, and fewer or more of the individuals may be Family members. However, when the individuals and tasks listed for this typical connection are compared with the simplicity of the single visitor connection, the possible range of complexity which may exist in an economic connection is apparent.

Many of the things a runner may do are briefly indicated in the above description of a typical narcotics connection. Now, if the money bulls are paid for running contraband is considered, it will be possible to project from that amount to the much larger actual value of the goods that they bring in. This may not be a precise method of valuation; however, it does suggest the volume of contraband that is brought in by the runners—and they account for a major portion of the smuggling. As many as 30 bulls may be running for prisoners at any one time. Usually a bull will net about $10,000 for a year of running. This is always undeclared, tax-free income. After about a year, the possibility of the bull getting busted increases; so a bull usually will back off and quit for three or four years, until he finds himself in a financial pinch or is pressured into resuming such activities by prisoners. The irregular timing of the runs makes this activity relatively safe for about a year. However, roughly 10 percent of the bulls who run do get caught. Those who are actually caught and convicted in court are usually the ones who (through their ignorance) have been dealing with inmates. When pressed, inmates are often willing to testify against the bull in court, in order to further their own ends. However, if the bull is caught running for a convict, staff can never expect to base any part of their case on the testimony of the convict; for convicts will not testify. The one exceptional convict who did testify against a bull in court lost his right to be considered a convict ever again.

Occasionally, a bull who is running will net as much as $50,000 or $60,000 in a year. When this happens, the bull usually quits his job. Once a bull brought in about $300,000 worth of narcotics at one time (a several months supply for the prisoners). He received $60,000 for his effort. He quit a short time later; and if his considerable earnings from earlier that year are included, his running probably netted him close to $100,000 that year.

Since it controls most cash money, cigarette money, and contraband goods, Family is able to manipulate and regulate the value of prisoner money. Since ducats have an actual cash value, their use for the purchase of cigarettes at the canteen establishes an actual cash value for cigarettes too. Normally, there is a definite exchange rate between cash and cigarette money. Either type of money can be used to buy contraband goods at their normal price. For example, $35 worth of goods can be paid for with cash, or with ten cartons of cigarettes worth $3.50 a carton, or with some combination of the two. However, Family is able to set the value of either type of prisoner money. Members refer to this manipulation as the "turning" of money. When Family turns money, it is able to decrease its effective value or purchasing power. For example, Family is able to force prisoners who have only cash money to exchange their cash for cigarettes. This is done by Family's refusal to accept cash money as payment for contraband goods which it controls. All prisoners with cash money, if they want to purchase contraband goods, must pay an inflated exchange rate for cigarette money—as much as twice the normal rate. During this process, the canteen price of cigarettes remains the same—$3.50 worth of ducats for a carton. Also, the price of contraband goods remains the same—$35 worth of goods still costs 10 cartons. The only difference is that cash is not accepted. Prisoners must turn cash into cigarettes; and if the value of cash has been cut in half by Family, it will take $70 cash to exchange $35 worth of cigarettes. In effect, a prisoner with cash must really pay double the price for the same goods. Or, seen another way, Family acquires half of the prisoner's money when it exchanges his cash for cigarettes. Since Family controls the exchange process, it is obvious that a considerable amount of cash comes to Family quite rapidly; and the cash reserves held by prisoners are rapidly diminished.

Family's capital, organization, and activities have allowed it to become identified with, and have exclusive rights over all significant three-for-two loans. The volume from this business may not appear to be as great as that involved in drugs, because three-for-two profit does not come in large, isolated sums as drug profits do. However, the vast sources of daily profit from three-for-two loans create a steady flow to Family; and the volume involved is incredible, being greater than the profit from drugs. . . .

About two-thirds of the convicts either directly or indirectly work three for two for Family. The convicts use Family money— either cash or cigarettes. For their efforts, they receive one half of the profit, with the other half going to Family. In addition, many Family members work three for two. The loans they make usually are large ones, being made directly to convicts. With these loans, all the profit goes to Family.

The time allowed for repayment of a loan varies. With smaller loans, the time may range from one or two weeks up to a month— usually according to when the prisoner makes his draw, which allows him to make repayment. The average time for small loans would be about three weeks. With larger loans, longer repayment terms may be worked out.

Family's high economic rank affords its members considerable advantages over other prisoners. . . . For example, Family takes great care to deal fairly with convicts, allowing them to realize a reasonable share of the profits from the extensive prisoner economic activities. In addition, since Family essentially is a Chicano organization, it takes an interest in Chicano activities inside and out. In particular, Family exhibits a keen concern for the well-being of all deserving Chicano prisoners. Therefore, it has expanded its concern and authority to a group much wider than its membership. In a forceful, yet benevolent manner, Family has set up a redistributive system that endeavors to mitigate some of the individual and group needs of worthy Chicano prisoners, with some help being given to nonprison Chicanos and Chicano causes, and occasionally to deserving non-Chicano convicts. This redistributive system is known as the "Chicano Fund."

In order to accumulate money for the Chicano Fund, Family has imposed a type of voluntary taxation on almost all Chicanos who receive a monthly draw or some sort of income. Most Chicanos who enter prison have at least heard of Family. When approached by Family about the Chicano Fund, most Chicanos with some income are glad to voluntarily and routinely contribute a portion of it—such as $5 out of a $35 monthly draw. They understand that the contributors, as well as others covered by the fund, are given protection, goods, and services by Family. . . . The Chicano Fund is a communal fund which normally is used to help those deserving Chicanos who have nothing. However, even those with adequate incomes may need to draw upon the fund in emergencies. For example, if one of these individuals is thrown in the hole, he might appreciate Family stepping in for him and taking care of his normally manageable debts and any other emergency items. This enables him to come out of the hole in no worse shape than when he went in. Since some Chicanos feel that they would seldom, if ever, need help from the fund, resentment and misunderstanding can develop. A few of them may refuse to contribute; but, since they are expected to contribute, Family will take the "voluntary contributions" from them if necessary.

The convicts' wholesale and retail methods of distributing goods resemble those used by Family. However, convict distribution is on a lesser scale and does differ in some significant ways. For example, some convicts may have their own connections for bringing in goods, but most convicts normally rely on Family to produce the majority of the goods that they distribute either as middleman jobbers or as retailers. When they purchase goods from Family on a wholesale basis, they lose the profit involved in bringing goods in from the streets. Also, convict sales often are on a smaller scale than those of Family. Usually convicts are further down the lines of distribution than Family. Most are at least one step removed from the connection to the source of goods and at least a step closer to the inmate consumers. Those convicts who do directly bring in goods would rarely wholesale the entire shipment out to other convicts as Family does, for they would lose the considerable profit involved in retailing the goods. If convicts do wholesale goods, they are most likely to do it on a smaller scale, working with lesser amounts. They function much like a middleman jobber, being neither the wholesale producer (as Family is) nor the retailer. Also, convicts generally conduct a much higher percentage of retail sales than would ever be found in Family distribution activities. In their retail sales, convicts not only deal with other convicts, they also deal directly with gunsels and a small number of dependable inmates—up to a limit. And, as Family does, convicts set aside certain goods for their own consumption.

Gunsels play a very important role in the distribution of goods. Except for the canteen goodies that are sold by inmates from stores set up in their cells, gunsels serve as the major link between the convict retailers and most inmate consumers. Because they tend to consume almost everything that they make, gunsels are always broke. Their immature, independent nature, coupled with their incessant, risky hustling, makes them a very poor risk in any long-term operation, especially if credit is involved. These factors preclude gunsels from being able to purchase a volume of wholesale goods to sell on a retail basis. Nevertheless, with their nerve, their guts, their ability to hustle, and their willingness to take risks, they make excellent salesmen. The convict retailers have no retail stores; of necessity they maintain covert markets. The gunsels serve as salesmen for the convicts' secret markets. Instead of working in a store, the gunsels work a territory—the prison. Each gunsel is a kind of traveling salesman who acts as a representative for several convict retail businessmen. The gunsel serves as the link between the covert markets and the inmate customers. The gunsel, not the customer, goes to the market. The gunsel receives no salary from the convict—just a percentage of the money paid for goods or services. He may be able to make more, though, by hustling the inmate to pay a higher price than the convict is asking. Although the gunsel may take advantage of inmates, he is quite proud of the fact that he will never snitch on a convict. Therefore, in a market system where the owner of retail goods or services does not want to be known by the consumer, the gunsel salesmen also serve as effective buffers.

Inmates may not be deemed worthy of being included in the reciprocal or redistributive systems. However, in the market exchange system they are "allowed" to play two roles. The first role involves the relatively small number of inmates who are permitted to run stores in their cells and sell canteen goodies. They, too, form an important link between the convict wholesalers and retailers and the inmate consumers; but the volume of canteen goodies they sell is small when compared with the volume of contraband goods and services sold by gunsels. Even though it is on a lesser scale, a considerable volume of canteen goodies is sold through these stores. The inmate salesmen are allowed to share in a bit of the profit from these sales. And, although considered inferior when compared with gunsels who almost never snitch, these inmates also serve as buffers between the convict wholesalers and retailers and the inmate consumers. Convicts are quite willing to let them fill this role; for inmates, not convicts, are the ones who frequently get busted for running stores.

The second role that inmates are allowed to play is vitally

important. In fact, they are not only allowed, they are encouraged to be the retail customers on the end of the line. Since they are the terminus, they cannot distribute goods or services any further. Nevertheless, they are actively persuaded to supply their cigarettes from the canteen to Family and convicts—in the form of cigarette money used to purchase contraband goods and services. The monthly amount most inmates spend may be small, but there are so many inmates that the total sum is great. It is the high prices they pay for retail goods and services that enable the *many* persons involved in the production and distribution of these goods and services to make considerable profit from their efforts. In fact, the total profit is so great that Family members and convicts can consume major portions of certain types of goods and still realize a sizable net profit.

Hustle

The hustle is obvious in any job that puts a prisoner in contact with usable, stealable items that are in demand, such as clothing, soap, towels, food, or even information if nothing else is available. With clothing for example, state-issued sweatshirts that are stolen from the gym department sell for 5 packs of cigarettes apiece, and there is a heavy demand for them in the late fall and winter. And, if a prisoner gets tired of the ill-fitting clothes he routinely has to pick out of the freshly laundered pile that supposedly is his size, he may arrange to have some tailored blues of his own. First, he buys shirts and pants for one package of cigarettes each. Then he has them tailored to fit by a prisoner who works in the clothing factory. The charge for this service is 2 packs for each shirt and 3 packs for a pair of pants. Usually a prisoner will buy 3 or 4 sets so that he can rotate them while they are being "bonarooed"—given special starching and pressing service at the laundry. The charge for this service is one pack for each garment. The many prisoners involved in this extensively used service all get their cut of the money. The prisoner will not be bothered by bulls simply because he is wearing bonarooed blues. Trouble would occur only if a prisoner who is engaged in this service is caught bringing them from the laundry.

The hustle resulting from some prison jobs may be in direct competition with state-offered services. Even though the prisoners who do the hustling charge for their services, the superior quality of the prisoner services allow them to compete successfully with the state's free services. The bonarooing of clothing, noted above, is a good example of this type of competition. Another example would be the state's free shoe repair service. The drawback is that not only is there a 4- or 5-day wait, but there is no guarantee that a prisoner will ever get his shoes back. The prisoners offer a personalized service. One-day service is available for 5 packs of cigarettes; and, for a little more, one can have leather soles and heels put on. Also, routine haircuts are free. However, prisoner barbers sell special haircuts and talcum, and the large volume of their special business is not really surprising. The situation is not unlike that of the soldier who passes up a free scalping by an army barber to pay a civilian barber to give him a decent haircut. The vintage quality and lack of relevance of the majority of the books available in the library has led to another successful hustle. Prisoners who are attending school are required to read certain books for their classes, but other prisoners have discovered and profited from the relevancy and popularity of many of the books that are stocked in the education department's book room. In addition to the above examples, there are those prisoners who have a personal interest or ability (not necessarily from a prison job) that allows them to hustle and compete with state-offered services. For example, there are a few highly competent jailhouse lawyers who are in competition with, and much more effective than, the poor quality law library that is offered to prisoners for their assistance in legal matters.

Some prisoners have hustles that capitalize on the desire of many prisoners to fix up their cells. For example, a job in the paint shop allows a prisoner to prepare special cans of paint. These are sold to others who want to paint their cells. And a job in the woodworking shop enables the prisoner employees to make and sell many small items that prisoners use in their cells—such as small shelves, covered boxes, and toilet paper dispensers. A few gifted prisoners sell their art works to prisoners who want a painting on the wall of their cell. At times these prisoners are even commissioned to do a portrait of a prisoner's wife, girlfriend, or children. For some artists, this hustle may supplement their income from the legal sale of their paintings. However, a few may not even have money for a legal draw; and consequently, they are unable to legally purchase supplies from the hobby shop. They must use the supplies of other prisoners, and therefore their paintings can never be sold to the public through legal channels.

A wide variety of hustles cater to the thirst and hunger of the prisoners. For example, some prisoners just steal certain food items from the mess hall and wholesale them to other prisoners who cook or combine the ingredients into consumable products. Additional prisoners usually are involved in the retail distribution of this food. Or, other prisoners may be able to manufacture equipment that is used in the preparation of food or drinks. For example, instant coffee is sold at the canteen, but there is no hot water in the cells. Even the "hot" water that is passed around in the evening is not very hot. Therefore, many prisoners make and sell "stingers"—small electrical coil immersion heaters that are used to heat a single cup of water. The stingers enable prisoners to make hot coffee almost any time they wish. However, there is one drawback from which stingers get their name. Those who use them must take care to avoid getting "stung" by an electrical shock. At one time, the prisoners who worked in the office machinery repair shop actually had an assembly line set up to produce them. Also, the hot plates that prisoners produce are popular. They enable prisoners to cook a surprisingly wide variety of things.

14

MAKING IT IN A WOMAN'S PRISON: THE SQUARE, THE COOL, AND THE LIFE

ESTHER HEFFERNAN

THE SQUARE, THE COOL, AND THE LIFE

It is now possible to move directly into consideration of the three subsystems, the square, the cool, and the life, whose personnel are recruited from the noncriminal, the professional, and the habitual offenders. The titles of the systems are based on the inmates' own designation of the normative bases that underlie the system. In the terminology of the inmates, members of the noncriminal or homicide group are squares—a designation accepted by the members themselves, though with some reservations as to its connotations: "They call my view of church life and things 'square,' but they don't realize how much pleasure I've had in them." The square system's major goal, actually, is the preservation of "squareness," the maintenance of a conventional way of life within the inmate body. When this designation—or preferably the appellation, "good Christian women"—is accepted by others, one of the important functions of the system is achieved.

To be in the life has wide application in the underworld, including participation in prostitution, drug traffic, numbers, and shoplifting. However, within the institution the meaning shifts in an interesting way, as these five quotations imply:

Fighting comes from "little" things, but Occoquan is *our world,* just like there is an outside world and a world of midgets. We have ours too, and the "little" things become big. So what someone "said you said" may mean that you walk in the dining room and someone will slap you in the face, or you'll be cut in your bed.

You know, some of the people belong in here. Here they are something, out there on the streets, they are like a drop of water. They may not know it but they really want to be here. And maybe I want to be too.

Source: From *Making It In Prison* (New York: John Wiley and Sons, Inc. 1972), pp. 41–42, 87, 95, 113–114, 170, 172, 174 (editorial adaptations). Copyright © 1972 by John Wiley and Sons, Inc. Reprinted by permission of the author and publisher.

There are about six in a group. [Youth Correction cottage.] What one does, they all do. What they want, everyone must do—fighting, agitating, taking pills, going to "the hole." I tried to join at first. Now I avoid them and try not to get tangled. They call me a square because I don't think the same way about drugs. I don't want to go back on them. They joke about "reform." The girls are "institutionalized." They *want to stay here*, they don't mind losing time.

Those "familying" are the happiest around here, when they're not in arguments over "wives," because they're *living in here*, not thinking about the outside. They're gay like larks.

Some seem to have nothing outside and not want anything outside. *This is everything.* They get all involved and in trouble.

The first two quotations are from members of the life, the third, from a "deviant" member. The final two are from on-looking members of the square system. From these quotations it is clear that the prison has become the life for some inmates and being in the life implies a subsystem that must provide, in substitute fashion, a relatively total societal system from its own resources. If "this is our world," then, like a community, the system must provide for a diffuse number of goals.

If the square system's goal is the maintenance of a conventional way of life and the life an anti-society (perhaps really more derivative than "anti"), the professional's cool system is less pervasive, "keep busy, play around, stay out of trouble, and get out." The cool system's goal, like that of a bureaucratic organization, may be seen as manipulative efficiency—the provision of an "easy time" within the institution without endangering the possibility of a short stay. The emphasis is on unity to achieve a maximum of amenities: "There's a lack of loyalty because of selfishness, lack of interest in others; while we'd get a lot of things if we'd just stick together." The cool system is orientated toward inmate organization and integration, as shown by their concepts of deprivation. However, this does not imply affective involvement: "Stay on the fringe of things." "Don't let them get you involved." "Keep an interest in the outside." In other words, "Keep cool!"

ADAPTIVE SOCIAL STRUCTURES

Most persons would expect to find an extension of the outside economy within a prison, but the existence of a family structure in a single-sex situation is less frequently anticipated. . . . Perhaps someone might mention that her "play sister" was coming . . . or another would call to a fellow inmate, "Mommy, bring me something when you go to canteen." A little later a woman might trace for her a whole set of relationships—play mothers, play sisters, play brothers, play daughters, and "daddies."

> It's nice, with crazy combinations. _____ is my sister and a mother to another girl, but her daughter is my sister. Several of us have a mother in the laundry, "real back alley." I wouldn't want to tangle with her, she'll steal bleach for us and press our robes. She's older, but not old enough to be our real mother.

Some speak of "familying" with contempt: "It's just rubbish." "It's just to use you. It's 'Mommy, I'd like some candy,' not 'Mommy, what would you like?'" "I'm your play sister, now may I have a carton of cigarettes?" Other's eyes shine as they describe their play daughters, mentioning wistfully that their "daughters" soon will be out on parole and how they'll be missed. Nor will the economic aspect always be described negatively:

> Ah tells my mother, "I'm hungry." When we go to canteen, we get things for everyone. We always take care of each other. At night I makes two jars of tea and they make some tuna salad, plucking the onions and the eggs from the grapevine, and since I don't like tuna, they have "kippers" for me. And we have a lot of fun taking it to the movie and sitting around eating.

. . . the women playing the role of "daddy" or "stud" are often the objects of active competition and the recipients of extensive support. It was asserted, however, that some of the "husbands" would not hesitate leaving one partner to play an initially active role in attracting a new "wife" if she "had the looks and the money." Later in the relationship the "wife" would be expected to supply material support and services. In a few cases the "wife" remained the main recipient of gifts and canteen commodities. The woman who openly asserts the masculine role, or, in the institution slang, becomes a "broken down daddy," is not necessarily more highly rewarded.

> I ain't got no time for those who cut their hair short, quit wearing bras, and walk differently, who don't control themselves and act like women. They're not really abnormal, they're just putting on an act. If they're really so, they're not going to have everybody knowing it. They'll hide it.

From this description, which makes an explicit distinction between "playing" and the overt homosexual relationship, it becomes obvious that there are several different relationships involved.

To "have a man" or "have a woman" may imply the existence of a diffuse set of relational bonds, or it may represent a specific, monetary relationship. In addition the role's bonds may be limited to the supportive and affectual aspects of the husband-wife relationship or may include sexual relations. Despite the frequent mention of the presence of economic motivation by women condemning the practice, the intensity of the emotions exhibited between the women involved implies that there is a broader function. Since many of the physical attacks and violent arguments in the institution are traceable to some violation or suspected violation of "fidelity" on the part of one of the partners or the presence of a potential rival, the relationships are vital for those involved. A threatened or real disturbance of the marital bond provokes the strongest possible countermeasures available to the women.

The new inmate is usually quickly informed of the dangers of "talking to so-and-so's wife," and ignoring the advice may bring group reprisal in the form of petty harassment. The "blades," rumored to be carried by many of the women, make a continued violation dangerous. The existence of organized rather than individual enforcement of the "marital norms" implies that preservation of the family is a concern that transcends individual attraction and jealousy.

"Easy" and "Hard Time": Subsystem Norms

It might be expected that individual women within the various subsystems would vary in their acceptance of the conflicing norms. This is rather graphically illustrated by the comments of an inmate who had spent most of her previous commitment in and out of "the hole." In discussing "easy" and "hard" time with a group of fellow inmates, she remarked:

You know, everybody thought I was doing "hard time" before. They're crazy. That wasn't "hard time," that was easy. I just did what I felt like doing and said what I thought to everybody around. But the time I'm doing now—that's "hard time," 'cause I'm always having to hold myself in and "go along with the program." It's no "easy time."

However, this life member's definition of "easy time" would hardly commend itself to a cool, who would question the "easiness" of multiple days of solitary confinement and restricted diet and the continual loss of industrial and "good time" days. Nor would a square find conformity to institutional regulations and maintenance of positive relations with staff the epitome of "hardness." Each subsystem, if it actually represents an alternative normative orientation, should significantly differ from the other two in the formulation of and adherence to the patterns of "doing time."

The squares' orientation to conventional values and the image of a "good inmate" require adaptive patterns, standards of status evaluation, and forms of social control that are acceptable to staff. Perhaps more accurately, the squares accept those staff values that they perceive to conform with those of the larger society.

For the cool the appearance of conformity rather than conformity itself is a major aim; thus the actual structures of the cool system differ from those legitimated by the staff. The appearance of conformity without actually fulfilling official expectations achieves a maximum utility from both official and inmate structures. Nevertheless, to reach this goal, there must be constant control, with a stress on inmate integration to prevent the image of conformity from being disturbed either by overt violation of institutional forms or by inmate disclosure of illegal adaptive patterns. In addition, the cool's participation in inmate structures must be limited to ensure continued orientation to the "outside" and control "inside."

With counterpower one of the goals of the life, overt violation of regulations is required, at least periodically, to test the ability to force official action and to enhance the status of the system as a wielder of control. Covert exercise of power, which by its very nature is not recognized, cannot adequately fulfill system goals. Direct inmate confrontation with staff's power, however, necessitates a willingness to stay in prison, since the final sanction available to the authorities short of execution is continued incarceration. To the extent that the subsystem successfully provides a "life" inside, this frequently invoked and supposedly highly coercive control actually loses its effectiveness. Therefore the system's espousal of extensive evasion of institutional regulations requires as highly organized an economic, affective, and ideological system as possible. The prison system's reactions to the direct challenge of their official norms, in turn, reinforces the life's dependence on their own system for long-term support.

Staff: Square, Cool, and the Life

The existence of staff structures that parallel inmate structures became evident as the research continued. Staff members, like inmates, can be square, cool, or in the life. Although staff relations were not directly examined in this research, certain tentative observations may prove fruitful for speculation and future observation.

In many ways, prison expectations for the "good employee" and the "good inmate" are similar. A new member of the Department of Corrections, whether on the professional treatment staff or the correctional staff is introduced to the "official world" through an orientation program and testing based on the close reading of the department's *Perspectives for Correctional Practice* and the *Manual of Regulations and Orders.*

As the inmates find significant differences between the "official world" and the "inmate world," so also the employees find living "by the book" as described by the Department and the everyday world of prison employment similarly divergent. Several new employees commented in informal conversations on their initial bewilderment at this divergence. In a trisemester training session, one of the new officers, with some hesitation, asked the Superintendent: "What do you do when you see things that you know are against the rule book and the officers who are showing you the rules ignore them?" When the official manual of any formal organization presents a level of expectation, a singleness of purpose, or a multiplicity of goals impossible to attain, both deviance and conformity become necessary choices.

As the new employees move into the "real world" of the prison they meet patterns of staff adaptation that appear to parallel those of the inmates: the square, the cool, and the life. Just as inmate subsystems are related to inmate background and orientation to prison, these staff patterns reflect differing backgrounds and the subsequent development of several basic orientations to prison work. These orientations seem to subsume other traditional differences among staff, such as the distinction between custodial and treatment staff, between professionals and nonprofessionals, and race, class, and urban-rural cleavages.

For one group of correctional officers and personnel, prison work is primarily a job. Their major supportive relationships and status sources are outside the prison. They tend in some ways to be "ideal" employees, since they are impartial, generally obey the rules and regulations, and frequently are kind and considerate to the women. They "keep their mouths shut," have relatively little contact with the staff "I say, you say," and do their job well. Like the square, they are in the positions for which they were hired. This is particularly true for work supervisors. Glaser's finding that "the best liked officer most often mentioned as the source of rehabilitation by men who were successful on parole" was the work supervisor can be seen in this context as a confirmation of the supervisor's square status. One work supervisor in particular . . . was highly regarded by the women —the square found her understanding and supportive, and the cool and the life respected her, which was manifested in their care to conceal the advantages they took of her lack of knowledge of the "inner workings" of the inmate system. Since she did not try to "outslick" them, they tried as far as possible to protect her. Sometimes correctional officers in the dormitories functioned in a similar way. Without any involvement in contraband, they could and did play a maternal role in the affective supportive area in ways that paralleled that of the square inmate. As in the square's participation in "familying" there is role conflict involved, since a "fraternal" relationship with inmates formally was a violation of Department rules and potentially could involve the staff member in additional illicit relationships with inmates or in disciplinary action by superiors if "betrayed" by other inmates or correctional officers.

It would appear that the cool find their counterpart in the professional staff. The treatment staff, almost by definition, is externally orientated, since prison as a way of life violates the very premise of "rehabilitation." In addition, professional competency, control, and emotional detachment are valued role components for treatment staff—precisely the same qualities admired by the cool inmate. Perhaps this congeniality of approach rather than any inmate acceptance of treatment goals explains the relatively high cool participation in treatment activities. It might be noted that this mutual respect for "professional" competence may well atract the professional researcher to the professional criminal, since the articulate thief is a frequent source of valuable data.

15

THE SOCIAL MEANING OF PRISON HOMOSEXUALITY

JOHN H. GAGNON AND WILLIAM SIMON

The last half century has seen marked, if uneven, progress in most areas of prison management and perhaps even more marked progress in the creation of a new ideology of prison management. However, despite evidence of progress, there still remains a major area of behavior with which prison systems have been unable to cope. This is the problem of sexual adjustment that occurs in all institutions where one sex is deprived of social or sexual access to the other. It is in the area of sexuality that the prison is perhaps more limited than it is in other areas of activity, partially because of its very single-sex nature and partially because the society rarely provides clear guidelines for sexual behavior even outside the penal institution.

In the midst of the confusion about sexual standards and sexual behavior, the prison exists as the major single-sex institution in the society that has (unlike the mental hospital and other closed institutions) within its walls a population that is physically and, for the most part, psychologically, intact and is, at the same time, sexually experienced. The prison administrator is faced with a fundamental dilemma: He is aware of the sexual needs of the population that he is charged with holding and retraining, but he is also aware that he is not going to get much support or even a sympathetic hearing from the larger society if he focuses upon the problem of the sexual adjustment of his population.

SOME MAJOR CONSIDERATIONS

There are two major areas that require clarification before one can proceed to discuss the actual patterns of sexual adjustment among

Source: From *Federal Probation,* XXXII(March 1968): 23–29. Reprinted by permission of the authors and publisher.

prison populations. The first is an unfortunate tendency to view the sexual adjustment of prisoners as arising exclusively from the contexts of prison life. It is frequently assumed that any group of people who were incarcerated for any period of time would react sexually in the same way as those who are presently in prison. This is a major oversimplification brought about primarily because of a lack of information about the prior sexual and nonsexual lives of those who are imprisoned and the way in which this prior experience conditions a person's responses not only to sexual deprivation, but also to a general loss of liberty.

The second element that is important to specify is the range of sexual responses that are available to those imprisoned. With the exception of the small number of prisons that allow conjugal visits, there are only three forms of sexual behavior that are generally available to a prison population (except for animal contact for those males on prison farms). These are nocturnal sex dreams, self-masturbation, and sexual contact with other inmates of the same sex. The meaning, amount, and the character of these adjustments will be strongly dependent on the meaning that these same behaviors had for the inmate before he or she was incarcerated. Thus, the problem for the inmate is not merely the release of sexual tension, but the social and psychological meaning that such release has and the motives and beliefs that it expresses for him. The source of this set of values does not reside in the prison experience, but outside the prison in the community at large. Thus, the prison provides a situation to which prior sexual and social styles and motives must be adapted and shaped.

There are two major dimensions on which most sexual activity is based. One is that of age, with the primary break occurring between adolescence and adulthood. The other, perhaps of greater significance is the differential meaning of sexuality to the two sexes. Thus, the striking differences between the sexual orientations of men and women noted in the Kinsey volumes offer the best starting point for a discussion of sex in prison.[22] The discussion that follows focuses on the responses of adult male and female inmates to the prison experience, with only passing reference to institutions for adolescents as they represent continuities to the adult institutions.

MALE RESPONSES TO IMPRISONMENT

Male prison populations are not random selections from the larger society and do not reflect the usual distributions of the population in terms of education, income, ethnicity, occupation, social class, and general life style. The men who make up the bulk of the imprisoned populations tend to be drawn from deprived sections of the society or from families imbedded in what we have now come to call the culture of poverty. As a consequence, the sexual experiences of these men and the meaning that sex has for them differs in significant ways from other portions of the population that are less likely to be imprisoned.

A number of dimensions of these differences may be found in the work of Kinsey and his colleagues in which they report the substantial differences to be found in the sexual activity and attitudes of men who have differing amounts of education.[23] These findings are further amplified in the volume, *Sex Offenders,* where a comparison of imprisoned men and men of the same social origins without delinquent histories showed that the men with prison histories generally have wider sexual experience of all kinds than do men leading conventional and nondelinquent lives.[24] These variables suggest that at least the modal male prison population enters institutions with differing commitments to sexuality than would a middle-class or working class population. We can therefore suggest that the response of these latter groups to institutionalization will differ as well.

Prior Sexual Adjustment a Factor

Drawing on what we know about the dimensions of the prior sexual adjustments of men who go to prison, our first major sense of the experience is actually how little sexual activity of any sort occurs within the prison.[25] Thus, even after the shock of imprisonment has worn off (and often for the recidivist this occurs quickly), there is no sudden burst of sexual activity of any type. Confirming these impressions is the low order of complaint one hears about sexual deprivation, even when prisoners are presenting a list of grievances after a riot or outbreak of some sort. Part of this is surely due to the closeness of custody in the institution and the fact that men move and live in close proximity, and, except for certain moments of the day, there is very little privacy—not so much from the custodial staff as from inmates.

However, another cause of this reduction is that sexual activity is potentiated by or channeled through an existing set of social frameworks that do not exist in prison. The man in prison finds himself without the appropriate stimuli which suggest opportunities for sexual activity or situations that are appropriate for such activity. Without the existence of these social cues, the biological imperative of sexual arousal is never even elicited.[26] The absence of females, the sheer sensory monotony of the prison environment, the absence of those social situations that call for sexual responses (being out on the town, going drinking, etc.) serve as effective inhibitors of sexual responsiveness. The most successful aphrodisiacs seem to be an absence of anxiety, the presence of available sexual cues, an adequate diet, and plenty of rest. Of these, only the latter two are commonly in the prison environment and in some cases only the last is.

The other source of sexual cues is fantasy, those remembered or desired sexual experiences that commonly serve as the basis for masturbation. However, as a result of the social origins of the bulk of the prison population, there is a major taboo against masturbation and a paucity of complex fantasies that would sustain a commitment to sexual experience.[27] Thus, unlike the middle-class male who learns and rehearses sexual styles in the context of masturbation, the usual prisoner is drawn from a population in which sexual experience is concrete and not symbolic; in which there is a taboo on masturbation; and, finally, in which much of heterosexual experience is structured around the need to have sexual encounters that validate his masculinity among other men. In this environment it might be said that men have sex in order to be able to talk about it.

The Kinsey evidence is that even among lower-class men who do masturbate there is often no conscious fantasy accompanying the behavior, and it serves primarily as a mechanical release of felt physical tension. This is quite unlike the middle-class situation in which masturbation occurs at relatively high rates accompanied by fantasies of sexual experience. These fantasies then begin to facilitate further masturbation and a continuing commitment to this sexual outlet. This adjustment rarely happens in the lower-class environment and, along with the sensory poverty of the prison environment, accounts for the ease with which strong commitments to sexuality are abandoned. Thus, prisoners may complain about sexual deprivation in terms such as "I would really like to have a piece" but often this is a continuation of lower-class male talk about sex, not a passionately felt drive that will eventuate in sexual activity.

Male Homosexuality More Than Outcome of Sexual Desire or Need for Physical Release

Since most prisoners do not seem to feel an overwhelming sexual need, male homosexuality in this context must be seen as something more complex than merely the outcome of sexual desire or the need for physical release. There are varying estimates of the number of males who have homosexual contact during their periods of imprisonment, but the range is probably somewhere between 30 and 45 percent, depending upon the intensity of custody in the institution, the social origins of the population, and the duration of the individual sentence.[28] It seems quite clear that the frequency of homosexual contact is usually quite low, even among cellmates; and in no sense does it approach the rates of heterosexual or homosexual behavior of these same prisoners on the outside, except possibly for those prisoners who come into the institutions with well-developed homosexual commitments and who become the "passive" partners in homosexual liaisons. In some prisons, usually those with a very low order of custody inside the walls, high rates of homosexual behavior may be achieved; however, these are not the prevalent conditions in most prison systems.

It must be pointed out that homosexuality in prison is quite a different phenomenon than homosexual experience in the outside community. Thus, the image of homosexuality as consisting of masculine-seeming men who are always "active" and feminine men who are always "passive" in the sexual performance derives primarily from both journalists and scientists observing homosexuality in prisons and then extending their observations unchecked to the outside world.[29]

Homosexuality in the prison context is partly a parody of heterosexuality, with the very sexual activity suggesting masculine and feminine role components. We now know that this is a basic oversimplification not only of homosexuality in general, but heterosexuality as well. It is, however, in the prison environment where this parody is most likely to occur, for the crucial variable is that many of the men who take part in the homosexual performances conceive of themselves, and wish others to conceive of them, as purely heterosexual.

Thus those prisoners known in prison parlance as "jockers" or "wolves" think of themselves as heterosexual; and, as long as there is no reciprocity in the sexual performance (aiding in the ejaculation of the other male) or the penis is not inserted in their mouth or anus, other inmates will continue to conceive of them in the same way. Thus the homosexual world of the prison is roughly divisible into aggressive "active" males (jockers, wolves) and "passive" males. The latter group commonly includes males who are heterosexual on the outside but who are coerced, either by fear or debt, to be homosexual (usually labeled "punks") and males who have already well-developed preferences for males from their outside experience and who enter prison as homosexuals.[30] The relationships of these males is usually highly stylized both socially and sexually, the aggressor providing protection, a measure of affection and perhaps gifts (in the case of older inmates), and the passive inmate providing sexual access, affection, and other pseudo-feminine services. In the cases of long-term inmates these relationships may be conceived of as pseudo-marriages, resulting sometimes in a greater degree of sexual reciprocity; however, such reciprocity results in a decline in other inmates' estimates of the aggressive male's masculinity.

Search for Meaningful Relationships

The sources of this homosexual activity for the predominantly heterosexual and aggressive male seem to be twofold. One element is certainly a search for meaningful emotional relationships that have some durability and which serve as a minimal substitute for affective relationships that they normally have on the outside. This is not unlike the chance homosexual contact between men during combat or in other situations of all-male communities under circumstances of fear and crisis. It represents an attempt to counter the effort of the prison to atomize the inmate community in order to reduce the potential for collusion, which could result either in conniving for goods and services or in attempting escape.

One of the collective responses to this attempt is the development of a resistant inmate community, and at the individual level one of the responses is the establishment of homosexual liaisons.

A second motivation underlying many of these relationships transcends the level of affectional need and essentially becomes a source for the continued validation of masculinity needs and a symbol of resistance to the prison environment. The male whose primary source of masculine validation in the outside community has been his sexual success (rather than work, family, etc.) and who has conceived of himself as aggressive and controlling in his responses to his world finds himself in prison deprived of these central supports for his own masculinity. In reaction to this he enters into homosexual relationships in which he can be conceived as the masculine, controlling partner and which for him and for other males in the system validate continued claims to masculine status. A complicating factor here is that some men suffer a profound psychological crisis when the supports for their masculine identity are removed. In these cases both severe homosexual panics or falling into "passive" homosexual roles are likely to result.

In general, these homosexual relationships are developed not through force, though there is evidence of homosexual rape, especially in poorly controlled detention institutions where the powerful threat of imprisonment to masculinity is first felt, in penal institutions that are inadequately controlled, and in juvenile institutions where the sexual impulse is less well-ordered and tends to be confused with aggression by the adolescent male. In most cases the "passive" partner drifts into the relationship through falling into debt, being afraid of the environment, and feeling that he requires protection, or because he already has a well-developed commitment to homosexuality that he cannot or does not want to conceal. Once an inmate has fallen into this role it is extremely difficult to shift out of it, and, if a current relationship breaks up, there will be pressure to form a new one. Even in a reincarceration there will be a memory of his role from prior institutionalization and there will be pressure to continue. It is as if the prison required as one of its role types the "passive" homosexual, and, if a number of them are removed, there is pressure to restore to equilibrium the relationship between those playing aggressive-masculine roles and those playing passive-feminine roles.

Problems Facing the Prison Administrator

This conceptualization of the pattern of homosexuality in the prison for men suggests a number of problems that face the prison administrator in dealing with sexuality. It means that as long as the prison is an environment which is largely devoid of situations where legitimate affectional ties can be established there will be a tendency for the formation of homosexual relationships, especially among those men serving long sentences who have concomitantly lost contact with meaningful persons in the free community. If in addition the prison does not allow legitimate attempts of the inmates to control their own lives and does not give an opportunity for expressions of masculinity and self-assertion that are meaningful among men at this social level, there will be homosexual relationships created to fulfill this need. The proposal for conjugal visits does not meet this problem, in part because it is available for only the very small number of inmates who have intact families. There is little evidence that the society will tolerate sexual relationships for prisoners when these relationships are not sheltered under the umbrella of a marriage.

What is clear is that the prison is not a seething volcano of sexual passions, and that as a matter of fact most males survive the deprivation of the sexual outlet and usually even survive transitory homosexual commitments to return to relatively conventional heterosexual lives on the outside.

What the sexual problem in the male prison does represent is a series of land mines, some for the administration, more for the inmates. In the case of the inmates, men get into relationships which have some potential for shaping their future commitments to sexuality; relationships which leave them open to exploitation; and, especially for those who take the passive role, the possibility of distortion of their self-conceptions. Further, there is some tendency for these relationships to create problems of sexual jealousy. When a relationship deteriorates or when a transfer of affection takes place, there is a distinct possibility of violence. The violence that does occur often is extreme, and at this point becomes a serious matter for prison management.

The dilemma for the prison manager is that often he is not aware of the relationships until they erupt into violence. Attempts at intervention in this process through getting inmates to aid in the identification of those involved may result in serious scapegoating of these persons out of the sexual anxieties of the other prisoners. The segregation of these prisoners has also been attempted. However, one major difficulty with this measure seems to be that when the most obvious homosexuals are removed from the situation there is a tendency to co-opt other persons to take their place. This tendency is also noted when the aggressive male is removed, though the policy has usually been to remove only those men who are conventionally obvious, that is, who are excessively effeminate.

Probably the only long-term solution is to adopt the policy of home visits at intervals during incarceration and to provide alternative modes of self-expression for those social and psychological needs which, because of the current structure of the male prison, result in homosexuality.

FEMALE RESPONSES TO IMPRISONMENT

As we have noted before, the major dimension which differentiates between the sexual adjustment of persons in the larger society is gender; that is, men and women differ fundamentally in their sexual commitments. While this is obvious, the consequences for the differential sexual adaptation of the males and females in prison are not.

By and large, there is in society a bias against committing females to prison, especially when any alternative is available. Thus the women's prison often has within it women who have either committed major crimes (most commonly homicide) or had long careers in crime and who have been strongly recidivistic. Thus in a certain sense the female institution is composed of some women who have had no prior link to delinquent life-styles and a larger number who had long-term ties with such a life.

Women have Fewer Problems than Men in Managing Sexual Deprivation

However, the sexual adjustment of these women to imprisonment is strongly linked to the general goals to which most women are socialized in the larger society. Probably the most significant difference between men and women in this regard is that women are socialized in the language of love before they learn about sex, while men are socialized in the language of sex before they learn about love. The consequence of this is that women commonly show considerably fewer problems managing sexual deprivation than do men, and while there is little evidence, one might expect that the frequencies of any sexually ameliorative behaviors, such as masturbation and homosexuality, are considerably less frequent for women than for men in prison. There is considerable evidence that such behaviors are less frequent among women in the free society than among men, and one should not be surprised that such continuity would be found inside the prison. In addition, women seem to tolerate the absence of overt sexual activity far better than do men, and thus the rates of overt sexual behavior in the female institutions should be considerably lower than those found in male institutions.

Women Tend to Establish Family Systems

The typical response of women to the depersonalizing and alienating environment of the penal institution differs substantially from that of males. Nearly universally in juvenile institutions, and in some observed cases in institutions for adult females, female prisoners appear to form into pseudofamilies with articulared roles of husband and wife, and then, especially in juvenile institutions, extend the family to include father, mother, and children, and aunts, uncles, and cousins.[31] These family systems seem to arise from three sources. One source is a process of compensation; the majority of females in these institutions are from severely disordered homes, and the creation of the pseudofamily often compensates for this lack. A second source results from the socialization of women who, unlike males who form gangs in self-defense, tend to form families, the basic institution in the society in which they have stable and legitimate roles. Finally there is the fact that the pseudofamily operates to stabilize relationships in the institution and to establish orders of dominance and submission, the primary model which women have in family relationships with father, husbands, and children. Since all social systems require some form of articulation which is hierarchical in nature, it is not odd that women model their experience on the institution that they know best in the outside community. There is some evidence that the pseudofamily is not as prevalent in institutions with older females, and it is possible to speculate that in these institutions dyadic friendship patterns are more frequent and may be more similar to those in male institutions.

Inside the context of these familial structures there is the potential for and the acting out of overt homosexual contacts. In the two most recent studies of female prisons there are varying estimates of the number of women who are involved in homosexual practices, but this variation is probably a function of differing definitions, with one limiting the estimate to overt physical contact (yielding a rate of about one-half) and the other probably referring to the proportion of the population who are currently involved in roles in pseudofamily structures (yielding a rate of about 85 percent).[32]

Deprivation of Emotionally Satisfying, Stable, Predictable Relationships with Males

A minor part of the overt female homosexual contacts may arise from deprivation of sexuality, but the primary source is the deprivation of the emotionally satisfying relationships with members of the opposite sex and the desire to create the basis for a community of relationships that are stable and predictable. The overt homosexuality derives somewhat from the conventional sexual content role definitions of husband and wife, but also partially from the fact that a certain proportion of females who come into these institutions may well have experience with lesbian relationships through experience with prostitution in the free community. This is not to say that female homosexuals becomes prostitutes, but rather that among prostitutes homosexual relationships are sought because of the degraded conditions of contacts with men. The processes of induction into homosexual activity in the women's prison is often based on the same principles that one observes in male institutions as part of a search for affection and stability in personal relationships. The homosexual relationship offers protection from the exigencies of the environment and the physical homosexual contacts are less sought for the physical release that they afford than for the validation of emotionally binding and significant relationships.

CONCLUSION

From the arguments posed above it is suggested that what is occurring in the prison situation for both males and females is not a problem of sexual release, but rather the use of sexual relationships in the service of creating a community of relationships for satisfying needs for which the prison fails to provide in any other form. For the male prisoner homosexuality serves as a source of affection, a source of the validation of masculinity, or a source of protection from the problems of institutional life.

In a like manner, the females tend to create family structures in an attempt to ward off the alienating and disorganizing experience of imprisonment; the homosexual relationships are merely part of the binding forces of these relationships.

The problem for the prison administrator then becomes considerably more complex than merely the suppression of sexual activity— it becomes a problem of providing those activities for which the homosexual contacts are serving as substitutes. The inmates are acting out their needs for self-expression, control over their own behavior, affection, and stability of human relationships. The homosexual relationship provides one of the few powerful ways of expressing and gratifying these needs. Unless these needs are met in some other way, there is little opportunity for adequate control of homosexual activity in the prison environment. It might be hypothesized that any attempt to become more coercive and controlling of inmate behavior in order to reduce homosexual contacts may result not in a decrease in activity, but perhaps in an increase. By increasing coercion one increases the pressure to divide inmates from one another, and one decreases their capacity for self-expression and self-control. As the pressure builds there may well be a tendency for homosexual relationships to increase in importance to the inmate population as a reaction to the intensity of the pressure.

Imprisonment and the concomitant sexual deprivation of inmates obviously has some serious consequences, at least during imprisonment, and has a minor potential for complicating postinstitutional life. Little systematic research exists that links the prior nonprison experience of the prisoner, both sexual and nonsexual; methods of institutional management; and the consequences of the interaction of these two elements for the inmate's future functioning. The fact that many inmates adjust easily to the climate of deprivation in the prison may be a measure of their pathology and inability to get along in the outside community rather than a measure of healthy functioning. Just because we manage to make people conform to a climate of deprivation, both sexual and nonsexual, is no reason that we should.

16

COLLECTIVE BEHAVIOR AT ATTICA*

ROBERT MARTINSON

An accurate rendering of changes in the profiles of social disturbance in the prison is made difficult when the standard abstractions of "collective behavior" are mixed with the dominant motif of the "total institution." Long before the events at Attica, I had begun to question versions of inmate behavior tied to the "custody-treatment" dimension or to Sykes and Messinger's utilitarian notion of the "pains of imprisonment," or indeed to any concept of the prison which views it as primarily an autonomous "community."[33]

Unfortunately, penological history provides almost no help. Except for histories of prison reform movements, there is such a poverty of scholarship that the prison appears as a historyless administrative unit, broken from time to time by riot. History is most at home when it traces processes of social conflict which develop, in which the incipient becomes the full-blown. So the historian has left this seemingly dreary landscape to the tender mercies of the sociologist. Thus we are burdened with timeless abstractions about the "inmate subculture," the "inmate code," and so forth.

TYPES OF PRISON DISTURBANCE

The poverty of penological history is an illusion. There are changes over time in the profile of prison disturbance. To advance the discussion, I will suggest two main historical types and argue that Attica exemplifies a third. Let us call these types: (1) the mass escape; (2) the prison riot; and (3) the expressive mutiny.

(1) Mass escape as a mode of prisoner behavior was associated

Source: *Federal Probation*, XXXVI(September 1972): 3-7. Reprinted by permission of the author and publisher.

*This article is a slightly edited version of a paper presented to the Eastern Sociological Association meetings, Boston, April 22, 1972.

with a prebureaucratic society and in America with the frontier. To escape from a dungeon is a dangerous enterprise. Mass escape required shared ingenuity and motivation, some common hope of taking up a new life, concealing one's past, even leaving one's home territory. In this early epoch, the prison was unashamedly brutal and was designed for incapacitation and severe punishment. Prison revolt was commonly put down with deadly fury by officials and guards backed up by deputized locals since every disturbance implied the real probability of a mass breakout followed by spoilation of areas adjacent to the prison.

(2) Prison riot—which dominated the 19th and early 20th centuries—involved a struggle to improve conditions *within* the prison rather than an attempt to escape from it. Within the armed perimeter, power struggles occurred over the meager privileges prison had to offer. Such riots were often nicely timed to provoke the intervention of the prison reform movement and sometimes led to changes in paroling practices, better food, less punishment for breaking prison rules or fewer rules.

In the 20th century riot increasingly tended to run in cycles. The riot cycle implied swift communication and contagion reflecting the creation of state systems of corrections, standard penological practices, and a nationwide convict subculture.

The most recent cycle of riots (1952-1953) began in the disciplinary cellblock of the world's largest prison in Jackson, Michigan, and spread to dozens of prisons in the United States and abroad. One hypothesis maintained that these riots were sparked by inner-prison struggles for control between the "custodial" and "treatment" points of view among the staff. These struggles threatened to change the inmate status quo and led to a preventive counterrevolution led by a corrupt inmate priesthood which preached the inmate code as a means of retaining privileges.

(3) Unlike the riot, the expressive mutiny is not primarily focussed on winning power, maintaining privileges or improving conditions within the prison. It aims to communicate the inmate's plight to the public so far as he understands it. It is a new form of disturbance not merely a temporary reflection of new left influence among a group of politicized black convicts. The prison is used as an arena in which to stage dramatic renditions of inhumanity and rebellious gestures of inchoate despair and apocalypse. Demands for improvements in prison conditions appear side by side with borrowings from the Black Power movement, the student movement, and the revolutionary sect. The entrepreneurial spirit of the escape artist is replaced by the organizational methods of the militant.

Clearly, convict disturbances take different forms over time reflecting both prison conditions and dominant attributes of society.

THE AGE OF TREATMENT

To understand the causes of the expressive mutiny, one must trace the evolution of the New Penology from its beginnings in the latter half of the 19th century to its total victory over corrections in the decades of the 1950's and 1960's.[34]

Treatment began with the growth of new professions—social welfare, probation, parole, psychiatry—which entered the prison (along with teachers, vocational instructors and counselors) in the decades preceding World War I. Its greatest innovation and most hated product was the indefinite sentence. Its second major stage was victory over correctional administration and the permeation of entire systems with the philosophy and practice of correctional treatment. The "correctional therapeutic community"—as it came to be called in California—in its common form, went no further than individual and group counseling, an intense "bull session" which syphoned off inmate discontent into relatively harmless verbal abuse. In its most extreme form—the California Adjustment Center—treatment combined "max-max" confinement with a future of indeterminateness. Even parole—under this system—was increasingly perceived by inmates as a trap instead of a privilege.

More important than the victory of treatment has been the secular decline in opportunity for the ex-offender in a modern technological society which demands uncoerced, skilled, and motivated activity from its employees. I have defined correctional treatment as a "redoubling of efforts in the face of persistent failure."[35] Inmates once believed in these efforts. This belief plus the introduction of treatment programs, group counseling, parole outpatient services, and so forth, managed to keep the lid on our volatile dungeons for two or three decades. Attica may be seen as a typical disturbance of the Age of Treatment and an indication of the beginning of its decline.

SOME CHARACTERISTICS OF COLLECTIVE BEHAVIOR

The idea that the inmates at Attica revolted against brutality or repression is untenable. Empirically, the so-called "pains of imprisonment" were lessening, certainly not increasing. The precipitating cause of the revolt was the disintegration of discipline combined with the "hope" aroused by the new reform administration of the New York prison system. For those who like to exercise the sociological imagination, the expressive mutiny might be described as a temporary burst of chiliastic fervor and action physically constrained within by the architecture of penology. Many prisoners at Attica locked themselves into their cells or attempted to "escape" the militants into the hands of the guards and officials. Their behavior reflected fear and rejection of modes of political and ideological protest which have no direct and visible payoff for inmate welfare.

I must rely on newspaper reports in briefly describing four characteristics of inmate collective behavior at Attica.

(1) Militant Inmate Leadership

The prison riot was frequently sparked by violent "psychopaths" and normally disintegrated into chaos within a few hours or days. The militant leadership at Attica locked up this kind of emotionally unstable element and through its energy (and the willingness of the officials) maintained a negotiating stance through 5 days of turmoil. Still, like the traditional prison leadership, there was a good proportion of armed robbers as one would expect from previous research. Also, three white inmates were apparently executed after a drumhead court lasting a few minutes because they were regarded as "rats." Fierce adherence to the "rat complex" is a characteristic of convict leadership.

The militant group at Attica was a convict elite, banded together in self-protection, with its own "leadership table," set apart from the other inmates. Factional and strategic differences within the leadership group were jealously guarded. Officer Morris, a hostage, may overstate the matter when he calls the rank-and-file "hostages," but elements of apathy, terror, and uneasy support were probably intermixed. He says:

It was my opinion they thought they were going to start a revolution. They would never have agreed to any settlement. They wanted the troopers to come in and kill a lot of people to start things in the street. . . . I'd say about 50 of the men wanted this and another 150 went along with it because they were members of the group. . . . I'd say there were about a thousand inmates in the yard that didn't want to be in the yard—I think they were hostages the same as I was.[36]

The insurrection took palce after an "influx of newcomers" previously "involved in riots" who tended to form ". . . a number of organized factions: Black Muslims, Black Panthers, Young Lords." I am quoting Officer Rhodes, another hostage:

The Muslims preached peace and loving . . . but the Black Panthers and Young Lords wanted to go into it like a small war. I was talking to a Muslim [this was before the outbreak] and he said they were planning to take a lot of hostages but there wouldn't be any brutality.

Of the 2,200 inmates at Attica, 1,200 were in D-yard, some forced to participate by the militant leadership group. According to one estimate, about 800 of these 1,200 ". . . wanted no part in the revolt."

The leadership shared an essentially prepolitical idea of revolution as a big ghetto riot sparked by starting "things in the street." Most covered their faces to make reprisals and indictments more difficult when the end came as they knew it must. Using John Irwin's terms, this group appears oriented to "convict" rather than "thief" values. The Panther style, the "macho" posture and the Black Power rhetoric are clear borrowings from outside militant groups.[37]

(2) Ecstatic Solidarity

Even the most apathetic inmates in D-yard were drawn in by the collective enthusiasm, and potential critics silenced by the unitary public reality. This state of "negative bondedness" is similar to that found among Freedom Riders in a maximum security cellblock in the Mississippi State Penitentiary at Parchman.[38] This study led me to conclude that there is a ". . . special quality to the social bondedness of the closely confined." I called it "ecstatic solidarity." D-yard was not an ordinary cellblock, but this concept may help explain seemingly irrational features of behavior during these 5 days.

An initial ideological solidarity grew slowly among the leadership cadre. I quote Officer Aldrich, a hostage:

> They started an Afro-American class in the school about six months ago, taught by an inmate, which was bad in my opinion. Anytime you went in the room they would change the subject. We thought they might be planning things. We couldn't sit in the class all the time because we only had one officer on each floor, with over 100 inmates.
>
> We had been noticing large gatherings of inmates, especially Muslims, in the yard and we reported it. At one time they called the big shot of the Muslims, [Norman] Butler, down front and discussed it with him because inmates weren't allowed to congregate that many at a time . . . this was finally allowed.

Various disparate groups had linked up by the time the revolt occurred. Social control in a prison is always tenuous, of course, and the combination of lax discipline, inmate organization, and hope for change made insurrection a likely outcome.

D-yard was an intense cauldron of public behavior since everything taking place was directly observable and constantly monitored by armed guards on the walls equipped with rifles with telescopic sights. The yard was broken by the leadership table and the marked-off "compound" for the hostages. On display, the inmates had to regard their every action as, willy-nilly, relevant to staff. They were an audience for their own actions, and simultaneously actors in a pageant displayed provocatively to guards and reporters and, ultimately, the world at large. The leadership table was, intermittently, a focus for cognitive attention, a center for action, a negotiating session, and a court of last resort. During harangues and speeches given by the "outside negotiators" the crowd aligned temporarily into a mass meeting except that it was still under close observation.

This unitary sociation broke down during the lulls between mass meetings and social order became more tenuous. Warren H. Hansen, a doctor and observer, reports an episode which took place on Saturday, September 11:

Suddenly, a band of blacks dressed in a bizarre array of costumes (including priests' vestments taken from the prison chapel) and brandishing makeshift weapons (including assegais, bats and clubs) approached the hostages' compound. One guy had a spear about 10 feet long. Hell, he was showing his teeth and jumping up and down like a Watusi. The hostages' security guard kept off this band of men until Brother Richie arrived and, after a long discussion persuaded the surrealistic vision to go away.

This episode may appear bizarre to an outside observer, but I can recall similar episodes of pageantry (minus the threat of violence) in which the Freedom Riders in Parchman paraded down the corridor of their cellblock dressed in sheets, miming integrationist morality plays for the benefit of the indignant guards.

Ecstatic solidarity in D-yard was tenuous and tiring and had to be constantly reinforced by the ideological injunctions of the leaders and the "outside negotiators." It was partially and differentially shared by larger numbers depending on the moods of enthusiasm, despair, and hostility which break over mass gatherings as events unfold.

From these accounts, written for nonscientific purposes, one should be wary of interpreting inmate enthusiasm or silence as support for the actions and strategies of the militant leadership. Many con-wise men (probably a majority) may have had private doubts about what was being said and about the outcome. But, there are only two classes in a prison, and the convict body (even in normal times) is constrained to say nothing in public favoring the "screws." It would have taken extraordinary personal courage to disturb the public "reality" imposed on collective life by the "spokesmen" and their cothinkers from outside, especially after the execution of the three white inmates.

(3) Magical Thinking

Richard McCleery's leading study indicates that the belief systems of "incorrigibles" are characterized by authoritarianism, personal "toughness," the inmate code, belief in a rigid leadership hierarchy, and a doctrinaire adherence to criminal values.[38] Normally, however, convict leaders are "moderates" and seldom do they seek out Armageddon as they appeared to do at Attica.

A *New York Times* chronology states: "Rebel leaders had often expressed a willingness to die, but many inmates in the yard thought that gas, fire hoses, and rubber bullets were the worst they had to fear."[39] In addition, prisoners apparently believed that they would receive amnesty and perhaps deportation to a foreign country. Clark Whelton reports that a prisoner asked one of the members of the outside negotiating committee: "What's this I hear about foreign countries?"[40] The answer: "There are four Third World and African country people across the street from this prison, prepared to provide asylum for everyone who wants to leave this country for this purpose. (Shouts and pandemonium from the inmates)." The speaker later explained his final speech this way: "I thought if they were going to die, at least they should know that people were with them all over the world." But if the inmate rank and file thought they were going to die why did they act on the belief that they faced rubber bullets?

Another committee member added, after the hostages and inmates had been killed by very unrubber bullets, "I knew I should have . . . gone to the microphone and said: 'they're saying things here that they may believe, but there's no hope that you're gonna get complete amnesty.' I didn't have the courage to say that to that particular crowd."

Inmates are normally aware that taking hostages is an act of war and that officials feel little hesitation in using deadly force. Twenty-six of their 28 demands had been accepted by Commissioner Oswald. Yet they played the game of preparing to cut the hostages' throats to the end. Did the bonds of "ecstatic solidarity" so intensify the currents of magical thinking that many inmates literally ceased to be themselves?

(4) Social Bluff

When the showdown came, the hostages' throats were not cut despite the elaborate preparations and reiterated threats. The State police acted as if they were convinced that the inmates were not bluffing by unleashing a deadly hail of shotgun pellets the moment they enetered D-yard. (I doubt one could make a convincing case that the leaders meant what they said but were frightened or deterred.)

The everyday world of the prison is an interpersonal jungle and bluff in the form of "front" is a familiar form of brazen effrontery in which the winner maintains his "cool" and the loser has himself locked securely in a cell. In social bluff, the rhetoric of intransigence is essential, for the game is lost if contrary verbalizations surface. It appears that an element of social bluff is needed to explain the final denouement.

Social bluff is treated humorously in the works of Tom Wolfe, who provides telling examples of how poverty officials elicited stereotyped threats from clients who quickly caught on. For a good salary, one of the officials—the Flak Catcher—assumed the ignoble but socially useful role of a good natured but truly frightened bureaucrat. Day-after-miserable-day he sallied forth to be "Mau-Maued" by the demonstrators who assumed the role of angry blacks with theatrical triumph.

When social bluff enters the prison, comedy is replaced by tragedy. The outside negotiating committee was dominated by persons suggested by the militant leadership. This committee had a middle group of poverty lawyers and politicians. The members chosen by the Governor had no influence on the currents of enthusiasm which dominated D-yard. This unprecedented committee apparently played a major role in convincing the prison officials—and perhaps the Governor—that the inmate leaders were in deadly earnest, and not bluffing, in their threats to kill the hostages.

CONCLUSION

The combination of ideology, militance, magical thinking, and social bluff which shaped collective behavior at Attica indicates that the inner, autonomous process of the prison is a myth. Unfortunately, the official investigating committees may concentrate on these purported inner "causes" and thereby come up with little of value.

By using the term "mutiny" I underscore sociologist Erving Goffman's permanent contribution. His idea of the "total institution" is still useful for the understanding the prison. Ultimately, however, the prison is not a "place" at all any more than a factory is a set of machines in a building. The prison lies at the intersection of penal law, judicial action, correctional administration, penal architecture, prison reform movements, legislative enactment, professional treatment ideology, social research, generalized public beliefs, and broad political moods. All of these would have to be taken into account before a final version of the events at Attica can be understood.

17

TASK FORCE REPORT ON VIOLENCE

CALIFORNIA DEPARTMENT OF CORRECTIONS

INTRODUCTION

Violent behavior has always been a major concern of the California Department of Corrections. This is the fourth major study of the problem completed during the past ten years. ,Violence in prison ranges in scope from large groups of inmates striking out at each other or at the institution administration to individual actions in which one prisoner seeks revenge against another.

The nature of the violence problem in California prisons has changed dramatically over a short period of time. As recently as 1965, a major report on prison violence made no mention of the large, well-organized gangs or of the revolutionary groups that have been serious sources of prison violence in the past four years.

The way in which violence is expressed has also changed. Confrontations involving large groups of inmates as in the 1967 racial disturbance at San Quentin have been replaced by the hit-run tactics of guerrilla warfare. Assaults on employees prior to 1970 were typically the unplanned results of escapes or other incidents that prison staff were attempting to control. Since 1970, violence against staff has had an increasingly deliberate, ideological character.

From 1960 through 1968, the number of violent incidents and the rate per 100 inmate population fluctuated without any particular trend. Beginning in 1969, both the number and the rate of incidents increased steadily through 1973. The following table shows the increase in all incidents with focus on the most dramatic types of violence—stabbings involving inmates and assaults on employees.

The Department of Corrections' response to the violence of 1970 and 1971 was to maintain generally normal institutional operations,

Source: From the Task Force to Study Violence, *Report and Recommendations*(Sacramento: California Department of Corrections, May 1974), mimeo., pp. 1-15.

TABLE 12

Calendar Year	Total Incidents*		Inmates Stabbed		Employees Assaulted	
	Number	Rate Per 100 Average Institution Population	Total	Fatal	Total	Fatal
1969	303	1.08	56	12	32	—
1970	366	1.36	66	7	59	2
1971	466	1.96	110	13	67	7
1972	592	3.04	168	32	55	1
1973	778	3.64	179	15	84	1

*All incidents, including stabbings.
Note: Lock-up of 4 medium prisons, December 1, 1973, affected 1973 figures.

but with increased staff, installation of alarm systems and some structural modifications to increase safety of operation.

During 1973, the Director of Corrections took three major actions in response to a continuing increase in violence. In the summer of 1973, aggressive leaders of the Mexican Mafia and the Nuestra Familia gangs were segregated from the general prison population in an effort to control the extensive violence originating in the rivalry of these two groups.

In November 1973, the Director created the task force to study violence and directed that a thorough study of all aspects of prison violence be made to determine what solutions could be applied to the problem.

However, continuing violence made immediate action necessary and on December 1, 1973, the Director of Corrections ordered an unprecedented general lock-up of all inmates at San Quentin, Folsom, Deuel Vocational Institution and the Correctional Training Facility. The California Medical Facility was also under a general lock-up for a few days, but violence at this specialized institution involved a smaller segment of the inmate population than at the other four institutions.

These control measures resulted in an immediate reduction in the amount and seriousness of violence, but temporary closing of all but essential institution operations was necessary. As of June 1974, the four institutions continue in the process of cautiously reopening inmate programs and activities to the extent that safety requirements will permit.

The discussion section which follows the summary of recommendations will consider in greater detail the problems of current prison violence and methods of control.

SUMMARY OF RECOMMENDATIONS

Safety and Security Recommendations

1. The task force endorses a policy of separately confining and closely controlling violent inmates so that those who require less strict management can serve their sentences and participate safely in an extended range of constructive activities.

2. Control of destructive inmates in secure housing requires:
   a. Classification and review procedures that insure the limiting of such confinement to inmates who present a definite, direct threat to safety and security.
   b. Frequent inspection of security housing units to maintain the highest possible levels of living conditions, including cleanliness, adequacy of clothing, frequency of exercise and bathing, and access to correctional counselor and psychiatric services.
   c. Availability of increased amount of reading materials, radio and television programming, educational courses and other self-help programs.
   d. Knowledge by each inmate in security housing of the choices open to him and what he can do to accelerate release from such housing.

3. Increased resources must be invested in recruitment, selection, training and supervision of correctional officers:
   a. The equivalent of one full position at each institution should be assigned to the recruitment and selection of capable officers with emphasis on increasing the recruitment of minority officers.
   b. Solutions should be sought for the major problem of obtaining housing for entry-level employees in remote or high-cost areas.
   c. Increased resources should be assigned to correctional officer training with emphasis in the following areas:
      (1) Early development in each officer of an objective, professional job capability in which a thorough understanding of Departmental policies and procedures is applied in a manner that maintains human dignity.
      (2) Accelerate development of employee understanding of inmate problems and perspectives through the use of inmates or former inmates in training process.
   d. The direct supervision of correctional officers during the probationary period should be increased to insure that this time is an active part of the selection process and not merely passive confirmation of initial testing.
   e. The correctional officer must be an active manager of inmates:
      (1) There should be increased involvement of the correctional officer in management decisions made about inmates in his charge.

(2) There should be a continuing program of testing management innovations in suitable small institutional units.

f. Supervisory effectiveness and accountability must be increased:
  (1) Every officer and particularly every probationary officer should have one supervisor who is accountable for his training progress.
  (2) Administrative staff at all levels must increase their contact with line employees at the employee's work station.
  (3) Administrative and supervisory staff should work in line positions periodically to increase their sensitivity to employee problems.

4. The Department should have an on-going design program in which there would be a continuous development of institutional unit plans that allow for safe, humane housing with maximum program involvement for prisoners at all levels of difficulty.

5. Incident reports should contain a check-off section so that there can be a department-wide monitoring of incidents in terms of basic causes, locations, types of weapons and other data relevant to control and detection of trends.

6. The Department should explore the possibilities of an index of violence for institution populations with an objective of detecting climinates or population mixes conducive to violent outbreaks.

7. The Department should establish a fact finding group composed of Departmental employees trained in conflict resolution techniques that can be sent to problem areas to help resolve situations in early stages of development.

8. A most important improvement in institutional climate should be achieved by making available to every inmate full employment and training at private industry standards of production coupled with levels of pay and other means of compensation sufficient to be genuine incentives.
  a. Top inmate pay should be raised at least to the level of the maximum canteen draw.
  b. Authorization should be sought for pilot projects in paying inmates at industry wage standards.
  c. The Department should initiate exploration of means of modifying present restrictions on industrial operations.

9. Major immediate efforts must be made to improve the quality of communication between staff and inmates and between both groups and the correctional administration:
  a. There needs to be greatly increased contact on-the-job between line employees, inmates and administrators.
  b. Motivated inmates should be used in the training and orientation of employees.
  c. There needs to be active encouragement, including pay provisions, of employee-inmate discussion groups, "bull" sessions, planning committees, and special interest groups.

  d. Each institution should have a continuously operating rumor control system using written newsbriefs and the institutional radio system to provide employees and inmates with immediate news of incidents, policy changes and events of interest on a daily basis or as needed.

  e. The Department should evaluate current innovations in staff-inmate problem-solving groups and should initiate pilot projects to test other means of providing healthy inmate-administration communication.

10. Each institution should have a Special Problems Person at the Correctional Administrator level who would function with one or more staff assistants as appeals person, referral service and problem-solver with emphasis on increasing line employee ability to deal with the human problems of inmates.

11. The scarcity in institutions of nearly all goods and services must be changed by making it possible for every inmate to earn extra benefits:

  a. All inmates doing useful work should be paid with more adequate pay going for dirty, difficult or high production work as opposed to easy jobs such as inmate clerk positions.

  b. Fiscal incentives should be provided for reduction in waste of state property.

  c. A pilot study should be initiated in a smaller institution of the effects of giving inmates a monetary allowance instead of state-supplied goods so that they could purchase clothing and supply items of their own choice.

12. The present drab, grey, dirty, monotonous look of most prisons and their prisoners needs replacement by a less deadening and more varied visual environment:

  a. The institution should permit personalization of living quarters and should provide or sell the necessary paint and materials.

  b. Restrictions on inmate dress and grooming variations should be removed except for those absolutely required by security and sanitation.

  c. Institutions should be repainted in accordance with modern color standards, including use of both interior and exterior murals.

13. The Department should increase the resources allotted to involving families in the inmate's programs and planning for the future:

  a. Family visiting facilities in security areas should be increased so that most medium custody inmates can participate.

  b. The Department should initiate a pilot program at one institution permitting an inmate's fiancee to visit overnight.

  c. Sufficient counseling staff should be provided so that institutions can take the initiative in routinely contacting inmate families for planning and problem-solving with the inmate.

  d. The institution should aid in the transportation of inmate visitors from common carrier terminals to institutions and from urban areas to rurally located prisons.

14. There should be increased supervisory emphasis on effective, timely and considerate handling of personal services to inmates, such as mail, visits, phone calls, death messages, and the handling of personal property.

15. The task force affirms the value of properly supervised inmate activity and interest groups as a means of education, increasing self-esteem and channeling aggression with the following precautions:
    a. Paid sponsorship and supervision must be provided for the safe operation of such groups.
    b. The activity program must be administered by a member of the institutional executive staff and not delegated to employees with limited power and experience.
    c. The number of outside guests should be no more than can be effectively supervised by the staff available, with each guest contributing to the group activity rather than being involved in private contacts with individual inmates.
    d. Screening of guests prior to approval should be done carefully without regard to the amount of time this may take.
    e. In-service training should include presentations of the activities and goals of inmate groups by inmate participants.

16. The Department should re-emphasize the value of an effective, comprehensive re-entry program in keeping inmates attention focused on their future in the outside world rather than upon the artificial prison world.

Increasing Inmate Self-Determination

17. The variety and range of incentives that inmates can earn through their own actions should be increased. All programs and activities should be organized around a series of short-range goals that can be reached by inmates who perform specific and well-defined actions.

18. The inmate's ability to predict and to modify the length of sentence must be increased:
    a. Inmates should receive at least a tentative release date as soon as possible.
    b. Each inmate should have a written statement of the steps he can take to retain, advance or lose his release date.
    c. Inmates need to know more accurately how much additional time they may serve as a consequence of unsuitable behavior, the threat of a life sentence being unreasonable for minor infractions related to the special conditions of the prison culture.
    d. Inmates without parole dates should be informed of the realistic requirements he must meet in order to obtain a release date.

19. Inmate participation in classification decisions should be increased:
    a. The classification process should be individualized with program plans being made with the inmate, not done to him.

b. Information on which decisions about an inmate are based should
be available to the inmate, subject only to safety considerations.

c. Inmates should receive clear written statements concerning what
they are expected to do in the institution including an estimate of
the things they must do or the time they must wait before moving from one custodial or program classification to another.

General Recommendation

20. The Department of Corrections should establish a permanent committee to coordinate the planning and implementation of the task
force recommendations. The committee should include fiscal and
legislative representation.

DISCUSSION OF RECOMMENDATIONS

General Discussion

The task force recommendations contain no previously unknown
solutions to the problem of violence and no radically innovative programs are suggested. Nearly all the recommended programs are in
operation to some degree at one or more institutions. The task force
findings serve to reaffirm the value of some programs, to encourage
fuller implementation of others, and to suggest assignment of increased resources in certain areas.

Remedies for the basic causes of prison violence are no more
easily available than are solutions to the problem of violence in the
outside society. That the violence in both areas may have common
sources is suggested by the fact that the rise in California prison violence during the past five years is matched by a similar increase in the
community. The appearance of revolutionary violence in the prisons
was preceded by similar acts in the community. The tensions between
races and cultures are not apt to be alleviated in the prisons much before they are remedied in the outside society.

The understanding that prison violence has causes both within
the correctional system and in the larger outside community must
accompany attempts to cope with the problem. There is no doubt
that frustrations inherent in prison life are responsible for some violence and that prisons sometimes provide situations in which violence
can easily occur. Critics of the correctional system over-emphasize
this one type of causation, ignoring the fact that an earlier source of
attitudes leading to prison violence is in the family and community
experiences of the inmates; some 71 percent of the inmates received

in 1973 by the California prison system having had a history of violence prior to their incarceration. Instead of creating unique kinds of
hostility, the compact prison setting concentrates the tension and
anger that exists in a more dilute form in the outside community,
racial tensions being one example of this process. In some cases,
there may be a direct carrying of violence from the community into
the prison and from the prison back into the community as has been
demonstrated in the activities of groups advocating violent solutions
to social problems.

Changes in social situations and in community attitudes also have
a bearing on prison violence. Correctional management is going
through a continuing crisis that contains many of the same elements
found in similar upheavals in the universities, the military, and the
community. There has been questioning of long-accepted principles
and practices, probing into the operations of the system by interested citizens who range from cautiously conservative to irresponsibly
violent, involvement by the courts in changing management procedures, and demands by those who form the base of the system for a
greater voice in decisions affecting them, all of these elements being
intensified by the slowness of the system to react with adequate measures. The impact of these factors on correctional staff has been to
create confusion about their roles and uncertainty about their
authority.

Some specific social changes have complicated the management
of correctional institutions. The increased use of community-based
correctional programs, such as probation, has reduced the percentage
of convicted felons sent to prison from 30 percent to around 10 percent. As contrasted with ten years ago, the prisons now receive fewer
property offenders, more armed robbers, fewer skilled craftsmen,
fewer genuine first termers and more "state-raised" offenders who
have been in the criminal justice system for most of their lives and
who have failed to respond to a variety of community and institutional programs.

Another change reported by both penologists and prisoners is an
age factor that divides both staff and inmates into younger and older
segments. As one report states: "The old ways of doing time have
broken down and younger prisoners do not agree with older on how
to do time." Younger prisoners are less apt to reach an accommodation with officers, are more apt to seek confrontation and are more
inclined to violent radicalism. The prisoner of 20 years ago upheld
the American political/economic system even as he was looting it;
whereas, increasing numbers of young prisoners today express interest in ideologies advocating violent destruction of the present system.

Not only are the social components of prison violence complex, but both the immediate causes and the ways of expressing violence vary. For the purposes of this report, prison violence has been placed under four major headings, each representing a different aspect of the problem and each probably requiring a different solution.

(1) Violence As A Function Of A Closed Prison Society

This includes violence associated with gambling, debts, homosexual behavior, crowded living conditions, poor institutional design, inability of employees to supervise properly, life style and cultural-racial incompatibilities, time-setting policies and the cumbersome way a bureaucracy attempts to meet human needs. Expression of this type of violence ranges from general prisoner uprisings and large-scale racial disturbances to individual acts of vengeance. Prisoners are usually the victims.

Improving the prison environment, increasing incentives, improving staff training and reducing inequities can reduce this type of violence, although the realities of incarcerating difficult people against their will make it unlikely that it can be eliminated entirely.

(2) Violence As A Function Of Organized Gangs

While the elements listed in category (1) may contribute to the creation of gangs and cliques, once established a gang may take on characteristics that persist for years under a variety of leaders. A quasi-military organization structure may be used to lend continuity to the gang and provide for assumption of power by second-level leaders if the top leadership is segregated. Although membership in aggressive gangs and cliques involves probably no more than 2 percent of the total male felon population, the tight organization and discipline of these groups enable them to dominate much larger populations of unorganized inmates. Inmates have been the primary targets of the gangs, whose activities are the largest single source of assaults and deaths in the institutions. Gang actions have been the cause of death and injury in some otherwise violence-free institutions, such as the California Conservation Center at Susanville. Gangs are organized around racial/ethnic lines with the Mexican-American groups having the largest membership.

Because of the racial/ethnic orientation, any friction between gangs has the potential of growing into a large-scale racial conflict. Strict controls and segregation of gang leaders and enforcers is necessary to control their violence. System improvements may serve to limit recruitment of followers. It must be noted, however, that gang activities in urban areas have been increasing in recent years so that the impulse to form gangs may be independent of benefits available to inmates.

(3) Violence As A Function of Revolutionary/Retaliatory Ideology

This source of prison violence involves very small groups whose very existence as well as membership may be unknown to prison staff until an incident occurs. These groups are less stable than the organized gangs, forming and disbanding in secret under different names and with different participants. Continuity is provided by a common ideology with heavy emphasis on the rhetoric of revolutionary violence. Group leadership is sometimes politically sophisticated, but more often is not. There is active encouragement from like-minded groups in the outside community who provide moral support, legal aid, free literature, and attractive visitors for politically cooperative prisoners. Attempts have been made to turn the organized gangs into politically violent groups with employees as their targets instead of inmates. Both inmates and employees have been victims of revolutionary/retaliatory violence. Most, if not all murders of prison employees since 1970, can be attributed to this source of violence.

Reduction of this problem appears to involve strict control of aggressive leaders. System improvements may serve to limit recruitment of supporters.

(4) Violence As A Function of Individual Emotional Disturbance

Although contributing little to current violence in most institutions, this source of violence contributes significantly to the number of assaults at institutions handling psychiatrically disturbed inmates.

In large crowded institutions, the actions of an inmate in an irrational state can trigger violent responses in other inmates. The clumsy handling of a disturbed inmate by poorly trained staff can also create a dangerous situation. One penologist suggests that some violent inmate groups have formed because of an inmate leader's ability to instill his paranoid delusions into other prisoners.

Proper staff training, adequate physical facilities, good diagnosis and availability of psychiatric treatment resources are means of reducing this type of violence.

SPECIFIC PROGRAMS IN CORRECTIONAL INSTITUTIONS

INTRODUCTION

In the United States, as in other parts of the world, there has been considerable unrest in the prison establishment. There have been manifestations in the form of riots as well as movements and pressure groups. There were riots in the past, but these were usually attributed to the fact that an essentially good system was not working properly. It was generally accepted that the "model" (or theory) was perfectly correct and effective, as well as morally sound, and that the fault was only in the application of the theory. Prisoners could and indeed should be reformed; and there was no great difficulty in reconciling the ideas of punishment with those of rehabilitation.

The courts, following the general stream of thought, refused until quite recently to become involved in such concerns as prisoners' rights, matters of parole or conditions in jails. However, a number of landmark cases and decisions have recently set a very different trend. There are also many cases pending that relate to various aspects of prisoners' rights; the Constitution and its Amendments are the basis for many of these actions. Social action groups are devoting more time and effort to the preparation of arguments, briefs and pamphlets advocating that certain conditions be viewed as "rights" of prisoners. When privileges have been granted, demands have followed to formalize these into codes of "rights" and to provide for their protection by law.

The distinction between a privilege and a right, although relatively clear in philosophical terms, is, in practical situations, often a matter of debate. Until recently it could be doubted that prisoners had any rights. The development of a prison system has come to be accepted as a necessary means of social control, but the ethical implications of that system have been inadequately studied. Not too long ago, following a finding of guilt, offenders were disposed of by beheading or hanging. If they were lucky, they were whipped or maimed and then set free. Prisons were used to hold persons prior to trial: the idea of incarceration as a punishment (or as a "treatment") that is expected to lead to reform is approximately 200 years old.

The reasoning that the guilty offender was "lucky" to get away with his life has undergirded the strong resistance to change exhibited in the thinking and action of the courts and of all others concerned with the disposition of criminals. In recent years, however, there have been several attempts to confront fundamental issues. Some of these efforts are reflected in this book.

The recency of these trends cannot be too strongly emphasized. As late as 1871 the "lucky-to-be-alive" concept was clearly evinced in a Supreme Court ruling that referred to the offender as the "slave of the state."[1] The transition from the earlier thinking to the "treatment" philosophy only reinforced the reasoning that the courts should avoid arguments about prisoners' conditions. Professionals versed in the rationale of "treatment," rather than the courts, now became the authorities.

The idea that an offender has a "right to know" the reasons for decisions made about him is one aspect of the issue of rights and privileges of offenders that has already had a considerable impact and seems likely to have a continuing effect. "Theirs [is] not to reason why . . ." is no longer accepted as an appropriate attitude toward the status of the offender, petitioner or prisoner. Several legislatures have required that reasons be given for rulings made by various decision makers in the criminal justice system. Books highly critical of determinations made without any statement of policy have been published. Model acts, pamphlets and other media resources are widely available, as are documents recording important individual and class action cases. Among the latter cases, the dissenting opinions should not be disregarded.

The first reading in this section, by the National Council on Crime and Delinquency, presents the argument for legislation on prisoners' rights and proposes a "model act." The difficulties involved in distinguishing between rights and privileges may be noted in the second selection, "Classification of Offenders," by the National Advisory Commission on Criminal Justice Standards and Goals. One of the main ways in which prisoners' privileges (and rights?) may be influenced by the penal administrator is through the classification system.

Veteran correctional administrator Paul W. Keve examines prison work, and Professor Daniel Glaser investigates educational resources in prisons. Readers may find that these articles provoke a variety of ethical questions. For example, should compulsory education in penal institutions be restricted to minors, as in the community at large, or could a case be made for extending the age limit? If so, to what age? If a person in prison may refuse work, may he also refuse to attend classes?

A prison is a community, and as such is not immune to problems and disturbances. What kinds of disciplinary procedures should be utilized? What kinds of safeguards are necessary for the control of crime

---

1. Virginia Supreme Court: Ruffin v. Commonwealth, 62 Va. 790, 796, 1871.

within the prison? These issues are touched on in the selection by Professor Daniel Glaser.

There are as many ideas on how to run a prison as there are on how to conduct a business, a school or any other venture. A few ideas have gained some currency, among which are inmate self-government and a form of participatory democracy. Kentucky correctional administrator J. E. Baker explores these examples of current thinking and practice in his article.

We are familiar with the concept of the "right to work" in the context of unrestricted access to employment. The function of work in prisons has been seen in different lights in different countries of the world. In some countries it has been held that incarcerated offenders should work to pay for the costs of their imprisonment. The type of service might vary from "labor camp" activity to work performed inside the prison for a nearby manufacturer. In still other countries where there are strong labor unions, the work available to prisoners has been severely restricted on the grounds of "unfair competition" with the free labor force.

Some theoretical and practical difficulties relative to the utilization of labor are considered in the selection by sociologist Elmer H. Johnson.

The relationship between life inside and life outside of prison has been a focus of attention for many investigators. Since almost all offenders are at some time released, whether by parole, statutory release or other measures, new ideas to ease the transition are continually being developed. One recent attempt to involve the inmate in planning for his own future is known as Mutual Agreement Programming, and is described by the American Correctional Association. The method was begun experimentally in 1972 in three states (Arizona, Wisconsin and California) and is now flourishing in Wisconsin, Michigan and a dozen or so other states.

A note of warning about the enthusiasm that so often attends any new method of dealing with offenders is sounded in "Prerelease Program Evaluation" by California correctional officials Norman Holt and Rudy Renteria.

A different approach is presented in the State of Minnesota report on an "Ombudsman for Corrections." It implements the concept of fairness and equity in our dealings with offenders by providing a mechanism for handling issues and complaints that are not readily addressed by bureaucratic systems.

Size was at one time considered a vital factor in effective administration. Some ways of coping with the problem of size are described by Robert B. Levinson and Roy E. Gerard of the Federal Bureau of Prisons.

18

MINIMUM STANDARDS FOR THE PROTECTION OF RIGHTS OF PRISONERS

NATIONAL COUNCIL ON CRIME AND DELINQUENCY

THE NEED FOR A STATUTE

Over the years we received many communications from prisoners and from their relatives and friends. Most of them were requests for help: e.g., assistance of counsel, assistance in understanding what had happened and what procedures were to be expected, help in their being considered for parole, and help in obtaining a job so that the prisoner could be released on parole.

Nowadays the communications sent by prisoners (or their attorneys) to us—and to others, including the courts—are of a different order. Especially in the last half-dozen years they have been demanding recognition of the rights of prisoners as persons and citizens (citizenship is not lost upon conviction) and a halt to abuses against them. In the past little attention was paid to prisoner complaints of abuses and violations of their rights. Courts adhered to what a leading article in the *Yale Law Journal* in 1963 called the "hands-off doctrine," citing a United States court which said: "Courts are without power to supervise prison administration or to interfere with the ordinary prison rules or regulations."[1]

The "hands-off" doctrine is no longer an inviolate rule. Courts have begun to supervise prison administration to protect prisoners against abuse and to protect their basic rights, the sources of which are specific provisions of the Constitution. Thus the right to practice one's religion in prison has been protected, the most significant cases being those brought by Black Muslims. The cases are significant also in that the prisoners who violated institutional rules regulating the

Source: From "A Model Act to Provide for Minimum Standards for the Protection of Rights of Prisoners", *Crime and Delinquency* 18, 1(January 1972): 4-14. Reprinted by permission of the National Council on Crime and Delinquency.

practice of religion and other matters were punished by whipping or solitary confinement or both. The conditions of solitary confinement were often horrendously cruel. In numerous cases, the courts enjoined solitary confinement, sometimes retaining jurisdiction while awaiting compliance by the prison administration with the court-ordered changes. The Eighth Amendment prohibition against cruel and unusual punishment was applied in these cases; a federal court, for example, ruled that any whipping of a prisoner was a violation of the Eighth Amendment.

Newer cases deal with a different order of prisoner rights. They apply the spirit of *Coffin v. Reichard,* a federal case which declared that "a prisoner retains all the rights of an ordinary citizen except those expressly, or by necessary implication, taken from him by law."[2]

Thus censorship, often needless and degrading, as well as burdensome to the institution, has now come under examination. A federal court said recently that prison authorities "possess no power of censorship"; it held that they could not bar *Fortune News,* the newsletter of the Fortune Society, an organization aimed at creating greater public awareness of the prison system. It said:

> Only a compelling state interest centering about prison security, or a clear and present danger of a breach of prison discipline, or some substantial interference with orderly institutional administration can justify curtailment of a prisoner's constitutional rights. . . . Censorship is utterly foreign to our way of life; it smacks of dictatorship.[3]

Another court has ruled that "the reading of any outgoing mail from the inmates is . . . in violation of the First Amendment . . . unless pursuant to a duly obtained search warrant." For security reasons it allowed opening of incoming mail, except for mail from attorneys, courts, and public officials.[4]

Generally, however, the courts tend to be cautious about supervision of prisons and, more often than not, reiterate the hands-off doctrine. The breach is widening, but the flow of cases is not gushing.

What the Act Does

To establish the principle of *Coffin v. Reichard,* Section 1 of the Model Act contains language corresponding to that quoted above where the case is referred to.

As an agency concerned with prison reform, we believe that courts concerning themselves with prison abuses are acting properly, not only because they are legally sound in applying the Constitution and in interpreting the nature of imprisonment but also because the abuses of rights are serious. Recent events or disclosures include mass murder of prisoners, widespread self-multilation in protest against inhuman conditions, and destructive riots. The courts have a responsibility to deal with these conditions, and needed prison reform is occurring as a result of the decisions.

Such action by the courts also supports administrative efforts to correct abuses. Some administrators and wardens have made changes to eliminate abuses without any prodding by courts; but change is difficult, and custodial staff may resist changes that reduce their power. It sometimes also happens that a well-prepared suit and a full hearing may reveal not only abuses but their remedies. Sometimes a prisoner's suit results in a court-supervised conference between complainant and defandant at which agreement on changes is followed by dismissal of the suit.[5] The model statute is intended to encourage administrators to make changes without suit, but where this does not occur, it gives courts the necessary jurisdiction.

Briefly this act states the most onerous abuses occurring in prisons and specifies the courts' powers to deal with them. To those who say that its enactment would further burden the courts, there are two answers:

1. If the abuses exist and the violations of rights are amenable to law, the courts *must* take jurisdiction, just as they do with persons who are not in prison and whose litigation also "burdens the courts."

2. What burdens the courts is not their power to correct an abuse but rather the abuse itself. When the abuses cease or become less heinous, fewer writs will be brought to the courts. But for as long a time as attention is needed, it will be far better to have writs than riots. In 1970 a combination of court decisions and prison riots led the New York legislature to enact a law whose language is somewhat similar to ours:

No inmate in the care or custody of the department [of correction]
shall be subjected to degrading treatment, and no officer or other employee
of the department shall inflict any blows whatever upon any inmate, unless in self-defense, or to suppress a revolt or insurrection.

The act also goes on to set humane standards for inmates held in confinement in a cell or room apart from other inmates.[6]

Solitary confinement has been the subject of a number of suits, and in many instances prisoners have been ordered released from solitary. In some of these cases the courts have laid down rules that must be followed with respect to conditions in solitary. Solitary confinement has not been declared unconstitutional by any court; nevertheless, it is a destructive experience, probably producing the very opposite of what is intended and surely not rehabilitative. It is justified only where a prisoner requires temporary restraint because of his destructive, irrational pattern at the moment. Section 3 establishes the standards governing its special use.

As already noted, a number of courts have used injunctions and other means of redress.[7] Section 6, which deals with remedies, also authorizes a court to prohibit further commitments to an institution.

Many observers of the relationship between courts and prisons have noted that what the court expects in ordering a commitment—namely, a rehabilitative program—may be quite different from what actually occurs in the institution. Some advocate that, to deal with this discrepancy, judges should be required to visit the institutions to which they commit persons. Though this may well be desirable, it will not of itself provide a remedy. A judge may decide not to commit to a particular institution whose faults he has become familiar with, but other judges will not come to the same conclusion. What Section 6 provides is that where a court makes a finding of a pattern of violation of rights, it may declare the institution "off limits" for further commitments until certain conditions are corrected. Some administrative agencies such as state departments of correction have this power with respect to local jails.

Under some correction acts local jails may also be ordered closed, and Section 6 also gives this power to a court when the necessary findings have been made. Recently a court exercised this power where the conditions were grave; it did not close the institution but allowed it a few months to correct the abuses, meanwhile retaining jurisdiction.

In 1970 the atrocities in the Arkansas prison system led to a decision that the entire system was unconstitutionally operated and could be closed. The prisoners' petition maintained that any confinement in the system was cruel and unusual punishment. The federal district court held:

> As far as the Court is aware, this is the first time that convicts have attacked an entire penitentiary system. . . . The Court sustains the claim that conditions and practices in the Penitentiary System are such that confinement of persons therein amounts to a cruel and unusual punishment prohibited by the Eighth and Fourteenth Amendments.

The decision did not order the immediate closing of the institutions; instead the court, retaining jurisdiction, gave the authorities time to eliminate the abuses.[8]

In Philadelphia the Court of Common Pleas found that conditions in the city's Holmesburg Prison were bad enough for the entire institution to be condemned. It ordered the transfer of two prisoners who had filed writs of habeas corpus, and it held jurisdiction for thirty days to enable the prison administration to eliminate the abuses, in default of which it would hear petitions from any prisoners. "Conditions in the prison," it said, "constitute cruel and inhuman punishment.[9]

Another court, in New Mexico, ordered release from the Gallup Detention Center to bring the number of prisoners down to sixty and issued an injunction barring any commitments that would raise the number to more than sixty.[10]

In most instances it is the prisoner's petition to a court that uncovers inhuman treatment. Filing such a petition and presenting sufficient proof face many obstacles. A simpler procedure for prisoner complaints—one that would be more accessible to prisoners and closer to the prison administrator—is established in Section 5, which provides for an autonomous "ombudsman" agency empowered to receive and act on prisoner grievances.[11]

Discovery can also be aided by citizen visitors to institutions. The use of prison visiting has been cited by Chief Justice Warren E. Burger, who noted on one occasion that in the Netherlands a team of trained people visit prisons regularly to "flush out the rare case of miscarriage of justice and the larger number of cases in which the prisoner has some valid complaint."[12] Addressing the Association of the Bar of the City of New York, he commented that lawyers also assume responsibility for reform of prisons:

Where do you begin? The same way you prepare a case. By getting all the facts, visiting the scene if necessary, and then organizing the evidence. In this area most of the facts are available at the prison and from prison authorities. A visit to most prisons will make you a zealot for prison reform. If you will form a fact-finding party of one judge and two or three lawyers you will soon discover that 75-80 per cent of all prisoners are in substandard institutions.

A prison visiting program has been instituted by the Young Lawyers Section of the American Bar Association.[13]

What the Act Does *Not* Attempt to Do

The purposes set forth above, though important, are quite limited. The act does *not* undertake specification of prison treatment programs that are desirable or should be mandatory, which is the purview of the statutes governing a state department of correction and the administration of prisons. Thus NCCD's Standard Act for State Correctional Services lists numerous programs—vocational training, religion, medical services, etc.—that should or must be given by state departments.[14]

These statutes are the proper locale for a direct statement of practices that are prohibited (e.g., corporal punishment, forbidden in the Standard Act for State Correctional Services) and practices that must be regulated (e.g., solitary confinement—specifically, the conditions governing its use).

Some of these statutes also have provisions for inspection of institutions and their closure by administrators. The Model Act does not attempt to add to or affect such provisions. Administrators and wardens have the primary obligation to conduct satisfactory institutions, and the statutes should support their power to do so. When they fail, the Model Act is applicable.

Although the Act recognizes suits by prisoners, it does not undertake to detail any procedural requirements, and it does not deal with assistance of counsel to prisoners in preparation of suits. Such assistance is now most unsatisfactory. "Jailhouse lawyers"—inmates with claimed expertise of a kind—are often the only help a prisoner has, and the courts have not yet required any more. Unfortunately, the drafters of model legislation for public defender services have failed to include the obligation to assist prisoners.

In one prisoner's suit a United States Court of Appeals addressed itself to the clogging of the courts by many prisoners' petitions, most of them perhaps without legal merit, so poorly drawn that the time of the courts and others is wasted but nevertheless leaving unanswered the question of whether legal assistance might have disclosed a meritorious claim. The Court said:

> In the last analysis, however, the problem of petitions for collateral review that are frivolous, incoherent, false because copied slavishly from winning patterns, or otherwise lacking real merit, seems likely to plague the courts until a system is established for providing legal counsel to . . . prison inmates on a reasonably broad basis.[15]

AN ACT
TO PROVIDE FOR MINIMUM STANDARDS FOR THE PROTECTION OF RIGHTS OF PRISONERS

§ 1. Declaration of Purpose and Intent

The provisions of this Act shall be liberally construed to promote the intent of the Legislature as follows:

(a) The central principle underlying all rules, regulations, procedures, and practices relating to persons imprisoned in accordance with law shall be that such persons shall retain all rights of an ordinary citizen, except those expressly or by necessary implication taken by law.

(b) Such rights include but are not necessarily limited to nutritious food in adequate quantities; medical care; provision for an acceptable level of sanitation, ventilation, light, and a generally healthful environment; housing, providing for not less than fifty square feet of floor space in any confined sleeping area; reasonable opportunities for physical exercise and recreational activities; and protection against any physical or psychological abuse or unnecessary indignity.

(c) Persons in control of custodial facilities for prisoners shall be held responsible for maintaining minimum standards and shall make use of every resource available to them to prevent inhumane treatment of prisoners by employees, other prisoners, or any other persons.

(d) Measures shall be instituted and maintained within such facilities to protect against suicide or other self-destructive acts.

(e) All reasonable methods shall be used to protect against the theft or destruction of such personal property of prisoners as may be permitted in the institution.

§ 2. Inhumane Treatment Prohibited

Inhumane treatment includes but is not limited to the following acts or activities and is hereby prohibited:

(a) Striking, whipping, or otherwise imposing physical pain upon a prisoner as a measure of punishment.

(b) Any use of physical force by an employee except that which may be necessary for self-defense, to prevent or stop assault by one prisoner upon another person, and for prevention of riot or escape.

(c) Sexual or other assaults, by personnel or inmates.

(d) Any punitive or restrictive measure taken by the management or personnel in retaliation for assertion of rights.

(e) Any measure intended to degrade the prisoner, including insults and verbal abuse.

(f) Any discriminatory treatment based upon the prisoner's race, religion, nationality, or political beliefs.

§ 3. Isolation in Solitary Confinement[16]

A prisoner may be placed in solitary confinement—segregation in a special cell or room—only under the following conditions:

(a) During such confinement, the prisoner shall receive daily at least 2,500 calories of food in the normal diet of prisoners not in isolation.

(b) The cell in which the prisoner is confined in solitary shall be at least as large as other cells in the institution and shall be adequately lighted during daylight hours. All of the necessities of civilized existence, such as a toilet, bedding, and water for drinking and washing, shall be provided. Normal room temperatures for comfortable living shall be maintained. If any of these necessities are removed temporarily, such removal shall be only to prevent suicide or self-destructive acts, or damage to the cell and its equipment.

(c) Under no circumstances shall a prisoner confined in solitary be deprived of normal prison clothing except for his own protection. If any such deprivation is temporarily necessary, he shall be provided with body clothing and bedding adequate to protect his health.

(d) A prisoner may not be confined in a solitary cell for punishment, and may be so confined only under conditions of emergency for his own protection or that of personnel or other prisoners. Confinement under such circumstances shall not be continued for longer than is necessary for the emergency. A prisoner's right to communicate with his attorney or the person or agency provided for in Section 5 to receive complaints shall not be interfered with.

(e) No prisoner shall be kept in a solitary cell for longer than one hour without the approval of the highest ranking officer on duty in the institution at the time.

(f) No prisoner may be kept in a solitary cell for any reason for longer than forty-eight hours without being examined by a medical doctor or other medical personnel under the doctor's direction.

(g) A log in a bound book shall be maintained at or near any solitary cell or cells, and employees in charge of such cell or cells shall be responsible for recording all admissions, releases, visits to the cell, and other events except those of the most routine nature.

§ 4. Disciplinary Procedure

It is the responsibility of any person or persons in charge of the management of an institution for the confinement of prisoners to develop and describe in writing a fair and orderly procedure for processing disciplinary complaints against prisoners and to establish rules, regulations, and procedures to insure the maintenance of a high standard of fairness and equity. The rules shall prescribe offenses and the punishments for them that may be imposed. Any punishment that may affect the sentence or parole eligibility (such as the loss of good-time allowance) shall not be imposed without a hearing at which the prisoner shall have a right to be present and a right to be represented by counsel or some other person of his choice. A permanent record shall be maintained of all disciplinary complaints, the hearings, and the disposition thereof.

§ 5. Grievance Procedure

The director of the State Department of Correction (or the equivalent official) shall establish a grievance procedure to which all prisoners confined within the system shall have access. Prisoners shall be entitled to report any grievance, whether or not it charges a violation of this Act, and to mail such communication to the head of the department. The grievance procedure established shall provide for an investigation (aside from any investigation made by the institution or department) of all alleged grievances by a person or agency outside of the department, and for a written report of findings to be submitted to the department and the prisoner.

§ 6. Judicial Relief

A prisoner or group of prisoners[17] alleging abuses in violation of this Act may petition [appropriate court] for relief. The court may afford any of the following remedies:

(a) It may make a finding that the allegations are without merit.

(b) It may issue an injunction, prohibitive or mandatory, or utilize any other appropriate remedy in law or equity.

(c) It may prohibit further commitments to the institution.

(d) If the abuses are found to be extensive and persistent, it may order the institution closed subject to a stay of a reasonable period, not to exceed six months, to permit the responsible authorities to correct the abuses. If the abuses are not corrected to the satisfaction of the court, it may order those prisoners who have a history of serious assaultive behavior to be transferred to another facility, and it may order the discharge of other prisoners.

§ 7. Visits to Prisoners and Institutions

The director of a department responsible for the operation of an institution or a system of institutions for the confinement of prisoners shall establish rules and regulations permitting attorneys of record, relatives, and friends to visit and talk in private with any prisoner in an institution at reasonable times and under reasonable limitations. The institution may be visited at any time by members of the state legislature, judges of the criminal or appellate courts, the attorney general, and the governor.

Any other citizen may make application to visit an institution and talk in private with prisoners if the applicant establishes a legitimate reason for such visit and if the visit is not inconsistent with the public welfare and the safety and security of the institution. The director may reject any such application if the visit or any aspect thereof would be disruptive to the program of the institution.

If application for a visit is denied, the person may apply to [court of general jurisdiction] for an order directing the head of the institution to permit the visit. Such order shall be granted after notice and hearing if it is found that (a) the person is a representative of a public concern regarding the conditions of the prison, (b) he is not a mere curiosity seeker, and (c) it is not established by the head of the institution that the visit, or any aspect of it, would disrupt the program of the institution.

19

CLASSIFICATION OF OFFENDERS

NATIONAL ADVISORY COMMISSION ON CRIMINAL JUSTICE STANDARDS AND GOALS

Theoretically, classification is a process for determining the needs and requirements of those for whom correction has been ordered and for assigning them to programs according to their needs and the existing resources. Classification is conceptualized as a system or process by which a correctional agency, unit, or component determines differential care and handling of offenders.

Most correctional classification schemes in use today are referred to as classification systems for treatment purposes, but even a cursory analysis of these schemes and the ways in which they are used reveals that they would more properly be called classification systems for management purposes. This judgment does not imply that classification for management purposes is undesirable. In fact, that may be the only useful system today, given the current state of knowledge about crime and offenders. It is important, however, that corrections begin to acknowledge the bases and purposes of classification systems that are in use.

There is another problem with trying to answer the question: Classification for what? While it is often conceded that no generally valid and useful system of classification for treatment now exists, there seems to be broad agreement within the corrections field on the desirability of finding such a system. It is also pointed out that a number of serious and dedicated social science researchers have been working for years on developing "treatment-relevant typologies" of offenders, and there is a possibility that they will reach a consensus on the basic components of a classification system and types of offenders fairly soon. It is one of the ironies of progress that just as the

Source: From *Corrections* (Washington, D.C.: U.S. Government Printing Office, 1973), pp. 197–209(editorial adaptations).

development of "treatment-relevant typologies" at last appears likely, there is growing disenchantment with the entire concept of the treatment model.

DEVELOPMENT OF CLASSIFICATION

Classification may be said to have developed in response to demands for the reform of corrections that began to be heard in England in the mid-16th century. Blasphemy, gambling, drunkenness, lewdness of officers and keepers, and their cooperation in supporting prisoners' vices were reported as commonplace in the jails and prisons. To overcome these practices, committees from time to time recommended that neophytes should be separated from hardened offenders, and that prisoners should be separated by sex, age, and type of offense. Crude as it was, this was the beginning of classification.[18]

The first practical efforts toward classification were based less on theoretical concepts regarding the cause of crime and possible ways to correct it than on the practical necessity of managing people. The early classification schemes did, in fact, eliminate many abuses of the Bedlam type of institution that preceded the modern prison. But like most innovations, this solution itself generated problems.[19]

Segregation as Classification

Traditionally, administrators of correctional agencies have taken the position that men and women and youths should be separated from each other. The "Standard Minimum Rules for the Treatment of Prisoners" adopted by the First United Nations Congress on the Prevention of Crime and Treatment of Offenders, August 30, 1955, provides an example of an allocation scheme that is characteristic of what is normally accepted as classification.

> Separation of Categories. The different categories of prisoners shall be kept in separate institutions or parts of the institution, taking account of their sex, age, criminal record, the legal reasons for their detention, and the necessities of their treatment. Thus, (a) men and women shall so far as possible be detained in separate institutions. In an institution which receives both men and women, the whole of the premises allocated to women shall be entirely separate; (b) untried prisoners shall be kept separate from convicted prisoners; (c) persons imprisoned for debt and other civil prisoners shall be kept separate from persons imprisoned by reason of criminal offense; (d) young prisoners shall be kept separate from adults.[20]

Specialization not Classification

One of the obvious trends in the history of American jails and prisons was the development of specialization as various groups of prisoners were withdrawn from the first penal institution, the jail, for incarceration in specialized institutions. Vagrants were placed in houses of correction. State institutions, under various names, were established for juvenile delinquents, insane offenders, young adults, women, Negroes, defective delinquents, misdemeanants, the sick, and others labeled as criminals.

Although the trend toward specialization may be desirable, the principle cannot go unquestioned because the most prevalent example is assignment of offenders on the basis of the seriousness of their offense rather than the availability of programs or their individual needs. State institutions generally care for felons, county and municipal institutions for misdemeanants. This differentiation is far from satisfactory, for current knowledge dictates that offense is not a suitable index of an offender's character, dangerousness, or needs.

Rise of the Treatment Model

The adoption of the treatment model in corrections has been trenchantly described in *Struggle for Justice*, prepared for the American Friends Service Committee:

... the concept of reformation as something achieved through penitence or the acquisition of working skills and habits has been de-emphasized because of developments in social and behavioral science. Varying scientific or pseudo-scientific approaches to crime, although in conflict with one another and unconfirmed by hard scientific data, view criminals as distinct biological, psychological, or social-cultural types.

Such theories all share a more or less deterministic premise holding that man's behavior is caused by social or psychological forces located outside his consciousness and therefore beyond his control. Rehabilitation, therefore, is deemed to require expert help so as to provide the inmate with the understanding and guidance that it is assumed he cannot achieve on his own.

The individualized treatment model, the outcome of this historical process, has for nearly a century been the ideological spring from which almost all actual and proposed reform in criminal justice has been derived. ... Like other conceptions that become so entrenched that they slip imperceptibly into dogma, the treatment model has been assumed rather than analyzed, preached rather than evaluated.[21]

Adoption of the treatment model has had major implications for correctional operations. As it gained prominence, the stated purpose of classification moved from segregation of various categories of offenders from each other to that of implementing different rehabilitative strategies. Under the new model, prisoners are received in the correctional system, diagnosed, classified, and assigned to treatment based on their classification.

In the process of trying to implement this model, correctional systems turned to the social work profession for assistance and introduced the caseworker into the penal situation to diagnose and treat the offender. This attempt to incorporate casework theory into penal institutions has been warped, however, by a failure to absorb two of the most basic tenets of social work. The first of these is that, for casework to be effective, the individual must perceive that he has a problem and be motivated to seek help; this is the principle of voluntarism. The second is that the goals of the casework process must be established by the client; this is the principle of self-determination. In its zeal to "help" those in charge, corrections made the assumption that all offenders are "sick" and that all can thus benefit from casework services. With this assumption apparently came the belief that the two basic social work principles could be ignored. The result has been a treatment system in which virtually all offenders are forced to accept "help" (or at least subjected to classification for treatment as if they were going to get help) and in which the goals of that help are set by correctional staff.

The fact that there is so little knowledge about causes of criminal behavior and how to eliminate it means that systems of forced treatment based on that small amount of knowledge will necessarily be extremely subject to abuse. Furthermore, since the overriding goal of institutions remains that of maintaining order and control, it is not surprising that in large measure classification schemes are based on this objective and are used to the extent that they coincide with it.

For the offender, on the other hand, the main goal is release. Thus his secondary objective becomes that of trying to figure out what he is supposed to do to obtain release and then do it, or appear to do it. Most get bogged down on the first part; that is, trying to figure out what they are supposed to do. Given the fact that the offender is classified and assigned on the basis of subjective judgments by the treatment staff and that their judgments tend to shift as it is administratively convenient to do so, the individual can feel no confidence that whatever course of behavior he may try to follow will in any way help him to reach his goal. Furthermore, he is likely to be judged less on his behavior than on his "attitude," his demeanor, his degree of "contrition," his "desire to change," or some other subjective factor.

In addition, "diagnosis" and "treatment" concepts tend to lead staff to focus on intrapsychic problems when most offenders' crimes are probably at least equally related to such environmental factors as poverty and lack of education or other opportunity. And when the problem actually is mainly internal and psychological, correctional institutions are seldom an effective place to deal with it.

SOME CLASSIFICATION PROBLEMS

Running a Smooth Ship

It is around the problem of agency and personnel convenience, or "running a smooth ship," that a classification system supposedly geared to offenders' needs runs headlong into preoccupation with administrative order and convenience. Organizationally, it is difficult for correctional programs responsible for offering services to many persons to individualize services for a specialized few. In public education, this problem frequently is expressed by the classroom teacher, who says he cannot deal with the disturbing or distracting child because he upsets the routine designed to accommodate the other 29 students in the classroom.

Traditionally, security and custody have been primary concerns in establishing the direction of a correctional program.

A classification system or scheme cannot be adapted to an organization until the agency has spelled out its goals realistically and in a language clearly understood by offenders and staff. Within the framework established by these goals, a classification system can be devised to select those persons whose needs can be met within the agency's goals.

Involving the Offender

Offenders should be involved in assessing their own problems and needs and in selecting programs to resolve them. Almost without exception, classification systems exclude the offender himself from their operations. He is an object, subject, or ward; seldom is he given an opportunity to participate in assessing the problems he presents to himself and others. His conception of the classification process imposed on him greatly affects results of programs offered him.

Even superficial analysis of most current classification programs in correctional services would indicate that decisions regarding offenders' needs are made on the basis of court policy, agency policy, and management convenience. So much emphasis is placed on the attitude of the committing court, the public relations of the agency, bedspace requirements, and release quotas that correctional staff seldom involve the offender in determining what might meet his needs for growth and development.

Difficulties in Application

One of the difficulties with classification is that, even after agency goals have been clearly established and commitment has been made to a specific classification program, there continues to be a wide range of latitude for response to overall decisions by agency personnel. Because of this latitude the classification process frequently breaks down.

Correctional staff by necessity are concerned with making judgments as to appropriate levels of custody, needs for education or vocational training, suitability for counseling, and readiness for parole. In making these judgments, the staff plan the offender's education or training program on the basis of academic achievement scores, vocational preference inventories, and other devices that really provide little information on how to change an offender into a nonoffender. Security classification decisions are made on the basis of escape records, coupled with an appraisal of the seriousness of the commitment offense, even though this information never has been proved a reliable indicator of the inmate's custody requirements or potential for future violence.

Amenability to a counseling program is determined by the availability of the program, the offender's willingness to participate, and the counselor's willingness to make his services available. In practice, it has been demonstrated that certain forms of counseling are of little value to some inmates and actually detrimental to others.

Need for Comprehensive System

A major difficulty with present classification procedures is the need for lengthy interviews with each subject. It is extremely difficult to impart to staff the degree of knowledge needed to make reliable evaluations and program plans. Additionally, many classification decisions at reception centers have not proved accurate or consistent from one center to another. Persons wishing to use a given classification system in another geographical area experience difficulty in arriving at meaningful program plans from interviews. Consequently, many correctional adminstrators and researchers are seeking ways to standardize and computerize the classification approach.

A uniformly applied classification system can lead to more effective management, assignment, and programming decisions. It can add precision to evaluative research in the corrections field. Current evidence indicates that the most efficient ways to combine data for making classification decisions and for predicting problems are based on actuarial or mechanical (computer-based) methods combined with sequential classifications rules.[22]

Corrections personnel from necessity have become interested in the possibility of dealing with programs and persons simultaneously; that is, utilizing a classification system that would make it possible to match subjects and programs. Experience suggests that when such differential programming is inaugurated, the overall success rate achieved by offenders may be increased, particularly when the offender is included in determining the direction and extent of his own program.

Ultimately, the full utilization of classification systems requires a better application of technology. For too long, the correctional system has maintained an archaic system of keeping offenders' records. This traditional paper system provides relatively little useful information on the offender but a great deal of information about the prejudices and perceptions of correctional workers. Effective utilization of objective data, made more usable by modern electronic data processing, could substantially move the art of classification to its next level, wherein the primitive art form is converted into a rudimentary science.

In considering the significance of classification systems, it is important to recognize that the process begins in the community and that judges, probation officials, and intake workers of voluntary social agencies make decisions important to classification every day. In most cases, these decisions are made on the basis of subjective data, formulated within a framework that has little consistency with or meaning to the total correctional system. Any classification system must consider influences and input from the entire justice system and not just a single component such as corrections.

A basic problem with classification procedures today is that usually they are not conducted until after an individual's basic dispositional and program assignments have been made. Persons assigned to an institution are classified among themselves; persons assigned to probation are classified among themselves, etc. Thus one of the most productive and relevant opportunities for use of a classification system has already been bypassed. For classification to have any real meaning, it should take place before the offender's commitment to a formal correctional agency.[22]

It is imperative that classification systems be developed for the whole of the correctional system. Classification systems that operate effectively at the community level will help select those offenders whose needs can be met best through specific programs in the community setting. They will allow only those who need 24-hour control to pass on to correctional institutions.

CONTRIBUTIONS OF CLASSIFICATION

Classification systems can be useful in a number of ways. Foremost is the requirement that the agency or program adopting a classification scheme conceptualize the problem with which it is dealing. . . . In effect, it should render rational that which otherwise is a random operation.

Another advantage is that classification can make handling large numbers of offenders more efficient through a grouping process based on needs and problems. From an administrative standpoint, classification systems can provide for more orderly processing and handling of individuals. From a financial standpoint, classification schemes can enable administrators to make more efficient use of limited resources and to avoid providing resources for offenders who do not require them. From a research standpoint, they can permit comparative studies.

One of the basic characteristics of an effective classification system is its potential usefulness as a communications device. No part of the correctional system is an end in itself. The goal of developing a continuum of assistance, care, and supervision cannot be accomplished until the various parts of the system are able to communicate intelligently.

Organizationally, the classification system can be used to link administration, staff, and offender with a program providing planned experiences for the offender. These experiences must reinforce each other to move the client toward a planned program objective. This feat is not possible unless there is a basic theoretical plan that can be translated into program strategies and communicated in language common to all persons involved with the offender.

Essentially, classification should insure a more effective pooling of relevant knowledge about the offender and the development of a more efficient method by which all important decisions and activities affecting him may be coordinated.[24] Ideally, it should provide offenders with a means for changing themselves rather than subjecting them under coercion to so-called "treatment."

An ideal correctional system would match offender types successfully with program types. Society must be protected against incorrigible offenders, but it should not aggravate the problem by locking up those who would do better in the community. A need to isolate offender types works both ways. An effective classification process would identify offenders who must be kept out of community programs, as well as those who should be kept in them. It would acknowledge that a screening process is sufficient for the decisions needed for most offenders and that classification as theoretically conceived is needed only for a comparative few.

CLASSIFICATION FOR MANAGEMENT PURPOSES

The term "management" means effective control of offenders to avoid further law violations while the agency is responsible. In contrast to management, the term "treatment" refers to attempts to change the individual offender or aspects of his environment to assure long-term lawful behavior, beyond the period of direct agency responsibility.

In a community setting, management primarily involves control of offenders to prevent further law violations while protecting society and the offender. This protection means, for example, that high surveillance should be employed only for those who require it to prevent further offenses, low surveillance for those who represent little or no threat to others. All these management decisions require an implicit or explicit classification system. The difficulty with an implicit classification system, of course, is that it offers no way of checking the system's accuracy. There is no built-in self-correcting process.

Prior probability (base expectancy) approaches are examples of classification systems useful for management purposes. Decisions on whether groups of offenders are to be handled in the community or in an institutional setting can be made most rationally by considering, among other things, the risk of further violation. Surveillance level on probation or parole and related aspects of caseload may be determined in part by knowledge of violation probability. Prior probability classification systems may be used not only as an aid to administrative decsionmaking but also as a check on whether or not management decisions have a desired effect.[25]

A number of studies using this approach in conjunction with psychiatrically oriented classification systems have implications for selection of settings in which various offender subgroups can be handled best. The Borstal studies described by Simon and the Highfields study[26] are examples of research testing the differential response of selected offenders exposed to different correctional settings.

Courts, like other components of the justice system, are reluctant to depend on assessment devices that may suggest action contrary to their own experiences and beliefs. Judges, like parole boards, correctional administrators, and caseworkers, continue to base decisions on hunch, prejudice, and personal belief rather than fact or the need of the offender.

Understandably, criminal justice workers need to be reassured that classification devices are reliable before they are willing to stake part of their success or professional status on how such devices work. Base expectancy (a probable success prediction device) is a classic example of increased mechanical efficiency for large numbers but has only marginal reliability for individual prediction.

The case management system (RAPS) used by the Federal Bureau of Prisons is a modified operational version of this classification approach, although not a prior probability approach in the pure sense.[27] RAPS was initiated several years ago in an effort to develop a descriptive method of classifying inmates in order to allocate resources rationally. Need assessment now is based on four coded elements. "R" is for rating and represents the professional opinion of staff: "A" refers to the age of the offender; "P" refers to the number of prior commitments; and "S" to the nature of the sentence.

Originally, offenders were placed in categories labeled "intensive," "selective," or "minimal," according to staff judgment of the likelihood of change. The bases for these judgments were subjective and, predictably, there was considerable variation in decisions.

The three categories used early in the RAPS program have been replaced by Categories I, II, and III. Category I denotes the greatest expenditure of resources above the essential level; Category II denotes some expenditure above the essential level; and Category III denotes expenditures at the essential level. The revised system is designated to allocate available resources among offenders on the basis of objective assessment of relative need.

The bureau is developing a computer application using objective criteria for determing offender categories. Need assessment is based on the RAPS elements. Each element is given a numerical rating, and the ratings of the four elements are combined to give a code that determines the appropriate classification for each offender and the extent to which available resources will be used for him.

The RAPS system is in the process of evolutionary development. Evaluation of its ultimate value as a correctional classification tool and means of allocating resources will require further testing and experimentation. RAPS is an example of a classification system elaborately designed for the management of offenders rather than for attempting to relate the causes of crime to treatment methods and resources.

Using Warren's interpersonal maturity classification system for juveniles, Jesness conducted a study in which inmates of a boys' training school were assigned living units on the basis of delinquent subtype. An attempt was made to develop and describe the management techniques most useful in dealing with each subtype. Warren and the staff of the Community Treatment Project have developed a treatment model defining nine delinquent subtypes and prescribing both differential management and treatment techniques for various subtypes in the community.[28]

Classification for Risk

It is stated . . . in many . . . documents on corrections that perhaps the greatest contribution to corrections today would be development of a scheme or system that would effectively differentiate among offenders as to their risk of recidivism or their potential dangerousness to others. It is argued that such a scheme, applied at the time of sentencing, would greatly increase sentencing effectiveness, cost-effectiveness of correctional programs, and safety of the community.

Although this theory is basically sound, it presents a number of problems. Not the least of these is that sentencing decisions are not made solely on the basis of risk or a desire to protect others. Society also expects the courts to maintain individual liberties, satisfy a common notion of justice in the sense of equal and consistent treatment, maintain an image as "fair" institutions, maintain the declarative and condemnatory functions of the criminal law, seek a deterrent effect, and operate in ways that are reasonably cost-effective. Many of these goals are by no means fully consistent with the goals of protecting society and reducing recidivism. The dilemma created by these conflicting goals of the criminal sanctioning system has been well described . . . by Martin A. Levin.

. . . from what we know about the type of offenders who are most likely to fall into the recidivating group, one clearly could derive the following policy to reduce recidivism: *Incarcerate for the longest terms the youngest offenders, especially if they are black or have a narcotics history.* But such a policy, however effective it might be in reducing recidivism, is obviously unacceptable if the court is to remain in our eyes a fair and nondiscriminatory institution which exercises a due regard for equality and individual liberties. Conversely, the same findings of social science with regard to reducing recidivism would dictate that judges *incarcerate for the shortest terms possible under the law whites over 40 who have com-*

mitted murder or sex crimes! These groups have extremely low recedivism rates, and such a policy would also save the state money in incarceration costs. But there is little doubt that most people would consider such a policy wrong—both because it discriminates against the young and the black and because it does not sufficiently express society's disapproval of such grave crimes as murder or rape.[29]

Thus, society is faced with a number of crucial social policy determinations. Given the facts stated above, a common response is to declare that the public policy must be to continue to incarcerate large numbers of offenders for purposes of punishment, retribution, deterrence, or condemnation, even though they do not present a high risk to the safety of others.

There are other alternatives that can be entertained, however. . . . Just as society devised . . . imprisonment as a response to the ineffectiveness and brutality of cutting off the hands and feet of offenders, so other forms of sanction can be tried. . . . An institutionalized response to crime is a necessity; incarceration is not.

This may be a major challenge to classification in the future—to find alternatives to incarceration for various types of offenders which will better serve to punish, to deter, to express disapproval, or to reduce the probability of recidivism.

CLASSIFICATION STUDIES INCREASE KNOWLEDGE

Offender typologies are an important basis for integrating and increasing knowledge in the corrections field. Currently, there is considerable interest in the possibility of systematically developing differential programming for various offender types.

The British Home Office has been attempting to develop a typology based on the nature of offenders' problems. Probation officers have identified such problems in terms of personal inadequacies, psychological disturbance, or social stress. The study seeks to determine how each type of problem interacts with the others, with the "treatment" given, and with the probability of reconviction.[30]

O. S. Belle of Manitoba Penitentiary, Canada, is studying prosocial and antisocial inmates.[31] Several studies have been conducted utilizing the Schrag model, which includes grouping inmates into prosocial, antisocial, asocial, and pseudosocial types on the basis of their attitudes toward others. A number of studies have used the Quay classification of juvenile offenders into psychopathic, neurotic, subcultural, and immature-inadequate categories.

McCord, McCord, and Zola proposed six different treatment plans for six different offense types.[32] Gibbons suggested differential treatment methods for a variety of subtypes defined by their social role.[33] Freeman, Hildebrand, and Ayre describe a typology with corollary treatment techniques.[34] The underlying dimension of this classification scheme is a continuum of levels of emotional maturity or ego autonomy.

MacGregor develops a typology of family patterns that sets forth propositions by which families may be classified for treatment planning.[35] Hunt and Hardt relate developmental state to delinquent behavior and delinquency orientation.[36] The authors have made some specific speculations on the implications of their theoretical models for specific differential treatements for delinquents.

The work of Warren and her associates in the California Youth Authority's Community Treatment Project is based on the theory of levels of interpersonal maturity,[37] a formulation describing a sequence of personality integrations in normal childhood development. The theory identifies seven successive stages of interpersonal maturity, characterized in terms of social and psychological development, ranging from the interpersonal reactions of a newborn infant to an ideal social maturity level.

Theoreticians, practitioners, and researchers are constantly seeking some meaningful grouping of offenders into categories to offer (1) a step in the direction of an explanatory theory with a resulting aid to prediction that follows from understanding, (2) implications for efficient management, (3) effective differential programming strategies, and (4) greater precision for maximally effective research.[38]

CURRENT CLASSIFICATION PROCEDURES

Classification procedures generally are carried out through one of four organizational arrangements: classification units within an existing institution; classification committees; reception-diagnosis centers; and community classification teams.

Classification within an Existing Institution

The first organizational alternative involves classification clinics or reception units in the institutions to which offenders are committed. In the State systems using this arrangement, there are certain minimum requirements for "diagnosis," orientation, and protection from contagion through quarantine,[39] although the necessity of the latter is being increasingly questioned.

The reception unit is primarily a diagnostic section, administered by professional personnel whose functions are to make diagnostic studies and treatment recommendations. For this process to be of value and utility, it is considered essential that upon admission there be thorough study of offenders by competent staff; differentiation based on methods enhancing utilization of available programs; treatment based on careful study of individual inmates; an effective orientation program for all inmates; and finally, development of systematic research to explain criminal behavior and determine appropriate treatment programs.

The classification unit system suffers from a number of defects that virtually deprive it of usefulness. Reports typically are submitted to administrative authorities, who may or may not follow the recommendations. Even when high-quality diagnostic work is produced, the results may not be applied, because diagnosis has not been linked directly or operationally with available programs. The system also becomes the victim of institutionalization. Procedures usually are rigid. Too many inmates are kept too long in the reception unit and process. The procedures take on the character of an assembly line, with little selectivity in adapting the process to the individual inmate. Invariably the research component is completely lacking, and there is no check on whether the process really is fulfilling its purpose.

The Classification Committee

The second organizational arrangement is the institutional classification committee, which studies individual case records and collectively makes judgments as to the disposition of inmates in the institution. Professional personnel on the classification committee help develop the diagnostic evaluation and have a direct responsibility for translating this material into recommendations for inmate programs.[40]

Although the committee's composition may vary, it generally consists of individuals whose knowledge and skills are relevant to the offender's particular problem. It may include social workers or sociologists, the supervisor of education, a vocational supervisor, a recreational supervisor, a chaplain, a medical officer, a psychiatrist, or others. The committee determines inmate security ratings, assigns individuals to educational and vocational training programs, and decides where they will work in the institution.

Like other classification systems in use, the committee procedure becomes institutionalized, and decisions are made with little more consideration than the old deputy warden or yard captain used to give them when he alone had full authority over these matters. Since the classification committee processes all inmates, it works under the pressure of limited time and is necessarily restricted in its discussion of issues and interactions with individual inmates. The committee members are departmental representatives of administrative divisions and seldom know the inmate whose case is under consideration. Therefore, their decisions are based primarily on information in case records.

The demands of time, program routine, and workload—and the institutionalization of personnel themselves—prevent effective performance of service. The result is that a large number of ranking institutional personnel are tied up in a process that accomplishes very little in effective programming for the individual inmate, although the system in its way does promote the orderly management of large institutional populations.

In concept, the effectiveness of a classification committee in carrying out its responsibilities presupposes considerable interaction with the offender, yet rarely does he have an opportunity to react meaningfully with the committee. Even when a brief interview between the inmate and the committee is permitted, the offender is asked to respond to a few perfunctory and ritualized questions and is given little if any opportunity to initiate questions that might reveal a great deal about the way the offender perceives the world and himself. And contrary to the concept that classification decisions must be based on the needs of individual inmates, committees habitually base their decisions on administrative needs and convenience.

Reception-Diagnostic Centers

A third organizational arrangement for the classification function emerged during the late 1940's and early 1950's with development of reception centers.[41] By this method of operation, all offenders are committed to a central receiving institution for study, classification, and recommendations for training and "treatment" programs, and the institution to which the individual should be assigned. The process presupposes a plan and theory of classification consistent throughout the system. Such an approach places a major responsibility for collecting diagnostic information on one facility, thereby requiring a high degree of specialization.

While the reception center concept was progressive for its time, it has become obsolete. The system is administratively convenient and efficient in that a limited staff can provide services for a large number of offenders. However, this very administrative efficiency is largely accountable for its obsolescence.

Traditionally, the reception and diagnostic center has provided summary reports including information on social background, criminal history, initial adjustment to custody, medical examination, psychological assessment, vocational skills, educational level, religious background and attitudes, recreational interests and abilities, and psychiatric evaluation. Today, it is not necessary that any of these components of the diagnostic report be completed in a diagnostic or reception center. A number of the items usually are produced by probation and parole officers in the community. Although medical examinations and psychological and psychiatric evaluations require professional services, these services also are available in the local community through both contract and public agency programs.

The reception center, because of the ceaseless repetition in the nature of its work, becomes even more institutionalized than other forms of the classification process. Schedules are adhered to rigidly, and offenders are kept too long in the centers waiting for the diagnostic skills or services of a limited number of persons. The process itself is uniformly extensive and thorough for most offenders, and more information is produced than can be used effectively for classification purposes, considering the current lack of correctional knowledge and resources.

The futility of much of this work is evident in the separation of the study and diagnostic process from operational units. Independent institutions usually do not rely on information developed at the diagnostic center and may repeat clinical evaluations and studies.

The anonymity of inmates in the reception center is pervasive. The impersonality of the assembly line procedure permits them little opportunity to feel that they have any role or individual involvement in the process.

Reception and diagnostic centers use whatever resources are available to them in choosing the "rehabilitation" approach for a given offender. Typically, decisions are based on the recommendations of an intake worker who has subjectively weighed a collection of opinions and perhaps employed a few education, attitude, and aptitude tests. The basis of the intake worker's judgment may or may not be clear in his own mind. In any case, institution and personal bias are involved, because the worker rarely is apprised of the result of his recommendations. Even if he is, only an experienced worker is capable of rendering such judgments in a manner beneficial to the correctional system. Only when explicit criteria form the basis of recommendations is the system's management able to check assumptions, analyze relationships, and pass along pertinent data to inexperienced workers.

The central diagnostic facility is also in conflict with current theory over the importance of developing and programming correctional efforts at the community level. Many theorists in the field argue that a valid classification system, universally applied throughout the whole of corrections, would be more useful.

Community Classification Teams

Another organizational arrangement for classification that is now emerging suggests that with development of a realistic classification system used throughout a correctional system, the classification function can involve a much wider range of personnel and resources than previously supposed. For instance, a classification team consisting of parole and probation officers might collect the social history, while local practitioners could provide necessary medical and psychiatric examinations. State and local institution personnel, in cooperation with the other members of the community classification team, in turn would review the appropriatte correctional programs available to meet the offender's needs.

The community-based classification team concept is superior to current practice. It has already begun to emerge within the correctional system and may be generally realized within the next 5 years. Indeed, to the extent that community correctional programs become the pattern, offenders should not have to be removed to a State diagnostic center or institution for review and study. The classification process itself can be adapted to the needs of offenders, most of whom, for the purposes of community-based programs, require little more than screening for risk and matching to resources.

A Uniform Classification System

A widely accepted classification system could serve a vital research function. At present, persons in the corrections field are frustrated in their attempts to build an empirically based body of knowledge, partly because research findings are not comparable. Availability of a reliable, valid, commonly accepted classification procedure that is simple to apply could improve this situation vastly.

The need for an efficient, reliable classification system generally is conceded by practitioners and researchers alike. Such a system would lead to more effective assignment and management decisions. It would enable correctional administrators to guide inmates into programs that have been found appropriate for others with the same characteristics. It also would help minimize the "shotgun" approach that assumes that all inmates derive equal beenfit from program innovations.

Cross-Classification Approaches

Sociologists and psychologists continue to be in conflict over the appropriate theoretical basis for various approaches. Sociologists accuse psychologists of taking insufficient cognizance of environmental factors, while psychologists accuse sociological typologists of having insufficient regard for intrapsychic factors. Nevertheless, a few investigators are attempting to link theoretically the sociological and psychological situational variables necessary for a satisfactory classification system.

In an effort to explore the feasibility of developing a more uniform basis for classification, a conference on typologies was held in 1966 under sponsorship of the National Institute of Mental Health. Conference participants, including many of the foremost theorists in behavior classification and typology, identified many areas of agreement. On the basis of review and cross-tabulation of a number of classification systems, preliminary consensus was reached on the validity of six broad bands that cut across the various sytems. These six bands distinguish the following major types of offenders: asocial, conformist, antisocial manipulator, neurotic, subcultural identifier, and situational.[42]

The fact that cross-classification is possible is even more impressive when one considers the varieties of methods used for deriving the subtypes—theoretical formulations, empirical observation methods and multivariate analysis procedures. Additionally, it is important that similarities are evident in the descriptions of the etiological and background factors and the "treatment" prescriptions for similar subtypes, as well as in the descriptions of offender characteristics across typologies.

There is evidence at both the theoretician and practitioner level that the field is ready to move toward developing programs based on categorizing the range of problems represented in the offender population. Not only is there a ready ear for conceptualizing, but it also appears that a time of consensus among typologists, in which a rational correctional model may be begun, is approaching.

20

TOWARD MORE CORRECTIVE WORK IN PRISON

PAUL W. KEVE

EMPLOYMENT IN PRISON SHOULD, AS FAR AS POSSIBLE, BE CHARACTERISTIC OF EMPLOYMENT OUTSIDE

In its simplest terms this is a proposal to allow each inmate to apply in a formal manner for the prison job he wishes to have; to be hired for that job if an opening is available and if he is qualified; and to be paid full wages commensurate with the going rates in the outside community. It would then follow that he would also be charged for the services and goods provided by the prison. He would pay rent on his cell, he would pay for his laundry and medical expenses, and he would pay admission to movies or other entertainment. A weekly meal ticket could be purchased, and in going through the cafeteria line each man would select whatever food items he wishes and his meal ticket would be punched accordingly. He could eat sparely or lavishly as he might wish.

The prison might well contain a branch bank and prisoners could maintain both checking and savings accounts. Even loans would be arranged under certain circumstances. Probably specie would be used for legal tender within the institution instead of real money.

Some of the value of this approach can best be appreciated by comparing it with the more conventional prison operation. Ordinarily a prisoner is assigned to a specific job in prison and if at any time he rebels against it he is subject to disciplinary measures for refusing to work. In the dining room he is allowed to take what he wants to eat but is usually subject to a rule that he must eat all he takes, or be subject to discipline. These are rules that have been taken for granted and regarded as virtues as long as there have been prisons. But these conditions unnecessarily reverse the social situation of the outside world. For the rest of us there is no law that says we must work. We are punished for offenses which may result from not working—nonsupport of family, nonpayment of debt, etc.—but if a person can meet his legal obligations without working he is under no legal requirement to go to a job every day. Similarly, though it is considered virtuous to avoid wasting food, there is no requirement in the outside world that a person must clean his plate. In prison we tend to forget what is normal and impose these rules to enforce what is not necessity but only virtue, and with every such rule we create a new group of rule breakers, keeping us busy punishing people for actions that are bad only in an artificial, institutional sense.

Much of this could be avoided by instituting a normal economic system in the prison. Let the prisoner obtain a job by applying and qualifying for it. If occasionally he is not in the mood to work let that lapse be treated as casually as if it were in the outside community. The penalty would be the same that faces us outside. He would suffer only from the loss of wages and from the loss of such goods and services that the unearned money could have purchased. If his job absenteeism is excessive, he would additionally suffer the possibility of being fired. If his poor job management results in substantial economic failure, he could be evicted from his private cell and left to sleep on a cot in some open space (the equivalent of the park bench) without privacy.

In those cases where this kind of irresponsibility is persistent, extra counseling would be necessary to help the prisoner with this problem. It is here, while we have him in prison, that we should make the most of our opportunity to discover what problems he has in this regard and to give him realistic help with them.

The introduction of such a system will instinctively be resisted by many prison employees and administrators who will marshal a variety of arguments against it just as every prison improvement has been instinctively opposed since such institutions began. But the idea is beginning to be talked about and in fewer years than might be expected it will become commonplace. The most obvious impediment to it from the legislator's viewpoint will be that it will require an enormously increased prison budget. Legislatures now finance prisoner pay up to about a dollar a day in some of the more generous states; other states finance as little as five cents a day and some provide no wages at all. To move to full union-scale wages would be an enormous jump. But the jump will be made tolerable by the return of a substantial part of the wages paid. For instance, the inmate would be charged the full cost of his food, which the state now gives

him free. In addition to paying cell rent and paying for various services, he would be required to send part of his pay to any dependents
he has and this would offset welfare costs to that extent.

An obvious objection to the plan is that it simply will not work
for some prisoners. This is true. Every prison has a few physically
incapacitated men who cannot work, and there are always those who
are so maladjusted that they are frequently in segregation or otherwise not available or not reliable enough for regular work. This is
similar to life on the outside where a percentage of people must always be incapacitated for some reason, but still the world of work
goes on for those who can and will work. In a prison it may be
necessary for the full wage work program to be applied only to certain cell blocks or wings, with other parts of the prison reserved for
the prisoners who cannot fit into this type of regimen.

One setting in which the full wage plan (the Swedish correctional
system refers to it as the "market adapted wage") will be especially
appropriate is the large urban jail which houses a substantial number
of unconvicted prisoners awaiting trial. Usually it is assumed that
such prisoners, being unconvicted, cannot be required to work, and
this has sufficed as an excuse to provide little or no opportunity for
them to work even if they want to. But there is no reason to refuse
such a man the opportunity to work and support his family. He is
not in jail either "as" or "for" punishment. He is there only to
guarantee his presence at trial without new offenses in the interim.[43]

A possible answer to the work problem for this group would be
to invite a private industry to set up and operate a shop within the
jail. It would have to be some kind of assembly work that could be
taught quickly and would not be too badly hurt by frequent turnover of workers. If this existed within the institution the unconvicted men could be hired by the entrepreneur operating the industry
and could make full wages while awaiting trial. The family would
continue to be supported and the terrible effects of prolonged idleness would be averted. There would be no "work relevance" issue as
we constantly have the license tag shops and some of the other typical prison jobs. If the work is in a production shop and pays full
wages it is relevant.

It will not be easy to come up with the details of the successful
operation of such an industry in a jail, but as long as any jail with a
sizable population exists something of this kind is an important anti-
dote to the degenerative character of jail life. Yet there is one answer
that is better: no jail at all. It is proving quite realistic to develop pretrial release programs that will retain safely in the community a high
percentage of persons who now are jailed to await trial.

Another change needed to normalize prison employment is the

discontinuance of "state use" laws. To appease both the manufacturers and the unions, we play this little game of pretending that competition with private industry is avoided by allowing prison industries to sell only to other governmental institutions and offices. It is an empty gesture. Every item sold to a government agency is one less item bought from private industry. If we eliminate the restrictive laws and allow prison industries to compete on the open market, it will not result in any more competition than there is now, and it will make possible more realistic employment for training prisoners. Outside industries have little to fear from a shop that can never increase its production beyond the level that can be sustained by a static prison population.

21

THE EFFECTIVENESS OF CORRECTIONAL EDUCATION

DANIEL GLASER

Nobody knows conclusively and precisely the effectiveness of correctional education. Statistics vary from one study to the next. When one defines "success" for research purposes as the absence of post-release felony convictions or parole violations, some studies indicate that inmates who were in prison school succeed more than those who were not, while other studies have the opposite finding.[44] Analysis usually indicates that these results are due largely to the selection of inmates for prison school, rather than due just to the effects of the school.

Despite these sources of contradictory findings in gross comparisons of releases, there is some evidence of a favorable impact from correctional education. If one compares only inmates of similar age and criminality, and only those confined for long terms, those in prison school for an appreciable portion of their term have higher post-release success rates than those in prison school only briefly or not at all. Furthermore, inmates who advance their grade level while in prison have higher success rates than those who do not. Even these findings may be accounted for partly by the selection of students for school, or by the initial attributes of those who advance in grade level as compared with those who do not, rather than being purely effects of the schooling. We can only become highly confident in the conclusiveness of research on prison education if many more prisoners eligible for a prison school program than are assigned to it, and those assigned are selected by a purely random process, the remainder serving as a control group. However, this controlled experiment approach to research on prison education is only part of the last of four needs distinctive of prison school programs which I wish to dis-

Source: From *American Journal of Correction* 28, 2(March–April 1966): 4–9. Reprinted by permission of the American Correctional Association.

cuss, in considering how we can increase the effectiveness of correctional education.

BROADENING THE CHALLENGE

The first requirement for more successful education with the types of pupil predominant in prison is to increase the challenge of prison education. There should be a broader range in correctional pedagogy between that which frustrates the potential student, because he fears he will fail at it, and that which dulls his interest, because he finds it boring. This challenge area is narrow, for many students, and difficult to locate. We have some clues as to the cause of this narrowness from recent studies of so-called "culturally deprived" school populations. There also are clues, from recent experiments with special education methods, as to how education can be made more challenging.

One conclusion that is emerging from a variety of sociological studies is that the educability and the delinquency of youth are not just functions of his home, not just the heredity or the cultural environment provided by his parents. Instead, they reflect his neighborhood. The average income of a neighborhood within a large city is closely related to the average school performance in the neighborhood, and even to the prevailing attitude toward schooling there, and to the delinquency rates. Within any neighborhood the children of parents of different income do not differ in delinquency and in school achievement as much as over-all rates for neighborhoods differ according to the average income of each neighborhood.[45] Thus, youth reflect the school conditions of their neighborhoods, in addition to their individual school problems, although correctional education has tended to focus on the individual attributes.

The differences between schools from neighborhoods of diverse income are illuminated dramatically by the data presented in Patricia C. Sexton's book, *Education and Income*.[46] This New York University professor, and wife of an Assistant Director of the U.S. Office of Economic Opportunity, classified school districts in a large metropolis according to the average family income reported for their areas by the U.S. Census. In districts where the average family income was below $3,000 per year, the income range from the Office of Economic Opportunity employs as a working definition of "poverty," the average achievement test score in the fourth grade was 3.5, while in school districts where family income averaged $9,000 or more per year, the average test score was 4.8. For eighth grade classes, the average test score in the povertous districts was 6.8, while in the richer districts it was 8.7.[47] The further one advanced in the school level, the farther behind was the achievement in the poorer districts. These are the differences in composite score on the Iowa Achievement Tests; the differences were somewhat greater than this in the scores on reading ability, and not as great in tests on arithmetic.

Reading ability deficiency seems to be the key problem, for it is this deficiency which increasingly differentiates those who complete high school from those who drop out, as well as those who progress in college from those who never enter, or who enter but fail to remain long. As Mrs. Sexton says: "lower-income students are poor readers very often because their parents cannot or do not read to them at home, because they do not have books in their homes, and because even if they had books, their environment would not be conducive to reading. They are poor readers because they usually do not use public libraries, have never been taught to use them, have never been properly encouraged by libraries to enter and make themselves at home." On the average, a tenement flat with residents totaling two or more people per room, with small rooms and a loud television set, with no books or magazines, and with illiterate adults, is less conducive to a student's realization of his reading potential than is a home with more rooms that residents, and with magazines, books, and educated adults.

It is well established that deficiences in reading ability, and in accompanying verbal fluency, are reflected in intelligence test performance. Remedial reading instruction and motivation to do well tend to raise I.Q. scores, yet the myth that these scores reflect only inherent ability often has the vicious effect of barring some students from the remedial reading classes which might raise their intelligence test performance. Compounding these difficulties further are other problems which statistically distinguish schools in low-income neighborhoods: these schools receive a disproportionate share of the least educated and experienced teachers; they are the most overcrowded and the most poorly equipped of the city schools; they have the most frequent use of punitive discipline and the least extensive distribution of special awards for superior scholarship. In Mrs. Sexton's study it was even found that these schools in the lowest income neighborhoods had taken less advantage of the opportunity to secure free lunches for students, from surplus foods, than had schools in neighborhoods of somewhat greater income. In summary, the schools in the districts of lowest income level tend to be administered in a manner which is least responsive to the distinctive needs of these districts.

The psychological effects of the child's total experience in low-income neighborhoods, as compared with experience in high-income neighborhoods, is indicated by the responses which fifth grade students in these two types of setting gave to a questionnaire on perspectives towards daily social living. To the question, "Do you often think that nobody likes you?," 62 per cent of the fifth-graders in low-income areas said "Yes," as compared with only 19 per cent of those in high-income locations. Only 4 per cent of the students in higher-income settings responded affirmatively to the question. "Do you have just a few friends?" as compared with 42 percent of the lower-income students. To the question, "Are people often so unkind or unfair that it makes you feel bad?," 62 per cent of the lower-income fifth-graders said "Yes," as contrasted with only 15 per cent of those from families of higher income. The affirmative responses to the question, "Do people often act so badly that you have to be mean or nasty to them?" were 46 per cent in the poorer settings and only 8 per cent in the richer districts. And just one more of many additional examples that could be cited: 46 per cent of the low status background children, as compared to 15 per cent of those from high status, answered "Yes" to the question, "Is it hard to make people remember how well you can do things?"

What we see is that students in the schools of poorer neighborhoods, who predominate in our correctional populations, tend to have a background from early childhood of feeling that others are hostile and unappreciative toward them, and that they have to be hostile in response. These characteristics tend to be most pronounced among our prisoners, since they so frequently were the most maladjusted even in schools which in entirety tended to be much less conducive to academic pursuits than were schools in average or higher-income areas. With increased public awareness of this cumulative problem in students from so-called "culturally deprived" settings, there has been widespread experimentation with special methods of instruction to give such students a sense of acceptance and success in their schooling. The problem is to make studying a more rewarding and exciting activity for them.

Perhaps the best-known approach to this problem is that of programmed learning. By breaking instruction into bits, in well-planned sequences, programmed texts or teaching machines start students with learning tasks that they can master with ease. The programs also permit students to advance to more difficult tasks only when they have mastered the prerequisite learning. Thus students from the backgrounds which distinguish the correctional population have much more experience with success when studying by programmed methods, than most of them encounter with conventional teaching and studying procedures. It is especially significant in prison to have each individual progress at his own rate, because prisoners come to the school at all times of the year, and with a great variety of prior curriculum exposure and mastery. If all are given the same lessons at the same time, even in classes that have been grouped as well as possible by prior school record or by test scores, parts of each lesson will be frustrating to some students and boring to others. The best students will learn well by any teaching method, but poor students, or students that are easily distraught with schooling, tend to do distinctly better with programmed instruction than with conventional pedagogy. That is why conventional aptitude tests are less accurate predictors of subsequent achievement with programmed instruction than with ordinary teaching.

While programmed instruction is a major resource for increasing the challenge in our prison schools, it will not solve all of our problems here. Some academic and vocational subjects are not so readily taught by programmed methods, or, at least, have not yet been subjected to good programming. More important, there is a second major need in school programs for correctional populations which programs alone do not solve. This is the need to alter the social experience which offenders have associated with schooling.

CHANGING THE SCHOOL'S SOCIAL RELATIONSHIPS

As we have seen, the typical prison school student needs distinctly individualized pedagogy if he is to experience a continuous challenge and reward in his studies, but he has a background of regimented mass education in crowded schools. His personal relationships to teachers have frequently been characterized by conflict. By contrast, his most rewarding social experience has often been among peers who share his problems, and who extol his hostility to school authorities. He has learned to expect to feel that he has failed, and to fear derision, if he copes with a school learning problem in a social setting. With this background, it often is difficult to get studying by a prisoner energetically initiated and maintained in a prison school, even with programmed devices or other optimum lesson material.

One of the needs of the student who has felt persistent failure in school is a need to feel that he is regarded as personally important, and to feel that he is well liked. Much has been written of the need to make reading matter for slum children have some relevance to their life experience, but this is more than a matter of the illustrations and of the plots of the stories. In special schools for youngsters for whom learning to read has been a painful experience, to be resisted, one successful technique is to have a teacher provide a period of individual instruction in which she sits at a typewriter and types out a story that the student tells her. The story may be about himself, about what he has done that day, or anything that he wishes to make up. The teacher types it in approximately the boy's own words, perhaps improving the grammar and sentence structure slightly, and possibly abbreviating it somewhat. This now is given to the student as his reading lesson; he is likely to be interested in it, since it deals with the most fascinating subject for most of us, ourselves. In this fashion not only does rapid progress in reading ability frequently occur, but it can change attitudes toward reading. This can spread to other reading and to writing by the student, on his own, when the teacher is not available. In addition, the story-typing exercises may provide a useful vehicle for a counseling relationship between the teacher and the student, for the teacher who is skillful with questions and other reactions to the stories may thereby influence the student's thinking about himself.

While staff time for one-to-one instruction of this sort is limited, a small amount sometimes goes a long way. Also, it frequently is possible to augment staff by having students help each other. I am not referring to inmate teachers in the usual sense of handling a class, but to mutual aid by fellow students in the same class. A pleasing game may be created where one student writes or types what another dictates, especially when priority in the writing role is a reward for those who are slightly superior in the learning. This obviously has limitations, but the general principle of having people learn by teaching others in the same class can be adapted to many situations where a more personal tutorial relationship is needed than staff alone can provide. In scattered after-school study centers established in the last few years to cope with the problems of slum schooling, students from the same neighborhood are hired as "homework helpers."

Being from the same background and close to the same age—preferably slightly older—may make an inmate distinctly acceptable as a tutor for those prison pupils who would be uneasy with a staff member as tutor. At Draper Prison, in Alabama, where impressive achievements with programmed learning are reported they have established an inmate Service Corps in the prison school consisting of the more advanced students, who spend part of their school time as tutors for the less advanced. College student interns also are reported to be a good teaching resource at Draper.[49]

KEEPING CORRECTIONAL EDUCATION HONEST

One unfortunate solution to problems of conflict and inadequacy in some slum schools has been to make the education fraudulent. Peace sometimes is achieved in such schools at the expense of education, for there often is consensus of pupils and teachers that both teaching and learning should be minimum effort activities. So-called "social promotion" from kindergarten to high school has allegedly been encouraged in slum schools by large city school administrators as a way of avoiding pressures for equal educational services in minority group ghettos.

Many prison school pupils come from this kind of school background. They are not retarded in grade completed, but are revealed by test to have an educational achievement grossly below that for the grade in which they were last registered. They are used to school being a place where one "gets by" without real effort, and regardless of whether or not learning occurs. They come from a background of boredom in school to a situation where schooling, if it were suddenly to be as demanding as their prior grade warrants, would be most frustrating. Realization of this deficiency can be most humiliating, and resistance to school will be evoked if they are placed in a grade well below that which they thought they had achieved. Yet studies which begin at the point where their knowledge stops may be essential. Resulting ego shock can be reduced by avoidance of grade designation; to falsify grade levels by exaggerating them is to assure future ego shock from failure.

Some prison schools play the social promotion game or, at least, maintain the atmosphere of social promotion slum schools. These are places where the teachers merely serve time, along with their students. By not caring whether or not the students learn, or even whether the classroom discussions are perpetually bull sessions irrelevant to the subject-matter of the course, some prison education directors make their lives extremely soft. The inmates who have found such a school an easy way to do time will see to it that the school looks like a constructive enterprise: they will keep it orderly, and will help the Supervisor of Education make impressive charts on inmate participation in school. He may get promoted for this, and become the type of warden who merely serves time, while the inmates do not achieve a significant rate of progress. It may be that prison schools of this sort accounted for our finding, in some federal prisons, that inmates not in school had better post-release records than those in school; inmates out of school and in prison industry may have worked at a pace that prepared them better for outside employment conditions than did such added abilitites as they learned in the school.

Other kinds of corruption in prison schooling are stimulated by the fact that most correctional systems, appropriately, let their inmates know that participation in prison school will be rewarded. The main reward, an uncertain one, is that schooling may impress the parole board favorably. Although the validity of this belief varies, it usually is cultivated assiduously by prison staff. More dependable rewards may result from the fact that completion of a certain grade, or procurement of a diploma, is made prerequisite for admission to the most popular skilled trade courses or work assignments. The federal minimum security prison at Seagoville, Texas, requires involvement in self-improvement activities such as schooling in order for an inmate to be assigned to any paying job, such as one in prison industries, or to receive Industrial or Meritorious Service good time. All of these incentive systems motivate the prisoner to use his time constructively, but they also motivate many inmates to try to convey a fraudulent impression of school achievement.

On the whole, I suspect there is no more cheating in prison schooling than in many universities, where files of old examinations and term papers are the major character-building contribution of some fraternities. But one depravity does not justify another. In prison the cheating takes many forms. Copies are made of correspondence course lessons, and are sold for cigarettes or other commissary goods. Sometimes a bright inmate will complete a whole course for another inmate for a carton or two. Clerks in the prison school, and inmate teachers, can be pressured or bribed to falsify records of course completion or, minimally, to check examination papers before they are graded officially.

Wherever this sort of thing can occur, we are dealing with a lazy prison school administration. If staff will insist on supervising all final or other key examinations themselves, if they will base course credit primarily on such examinations, and if they will keep the records of major examinations and course completions entirely and continuously under their control, inaccessible to any inmate, a report on an inmate's educational achievement in prison will be dependable. Wherever inmates are involved in key examination supervision, or have access to key school records, corruption in prison education is not just an ever-present danger—it probably is a usually-present reality for some fraction of the inmates.

RESEARCH: THE KEY TO PROGRESS

Research is the bookkeeping of corrections. Unfortunately, many correctional enterprises operate without such bookkeeping. When this happens, like businesses without bookkeeping, they may soon be bankrupt. However, unlike business, corrections can provide a steady salary for its employees even when it is bankrupt.

While research is worthwhile in any school, it is not always as essential as it is in prison schools. Most schools can learn the answers to their questions by studying the published reports of research done elsewhere, in schools or with pupils comparable to theirs. In correctional education there is not enough research literature available to meet the needs of prison schools. In addition, each correctional system has unique features in sentencing and parole policies, and in the communities it serves, which make some of the knowledge it needs apply only to it. Procurement of this knowledge requires two kinds of research.

The first research need is follow-up data, on a routine basis, regarding the utilization of prison schooling in post-release life, and regarding its correlation with non-recedivism. Unfortunately, crime control in the United States is generally administered by completely autonomous agencies, each of which serves a successive stage of what should be a continuous process, but each of which is insufficiently concerned with agencies dealing with other stages. Parole supervision agents should routinely determine whether a parolee is working, and what kind of work he is doing. They could routinely record this on forms, on which they could also note the parolee's response to inquiry on what prison training he is using at his job. If these forms were sent back to prison, there would be a basis for evaluating the practical impact of much specific training, as well as correlating the relationships between prison education particpation or progress and post-release self-sufficiency.

Where almost all correctional institution releasees serve an appreciable period of parole or conditional release supervision, the record of post-release criminality can be procured from parole supervision records, and can then be correlated with the prison education record. Where many releasees do not receive parole, or a follow-up is desired on criminality beyond the parole period, we still are faced with the claim of the Justice Department that they cannot procure clerical help to provide post-release fingerprint report data for correctional evaluation research. However, a partially satisfactory substitute is the record on releasees returned to prison within the same state during a particular post-release period, supplemented by the record on inquiries from those states which routinely request information on prior prison record when they incarcerate someone who previously served time elsewhere.

The second type of research need was hinted at earlier. This is experimental research. It is invaluable both for measuring the effectiveness of a new correctional education enterprise, and to procure financial support for new enterprises.

If we secure for an educational program twice as many applicants or nominees as the program can handle, then select people for the program and for a control group by a purely random method, we can have much confidence that the difference between the subsequent record of any appreciable number in the program and those in the control group is a consequence of the program. There is no other procedure nearly as dependable, but it requires that separation of the treatment from the control group involves a purely random process, such as tossing a coin, using a table of random numbers, or separating by odd and even prison registry number. When this is done for an appreciable number of cases, we can be confident that any personality factors or other attributes apart from the education program which affect subsequent records, are as frequent in the experimental group as in the control group. When officials interfere with the purely random assignment of inmates to experimental and control groups, we have reason to suspect the validity of the research findings.

Of course, if a controlled experiment shows a program to be beneficial, or if it shows it to be ineffective or even harmful, it is still appropriate that research probe further. Experimental research is more conclusive than other research, but its findings still are not absolute and final. Sometimes the impact of a program comes from some unintended feature of it, rather than from the apparent features; it may be due only to the unusual personalities of the officials which the program employs, or to the unusual enthusiasm or caution distinguishing the administration of a new program. Only as we repeat experiments, in different settings and circumstances, and the results are consistent, can we gain extreme certainty about the validity of its findings. Of course, this is also true of experimental research in medicine and other fields; it is especially relevant in corrections, however, because of the many complexities which can confound the impact of correctional programs.

A final note on experimental research is that it provides an outstanding sales argument. Where support for a new program is not readily forthcoming, because of doubts as to whether it is worthwhile, this resistance will generally be reduced markedly should one propose that the program be introduced only on a controlled experimental basis. If favorable results then are yielded by the experiment, the administrator has a much stronger sales argument than he previously had. If the experimental findings do not confirm expectations regarding the program, it will be just as well that the program was introduced on a limited scale at first. The administrator can then cite this valuable knowledge in proposing that the experiment now be conducted with a different program, either completely different or a modification of the program that failed. Legislators usually are sufficiently familiar with science to realize that this is the only way in which knowledge in corrections can be made more precise and cumulative. Are correctional administrators this well informed?

CONCLUSION

Four needs of correctional education have been indicated: (1) to broaden its challenge for those who have been frustrated or bored in previous schooling; (2) to change the social relationships which its students associate with schooling; (3) to become honest or to remain honest; and (4) to conduct research. Some ways of meeting these needs were suggested. As these needs are met, all four of them, effectiveness in correctional education should become more clearly evident.

22

INSTITUTIONAL DISCIPLINARY ACTION AND THE SOCIAL PSYCHOLOGY OF DISCIPLINARY RELATIONSHIPS

DANIEL GLASER

PROCEDURES IN DISCIPLINE

The prison staff's policies regarding discipline may have far-reaching effects on staff members' relationships to inmates and, hence, on other prison programs. Discipline involves issues on which there is much staff disagreement and uncertainty. The immediate concern in discipline is with procuring conformity of inmates to the behavior patterns required of them for smooth functioning of the institution, but the *Manual of Correctional Standards* of the American Correctional Association asserts further:

> Discipline ... looks beyond the limits of the inmate's term of confinement. It must seek to insure carry-over value by inculcating standards which the inmate will maintain after release. It is not merely the person's ability to conform to institutional rules and regulations, but his ability and desire to conform to accepted standards for individual and community life in free society. Discipline must ... develop in the inmate personal responsibility to that social community to which he will return.[50]

One of the first issues that arises in connection with disciplinary policy is whether or not penalties should be determined by the type of infraction or by the behavioral patterns and circumstances peculiar to the inmate who commits the infraction. Modern criminal and correctional law holds that confinement should vary according to the characteristics of the offender; probation, the indeterminate sentence, judicial discretion in sentencing, and parole serve as alternative, complementary, or supplementary devices for achieving such variation. In applying these devices in the spirit of the so-called "new penology,"

Source: From *The Effectiveness of a Prison and Parole System* (Indianapolis: Bobbs-Merrill Company, 1964), pp. 116–129 and National Institute of Mental Health, *Strategic Criminal Justice Planning*(Washington, D.C.: U.S. Government Printing Office, 1975), pp. 84–87 and 144–149. Reprinted by permission of the publisher.

the nature of a man's offense is only one of many pieces of information considered in attempting to achieve an understanding of the offender as a person.

Despite this trend, it is still widely contended that within the social world of the prison, the effective motivating of all inmates in order to achieve conformity to institution rules requires that similar penalties be imposed on all who commit similar rule infractions. Nevertheless, in spite of this principle, federal prisons hold with the modern trend, and penalties are not closely dependent upon the infraction. They are initially uncertain, and are determined largely by the offender's total record and by his attitude while in disciplinary status.

The disciplinary agency in a federal prison is called the "adjustment committee." It was formerly called the "disciplinary court," and though this designation sometimes recurs in prison parlance, it is frowned upon by senior staff members. The committee is usually presided over by the associate warden for custody and has two additional members: one is either the associate warden for treatment or the chief of classification and parole, and the other, the senior custodial captain or lieutenant. A prison psychiatrist or other medical officer may be asked to participate as an adviser in some cases. When the committee believes that an inmate's conduct warrants his removal to a segregation cell, he is sent there not for a given number of days but for an indeterminate period of time during which officers representing the committee are able to talk to him several times each day, a physician may check him, and the chaplain usually visits him. These visitors are consulted by the members of the adjustment committee, and the man will be released from segregation when it is believed that his "attitude" warrants this action.

The duration of disciplinary segregation is much briefer in federal prisons than in most state prisons; the median period in federal prisons seems to be two or three days. Also, although many state prisons serve a restricted diet to men in disciplinary confinement and deny them reading and writing matter, men in segregation in federal prisons now receive the regular inmate food (but without seconds); they may have a Bible, and they may write and send letters, but not receive them. Like other prisons, the federal prisons also have a few completely stripped and closed "isolation" cells to be used for inmates extremely noisy, abusive, or suicidal. These are located among the regular open cells which are normally used for disciplinary segregation. Such isolation cells are usually empty.

If an inmate, when not being dealt with for a specific rule infraction, is considered seriously disturbed, assaultive, homicidal, or suicidal, or seems to be in extreme fear of attack from other inmates, he may be placed in a nondisciplinary maximum-custody unit. This is often called "administrative segregation." It exists in almost all prisons. Such units resemble the regular disciplinary section of a prison in that the men are kept almost continuously confined in cells and have their meals brought to them. Unlike the men in disciplinary segregation, men in these units may have personal possessions in the cells and may obtain study material and some types of art and game material. There may be variations in the extent to which the inmates are restricted to their cells, but usually they are taken from the cells individually and are always accompanied by a custodial officer. In large prison systems inmates believed to require a long term of such surveillance are transferred to the institution designed primarily for maximum custody (in the federal prison this was formerly Alcatraz, but it is now the federal prison at Marion, Illinois), where they can eat, work, and play in small groups within closed sections of the prison.

A number of lesser penalties are used more frequently than segregation in most federal disciplinary practice. The inmate may be temporarily restricted to quarters without being transferred to the segregation unit, he may be barred from a particular activity temporarily, he may be warned, or he may be asked to apologize to an injured party. In addition, the "good time" deducted from a sentence for conforming behavior during confinement and other rewards he may have earned are withheld if the prisoner misbehaves. Very serious misconduct may even result in revocation of previously granted good time. In general, time off for good behavior is much less automatic and secure in federal prisons than in many state prisons (indeed, no inmate receives more than 180 days of good time unconditionally; and all good time may be canceled for postrelease misbehavior and have to be served again). Finally, where an infraction in prison constitutes a clear felony, especially an assault to kill or to do bodily harm, the prisoner is taken into the court in whose district the prison lies where he may receive a new sentence.

HYPOTHESES UNDERLYING DISCIPLINARY POLICY

The relationship of disciplinary policies to inmate-staff relationships is an area in which conflicting hypotheses may reasonably be formulated. For example, one point of view can be summarized by the hypothesis: Disciplinary penalties which are determined by the offense rather than the offender, and interpreted "by the book" rather than with flexibility, create shared expectations in staff and inmates as to what penalty is mandatory; the person guilty of the offense, therefore, knows the penalty is prescribed by agencies beyond the control of the officers confronted with his offense, so he does not become hostile toward the staff because of it. This implies that when the offender commits an infraction he knows what penalty to expect if he is caught, and he feels that the staff is obliged to impose this penalty on him should they catch him, regardless of how friendly they may feel toward him.

Some years ago I presented what I thought was a fairly strong argument for the foregoing definite penalty hypothesis.[51] Examples of its success in reducing specific types of infraction have been cited. At one state institution for "young and improvable" offenders, a penalty of seven days of isolation always was imposed on every inmate involved in a fight, unless he not only did not start it, but made every possible effort to retreat from it and not fight back, or unless other clearly extenuating factors were present. More severe penalties were imposed for anyone clearly established as the initiator of the fight and for anyone using any kind of weapon. It was evident that most new inmates with a history of ready fighting got into fights only once or twice, then learned to avoid them. Inmates remarked that they learned to walk away from provocations in prison which they previously would have reacted to by immediate fighting. In terms of psychological learning theory, old habits seemed to be extinguished and new conforming behavior reinforced by this punishment and by the rewards of "extra privileges" and favorable assignments.

Despite this kind of support for the definite penalty hypothesis, the arguments of federal officials and readily available observations in federal prisons provide a strong case for two quite opposite hypotheses. One hypothesis stresses flexibility of rules. It asserts that objectionable behavior by men in prison is so diverse that no set of rules could encompass it without being long, complex, and difficult to apply, or so arbitrary that it would arouse resentment by dealing similarly with highly diverse acts. It follows that strain in inmate-staff relationships is minimized by a policy of flexible rules interpreted to fit each case which takes into account primarily the effect of each penalty on the future behavior of the offender. The other hypothesis asserts that the administration of disciplinary penalties is most effective if it: minimizes alienation of the rule-violating inmate from staff and maximizes his alienation from inmate supporters of his infraction; promotes in him a clear regret over having committed the infraction; but provides him with a perception of clearly available opportunities to pursue a course of behavior which will restore him to good standing in the prison and give him a more favorable self-conception than he had as a rule violator.

It has become particularly evident in federal experience that an incapacitating penalty such as solitary confinement in idleness rapidly loses effectiveness as it is prolonged. The first one to three days of such an experience seems to have a greater impact than any subsequent day. Even the first day or so seems useful only in influencing the inmate's communication to the staff. For most infractions serious enough to warrant segregation, a few hours of segregation, or an overnight stay in the case of infractions occurring in the evening, is sufficient to permit the staff to complete its investigation of the infraction and of the offender's attitude. By talking with the inmate during this period staff members are usually able to evoke in him a willingness to cooperate in a somewhat restricted program, but one which will enable him to earn back at least as satisfactory a prison status as he had previously. If this type of response is not awakened, the inmate is likely to be transferred to a close-custody institution or to be held for some time in a maximum-custody unit.

When prison staff personnel perform both counseling and disciplinary functions, it is impossible for the latter not to affect the former function. An impersonal view of punishment by those punished seems to exist, if at all, only when a person is punished by nature rather than by another human being. For this reason, a deliberate effort to integrate discipline with counseling is appropriate. It follows, therefore, from the concept of rehabilitation as a change which occurs in a man's inner values, that discipline rehabilitates inmates providing that the rules become internalized as their personal opinions. Also, habits are best extinguished if they are not merely punished, but if alternative behavior is reinforced by reward.

Clearly the two hypotheses, on flexible-rules and on constructive-penalty, depend upon the existence of a prison staff of high calibre. Flexible handling of disciplinary infractions requires keen judgment and an ability to suppress hostile impulses and prejudices. An impressive feature of the best federal prison discipline (not found at all federal prisons) is the imperturbability of the staff after a major individual infraction such as an escape has occurred. Instead of an hysterical tightening of the whole institution for some days taking place, and the establishment of new restrictions on everyone, a reaction which would occur in most prisons, the best federal prison officers quietly and efficiently execute an appropriate "escape plan." The plan varies with the place of the escape and the time it is discovered, but usually one officer notifies police officials and the FBI, another prepares extra photographs and fingerprints for these agencies, a third calls aside likely informants for interrogation as to the course and probably destination of the escapee, and others make appropriate patrols of the institution grounds and surroundings. There are few escapes per year, almost all are "walkaways" from outside jobs, and the escapees generally are caught in a day or two. Often most of the prison is unaware of the escape until they learn of it through news media, usually after the escapee is captured. Escapes are reviewed locally and in Washington, and sometimes at the national meetings of federal wardens that are held every few years. However, remedies which would have prevented a particular escape but would grossly limit prison programs and impair inmate-staff relationships are invariably rejected.

Essentially, one might say that the flexible-rules and constructive-penalty hypotheses call for a government of men, not laws, in the prison, which might seem against the American governmental tradition. However, it is appropriate to deviate partially from this tradition in a prison which achieves its primary goal, that of rehabilitating offenders, through relationships between staff and inmates. With a good staff it is possible to achieve a consensus among most staff members and inmates as to what handling of infractions is fair and constructive, even when the handling is flexible. Of course, any American prison staff still has some limits to its behavior set by both statutory law and administrative regulation. The issue is how much latitude these laws and regulations should allow.

The ideal of a "government by laws, not men" developed in a period of rebellion against the abuses of tyranny. Prison staffs have the power to be tyrannical, and where they lack the qualification and training to use this power wisely, a government by rigid laws may be most appropriate. In other words, the very specific regulation of discipline by rules suggested in the definite-penalty hypothesis might be preferable in a prison with a staff incapable of handling its authority with the wisdom which is demanded by the flexible-rules and constructive-penalty hypotheses. Indeed, in a prison operating under a punitive tradition with poorly selected, sadistic, or relatively untrained or improperly trained personnel, introduction of the flexible disciplinary policy suggested by the flexible-rules hypothesis could be disastrous. However, when staffs exist such as those in federal prisons and in some of the best state prisons, flexible disciplinary policy will enhance prison order and augment the rehabilitative influence of inmate-staff relationships.

It is probable that the flexible approach is more advantageous than a rigid-rule policy in dealing with major infractions which traditionally receive automatic and severe penalties. Nuisance infractions involving little serious threat to prison order, such as those from careless habits in putting away equipment or clothing or doing work incorrectly, might be administered under the fixed rules of the definite-penalty hypothesis without seriously violating constructive-penalty objectives. This assumes that the penalties imposed would not be such as to alienate the offender from the staff if imposed uniformly, and that the infractions are not likely to receive appreciable inmate support.

It should be stressed that order in a prison is a collective event reflecting the overall patterns of relationship between staff and inmates as well as intra-staff and intra-inmate relationships.

THE SOCIAL PSYCHOLOGY OF DISCIPLINARY RELATIONSHIPS

It is not surprising that a state of war between staff and inmates often is evident at correctional institutions, since for many inmates a reputation for nonconformity can become a source of pride, perhaps something to "live up to." This occurs with adolescents when the act of disobedience is one that produces a sense of manliness, of adult autonomy or of toughness, a perception especially encouraged by their associates. An official policy of segregating individuals considered custodial problems into groups with others who have been intractable amounts to labeling, and will probably have the effect of improving their self-image. This is suggested by the findings of Fiedler and Bass (1959) that both military and civilian offenders viewed themselves more favorably when incarcerated than when on probation in the free community; they tended to evaluate themselves from the standpoints of the people they were with. When criminals are deemed so dangerous as to require confinement, a minimum of regimentation and mass treatment and a maximum of contact with people who are not criminals may help to counteract the criminalizing effects of incarceration.

Even when offenders view crimes they commit against fellow inmates, such as robbery or other predations, as aberrant when committed by others, they are often able to discredit and reject the condemnatory labels that they themselves receive. This rejection reflects the process called "neutralization" by Sykes and Matza (1957), "conventionalization" by Lofland (1969) and "rationalization" by Freud. In the case of the individual criminal the process involves applying favorable labels and interpretations to his own acts, which are viewed as having special justifications not applicable in all such offenses. A common device is to blame the victim for having provoked the act. The victim may be described as morally inferior or stupid and therefore deserving of mistreatment, or as being so well off that the stolen goods "won't be missed." The latter rationalization is usually invoked when the victim is the government—"The Establishment"—rather than an individual. Sometimes perpetrators explain that their crimes are due to lapses from their normal mental conditions, such as drunkenness, desperate straits, the wrongs they have suffered or temporary psychological moods or ailments.

Persons who are accused of wrongdoing customarily condemn their condemners by claiming that the accusers are themselves dishonest or corrupt. People convicted of crimes tend to "collect injustices," as Matza (1964) puts it. They harp on every alleged or actual defect in the criminal justice system and feel ethically superior by comparison. "Censoriousness" was Mathiessen's (1965) term for the tendency of those imprisoned for violating society's norms to preoccupy themselves with the norm violations of their keepers; as he phrased it, these are "the defenses of the weak."

People who work with prisoners and achieve good rapport with them—especially outsiders such as researchers from a university, employees of social work or religious organizations serving prisoners, or other sociable visitors of inmates—can expect to be plied by some prisoners with endless repetitive accounts of the moral and other defects of various criminal justice officials. The most articulate inmates—usually known in the institution as "politicians" and disproportionately employed in front offices, prison hospitals and prison newspapers—are especially preoccupied with and adept at such communication. Although these criticisms are often based on fact, the avidity with which they are recounted reveals their real raison d'être. One should note: (a) that this phenomenon of censoriousness has existed in prisons for decades, long before organized groups of inmates began to seek political support from outside the institution; and (b) that censoriousness is a major factor in neutralizing the sense of guilt or remorse that criminal justice officials often hope to inspire by punishing offenders.

The individual's human need to feel secure about his moral worth and to be free of an oppressive sense of guilt is expressed in his rejection of labels and in his attempts to justify his crimes on moral grounds. Talcott Parsons (1951, Ch. 7) argues that these stresses generate motivation to uphold strongly polar positions with respect to the dominant people or to the rules of one's society—either a dedicated deviance or a rigid conformity can reduce ambivalent feelings about one's morality. The extreme deviant reaction is discernible in the rebelliousness and expressive destructiveness of the crimes of adolescents, notably their vandalism, much of which is directed against school property. The opposite extreme is represented by persons in authority who insist upon complete dominance over subordinates and on the absolute enforcement of rules in all cases, and who derive from this rigid stance a sense of their moral superiority.

When criminal justice employees with such a compulsive enforcement perspective confront an adolescent who has intensely rationalized his or her commitment to law violation or rule breaking, hostility rapidly escalates and the opposing views become still more polarized. Those familiar with correctional institutions soon learn that punishment of disobedient inmates tends to be much more extreme in juvenile and youth facilities than in prisons for adults; in some cases it is necessary to regulate the severity of disciplinary penalties. This attitude develops because stubborn rebelliousness, as an assertion of autonomy and of what is perceived by them as their manly or womanly strength of character, is more common among young offenders than it is among older ones. Similar conditions are fostered by large institutions where inmates are highly regimented, since responsibility for large groups of prisoners by individual staff members is especially conducive to stereotyping of inmates by staff, and of staff by inmates. The separate cohesiveness of staff and of inmates is thus promoted. Hostility between offenders and criminal justice personnel reaches passionate levels whenever the most actively and compulsively alienated offenders enter into escalating exchanges of hostile gestures with the most actively and compulsively conformist members of the staff.

An alternative to overt and aggressive defiance is surreptitious evasion of laws and rules, as well as manipulative deception of officials. This gives the offender a sense of "smartness," of having "conned" the authorities, and is thus quite as compatible with an extreme commitment to law violation as open rebelliousness. This alternative is what Parsons calls the "passive alienation" form of polarized defiance, as contrasted with the "active alienation" mode manifested in open defiance. Those mature offenders who continue to feel that nonconformity with the law enhances prestige tend to become more passive, hence evasive, in their law and rule violations and in their dealings with personnel of the criminal justice system. These offenders are well represented by the inmate politicians among prisoners with recidivistic records, who are astute at "conning" correctional officials in order to secure "front-office" jobs. Case study predictions of post-parole success for these offenders are seldom realized. Such adult offenders are presaged by what Warren (1967, 1969) has called the "manipulative" type of delinquent. These individuals believe that they have a stake in nonconformity and that they raise the ante each time they manage to "con" some official or other. In the same way, the actively alienated become more deeply committed to crime as a result of the self-acclaim and peer praise they gain through openly defiant acts.

A passive form of compulsive conformity is also pointed out by Parsons. This kind is illustrated by the ritualistic perfectionism of some officials who devote themselves to the dogged checking and enforcement of every detail of bureaucratic procedural requirement, regardless of circumstances. A condition of escalating polarization tends to be produced whenever staff and offenders exhibiting either the passive or the active forms of extreme conformity or extreme alienation confront and interact with one another; both represent passionate and moralistic commitments to their own positions.

REDUCING INMATE VIOLENCE

A general statement on correctional strategies for reducing the assaultiveness of offenders can be formulated as follows:

The modification of assaultive conduct requires that offenders gain experience and reward through nonviolent resolution of differences, identify with persons from nonviolent subcultures and share in group pressures directed against violence.

The ultimate success of this broad strategy depends on the attainment of five intermediate objectives:

1. Minimize as much as possible the concentration of persons from violence-prone subcultures in the same groups and facilities.

Many large correctional institution systems become locked into the simplistic practice of countering the violent acts of inmates chiefly by housing together those who have displayed similar degrees of violent behavior. As a result, the most violent offenders are concentrated in one institution, or in separated parts of one or more institutions. The degree of custodial security considered essential for safety varies among institutions. Too great an emphasis on security yields side effects that may actually increase violence and reduce safety for inmates and staff alike. Prisoners released from high security prisons may also pose a greater threat to the community than others.

The possibility of readily transferring problem cases discourages officials from coping imaginatively with inmates who exhibit violent behavior during confinement. Little thought and exertion are required to move such prisoners to increasingly secure facilities and, ultimately, to continuous solitary confinement in "adjustment" or "administrative segregation" centers, whereas true change demands dedicated effort.

Furthermore, the transfer process results in extreme concentration of inmates who come from subcultures that are prone to violence. There is scant opportunity to learn values and skills that encourage the nonviolent achievement of influence and resolution of conflict in a group that ratifies violent behavior and gains prestige from engaging in it. Extreme custodial grading thus transforms maximum security institutions into centers of continual violence or renders them, as an unimaginative recently retired warden of one such prison asserted, "unmanageable."

Safety requires that dangerous prisoners be confined in facilities that provide the following safeguards: secure perimeters, architectural features that permit inmate interaction with others to be continuously observable, and prompt access to superior force when necessary to suppress violence and remove the participants to temporary isolation. Segregation of the violence-prone as a control measure need not prevail to the extent that is now the case in many states. However, additional attempts should be made to change the attitudes of violent inmates.

2. Increase participation of persons from violence-prone subcultures in open formal group activities.

A frequent achievement of street workers with delinquent gangs and of group counselors in correctional institutions and halfway houses has been a decrease in the number of violent acts committed by their charges. (However, these correctional and crime prevention specialists have not greatly affected rates of property crime.) The success of street workers in "cooling" incipient "rumbles" between street gangs has often been reported (e.g., in New York City Youth Board publications). Group counselors at institutions describe numerous occasions when tension among residents has been "talked out" at group sessions. Disturbances have often been prevented by patiently nurtured inmate self-government groups that had been assigned responsible roles in correctional institutions, notably in recent years at the Washington State Penitentiary at Walla Walla. Unfortunately, none of these efforts aimed at reducing violence—street work with gangs, group counseling and inmate governing—have been subjected to systematic study.

Hostility expressed verbally in formal groups can be talked out if the norms of orderly discourse are well established. Loud threats, abusive language and physical aggression are seen as violations of the norm, and tend to discredit the user. More or less formal organizations of many types foster peer support for orderly verbal expression in place of the physical manifestation of hostility, and provide experience in giving and receiving nonviolent messages. In some so-called encounter groups speech and gestures become highly provocative, but norms still preserve a nonviolent atmosphere and permit verbal resolution of conflict. A large variety of formal groups among institutionalized offenders may, as a side effect, stimulate interest in nonviolent activities and skills—e.g., art, chess or sports clubs or service organizations such as the Inmate Welfare League, Alcoholics Anonymous and the Lifers With Hope Club—provided they are conducted democratically, with maximum membership participation in decisions and tasks.

Paranoid assaultive subgroups existing within the violence-prone subculture represent a challenge to those responsible for maintaining order. These subgroups not only subscribe to widely prevalent norms supporting violence, but buttress them with a distinctive ideology to rationalize their choice of target or their method of attack. The psychiatric definition "paranoid" is applied to this subgroup because their ideology is based, at least in part, on delusions about the justification for their assaultive conduct.

It is usually quite frustrating to argue with core members or leaders of a well-established paranoid group. Fringe members or sympathizers may be persuaded to shift their support on the basis of evidence or logic. Dedicated group members, however, base their conception of their own moral worth on the claims of their ideology, which is symbolized by their leaders. The ardent supporters have a personal stake in resisting change, and see those who challenge their views as threats. Therefore, they resort to unwarranted *ad hominem* insults, to ignoring evidence or argument they cannot discredit, or to other questionable argumentative devices. The ideology of paranoid groups includes delusions and distortions intermixed with some concepts that are sound, or at least not readily disproved. It is useful in ideological disputes to identify the verifiable, the uncertain and the clearly fallacious.

The principles advanced as a means of effecting change in subcultures prone to violence may also be applied to paranoid assaultive groups, which represent special cases within the subculture. In psychological terms, if group activities and attitudes are to be changed, positive reinforcements must be withheld and a gratifying alternative lifestyle must be encouraged. Fringe members are more receptive to such measures than core members and leaders. It is helpful to disperse the group so that its members mingle with offenders of varying backgrounds and affiliations and encounter other views and attitudes.

The end result of segregating a group, dealing with its members collectively and tagging them all with the same label is the reinforcement of the group's solidarity. Treating the leaders as spokesmen for a larger group rather than as individuals intensifies their sense of importance and the gratification they derive from affiliation with the group. The alternative approach is to recognize each offender as an individual with unique capabilities and to guide him into legitimate activities that reward these aptitudes. Often the sound idealism that may be a component of a paranoid ideology can be channeled into constructive activities for a legitimate cause in a legitimate manner and with a nonviolent group.

It is assumed here that members of paranoid groups held in correctional custody have been confined because they were convicted of criminal acts, and not because of their ideologies. It is also understood that the political views of most prisoners are neither paranoid nor violence-oriented. Our discussion thus far has shown that any feasible form of participation of prisoners in legitimate political organizations is not just a civil right but is in most cases an experience that will strengthen motivation for the avoidance of further crime. These observations support a third objective:

3. Foster formal and informal interaction of persons from violence-prone subcultures with persons from nonviolent subcultures.

Participation of inmate or delinquent gang representatives in outside organizations such as sports, study groups and service clubs facilitates interaction among persons from diverse backgrounds and thus promotes acculturation. Opportunities for these experiences are often provided to correctional institutions by visitors from community groups. A number of religious organizations, notably the Quakers, have long traditions of systematic visiting of penitentiaries. A growing number of colleges and universities near prisons have extensive programs of student participation in collaborative learning, recreation and service activities with inmates. The programs of Whitman College at the Washington State Penitentiary at Walla Walla are an outstanding example. The visits of ex-offenders, however, may be a more effective first step in reaching hard-core offenders. Ex-prisoner organizations have become increasingly involved in this mission.

Inmates value association with outsiders as a respite from their isolation. Some students and faculty members of nearby colleges become deeply committed to prison visiting as an ongoing voluntary activity. Some universities include student teaching or counseling of offenders in the academic credit progrm. Other students and faculty members are fascinated by prison service projects only while they have the appeal of novelty. Even so, these people are able to contribute new perspectives to inmates in informal interaction, and they are replaced as participants each year by new classes.

Sound correctional planning assigns officials specific responsibility for assuring a maximum amount of visiting between the prison and educational or other community establishments; this can be part of an overall assignment to encourage and coordinate volunteer services for offenders and to involve violence-prone inmates in formal open group activity with persons of nonviolent background. Such activities can provide a learning situation.

4. Penalize groups as units for the violent acts of their individual members, and reward them for nonviolence, to foster the transference of group norms of nonviolence to individual conduct.

One of the least effective ways of dealing with group disciplinary problems is to restrict penalties for individual offenses to individual offenders. This practice is mandatory in a free society, but in many closed institutions as well as in classes, clubs and teams in the community, more effective control is often achieved by establishing at the outset that the whole group will be penalized for the separate misdeeds of its members. When violence is the problem such a policy, if enforced fairly and instructively, can foster nonviolent attitudes in members of groups varying greatly in age and background. Even those who have shared the experience of living in a violent subculture can be so affected. Prisoners are motivated to cooperate in controlling violence. This paves the way for group acceptance of a policy of "cooling it" when quarrels occur. In the violent subculture, an individual who is singled out for punishment for engaging in physical assault becomes a hero to his peers. However, in the group learning to live by a nonviolent code, assaultive conduct by one of its members is viewed as a threat to the welfare of the whole group.

Nonetheless, penalties imposed on groups for the violent behavior of individuals are often resented by those who were not involved in the assaults. In time, however, most inmates come to appreciate a group penalty policy that affords them protection from victimization by assault. Staff must be aware of the possibility that the group itself may become violent toward its violent members. The problem of persistent violence can be referred by officials to the group, as a challenge to its collective responsibility. The group would then mobilize efforts to identify and correct the causes of violence. Prison officials who complain that the inmates of their institutions cannot assume responsibility may in fact be attempting to rationalize their own unwillingness to assign responsibility to prisoners.

It should be obvious that violent, unfair, unexplained or cruel penalties, whether directed against individuals or against groups, can only aggravate violent tendencies. Furthermore, the repeatedly validated psychological laws of reinforcement indicate that group rewards based on peaceful resolution of difficulties, if timely and relevant, will be more effective in changing norms than group punishments for violence.

Tangible rewards for nonviolence become unnecessary when "virtue is its own reward," that is, when nonviolent methods of handling disputes clearly produce more mutually acceptable settlements of differences and a heightened sense of the group's effectiveness than violence. To assure the success of a system of open formal group procedures and group penalties or rewards staff must exhibit consistent support of such methods and adhere to a framework of reasonable rules. Officials must demonstrate and maintain orderly discourse, and not allow themselves to be "conned" or bullied. These standards require more effort and thought by staff than does arbitrary authoritarian domination. However, inmates who have learned from experience that group decison methods can effectively assist in maintaining an orderly institution are more likely to be guided by nonviolent norms and to use related skills after release than those who experienced a discipline imposed by fiat alone.

5. Reduce the prestige of violence.

In a society in which the mass media, especially movies and television, publicize and idolize violent people, both real and legendary, criminal justice agencies can do little to alter significantly the widespread delusion that prestige and glamor can be acquired by outrageous conduct. Nevertheless, it is incumbent on these agencies to combat these notions to the extent of their ability. At the very least, criminal justice agencies must in no way promote the concept that prestige can be won by violent acts.

The fact that weight lifting is the most readily available hobby and exercise for prison inmates blatantly advertises a woeful lack of imagination and leadership on the part of correctional administrators. So also does the fact that boxing is the form of organized athletics and of television sports watching most often provided for inmates. These activities may indeed reduce the tensions of prison life and relieve inmate boredom. They may even encourage good behavior, if deprivation of such privileges is used as a penalty for serious rule violation. Unfortunately, the emphasis on such pursuits in fact reinforces values learned in subcultures that are prone to violence. In practice, the most muscularly developed of the weight lifters frequently bully other inmates into homosexual enslavement and extort other favors. Fear of powerful strong-arm individuals leads to the manufacture of knives by inmates who are not able to defend themselves by muscle alone, and escalation of arming and of organized violence ensues.

In many correctional institutions these practices are so deeply entrenched that they cannot quickly be eradicated. When officials are indifferent to the exploitation of weak inmates by stronger ones, the latter may, by terrorism, achieve a semblance of order. However, although order may appear to prevail, rehabilitation is seriously retarded. Official attempts to alter such a situation abruptly may invite riots, because they challenge the power of an inmate leadership that has attained its influence through actual or threatened violence. The pernicious effects of a violent, menacing environment may be minimized, however, by emphasizing more suitable types of physical activity and by providing nonviolent outlets for inmate expression. These alternatives may include team sports in which all are required to take part, and the already discussed inmate participation in democratic organizations. As more constructive alternatives are developed, weight lifting, boxing and other activities that contribute to violent attitudes can be phased out. An inordinate preoccupation with physical culture and boxing skill can be a psychological trap for the inmate. Such pursuits may enhance prestige and self-esteem at the moment, but they consume time required for more constructive efforts. Social and vocational skills acquired in prison can contribute to the released offender's successful adjustment to community life.

23

INMATE SELF-GOVERNMENT
AND
THE RIGHT TO PARTICIPATE

J. E. BAKER

In penology there yet persists the dream of finding a specific for the treatment of the myriad ills consigned to prisons by society. Historically the most intriguing attempts to create such a specific are those concerned with inmate self-government.

Of all concepts in corrections, inmate self-government is most likely to arouse partisan feelings. Other issues arising from time to time have been debated and resolved in orderly fashion by an incorporation in practice or at least an acceptance in principle. This has not been the case for self-government plans. The pros and cons of the matter as expressed today are essentially the same as those several decades ago. The static quality of the debate is interesting and significant for several reasons. First, it indicates little thoughtful examination of the inmate self-government concept and a paucity of fresh thinking. Reasons for or against self-government apparently stem from the psychological truism that we observe and remember selectively in accordance with our developed expectancies. Such selectivity tends to affirm the correctness of the expectancy.

Second, it appears that attitudes toward self-government are based primarily on accounts of such arrangements as advocated or practiced many years ago. Apparently, there has been no organized attempt to apply recent theoretical studies of institutional social processes or the results of experimentation in inmate social organization to the concept of self-government.

Third, advocates of self-government tend to regard it as a method or model of treatment which can be applied across the board to all inmates in all institutions.

Source: From *Journal of Criminal Law, Criminology, and Police Science* 55, 1(1964): 39–47 and *The Right to Participate: Inmate Involvement in Prison Administration* (Metuchen, N.J.: Scarecrow Press, 1974), pp. 244–252 (editorial adaptations). Copyright © 1974 by J. E. Baker. Reprinted by permission of the author and publishers.

Fourth, in contrast to other concepts which have intermittently appeared on the correctional scene, there apparently has been no real application of scientific principles in determining the efficacy and efficiency of self-government.

There appear to be very few neutral or uncommitted persons on this subject. Opinions are quite definite and can be summarized as follows:

Positive: Inmate self-government or inmate council systems are a part of the "new penology," hence are therapeutic in nature. Since we are nothing if we are not therapeutic, then we are "for" self-government. We know self-government will work if insidious forces do not undermine it.

Negative: The entire history of self-government proves how unsound it is. It never lasted anywhere. That is proof enough of its unworthiness. If inmates were smart enough to govern themselves they would not be in prison in the first place.

As can be readily seen, nothing in the position of either camp is in the nature of a reason. In either point of view we recognize familiar stereotypes not defensible on an intellectual basis.

In an attempt to provide a better perspective on inmate self-government, we have examined past experiments and experiences and have solicited the views of present correctional institution administrators. Our summaries and discussions are concerned with suggestions as to the reasons for the rigidity of opinions about the concept of self-government through inmate councils. In addition, we offer some views on the prospects for these groups in correctional institution practice.

No claim of completeness is made for the historical review of self-government experiences. Undoubtedly there have been other experiences about which no accounts have been published or which have not come to our attention. However, the review is a representative sampling of self-government experiments in correctional institution history.

PAST EXPERIMENTS AND EXPERIENCES

The earliest reference we found to an inmate self-government system in American penal institutions is that of the *Walnut Street Jail,* Philadelphia, in 1793. Our information is meager, mentioning only that the prisoners established rules to provide harmonious living with each other. As an example, a regulation pertaining to cleanliness was cited. It provided that no man should spit elsewhere than in the chimney. Punishment for violations was exclusion from the society of fellow prisoners. It is stated this was found to be sufficient.[52]

At the *New York House of Refuge* in 1824, a reformatory for delinquent children, the first Superintendent, Joseph Curtis, introduced a modified form of self-government. Rule violators or those charged by others with committing an offense were tried by a jury of boys. The Superintendent was the Judge. If the accused was found guilty the number of lashes to be given was announced by the foreman of the jury and administered by the Superintendent.[53] The system had no other features of consequence. Curtis was Superintendent for approximately one year. The system terminated at his departure.

Another reformatory for delinquent children, the *Boston House of Reformation,* established in 1826, was the setting for an early experiment which was broader in scope and lasted throughout the several years tenure of its originator. A young Episcopal minister, the Reverend E. M. P. Wells, became Superintendent of the institution in 1828 and promptly attracted considerable attention by his rather intensive education programming. Inmates were given a voting participation in the administration of the school. Corporal punishments were entirely excluded. Monitors were appointed from among the youngsters at the beginning of each month, and the head monitor presided over the institution in the absence of the officers.[54]

While his contemporaries had some reservations about his program, there was a consensus as to the outstanding nature and ability of Wells himself. Disagreement with the Boston Common Council after an official inspection visit in 1832 led to his resignation soon thereafter.

In his autobiography published in 1912, Zebulon R. Brockway reports that while he was Superintendent of the *Detroit House of Corrections* during the 1860's, he experimented with engaging prisoners in monitorial and mechanical supervision and in educating their fellow prisoners.[55] He claims this was ennobling to the prisoners so assigned. While we would not seriously doubt Mr. Brockway's claim of a self-government group during the 1860's, it does seem rather odd that he had never previously mentioned it.

The Mutual Aid League organized at the *Michigan Penitentiary* in 1888, under Warden Hiram F. Hatch, is the earliest contemporarily reported record of any inmate self-government system among adult prisoners.[56] The set of principles involved in this arrangement anticipated by many years those widely publicized three decades later in Osborne's Mutual Welfare League. In an unsupervised meeting an inmate committee drew up a constitution, naming the organization *The Mutual Aid League of the M.S.P.* This constitution set forth the usual ideals of self-government and group advancement. Meetings were held monthly with the Warden as presiding officer. Reports indicate he attended meetings "without guards." Warden Hatch received considerable criticism from contemporaries, which he answered by referring to a favorable record in the maintenance of prison discipline.[57]

The story of *The George Junior Republic* founded in 1896 by William Reuben George (1866–1936) is a familiar one and needs no recounting here except its mention as a rather early experience in institutional self-government. In 1908 the National Association of Junior Republics was organized and continues to the present. For this study, the George Junior Republic has special importance, since two of the later strong advocates for inmate self-government in penal institutions were associates of the founder. They were Thomas Mott Osborne, Member, Board of Directors, and Calvin Derick, General Superintendent.

Calvin Derick utilized the pioneering work of George when appointed Superintendent of the *Ione Reformatory in California* in 1912. He outlined and formulated a program using inmate self-government as the keystone of its arch. It is significant to note the Ione experiment represents the first acknowledgement and endorsement of inmate self-government by any state. At the inauguration of the second president of the self-government group, Governor Hiram Johnson of California went to the school and placed the stamp of his approval upon the experiment.[58]

The purported sole purpose of this system of self-government was to furnish a medium in which the boys might develop a civilization of their own with as many degrees and gradations as necessary to meet their needs and interests, the ideal being to come as close as possible to standards of civilization.

In his annual report for 1915, Frank Moore, Superintendent of the *State Reformatory, Rahway, New Jersey,* explains the failure of a self-government plan begun in 1914 and abandoned at the end of the year: "[A]fter giving the question sober consideration the inmates of the Reformatory felt that it was better for them that the institution should return to the original plan of being governed by the appointed authority of the institution and hence the council disbanded."[59]

In December, 1913, *The Mutual Welfare League* was founded at New York State's Auburn Prison by Thomas Mott Osborne. The stated purpose and objective of this inmate self-government group was to alter concepts of confinement then practiced routinely in the majority of penal institutions.

It was Osborne's contention, based on his experience with the George Junior Republic, that self-government was the practical remedy for the evils of the prison system. After a voluntary one week term of confinement at Auburn Prison he developed, with inmate assistance, the methods of implementing a self-government plan in an institution for adult offenders. A cardinal principle was that prisoners must work out their own plan, rather than have an outside plan presented to them. Osborne noted: "This was real, vital democracy; this was solving the problem in the genuine American spirit."[60]

It is significant to note that Warden Rattigan, of Auburn, with the approval of the New York State Superintendent of Prisons, proposed to hand over all infractions of discipline to the League except in five instances: assault on an officer, deadly assault upon another inmate, refusal to work, strike, and attempt to escape.

Prisoner cooperation was the foundation of the League. Its operations were based on the premise that the prison could be treated as a community. Tannenbaum espouses this by his comment: "Prisoners possessed among themselves a public opinion that if properly harnessed could be made effective in the enforcement of public policy and the development of public morale, which would make discipline both easier upon the warden and more effective with the men."[61]

Osborne became Warden of *Sing Sing Prison* on December 1, 1914. He immediately organized a Mutual Welfare League which has been described by Wines as follows:

> The real instruments of self-government at Sing Sing were the committees. It was these that effectively expressed the wishes of the prisoners and took the initiative in getting things done. The Warden's day was filled with appointments with committee chairmen who wanted assistance or advice. The chairmen quickly came to realize that a great deal of power lay in their hands if they knew how to wield it. Not only were they trustees of the wishes of their fellow-inmates, but the prison officials came to regard them as responsible makers of institution policy. Some of them became adept in the art of getting what they wanted without appearing to ask for much. Aside from the specific things they accomplished, their activity was beneficial in two ways: (1) It taught them some of the difficulties of administration, thus enabling them to pass that knowledge back to their constituents; and (2) It enabled the prison authorities, by means of the understanding thus promoted, to rely upon cooperation where before they would have received only suspicion and distrust.[62]

Later, Osborne organized a League while serving as Commandant of the Naval Prison, Portsmouth, New Hampshire.

At the *State Reformatory, Cheshire, Connecticut,* a self-government experiment was begun in 1915 and abandoned in the following spring. While we have no adequate description of its operation, Mr. Charles H. Johnson, Superintendent during the last eight months of the self-government regime, made the following report:

The reason for the dissatisfaction in the organization was that it lent itself readily to so much misrule and dishonesty that the inmates were tired of it. . . . It was finally decided at a gathering of the inmates that the management of the institution should be placed with the Superintendent and the officers appointed by law.[63]

In 1927 Howard B. Gill, Superintendent, *State Prison Colony, Norfolk, Massachusetts,* inaugurated a program of individual directional inmate treatment called the Norfolk Plan. This approach utilized balanced programs in the following broad areas: (1) inmate classification, (2) group system of housing and supervision, (3) community organization on a basis of joint-responsibility, and (4) individual programs for treatment.[64]

Based upon a classification of prisoners into groups of fewer than 50 men the development of a complete program for the period of confinement was directed by a House-Officer acting as a resident caseworker. Such an officer lived with the inmates for 24 hour periods on an alternate schedule.

The third phase of the Plan, an inmate organization known as the Council, occurred as a direct outgrowth of the group system of housing and supervision. Together with the staff, the Council constituted the community government of the institution.

In an address before the Conference on the Treatment of Criminal Deliquency at Cambridge, Massachusetts, December 4, 1930, Gill reported as follows:

. . . This is not to be confused with the strictly penal administration of the Colony which is in the hands of the Superintendent and his assistants. Also in contrast to inmate organizations in some institutions which are founded on the principle of self-government in the hands of inmates only, this community organization operates on the principle of joint responsibility in which *both* officers and inmates take part.

. . . In general the plan has worked, although it is neither an 'honor system' nor 'self-government,' because it is founded frankly on a basis of results for both Staff and men. . . . Neither officers nor men give up their independence or their responsibilities, and each continually checks the other to insure square dealing; but both agree that cooperation works better than opposition where men must work and eat and live together, whatever the circumstances.[65]

Summary

Two features of these past experiments stand out, both containing the seeds of self-destruction—inmates functioning as disciplinarians, and the dependence of the systems on a lone individual for sponsorship.

Discipline is a part of the treatment which must be retained in toto by prison personnel. Its proper administration requires a degree of objectivity which is not to be found in the object itself. This feature of the past experiments calls for an altruism psychologically not possible in the faulty ego structure of the socially disadvantaged and damaged person.

Involvement in the disciplinary process appears to have been a point of departure for these systems. One need not ponder long the question as to why. Examine only briefly the accounts of the early prisons, and the stark naked brutality of disciplinary practices assaults your senses. Revolting as they are to us today, these were the accepted methods of dealing with deviancy. The untrained personnel of the old prisons were ill equipped to handle discipline problems. To the originators of the early experiments apparently this was the area in most urgent need of change. Also, this was an area offering the best prospects for effecting a positive change. All the administrator need do was to reassign the responsibility for discipline from staff to inmates. This he could not do in other functional areas without a complete breakdown of operation. For this reason, it is believed, the self-government idea became equated with the handling of disciplinary matters.

Only at Gill's Norfolk State Prison Colony was staff support enlisted. It is apparent that it was not wanted by the other experimenters. Those employees affected by self-government were often placed in situations subordinating them to inmates. Little comment is necessary regarding the administrative crassness of this arrangement. Modern management recognizes the need for interpretive communication in advance of the implementation of an innovation. The presence of untrained and incompetent personnel intensifies that need. We can speculate as to the many positive changes which might have resulted had administrators of yesteryear focused their efforts on staff development.

THE EVOLVING PERSPECTIVE

As we review the scene from 1793 to 1973, it appears that the concept of offender participation in prison management as embodied in the advisory council has seldom been utilized in more than a superficial manner. Many administrators regard the advisory council as simply a device for the communication of inmate complaints to the administration. This narrow view has produced the term "gimme" groups.

The various rationales for the existence of advisory councils range from the pragmatism of providing an administrative peephole through which inmate plots may be discovered to the altruism of learning democracy by experiencing it. Some practitioners accept the view that the inmate must be a part of the service process rather than simply an object of service, but have done little to translate the view into action.

The history of advisory councils, since 1930 in particular, reveals that often the first step taken to create a positive relationship between inmates and staff has been the organization of an advisory council. Additionally, advisory councils have been organized following a crisis situation, such as a riot, as an agency to bring order out of chaos. In many respects, an advisory council formed under such conditions may be likened to a peace tribunal to which each side may send its most enlightened and capable representatives to determine upon what terms and by what means future difficulties might be averted.

Then, on the other hand there are institutions where an advisory council has never been organized for any reason or under any circumstance. There is no evidence that the presence or the absence of an advisory council has had any marked influence on the destiny of an institution. The best evidence which can be adduced from the past and the present is that open communications between inmates and staff does seem to facilitate the adjustment of both groups.

Why do some correctional administrators look with disfavor upon inmate advisory councils while others turn to the concept for succor in periods of program malaise and in the aftermath of disaster? Further, why, during the course of our surveys, did many administrators qualify their admissions of no councils with statements reflecting a belief that councils offer many advantages to an institution program, that serious thought was being given to establishing a council, or that the organization and operation of a council had not been ruled out for the future. Certainly these reflect more than a suggestion of uncertainty about not having a council.

Many administrators are obviously concerned that some inmates will use membership on an advisory council to their personal advantage and at the expense of sound administration. It has been postulated that since many inmates have grievances they may tend to regard the advisory council as a forum for the expression of those grievances. All of this may well be true. Also true is the fact that some staff members may have views similar to those of the inmates and in that light define their own role as one of advocacy and align themselves with the inmates. So, both inmates and staff can use an advisory council to their personal advantage and at the expense of sound administration.

The foregoing should be regarded by the administrator as a challenge to his correctional management skill rather than as a reason not to have an advisory council if he believes that such a group will be of value. The administration simply needs to recognize that this attitude may underlie the approach by some inmates and some staff members to the advisory council concept. A necessary part of the development of both groups is to recognize the defined role of an advisory council. And only management can make that definition.

Opponents of the advisory council point out that some inmates will use their advisory council membership to create centers of personal power which can subvert the authority of the administration. There is no doubt that politics can be involved, since prisoners are people and people do engage in politics of one fashion or another. Properly designed and monitored procedures can do much to reduce the creation of power centers—for instance, frequent elections and rotation of positions in which power may be implied or inherent, such as committee chairmanships.

If the decision is to have an advisory council, the purpose and scope of the group's function must be fully communicated to and understood by both staff and inmates. This should be accomplished before a group is organized. The method most frequently employed for this communication is the drawing up of a constitution and a set of by-laws. Another approach is the issuance of a directive by the central authority setting forth the official policy regarding advisory councils—or staff-inmate communications, or inmate organizations—and providing organizational and procedural guidelines. These approaches are adequate, but each lacks any means or method of insuring that the intent of the decision maker is effected.

Despite the best structuring, the most careful planning, or the most meticulous implementation, there is no absolutely certain method by which the intended purpose of an advisory council, or any program for that matter, can be assured. But we do know that people respond when their personal interest is involved. A staff response of acceptance and support for an advisory council can be facilitated if management makes it explicit that such acceptance and support are factors in personnel performance expectations.

If an advisory council is organized, it is assumed that the administrator is serious about it, that he is accepting the group as an element in the organizational structure, and perhaps even recognizing the inmates as members of the staff, even though in a subordinate status. Granted all of this, it is his intention then that the advisory council function as an integral agency of the institution. He recognizes that in order for this intent to be translated into reality, the involvement of staff at all levels is necessary. A fatal defect of most of the early experiences with advisory councils, and with many of those that came after 1930, was the dependence of the organizations on a lone individual. When that person departed the scene, the council ceased to exist. To avoid this, the base of personnel involved with council activities should be broadened. A warden and his associate wardens should be actively interested in council functions, of course, but can best demonstrate that interest by insuring budgetary support, for instance, leaving operational contacts to other staff. Whatever staff works directly with the council should be empowered to make decisions and take actions, at least within limits in certain areas.

The question is often raised as to what are the proper functions of an advisory council. The answer lies in the purpose for which the organization is formed. Almost without exception, the expressed purpose of a council is to effect or to improve inmate-staff relationships, and consequently insure the proper functioning of the institution, by providing a free-flow channel of communication. With this as a basis, there is really no function of the institution from which the input of council views should be excluded; even in those involving personnel recruitment, selection, and retention, management should be alert to the possibilities for staff development inherent in effective communication. Staff can learn much about itself by being attentive to the nuances of that communication. The point is important enough for a short digression.

Of all the techniques for changing behavior, the impact of one human being on another is probably the most effective. This imposes a tremendous responsibility on the correctional workers, since the direction of that change may rest in the hands of the worker. It is this aspect of correctional work which lifts it from the ranks of ordinary pursuits and makes of it, if so perceived by the worker, one of the most noble of all endeavors. The correctional self-potential of employees can be better realized when they are in a communication with inmates that will provide the kind of feed-back upon which progressive modifications of role can be based. The advisory council is one means by which this meaningful exchange can be accomplished.

All functions of the advisory council should be continuously monitored and frequently evaluated. Top management should be actively involved in this evaluation, according it the same serious consideration given to other program evaluations. This brings us to what the author regards as the most powerful of all rationales for the inclusion of inmates in both the program and the programming of corrections: the use of council membership as a treatment method. To do so offers an opportunity for effecting attitudinal changes through which more satisfactory modes of coping with social-role demands can be realized. A properly organized and functioning advisory council can be an excellent vehicle for the abundant energies and unusually high abilities of many offenders that are not amenable to conventional treatment forms. Some men need an experience of working for the welfare of others. Others require ego-satisfying assignments in which they can escape the feeling of being engulfed in the crowd.

Council membership often changes recalcitrants to rather agreeable persons; often, too, the inward viewpoint of the self-centered personality is redirected outward to a genuine interest in others. The use of membership in an advisory council as a part of the development plan for a particular inmate certainly will call for a different method by which council members are selected. One method would be to appoint members to the council. There are reasons against this so obvious as to make discussion of them unnecessary. However, in that connection the best accepted and most dynamic advisor council the author has ever known had 75 percent of its members appointed by the staff sponsor. The reason for this was that a series of vacancies created by transfers of elected representatives to other housing units or to other institutions, and the brevity of the unexpired portion of their terms made special elections not feasible. Such appointments were provided for in the council constitution.

Probably the best method is to use the individual's council membership as a part of his treatment development plan, after he has attained membership through the regular ballot process. Those persons for whom it is believed that advisory council membership would be beneficial can be encouraged to seek election. In this regard, classes in the principles of legislative duties, responsibilities, and techniques can be included in the educational program.

It has been the experience of the author, and of many others, that placement in a formalized situation, such as an advisory council, can have a salutary effect on dominating or aggressive individuals—those who demonstrate a big-shot complex. In such a situation where discipline and ability, rather than toughness or muscle are the factors important to personal stature, a distinct toning down process can occur. Conversely, those who are shy and withdrawn in the confinement situation, where a high value is placed on physical powess and who have lost confidence in themselves because of this, can attain some degree of stature and regain a large measure of self-esteem in a formalized structure where calmness and logic are superior to the strident voice and the balled fist.

An advisory council, properly utilized, has a two-way function. It is an agency for communicating to inmates the responsibilities which the administration expects of them and to present a picture of administrative problems in the areas with which inmates are concerned. For instance, by showing them the budget and soliciting their suggestions as to how a better job might be done with available resources, a structure is created which provides for an encourages thoughtful, constructive feedback. This approach involves the same psychological principles basic to management efforts to provide employee job satisfaction—call it morale.

Whether or not the formalized structure of communication is an advisory council or some other method is really not important. What is important is that correctional administrators recognize and believe that communication with their charges is vital to the proper functioning of the correctional process. Just as the advisory council was an outgrowth of self-government, there is much evidence of the evolvement of other forms of organizations in which the inmate is being recognized as performing an essential role in the correctional system.

For example, in Wisconsin, the inclusion of inmates on a committee to make recommendations on correctional grant requests to the Council on Criminal Justice is definitely a new direction in inmate participation. An evaluation of the experience will be of interest. The Residents' Advisory Council on Corrections at the Federal Correctional Institution, Fort Worth, Texas, in which offenders are engaged in discussing correctional philosophy and current practice, is a good example of furthering the social education of the participants.

Further, it is interesting to note the increasing number of jurisdictions in which the central authority has issued official statements on the establishment of formal systems of inmate-staff communications. When a vehicle for this has been suggested, or mandated in some instances, it has usually been an advisory council or similar organization. Guidelines for organization and implementation usually accompany the official statements. The implication of these statements is the growing recognition of the value of communications. Such a recognition is undoubtedly a reflection of an increasing number of professionally oriented persons occupying top management positions, and a manifestation of the results of efforts made during the last several years, through LEAA funded programs, to provide for the professional development of correctional administrators.

A further implication of the foregoing is that throughout the nation, at all levels of government, there is a gorwing relization that simply because of his confined status, the offender should not suffer the loss of all rights. With increasing frequency the courst are mandating changes in prison procedures. It is high time for corrections to acknowledge an additional right, and to guarantee that right, not under the compulsion of a court decree, but on the basis of professional wisdom. Every person in a correctional confinement facility should be assured of: *the right to participate in matters relating to his personal welfare by contributing his point of view.*

The author has previously stated that perhaps correctional administrators would be well advised to look again at the modern counterpart of self-government, the advisory council, and to consider it in its proper perspective as a part of social education, and as a morale-raising device for the entire institution through its facilitation of two-way communication.

24

PRISON INDUSTRY

ELMER H. JOHNSON

Inconsistency of goals and the masking of genuine motives under the guise of prisoner "rehabilitation" are particularly marked in the history of prison industries.

On one hand, it has been argued that the prisoner should work to pay for his keep and ease the burden of supporting the criminal placed on taxpayers who were his prey. A similar attitude has been applied to the insane and mentally defective, but recent decades have left the prisoner as the prime target. A second argument has been that "hard labor while wearing stripes" is an efficient means of deterring future crime or of balancing the scales of retribution by imposing work as punishment. A third argument is that prison labor instills habits of industry. The imposition of menial drudgery has been defended as "therapeutic" in this superficial sense. A fourth argument defines habits of industry and marketable job skills as essential ingredients in preparing the released prisoner for social-psychological integration into a free society in which job status is the basis of responsible social participation.

On the other hand, correctional institutions face many impediments in realizing any of these purposes. Under the *principle of less eligibility,* the inmate is considered less worthy of satisfactory employment and training than the worst-paid noncriminal. This principle was supplanted by what Mannheim calls the *principle of nonsuperiority;* namely, the earlier principle was slightly liberalized to contend that the condition of the criminal should not be superior to that of the worst-paid noncriminal. Consequently, the restriction of prison industry was stimulated by a psychological perspective conflicting with the pure economics of reducing prison operational costs.[66]

Source: From *Crime, Correction and Society* (Homewood, Illinois: Dorsey Press, 1968), pp. 558–566. Reprinted by permission of the author and publisher.

CONFLICT AMONG GOALS

The several objectives frequently conflict with one another. Labor as a punitive device stigmatizes labor for nonpunitive purposes. It strengthens inmate resentment against the prison and its officials, complicating vocational training, which requires instructor-student rapport. Conversely, employment for the sake of vocational training aborts the deterrent effect of punitive labor. Efforts to maximize economic return from industries require emphasis on output, rather than on correction of faulty attitudes of the prisoner-worker. Work pace must not be interrupted to counsel prisoners or to afford the personalized instruction necessary for on-the-job training. Industrial foremen usually are selected for their qualification in meeting output quotas, rather than for their instructional skills. Maximum output usually demands concentration on a few products to exploit the possibilities of minimizing per unit costs. Cost factors favor the use of power machinery which reduces the economic advantage of prison labor and reduces the contribution of prison industries in overcoming prisoner idleness. The increased volume of output raises the issue of competition with free labor. In keeping with the objectives of individualized treatment, vocational training requires a wide variety of products to extend the range of skills taught. On the other hand, because the prisoners generally are either unskilled or semiskilled, the industrial manager is limited in the range of products appropriate for his labor force.

Wardens agree that the most difficult prison to administer is the one in which prisoners languish in idleness. Absence of work leads to moral and physical degradation and corrupts institutional order. However, aimless drudgery is of little advantage. Consequently, official statements of industrial goals recognize rehabilitation of prisoners to varying degrees. As Grunhut has noted, the attainment of rehabilitation through labor is supposed to be through *training FOR work* and *training BY work*.[67] Work has the virtue of relieving boredom. Under the concept of training by work, it is assumed that habits developed through regular employment will persist automatically. In contrast, training for work would employ this more superficial and immediate motivation to work as the first stage of a more sophisticated process of stimulating the prisoner's interest in employment on a long-term basis. Inmate employment becomes only one facet of a multifaceted effort to change the prisoner's attitudes and values. Wages and consideration of the inmate's individual qualities in job assignment can be inducements to promote work motivation.

EVOLUTION OF LABOR SYSTEMS

Systems of prison industries have been based on the so-called "sheltered market" and on the open market. Generally, contemporary prison industries employ the "state-use" and "public works and ways" systems for a sheltered market. The four open-market systems are lease, contract, piece-price, and state account. These four systems are chiefly of historical interest.

The *state-use system* produces goods and renders services for agencies of the state and their political subdivision. *Public works and ways* involves road construction and repair, reforestation, soil-erosion control, and the like. The *lease system* turned care and custody over to an entrepreneur for a stipulated fee. Under the *contract system,* the state retained control of inmates but sold their labor to an entrepreneur at a daily per capita fee. The entrepreneur furnished the raw materials and paid the prison a stipulated fee for each unit of finished product under the *piece-price* arrangement. The state became the manufacturer under the *state account system* and sold its products on the open market.[68]

Sources of Opposition

When reformers sought to develop prison labor programs for purposes other than punishment, they encountered hostility from organized free labor and from some businessmen and industrialists. The development of group cohesiveness has been a major problem for organized labor in the United States where workers have been prone to identify themselves with the lower middle class. The workers have lacked the spontaneous class solidarity upon which European unions were based psychologically. Selig Perlman describes the experimentation which culminated in the job-conscious unionism of the American Federation of Labor about 1890. Recognizing the strength of property rights in American society, unionism adapted the concept of property rights to claim the union's right to control jobs. Job opportunity was viewed as limited. The worker's adherence to the union was won through establishing "rights" in the jobs for the individual and for the work group through agreements regulating priority and seniority in employment.[69] Since organized labor regards as exclusively its own the rights so painfully acquired, labor unions have been sensitive to the extension of job rights to nonmembers. Under the principle of less eligibility, the prison inmate was regarded as an inappropriate competitor for the jobs of free labor.

Labor unions and employer's associations have found a common cause in protesting the "competition" of prison labor. As early as 1801, a New York law required boots and shoes to be labeled with the words "State Prison."[70] The prosperous contract industries attracted major opposition in the northern industrial states in the 1880's. There were a series of investigations into the contract and lease systems in 11 states during the 1870's and 1880's. Manufacturers in certain industries organized a National Anti-Contract Association in 1886.[71] In 1887 contracting of federal criminals was made illegal. Brockway proposed the piece-price system as an alternative to counter the growing opposition to the contract system.

From Lease to State-Use

During the 1830–70 period, the lease and contract systems provided employment and the funds to establish the American penitentiary, but the zeal to make prisons self-supporting had killed the idea that prisoners should be denied opportunities to communicate with each other. Some prisons had been turned over to economic exploiters, jeopardizing security and treatment. The priority of profit making tended to jeopardize parole of skilled prisoners, control of contraband, and the warden's authority. To keep production costs down, the contractor tended to discourage absenteeism necessary for inmate participation in rehabilitation programs. Mass production of a limited variety of articles was favored over the diversity appropriate for vocational training on an individualized basis. Competition with free industry was direct. Just as many prisons were freeing themselves of the objectionable features of the contract and lease systems and achieving steady employment, the opponents of prison industry succeeded in barring sale of prison-made goods on the open market.[72] As one major exception to the general trend, Minnesota established a model state account system in the early 1890's when it took over production and marketing of farm machinery and bindery twine from contractors.[73] The political power of Minnesota farmers and the absence of production of farm machinery in the state explains the continued sale of prison-made farm machinery on the open market, a rare phenomenon today.

The state-use plan was suggested in 1887 and was endorsed in 1900 by the United States Industrial Commission.[74] Legislation struck at the interstate commerce in prison-made goods, with the result that the state-use and public works and ways sytems have become paramount. The Hawes-Cooper Act of 1929 deprived the goods of their interstate character and made them subject to state law. The Ashurst-Sumner Act of 1935 prohibited transportation of goods into states forbidding their entry and required the labeling of prison-made goods shipped in interstate commerce. In the face of mass unemployment during the depression, every state had passed legislation by 1940 to take advantage of this opportunity to ban prison-made goods of other states.[75]

GOALS OF WORK PROGRAMS

Two divergent trends have shaped prison labor programs. One trend reflects the attitude that prison labor should be looked upon as different from labor in general. In keeping with the punitive ideology, the prisoner is thought of as part of the abnormal world of repressive confinement. Labor is seen as a punishment and as an obligation imposed on the prisoner. The prisoner's "hard labor" is deprived of the dignity and incentives of labor in general. His work becomes an activity which isolates him from the rest of society. The deterrence and rehabilitative rationalizations for punishment prescribe hard work at the lowest levels of skill. Even with the rise of humanitarian concern for the lot of the prisoner, the opportunity to work was advocated in the spirit of charity to help the prisoner avoid the moral and physical degradation of idleness; even the humanitarians did not seek to end the differentiation between labor behind bars and labor in the community.

The second trend has been toward improvement of prison labor conditions and increased concern that prison employment should play a part in rehabilitation of character. The aim is to prepare the inmate for a constructive life after release, and prison labor is viewed as an activity intended to reduce the alienation of the offender from society. Vocational instruction is used to develop occupational skills and work motivation. The tasks are related to the inmate's self-interest. The rhythm of work and the conditions of employment are as similar as possible to those in the free world.

A third approach is utilitarian in that some administrators consider prison labor as something to be used to help balance the prison budget. The increasing acceptance of the state-use system is an adjustment of prison administration to the pressure by critics of prison competition with free labor. Being able to cite reduction of governmental costs through prison industries is an additional factor in meeting criticism. However, when given undue priority, the utilitarian approach can negate rehabilitative efforts as the price for budget balancing.

Lopez-Rey argues that within certain limitations prisoners should share the fundamental human rights to work and to earn equal pay for equal work. The limitations stem from the juridical situation of the prisoner which denies him the right to select his work, to refuse a certain task without justification, and to change his place of work. Aside from these limitations, Lopez-Rey would organize prison labor to be as similar to free labor as circumstances would permit. He would bring private industry into the prison to provide the equipment and wage scales of free labor. He argues prisoner self-respect and self-responsibility would emerge as basic elements in rehabilitation of prisoners. Therefore, he contends, many of the existing psychological and psychiatric services would become unnecessary.[76]

Labor and Rehabilitation

Usually there are four activities related to training and employment of inmates. First, the maintenance activities are concerned with the feeding and clothing of prisoners, with providing heat, power, light and other operational requirements of the institution. Second, farms reduce the food costs and afford employment. Third, the industrial department provides employment, possible opportunities for on-the-job training, and a means of reducing the costs to the taxpayer of prison operations and of government in general. Fourth, the educational department contributes to improvement of work skills to promote postrelease employment and to upgrade the quality of prison industrial production.

In merging labor and rehabilitation purposes, a prime problem is to overcome conflicts among the four activists. Ideally, prison industries would be provided well-trained and motivated workers through prisoner classification and vocational training programs which would wed job requirements with inmate self-interest. Unfortunately, most prisons do not integrate vocational training, inmate vocational interests, and choice of industrial specialities to coincide with a vocational training program consistent with the job market for released offenders. Even for the adequate workers among the prisoners, industries must compete in the face of higher priority usually given maintenance activities.

Industrial supervisors have been habituated to using excessive numbers of prisoners because their quality as workers usually depresses productivity. This habit is reinforced by another major problem. Releases on parole or completion of sentence create a high rate of turnover, especially for prisoners most likely to be efficient workers because their characteristics are consistent with early release.

In too many instances prison-made goods are inferior in design and workmanship to the products of private enterprise. The state-use industries have not been able to capture a significant share of the market offered by other governmental institutions because of quality inferiorities and because of the stigma attached to prison-made goods. This failure has contributed to the small scale of industrial operations—too small to support standards of cost reduction and continuity of production essential to giving the inmate familiarity with work situations in the free community.

As a whole, prisoners have inadequate educational attainment, vocational skills, and work habits. To use the bulk of them for anything above unskilled labor, vocational and academic training is required to prepare them for industrial tasks. This preparation consumes a portion of the sentence, reducing the period when a skilled worker will be available for full-time work assignment.

To make prison industrial work a real asset to vocational training, plants must be modernized by eliminating useless jobs, by insisting that each shop be operated on the basis of present-day methods, by emphasizing quality of products, by stressing the goal that men be helped to develop themselves, by holding job training to rigid standards, by recognizing that some inmates are incapable of training, and by emphasizing the recognition of individual differences.[77]

If his labor is to contribute to production goals and his own long-term interest, the industrial program must motivate the prisoner, encourage development of good work habits, and fit him to tasks appropriate to his intelligence, educational potential, age, and ability. To achieve these difficult objectives, Springsted advocates training of industrial supervisors in orientation of new workers, constructive handling of grievances, and recurrent problems for counseling.[78]

It is difficult to strike a proper balance between vocational training for prisoner rehabilitation and the achievement of high production for its own sake. However, even if prisoner rehabilitation were the only aim, the administration would encounter difficult problems: Should an inmate scheduled for early release be given priority in assignment to a wage-paying task so that he may gain funds to support himself and his dependents on the outside? What kinds of work should be given to the physically handicapped? What limitations should there be on the prisoner's expenditure of his earnings? Should a long-term prisoner be permitted to become so wedded to a particular job that he loses interest in other prison programs more in keeping with his needs?[79]

Trade advisory committees and councils provide the means for organized labor and management to participate in vocational and industrial training programs of prisons. A *trade advisory committee* may be set up for each vocational area, whereas a *trade advisory council* represents all trade training within a correctional institution. California has used this plan to obtain expert advice on training standards, procedures, equipment, trainee evaluation, postrelease placement, and instructor requirements. Increased support of prison industries by union and management has been an additional advantage.[80]

Wages for Prisoners

When labor is forced and unrewarded, there is little incentive for diligence and development of skill. As an incentive and reward, money is as effective within an institution as it is in the free society. It is part of the American cultural norms shaping the personality that the offender brings into the institution. Therefore, money is a familiar incentive to him, one that will continue to operate after he is released. Money has great exchange power because the individual can convert it into the specific reward he values most among purchased goods and services. By using money, the institution skirts the difficult problem of fitting a reward to the interests of each inmate. Money serves as a bridge between self-interest and the ability to cooperate with others within a social organization.

The inmate should bear the financial burden of supporting his dependents, rather than adding them to the public welfare programs. He would have a "nest egg" to support himself during the crucial early period of release before he finds employment. With funds available to ease the released prisoner's adjustment, disintegration of families would be prevented. The inmate's sense of responsibility for his family would be nurtured during his confinement. Wages symbolize the state's interest in the inmate's personal welfare.[81] Lack of money contributes to inmate subterfuge, disorder, and labor inefficiency. Leavenworth Penitentiary has rewarded prisoner-workers with a "paid vacation" after two years of good conduct. Wages were continued during a period of absence from work. Improved worker morale and job tenure were reported.[82]

Objections have been raised against inmate wages. Deprivation of earning capacity is viewed as part of punishment. Easing of the lot of the prisoner's family would reduce the deterrent effect of imprisonment. The cost of prison operations already is too great without the additional expense of paying wages.[83] To pay wages to convicted criminals has been opposed as a travesty on social justice when thousands of honest citizens are unable to find employment.[84]

In a national survey, 20 states, the District of Columbia, and the Federal Bureau of Prisons reported payment of wages to from 90 to

100 percent of their inmates. In five states, no more than 10 percent earn money. Six states did not permit inmate earnings in prison. Of 33 states supplying such information in another survey, wages ranged from 4 cents a day to a high of $1.30 a day.[85]

SUMMARY

In a society emphasizing work as the major status determinant, prison industry has important potentialities for making the correctional institution a means of rehabilitation. The trend toward opening new forms of communication with the free community holds promise for reducing the serious discrepancy between the prison and the outside society as universes of social experience. However, if the trend is to have significant results, issues related to prison labor must be resolved. We have reviewed those issues.

25

MUTUAL AGREEMENT PROGRAMMING

AMERICAN CORRECTIONAL ASSOCIATION

WHAT IS MUTUAL AGREEMENT PROGRAMMING?

Mutual Agreement Programming is an innovative approach to corrections designed to encourage greater humanity and efficiency in the criminal justice system. It is based on the following principles:

1. The period of imprisonment can and should help prisoners acquire the skills, self-discipline, and self-respect needed to be responsible citizens and employees in the open community.
2. Inmates can and should determine their individual rehabilitative needs and can be motivated to behave responsibly to meet them when they are treated as active participants, and given appropriate resources.
3. Institutional and parole authorities can and should explicate and coordinate their goals, programs, and expectations so that an inmate's behavior during imprisonment can contribute to and be recognized as contributing to his readiness for release.
4. The conditions and date of parole can and should be made explicit so that inmates can know what is expected of them to earn release, and when release will occur if they fulfill their obligations.
5. Inmates, institutional staff and parole officials can and should be held accountable for developing, delivering, and participating in rehabilitative programs designed in concert, with all parties meeting specified goals appropriate to their roles.
6. For those prisoners able to return responsibly to the community, parole release is a humane and economical alternative to institutionalization. Expediting the parole process (particularly when parolees have acquired marketable job skills through prison training programs) is possible and desirable.

Mutual Agreement Programming is a method of preparation for an inmate's parole release. It calls for the inmate and corrections personnel developing together and formally contracting to complete a

Source: *Mutual Agreement Programming* (College Park, Maryland: American Correctional Association, June 1974), pp. 1-6, 21-23 (editorial adaptations).

rehabilitative program that they design to meet what they agree are the individual inmate's needs and opportunities. Inmate participants in the Mutual Agreement Program negotiate their contracts with representatives of the prison and the parole board. A definite parole date is specified in the contract, contingent on the inmate's successfully completing particular objectives in one or more of these areas: education, skill training, treatment, discipline, or work assignment. Each prisoner is responsible for developing the original written plan on which negotiations are carried out, and for meeting the specific and measurable objectives outlined in his contract. Thus, he works to effect his own release. The use of a formal, negotiated, legally binding contract encourages all parties—institutional and parole personnel as well as inmates—to be responsible and accountable for the program's fulfillment.

Mutual Agreement Programming has been designed to accomplish several interrelated goals:

1. Give inmates greater opportunities to assess and plan for their needs and assume responsibility for their behavior;

2. Improve communications and coordination throughout the corrections system (especially between prison and parole staffs) and establish linkages with relevant community resources;

3. Better prepare prisoners to be responsible citizens and employees after release, through improved job training and coordination with post-release job placement;

4. Expedite the parole process by making the conditions for parole explicit, and setting firm parole dates wherever possible. When parole dates are firm, inmates have concrete goals to work for, and both training and job placement can be arranged more realistically and efficiently.

MAP was developed by the Parole-Corrections project of the American Correctional Association, under U.S. Department of Labor funding. It has been used on an experimental demonstration basis over the past few years in Wisconsin, Arizona, and California (and in Michigan without federal funds), and is being considered for adoption in a number of other states.

Mutual Agreement Programming is still being tested and refined. But experience with the Program in several states has shown it to be workable and acceptable to inmates and corrections personnel alike. For a program that is novel in its use of contracts, and in its approach to establishing the conditions and date of parole, this acceptance is an essential first step. It appears from what is known that MAP participation can motivate prisoners to behave responsibly and constructively in prison; it is expected that MAP participation will help these same individuals, as ex-offenders, find and keep better employment than they might otherwise obtain and that, as a result of better employment and preparation for post-release realities and responsibilities, recidivism rates will be lowered.

HOW WAS MAP DEVELOPED?

Although the various criminal justice agencies are sometimes called the "criminal justice system," there has been little if any coordination and communication among them, particularly between institutional and parole authorities. As a result, inmates have often been unaware of what they must do to earn release by the authorities, and have been uncertain of the time they must serve until parole. Lack of agency coordination has also meant that inmate training programs designed to insure work skills and better job placement after release have not been used to full advantage. For example, although the U.S. Department of Labor, since 1964, had been funding inmate training programs in over 40 states and federal jurisdictions (under the Manpower Development Act [MDTA], Section 251), there had been a long and unpredictable time-lag between training achievements and release decisions. Training programs were not coordinated with an inmate's possible release date, and parole boards did not necessarily consider such training in release decisions. It became apparent that for the inmate programs to be fruitful and financially justifiable, some means was needed which would establish firm parole dates and criteria for parole, and would allow a man to be released when training was completed and placed in a training-related occupation.

The Parole-Corrections Project was therefore funded in 1971 by the Office of Research, Manpower Administration of the Department of Labor to develop and implement a method to overcome some of these problems, under experimental research conditions. The Project staff was responsible for developing a theoretical framework for change and a prison-based practical method for bringing it about. Project staff was also charged with obtaining evaluative data to determine the results of an experimental demonstration of the method. The Project's findings are expected to aid in increasing agency communication and effectiveness in rehabilitation, in developing and specifying parole selection criteria, and in formulating parole and corrections policies. They should also assist in setting U.S. Department of Labor policy, such as establishing the most effective point for federal funds in the delivery of services to inmates.

The most difficult question facing those developing state models were the following:

1. At what point during imprisonment should MAP begin?

2. What should be MAP eligibility criteria?
3. How could the Program be established within the narrow time limits of the Project's implementation phase?
4. What kinds of approval would be needed by agencies and individuals involved in developing a workable state model?

For each state, the answers had to be worked out in accord with local custom, expectations, and law. Parole board members debated the point of optimal (from their perspective) intervention to see an inmate for a contract. Even though they preferred to do this right after diagnostic testing was completed, the sequential timing of the Project, as well as state eligibility requirements, precluded this in most cases. The solution agreed upon was to involve inmates who were within a given number of months from their minimum eligible parole date, and could be legally released on parole before the Project was complete.

Inmate selection criteria were always a concern for both institutional and parole authorities, who had local politics, philosophies, and statutes with which to contend. Although Project staff urged the fewest possible limitations, the final discretion for establishing criteria rested with parole board members, since they ultimately are responsible for determining parole readiness.

Because Mutual Agreement Programming involves a legal contract between three parties, legal counsel was important during model development to assure the legality and applicability of the contract form, and to research all statutes which might bear on the Program. For instance, minimum parole eligibility statutes had to be taken into account in locating eligible participants. In one state (Wisc.) it was found that sentencing judges and district attorneys must be notified before an inmate is considered for parole. By contrast, in another state (Ala.), a unanimous decision of the three-member board was sufficient to release an inmate at any time, regardless of his minimum parole eligibility date. There was also a chance that in some states, the law might not allow an inmate to enter into a contract, or that the contract might not be recognized in court. For these reasons, Project staff not only consulted with agency legal personnel, but contacted other local attorneys in private practice or associated with law firms. The wording of the contracts themselves (see Appendix A) was especially important to insure their legality. (Nonetheless, despite careful wording, problems later arose, both in Arizona, and California, where unilateral changes were made in contract wording without Project staff agreement or further legal consultation.)

All in all, the Project's first phase proceeded cautiously, recognizing the importance of involving all major and collateral agencies and individuals in the planning process. However, their inclusion slowed down model development, especially in the larger states. There was no solution to this except to compromise, to resolve differences, to establish a semantic base, and keep individuals and agencies from losing interest. After intensive negotiations with several states, final individual models were developed for Wisconsin, Arizona, and California.

TOWARD THE FUTURE

Mutual Agreement Programming, although still in an experimental stage, is coming of age. The concept of a contract which is legal and binding on its three parties—inmate, institution, and parole board—is now an accepted correctional approach in many states, and is under consideration by others. From the point of view of institutionalization, it is a success, with two of the three model states adopting it statewide, and one other state, Michigan, having tested and adopted the Program without federal assistance. Another state, Maryland, is experimenting on a small scale with MAP at Hagerstown Reformatory.

MAP has been successful in other ways as well, causing the initiation of new training programs and the expansion of others, as well as opening up new resources in the community for the inmate and parolee. It has also stimulated legislatures to consider revising old legislation and drafting new corrections-related reforms. Perhaps its most important effect has been to show that a federal agency with a moderate sum of money can induce change in the criminal justice system, and can do it without evoking antagonism or making enemies.

Looking forward to the future of MAP, its implications for corrections and parole are immense. At the very least, it will create articulated parole selection and release criteria wherever it is adopted. It is also likely to increase agency cooperation and effectiveness, and may improve the economic stability and community participation of the offender. Even more far-reaching may be effects and application of contractual relations to other parts of the system, for example to pre-trial and pre-sentence, post-conviction, and parole itself, and in the administration of good-time regulations. The first step in this new direction has been taken in New York State, where the MAP concept is being applied to the probation process. Developed by staff of the State Division of Probation of New York, in collaboration with four county probation directors, the Mutual Objectives Probation Program is in the process of implementation on an experimental demonstration basis. This experiment may point the way to successive contractual agreements with offenders, during prison, parole, and probation, which specify realistic behavioral steppingstones leading to gradual constructive reintegration into the community.

To date, the contract model has been shown to be feasible, with potential for widespread application. This is not to say that it is either the only or the best available alternative to current prison programming and parole granting practice. But it is a humane, efficient alternative definitely worthy of consideration. At its heart is a new approach to the prisoner and those responsible for him that frees both of a "double-bind" previously endemic to the prison system. As described by Prof. Ronald Scott, of Virginia Commonwealth University at the Second National Workshop on Corrections and Parole Administration in March, 1974:

It is my contention that the correctional system today systematically deprives the correctional client, or inmate, of responsibility, while at the same time making the correctional worker accountable for objectives over which he has little, or no control. The correctional game, as it is played today, is one in which there are no winners; one in which everyone—correctional workers and inmates alike—are losers.

In Prof. Scott's view:

MAP is exciting, I believe, precisely because it does not fall victim to the kinds of 'double binds' of other treatment approaches. In MAP, treatment responsibilities are clearly designated, and accountability can be assessed; and neither the worker nor the client is left with unachievable responsibilities. MAP in fact approximates [a] 'new' medical model . . . Diagnosis of problems and development of appropriate treatment programs, in MAP, is done by the correctional worker and the correctional client together, with the client supplying information about symptoms and goals, and the worker supplying information about possible underlying causes and appropriate treatment alternatives. The correctional worker (that is, the correctional system) assumes the responsibility of providing the needed treatment resources, whether in terms of education, trade training, counseling, opportunities for interpersonal development, release resources, etc. *Enactment of the agreed treatment program, however, is the clear responsibility of the inmate.* If the resources are made available, failure because of the inmate's nonparticipation is *his responsibility, and his responsibility alone.*

It seems to me that such an approach to correctional treatment begins the process of resolving the mutual double binds of the correctional worker and correctional client as they exist today. Furthermore, such an approach would make it easier to program the offender for responsible behavior. Finally, such an approach would permit assessment of the actual degree to which correctional workers (whether administrators, workers, or systems) had met their achievable responsibility. It seems, in short, like a better way to play the correctional game—one in which the rules for each player are clearer, and one in which each participant—worker and inmate—in short, society itself has a chance to win.

26

PRERELEASE PROGRAM EVALUATION: SOME IMPLICATIONS OF NEGATIVE FINDINGS

NORMAN HOLT AND RUDY RENTERIA

There seems to be a growing awareness in the field of corrections that a disproportionately small amount of institutional resources are devoted to preparation for release. Glaser remarks:

> In federal and state prison I have repeatedly noted much more contin-
> uous concern with maintenance of high standards in the orientation classes
> for newly admitted prisoners than in the prerelease classes. The latter seem
> to operate in spurts, being elaborately developed for some periods and
> then diminishing or disappearing altogether. They often decline when staff
> in charge of these sessions leave the institutions or become involved in
> other programs. Usually no one strongly complains about the interruption
> of the prerelease programs, so they readily slow to a halt or near halt.[86]

In an issue of *The Prison Journal* devoted to prerelease, Jansyn observed that:

> Preparation for release is a widely discussed matter, but the extensive
> literature is not matched with equal concern in practice. By comparison
> there is not a prominent literature on admission and orientation, but this
> preparation for life in the prison is conducted under higher standards than
> the preparation for life in a free society.[87]

The modern, well-equipped reception centers which dot the correctional landscape are hardly matched by equally endowed prerelease facilities.

THE PROBLEM

While resources devoted to prerelease programs are, by comparison, admittedly meager, the proportion devoted to evaluating the
effects of these programs is virtually nonexistent. There are a number of good descriptive reports[88] and impressionistic accounts which

Source: From *Federal Probation*, XXXIII (June 1969): 40–45. Reprinted by permission of
the authors and publisher.

serve the important function of sharing experience but hard data is scarce.

An important exception is Baker's research with prerelease in the United States Penitentiary at Lewisburg, Pennsylvania. The results of a questionnaire administered to inmates before participating in the program is summarized by Baker:

A summary analysis of responses revealed the average prerelease inmate to be principally interested in finding a job and having money to meet release needs. He also had a strong wish for assistance from the institution. As he viewed the situation 90 days prior to his release, his principal and immediate postrelease interest was to "settle down and stay out of trouble." His anticipated major problems were finding adequate employment and/or financial assistance.[89]

In the postrelease questionnaire, however, the relationship between the prerelease program and experience on parole is treated in a very general way so that it is difficult to tell what, if anything, it was about the programs that was successful. Baker expresses this difficulty: "We do not know to what extent the postrelease adjustment is the result of institutional training and experience, prerelease preparation, supervision by the probation officer, acceptance by and encouragement from the family, a break in finding the right job, or any combination of a host of other variables."[90]

It should also be pointed out that in using a self-reporting technique, Baker loses some degree of validity that might be reduced with a less obtrusive measure of success. Evaluations of this type by inmates are subject to considerable bias.

This article reports the results of research on a prerelease program in which we attempted to overcome these difficulties by using a variety of methods.

THE PRERELEASE PROGRAM

The program on which this research is based began in the fall of 1965 as a major undertaking by one of California's smaller institutions for adult male felons. The institution serves mainly as a screening and training facility for the Correctional Forestry Camps in Southern California. Thus program development faces the dual problem of transience and the small number of potential participants. Despite these difficulties it was described in an independent statewide survey at that time as "the most ambitious prerelease program in California."[91]

Utilization of community resources was a prime objective. The program was given this emphasis because better community relations was viewed as an equally important goal. Three months before the classes began the correctional counselor responsible for the program was detached to develop contacts with local businessmen, government officials, labor leaders, and key personnel in public and private agencies. With a few exceptions the community was described as enthusiastic. Public agencies seemed the most interested. During this planning phase extensive contacts were also made with parole and institution personnel throughout California. In addition, much information was supplied through correspondence with knowledgeable persons in both the federal and other state correctional systems. Following the preliminary contacts a meeting was held at the institution for all interested resource persons. This provided the opportunity for them to meet the institution staff and ask any unanswered questions. These same community leaders provided most of the material for the program.

Most of the program contents were developed from literature supplied by larger, more progressive institutions. It thus contained much of what is considered to be "the state of the art" in prerelease programming. Below is a typical schedule for the course.

Five such courses, each lasting about 5 weeks, were offered over an 18-month period. The participants consisted of 100 inmates with parole dates or the status of "Release Upon Approved Parole Plan."

Class	Instructor	Date
Orientation	Staff	June 27
Conditions of Parole	Parole agent	June 28
How To Get a Job	CSES representative	June 29
Educational Opportunities	Local school administrator	June 30
Welfare Dept. Assistance	San Bernardino Welfare representative	July 1
Holiday		July 4
Setting Up a Parole Placement	Parole agent	July 5
Wardrobe Tips	Local clothier	July 6
Motor Vehicle Operation	DMV representative	July 7
How To Keep a Job	Local businessman	July 8
How To Fail on Parole	Staff	July 11
Problems Faced By Parolee/Agent	Parole agent	July 12
Tips on Buying a Car	Local car dealer	July 13
Budgeting and Borrowing	Local bank official	July 14
Legal Problems	Attorney	July 15
Release Anxieties	Staff	July 18
Laws Unique to Parolee	Parole agent	July 19
Union Management	Union Representative	July 20
Purpose/Function of Law	Local law enforcement official	July 21
Salvation Army Program	Salvation Army representative	July 22
How Staff Sees Inmates as They Go to Parole	Staff	July 25
How To Succeed on Parole	Parole agent and parolee	July 26
Family Responsibilities	Staff	July 27
Social Security	Social Security representative	July 28
Summary/Conclusion	Staff	July 29

Seventeen were released earlier than anticipated so that 83 completed the full course.

METHOD

Several different procedures were used to collect data. The same fill-in questionnaire was administered to participants in the first four courses on the first and last day of instruction.

The fifth group was given a "true or false" test during the first and final classes. These questions were developed from lesson plans and handout material submitted by the instructors. An inmate research clerk joined the fifth class as a participant observer, unknown to the instructor or others, and wrote up extensive notes. In addition, focused interviews were conducted with three members of this course. And finally, following the fifth course, all other inmates in the institution with parole dates were asked to complete a short questionnaire asking what, if anything, they would like considered in a prerelease course.

FINDINGS

Table 13 gives the results of the information and attitude questionnaire. In general, there appears to be very little difference between the pre- and postquestionnaires. This strongly suggests that only a meager amount of learning or attitude change took place.

TABLE 13
Questionnaire Responses of 70 Inmates Before and
After Instruction in Prerelease Course

| | After Instruction | | |
| | More or Better Ideas | Fewer or Poorer Ideas | Same Ideas |
Subjects Covered			
1. Where to find employment	30%	30%	40%
2. How to get a job	22	21	57
3. How to keep a job	29	21	50
4. What do you want out of a job	26	16	58
5. How parole agent can help you	34	18	48
6. What parole agent expects	18	4	78
7. Biggest problem after release	17	11	72
8. Ingredients of successful marriages	16	7	77
9. Expectations from family	16	6	78
10. Expectations toward family	16	14	70
11. Plans for recreation	37	29	34
12. Plan to be doing in 5 years	10	17	73

In a study of attitudes toward parole agents after instruction, 14 percent had a more positive attitude, 29 percent were more negative, and 57 percent showed no change. In the study of postinstruction attitudes toward budgeting money, 14 percent were more positive in their attitudes, 7 percent were more negative, and 78 percent showed no change.

On the participants' opinion of the prerelease course, 69 percent disclosed a positive attitude, 19 percent a negative attitude, and 12 percent expressed no opinion.

On almost every item less than one-third do better after the course. The number doing better only exceeds the number doing worse by an average less than 8 percent.

The responses to items 7 and 10 in table 13 were typical of the lack of change. Item 7 asked, "What will be your biggest problem when released?" Seventy-one percent had no better idea after completing the class. Eleven percent of the inmates moved from "some idea" to "no or poor idea" while 17 percent seem to have a better idea. When asked what they expected from their families (item 10), 70 percent had no more of an idea after the class than before. Fourteen percent had a poorer idea while 16 percent had more of an idea the second time.

The largest information gains occur for questions about parole (16 percent and 14 percent); but 29 percent also report more negative attitudes toward parole agents. Whether this represents a net gain is debatable. On the average, the majority of inmates (60 percent) showed no changes.

Most of the participants, however, made positive remarks about the courses (69 percent). Although such positive reactions often are given as proof of a successful program, their true meaning is difficult to ascertain. In this program inmates were released from work assignments and, since classes were shorter, participants ended up with more free time. It could have been this benefit to which they responded.

The relationship between prerelease instruction and questionnaire responses was so weak that we were prompted to construct a new instrument. We felt that the negative findings might have resulted from difficulty in written expression. Thus the "true or false" test was constructed with considerable care. Table 14 gives the results of this second instrument.

Here, again, there is very little difference in the number of questions answered correctly before and after the course. The average scores are almost identical. The average percentage of correct answers on the first test was 49.2 and 50.5 on the second test. As on the

TABLE 14
Comparison of Test Results of 13 Inmates Before
and After 5 Weeks of Prerelease Instruction

Subjects Covered	Number Who Did Better After Course	Number Who Did Better Before Course	Number Scoring Same on Both Tests
All subjects combined	8	4	1
Purchasing a car	7	5	1
Motor Vehicle Code	6	3	4
Educational opportunities	8	3	2
Budgeting money	4	5	4
Buying a wardrobe	2	8	3
Securing employment	2	6	5
Relations with police	3	2	8
Condition of parole	9	4	0

TABLE 15
Percentage of 100 Inmates with Parole and Discharge Dates Who
Wanted Various Subjects Covered in a Prerelease Course

Did not want to participate in any prerelease program	47%
Would like to participate in such a program	53
Parole agents to discuss problems of parole	47
Parole agents to discuss conditions of parole	43
Driving privileges	43
Parolees to discuss their parole problems	36
How to buy a used car	36
California Department of Employment	32
Labor Union policies	30
Applying for a job	29
Purchasing clothes	27
Income tax	26
Vocational rehabilitation	25
Social Security benefits	23
Family Welfare Aid	22
Certificate of Rehabilitation	20
Budgeting your money	20

questionnaire, the classes on parole stand out as learning experiences. They also do somewhat better on questions about educational opportunities and the Motor Vehicle Code. The classes on buying clothes appear to have been a wasted effort.

For several months following the fifth course inmates, whose time was set, filled out questionnaires asking what subjects they wished covered in a prerelease program. Respondents were asked to select from a list of 15 subjects commonly offered those which interested them. Item 1 asked them whether they wished to participate in a program at all. Table 15 shows the relative frequency with which the subjects were selected.[92]

About half of the 100 inmates did not want to participate. Those who did, requested an average of nine subjects each. Here again, we see the relative importance inmates placed on the subject of parole. All but six wanted to talk with a parole agent.

Paralleling Baker's findings, the next subject of most interest was information about jobs and transportation. The number interested in job information suggests that as much as 50 percent of those wanting any instruction are uncertain about their job plans.

The Certificate of Rehabilitation seems to attract the least interest. For each item there is a small but substantial group interested. For the average area about one-third were interested. One-third of those making additional comments asked about early release procedures.

DISCUSSION

Thus far we have reported the results of three data collection instruments. On the information questionnaire the answers were not much better after 5 weeks of instruction than before. Similar results were obtained with a "true or false" test. In this section we shall bring to bear the observation and interview material in trying to explain the program's apparent lack of effect.

The major difficulty appears to have been poor motivation. Many of the inmates were ill-prepared for a learning experience. This was related to several factors. First, although not all eligible inmates participated, there was no real selection of participants in the first four classes. These were composed of inmates most readily available —those already in the Center and lacking crucial work skills. In this institutional setting inmates who are readily available represent a disproportionate number of program failures. Center inmates also have the time and are in the location to get prerelease information through less formal channels. Thus, compared with camp men, as a group they would be expected to profit less from classroom instruction. This interpretation is supported by the somewhat better showing in the fifth course. Participants for this course were brought in from outlying camps—the program successes.

Secondly, several of those interviewed were anxious about some pressing individual problem and had little energy left over to concentrate on more general matters. One inmate had kept his imprisonment secret from certain family members but was now in the position of having to make it known. Another inmate, a parole violator who had lasted 2 weeks on his previous release, still had no job prospects although this was a crucial ingredient in his past failure.

Thirdly, the program sought to meet the needs of inmates in general and thus met the needs of none in particular. The average inmate, if he was interested at all, was interested in only about half the subjects. Third termers found out about the conditions of parole, single men heard about Aid to Needy Children, and a halfway house was described to men with well-formulated residential plans. In addition, the subject matter might have been more relevant if inmates had participated in the planning stage of the program.[93] The subjects offered reflected what staff judged to be the inmate's needs.

Fourthly, the quality of the presentations by staff and outside personnel was uneven. The instances of poor presentation were, in part, the price paid for community involvement. Willing volunteers are not always the best prepared. Staff assignments, on the other hand, are too often made on the basis of availability rather than suitability. Parole agents who are available for a last minute assignment to a prerelease class are not likely to be the most inspiring.

But there would seem to be a deeper, underlying reason for the uneven quality of the classes. When the prerelease program is an institutional operation there is no real payoff on the investment. Neither the institution nor staff involved are rewarded on the basis of how the inmate utilizes the prerelease information on parole. Whatever benefits the program has are received by the parole division. Typically, institutions lack even systematic feedback on the parolees' use of prerelease material. By contrast, orientation programs have a very immediate and concrete payoff in the form of a smoother running institution.

Fifthly, attendance at all classes was mandatory for those placed in the course. Under these conditions the data in table 15 indicate that about two-thirds of the participants will have no interest in the subject matter during any given class and half will be attending under duress.

The alternative would be to have at least part of the course voluntary. Classes on legal and administrative matters might require attendance, for example, while inmates could attend others as needed.[94] Another possibility is to have the inmate, with his counselor, make up a schedule based on his individual needs but have attendance required once he has made his selection.

The principal argument against having participation voluntary is that not enough inmates would show up. It is generally felt that a prerelease class is not worth conducting unless there are 15 or 20 inmates. By contrast, how many orientation sessions have been can-

celled because of too few new arrivals? Most institutions would probably continue orientation as long as there was one new prisoner.

In conclusion, this study illustrates some common pitfalls in prerelease programming and suggests some broad directions that future
programs might take with profit. The plain fact is that our knowledge of the effectiveness of such programming is meager. If there is
any overall lesson to be learned from our data it is that one must
avoid getting overly committed and bogged down with traditional
prerelease programs. The subject matter's utility and effectiveness
should be under constant review. By contrast, we have seen how a
prerelease program can provide a fertile ground for program experimentation. We have tried also to demonstrate with this report the
importance of building evaluation techniques into the program's
development.

27

OMBUDSMAN FOR CORRECTIONS

STATE OF MINNESOTA

The Minnesota Ombudsman for Corrections . . . began in July 1972 as a bold experiment [and] has matured into an established program which now functions as an important adjunct to the state corrections system. A major independent evaluation of the Ombudsman program, completed in November 1974, was quite positive in its findings, conclusions, and recommendations.

The Ombudsman program operated during its first year as a federally-funded project. In may 1973 an Act was passed by the Minnesota Legislature creating the office of the Ombudsman for Corrections as an independent state agency. The office is part of the executive branch of government with the Ombudsman appointed by and responsible to the Governor.

The basic goal of the Ombudsman office as set forth in law is to "promote the highest attainable standards of competence, efficiency, and justice in the administration of corrections." This broad objective is accomplished by providing an external grievance mechanism to be used when corrections' internal procedures fail to formulate and/or implement reasonable standards, rules, regulations and goals. The effectiveness of such an external agent depends in large measure upon its style of operation. The ombudsman must maintain high credibility among both staff and inmates. Credibility is the by-product of case-by-case analysis, which over a period of time, establishes an operating standard dedicated to thorough fact-finding, detailed research, and sound evaluation.

The Ombudsman maintains high visibility within the state correctional system. However, he functions with a low profile insofar as every effort is made to resolve situations of conflict within the

Source: From *An Annual Report of Operation of the Ombudsman for Corrections for the State of Minnesota*(Saint Paul: State of Minnesota, 1975), pp. 1-5 (editorial adaptations).

framework of the Department of Corrections. This mode of operation has proven successful. The Ombudsman has not yet elected to utilize public pressure or the Governor's office to assist in the adoption or implementation of any recommendations made to the Commissioner of Corrections. The ombudsman has written guest editorials dealing with crucial corrections' issues which have been printed by local newspapers.

This report provides an overview of the Ombudsman's activity in fiscal year 1975. It will discuss the organization and function of the Ombudsman office focusing specifically on the type of complaints received and the method by which each was investigated.

COMPLAINT PROCESSING PROCEDURE

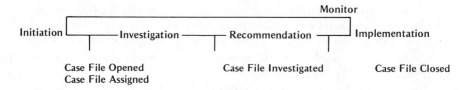

Initiation

Complaint Received. The Ombudsman may, on his own motion or at a request from any source, investigate any action of the Department of Corrections.

Complaints can be initiated by three basic methods:

. . . Ombudsman may initiate an investigation,

. . . complainant may file complaint personally, by telephone or by mail,

. . . a person on behalf of another may file a complaint personally, by telephone or by mail.

Investigation

After reviewing the case file, the investigator will proceed in the following manner:

. . . Personally contact the complainant to get a detailed account of his/her grievance. Determine exactly what steps the complainant has previously taken to resolve his/her problem.

. . . Explain to the complainant the function of the Ombudsman office and how it relates to his/her specific case.

. . . Prepare a list of staff, inmates and appropriate others to interview.

. . . Prepare a list of documents, reports and other written material to review.

. . . Notify selected officials of the Department of Corrections that an investigation is being undertaken when appropriate.

. . . Conduct interviews and review documents, thus gathering all necessary and pertinent information.

. . . Formulate a conclusion on the basis of accumulated evidence.

. . . Notify complainant concerning conclusions reached.

Recommendation

If the investigator, in conjunction with his/her client, concludes that a recommendation is warranted, such recommendation will be submitted, in writing, to the appropriate official of the Department of Corrections. The Ombudsman will be made personally aware of all cases involving recommendations and shall determine which ones require his signature.

The Ombudsman may publish his conclusions and recommendations.

Implementation

The Ombudsman may request, within the time he specifies, to be informed of any action taken on a recommendation or the reasons for not complying with it.

The Ombudsman shall inform the complainant of any action taken on his/her recommendation.

The Ombudsman shall monitor the implementation of recommendations accepted by the Department of Corrections.

FUNCTIONAL ANALYSIS PROGRAM ACTIVITIES

The Ombudsman for Corrections has been organized along functional lines to facilitate management, budgeting, and reporting the activities of the office. The function has been divided into three program or activity areas.

INVESTIGATION OF COMPLAINTS

1) Inmate Complaints

Most of the Ombudsman's activity relates directly to the investigation of complaints from individuals who are incarcerated in the eight institutions under the supervision of the Department of Corrections. In addition there are contacts with corrections' clientele who reside at the Minnesota Security Hospital, with participants in various community corrections programs, and with persons who have been placed on parole by the Minnesota Corrections Authority.

The institutions, as in the past year, continue to provide the greatest workload for the Ombudsman. During fiscal year 1975 they accounted for 91.6 percent of this activity area as compared to 92.7 percent for fiscal year 1974. This high percentage is expected since the Ombudman's office was established primarily to investigate complaints that are a direct consequence of a person's institutionalization.

In each of his investigations the Ombudsman seeks to provide individual relief to a person who has registered a justified complaint. In addition the Ombudsman reviews each complaint to determine the need for change in the policies of the Department of Corrections or an individual institution. Thus the resolution of an individual complaint may result in a major policy recommendation to the Department of Corrections. Such a change resulted from a complaint registered by an inmate at the Minnesota Correctional Institute for Women. The inmate objected to being restrained by male staff members during a pelvic examination by a female nurse in search of drugs. As a consequence of the Ombudsman's discussions with the institution superintendent, the deputy commissioner, and the commissioner of corrections, a new policy was formulated which set guidelines for three kinds of personal searches. This policy states that "all searches are to be conducted by female staff in a closed room." It further stipulates that if it is necessary to restrain a resident who is out of control, prior to the search, "male staff will only be used until female personnel are assembled."

The Ombudsman may obtain individual relief for his client but such singular action is insufficient if the conditions that resulted in the complaint remain unchanged. Therefore, in certain instances, the Ombudsman seeks changes in policy and/or procedure in an attempt to gain relief for all inmates similarly situated.

2) Staff Complaints

The Ombudsman does investigate complaints from staff members of the Department of Corrections. As expected, however, the staff does not make extensive use of the Ombudsman to assist in the resolution of its grievances. During fiscal year 1975 twenty-four complaints were registered by staff members. This figure represents an increase of seven from the previous year's total of seventeen.

The fact that only 1.8 percent of all complaints investigated last year came from staff members can be attributed to at least three reasons. First, staff has ready access to union and civil service assistance. Second, staff generally view the Ombudsman as an agency established primarily to assist inmates. Third, the Ombudsman has made only limited attempts to acquaint staff with the availability of his services. In so doing, it is always clearly understood that the Ombudsman becomes involved in a grievance after all other channels have been utilized.

3) Special Investigations

The Ombudsman has the authority to initiate investigations on his own motion. Under this provision five special investigations were conducted during the past year. Three of these involved inmate deaths at the Prison. In each case a report was issued which reviewed the victim's personal history, reconstructed the circumstances of his death, suggested the cause of the death, and offered recommendations to the Department of Corrections.

The fourth and fifth special investigations focused upon juveniles. One of these examined the parole process and programs of the three major juvenile institutions. The other dealt with revocation hearings. Complaints received from groups of individuals are also placed in this activity area. During fiscal year 1975 twenty-four such complaints were investigated. This figure represents an increase of five cases over the number processed in fiscal year 1975. These frequently came from the permanently established groups at the institutions such as the Indian Folklore and Afro-American organizations. The complaints often related to an institution's policies which affect the group as a collective unit or which affect a segment of a group's membership.

PUBLIC INFORMATION AND EDUCATION

The Minnesota Ombudsman for Corrections concept is unique in the United States. To date the penal systems of thirteen other states have "conflict mediators" called Ombudsman. However, the Minnesota program is the only one which has the status of an independent state agency with substantial statutory authority.

Keeping all segments of the Department of Corrections abreast of the Ombudsman program is an ongoing effort. The Ombudsman or members of his staff are regular participants in the Department of Corrections Training Academy which provides training for correctional counselors. Such contact is viewed by the Ombudsman as an important part of his function. The Ombudsman program will continue to be effective only if it maintains a high level of credibility. Maintaining open channels of communications with the Department of Corrections and the public-at-large fosters the development of mutual confidence.

ANALYSIS OF COMPLAINTS

The Ombudsman may investigate upon complaint or his own motion the action of any division, official or employee of the Minnesota Department of Corrections, the Minnesota Corrections Authority and the Board of Pardons. The Ombudsman's services are directly available to any person under the jurisdiction of the Minnesota Department of Corrections and includes all persons in state correctional institutions and all persons on parole or probation under the supervision of the Commissioner of Corrections or the Minnesota Corrections Authority.

During fiscal year 1975 the Ombudsman dealt with a total of 1343 complaints. Upon investigation, each complaint was placed in one of the following categories:

Parole—Complaints concerning any matter under the jurisdiction of the Parole Board. For example, work release, temporary parole, and special review, etc.

Medical—Complaints about the ability to get treatment from staff physician or other medical source.

Legal—Complaints that require legal assistance or problems with getting proper response from the public defender or other legal counsel.

Placement—Complaints about the facility, area or physical unit to which an inmate is assigned to live for a part of or all of his sentence.

Property—Complaints dealing with the loss, destruction or theft of personal property.

Program—Complaints relating to the inability to get involved in a meaningful training or rehabilitative program requiring classification team's approval, i.e. drug, alcohol, vocational, etc.

Racial—Complaints concerning the use of race as a means of invidious classification or treatment.

Staff—Complaints, other than racial, about an inmate's relationship to a staff member.

Rules—Complaints about administrative policy establishing regulations that an inmate is expected to follow, i.e. visists, disciplinary hearings, dress, etc.

Threats—Complaints concerning threats of bodily harm to an inmate from other inmates.

Other—Complaints not covered in the previous categories.

The Ombudsman's policy of visiting the major institutions on a regular and frequent basis is reflected by the fact that nearly 45 percent of the cases were initiated through direct personal contact. While the number of written contacts decreased by 16 percent compared to last year, the number of telephone contacts increased by 12 percent. This is attributable mainly to a Department of Corrections' policy change allowing inmates greater accessibility to telephones.

Once a complaint has been received, the Ombudsman seeks to interview each complainant within the shortest period of time possible. . . . approximately 70 percent of the complainants are interviewed the same day their complaint is received by the Ombudsman. This figure represents the Ombudsman's effort to maintain high visibility by having his staff personally respond quickly to complaints. It also is the result of his effort to increase his efficiency by assigning a staff member to be responsible on specified days for receiving telephone complaints made to the office. The "intake officer" for each day interviews every person who calls with a grievance. This new procedure accounts for approximately 20 percent of the "same day contacts."

After initial contact with the complainant, the Ombudsman's investigation is conducted as thoroughly and as quickly as possible. . . . 70 percent of the complaints were closed within 30 days. Many complaints, however, are neither quickly nor easily resolved. Most of those held open longer than 30 days are "treatment" oriented and generally are categorized as parole, program, or placement.

In an effort to measure their success, the Ombudsman and his staff determine the extent to which each complaint is resolved. The basic standard is simply whether or not the Ombudsman did all he could as well as he could within the limits of his jurisdiction. In so doing, the Ombudsman is concerned with procedure as well as with the results or consequences of procedure. For example, the Ombudsman may monitor a disciplinary hearing and conclude that an inmate had been accorded the full measure of due process to which he is entitled. Upon a finding of guilt and the assessment of a fair penalty the Ombudsman may well close the case in the full resolution category. However, the inmate who must pay the penalty may be highly dissatisfied with the result irrespective of the actual process by which the result was determined.

The extent to which each complaint is resolved is difficult to quantify or measure in any exact terms. However, the fact that 58.5 percent of this year's cases closed were recorded as fully resolved falls very close to last year's figure of 56.4 percent. A total success figure in the 50 percent range seems to be the emerging standard. This may seem low at first glance but probably meets reasonable expectation. In fact, an independent evaluation of the Ombudsman program concluded that a figure in the area of 50 percent "is probably about what one would hope to find given the nature of the Ombudsman's role. The Ombudsman is not an administrative head issuing orders to subordinates which one would always expect to find carried out. He is, rather, an external agent agitating for positive change. Given this role, one would hope to find that a significant number of his recommendations had been implemented in order to show that some of his suggestions had been worthy of implementation. If, on the other hand, one found that all or nearly all of his recommendations had been implemented, one would have cause to wonder as to whether the Ombudsman was as active and aggressive as his role implies he should be."

Few complaints registered with the Ombudsman's Office are dismissed . . . less than one percent of the 1304 complaints closed last year were found to be completely without merit. The legitimacy of each case is measured primarily by its inclusion into at least one of five criterion. A complaint is legitimate if it concerns issues or actions which are proven to be 1) contrary to law or regulations; 2) unreasonable, unfair, oppressive or inconsistent with any policy or judgment of the Department of Corrections; 3) arbitrary in the ascertainment of facts; 4) unclear or inadequately explained; 5) inefficiently performed.

Approximately 12 percent of the complaints received by the Ombudsman were referred to other agencies for final resolution . . . 157 cases were referred last year. Of this number, 81 went to the Legal Assistance to Minnesota Prisoners (LAMP) office.

28

FUNCTIONAL UNITS: A DIFFERENT CORRECTIONAL APPROACH

ROBERT B. LEVINSON AND ROY E. GERARD*

Accepting the proposition that there will always be a need to confine some of society's law violators, advocates for prison reform have persistently stressed the need for humane, rehabilitation-oriented institutions. Cogent arguments have been made regarding the need for facilities with more adequate staff/inmate ratios. This is seen as a major achievement towards reducing the anonymity of offenders; as a critical component in staff coming to view those incarcerated as people and, thereby, fostering a more healthy institutional climate. Limitations on manpower and other resources suggest the need for the most efficient use of those means that are made available. With these considerations in mind, the Federal Bureau of Prisons has initiated a program to restructure the organization of its institutions into Functional Units.

FUNCTIONAL UNITS

A functional Unit can be conceptualized as one of a number of small, self-contained "institutions" operating in semiautonomous fashion within the confines of a larger facility. The concept includes the notion of: (a) A relatively small number of offenders (50–100); (b) who are housed together (generally throughout the length of their

Source: From *Federal Probation*, XXXVII(December 1973): 8–16. Reprinted by permission of the authors and publisher.

*The authors wish to acknowledge the assistance given them in the development of this article by many individuals, both within and outside the Federal Bureau of Prisons. Particularly helpful were: Norman A. Carlson, director, Federal Bureau of Prisons; the staff (and especially John A. Minor, supervisor of case management) at the Kennedy Youth Center, Morgantown, West Virginia; and Dr. Herbert C. Quay, chairman, Division of Educational Psychology, Temple University.

institutional stay or as they near completion—12 to 18 months—of a long term); (c) and who work in a close, intensive treatment relationship with a multidisciplinary, relatively permanently assigned team of staff members whose offices are located on the Unit; (d) with this latter group having decision-making authority in all within-institution aspects of programming and institutional living; (e) and the assignment of an offender to a particular Unit being contingent upon his need for the specific type of treatment program offered.

While it is preferable to identify a Functional Unit with a single living unit (ideally, one with differentiated quarters within the building), this is *not* a requirement. Given that the above conditions (a–e) prevail, a Functional Unit can encompass two living areas if this more adequately "fits" institutional architecture.

DECENTRALIZATION

The consequence of organizing a total correctional institution around the Functional Unit concept is to decentralize the facility's organizational structure. This means a "flattening out" of the typical hierarchal pyramid; thereby placing those having the most immediate and direct contact with the residents in close proximity (organizationally) to top-level management. Specialists (such as caseworkers and educators) continue to function at a line and at the supervisory or Department Head level in both the centralized and decentralized institution. In the centralized facility the generalist, who manages activities which cross departmental lines, is represented on the table of organization at the associate warden (AW) level; in the decentralized institution both the unit manager and the AW are generalists (with the latter functioning in the more "pure" managerial role, while the former individual still gets involved to some degree in the delivery of direct services).

The result of this restructured table of organization is a smaller gap between those who have the most contact with the resident population and the policy, decision-making executive staff. However, decentralization and the establishment of Functional Units can be a mixed blessing.

Perhaps the most difficult aspect of implementing a Functional Unit approach is "getting there." The transition stage—moving from a centralized organization to a decentralized structure—presents a complexity of problems that are not found in either the totally centralized or totally decentralized institution. One problem in the transitional facility centers about the ability of the associate warden to coordinate the programs of the decentralized units with the rest of the institution's centralized operations. Program information has difficulty filtering-up to the associate warden. The relationship between the manager of the Functional Unit and the department head who ordinarily would be supervising "his" staff members in each Unit becomes one fraught with complications. Unit managers do not relish "interference" with the running of their unit. There tends to be a lack of communication between the various departments and the units. As a consequence, program coordination becomes more difficult. Faced with these problems, the warden must make a definite decision concerning decentralization and Functional Units.

FUNCTIONAL UNITS: ADVANTAGES

The advantages of Functional Units can be clustered under three headings: correction, care and control.

Correction

The semiautonomous nature of the Functional Unit permits maximum flexibility, both in the initial designing of programs and in later modifications required to meet changing population characteristics. Functional Unit programs may be individually altered, removed, or added with only the most minimal disturbance to the facility's basic organization.

It places services close to the users, thereby allowing decision-making in regard to planning, implementing, managing, and evaluating programs to be in the hands of those most knowledgeable about the resident population.

The Functional Unit concept fosters decentralized case management. This provides continuity of program responsibility by the treatment team, easier recognition of, and greater likelihood for, program assignment to meet the offender's needs. Program fragmentation (which traditionally occurs along department or disciplinary lines) is reduced; which, in turn, results in improved interpersonal relationships among staff members and between staff and residents. Under this organizational structure, those incarcerated receive better treatment, thereby improving their chances of being ready for earlier parole and making a more successful community adjustment.

The staff also benefits by becoming a more integral part of the treatment effort; additionally, they have their immediate supervisors in close proximity. These circumstances lead to greater cohesiveness and better morale.

Care

Functional Units lend themselves to differential allocation of resources. This permits more efficient management of available resources since money, manpower, and material can all be distributed in accord with program needs. That is, special physical facilities (e.g., maximum-security features) and specially trained staff can be optimally utilized with those offenders for whom they are most appropriate. Differing staffing patterns and types of housing can be established for other types of residents for whom the aforementioned features would be inappropriate.

Staff development is also encouraged by adopting the Functional Unit plan. The semiautonomous functioning of the Unit (treatment) Team which requires lower level staff members to plan, implement, and manage programs, provides an opportunity for these individuals to develop managerial skills. This allows for easier identification of training needs leading to better staff development.

Since all staff members become a more integral part of the Functional Unit's treatment plan, a greater organizational cohesiveness develops. Further, the close working relationship between line and supervisory staff fosters enthusiasm and better morale.

Control

The Functional Unit concept involves maintaining residents in small, independent treatment-relevant groups. This substantially reduces the amount of movement within the facility. Since transfers between units are discouraged, "problem cases" are not passed around. It also permits a more easily achieved physical control of residents since there is a closer working relationship between those incarcerated and the institution staff. The yield is a maximum effort from both groups towards achieving positive goals.

Maintaining control is also aided by the friendly rivalry which tends to develop between Functional Units. Both staff and residents come to feel a sense of pride in "their" unit and its accomplishments. Rather than offenders finding a common cause in organizing against the staff, competition develops along more desirable lines; e.g., which Unit has the best record in achieving some positive goal. The resulting learning can be shared among Units for the benefit of all.

FUNCTIONAL UNITS: DISADVANTAGES

The group which most acutely feels the impact of the Functional Unit approach is management—particularly at the department head level. The roles of department heads change as traditional lines of authority are restructured. They need to develop or utilize new and different skills; such changes are often agonizing to undergo.

This change is reflected in a different set of responsibilities for department heads. Their role becomes one of monitoring policy implementation and maintaining performance standards across all of the institution's Functional Units. Other duties and responsibilities are detailed below, but the main point is that some department heads may find their altered role much less satisfying.

The loss of a direct line of authority between the department head and "his people" is reflected in the different table of organization of a decentralized facility. The redesigning process can raise a number of problems for personnel, not only at the department head level, but also at the associate warden level. The redefining of areas of responsibility, the need to clarify vague supervisor-supervisee relationships, the role of the specialist vis a vis the generalist, the writing of new position descriptions and program designs and the implementation of new procedures, all pose difficulties for staff. Feelings of loss of authority or status may result in staff morale problems at the upper echelon level.

FUNCTIONAL UNITS: TYPES

It is possible to organize Functional Units around a variety of dimensions; these, then, become the core concept of the Unit's program and help identify selection criteria.

For example:

(1) *Problem area.*—drug treatment units, mental health, alcoholism treatment units, etc.
(2) *Personality types.*—the I-level subtypes described by Warren, *et al.* (1971); Quay's (1972) Behavior Categories, etc.
(3) *Work/Training.*—grouping together offenders programmed for work or academic training and/or integrating both vocational and educational training with an appropriately designed counseling program.

Implementation of the Functional Unit concept presupposes a "sorting out" process (Admission and Orientation Program) which results in a meaningful assignment of residents to Unit programs. Thus, the classification procedure becomes a crucial diagnostic process—involving both staff and offender—attempting to "match" each resident with the most appropriate total program to meet his treatment needs.

FUNCTIONAL UNIT: STRUCTURE

The concept of a Functional Unit is realized in direct correspondence to the degree that the offender's total correctional treatment plan is designed and implemented by a single, small, integrated group of staff members. This requires a multidisciplinary Unit Team, i.e., caseworkers, clerical support, correctional counselors, correctional officers, educators, and mental health personnel. Depending upon the number of staff and residents in the Functional Unit, an additional staff member—the unit manager—is needed; he is a "generalist" and may be drawn from any of the fields represented on the Unit Team.

To a considerable degree, staff activities (next section) are dependent upon the manner in which Functional Units are integrated into the total institution. In a decentralized facility the unit managers function as program directors. As such, they are responsible for the total operation of their Unit and report directly to the office of the warden. The role of the department heads changes (see appropriate section below) to that of functioning in a coordinating role between the warden and the Functional Units and between Functional Units. Figures 7 and 8 represent different "model" tables of organization.

The table of organization shown in figure 7 has the department head functioning in a staff role rather than in a direct supervisory relationship. In this model, the associate warden for programs, AW(P), and the associate warden for operations, AW(O), play their traditional roles.

In figure 8 the unit managers as well as the program/training areas, (education, V.T., etc.) all report to a Program Management Committee—composed of five department heads[95]—which functions in the role similar to that of an AW(P). The AW(O) continues to be responsible for coordinating support services throughout the facility in order that the treatment programs can function smoothly.

The within-Unit structure and its relationships need to be made explicit. Utilizing the staffing pattern for a 100-man Unit—figure 6— the administrative lines of authority are shown in figure 9.

FIGURE 6
Functional Unit—Ideal Staffing Pattern

Staff/Unit Size	50 Residents	100 Residents
Unit Manager	a/	1
*Caseworker	1	2
Clerical	1	2
*Correctional Counselors	2	4
Correctional Officers	4+	4+
*Educators	1	2
*Mental Health	1	1

a/ One of the asterisked staff serves dual role as specialist and unit manager.

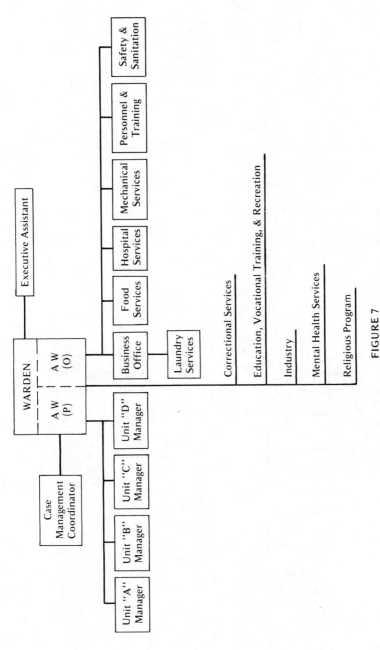

FIGURE 7

Functional Units in a Decentralized Facility

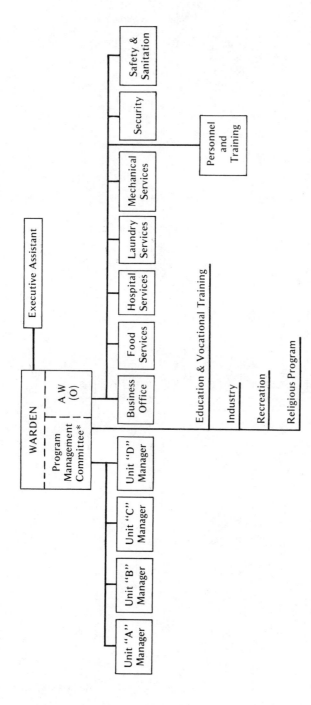

FIGURE 8.

Functional Units in a Decentralized Facility

*Consists of the following five department heads: chief, C&P; chief, correctional supervisor; coordinator, mental health services; superintendent, industries; supervisor, education.

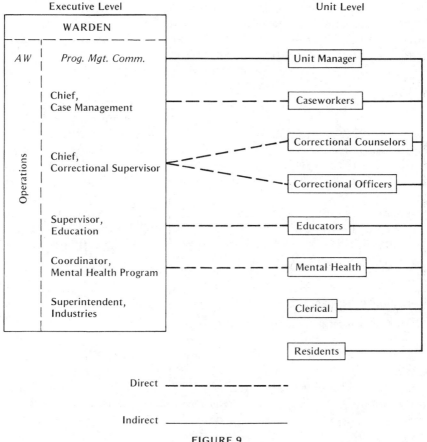

Executive Level   Unit Level

FIGURE 9
Administrative Lines of Authority

Lines of administrative authority flow upward through the unit manager to the office of the warden (i.e., the AW(P) or the Program Management Committee). That is, members of the Unit staff are responsible to the unit manager. He, in turn, is responsible to the office of the warden. The department heads function in a staff role to the warden and have only an indirect relationship with the personnel in the Unit staff.

FUNCTIONAL UNIT: STAFF ACTIVITIES

The staff members on the Unit Team are responsible for all aspects of resident program planning and monitoring. This includes initial orientation, admission evaluation, program assignment, implementation of the "in-Unit" treatment program (e.g., counseling, therapy, recreation, leisure-time activity, etc.), coordination and liaison with "out-of-Unit" activities, both formal and informal program and progress reviews, "promotions" and "demotions" (i.e., handling discipline), Parole Board recommendations, prerelease programming, and so on.

In addition, the Unit staff is accountable for the physical condition (i.e., sanitation, orderliness, etc.) of their living unit. They are also responsible for maintaining control in their Unit and for observing necessary security measures. In short, each Unit is comparable to a small institution which the staff in the Unit "run." Within the guidelines formulated by both the executive staff at the facility and those issued by the Central Office, the Unit staff are free and expected to formulate a treatment approach appropriate for their "type" of offender. This Unit program, in its initial form, is a written proposal subject to review by local executive-level administrators and approval by the Central Office, prior to its implementation.

The Unit Manager

The unit manager's function is to orchestrate the development and implementation of an effective treatment approach in his Unit. He is the administrative head of the Unit and, as such, the direct-line supervisor of staff assigned to the Unit Team. In addition to overseeing the within-Unit program, the Unit Manager has important liaison functions throughout the institution. In many ways, he functions in the traditional role of a department head, e.g., attending a variety of administrative meetings (budget, training, warden's staff, etc.), thereby "linking" his Unit into the total operation.

The manner in which manpower resources will be expended in the Functional Unit are the responsibility of the unit manager. In establishing work schedules the unit manager should be guided by a number of operating principles: The purpose of the Functional Unit is to find ways to best help offenders, not to set up the most convenient working schedules for the staff. Accordingly, staff should be on duty at those times when residents are most available; e.g., evenings and weekends. Further, since those who are incarcerated are in the institution all year, program activities should not cease during holiday season because all the staff have scheduled themselves for annual leave. It is the responsibility of the unit manager to see to it that staff are available to conduct programs on an extended "treatment day" basis throughout the year.

The unit manager is accountable for the program activities which occur in his Unit and should be knowledgeable concerning not only "what's happening" with residents, but with staff as well. It is his responsibility to recognize and remedy program deficiencies. Accordingly, he must be knowledgeable about the treatment philosophy being implemented and capable of either providing himself, or seeing to it that others supply needed staff training. In order that he might be aware of his Unit's level of performance, the unit manager must place a high priority on the development and implementation of program assessment and monitoring methods. As a "mini-warden," accolades for conducting an effective Unit are his due as much as blame for program inefficiencies.

The Caseworker

The caseworker's (and social worker's) responsibilities in a Functional Unit include all the traditional duties required to move an individual through a correctional institution. They include awareness of Central Office policies, possessing the technical expertise to assess correctness of reports, knowledge about Parole Board procedures and the legalities involved, etc. In addition, since caseloads are small, the caseworker takes an active role in direct treatment intervention. That is, he or she will not only function as a full-fledged member of the Unit Team in all aspects of the programming process as it relates to residents on his caseload, but he will also conduct counseling sessions or whatever other treatment modalities make up the Unit's therapeutic approach.

The Correctional Counselor

The correctional counselor serves as a crucial member of the Unit's treatment team. He becomes the prime contact between this small group of 25 residents and the rest of the Unit and the institution. His role includes being a direct implementer of the agreed-upon treatment modalities, a fully functioning member of the Unit Team, a liaison between outside-the-Unit activities (e.g., work assignment) and their implications for the Unit Team, an organizer and/or monitor of recreation and leisure-time activities, and so on. In general, he will have the most immediate, prolonged and intensive relationship with many of the Unit's residents, of any member on the Unit staff. Therefore, he needs training and orientation in the Unit's philosophy and methods of treatment implementation. His supervision is the responsibility of the unit manager in consultation with the chief correctional supervisor; his training is the responsibility of the Unit Staff, other institution personnel, and outside consultants with whom the Unit contracts. It is the responsibility of the unit manager to see to it that these staff members receive training in the skills required to conduct the Unit's program. He must also be the responsible individual to insure that the correctional counselor's skills are utilized appropriately and that the latter *not* become the "ever-ready" substitute to fill in for absentee staff in other institutional areas.

The Correctional Officer

The correctional officer has the prime role in maintaining security controls in accord with established policies and consistent with the therapeutic nature of the Functional Unit's program. His is the most difficult and least recognized function in any correctional treatment program; yet he is among the most influential in setting the "tone" present in the Functional Unit. Because of his day-to-day interaction with the Unit's residents, he becomes a central figure in the establishment and efficient functioning of the "therapeutic community." Therefore, he needs to be oriented to the mission and goals of the Unit; he should be an active participant in Unit activities; and he should be viewed as a valuable contributor to the Unit Team of information about an offender's level of progress. In view of the correctional officer's important role in the Functional Unit, care must be exercised to insure that shift rotation is conducted in such a manner that it is not disruptive to program integrity. That is, an orderly, consistent pattern of correctional officer rotation should be established (e.g., relief, morning, day, evening). Every opportunity should be taken to rotate officers within the Unit rather than from the day shift in Unit "A" to the Evening shift in Unit "B." Promotion opportunities exist in the direction of either moving up the correctional officer's career ladder or moving into the counselor/unit manager sequence.

The Educator

The role of the educator (academic or vocational training instructor) in a Functional Unit has two major focuses: (1) To function as an education/vocational training guidance counselor—40 percent of his time; (2) to monitor and/or conduct academic or vocational training, ideally within the Unit, but more likely in a central school or VT shops building—60 percent of his time. In addition, he is a full member of the Unit Team and a contributor to this group of information relevant for program assignment. Depending upon the specific needs of the Unit's residents, it is the educator's responsibility to recommend training alternatives in order to help each individual reach goals mutually agreed upon in collaboration with the Unit Team. He may also be required to develop special "classes" which provide the Unit residents with information of relevance to the intent of the Functional Unit's program (e.g., "The Social, Psychological, and Physical Effects of Alcoholism" for an alcoholism treatment unit).

The Mental Health Staff Member

The mental health staff member (psychiatrist, psychologist, psychiatric nurse) on the Unit Team has a multifaceted role. He is expected to be involved in the admission and information gathering process prior to classification; he is a member of the decision-making Unit Team; he monitors, supervises, and/or conducts therapeutic sessions; he serves as a consultant and trainer for other staff members; and he helps to design and implement program evaluation studies. As with other staff, the mental health worker plays a significant role in the development of the Functional Unit's treatment program. He is expected to become a member of the Team in every sense; his activities should be well integrated into the Team's functioning in order that the Functional Unit operate as efficiently and effectively as possible.

If there are too few mental health personnel so that the staff pattern in figure 6 cannot be adhered to, an alternative structure has the mental health staff serve in a consultative role to the Functional Units. Under these conditions, mental health remains centralized and functions more in a staff role. However, to the extent possible, available mental health staff resources should be "assigned" to a specific unit even though each staff member may cover two or more Units.

Clerical Help

Clerical support is critical to the operation of a Functional Unit. Not only is there a high correlation between the smooth flow of paper and an effectively functioning Unit, but delays and disruptions in this area have marked negative influence on the therapeutic effort, and staff and resident morale. Further, the need to document program activities and accomplishments, to describe the Functional Unit's program, to prepare brochures to help orient new staff, and to type articles and studies for publication, all argue for capable and adequate clerical support. Message-taking, intra- and interunit communication, and administrative functions such as budgeting, time-keeping, etc., all become clerical functions without which the Unit flounders. Further, by including these staff members in training activities, they can become additional treatment resources with the Unit.

The Residents

The residents are the *raison d'etre* of Functional Units. Whether they are referred to as prisoners, inmates, residents, or students the purpose of the Functional Unit is to provide better, more intensive, more appropriate, and more effective methods to help them cope more successfully with the problems of living following their release. In achieving this end, programs must be designed which recognize the humanness of those they plan to help. Offenders must be involved in decisions which significantly affect them. Ways must be found to offer opportunities for Unit residents to take intramural roles of increasing responsibility both for their own activities, as well as for the smooth functioning of the Unit. In the area of decision making, as it relates to a particular individual, he should be viewed as a member of the Unit team and have a voice in program decisions affecting him. The "climate" of the Functional Unit should convey a clear respect for the dignity and uniqueness of each of those entrusted to its care.

THE DEPARTMENT HEADS' ROLE

In a totally decentralized institution—one comprised entirely of Functional Units—the activities of department heads must, of necessity, change. As indicated in figure 9, they no longer have a line-authority relationship with "their people" in the Units. Their function becomes one of a staff role and resource person to both the warden and the unit managers.

As individuals, the department heads consult with and monitor the performance of Unit staff members from their area of expertise. Coordination between Functional Units is their prime area of concern; monitoring adherence to policy and standards is of almost equal importance.

Under one model the department heads[96] could function as a Program Management Committee. In this capacity they operate as: an "appeals board" to review Unit Team decisions; as a policy-recommending, standards-developing group; as an Advisory Council on Treatment; as the Warden's Advisory Research Committee; as a Special Projects Task Force, etc. Either a permanent or rotating chairman of the Program Management Committee could be appointed by the warden.

One of the dangers in a decentralized facility is that the Functional Units may become totally "out of step" with one another, so that the institution appears to be headed in all directions at the same time. The Program Management Committee, therefore, should meet regularly with the unit managers, thereby bringing a broader perspective to program implementation. Despite the change in their role, department heads still have the responsibility to monitor staff activities in their area of expertise, to see to it that standards are maintained and policies adhered to. The warden can expect them to maintain high quality programs, to handle staff problems, and to keep him fully informed.

In those instances where some programmatic areas remain centralized (e.g., vocational training) the department head may function to some degree in the more traditional model; however, even here he will share with the unit manager some of his former authority (e.g., rating VT instructors who also function as part of a Unit Team).

THE NONDECENTRALIZED FUNCTIONS

Up to this point, the article has dealt almost exclusively with those aspects of institutional functioning which are most directly affected by the Functional Unit concept. There remain a number of areas which function much in the same fashion as in a centralized facility. The Business Office, Food Service, Health Services, Laundry, Mechanical Services, Personnel and Training, and Safety and Sanitation, are not significantly affected by this change in organizational structure.

Perhaps the greatest change affects the Correctional Services. In effect, three different areas emerge: the correctional counselors (based in the Units and closely tied to the unit manager); the living quarters correctional officers (based in the Units but more closely tied to the Correctional Services Department), and security officers (based outside the Units and closely tied to the Correctional Services Department). Security operations refer to manning towers, operating the control room, inside patrol, etc. These are characterized by having almost no direct contact with inmates. A second type of security function does have inmate-contact involved—e.g., detail officer; hospital, kitchen, or school officer. Assignments to these latter areas could be distributed among the Units with the number of correctional officers attached to the Units being increased; rotation through these outside-the-Unit situations, then, becomes part of the regular correctional officer rotation sequence.

Thus, the corrections force is required to function in a variety of ways and lines of authority may not always be clear. Care has to be taken to explicate how these separate, but equally important functions will be smoothly integrated, a problem similar to that faced in the dual role played by the education staff.

EVALUATION

In any undertaking there needs to be a built-in feedback or evaluation system so that both those conducting the program, as well as those overseeing its operations, have data concerning its level of accomplishment. The development and implementation of assessment methods should be an integral part of a Functional Unit Program Plan.

The Unit Program Plans can become part of a total Master Program Plan for the entire facility. This document details the correctional philosophy, mission, goals and objectives of the total institution in an attempt to describe what a particular institution is trying to accomplish and how all its components contribute towards those ends. Included in the Master Plan is a measurement and/or evaluation system so that periodic progress reports can be assembled which will provide information regarding the degree to which the facility is meeting its stated objectives. It is the unit manager's responsibility to accord program evaluation high priority in the total activities of his program. While he, himself, may not be knowledgeable in the design of evaluation techniques, such expertise should be accessible either on his own staff or through contracting with appropriate consultants.

CONCLUSION

The foregoing represents an attempt to describe the concept of a Functional Unit in operational terms. Since the experience of the Bureau of Prisons with this type of Unit (and particularly with totally decentralized institutions) is very short, these ideas will no doubt undergo growth and continuing development. This article will have served its purpose to the degree that it provides all concerned with a common frame of reference in discussions about Functional Units, and to the degree that it exposes others to a different approach in the delivery of effective correctional treatment services to incarcerated offenders.

REFERENCES

Quay, H. C.
  1972   "Patterns of Aggression, Withdrawal, and Immaturity," in Psycho-
          pathological Disorders of Childhood, H. C. Quay and J. S. Werry
          (Eds.). New York: Wiley & Sons.
Rowitz, L. and Levy L.
  1970   "The State Hospital in Transition." *Mental Hygiene* 55, No. 1.
Warren, Marguerite Q.
  1971   "Classification of Offenders as an Aid to Efficient Management and
          Effective Treatment." *Journal of Criminal Law, Criminology, and
          Police Science* 62, pp. 239–258.

IV

FUSION OF INSTITUTIONAL AND COMMUNITY PROGRAMS

INTRODUCTION

Lloyd E. Ohlin, Roscoe Pound Professor of Criminology at Harvard, recounts how the "rhetoric of rehabilitation" used by American prison reformers regularly exceeded their achievements. He contends that, as the United States enters its third century, new conflicts over correctional policy are highly probable but may be very constructive. These potential conflicts he ascribes especially to the reduction of inmate opportunities for meaningful employment; the futility of most treatment programs under these circumstances; public pressure for policy evaluation; and the possibility that 90 percent of prisoners could be safely released from penitentiary confinement, with the remainder held in facilities that would be much smaller and different from those now in use.

A defense of the opinion that community-based correctional programs should drastically modify or replace traditional modes of confinement is detailed by the National Advisory Commission on Criminal Justice Standards and Goals. The Commission also specifies the roles and responsibilities of correctional administrators and citizens in effecting this transformation, and describes several types of community adjuncts to correctional institutions.

These new developments imply not only provision of correctional services outside of institutions, but also involvement of noncriminal community residents in programs for offenders.

The varied career of Vincent O'Leary, of the School of Criminal Justice of the State University of New York at Albany, has included supervising parole services for the states of Washington and Texas, and directing training and research programs concerned with correctional innovation in a series of national institutes. Professor O'Leary describes four patterns of citizen involvement in corrections: (1) direct service to offenders; (2) recruitment of public support for correctional programs; (3) expansion of opportunities for prisoners in schools, businesses and community life in general; (4) provision of personal friendship and support for individual offenders after release as well as during confinement.

Norman Holt, formerly a correctional counselor for juveniles and now a research analyst in the California Department of Corrections, describes the phenomenal success which that state and others have had in furloughing prisoners a few days prior to parole. Not only do almost all releasees conform to the law while temporarily living in the community, but they arrange constructively for the employment, housing and other needs they will have when paroled. A major factor in such achievements, he indicates, is staff emphasis on pre-furlough planning by the inmates.

Psychologist Robert Jeffery and political scientist Stephen Woolpert provide a sophisticated evaluation of furloughs in a different setting— a jail—and of a different type—work furloughs. Under this system prisoners leave daily to work in the community and return to confinement at night. Not only was there less recidivism among releasees after the work furlough program was introduced, but the decline in crime apparently due to this program was greatest among those usually considered more likely to commit crimes—those unskilled, unmarried and under 35.

Sociologist C. Ronald Huff provides perhaps the first social science study of a new form of community involvement in correctional institutions—prisoner unions. Most of these have outside branches and some are affiliated with established labor unions. These organizations may greatly increase the bargaining power of inmates in dealing with prison administrators, and could conceivably enhance their postrelease opportunities as well.

The National Advisory Commission on Criminal Justice Standards and Goals portrays a future in which institutional confinement of juvenile and youthful offenders will be strongly discouraged. Consequently, those who will be incarcerated will be older, more experienced in crime and less tractable than most prisoners are today. The Commission recommends much smaller prisons, located closer to urban areas than is currently the case. They note the absence of effective standards for the development of these new facilities.

29

CORRECTIONAL STRATEGIES IN CONFLICT

LLOYD E. OHLIN

In the United States today, the assumptions underlying our correctional policies are being subjected to searching criticism and radical proposals for change. During the two hundred years in which these policies developed, it is difficult to identify a period of comparable turmoil, uncertainty, and sense of urgency about the need to achieve consensus on basic objectives and new policies. It is possible that the historic declaration of principles for correctional agencies that emerged from the meeting of the National Prison Association in Cincinnati, Ohio, in October, 1870, marked such a time.[1] That conference repudiated the silent, lockstep system of punishment, rigid discipline and hard labor accepted as a model for most of the nation's prisons at that time. Developed most fully at Auburn, New York, about 1823, the system confined inmates in separate cells at night but brought them together in congregate workshops to labor in silence during the day. These penal practices gained dominance over the alternative Pennsylvania System based on confinement of prisoners in single cells for work or repentant reflection in solitude.[2]

The conference called for a new era in corrections. The new system must be less concerned with punishment and more with the rehabilitation of prisoners through programs for vocational training and education for law-abiding pursuits. It sought to incorporate new correctional strategies such as the indeterminate sentence, the classification of prisoners based on a progressive system of "marks," and the encouragement of each inmate's sense of self-respect. It borrowed extensively from the correctional policies instituted by Sir Walter Crofton while director of the Mountjoy Prison in Ireland. The Irish System of Intermediate Stages permitted a prisoner to work his way toward release by earning favorable "marks" in a graduated set of

Source: From *Proceedings of the American Philosophical Society,* 118, 3(June 1974): 248–253. Reprinted by permission of the author and publisher.

programs from secure confinement to work release and parole. The Irish System was based primarily on ideas developed by Alexander Maconochie at Norfolk Island, Australia, from 1840.[3]

The conference marked a turning point in penological thinking. Henceforth, correctional policies were to pursue the reformation of the offender more through retraining than the deterrent effects of punitive discipline and hard labor. Shortly thereafter, in 1876, the new strategies found expression in the new reformatory in Elmira, New York, for youthful first offenders. In most respects this new institution was patterned on the older prisons of the Auburn model with solitary interior cells and congregate workshops. It introduced the mark system for assigning prisoners to three grades based on good conduct. But, more importantly, it established the indeterminate sentence system, providing for a maximum period of confinement and the privilege of early parole for good behavior.[4]

The innovative proposals of this period have shaped the development of our correctional practices for adult felons ever since. The vast majority of adult prisons in the United States today are still seeking to implement the principles of correction articulated in 1870.

Nevertheless, the judgment of history must be that the rhetoric of rehabilitation so enthusiastically espoused by the reformers of the late nineteenth century has far outrun achievements. The grading system deteriorated into a negative rather than a positive reward system. Good time allowances and parole eligibility are automatically granted to prisoners on admission but can be lost by bad conduct. Thus the grading system has been converted into a mechanism for custodial control rather than a source of motivation for self-improvement. Similarly, the administrative discretion lodged in the indeterminate sentence and parole system gradually displaced more punitive measures for coercing inmate conformity to prison routines and discipline. This administrative control over the length of confinement is a powerful means for preserving prison order and at least simulated compliance by inmates with treatment programs. However, the exercise of this discretion is nonreviewable by the courts and its frequently arbitrary application generates great anxiety and hostility among inmates that obstruct treatment efforts.[5]

Thus, it is now apparent that implementation of the reforms called for in 1870 has had the effect of preserving large penitentiaries as instruments of punishment and incapacitation of offenders rather than their rehabilitation. One good reason for this result may be deduced from the following account of the 1870 convention:

> The convention was in the hands of reformers who had arrived with prepared speeches while the traditions had no spokesman. Overwhelmed

with inspired addresses, with prayer and song and much exhortation, even the hard-headed wardens were carried up for a mountain-top experience. In their enthusiasm for the ideal they rose above the monotony of four gray walls, men in stripes shuffling in lock-step, sullen faces staring through the bars, coarse mush and coffee made of bread crusts, armed sentries stalking the walls. They forgot it all and voted for their remarkable Declaration of Principles.[6]

Nevertheless, the reform measures and their accompanying rhetoric of rehabilitation have been consistent with the gradual public acceptance of more humanitarian ideologies of treatment in human services. It has proved most difficult to assess the benefits these reforms may have brought, but we are now beginning to apprehend the costs more clearly.

There was something uncompromisingly honest about the ideologies in justification of the early prisons prior to 1870. Because crimes had been committed, offenders were to be subjected to punishment, hard labor, and solitude to encourage repentant thoughts. This is what the convicted felons expected and got. In contrast, proponents of the rehabilitation ideology, oblivious to the inevitable deprivations of large prisons, held out promises of self-development opportunities which could never be realized under these conditions. The new philosophy created a credibility gap of serious proportions. The rehabilitation aims, so congenial to humanitarian and professional ethics, then and now, contrast radically with the facts of everyday life which most convicts experience. The turmoil in our prisons today is attributable in considerable measure to the low public visibility of this gap between the manifest goals of rehabilitation and the reality of prison life.

To come back to our starting point, the search today for a realistic philosophy and set of correctional strategies is more radical than the proposed reforms of 1870. This search now challenges what was then taken for granted, i.e., the confident reliance of correctional policies on confinement in large congregate prisons and equal confidence in the achievability of the rehabilitative ideal within the coercive context of criminal sanctions.

To discover a comparable period of critical reexamination of accepted premises in correctional policies I believe we must look even further back in history than the 1870 reform proposals to the origins of the Pennsylvania System in the late eighteenth century in Philadelphia. In a recent article Thorsten Sellin traces the emergence of the prototype institution of this new system, the Walnut Street Jail, from its antecedent British forerunners, stimulated by the observations and reform ideas of John Howard.[7] At a meeting in Benjamin Franklin's home in March, 1787, a small group discussed proposals presented in a paper by Dr. Benjamin Rush for new measures in the treatment of convicted offenders. Shortly thereafter the Philadelphia Society for Alleviating the Miseries of Public Prisons was formed. Their proposals to the legislature resulted in a law of April 5, 1790, to remodel the Walnut Street Jail in accordance with the principles of solitary confinement and hard labor.

These events are of particular significance because they established the first enduring effort in the new nation to adopt a consistently new approach to correctional treatment. Fines and imprisonment were henceforth to take the place of mutilation, physical punishment, and other measures of social stigmatization. Imprisonment as punishment was to be humane and to allow for redemption and reformation. The facilities should provide for the segregation of men from women, witnesses from offenders, and categories of convicted persons according to their dangerousness. From payments for their labor at trades in the workshop the costs of maintenance were deducted, and good conduct could lead to a pardon by the governor.

The point is that these reforms represented a radical departure from practices prevailing throughout the former colonies in the treatment of convicted offenders. They invoked new conceptions of the offender, the goals of correctional treatment, and strategies for achieving them. We are in desperate need today of just such a radical reappraisal of our policies and goals. Let us review briefly how we arrived at this state of affairs. Why do so many leading criminologists now feel that our most widely institutionalized correctional policies are bankrupt and unable to serve us effectively in the future?

It is, I believe, axiomatic that no major social institution can long remain out of phase with the social and cultural developments that prevail in the rest of the society. Yet that is what appears to have happened to our correctional establishment and other agencies of criminal justice as well.

Looking back, the early success of the Pennsylvania penitentiary system seemed to stem from its embodiment and reflection of the prevailing cultural conditions and trends of the time. These included the Quakers' faith in the virtues of penitence, their humanitarian repugnance for public displays of human degradation, and the economic viability of a piecework system of production within trade-oriented shops for both skilled and unskilled workers. Almost everyone else worked long hours anyway, and the labor of convicts paid for their keep and the support of their families, while inculcating useful habits of industry.

The Auburn Model of congregate workshops gained ascendancy because it could more efficiently incorporate and operate profitably the machine technology of small factories and, later, prison indus-tries. Unskilled labor could readily be harnessed to simple production tasks and the correctional system could achieve the ends of deterrence and custody without burdening the taxpayer. In the rural south the leasing and contracting out of prison labor served the same ends.

This industrial period of prison management ended in the depres-sion years of the 1930's when the rising political power of labor, high unemployment, and declining business markets forced a halt to the use of convict labor in competition with private enterprise. By 1935 a combination of federal and state legislation had destroyed the eco-nomic potential of the industrial prison.[5] Since that time the increas-ing technological complexity of industry, the declining utility of unskilled labor, and state laws restricting the sale of prison-made goods have virtually wiped out the economic productivity of convict labor in large prisons.

For the past forty years advocates of the penitentiary system have searched for correctional strategies which could provide an equally strong claim for its maintenance as its industries once fur-nished. The economic costs of this system constitute an increasingly heavy burden on tax dollars. For example, it is now commonplace in Massachusetts to note that the average annual cost per capita for in-mates in state prisons could pay for an academic year at Harvard and a summer of travel and study abroad.

The search for alternative programs has taken two somewhat related paths toward achievement of the goals of rehabilitation. The first has involved attempts to convert the production facilities of the prisons into vocational training and remedial education programs in accordance with the philosophy espoused in the 1870 declaration of principles in Cincinnati, Ohio. By and large this solution has failed. The vocational training capacity tends to fall rapidly behind the ad-vances of private industry owing to obsolescent machinery and anti-quated instruction. It is simply too costly to keep up-to-date, and inmates become apathetic about involvement with little prospect of payoff. Comparable problems of inmate motivation beset academic instruction. It appears that the costs of maintenance and custodial security are so high in themselves that correctional needs cannot compete for the tax dollars necessary to build an effective vocational and educational program that might engage the interest of a substan-tial number of inmates.

The second path has been to convert the prisons into centers for psychological and social therapy to deal with the personal and social adjustment problems of the inmates. Here again the costs of mount-ing an effective treatment effort in prisons of 500 to 3,000 or more men have prohibited any substantial progress, even if one assumed that treatment could yield enduring effects, except in rare cases, under such conditions.

Thus it seems inescapable that the concept of the congregate prison as a correctional solution is out of touch with the reality of our times. It is too costly to maintain and destructive in its consequences. The idleness and boredom have no foreseeable remedy. The rhetoric of rehabilitation may induce public acceptance of the system but it generates inmate anger and charges of hypocrisy. The large prison now serves primarily the ends of custody and punishment through the deprivation of liberty, material comforts, personal autonomy and initiative, and affectional relationships. A recidivism rate of two out of three releases raises serious question about its special deterrent effect on individual felons, and its general deterrent effect on the public at large seems to be beyond reliable estimation.

The search for alternative correctional policies is a continuing and thriving enterprise that has been described and promoted by recent national crime commissions. President Johnson's Commission on Law Enforcement and the Administration of Justice reported in 1967 its assessment of the state of correctional practice and recommendations for future development.[9] These have been supported and elaborated most recently by the reports of the National Advisory Commission on Criminal Justice Standards and Goals in 1973.[10] These reports reflect quite well for the most part current progressive ideas about change. Briefly summarized the recommendations propose six major changes as follows:

1) Decriminalization

This involves change in the existing criminal code to exclude criminal sanctions where problems might better be dealt with through other processes of formal or informal social control. The most relevant offenses are drug abuse, alcoholism, abortion, consenting sexual offenses between adults, and child status offenses involving truancy, runaways, or incorrigibility.

2) Diversion

Many offenders are stigmatized by criminal justice proceedings when their problems could be solved more effectively by diversion and referral to alternative social services or simply termination of proceedings. This recommendation assumes resort to criminal sanctions only where other modes of less punitive treatment are very likely to fail or already have been tried.

3) *Deinstitutionalization*

Our current correctional policies fail to discriminate sufficiently among offenders as to the danger they might pose in the community to the safety of persons and property. Consequently, many offenders are needlessly committed to confinement in high security prisons. The resulting alienation and escalation to more serious criminal careers might be mitigated, according to the best research evidence available, by phasing out the large centralized prisons and creating small, locally based residential and non-residential treatment services.

4) *Better Treatment Opportunities*

The movement to establish community-based services should help to enrich treatment alternatives. Part-time professional assistance and volunteer aid should be easier to procure. The capacity to purchase services together with strong quality control procedures may tap more deeply the potential resources for service latent in all communities.

5) *Civil Rights of Offenders*

To ensure greater protection for the civil rights of offenders in the criminal-justice process is to promote greater respect for law and the principles of fairness and "just deserts." To achieve this will probably require new forms of advocacy for offenders in the correctional process through individual and collective representation. Current practices moving in this direction are projects for legal assistance to prisoners, prisoner unions and representative councils, and the independent office of a prison ombudsman. The previous hands-off policy of the courts, in deference to the discretion of correctional authorities, is breaking down. Court intervention into the disciplinary and classification processes within prisons is growing rapidly under the pressure of test cases that raise fundamental constitutional issues.[11] The past refusal of prison authorities to codify their own procedures in order to preserve maximum administrative discretion has left them especially vulnerable to such intervention.

6) *Policy Evaluation*

We appear to be entering a new period of skepticism in which the citation of personal experience and a few exemplary cases constitute insufficient proof of the assertions they are designed to defend. As the technology and sophistication of social indicators, econometric analysis, and psychological measurements have increased, more stringent demands are being imposed for proof of the effectiveness of new programs or policies. Increasingly large sums of federal money from the Law Enforcement Assistance Administration in the U.S. Department of Justice are becoming available for new correctional programs. The mandatory evaluation requirements attached to such grants may force these new programs to consider their consequences more quickly and unequivocably.

The theoretical premises of these six major policy recommendations are readily apparent. They assert that criminality is not simply a devilish possession to be exorcised from the individual offender. Nor is it simply a failure of character to learn right from wrong that might yield to instruction, an emotional sickness responsive to psychiatric therapy, or a deficiency in educational and vocational attainments. It is instead an interactional product of both social circumstances and individual tendencies that must be confronted within the communities and social systems from which these criminal acts emerge. The answer lies in part in the alteration of social conditions and partly in the accommodation of persons to them.

To implement these recommended correctional policies will be a formidable task attended by much painful social conflict, riot, fear, and acrimonious debate. It seems to me that these confrontations are inevitable if the needed changes are to be brought about. Social conceptions of the roots of crime are deeply ingrained through early instruction and thereafter taken for granted. To change these definitions through reeducation will take many years, unless at the same time radical change also takes place in the institutional arrangements for coping with the criminal offender. The road once determined and the change swiftly begun may produce more hardship and turmoil for us all in the short run but more effectiveness and tranquility thereafter.

I do not underestimate the painful conflicts which major social changes produce. We are now experiencing a new wave of prison riots similar to those attending the attempts to introduce new treatment concepts in prisons after World War II. But now new related sources of conflict are also at work. The civil rights struggles of the 1960's, the recoil from the Vietnam war, and radical protests against the establishment have challenged the power and intentions of authority in many of our basic social institutions. The issues in these struggles, not surprisingly, have permeated our prisons and they are forcing reexamination of basic assumptions about crime, criminals, and criminal justice practices.

With an associate, I am now analyzing results of our study of prison riots that took place in 1951-1953 and 1968-1972 drawing on case histories and questionnaire returns from all but two states.[12]

It is abundantly clear that we are in a period of great turmoil in prison policies. However, the study suggests that riots occur when the communication of grievances to a potentially sympathetic outside world is cut off. Where some effective balance of power to communicate with supportive interest groups on the outside is maintained between inmates and staff, then negotiation, well-organized strikes, and protests take the place of riots. Though the results of our study are not yet final, they already testify to the importance of effective communication as a cushion for change.

The prospective changes from prisons to community-based correctional services will involve conflict over many issues. There now exist deeply entrenched vested interests on the part of staff, local communities, politicians, and other parties in maintaining the status quo. Radical reform measures will generate from these sources strong resistance and sabotage of efforts for change. They may produce riots because of pervasive uncertainty by both staff and inmates as to the sources, strength, and direction of final authority. In any case the changes essential to the development of community-based correctional policies will involve much searching reexamination of basic values and beliefs about crime, criminals, and control measures. The vested interests of the existing system in large institutions will make the change to community-based reintegration services a most difficult political process.

I am aware that this picture of past disillusionments and future conflict is a sobering one, but in many ways I think that is a healthier and more promising attitude with which to approach these difficult problems. Among many professionals in the human services there is emerging a more realistic assessment of the limitations of coercive treatment within the humanitarian principles of a democratic society, along with a more acute appreciation of the harmful consequences of excessive official intervention. The abandonment of the large penitentiary is a step in this direction. The evidence now available makes it clear that public security will not be endangered if we start by finding other less destructive alternative measures for 90 per cent of those now confined in these facilities. At the least we can begin by reorganizing juvenile services with this present generation of youthful offenders, a process already underway in several states. The remaining 10 per cent will require confinement in small intensive security units to guarantee public safety. Changes in this direction are indicated on the grounds of experience, social justice, and economic necessity, so I expect they will come in time. With better applications of existing knowledge these social changes may be made less costly for us all.

30

CORRECTIONS AND THE COMMUNITY

NATIONAL ADVISORY COMMISSION ON
CRIMINAL JUSTICE STANDARDS AND GOALS

Revised public and professional expectations of corrections have
brought about a transformation in its means and ends during the last
several years. Tradition required institutions merely to hold prisoners
until ordered to release them. Now both the public and the correctional staff expect prisoners to be, at least, no worse for the correctional experience and, at most, prepared to take their places in society
without further involvement with the law. Tradition required probation and parole merely to provide some form of nominal supervision.
Now it is expected that the experience of probation and parole will
provide the offender with positive assistance in making a better
adjustment to his circumstances.

These revised expectations have led to an awareness that corrections must be linked to the community in every phase of operations.
These links are hard to forge because correctional agencies of all
kinds traditionally have maintained an isolation from other human
service agencies.

Dissatisfaction with incarceration as a means of correction has
grown to a point where some States have almost completely abolished incarceration for some classes of offenders. In other States,
experimental programs have been successful enough that once-over-
crowded prisons and reformatories now are unused. Clearly, the
future lies with community-based corrections.

The institution model for corrections has not been successful
in curbing potential crime. But at least it exists, with its physical
plant and identified processes of reception, classification, assign-

Source: From *Corrections*(Washington, D.C.: U.S. Government Printing Office, 1973), pp.
221–236 (editorial adaptations).

ment, custody, work, academic and vocational training, religion, and recreation.

The substitute models are talked about and are occasionally used. But community-based corrections is not well organized, planned, or programmed. This task is the challenge of the future. Required is a complicated interplay among judicial and correctional personnel, those from related public and private agencies, citizen volunteers, and civic groups. This interplay of the correctional system with other parts of the public sector and greater involvement of the private sector, including civic participation in dimensions not foreseen in the correctional world just a few years ago, requires leadership in the entire criminal justice field to collaborate in the exploitation of all possibilities for successfully changing repression to reintegration. Policymakers must understand the essential elements of a sound community-based correctional system as well as they now understand the orderly management of the prison.

DEFINITION

As used in this chapter, the term "community-based corrections" includes all correctional activities that take place in the community. The community base must be an alternative to confinement of an offender at any point in the correctional process.

Most persons confined to custodial control are potential participants in community-based corrections through work- and study-release programs, family visiting furloughs, and reentry programming. Finally, well-established parole services constitute the community-based programming core for offenders released from relatively lengthy custody.

This enumeration of major program components does not exhaust the potential of community correctional services, but the central principle of the definition is clear. Community-based correctional programs embrace any activity in the community directly addressed to the offender and aimed at helping him to become a law-abiding citizen. Such a program may be under official or private auspices. It may be administered by a correctional agency directly or by a noncorrectional service. It may be provided on direct referral from a correction agency or on referral from another element of the criminal justice system (police or courts). It may call for changing the offender through some combination of services, for controlling him by surveillance, or for reintegrating him into the community by placing him in a social situation in which he can satisfy his requirements without law violation. A community-based program may embrace any one or any combination of these processes.

The use of control and surveillance is basic to a sound community corrections system. Both policymakers and the public must understand that the elimination of incarceration does not eliminate control.

SIGNIFICANCE OF
COMMUNITY-BASED CORRECTIONS

The significance of community-based corrections will be assessed from three aspects: humanitarian, restorative, and managerial. The criteria of success in each differ markedly.

The humanitarian aspect of community-based corrections is obvious. To subject anyone to custodial coercion is to place him in physical jeopardy, to narrow drastically his access to sources of personal satisfaction, and to reduce his self-esteem. That all these unfavorable consequences are the outcome of his own criminal actions does not change their reality. To the extent that the offender can be relieved of the burden of custody, a humanitarian objective is realized. The proposition that no one should be subjected to custodial control unnecessarily is a humanitarian assertion. The key question is the definition of necessity, which must be settled by the criterion of public protection.

The restorative aspect concerns measures expected to achieve for the offender a position in the community in which he does not violate the laws. These measures may be directed at change, control, or reintegration. The failure of offenders to achieve these goals can be measured by recidivism, and their success is defined by reaching specific objectives set by correctional decisionmakers.

The managerial goals are of special importance because of the sharp contrast between the per capita costs of custody and any kind of community program. Any shift from custodial control will save money. But the criterion of correctional success is not fiscal. A major object of correctional programs is to protect the public. Therefore, any saving of public funds must not be accompanied by a loss of public protection. When offenders can be shifted from custodial control to community-based programming without loss of public protection, the managerial criteria require that such a shift be made. Otherwise public funds will have been spent without satisfying a public objective.

It is necessary here to note that public protection is not always the sole objective of correctional programming. Some kinds of offenders, especially the most notorious, often could perfectly well be released without jeopardizing public safety. But their release will not be countenanced because public demands for retribution have not been satisfied. Offenders in custody should be there predominantly because public protection seems to require it. Decisionmakers must disentangle these objectives to assure that use of community-based correctional programs is not denied for irrelevant reasons.

RATIONALE FOR CORRECTIONS IN THE COMMUNITY

The movement toward community-based corrections is a move away from society's most ancient responses to the transgressor. For thousands of years, society relied mainly on banishment, physical punishment, or the death penalty to accomplish the goals of criminal justice. The world is now too small for any society to eject anyone. Our culture has so changed that we no longer consider imposing capital penalties on the sweeping scale that seemed appropriate to our ancestors.

Out of the realization that the old ways were unacceptable there emerged the prison, a place for artificial banishment or civil death. Nearly two centuries of experience with the penitentiary have brought us to the realization that its benefits are transient at best. At its worst, the prison offers an insidiously false security as those who were banished return to the social scene of their former crimes. The former prisoner seldom comes back the better for the experience of confinement. The effectiveness of the prison as a school for crime is exaggerated, for the criminal can learn the technology of crime far better on the streets. The damage the prison does is more subtle. Attitudes are brutalized, and self-confidence is lost. The prison is a place of coercion where compliance is obtained by force. The typical response to coercion is alienation, which may take the form of active hostility to all social controls or later a passive withdrawal into alcoholism, drug addiction, or dependency.[13]

Mitigating Damages Done by Prisons

One of the tasks of corrections is to mitigate alienation. For generations this task has been attempted mainly by placing some offenders on probation instead of sending them to prison. When offenders have been incarcerated, parole has made it possible for them to serve part of their terms in the community, in the belief that assistance of a parole officer will help them to choose a law-abiding course.

There has been a growing realization that prison commitments for most offenders can be avoided or at least abbreviated without significant loss of public protection.[14] If the committed offender eventually returns to the community, it is best that his commitment removes him for as short a time as possible. The principle has evolved: incarcerate only when nothing less will do, and then incarcerate as briefly as possible. The services provided by probation and parole should strengthen the weak, open new channels to the erratic, and avoid openly reinforcing the intimidation that is latent in the relationship between the offender and the state.

The objective is to motivate each offender by the incentives that motivate most citizens toward orderly social life. In large part these incentives derive from an economic philosophy in which a day's pay for a day's work forms a unit in a prospect of lifetime security. Such employment is the necessary, if not sufficient, basis for conventional life in America. Emphasis on the employment of the offender is a response to the common-sense awareness that the unemployed offender is a probable recidivist.

But community-based corrections cannot be limited to the services of an employment office. A man who has committed a crime and been caught and convicted has suffered a blow to his self-esteem that may be masked by bravado or indifference. He has good reason to believe that conventional persons will reject him, and he therefore seeks out the unconventional. In the prison he has no choice; he must associate with the unconventional. In the community, probation and parole resources should make accessible a whole range of social support services as needed.

The difficulty of the task is obvious. Far more is required than the one-to-one contact between probation or parole officer and the offender. The offender's predicament stems from the combination of personal deficits and social malfunctions that produced a criminal event and a social status. Most personal deficits characterizing offenders are also commonly found in nonoffenders. The social malfunctions of unemployment, discrimination, economic inequity, and congested urban living affect most citizens. The offender, like other citizens, must find a way to live with his deficits and with the disorder around him. If corrections is to mitigate alienation, it must mobilize the community services that can make such an outcome possible.

To a much larger extent than has been realized, social support services must be given outside the official correctional apparatus and inside the community. Schools must accept and help reintegrate the delinquent instead of exiling him to reform schools. Unions and employers must open doors to adult offenders instead of restricting their employment to the most menial and insecure labor.[15]

Corrections cannot continue to be all things to the offender. The correctional structure must change from a second-class social system consisting of a correctional bureaucracy and a dependent population of offenders subject to official control and service. Although the pattern of the future is not yet clear, it seems to consist of a brokerage service in which the agency opens up to the offender community services where such services exist, or helps create new services for the entire community where none existed before. This enlarged theory of corrections will be unfamiliar to many correctional and community agency personnel, but it offers the only reasonable prospect for dealing more successfully with the serious problem of the recidivist offender.

Community-Based Corrections as Deterrents

There remain two additional public policy considerations in the rationale for community-based corrections: the deterrence or intimidation of the offender who is caught and the deterrence of potential offenders. It may be legitimately argued that the milder punishment aspects of community-based programs will not sufficiently deter either the actual or potential offender.

For the offender who has been under control, deterrence can be measured by whether he commits further crimes. Current measurements hardly support the contention that incarceration deters. But, regardless of this finding, no one should minimize the deterrent effect of noninstitutional control by the correctional system. Indeed, the deterrent effect of proper control within the community, coupled with realistic opportunities for the offender to make an adjustment there, may be expected to be considerable, not only on the basis of theoretical assumptions but also as indicated by preliminary studies which offer suggestive findings.[16] And the experience of simply being under official jurisdiction constitutes a punitive experience for nearly all offenders.

The deterrence of potential offenders has not been supported by evidence. Despite many attempts, especially in the controversies over capital punishment, no one has ever proved that the threat of severe punishment actually deters crime. Indeed, there is evidence that swiftness and certainty have much greater deterrent effect than a long prison sentence.[17] This raises the serious question of how just it is to adhere to a policy that can be supported only by assumption.

But even if we allow that some crime is deterred by the criminal justice system, the deterrent potentiality of the prison is grossly exaggerated. The argument should be framed properly in terms of the statistical chances of getting caught. In the case of most crimes other than homicide, the chances are much less than even. In most communities a criminal can reasonably assume that, even with repeated law violations, his chances of getting caught are relatively slight. The prospect of incarceration or other punishment is distant.

Documentation of the foregoing is available particularly with reference to the failure of imprisonment in primary deterrence; that is, the discouragement of further criminal activity by those punished at least once. Available studies suggest strongly that jurisdictions making extensive use of probation instead of prison do not experience increased recidivism.[18]

Similarly, studies of confinement length do not establish that lengthier prison terms result in decreased recidivism.[19]

Secondary deterrence—the discouragement of first-time criminal behavior by persons who may fear punishment—is a more elusive subject. However, the available statistical studies and analyses on varying punishment and prison confinement practices in different localities offer some basis for comparison.

We can conclude that, at the least, there is no established statistical base relating crime rates to the severity of dispositions imposed by courts in different locales.

ROLE OF THE COMMUNITY IN CORRECTIONS

The recent shift in our Nation's values—particularly in corrections' views of criminality—helps explain the rationale and current emphasis on citizen involvement and community programs. Within this general context, the various roles citizens play and corrections' responsibility to involve the public can be understood better.

Circumstances of the past decade have had dramatic impact on corrections. The poverty programs of the 1960's, which failed to win the war on poverty but made strong impressions on the Nation, are of particular import for corrections. The ideology underlying those programs suggested that persons of minority origin and low socioeconomic status systematically are denied access to higher status in American society. They thus are persistently overrepresented among those who experience mental and physical illness, educational failure, unemployment, and crime and delinquency.

Programs that attacked such systematic exclusion from higher status used varied techniques. Emphasis on cultural awareness attempted to promote dignity and pride among minority groups, inserted minority history into America's records, and resulted in new group cohesion, political clout, and often militant reactions with newly discovered strength. The "maximum feasible participation" emphasis of poverty programs, although ultimately failing to achieve what it called for, made official the acknowledged but often ignored rights of all Americans to have a say in their own destiny.

The disadvantaged began to assume positions on boards of public and private agencies designed to serve them but formerly run for them by persons of more affluent status. "New careers" provided alternative routes for low-income persons to social and economic mobility through revised employment and training schemes. The pervasive ideology proclaimed to the formerly powerless that "you, too, have power, if you choose to exercise it."

This trend, visible in civil rights concerns, in welfare activism, and in student unrest, has its counterpart in correctional systems, and for the first time the voices of the inmate and the ex-offender are being heard. There are prisoners' unions and racial and ethnic ex-offender groups in all American cities. This as yet undocumented movement offers powerful new allies for correctional reform if professionals in corrections choose to take that view instead of the frequent, defensive reaction to exclude.

Today American prisons contain, for almost the first time in our history, substantial numbers of young persons of middle and upper socioeconomic levels, largely through prosecution of the Nation's youth for drug use. Another new set of allies for correctional reform thus exists today: concerned parents and friends of such youths, along with a vast body of parents who fear that their children might be among those jailed or imprisoned in the future.

This group is perceived by correctional staffs as less threatening than minority group ex-offenders. The reforms they urge may be listened to with greater attention. But coalitions are to be expected. These young persons learn militant and disruptive techniques very quickly and will employ them if they observe that rational discussion does not accomplish the desired reform.

Corrections has a unique opportunity to enlist such potential supporters and to organize their widespread concern into constructive aid for improving the correctional system. This audience is a prime source for volunteers. These citizens have political influence and know-how about influencing policy at local and State levels. The corrections system must design and implement public information systems to present facts and interpretations. If the potential of this group in aiding the correctional cause is to be realized, agencies must inform the public of their needs and welcome participation.[20]

Social Service Agencies

Other social service agencies also have an impact on corrections. As community-based treatment programs increase in number and variety, correctional personnel and offenders will interact increasingly in formal and informal ways with professionals from other human service areas such as welfare, education, health, and employment. As institutional walls disintegrate, figuratively speaking, the boundaries between the various human service areas will disappear as well—and correctional problems will come to be the problems of a range of professionals serving communities.

Another group of allies thus is identified: colleagues in related fields, many of whom have had relatively limited contact with the world of corrections. While there has been some professional mobility between welfare and corrections, or corrections and rehabilitation work, such relationships will become closer and more common as community-based programs develop. Concerns for meeting human needs are shared; common problems are faced in various settings. Social welfare personnel, broadly defined, clearly are allies of corrections. Their special talents and experiences will add enormously to the strength of correctional reform movements.

RESPONSIBILITY OF CITIZENS

In a democratic nation, responsibility for provision of necessary public services is shared broadly by the citizenry. Decisions are made directly by public interest and demand for services, or indirectly by public neglect. In the case of correctional services, as with education, health care, and welfare needs, the decision regarding type and quality of service is determined ultimately by the public's will. An objective, therefore, in considering ways to improve criminal justice standards and goals must be attainment of an informed and concerned public, willing to insist on exercising its right to make informed decisions concerning correctional services.

Historically this objective has not been realized, and a massive public information campaign to bring about citizen involvement will be required to reverse the patterns of the recent past. In an earlier era, the community directly exercised law enforcement and correctional responsibilities: for example, the religious tribunals of New England, with punishments of banishment, public pillories, and even executions; and the citizen posses of the frontier West, with their "out of town by sunset" sentence or execution by hanging. These are well-documented examples of citizens acting to maintain public order and safety.

As the Nation developed in size and complexity, these functions were delegated to public servants, supposed experts with specialized knowledge and certain personal characteristics. The sheriff's staff and the police force replaced the posse; the court system replaced church tribunals and posse justice; jails, workhouses, and prisons replaced the public pillory, banishments, and summary executions. A professional criminal justice system came into being.

The immediate aim of adminstrators should be to consult as many public representatives as possible during all stages of a program from planning through operation. This should not be token participation for the sake of appearance, or confined to individuals and organizations representing a single community sector. It is especially important not to limit participation to persons associated with the power centers of the community or with whom corrections officials have closest rapport and can expect to be in least conflict.

The correctional administrator launching new programs faces a conflict that may be inherent in any effort to offer services for convicted persons: the limit on innovation beyond existing levels of public acceptance. The easiest programs to launch are those that do not require radical adjustment of attitudes toward the offender.

The Community as Policy-Maker

A variety of specialized policymaking roles currently are undertaken by citizens, often at the request of criminal justice officials. In such situations, lay citizens function in task forces or study groups and serve a general advisory role to the government. A by-product, perhaps more important than this advisory objective, is the creation of an ever-larger pool of citizens who have in-depth knowledge of corrections issues. They provide much-needed feedback to corrections, especially regarding lay thought and opinion.

It is important that meaningful roles be assigned without expecting the advisory body merely to rubber stamp the decisions that the correctional administrator has made. Community involvement that is only a facade will be discovered quickly. Therefore, administrators should carefully analyze, in advance of creating citizen committees, the areas in which their input is desirable, if not essential. Decisions to be left to the agency should be specified and communicated to the committee.

Frequently, advisory bodies are comprised of "leading citizens" representing only one element of the community rather than a cross-section. In recent years, the necessity of broad representation has been recognized, and most groups seek appropriate membership of minorities, ex-offenders, women, and special community interest groups.

RESPONSIBILITY OF CORRECTIONAL
SYSTEMS FOR COMMUNITY PARTICIPATION

Correctional systems themselves must assume responsibility for enlisting broad community support for correctional programs.

Agencies generally are responsible to administrative branches of government and only indirectly to the legislature and public. An unconcerned public has been relatively unaware of correctional issues. Correctional agencies have operated with little public scrutiny and in general have enjoyed that autonomy while simultaneously complaining about the lack of public support for their endeavors.

Given the realities of rising community concern and citizen involvement, these circumstances are likely to be altered drastically in the years ahead. It is in the general interest of correctional programs for citizens to exercise their prerogatives as participants in a democratic society. The correctional systems of today bear a heavy burden of responsibility for the lack of involvement with the community in past decades and should expend extra effort to make amends.

IMPLEMENTATION OF
COMMUNITY-BASED CORRECTIONS

A basic principle underlying the philosophy of community-based corrections is that all efforts consistent with the safety of others should be made to reduce involvement of the individual offender with the institutional aspects of corrections. The alienation and dehumanization engendered in jails, workhouses, prisons, even probation services, is to be avoided wherever possible. The less penetration into the criminal justice system the better.

A second basic principle is the need for extensive involvement with the multiple aspects of the community, beginning with the offender and his world and extending to the larger social system.

As a final basic principle, it is apparent that community-based programs demand radically new roles for inmates, staff, and citizens. This must be made explicit in altered job descriptions, new patterns of training, different performance expectations.

The principle implies changes in recuitment. Since corrections needs to relate increasingly with the various facets of the community, its work force must increasingly represent those facets. This means greatly expanded recruitment from minority and economically disadvantaged groups, with all that implies for location of services (such as prisons), for innovative training, and for new kinds of staffing patterns.

Community Alternatives to Confinement

Nonresidential Programs

Structured correctional programs, which supervise a substantial part of an offender's day but do not include "live-in" requirements, are another community-based necessity. The clients are persons who need more intensive services than probation usually can offer, yet are not in need of institutionalization. School and counseling programs, day treatment centers with vocational training, and guided group interaction programs are among the treatment modes used, many with related services to families.

Many such programs are described substantially in corrections literature.[21] Essexfields and Collegefields, community descendants of the Highfields residential program, were based on group dynamics theory and utilized peer group pressures to modify behavior. The Provo experiment in Utah used similar theoretical approaches. The programs, in brief, involved intensive daily programs of work or school and counseling sessions. Essexfields in Newark, N.J., used employment in a county mental hospital; Collegefields, a short-term project, used an academic program adapted for individual student needs, as the heart of the program.

Each of these projects has demonstrated success in treatment outcomes sufficient to warrant further experimentation. Each clearly showed that intensive programs in communities are at least as effective as, and usually somewhat better than, institutionalization and that offenders who otherwise would be in penal settings can be treated safely in the community. To date, these types of programs have been used most extensively with adolescent populations.

Foster and Group Homes

Juvenile judges frequently have felt it necessary to commit youngsters to an institution when circumstances in the parental home were totally unsuitable. Foster home development and more recently the group home, when used for aiding delinquent youths, are attempts to prevent unncessary institutionalization.

Foster homes, also extensively used to meet child dependency needs, are operated under a range of administrative arrangements, public and private, State and local, court and correctional.

Foster care appears to be considered a less useful tool than the more recently developed group homes. These quasi-institutions often are administered by agencies with house parents as paid staff, in contrast to foster homes where a monthly or daily room and board fee is customarily made to foster parents. The theoretical assumptions underlying the group home are related to child development stages. Most delinquency occurs in adolescence when family ties are loosening as adulthood approaches. Transfer to a new family situation, as in the foster home, is felt to be less desirable than the semi-independence from family that is possible in the group home, along with a supportive environment and rewarding experiences with adults.

The group home model usually has six to ten young people living in a home owned or rented by agencies and staffed by employed "parents" or counselors, supplemented by other necessary professional services obtained mostly through existing community resources. Correctional agencies in Minnesota and Wisconsin use such group homes extensively. California has systematized the use of group homes through a classification related to particular types of youth.

Evaluation of such efforts generally is positive. Costs are high relative to nonresidential treatment, but not as high in most cases as institutional care and, in the case of Boulder where community resources are extensively used, considerably less.

The Community Correctional Center

The popularity of the "community correctional center" concept in recent years has led to a bandwagon effect with rapid growth of a wide variety of programs. Definition, therefore, becomes increasingly difficult. For purposes of this report, the term is used to mean a relatively open institution located in the neighborhood and using community resources to provide most or all of the services required by offenders. The degree of openness varies with offender types, and use of services varies with availability and offender needs. Such institutions are used for multiple purposes—detention, service delivery, holding, and prerelease.

The lines between community-based and institutional programs are blurring substantially. Because of their newness, projects of this nature have generated little evaluation, minimum descriptive material, and few guidelines. They do, however, provide a flexible and theoretically sound design with potential for meeting varied correctional needs.

Many types of community correctional centers are in existence today, using such facilities as jails, parts or all of hotels or motels, floors or wings of YMCA's, surplus army barracks, and former fraternity houses. Some are used as alternatives to penal service, others as adjuncts to institutionalization. They serve many types of offenders, usually in separate facilities. An interesting variant in Minnesota is a "restitution" house where offenders live while working to earn funds to compensate victims.

Community Adjuncts to Institutions

The program activities discussed so far have been designed generally to serve as alternatives to the use of the institution. A major assumption throughout this report is that most persons committed to correctional authority can be served effectively and economically in community settings. The implications require a brief review.

It seems obvious that institutional populations will be made up increasingly of hard-core criminals and persons difficult to control. Prison will become the final resort. However, all but a very small fraction of institutionalized individuals ultimately return to the community, and it is therefore essential that institutional programs also involve the community.

The notion that isolating individuals from the community influences that made them engage in crime and that exposing them to the influences of prison will reform them is no longer accepted.[22] Instead, as this report so often notes, prisons have proved to be criminogenic in themselves. For this reason, administrators have been seeking alternative experiences for inmates.

Many of the programs in use today favor the traditional values of work, training, and education. While reintegration efforts must encompass standards that society accepts and endorses, correctional administrators should not impose their own value systems on the potential range of community programs. To do so may restrict the breadth and innovative character of what is offered.

Instead, the range of activities permitted in the larger community should be considered. For example, some offenders might participate with nonoffenders in private group therapy, consult with their own lawyers, conduct investigations in connection with their own trials, negotiate with community institutions, participate in school activities, attend social functions, and engage in athletics in the community.

Some of these ideas may seem unrealistic and foreign to today's conception of the inmate's role. However, the hypothesis is that the benefit to be derived when an offender's feelings of hopelessness and powerlessness are dissipated by virtue of his having a measure of control over his own destiny will far outweigh administrative anxieties and burdens.

The institutional custodial climate that so clearly separates the keeper from the kept should be replaced in significant measure by one of mutuality as staff and offenders work together in responsible citizen roles that are meaningful to both parties.

The concept of "bridging" is used to denote programs that establish links between imprisoned inmate, institution, and free society, to afford the inmate experiences expressly intended to maximize his reintegration potential. Inmates participate in training, work, education, or other activities that provide as many normal transactions and experiences with community persons and organizations as possible. The number and variety of community resources that can be developed for these purposes is virtually unlimited.

The bridging concept contains the reciprocal notions of inmates relating outward to the community and of opening the institution to community access. As bridging from the prison to the outside is intended to normalize interactions with community resources, so bridging into the prison is intended to transform traditional prison activities into more normal patterns of life. Families and neighbors, employers and teachers, ministers and counselors enter the prison, participate in its life, and bring the ongoing community life into the formerly insulated institution.

Bridging activities provide much-needed diversification of options for inmates. Staff and program can be augmented significantly by utilizing more fully the opportunities available outside the walls or by bringing them inside. Inmates have the opportunity to try out socially acceptable roles in a planned transitional process.

The dependence fostered by institutionalization can be reduced. Inmates are allowed to discharge a measure of social and personal responsibility by assuming financial obligations and a larger measure of control over their destinies, thus contributing to their self-esteem and an awareness of their stake in the community.

Citizens who participate in bridging activities become involved in correctional services and decisionmaking. Greater public participation should result in increased understanding of and support for these programs. Such public involvement also will prepare communities for a certain amount of conflict and failure, for bridging concepts imply risk of an unassessed nature. Expectations of total success will lead only to disillusionment, but realistic optimism for potential gains must be retained.

Work Release

Work-release programs began to be used extensively in the 1950's. The practice permits selected inmates to work for pay outisde the institution, returning each night. Prisoner employment is not new; the work gang for hire is a well-known feature in penal history. The work-release concept differs markedly, however, in allowing regular civilian employment, under specified circumstances, for selected low-risk inmates. Initially used mainly with misdemeanants, work release now is used widely with felons and youthful offenders. Other versions, similar in intent, provide for weekend sentences, furloughs, and release for vocational training or educational programs. All help to reestablish links to the community for the incarcerated.

In a few instances, commercial manufacturing operations have been introduced into prisons. Honeywell, Inc., has loaned a computer to a Massachusetts prison for use by inmates to do programming and data processing for various departments of State government, an up-to-date version of "state use." Union involvement in such efforts is crucial; it will add a much needed dimension to employment programs and represent a further potential resource for correctional programs.

Family Visits

Prisons are attempting in a variety of ways to assist the reintegration of offenders into family circles, as well as the work world. Prison visiting always has been allowed, frequently under less than favorable circumstances, with minimum opportunities for privacy and personal communication. Conjugal visits long have been the practice in Mississippi institutions[23] but have not been allowed elsewhere in this country until recently. A relatively new California scheme allows entire families to spend up to two days in cottage-like houses on prison grounds.[24]

Family counseling programs for inmates and families are available in many States. A family life education program in Hennepin County, Minnesota, is used with adult inmates, their families, and with juvenile probation caseloads.[25] Adlerian group counseling methods, with involvement of even very young children, underlie this attempt to assist the offender and his family.

Volunteers of America programs for youth involve families in somewhat similar ways, with special Sunday events such as picnics or parties to which families are invited for socializing.

In the Swedish penal system, where family visitation is taken for granted, some institutions even permit husband and wife to live together if both are institutionalized. Most interesting is their "holiday" policy—inmates, like other citizens, are entitled to a two week vacation at the beach accompanied by families.[26] Such programs seem startling to American observers but are sensible if assisting families through difficult days and preparing them for stable relationships are desirable goals.

Educational Programs

An educational bridging program is the Newgate model, in which mini-universities are established within prison walls to serve higher educational needs of inmates. Newgate programs are located across the country in State and Federal institutions.[27] Each uses different procedures, but the common thread is use of education as the major tool.[28] Opportunities for continuation of college on release are arranged, and extensive support given. Evaluation evidence developed thus far is positive; a serious limitation of the program, however, is its very high cost.

Students from Augsburg College, Minneapolis, as part of their regular curriculum attend classes held in the penal institution with inmates and prison officers as fellow students.[29] While a range of courses are taught in this "co-learner" model, the criminology course is of most interest—as a living laboratory with mutual benefits to all students.

Ethnic Programs

In recent years, with heightening cultural and ethnic awareness, various minority consciousness groups have formed in the Nation's prisons, many involving extensive contact with similar groups outside. Enriching in many ways and clearly of potential assistance to the reintegration of inmates with their community, such programs are sensitive issues in correctional circles. Prisons mirror the racial unrest of the Nation in aggravated form associated with the tensions of anxiety and fear, close quarters, lack of privacy, and hours of idleness. Cultural groups, strengthening the individual's awareness of his group identity and raising questions of discrimination, are potential sources of discord. But they are nontheless vital links to the self-help potential of such groups on the outside.

Prerelease Programs

The Federal prison system pioneered in the development of prerelease programs in the early 1960's. In several cities small living units were organized, usually in leased quarters, to which individuals could be transferred for the final months of a sentence as part of preparation for release. Special orientation programs and employment assistance were provided, with gradually increasing opportunities to exercise decionmaking. The purpose was to phase inmates into community life under supervision, with assistance as needed. Such centers are used increasingly in State programs.

The California system has reorganized its services to give its field staff (parole personnel) greater responsibility for inmate programming during the last 6 months of confinement, in essence converting that period into a release-planning phase. Arrangements have been made to permit temporary release at any time in the last 60 days before the official release date, thus permitting more flexible timing as plans are developed. Inmates within 90 days of release may make unescorted trips to home communities on 3-day passes to facilitate release plans, another way of easing into the often difficult postrelease period.[30]

Short-Term Return of Parolees

Related closely to prerelease planning is recent development in many States of programs permitting the short-term return of parolees who have made a misstep that is potential cause for parole revocation and return to the prison. Frequently, prerelease facilities are used for this function. The return to a relatively open institution allows the parolee a breather, more supervision than in the community, and time to plan a new and hopefully more effective reentry into the community. Research indicates that short-term returnees in California do as well on second release as those released after a long period of reimprisonment.[31]

31

SOME DIRECTIONS FOR CITIZEN INVOLVEMENT IN CORRECTIONS

VINCENT O'LEARY

The notion that the citizen can play a vital role in corrections is as old as the field itself.[32] One only has to recall the tremendously significant part played by religious groups in American corrections or to review the programs of the John Howard Association, the Osborne Association, and prisoners' aid societies through the years.[33]

But even with these contributions, it is fair to say that corrections and its clientele were, and still are, largely isolated from the community. As the National Crime Commission recently said: "Corrections it not only hard to see; traditionally, society has been reluctant to look at it."[34] And the growth of a professional service in corrections may have actually heightened its isolation. Government programs, for example, virtually replaced the large number of citizens who provided supplementary or direct parole supervision in a considerable part of the United States prior to World War II. Desirable as this professionalization may have been, it resulted in a loss of intimate knowledge and sense of responsibility by persons outside the correctional establishment.

Since the latter part of the 1950's, there has been an emphasis on reversing these trends, on bringing the citizen more directly into correctional affairs. The President's Committee on Juvenile Delinquency and Youth Crime, particularly, was instrumental in pressing for the enlistment of citizen groups in delinquency-prevention activities. This emphasis spring directly from that Committee's adoption, and relatively consistent application, of a theoretical position which contended that the essential task in delinquency-prevention and control was the reordering of society's opportunity system, particularly in education and employment. Though it actually gave little direct attention to the traditional correctional services—probation, parole,

Source: From *The Annals of the American Academy of Political and Social Science,* 381 (January 1969): 99–108. Reprinted by permission of the author and publisher.

or institutions—the Committee's programs had a carry-over effect and accentuated their need for more citizen support.

This emphasis on citizen involvement has been paralleled by a growing willingness by citizens to make a personal commitment to correctional programs. Recently, the National Council on Crime and Delinquency (NCCD) embarked on a large-scale effort to enlist citizens in work on the problems of criminal justice. The response was substantial, with a significant number of persons indicating specific interest in correctional services. This experience has been repeated elsewhere by groups such as halfway-house associations.[35]

Despite the growing awareness of the need to build citizen interest, few correctional programs appear prepared to engage in utilizing citizens successfully. In a survey of the twenty largest states, NCCD's staff found only limited utilization of citizens in correctional programs. Apparently, many more of them could be enlisted in correctional enterprises than are now being used. Possible explanations of this disparity can be traced to the history of corrections and to the nature of its bureaucracy and its ideology. In each of these, powerful forces can be identified which militate against an intimate participation by citizens.

Even those correctional agencies which have successfully tempered these forces often find difficulty in mounting effective programs. Usually, the chief reason is a failure to allocate the staff and financial resources required to carry them out. Another important source of failure is the lack of recognition of the varied roles which citizens might play. Each role appeals to a different kind of person. Each rests on different assumptions about the function to be served. Each requires a specific strategy for recruitment and training, and for obtaining the maximum contribution of each person. Failure to recognize these differences almost inevitably produces, for citizens in the programs, low motivation, low productivity, and low continuance and, for the correctional managers, frustration and disillusionment. An examination of four key citizen roles in corrections will help to point up the differing attractions and requirements of each role. Such a review will also illustrate the forces in the correctional system which tends to support or oppose them.

The roles are not mutually exclusive; the same person could play several simultaneously. They are quite distinct, however, and require quite different behaviors on the part of corrections if they are to be successfully engaged.

THE CORRECTIONAL VOLUNTEER

The first and most common role for the citizen in corrections is as a volunteer willing to assume responsibility, more of less formalized, for working directly with offenders. In fact, an important source of the growing perceived need for increased citizen participation is the inability of corrections to provide the manpower needed for the level of services increasingly demanded of it. Organizations such as the United States Children's Bureau, as an illustration, have consistently pointed out a tremendous shortage of probation officers in the United States. The idea of citizens providing this service on a voluntary basis was an obvious response to this continuing problem. It was an idea which has been seized upon by several agencies.

One of the most outstanding programs of this kind is sponsored by the University of Colorado. College students and other citizens are enlisted to work as assistant probation officers and in a wide variety of other activities.[36] Another outstanding program is in the Municipal Court of Royal Oak, Michigan, where probation services are largely dependent upon a staff of volunteers. The program has been so successful, that it has been adopted by the Methodist Church, and large numbers of citizens are now being recruited for probation-officer duties in misdemeanant courts.[37]

Programs like these could be vastly expanded.[38] The National Crime Commission made a strong plea for employing more citizens to reduce correctional manpower shortages. It maintained that "current demonstrations of the vitality of the volunteer in corrections argue strongly that he can be a strong ally in correctional programming."[39] A task force of the Joint Commission on Correctional Manpower and Training is working to develop ways to remove obstacles to the use of volunteers. One explanation offered for the reluctance of corrections to use volunteers is the professional strivings within the field. The argument is made that nonprofessionals are seen as diminishing the status of an agency and are therefore resisted.[40]

Another explanation can be found in the way in which correctional organizations typically function. Like most public organizations, correctional agencies tend to develop patterns of behavior aimed at sustaining the agency which may have little relation to external program objectives.[41] Alternative approaches to tasks tend to be evaluated by their efficiency in protecting the organization's welfare and minimizing the required expenditure of energy.

Such cross-currents must be understood if an agency is to use volunteers successfully. The introduction of volunteers can mean an expenditure of organizational energy on activities which may not "build the agency." The volunteer in corrections tends to be less sensitive to such needs and to make demands directed toward goals other than those of system-maintenance. Parole officers, for example, often will contend that they have great difficulty in dealing with

volunteers because they "refuse to understand the necessity of observing the administrative regulations of the parole department and
only think about the parolee."

Volunteer programs are too often encouraged in which the volunteer is actually granted little power or given tasks which largely tend
to support latent organizational needs. Thus, volunteer programs
ostensibly aimed at providing a needed service to inmates may do
little more than foster institutional stability and harmony. Administrators can easily support volunteer activities such as these, but
ultimately will pay the price in the quality of persons that they are
able to attract. A higher order of administrative skill, and dedication
goals larger than the agency's welfare, are needed if creative and able
volunteers are to be recruited and held.

The effective development of a volunteer program requires, foremost, a clear decision by correctional managers that they have an important function to serve in corrections. It requires a willingness to
invest volunteers with the power to use their skills and resources. It
requires a commitment of staff time and funds to develop an adequate
program of recruitment, screening, training, and supervision. It requires training for all agency staff who will be expected to deal with
volunteers.

THE SOCIAL PERSUADER

Another citizen-participant role is characterized by the person of
influence in the dominant social system who is willing to persuade
others to support corrections and its programs. This type of strength
is especially valuable in bidding for legislative support. It is critical
in mobilizing assistance to expand programs of community-based
corrections. Opportunities for offenders are also dependent upon the
extent to which corrections is able to enlist powerfully placed per-
suaders to intervene in the community's social structure.

The National Crime Commission made this type of citizen activity an important concern. It is recommended that regional planning
and liaison councils be set up to consider the effectiveness of correctional apparatus in various areas, to review future plans and projects,
and to make recommendations for change.[42] Public involvement is
needed to shape workable programs; more important, it is needed if
they are to be fostered and achieved.

A recent survey by the Harris Poll tellingly revealed how little
public involvement there has been in correctional affairs and the
resultant gap between its programs and public understanding of
them.[43] Increased efforts toward public education may help to nar-

row the gap, but they cannot substitute for citizens who have a direct stake in an agency's program. A few correctional departments have developed citizen advisory boards; a few sponsor events such as an annual conference for community leaders; almost none have a systematic, formalized, and well-developed program of substantial involvement of key citizens.

This lack may be explained by several reasons—the traditional isolation of corrections, a lack of aggressive leadership, or an acute absence of resources. It could be argued that another factor of major significance has been the resistance of corrections to sharing power over its program with those outside the system. That sharing is the price which must be paid for the involvement of persons of influence.

There is little reason to expect that corrections will be exempt from a generalized reaction against governmental bureaucracy. There has been a significant change in the perception of the nature of government since the 1930's. Then, the predominant idea was to free its experts and to provide them with resources so that they could perform their task efficiently. There has been a growing disenchantment with this view. As Frank Remington points out, we now find a considerable effort to restrict the power of the government expert and to hold him much more accountable for his actions.[44]

This thrust toward a decentralization of governmental actions and power is becoming common cause for the liberal as well as the conservative.[45] Governmental agencies of all kinds are under increasing pressure for direct participation by citizens in shaping their policies. Corrections, too, must learn how to share responsibility with the citizen.

It may find this more difficult than do other agencies because of its long tradition of isolation and because of its authoritarian strain. The talented correctional administrator, however, will discover—and some have already discovered—the administrative techniques and the organizational models which permit direct participation by citizens. Most of all, administrators will need to develop the habit of sharing information freely with citizens in the planning as well as the implementation stages of policy. At present, correctional administrators tend to share information only when a program is finally shaped and there is a need to sell it.

Perhaps the most dramatic effort aimed toward enlisting citizens to promote correctional change is the program of the National Council on Crime and Delinquency. Begun in 1954 with a grant from the Ford Foundation, its citizen-action program has grown until today there are citizen councils in twenty states. Typically, these programs have enlisted a relatively small group of persons with influence in a state. Each council is provided with a full-time consultant and the program resources of a national agency. From this base, a variety of programs has been developed.

Cause-and-effect claims are always perilous, but a conservative evaluation would indicate that the citizen-action programs of NCCD have been influential in bringing about change in the correctional programs of a number of states. In 1957, the work of an NCCD citizen group in Texas was pivotal in the development of a parole system for that state. More recently, a probation-subsidy bill was fostered by a similar group in California. In several other states, broad-scale revisions of entire correctional services were brought about because of citizen-action programs.

These programs primarily draw their strength from an appeal to a select group of persons of power in the community, rather than from a broad base of support. Persons of the desired status for service on state committees do not volunteer extensive amounts of time for direct services with clients. Instead, they prefer to work on problems in the context of their own social contacts. Above all, they require skillful and substantial staff assistance.

The success of these programs lies in their ability to enlist and maintain the interest of persons of influence. An NCCD staff member of considerable experience contends that the key to this depends upon the program being perceived by the citizen as: (1) important, (2) not achievable without his unique contribution, and (3) resulting in a visible payoff. These criteria may comprise a key to effectiveness for all types of citizen-action programs.

THE GATEKEEPERS OF OPPORTUNITY

The third citizen group to be discussed here are the custodians of access to important social institutions—employers, school administrators, and welfare directors. Corrections has sporadically dealt with these gatekeepers of opportunity, but only rarely in their roles as representatives of crucial social systems the modification of which is required for meeting the special needs of the correctional clientele.

The concept is not widely shared in corrections. Even though used too little, the roles of the social persuader or volunteer are at least generally recognized. It is easy to perceive them as necessary for helping to provide the climate and facilities in which the correctional expert can work, or to execute necessary, but nevertheless auxiliary, services for him. Note should be taken that, in either case, the work of the professional is central. The gatekeeper role develops from a different set of beliefs about the nature of the correctional mission and the pathways to its accomplishment.

Clarence Schrag describes three "revolutions" in the history of corrections.[46] The first, the age of reformation, replaced corporal punishment, exile, and physical disfigurement with the penitentiary. The second, the age of rehabilitation, assumed that criminals were handicapped persons suffering from mental or emotional deficiencies. In this era, individual therapy, aimed at healing these personal maladjustments, became the preferred style. In the third revolution—the age of reintegration—society becomes the "patient" as well as the offender. Much more emphasis is placed on the pressures exerted on the offender by the social groups to which he belongs and on the society which regulates his opportunities to achieve his goals.

The central task of corrections is to connect the offender with the opportunity systems of the community and to integrate him with the socializing institutions of society. To accomplish that task, corrections must change those systems and institutions to eliminate their tendency to reject him. No matter how many resources are provided to corrections, it cannot, by itself, solve the problems of reintegration. That requires the participation of the community. The problems of crime primarily arise in the interaction between the individual and his community. The solution to those problems requires a modification of the offenders' adaptive behavior and a substantial contribution by those responsible for the community's opportunity system.

Martin and Shattuck contend that the goal of the correctional agent should not be to arrange for the exemption of offenders from the consequences of belonging to a particular segment of society.[47] They would charge corrections with a responsibility to change the power relationship between society and the offender, so that all persons in the community to which the offender belongs would find similar opportunities. Social reconstruction becomes the other side of the coin of social reintegration.

The difference between a professional and a gatekeeper citizen, from a reintegration frame of reference, might best be described as the difference between an "inside" and "outside" treater who share responsibility in the process of reintegration. Each has a unique and necessary contribution to make.

This represents for virtually all of corrections a vastly different way of conceiving of the community. It requires an ability to identify important social systems and to design sophisticated strategies for changes in each. Needed is a special sensitivity to the forces working toward collaboration, and those resisiting it, in each of the target systems. Suitable tactics to enlist the gatekeepers of the systems must be undertaken.

Enlisting them requires, most of all, that they not be seen simply as individual citizens willing to help correctional clients. They are not to be coopted into the correctional milieu, but, rather, to be asked to use the power which adheres to their status toward a correctional end. Unexpected resistance to such requests can be expected, for the citizen is being addressed not as a single individual, but as a member of a social group, with all the referent group forces at play which are implicit in such membership.[48]

The social persuader can be an important ally. For example, the Washington State Citizen Council of NCCD became interested in creating employment opportunity for offenders. Because of their prestige they were able to enlist the active help of the governor and the co-operation of some of the largest employers in the state.

Another technique which could be widely emulated is the assignment of specific personnel to work with specific community groups and institutions. Several correctional agencies have assigned staff to develop apprenticeship and vocational training programs with the help of labor unions, with notable success. Parole agencies have designated staff to work specifically with employer groups. Schools have been similarly assigned to juvenile probation officers who have the task of dealing with the entire social complex they represent. Many more opportunities for this kind of specialization are available.

THE INTIMATES

A final group of citizens for whom corrections must develop more effective programs of engagement are those who are significant in the immediate world of the correctional client.[49] By and large, corrections has done little to engage the peer culture of the offender, and even less to engage his community. They may be the most powerful citizen groups of all.

The correctional theory of rehabilitation placed stress upon the personal characteristics of the offender: they were the primary targets for change. This view has been tempered. The peer group has increasingly become an important target.

We must be more aware of the group context and social occasions that give rise to delinquency and crime, to the continuing structures of interaction in which they are embedded. The implication is that, instead of trying to tear individuals out of the networks of interaction from which they now gain meaning, these networks themselves must become the targets of change. New rules, new styles of play, new rewards and punishment must be provided.[50]

A dilemma posed for corrections is how to deal with offenders' peer groups when they are not themselves subject to correctional restraint. There has been some experimentation in dealing with these groups within a correctional setting,[51] but few attempts have been made to move beyond *ad hoc* groups created in a correctional setting and to deal with the traditional community peer groups of offenders.

To undertake this task, corrections will probably need to work much more closely with community agencies directly involved with peer groups on a nonofficial basis. The gang-workers projects in New York City constitute one example of such an attempt.[52] The Youth Services Bureau concept advanced by the National Crime Commission may be another useful device. As envisioned, the Bureau would deal with all youths in a given community, whether adjudicated delinquent or not. It would thereby create a vehicle through which correctional authorities could work in dealing with the offenders in their natural context. The Joint Youth Development Committee in Chicago is an outstanding example of correctional agents working very closely with community workers in dealing with traditional peer groups.[53]

Relating to the offenders' broader community presents other problems. They are problems which must be overcome; the offenders' neighborhood and community, in too many cases, act as powerful forces against any program of reform. Gus Tyler describes the community of most offenders:

> These are the areas that compose the "other America," standing outside the affluent society and hungrily looking in. Denied the delights of economics and social democracy, this "other" and "under" world breeds its marauders who turn to crime and redistribute the wealth, to voice their frustrations and to express the mores of the disinherited, distressed and disturbed.[54]

Logic demands that the correctional worker be concerned with the well-being of the community of the offender if he is going to be of any realistic help to him. Martin and Shattuck argue that the correctional worker of the future, as well as being a therapist, must act as a community worker concerned and participating with citizens of the community to improve it. Moreover, they contend that the correctional worker should become increasingly an advocate for the community, advancing its general causes.[55]

Already some examples of this kind of citizen involvement are seen in a few correctional programs. The Forsyth County Domestic Relations Court, in North Carolina, has recently undertaken the reorganization of its staff on a test basis. One position being created is that of community-action specialist. Among the requirements for that person are the following:

To move through areas of high delinquency, interviewing clients and client families before the court to assess the contribution of neighborhood problems to delinquency in general, and specific delinquent acts in particular; to work with others active in community action, such as the police, poverty workers, etc., to develop and carry out planned efforts to change community conditions; to co-ordinate and expand the court's volunteer programs and develop new ways to engage people in the community in the treatment and prevention of delinquency.[56]

This notion of concern with the offender's community as well as with the offender has another important aspect when considering programs in the ghetto areas. Here the correctional agency can easily be perceived simply as the white man's chosen instrument of conformity, an instrument of an essentially racist policy. Agencies offering "help" can have little credibility in clients' eyes within that frame of reference. The problem, indeed, is very much the same as in correctional institutions, where the official structure is seen as antithetical to the inmate culture and is resisted as such. And, as in an institution, part of the solution to the problem must involve the breaking down of those divisions, if there is going to be a legitimization of constructive work with the representation of the dominant community.

Indeed, the notion of decentralizing probation and parole offices and correctional community centers to the ghetto areas, as is now widely recommended, will encounter some very difficult problems unless it comes to grips with the realities of those communities. And the first of these is the necessity to develop some identity of interest with them if community correctional enterprises are to be seen as anything but outposts of an implacable enemy.

Perhaps one of the most effective ways yet undertaken by correctional agencies in meeting these problems is through the use of "new career" personnel in correctional activities.[57] Some correctional departments are making special efforts to enlist citizens from the ghetto community as workers. The city of Seattle, Washington, has such a program; another is being undertaken in Austin, Texas. Such programs create career opportunities in corrections for the citizen of deprived areas and establish bridges between the correctional agency and the community, to permit effective work with the client groups in those areas. They may represent some of the most important citizen programs yet undertaken by corrections.

32

TEMPORARY
PRISON RELEASE

NORMAN HOLT

In 1968 the California legislature amended the penal code to enable the Department of Corrections to furlough inmates to the community in preparation for their eventual release. The amendment resulted, in part, from widespread and longstanding dissatisfactions with traditional prerelease programs. These dissatisfactions centered in the age-old correctional dilemma of trying to acclimate inmates to roles in the free community while holding them in total custody. Furthermore, research on the most ambitious prerelease program in California —a program which seems to represent "the state of the art"—revealed that it was not very effective.[58] Inmates going through the prerelease classes were learning very little. The furlough program's reasoning was that since bringing the community resources needed for the prerelease preparation into the institution had been tried without significant results, the logical alternative was to send the inmate out into the community where the resources were in the first place: to bring together in the community setting the inmate and the resources necessary for planning his release.

While the amended law, P.C. 2690,[59] requires only that candidates be within ninety days of their release date, departmental procedures permit inmates no more than two furloughs of seventy-two hours duration. Within these broad guidelines, each correctional institution was asked to develop its own procedures, subject to approval by the director of correction, for best use of the furloughs in preparing inmates for their return to the community. The program was inaugurated in most of the institutions during January 1969.

California's prerelease furlough program differs from most furlough programs in the United States in that it is not specifically in-

Source: From *Crime and Delinquency*, 17, 4(October 1971): 414–430. Reprinted by permission of the author and publisher.

tended for a select group who meet rigorous criteria.[60] Furloughs in certain other countries, however, have become so commonplace that participation is often viewed as a right rather than a privilege.[61] The figures on participation in the California program show the lack of restriction on the granting of furloughs. During the first six months of the operation of the program, 795 furloughs were completed, most of them by inmates who were leaving for the first time since their commitment or return as parole violators. Table 16 shows the program's growth over the period studied—from a slow first three months with a gathering momentum to a high of 249 furloughs in June. The June total is equal to about 1 per cent of all adult felons in the state's institutions. The institution most often using furloughs released about 5 per cent of its population to the program during the average month. Variations between institutions reflect, in part, differences in location and the number of inmates who are near their release dates.

DESCRIPTION OF THE PROGRAM

The Southern Conservation Center, which furloughed the largest number of inmates, is the focus of this program evaluation. The first inmate to be furloughed from it was released on January 19, 1969. The staff had decided at the onset to place the responsibility for applying for a furlough squarely on the inmates. The criteria for candidacy are quite clear and the practice in many institutions of

TABLE 16
Number of Inmates Released on Three-Day Furloughs
During First Six Months of 1969

Institution	Jan.	Feb.	March	April	May	June	Total
California Conservation Center	—	—	2	16	13	9	40
North Coast Branch—CCC	—	—	—	—	5	8	13
Sierra Conservation Center	1	1	5	41	34	37	119
Southern Conservation Center	4	26	34	50	38	46	198
California Correctional Institution	4	18	19	7	9	12	69
Correctional Training Facility	—	—	1	—	6	18	25
Deuel Vocational Institution	1	—	1	1	—	15	18
California Institution for Men	—	3	4	7	47	57	118
California Medical Facility	1	—	2	16	11	23	53
California Men's Colony	—	—	1	2	6	1	10
Folsom State Prison	—	1	—	—	5	1	7
San Quentin State Prison	2	—	9	36	30	22	99
California Institution for Women	—	—	—	3	23	—	26
Total	13	49	78	179	227	249	795

relying on caseworkers to make referrals seldom seems to produce enough eligibles. The second major feature of the program is the requirement that each candidate develop very specific and detailed plans of what he intends to accomplish in the three days to prepare himself for his return to the community.

As the inmate comes within ninety days of his release date, he formulates a preliminary outline describing both his plans for making the transition back to the community and, in specific terms, his plans for his furlough. Then he consults with his caseworker, who suggests additions or deletions and makes a recommendation for approval. Next the casework supervisor reviews the plan and forwards it to the program administrator for final action. The superintendent reserves the right to reverse decisions in exceptional cases.

METHOD

The data on which this evaluation is based came from three sources.[62] The furlough application forms indicated the inmate's plans and resources and staff recommendations. Upon each inmate's return to the institution, his caseworker interviewed him, using a two-page interview schedule that included six open-ended questions directed toward finding out the inmate's accomplishments and his reactions to his three days in the community. We can have some confidence that the inmates' reports were truthful because the caseworker doing the interviewing also was responsible for bringing the case up to date. For example, if a returning inmate told the interviewer he had secured employment, the interviewer was the same person who would notify the parole agent to confirm the offer. The caseworker conducting the interview in this institution is also most likely to be an officer in the inmate's dormitory and to have a small caseload (twenty men). This should increase the reliability of such information.

While we would expect that the inmates might exaggerate their accomplishments somewhat, there is also a bias operating in the opposite direction. The inmates were required to recall from memory all the things they did without referring to what they had written in their original applications. Undoubtedly some things were accomplished but forgotten. Still the data must be interpreted with some caution since interaction between prisoners and personnel is not noted for its candor.

The third source of data was a follow-up questionnaire sent to the inmate's family or sponsor asking for their reaction to his furlough and how they felt it was most helpful to him. This provided some collateral evidence of the accomplishments.

During the first two months, effort was concentrated on collecting data about furlough plans and processing. Intake interviewing and the administration of the follow-up questionnaire began in March. Thus, the data from each instrument do not cover the entire sample. In all, 165 inmates were released on 198 furloughs, 33 being furloughed twice.

PROCESSING APPLICATIONS AND PROVIDING RESOURCES FOR FURLOUGHS

A pool of about 150 eligibles existed during the first two months of the furlough program. Of these, only 63 candidates applied, suggesting an initial attitude of caution. The caseworkers recommended denial of only two requests; almost all (87 per cent) received final approval.

An average of about ten inmates per week, which represents two out of three of those receiving parole dates, are being furloughed at present. Those not receiving furloughs either failed to apply or had their requests denied. Most of those not applying live too far away to make use of the furlough, while others do not participate for fear that trouble might cause them to lose their parole dates.

About 10 per cent of the applications are denied, usually because the inmate lacks adequate resources. A few are approved for less than seventy-two hours, usually forty-eight hours.

The applicants had served a considerable amount of time since their commitment or return as parole violators. Table 17 shows that one-fourth of those furloughed had not been in the community for four or more years. The average inmate participating had been locked up thirty-four months, which is about equal to the state average.[63] Very few had served less than one year.

TABLE 17
Amount of Time Furloughed Inmates Served on Current Commitment or Since Violation and Time Left to Serve[a]

Months Served since Reception	Number (N = 165)	Per cent	Days Remaining to Serve before Parole	Number (N = 165)	Per cent
No information	6	4%	No information	21	13%
Less than 1 year	9	5%	14 days or less	8	5%
1 year to 2 years	36	22%	15 days to 29 days	21	13%
2 years to 3 years	46	28%	30 days to 44 days	20	12%
3 years to 4 years	28	17%	45 days to 59 days	32	19%
4 years or more	40	24%	60 days to 74 days	29	18%
			75 days to 90 days	34	20%
Median = 34 months			Median = 48 days		

[a]For those inmates who received more than one furlough, the figures represent the time to and from the first furlough.

The average inmate left on his first furlough forty-eight days before his parole date. This time was shorter during the first two months because of the slow start. One-fifth were released from seventy-five to ninety days before their parole dates.

It is surprising the amount of resources the furloughed inmates came up with even though they had been out of circulation for a considerable time. Table 18 gives the percentage breakdown of who supplied what. Most of the clothes and money were supplied by the inmate himself (inmates at the Center's forestry camps can keep civilian clothes), while transportation and a place to stay were usually provided by the parents. Wives supplied most of the resources for married men. Siblings supplied 10 to 20 per cent of the resources. The only way the institution had to supply resources was by providing a few inmates with their civilian clothing early. The average inmate budgeted $16 to spend in the three days, although those staying with relatives probably had access to additional funds. Only two inmates stayed at motels, and only seven used public transportation to and from the furlough.

FURLOUGH PLANS AND ACCOMPLISHMENTS

In an earlier study inmates with parole dates were asked what they would like presented in prerelease classes within the institution.[64] Half said they didn't want to participate in any prerelease classes.

TABLE 18
Who Supplied Resources for the Prerelease Furlough?

Source	Residence		Trans-portation		Clothing		Money	
	No.	Per cent	No.	Per cent	No.	Per cent	No.	Per cent
Parents	72	44%	54	33%	41	25%	50	30%
Wife	38	23%	34	21%	28	17%	26	16%
Brother, sister	21	13%	34	21%	17	10%	15	9%
Other relatives	12	7%	12	7%	5	3%	8	5%
Friend	10	6%	12	7%	2	1%	3	2%
Sponsor or social agency	2	1%	7	4%	—	—	2	1%
Institution	—	—	—	—	3	2%	—	—
Inmate himself	—	—	—	—	64	39%	54	33%
Public housing or transportation	2	1%	7	4%	—	—	—	—
Other, or no information	8	5%	5	3%	5	3%	7	4%
Total number	165	100%	165	100%	165	100%	165	100%

Median estimated expenses = $16.00

Those who did want to participate asked primarily for a parole agent with whom to discuss problems of parole (89 per cent), information about driving privileges (81 per cent), and information from the Department of Employment (60 per cent).

When the prerelease furlough was substituted for conventional prerelease classes, the inmates planned to go out into the community and do for themselves the same things they had asked for in the classes (Table 19). Slightly more than half of the applicants had no firm job offers and planned to go job hunting, while another 39 per cent planned to visit their future employer and confirm the offer. In short, 92 per cent planned to go out and do something about the general anxiety over employment that the earlier inmates could only talk about. Most (86 per cent) also planned to apply for a driver's license. While the majority of these anticipated actually getting a license, others with special licensing problems planned only to have an interview or to file an application.   The third most common plan was to contact the parole agent. Visiting with the family was listed by one-third of the applicants, and 21 per cent included such things as buying tools or clothes, arranging for a car or insurance, getting union membership in order, investigating the possibilities of going to school, and going fishing.

The activity most frequently planned for, securing a firm job for parole, appears also to have been the one most frequently accomplished. Table 20 shows that more than half of the furloughees left the institution with no job offers on file. Forty-seven per cent of these returned with jobs for parole, and 32 per cent looked but were not successful. In eighteen cases no evidence of job hunting was found; this does not mean that these furloughees made no effort, but rather that there is no record of job hunting.

Jobs were confirmed by 75 per cent of those with offers pending, while some chose to look for a different job. For both groups, 59

TABLE 19
Inmates' Plans for Their First Prerelease Furloughs

Plan	No.	Per cent
Look for a job (no offers on file)	85	53%
Confirm existing job offer	63	39%
Obtain or apply for driver's license	137	86%
Contact parole agent	72	45%
Get reacquainted with family	54	34%
Contact some social agency	7	4%
Other	33	21%
Total number of cases = 160[a]		

[a]No information on 5 furloughees.

TABLE 20
Success in Securing or Confirming Employment on Prerelease Furlough

Planned to Secure Job (No Offers Pending)			Planned to Confirm Existing Offer			Total	
	No.	Per cent		No.	Per cent	No.	Per cent
No evidence of job hunting	18	21%	No evidence of contacting employer	9	14%	27	18%
Looked for but didn't get job	27	32%	Looked for different job	7	11%	34	23%
Got job on first furlough	34	40%	Confirmed job on first furlough	41	65%	75	51%
Got job on second furlough	6	7%[a]	Confirmed job on second furlough	6	10%[a]	12	8%
Total	85	100%		63	100%	148[b]	100%

[a]As a percentage of those who had such plans for first furlough.
[b]No information was available on 5, and 12 had no plans to secure or confirm employment.

per cent secured or confirmed employment during their furloughs, while no record of contacts or applications could be found for 18 per cent of those who had this as part of their plan.

The achievement of the furloughed inmates in the area of employment must be emphasized. Those who confirmed or secured work could avoid that initial shock, on the first day of parole, of showing up for work at a place they've never seen for a boss they've never met.[65] Several inmates were able to work at their jobs one or two days for pay. Several others worked part of a day without pay in order to find out what the job entailed. One baker was able to confirm what was originally a very tentative offer by working half a day at a bakery to demonstrate his skill. Those who went job hunting without success at least broke the ice, perhaps making the transition to the workaday world easier.

Forty job offers were found which didn't exist before the furloughs. Many, if not most of these, were in cases where job placement would have normally been left to the parole agent. A certain amount of the agent's time and effort was thus saved. More importantly, however, it seems likely that inmates who secure their own jobs, if not securing more rewarding work more in line with their skills, will at least have more motivation to stay with them. "Get-out-jobs" are notoriously short-lived.

The lack of a valid driver's license is a perennial problem for new parolees. In Southern California the lack of a driver's license is often the equivalent of a lack of transportation. Employment frequently must await the license. Parolees have traditionally spent one of their first days on parole in applying for a driver's license.

Most furlough applicants (137) made plans to take care of their license problems. There is evidence that eighty-six inmates (63 per cent) followed through (see Table 21) but only 45 per cent appear to have actually obtained a license. While this means that there are sixty-one more licensed parolees than there would have been had they not been furloughed, the number probably could have been higher. Some simply failed the written examination. Others, because of compounding problems, were eligible to take only part of the test or only to be interviewed. A number reported that although they were able to get to the Department of Motor Vehicles office, they could not borrow a car in which to take the driving test. Probably more important is the fact that most inmates planned their furlough to include a week end so that they could spend at least one day (usually Sunday) with their families. This meant that they were applying for a license on the busiest days, Monday and Friday. As anyone who had been to a D.M.V. office on a busy day will attest, this can be a formidable task.

A mainstay of conventional prerelease programs is the parole agent's explanation of the conditions of parole. It has long been felt that the ideal prerelease arrangements would provide for face-to-face contact between the inmate and his future parole agent. Logistical problems, however, have commonly prevented many agents from traveling so far, so often, to see so few future clients. Ideally this face-to-face contact is what should happen under the prerelease furlough system.

Fewer than half of the applicants planned to meet with their parole agents on the first furlough (Table 22). Although this goal

TABLE 21
Number of Furloughees Who Applied for or Obtained a Driver's License

	Accomplished on 1st Furlough		Accomplished on 2nd Furlough		Total	
	No.	Per cent	No.	Per cent	No.	Per cent
Applied but no evidence that license was obtained	23	17%	2	1%	25	18%
Obtained license	53	39%	8	6%	61	45%
Total	76	53%	10	7%	86	63%

Note: All percentages are based on a total of 137 inmates who planned to apply for a license on their first furlough.

TABLE 22
Success in Contacting Parole Agent on Prerelease Furlough

	Accomplished on 1st Furlough		Accomplished on 2nd Furlough		Total	
	No.	Per cent	No.	Per cent	No.	Per cent
Attempted to contact parole agent but no evidence of success	7	10%	1	1%	8	11%
Contacted parole agent	66	92%	11	15%	77	107%
Total	73	102%	12	16%	85	118%

Note: All percentages are based on a total of 72 inmates who planned to contact their parole agent on their first furlough.

didn't have high priority during the planning stages, this appeared to change as the furlough materialized. Seventy-two inmates had planned to contact their parole agents on the first furlough; seventy-three actually made the attempt. The combined data for both the first and second furloughs show that thirteen more inmates than had planned to attempted to contact their parole agents. The contacts, however, were not necessarily face-to-face between the furloughee and the agent. Some were over the telephone, some were with the supervisor, and others undoubtedly were only with "someone in the office." Since the average agent in California spends about one day a week in the parole office, a meeting with the furloughee is no easy matter.

Many of the contacts took the form of a "get acquainted" interview, and the inmates generally reported a more positive attitude toward the agent and parole as a result. For example, one caseworker reported, "Seeing and knowing the parole agent is a real relief to this man. He feels much better about parole now." Another wrote, "The parole agent solved most of the problems by putting this inmate at ease. [The inmate] expected a monster but instead met an understanding official."

Some of the agents used the furlough to become more involved in the case. Several helped the inmates accomplish their prerelease plan by providing them with such things as job leads. At least one agent took an inmate, who had no transportation, to interviews for jobs. In another case a furloughed inmate who had just secured a job contacted his agent for an interview. The agent obtained the employer's address and arranged to see the inmate at his proposed residence. On the way over he verified the job offer; during the interview he

TABLE 23
Success in Accomplishing Other Tasks on Prerelease Furlough

Planned to Accomplish	Accomplished on 1st Furlough		Accomplished on 2nd Furlough		Total	
	No.	Per cent	No.	Per cent	No.	Per cent
Getting reacquainted with family (planned by 54)	61	113%	11	20%[a]	72	133%
Contact some social agency (planned by 7)	4	57%	1	14%[a]	5	71%
Other (planned by 33)	29	88%	8	14%[a]	37	112%
Median number of tasks accomplished (Number planned = 3)	3		3		3	

[a]As a percentage of those who had made such plans for their first furlough.

verified the residence, met the family, and let the inmate know what was expected.

Getting reacquainted with the family, like contacting the parole agent, was originally not part of most prerelease plans, but in retrospect this accomplishment took on new importance. The inmate's relationship with his family will be discussed later. Suffice it to say here that virtually all the inmates expressed appreciation for the way in which they were received and treated by their families. While most reported that simply being with the family and getting to know them again were the important things, many worked out specific family problems. Several furloughees previously estranged from their wives achieved a reconciliation with them. Several other inmates and their wives decided to dissolve unhappy marriages, and two made plans to legalize common-law relationships. In all, seventy-two inmates (Table 23) reported that getting reacquainted with their families was one of the important accomplishments on their furlough.

The number of miscellaneous accomplishments suggests that inmates have no problem finding things to do on their furloughs. The average inmate made plans to accomplish three things to prepare himself for his return to the community; the average furloughee accomplished three things.

INMATES' REACTIONS TO THEIR FURLOUGHS

Besides asking the inmates what they had done, the caseworker asked them five questions designed to get their overall reactions to their prerelease furlough.[66] Table 24 gives the frequency with which various answers were selected.

Over three-fourths of those interviewed reported that their furlough turned out better than expected. Only six said it was less satisfactory than they had anticipated, and most of these had encountered some special difficulty such as illness. The inmates' reasons for why the furlough seemed better than expected seem to be of two types. Most of the men were apprehensive about how they would be received by those outside, particularly family and friends, and were somewhat surprised by the positive reception and support they received. For example, one inmate reported, "I didn't know what to expect. I mean my attitude toward people and theirs toward me was better than I had envisioned." Another said the furlough was "better due to the amount of unexpected support received from my family, relatives, and friends. My release plans are now firmed up and are realistic. I know what I'm going to be doing now for sure."

Many also were surprised at how much they were able to accomplish and gave this as the basis of feeling the furlough was better than expected. For example, a caseworker recorded, "He reports that 'everything just fell into place,' says it was the best three days he has had in four years—he has been incarcerated only twenty-eight months—and [that he] 'accomplished more than I really intended.'"

When inmates were asked what, if anything, stood out in their minds as being particularly pleasant, approximately two-thirds (68 per cent) said, "Being with family or friends." Second most often mentioned was the freedom the furlough afforded; one inmate spoke of "getting a taste of freedom and the more relaxed atmosphere," and another reported that the most pleasant part of the furlough was "walking out of camp, getting in a car, and driving away."

In response to question 3, only 16 per cent said they thought that the furlough would make the rest of their sentence more difficult to do. Approximately two-thirds (68 per cent) said either that it would make it easier or that they didn't think it would make any difference. Those who felt it would make the remaining time easier usually explained that it had reduced their anxiety and concern because while on furlough, they were able to solve some particularly worrisome problem. For example, one caseworker reported an inmate was much less anxious because "he was able to work at his release job for two days and knows that he will be able to support his family and meet obligations." An inmate who patched up his marriage reported that the furlough had made things easier, "because things are straight at home now; there are no doubts in my mind." One inmate told his caseworker, "I'm just happy everything is arranged and I feel these

TABLE 24
Inmates' Reactions to Their First Prerelease Furlough

Questions	No.	Per cent
1. Would you say your leave turned out better than you expected, not as well as expected, or about the same as you thought it would?		
Better	103	78%
Not as good	6	5%
About the same	23	17%
Total	132[a]	100%
2. Was there anything about your furlough that stands out in your mind as being particularly pleasant?		
Being with family or friends	88	68%
Freedom	23	18%
Being away from institution	5	4%
Observing, experiencing change outside	2	1%
Other answers	12	9%
Total	130	100%
3. Has the leave made the thought of staying here (at the institution/camp) easier or more difficult for you, or doesn't it make a difference?		
Harder	22	16%
Easier	77	57%
No difference	15	11%
Don't know	19	14%
Other answers	2	2%
Total	135	100%
4. What would you say was the most difficult part of your furlough?		
Getting or processing furlough request	3	3%
Transportation	14	12%
Too much to do in the time	11	9%
Returning to institution/camp	48	40%
Accomplishing some part of my plan	13	11%
Other answers	30	25%
Total	119	100%
5. What advice or suggestions would you give the other inmates who will be going out on furloughs?		
Accomplish what was planned before relaxing (take care of business first)	72	56%
Use moderation and be careful	11	9%
Take enough money	3	2%
Have important papers handy	2	2%
Other advice	40	31%
Total	128	100%

[a]Totals vary because those not responding are excluded.

forty days will pass fast," and another said, "Doing time is easier now that I'm sure of employment and relationships with [my] family. The worry and stress is gone."

Most of the inmates felt that returning to the institution was the hardest part about the furlough. Some said that transportation was a real problem, while others reported that accomplishing some task on their plan was the most difficult part.

The majority of furloughees said that they would advise others going out to be sure to accomplish their plans before relaxing or beginning their recreation. Such advice included the following: "Take care of important business before doing [any] visiting with family and friends," "Do what you are supposed to do first!—then if there is time go on to other details," "Stick dead to your plans," and "Go out and take care of business." Other advice was to be careful not to violate any rules, and to stay sober. One furloughee recommended, "Do not drink, or, if you have to, do it at home and stay there." The furloughees also recommended such things as arranging appointments beforehand, making sure of transportation, and relaxing when meeting others.

EVALUATION OF THE FURLOUGHS

At the conclusion of the interview with each participant, the case-worker was asked to indicate whether he thought the inmate had used his time as constructively as possible. To obtain an independent evaluation, an additional rater read all the material on file for each case and, by comparing plans with accomplishments, rated the degree of achievement. In addition, the rater compared data for the first and second furloughs to decide which led to the most accomplishments. Table 25 presents the results of these evaluations.

Two-thirds of the furloughees were rated by their caseworkers as having used the time positively but with room for improvement. Positive evaluations included statements such as the following:

This man, as best I can determine, took full advantage of his furlough. He is ready to start work on the day that he is to be released. He has his driver's license, a job, and knows what to expect.

He went out there to take care of business and that's what he did. It is nice to see someone really enjoy freedom even if it is only for three days.

From all indications this individual used his furlough adequately. He returned to camp with a sense of relief and a better outlook toward parole.

He was able to accomplish such things as obtaining employment and finding a place to live. This relieved some of the anxiety he had about parole.

The most important thing that happened was reuniting with his father. He expressed real pride in his ability to obtain a job and establish rapport with his parole officer.

He had to use public transportation to make all his contacts and still

TABLE 25
Evaluation of the Use Inmates Made of Their Prerelease Furloughs

Program Supervisor's Evaluation of First Furlough			Independent Rater's Evaluation of First Furlough		
	No.	Per cent		No.	Per cent
Very positive (time used as constructively as possible)	80	66%	Accomplished more than proposed	12	9%
Positive (constructive use of time but inmate could have done more)	11	9%	Accomplished all, or as much as, proposed	57	42%
			Accomplished most of what was proposed	46	35%
Neutral	27	22%	Accomplished less than half of proposed	16	12%
Somewhat negative (time not used wisely)	1	1%	Accomplished little or nothing	2	2%
Very negative (furlough a waste of time or detrimental)	3	2%			
Total[a]	122	100%	Total[a]	133	100%

Independent Rater's Comparison of 1st and 2nd Furloughs		
Accomplished more on second furlough	6	24%
Accomplished about the same on each furlough	14	56%
Accomplished less on second furlough	4	16%
Accomplished little or nothing on second furlough	1	4%
Total[a]	25	100%

[a]Cases on which no evaluations were available were excluded.

accomplished all his plans. Returned to the Center half an hour early and in *good* shape!

Somewhat positive evaluations included such statements as "Moderately successful. He did find a job and contacted his parole officer, but he did a lot of 'resting' also."

In twenty-seven cases either the statements were nonevaluative or it wasn't possible to decide the direction of the evaluation. Only four of the 122 evaluations were negative. Three furloughs were felt to be a waste of time or actually detrimental. These evaluations included statements such as the following:

This furlough was probably a mistake. He did not obtain a driver's license and his time was used to put the bite on [borrow money from] his mother for a wardrobe, house rent, and old bills. It is hoped that parole to San Francisco will keep him away from Mother for a while.

Monday and Tuesday afternoon were spent at his dad's home doing little or nothing. He seems to have spent half of his leave vactioning.

(The latter inmate got a job as a butcher but failed the written part of his driving test.)

The independent rater judged 51 per cent of the inmates as having accomplished as much as or more than they had planned. Only 12 per cent were rated as having completed less than half of their plans, and two men were rated as having accomplished little or nothing.

The possibility of a second furlough created some problems for program planning. Two kinds of criteria could be used in determining whether a second furlough should be granted. It could be granted on the basis of program needs. However, if the individual were interested in a second leave, this would insure that the first furlough would not be used to the fullest, since by taking care of all the things needed for prerelease, the inmate wouldn't be able to justify another trip. Thus, undoubtedly some important things would intentionally be left undone. The other possibility was to grant the second furlough as a reward for accomplishments on the first. This had the advantage of providing a strong motivation for achievement. One disadvantage, however, was that it would leave no major tasks for the second trip, since most of the important tasks would have already been completed. The reward system, with room for exceptions, was chosen. It was reasoned that even though the furloughee had completed all the stated tasks on his first leave, his demonstrated ability to use the time constructively would undoubtedly lead him to find and accomplish new tasks on the second. With this system, however, it was anticipated that the second furlough would be less productive than the first.

The data in Table 25 suggest, however, that the second furloughs were slightly more successful; 24 per cent of the furloughees accomplished more, while 16 per cent accomplished less. Eighty per cent achieved at least as much the second time around. For example, on his first furlough one inmate obtained a driver's license, met a prospective employer, tried unsuccessfully to contact his parole agent, and spent the remainder of the time with his family. A change in residence plans shortly after the furlough, however, nullified the job offer. On the second furlough he secured another job, bought and registered a cheap car, acquired auto insurance, and packed his belongings in preparation for moving closer to his new employment. In several cases the caseworker mentioned that the success of the second furlough resulted from the inmate's being less nervous and anxious.

One inmate returned a day before he was paroled (on a release-upon-approved-parole plan). The caseworker still thought the furlough worthwhile in that the inmate had spent two days working on his job and thus had a jump in this area as well as some extra money.

THE PRISONERS AND THEIR FAMILIES

Upon each inmate's return, a short questionnaire was sent to his family asking them how the furlough had helped him, whether it turned out as they expected, and whether there was anything the institution could do to make his eventual return home easier.

Two major themes appeared in the families' responses. One was that the inmate's past behavior had been deviant but that he seemed to be a different, better person now. This reaction was indicated by such statements as the following:

We found out how mature he has become, and his outlook was bright for his future plans for release.

He understands the mistake he made. He realizes that what he did wasn't worth it. We had a very good talk and I explained just what I expect of him when [he] gets out.

Pat seems to have matured and straightened out his attitude and thinking. His brother gave him the use of his car and he was very prompt and careful with this privilege.

Willie has matured, though the hard way, but he is now a full-grown, mature young man who has found out that the honest way is the best and easiest way after all.

He has been returned to us a far better young man; his high school completed, ambitions are normal for a fellow his age, no bad habits, as far as I can detect, a desire to complete a college education. What else could we have hoped for?

The second major theme was the family's willingness to lend the inmate support. In assessing their reactions, however, it is important to keep in mind that the inmate was scheduled to return to the institution on the third day. Thus, the setting undoubtedly took on a "honeymoon" quality, with the inmate on his best behavior and the family extending itself to be receptive and helpful. An inmate's wife takes note of this:

During [these seventy-two] hours we spent more time together as a family than we ever have before. We have learned a great deal in the past two years through family group therapy and were able to put some of it into practice. I realize we both had *our best foot forward* during these seventy-two hours, but I think we know how much we need and love each other and our son.

The majority of respondents mentioned the inmate's getting together with his family as one of the more important things he did. Offers of family support included statements such as the following:

We were very happy to have him home after six years. I do hope LeRoy will do good. I'll try my best and do everything I can to help him.

My husband and him get along fine, and [he] thinks this time LeRoy has to try and do good and he will also help in everything he can.

He has a home with his mother and father as long as he wants to stay with us.

It gave him back his faith to know his family and friends still have faith in him and want to give him a helping hand.

The visit was better than I expected because everybody pitched in to help him. I thought there was going to be regrets because of what happened [his being in prison] but there were none. All the family were very nice to him.

I am his mother. My home is his too. I hope he comes home soon. He worked all of the time he was home—came home and went to bed early. He did real good—he is a good boy—just did wrong.

Seeing his family's happiness at his presence and our desire to make his visit pleasant seemed to restore his confidence and self-assurance.

Even some honeymoons go awry, however. One wife reported that her husband "was out drinking when his son was in the hospital on emergency. I don't think he is ready to accept responsibility. I think he needs counseling about responsibilities of marriage and family. I think something is bothering him. The visit ended in a quarrel."

A number of families also noted that the furlough assisted them in making the adjustment. After a six-year separation, a wife writes what the furlough meant to her: "It was like a preview of coming attractions in a theater and I feel very strongly that, because of this pass, our adjustment has already begun and will be much easier not only on Jim but on our children and me."

The value of the furlough in terms of the family's ability to play a constructive role in the inmate's future appears to lie in its contribution to getting the relationship off to a proper start. The extent to which the family perceives the inmate as a changed individual and responds to him with the expectation that he will act in a law-abiding manner should be an important element of social control. The uniqueness of the furlough, compared to the first few days of parole, is its short duration, which provides an incentive for all to be on their best behavior. This gives it the quality of a dress rehearsal.

DIFFICULTIES ON FURLOUGH

The furlough was the first time most of the inmates had been without close supervision in several years. As we noted earlier, these inmates are fairly representative of a cross-section of state prisoners, rather than being a specially selected group. They included a representative proportion of robbers and assaultive and narcotics cases, but fewer murderers. More than the average proportion of burglars, forgers, and thieves were furloughed. More of the furloughees were parole violators than first termers. The ethnic distribution parallels that of the institutions.

Table 26 shows the difficulties known to have been encountered by the furloughees. From both furloughs, 184 inmates out of 198 (93 per cent) returned sober, on time, and with no known difficulties in the community. Returning late was the difficulty encountered by nine of the fourteen inmates in trouble. This most frequently resulted from car breakdowns or unusual highway conditions. Some simply made poor estimations of the travel time. A number telephoned that they would be late. One of the five involved in more serious difficulty was arrested for drunk driving and is currently serving a jail term. Two others returned intoxicated. One of these was later found to have also been under the influence of drugs. The two remaining furloughees in trouble failed to return and were designated as escapees.

CONCLUSIONS

Donald Clemmer summarized a study of prisoners' prerelease expectations in the following words:

> While it may have been obvious through either poetic or common-sense interpretation, we now have an array of data that suggest that the environment of the prison as it is lived by its inhabitants combines, almost, to rule out hope and favorable expectations towards the life of these people upon their return to the free society.[67]

All the data presented so far indicate that the prerelease furlough program has gone at least some way toward reversing these unfavorable expectations. The program was designed to help inmates acquire

TABLE 26
Difficulties Known to Have Been Encountered on 72-Hour Furloughs

Type of Trouble	1st Furlough No.	2nd Furlough No.	Total No.
No known trouble	152	32	184
Returned late	8	1	9
Returned under the influence of drugs	1	—	1
Returned under the influence of alcohol	1	—	1
Arrested for misdemeanor	1	—	1
Absconded	2	—	2[a]
Total	165	33	198

[a]Both apprehended within eight hours.

the basic resources needed for their parole to the community, and this is what it has done. The great majority of furloughees accomplished the things they had planned: securing employment, acquiring a driver's license, getting to know the parole agent, establishing a residence, and cementing family relationships. The program has the double advantage not only of working but of costing no more than a little extra staff time.

Although there are no hard data on why the program works, we have several strong suspicions. First, the inmate is required to take the initiative in developing a plan. What he plans to do to prepare himself for release he will basically decide himself and do for himself. Thus, if he doesn't succeed he has no way to blame others. There is no way to cop out. It's strictly his decision whether or not to behave responsibly and do something for himself.

Second is the plan itself. The inmates are encouraged to set a few selected tasks and to concentrate their efforts on them. They generally have about a month to think about how best to accomplish their plans. This may well represent the most organized thinking that many of them had ever done. Furloughees continually express amazement at how much they were able to do. The use of a concrete plan parallels the procedures William Glasser has found so successful in reality therapy.[68]

Third, interviewing the inmate when he returns and asking the families about their reactions to the furlough experience provides some external control. In addition, the possibility of another furlough presents a strong built-in motivation for achievement.

Fourth, a climate of competition appears to have developed among the inmates to see how much they could do in three days. There is evidence that furloughees are advising other inmates to accomplish their plans before participating in recreational activities.

The fact that all but two furloughees returned is consistent with the experience of other furlough programs and therefore not surprising. Mississippi has operated a "Holiday Suspension Program" for some time. Over a twelve-year period, over three thousand inmates were sent home for ten days each and only fifteen failed to return.[69] Over a five-year period, one thousand men (between the ages of eighteen and twenty-four) were granted home leaves from two Michigan camps; only three failed to return.[70] What is surprising in the California program is the amount accomplished on the prerelease furlough.

In this paper we have tried to give an in-depth view of California's prerelease furlough program by focusing on its operation at one institution. No one in the community is known to have suffered any physical hardship or to have lost any property as a result of these 198 furloughs. Nor did the program require any additional funds or capital outlay; the institution actually realized a savings on clothing and food. All the data we have gathered indicate that the prerelease furloughs have substantial benefits in preparing inmates for their return to the community.

33

WORK FURLOUGH AS AN ALTERNATIVE TO INCARCERATION: AN ASSESSMENT OF ITS EFFECTS ON RECIDIVISM AND SOCIAL COST

ROBERT JEFFERY AND STEPHEN WOOLPERT

Sentencing of the criminal offender is the central activity of the criminal justice system. The majority of cases prosecuted in criminal courts result in a determination of the defendant's guilt. Whether prosecution leads to a formal trial or to a negotiated plea, the sentence is the culmination of the judicial process.

There are two basic problems in present sentencing practices. The first results from the contradictions inherent in a criminal system whose purposes include both punishment and rehabilitation. Punishment is believed to further the goals of deterrence, retribution and protection. It requires that an offender be denied access to opportunities and resources readily available to non-criminals. Rehabilitation, on the other hand, is intended to produce inmates who are ready to assume responsible roles in the community after release. It requires that an offender receive guidance, supervision and training in excess of that freely available to the average citizen. Thus, it is not surprising that judges often find it impossible to impose punishment and to prescribe rehabilitory measures at the same time. They must choose one at the expense of the other or strike a compromise which serves neither goal satisfactorily.

The second problem of sentencing lies in its future-oriented nature. A sentence "tries to predict how an offender will behave under certain circumstances and how other potential offenders will be-

Source: Reprinted by special permission of the *Journal of Criminal Law and Criminology,* Copyright © 1974 by Northwestern University School of Law, Vol. 65, No. 3, (September 1974): 405-415.

have."[71] The task of predicting the outcome of judicial dispositions is complicated by several factors. For example, although judges have considerable latitude in deciding the fate of convicted offenders, few have sufficient knowledge of behavioral laws (which are frequently at odds with conventional wisdom) to make socially optimal choices. Also, the failure of correctional officials to systematically evaluate various correctional programs has resulted in a paucity of descriptive data regarding the manner in which different individuals will respond to different rehabilitation efforts.[72] Moreover, judges seldom observe and are not held accountable for the impact which a sentence has on the subsequent behavior of an offender. Consequently, they are not strongly motivated to improve their performance. The net effect of these influences is haphazard sentencing practices that are rarely standardized even within a single jurisdiction.[73]

There is growing concern over the need to upgrade society's sentencing and correctional practices. This concern stems from a humanitarian interest in the living conditions in correctional institutions, from a desire to reduce the incidence of violent uprisings in prisons, and perhaps most importantly from the alarming rate at which those released from custody are subsequently incarcerated for new crimes.

Many believe that traditional punitive practices are counterproductive to rational social planning. This view is well expressed in the 1969 San Francisco Crime Commission Report:

Imprisonment is a most ineffective tool for rehabilitation. . . . Imprisonment is detrimental to the future adjustment of some offenders, and it is likely to embitter the convicted persons and turn them loose, more skilled criminally, to prey on society again. . . . The system of criminal justice should so operate that dangerous criminals are not released into the community, that less hardened persons may not be unnecessarily brutalized by jailing, and that the taxpayer does not bear needless or wasted cost.[74]

Similar sentiments are also expressed by social scientists,[75] whose empirical work suggests that punishing criminal behavior without providing pro-social alternatives may well produce more ingenious criminal activities rather than the pro-social adjustment that is desired.

Increased awareness of the many failures of jail and prison systems has resulted in an upsurge of interest in alternatives to incarceration. Although specific recommendations differ, the main thrust of recent proposals is that it is less expensive, more productive, and ultimately for society's benefit to keep offenders out of prison. Such proposals would move the bulk of the correctional effort to the community level.

This study focused on the effectiveness of one community based program, the work release or work furlough program. The work furlough program permits selected inmates to work at-large in the community during the day and to return during their non-working hours to the institution. In theory, therefore, it represents a mid-point between incarceration and probation.

There are three fundamental features of the work furlough program. First, while it is logical extension of the philosophy of individualized treatment, it differs from most other such programs (e.g., psychological and vocational counseling, medication, behavior modification) in that it decreases rather than increases the amount of direct control which the correctional system exercises over the individual's life. Second, in line with experimental evidence indicating that post-institutional setting events are the primary source of variance in recidivism rates,[76] the program does not focus on "rehabilitating" the offender while he is incarcerated, but rather on facilitating his reentry from a highly structured institution into society. Finally, work furlough, like many other community based programs, costs less to administer than total incarceration. Work furloughees assume a share of the administrative costs of the program, repay outstanding fines and debts, support their families and return to society in better financial shape than inmates released from total incarceration. Thus, work furlough is a method by which selected offenders may be better integrated into the community without increased risk to the community and at a measurable savings in cost to the community.

In practice, however, there is little reliable evidence of the program's effectiveness. Research conducted on work furlough programs[77] has generally concluded that work furloughees do as well or better than other groups of inmates after release. However, much of this work has been criticized on the grounds that adequate control groups were not used (i.e., regular inmates who shared the same social and criminal background). The criteria used to select work furloughees are not clearly defined or consistent, but correctional officials attempt to include those deemed most likely to benefit from the program and to exclude those who present the greatest risk. In evaluating such a program, it is essential to select control inmates using similar criteria.

This control problem is a persistent one in correctional systems research. While the soundest evaluation procedure would be to randomly assign inmates to different rehabilitation programs, judges and correctional officials are understandably reluctant to prevent an offender from participating in a progressive program when they think the program will benefit him. At the same time, they are reluctant to include an inmate in a program if they believe he will abuse the opportunity. Moreover, the punitive traditions of corrections work make it tempting to use programs like work furlough, which are highly valued by the inmates themselves, as rewards for inmates who "behave" in the regular institutional setting.

An alternative approach to the problem of selecting control groups for evaluation purposes is to find a group of inmates whose backgrounds are similar to the inmates in the program of interest. The problem with this procedure is that the two groups may still differ on some unmeasured factor (particularly when selection criteria are not clearly specified). Nevertheless, it is considerably better than comparing known dissimilar groups. In the present study, by comparing work furloughees with a carefully selected control group of inmates with similar social and criminal histories, the study hoped to avoid some of the criticisms of earlier work and thus determine more accurately the effect of work furlough on recidivism rates.

In addition, since there was no research providing any basis for evaluating the selection criteria used in assigning offenders to work release programs, the study also examined the recidivism rates of men with different social and criminal histories. The purpose was to determine whether present selection criteria screen out the least desirable inmates and include those most desirable for the program and if not, what factors might better determine acceptability.

The authors held only one clear expectation about the results of the research. It was predicted that work furlough inmates would fare better overall after release than the comparison group. This prediction was based on the assumption that a person leaving jail with a job and work experience would have less difficulty adjusting to society than a person with neither. The work furlough experience should provide an economic base for a prosocial adjustment.

METHOD

The present study examined the work furlough program in San Mateo County, California. The facility was established in 1966 pursuant to Section 1208 of the California Penal Code,[78] which permits convicted misdemeanants to continue or secure employment while serving their sentence.

There are two methods of admission to the program. Those with jobs prior to the execution of their sentence (approximately 50 per cent of the program population) may apply directly to the program administrator. Those without jobs are reviewed by a classification committee, which assigns eligible cases to the program on a provisional basis while they seek employment. The average program population varies between eighty and ninety men.

Inmates are confined to the work furlough facility except during working hours or while seeking employment. The program administrator supervises all inmate travel, expenditures and visiting privileges. A per diem maintenance charge based on the inmate's gross income is deducted from his earnings. Net weekly income among work furloughees ranges from $43 to $285, with a mean income of $114 and a median income of $97.

A basic policy of the California work furlough program is that participants must work in fair and competitive employment programs. Wages and working conditions must be on par with those prevailing in the area. Participants are not permitted to accept jobs which pay on a commission basis, which lack adequate job insurance programs, or where labor disputes are in progress. A minimum wage of two dollars per hour is required to enable the inmate to benefit financially from participation.

Although there is no formal job placement service, inmates are encouraged to find employment consistent with their skills, training, and postrelease expectations. The majority of the inmates continue in their jobs after release from the program.

The work furlough sample consisted of all those admitted to the San Mateo County work furlough program during the first four months of 1967 (n = 110). Of this group twelve were returned to jail for disciplinary problems, loss of job or other reasons. Since no information on incorrigibility was available for the comparison group, these twelve were retained in the sample.

The control group was selected from inmates in the San Mateo County jail system during the year 1965—the year prior to the establishment of the work furlough program. The group was drawn from the records of the Southern Municipal Court Clerk (n = 94). These men served their sentences in either the Sheriff's Honor Camp or the main jail.

Current selection policy excludes sex offenders, narcotics offenders and violent criminals from the work furlough program. Therefore, in the initial selection of the control group, the same general criteria were applied: minimum 30 day sentences, no narcotics, sex, or violent offenders.

Additional, less formal criteria which also determine eligibility for work furlough include employability, prior criminal record, and family ties in the community. In order to control the influence of these variables, two types of information were obtained for both groups: social background and criminal history. Social background data included age, race, marital status, and type of occupation. Criminal background data included number of prior convictions, nature of the current offense, length of sentence and time actually served for the current offense. This information was obtained from arrest records in the County Hall of Justice.

A series of statistical comparisons were made between the two samples on all of these variables (see Table 27). The groups were not perfectly matched. However, they did not differ substantially in any respect except length of time served. Furthermore, since work furloughees regularly serve a portion of their sentences in the main jail prior to their admittance to the program and also because approximately 10 per cent of the work furlough sample stayed for only a few days in the program before being returned to jail for rule infractions, it was decided to consider the two groups as adequately matched on this factor as well.

The fact that there was a two year time difference between the

TABLE 27
Comparison of Social and Criminal Backgrounds of Experimental and
Control Groups

Background Variable	Work Furlough (n = 110)	Control Group (n = 94)	Statistical Comparison
Social Background			
Mean Age	31.83 yrs.	30.12 yrs.	$t = 1.20$ ($.20 < p < .50$)
% Married	49.1	38.3	$X^2 = 2.42$ ($.10 < p < .25$)
% Skilled	29	23	$X^2 = 1.68$ ($.10 < p < .25$)
% Caucasian	62	51	$X^2 = 3.49$
% Minority	38	49	($.05 < p < .10$)
Criminal Background			
Mean Prior Convictions	6.36	5.96	$t = .50$ ($.20 < p < .50$)
Vehicle Code Violations*	42%	37%	$X^2 = 1.11$
Non-support	17%	22%	($.50 < p < .75$)
Other Violations**	41%	41%	
Mean Sentence	154.5 days	124.1 days	$t = 1.93$ ($.05 < p < .10$)
Mean Time Served	57.2 days	79.2 days	$t = 2.87$ ($P < .01$)

*Most common vehicle code violations are driving without a license (work furlough, n = 29; control, n = 18); Drunk Driving (work furlough, n = 12; control, n = 9); Others (work furlough, n = 10; control, n = 9).
**Most common others are disturbing the peace (work furlough, n = 6; control, n = 10); Assault (work furlough, n = 6; control, n = 10); Petty Theft (work furlough, n = 5; control, n = 5).

two samples introduced the possibility of additional uncontrolled factors. Unemployment rates were undoubtedly different in 1967 than they were in 1965, sentencing practices may have changed with the advent of the work furlough program, crime rates may have been different, and changes in law enforcement techniques could conceivably have contributed to changes in inmate populations. However, because the work furlough and control samples were similar in terms of the demographic variables measured, and also because no a priori reason could be found for predicting differential effects on the basis of year alone, it is a reasonable assumption that these factors would not bias the results. Undoubtedly, the majority of the men in the control group would have been eligible for work furlough if the program had existed in 1965. Had a control group been selected from inmates in 1967 this conclusion would have been unwarranted, since they would have already been excluded from the program, presumably for cause.

Having drawn the two groups, forms were sent to the California Bureau of Criminal Investigation and Information (C.I.I.) requesting criminal records for each individual. The C.I.I. records were examined and the number of arrests and convictions in each of the four years following release was recorded for each inmate. These figures served as the dependent variables in the study. Half of the records were scored independently by the two investigators. Agreement exceeded 90 per cent on the year-by-year arrest and conviction figures and on four year totals taken for each man.

One inmate was dropped from the work furlough sample because he died before the end of the four year period. Two control subjects were also dropped: in one case because C.I.I. records could not be located and in the other because the inmate had inadvertently been recorded twice under different names.

The post-release arrest and conviction data were highly skewed toward zero. There was also considerably more variance in the control group data than in the work furlough data. Therefore, nonparametric statistical tests were used throughout the analyses.

A. Overall Comparisons

Table 28 gives year-by-year and overall success rates for the two groups. Mann-Whitney U tests performed on these data revealed that in general, work furlough inmates fared substantially better after release from jail than the control group inmates. They were convicted of significantly fewer crimes in each of the four years following release and had significantly better arrest records in the first two years

TABLE 28
Percent of Inmates Not Arrested or Convicted of a Crime in Each of the Years Following Release From Jail

| | % Not Arrested | | | % Not Convicted | | |
Time Period	Work Furlough	Control	Significance Value*	Work Furlough	Control	Significance Value*
Year 1	51	25	z = 2.43	61	35	z = 2.52
	n = 109	n = 91	p < .01	n = 109	n = 91	p < .01
Year 2	68	51	z = 2.40	77	61	z = 2.50
	n = 106	n = 87	p < .01	n = 106	n = 87	p < .01
Year 3	65	59	z = 1.44	79	72	z = 1.76
	n = 105	n = 83	NS	n = 105	n = 83	p < .05
Year 4	70	60	z = 1.44	90	67	z = 2.85
	n = 105	n = 89	NS	n = 106	n = 89	p < .01
Four Year Total	23	13	z = 3.51	43	23	z = 3.57
	n = 109	n = 92	p < .001	n = 109	n = 92	p < .001

*Since a directional prediction was made regarding overall effects, the p values reported in this table are one-tailed.

and for the four years as a whole. The overall differences between the two groups were substantial since there was less than one chance in a thousand of the result being due to chance alone. Thus, the data strongly supported the contention that work furlough softens the impact of reentering society after a period of incarceration. The fact that arrest rates were reliably different only in the first two years, however, suggests that the benefits diminish over time. Many variables might contribute to this effect: family stability, job satisfaction and participation in other rehabilitation programs.[79] Apparently, variables other than initial program placement become more important over time.

Unfortunately, work furlough does not completely eliminate reentry problems. A Friedman two-way analysis of variance showed significant differences between years for both groups (Arrests: Work Furlough, $X_r^2 = 13.05$, p < .01; Control, $X_r^2 = 26.69$, p < .01; Convictions: Work Furlough, $X_r^2 = 10.02$, p < .02; Control, $X_r^2 = 17.60$, p < .01). Whether inmates served time in the work furlough program or in other county facilities, they were arrested and convicted more frequently in the first year after release. Comparisons with the Wilcoxen test indicated that work furlough inmates had significantly poorer records in the first year after release than in any other year. They also had significantly more convictions in the third year after release than in the fourth. The control group inmates did significantly worse in the first year following release than in any of the subsequent three

TABLE 29
Wilcoxen Test Values for Between Year Comparisons
of Arrest and Conviction Rates

Comparison	Work Furlough		Control	
	Arrests	Convictions	Arrests	Convictions
Year 1 vs Year 2	z = 3.36 p < .001	z = 2.98 p < .01	z = 3.02 p < .01	z = 2.35 p < .05
Year 1 vs Year 3	z = 3.32 p < .001	z = 2.52 p < .05	z = 4.63 p < .001	z = 4.25 p < .001
Year 1 vs Year 4	z = 3.31 p < .001	z = 4.11 p < .001	z = 5.25 p < .001	z = 4.01 p < .001
Year 2 vs Year 3	z = -.37 NS	z = -.23 NS	z = 1.63 NS	z = 1.44
Year 2 vs Year 4	z = .93 NS	z = 1.95 NS	z = 2.26 p < .05	z = 1.48 NS
Year 3 vs Year 4	z = .65 NS	z = 2.11 p < .05	z = .96 NS	z = -.27 NS

years. They also had more arrests in the second year than in the fourth. (See Table 29 for test values.) It appears that although the transition from incarceration to freedom is easier for work furlough-ees than it is for other inmates, the first year after release is still particularly difficult.

B. Criminal History

To determine whether work furlough has a differential impact on men with different criminal histories, the two sample were subdivided in terms of the offense for which the inmates served time, prior criminal record, and length of time served. Table 30 shows the four year success rates of inmates in these various categories.

The crimes for which inmates in the two groups were incarcerated were divided into three categories: non-support, vehicle code violations, and miscellaneous offenses. Comparisons between the work furlough and control groups for the different crime categories revealed that there was no difference between the two groups of inmates convicted of non-support. Work furlough inmates who were sentenced for vehicle code violations had significantly fewer convictions

TABLE 30

Percent of Inmates Not Arrested or Convicted of a Crime in the Four
Years Following Release as a Function of Present Offense,
Prior Criminal Record, and Length of Time Served

	% Not Arrested		% Not Convicted	
Subgroup	Work Furlough	Control	Work Furlough	Control
Present Offense				
Non-Support	26	27	37	36
	n = 19	n = 22	n = 19	n = 22
Vehicle Code	24	10	44	19
Violations	n = 45	n = 31	n = 45	n = 31
Miscellaneous	20	10	40	18
	n = 46	n = 39	n = 45	n = 39
Prior Convictions				
0 to 1 prior	39	31	61	44
	n = 18	n = 16	n = 18	n = 16
2 to 5 priors	33	18	54	25
	n = 39	n = 40	n = 39	n = 40
6 or more priors	12	3	29	11
	n = 52	n = 36	n = 52	n = 36
Time Served				
0 to 30 days	30	5	54	14
	n = 46	n = 22	n = 46	n = 22
31 to 90 days	14	11	26	24
	n = 42	n = 37	n = 42	n = 37
91+ days	29	27	52	33
	n = 21	n = 30	n = 21	n = 30

than the comparison control inmates ($z = 2.23$, $p < .05$), but did not
differ from their control counterparts in arrests. Work furlough inmates in the miscellaneous category were dramatically superior to
their control group matches, both in arrests ($z = 2.70$, $p < .01$) and
convictions ($z = 3.22$, $p < .01$). Thus, work furlough clearly reduced
recidivism for offenders convicted of disturbing the peace, assault, and
petty theft. The program appeared to have little effect on non-support violators.

To determine whether work furlough has a differential impact on
individuals with different histories of criminal activity, the two
samples were subdivided into three groups: individuals with less than
two convictions prior to the present offense, those with two to five
prior convictions, and those with six or more prior convictions. Comparisons between work furlough and control group inmates with
similar records revealed that there were no differences between the
two groups with zero or one prior conviction and that work furlough
inmates with two to five prior convictions did better after release

than their control counterparts (Arrests, z = 2.06, p < .05; Convictions, z = 3.44, p < .001). Similarly, work furlough inmates with six or more prior convictions fared better than control inmates with six or more prior convictions (Arrests, z = 3.25, p < .01; Convictions, z = 2.98, p < .01). Again, work furlough had differential effects. It reduced recidivism rates among men with moderate or extensive criminal records, but had no reliable effect on those sentenced for a first or second offense.

The following categories were used in analyzing whether length of incarceration was related to recidivism: zero to 30 days, 31 to 90 days, and 91 or more days in jail. Comparisons between work furlough and control inmates in the respective time-served categories showed that work furlough inmates serving less than 30 days did significantly better after release than their control counterparts (Arrests, z = 3.23, p < .01; Convictions, z = 3.36, p < .001). Those serving thirty to ninety days in work furlough did not differ from the comparable control inmates. Long term work furlough inmates did better than long term controls in convictions (z = 2.56, p < .05), but not in arrests.

C. Social Background

Table 31 shows the success rates of inmates in the two samples who differ in age, race, marital status, and job skills.

Three groups were selected in order to analyze the effects of work furlough on individuals of different ages: nineteen to twenty-five years, twenty-six to thirty-five years, and thirty-six years or older. Comparisons between work furlough and control individuals in the same age categories again revealed differential effects. Work furlough inmates between nineteen and twenty-five years of age did better than control inmates in the same age range (Arrests: z = 2.45, p < .05; Convictions: z = 2.89, p < .01). The differences between work furlough and control inmates in the older age groups were not statistically significant. Work furlough was thus more effective with younger inmates than it was with older ones.

One argument in support of work release programs is that they provide financial support for the family of the inmate. Recidivism rates were analyzed as a function of marital status to determine if this factor influenced the likelihood of police contacts after release from jail. Between-group comparisons showed that married work furlough inmates fared no better than their control group counterparts, while unmarried work furlough inmates did considerably better after release than unmarried control inmates (Arrests, z = 3.66,

TABLE 31
Percent of Inmates Not Arrested or Convicted of a Crime in the Four
Years Following Release as a Function of Age,
Marital Status, Job Skills, and Race

Subgroup	% Not Arrested		% Not Convicted	
	Work Furlough	Control	Work Furlough	Control
Age				
19 to 25 yrs.	33	18	56	26
	n = 39	n = 39	n = 39	n = 39
26 to 35 yrs.	21	5	42	18
	n = 33	n = 22	n = 33	n = 22
36+ yrs.	16	16	29	23
	n = 37	n = 31	n = 37	n = 31
Marital Status				
Unmarried	34	12	52	22
	n = 56	n = 58	n = 56	n = 58
Married	13	18	34	24
	n = 53	n = 34	n = 53	n = 34
Job Skills				
Unskilled	22	12	42	19
	n = 78	n = 69	n = 78	n = 69
Skilled	29	19	45	38
	n = 31	n = 21	n = 31	n = 22
Race				
Caucasian	26	23	49	34
	n = 68	n = 47	n = 68	n = 47
Minority	20	7	34	11
	n = 41	n = 45	n = 41	n = 45

$p < .001$; Convictions, $z = 3.78$, $p < .0001$). In fact, unmarried work furlough inmates did better than married control inmates (Arrests, $z = 2.11$, $p < .05$; Convictions, $z = 2.08$, $p < .05$). Thus, work furlough was clearly more effective with unmarried than with married inmates.

Because work furlough involves inmates working regularly while serving their sentence, it is relevant to analyze the success of men with different job skills. Professionals were combined with skilled workers and were compared with unskilled and manual laborers. Analysis revealed that work furlough was superior to previous rehabilitation methods for unskilled individuals (Arrests, $z = 2.92$, $p < .01$; Convictions, $z = 3.33$, $p < .001$), but not for skilled individuals. Thus, work furlough seemed to benefit unskilled inmates more than it did skilled workers.

The last social background factor investigated was race. Those inmates with Spanish surnames and those listed as "negro" by C.I.I.

were combined as minority group members. The remainder of the inmates were considered Caucasian. There were no Orientals in either sample. Between sample comparisons showed that minority group inmates did substantially better in the work furlough program than they did in the control group (Arrests, $z = 2.16$, $p < .05$; Convictions, $z = 2.78$, $p < .01$). Caucasian inmates in the work furlough sample had significantly fewer convictions than their control counterparts ($z = 2.16$, $p < .05$), but the two groups did not differ in arrests. These results suggest that work furlough benefited both Caucasian and minority group inmates, the effects being slightly more convincing for the latter group.[80]

To determine whether any single variable was responsible for the differential effects of work furlough on those with different backgrounds, Pearson's X^2s were computed separately for the work furlough and control groups on all pairwise combinations of age, marital status, job skills, race, prior convictions, current offense, and time served. Of the fifty-six contingency tables analyzed, eleven produced X^2 values reaching the .05 level of statistical significance. This was approximately the number that would be expected by chance.

In both samples age was related to the length of time served and the type of crime (Work Furlough, $X^2 = 7.90$, $p < .10$; Control, $X^2 = 9.81$, $p < .05$; Work Furlough, $X^2 = 10.46$, $p < .05$; Control, $X^2 = 10.65$, $p < .05$). Younger inmates served shorter sentences and were less likely to be incarcerated for non-support than older men. Younger inmates were also more likely to be sentenced for miscellaneous offenses than older inmates. Moreover, inmates tended to serve more time for non-support than for miscellaneous violations (Work Furlough, $X^2 = 13.69$, $p < .02$; Control, $X^2 = 20.45$, $p < .01$). Although no causality is indicated by these relationships, it appears that the beneficial effects of work furlough on inmates serving short sentences and those incarcerated for miscellaneous crimes may be due to its differential effectiveness with younger inmates.

Five relationships were evident in one sample but not in the other. Three of these were covariations involving race. Minority group members in the work furlough sample were usually older ($X^2 = 9.22$, $p < .01$) and had more prior convictions ($X^2 = 6.68$, $p < .05$) than Caucasians in this group. In addition, Caucasians in the control group were more likely to have job skills ($X^2 = 10.93$, $p < .001$) than were minority group members.

These relationships introduce some uncertainty about the analyses by race presented above. For example, substantial differences in the job skills of the different racial groups may explain why Caucasians in the control group had better post-release records than minority group members. Similarly, differences in age and job skills may partly explain why work furlough was more effective with minority group inmates than with Caucasians. In pursuing these possibilities, additional X^2s were performed comparing work furlough and control inmates in the same racial groups as a function of age, prior convictions and job skills. Since none of these covariations were statistically significant, however, it was impossible to verify these speculations. The differential covariations observed may have been due to chance.

Two other covariations were found only in the work furlough sample. First, a larger proportion of work furloughees incarcerated for non-support were unskilled than were work furloughees imprisoned for vehicle code violations and miscellaneous offenses. The second relationship noted was that younger work furlough inmates had fewer prior convictions than older ones ($X^2 = 12.90$, p < .05). To determine whether the marked effectiveness of work furlough on younger inmates held when prior convictions were controlled for, a comparison was made between work furlough and control inmates who were 19–25 years old and had two or fewer prior convictions.[81] It should be remembered that the work furlough and control inmates with small numbers of prior convictions did not differ overall. Forty-seven per cent of the work furlough inmates in the newly constructed category were not arrested in the four years following release as compared to 33 per cent of the controls. This difference approached, but did not reach the .05 level of significance (z = 1.70, p < .10). Seventy-nine per cent of the work furlough inmates in this group were not convicted of a crime in the four years following release. Only 39 per cent of the controls achieved this level of performance through all four years. This difference was significant (z = 2.29, p < .05). Apparently, the differential effects of work furlough on inmates who differ in age, marital status, job skills, and prior criminal record are not attributable to any one of these variables. The lack of a strong relationship between these measures would suggest that the effects are fairly independent. Unfortunately, the samples were not large enough to permit a meaningful multivariate analysis.[82]

DISCUSSION

Overall, the four year post-release arrest and conviction records of county jail inmates are discouraging. The 201 men in this study accumulated more than thirty-two years in jail sentences and twenty-seven years in prison terms. Only thirty-eight men (19 per cent) avoided arrest and only sixty-eight (34 per cent) were not convicted of a new offense in the four years following their release.

A comparison of the two groups, however, is more encouraging. The four year totals show the percentages of work furloughees with no arrests and no convictions (23 per cent and 43 per cent) to be nearly double those of the control group (13 per cent and 23 per cent). More notable perhaps is the *decline in these differences* over time. Between group comparisons for the third and fourth years reveal smaller differences in overall success rates than during the first two years. Thus, not only is work furlough effective in overall terms, but the positive effects of the program are felt most strongly during the immediate post-release period when recidivism rates are the highest.

Perhaps the major finding of the study is that work furlough is most beneficial to those having *the highest risk of failure after* release. None of the inmates in this study fared better in pre-work furlough facilities than in the work furlough program, but those who fared worst under standard institutionalization showed the most dramatic improvement in the newer program. The highest risk inmates were the unskilled, unmarried men under thirty-five years of age who had three or more prior convictions. Thirty-six per cent of work furloughees with these traits had no arrests in the four years following release, compared to 5 per cent of equivalent members of the control group. Fifty per cent of these work furloughees had no convictions compared to 10 per cent of their control counterparts.

With the evidence presently available, it is difficult to explain why work furlough was most effective with those who were least likely to succeed with regular treatment. The answer may be the fact that this program's main therapeutic function is to return people to work. In doing so it is probably most effective with people who would otherwise be unemployed and who might engage in illegal behavior. People who are already working would benefit less because their criminal activities are related to other factors.

There are other possible contributing factors. Work furlough is a special program so that inmates prefer it to total incarceration. Admission to such a program may therefore have psychological benefits in and of itself. If so, it is possible that high risk inmates benefit most from this positive, "labelling effect," since they presumably have fewer other sources of positive self-esteem. Moreover, information is unavailable on the types of jobs which the men on work furlough are able to obtain. In may be that skilled workers are unable to obtain work commensurate with their ability, thereby weakening the beneficial effect of employment on their post-release adjustment.

Although there were differential effects of work furlough on in-mates imprisoned for different offfenses, the effects were not obvi-ous. The fact that there were no differences between the two groups of non-support offenders suggests that economic factors may not be primarily responsible for these men's unwillingness to provide for their families. Many of these men (42 per cent) were again charged with non-support after they were released, despite the fact that work furlough provided them with jobs. This is about the same percentage as for the control group (36 per cent).

Vehicle code violations (primarily driving without a license and drunk driving) seemed to be more directly affected by the work fur-lough program, possibly because furloughees are required to get a valid license and insurance before using an automobile to go to work. Twenty-four per cent of the work furlough inmates serving time for traffic violations were arrested on the same charge after release, about half the percentage for the control group (45 per cent).

The marked effectiveness of work furlough with inmates in the miscellaneous category does not appear to be related to its effect on the crime *per se*. About the same percentage of inmates in both sam-ples were arrested for the same offense after release (Work Furlough, 27 per cent; Control, 31 per cent).

The most perplexing result of this study is the finding that work furlough was of greater benefit to those serving less than thirty days and more than ninety days than to those serving intermediate-length sentences. This effect may be merely the result of chance. The bene-ficial effects on those serving thirty days or less may result from the high proportion of young offenders receiving short sentences. Those serving more than ninety days, on the other hand, might benefit by establishing stable work habits and saving considerable amounts of money. It is also possible that the impact of incarceration on inmates' self-esteem and motivation varies in a U-shaped fashion with length of sentence, thus affecting the kinds of post-release adjustments which need to be made.

The impact of the work furlough program is not limited to those involved in it. The entire community benefits from the reduction in the social cost of crime and its punishment. The total cost of operat-ing the San Mateo County work furlough program is $12.16 per man-day. The equivalent figure for the main jail is difficult to determine, since jails incur the added costs of handling "one-nighters" and those unable to post bail while awaiting trial. It is estimated, however, that the base cost of maintaining a man in jail is about $2500 a year, or $6.85 per man-day.[83] But while the cost of operating the jail is borne entirely by public funds, work furlough receives a major share of its maintenance funds from the inmates themselves. In 1970, the mean per capita charge in San Mateo County was $5.50 per man-day. This reduces the public cost of the program to $6.66 per man day, 3 per cent less than the estimated main jail figure.

Perhaps the greatest savings to the community is derived from the decline in recidivism rates. Although the work furlough group was 18 per cent larger than the control group, the former totalled 29 per cent fewer arrests and 44 per cent fewer convictions during the four-year post-release period. This represents an enormous savings to the community in terms of police man-hours, pre-trial detention and court costs. The work furlough group received 2472 fewer days in jail sentences than the controls—a reduction of 35 per cent. At $6.85 per man-day, this is almost $17,000 in savings to the community. This figure does not include the considerable savings to state and federal authorities resulting from the fact that the work furlough group received lesser sentences than the control group.

There are two specific ways in which selection criteria for work furlough might be improved. The first would be to relax the general eligibility requirements for the program in order to make its benefits available to a larger proportion of jailed offenders. Persons convicted of narcotics, sex, or violent crimes are currently ineligible for the San Mateo work furlough program. While the risks involved in allowing such offenders to enter this program are obvious, the present data raise some interesting questions. Since inmates with the highest risk of future incarceration benefit most from the program, would not many of those currently ineligible respond similarly? If so, does this not warrant re-evaluation of the policy which excludes them?

Essentially, the issue is whether those currently ineligible for work furlough face the same kind of transition problems which other newly released offenders face, and whether work furlough provides them with adequate solutions to those problems. Without reliable evidence, the question remains an open one.

The second modification of selection criteria would be to revise the post-release prognosis for various types of offenders. For example, work furlough was considered especially beneficial in non-support cases, since the need to maintain an adequate income is related to the offense. Nevertheless, non-support offenders do not benefit as much from work furlough as do vehicle code violators. Moreover, neither of these groups show as much improvement as do those convicted of penal code violations such as disturbing the peace, petty theft and assault. It also appears that inmates with the worst social and economic backgrounds are most likely to respond to work furlough. The present data indicate that the young, single, unskilled offender with several prior convictions should be given special consideration for this program.

In sum, more research is needed in this area. First, there must be an effort to isolate the variables involved. In particular, more information is needed on the relationship between employment and the decision to commit different crimes. In addition, information is needed on how work furloughees obtain jobs, and on the possibility of mismatches between individuals' job skills and job opportunities.

An effort should also be made to determine whether the beneficial effects of work furlough are partially attributable to a positive labelling effect or whether recidivism could be reduced by simply giving offenders jobs and money without imposing any form of incarceration on them. Answers to such problems should rest in part upon evidence obtained directly from inmates regarding program improvements and post release problems in employment. The aim of such research should be to clarify the relationship between the penal system's conflicting goals of punishment and rehabilitation.

34

UNIONIZATION BEHIND THE WALLS

C. RONALD HUFF

During the past five years, the inmates of Ohio's correctional institutions have become increasingly militant and openly expressive of their frustrations and resentments regarding the criminal justice system under which they have been convicted and confined. The forms of expression utilized have included rioting, work stoppages, food boycotts, and, most recently, large-scale union organizing inside the walls. These activities have extended over two state administrations, one Republican and one Democratic. They have involved every adult correctional institution in the state. The evidence indicates that the leadership for the movement has come, for the most part, from inside, with outsiders serving in supportive or advisory capacities.

Why has this militancy developed (or at least surfaced) at this particular time? What are the goals of the inmates? What has been the reaction of correctional administrators to the prisoners' union movement? What legal issues are involved? This paper will address itself to these and other questions which naturally occur to any thoughtful observer. The questions which arise in connection with such a movement are, to say the least, very complex and not dispensed with easily. However, even at this relatively early stage, some informed observations and analyses can be made.

Source: Reprinted from *Criminology* Vol. 12, No. 2(August 1974) pp. 175–194 by permission of the author and the Publisher, Sage Publications, Inc. AUTHOR'S NOTE: This paper is based on part of the author's dissertation research at Ohio State University under the supervision of Professor Simon Dinitz. Appreciation is expressed to Professor Dinitz for his helpful suggestions and reactions. The author also gratefully acknowledges the cooperation of both the Ohio Prisoners' Labor Union and the Ohio Department of Rehabilitation and Correction. Finally, it should be noted that several of the sources contributing information used in this paper are not cited and must, unfortunately, remain anonymous due to their vulnerable positions and the author's ethical obligations to them.

THEORETICAL CONSIDERATIONS

As Martinson (1972) and others have noted, the nature of collective inmate action has undergone dramatic change since the early attempts at mass escape. Contemporary inmates are much more politically sophisticated and organizationally inclined. They no longer involve themselves in collective action for the exclusive purpose of communicating their displeasure to their immediate keepers. Instead, they are becoming aware that, in an age of instant communication through the mass media, their "audience" has widened considerably.

Any perusal of inmate literature today will demonstrate to the reader that the modern prisoner is often acquainted, formally or informally, with the basic tenets of labeling theory and with the results of studies focusing on self-reported crime, police and judicial discretion, and "white-collar" crime. Increasingly he feels that he has been singled out to bear the burden of punishment by a society that is, from most indications, characterized by a tremendous discrepancy between idealized behavior (as reflected in its laws) and actual behavior (as reported by its citizens). The belief that they are "political prisoners" characterizes the conclusion drawn by an increasing number of our inmates. They are aware that the attributes which disproportionately distinguish them from the free citizens outside the walls are race, income level, and social status—not behavior or mens rea.

Given this background of increasing political and criminological awareness of inmates (or at least a number of inmates, including the leaders), we can superimpose this on the conditions and receptivity (or lack thereof) of the correctional administrators and state officials. In the state of Ohio, the administration in power in 1968 had done very little to improve correctional faciliteis and programs, nor had it spoken of significant reform. What changes it did make focused largely on juveniles. Insofar as correctional institutions for adults, the status quo was essentially preserved. The strikes and riots which occurred at the Ohio Penitentiary in 1968 cannot, then, be attributed to "rising expectations" of inmates, except insofar as new wardens at some of the major institutions in the stae had reputations as being more inmate than staff-oriented. This was particularly the case at the Ohio Penitentiary, where the newly installed warden in 1968 was closely identified with the "social work" orientation, thereby alienating many of the more powerful figures on the custody staff. (This warden lasted a mere 46 days in his position—the shortest tenure on record in the history of the state.) Instead of "rising expectations," it would appear that the riots of 1968 (and the more recent developments occurring under a "reform" administration which made prison conditions a key issue during the gubernatorial campaign) had less to do with who was in power in the state capitol than with the political ideology and criminological sophistication of the leadership of the kept.

DEVELOPMENT OF THE OHIO PRISONERS' LABOR UNION

Despite the absence of published information, the historical development of the Ohio Prisoners' Labor Union can be described, based on in-depth interviews with inmate leaders and with the legal counsel for the union. Although the Ohio prisoners' movement was not the first in the nation, it has progressed more rapidly (as an organization and in inmate membership) than any of the others, given its brief duration.

The origin of the O.P.L.U. can really be traced to the aforementioned Ohio Penitentiary riots of 1968. There is a logically clear, though temporally separate, relationship between those events and the development of inmate councils, and, now, of the union. From the perspective of the inmates, most of the promises made by the corrections officials following the June and August 1968 riots (the latter of which saw five inmates killed in the prison yard by state troopers summoned to quell the disturbances) were broken, due in part at least to the pressure exerted by the guards, who perceived the loss of power they would experience as a result of the possible implementation of reform. At any rate, many inmates felt betrayed, and this feeling may have contributed to the second riot.

Late in 1968, after the second riot had occurred, inmate leaders at the Ohio Penitentiary wrote to the governor's office and *requested* that they be allowed to form a union which would approximate a trade union in form. The inmates wanted a regular mechanism for bargaining and resolving disputes; otherwise, they could only foresee more broken promises and more violence, in which case they would always be the losers. Permission to organize was *not* granted.

The inmates continued to discuss the idea of a union, but no concrete steps were taken until a new governor was elected. During the gubernatorial campaign (and as early as 1968, when he ran unsuccessfully for the Congress), this governor had made prison reform a key part of his platform and his image. He also had extensive support from organized labor and talked frequently of repealing the state's Ferguson Act (prohibiting strikes by public employees) and of the state's duty to negotiate with groups representing labor. After his election in 1970, the inmate leaders around the state organized a few work stoppages and then, in 1971, while the Ohio Citizens' Task

Force on Corrections was conducting an inquiry into all aspects of the correctional system, the political rhetoric of demands surfaced in a list of grievances and a *notification* (contrasted with the 1968 request) that the inmates of the Ohio Penitentiary intended to form a union. Given the dependency-producing nature of "prisonization," this event was a major departure and a crucial point in the development of the union.

The message was officially ignored, but the inmates continued to discuss the desirability of a union. In March of 1972, a hunger strike developed into a virtual statewide shutdown of the adult correctional institutions. At that point, another signal event occurred— informal negotiations among inmate leaders, the warden of the Ohio Penitentiary, corrections officials, and representatives from the governor's office. The agreements reached during these meetings were again broken by the state, according to the perception of the inmates (which is the important perspective here, in accordance with W. I. Thomas' observations about men's definitions of reality). However, partly as a result of the negotiations, regulations emerged specifying the "ground rules" under which the inmate councils, suggested by the task force and accepted by the Division of Corrections, would operate. These regulations were given a mixed reaction by inmates. At the Ohio Penitentiary, the idea of an inmate council was unanimously rejected because it was anticipated to be state-controlled, not self-determined. It was felt that such a group would be powerless and ineffective. The inmates at London Correctional Institution, on the other hand, accepted the idea and formed the first inmate council in the state.

In addition to inmate councils, other reform measures suggested by the Ohio Citizens' Task Force on Corrrections (1971) and adopted by the Division of Corrections included a legal assistance program; the abolition of censorship of first class mail; the hiring of ministers for the Black Muslim inmates at the Ohio Penitentiary and the Ohio State Reformatory; a recruitment program to attract black employees into the Division of Corrections; standardized grievance procedures for inmates; expanded visitation rights; use of furlough programs; the right of an attorney to visit an inmate in strict privacy upon the inmate's request; and a number of other very important changes, based on the task force's ten-month study.

There were no further significant developments until January of 1973. At that time, continuing discontent with the inmate councils, dissatisfaction with the two ombudsmen established by the Division of Corrections (also a task force recommendation); and displeasure with the results of the implementation of certain other task force recommendations led to a request that the American Civil Liberties

Union and a few young attorneys help organize a prisoners' union and get recognition. The leaders wrote to California, where the first prisoners' union had formed, and sought advice, which they received. The local legal advisers suggested that the first two steps which should be taken were: (1) organizing a local chapter at each institution and training leaders for succession (to counteract the "union-busting" tactics encountered in California); and (2) obtaining written authorization by petition from inmates requesting that the O.P.L.U. be their exclusive bargaining agent.

Thus far, the leadership which has developed among the inmates has been largely self-proclaimed. These leaders seem to differ in background and orientation, and, at some institutions, coalitions of leaders have formed. For example, at the new Southern Ohio Correctional Facility the Sunni Muslims (a very powerful group of Orthodox Muslims) and certain other factions of the population formed such a coalition. Racial separatism has been clearly reflected in some of these arrangements around the state.

Where the administration has not permitted inmates to meet for what might be union activity, the inmates (through legal advisers) have sometimes been successful in forming what amounts to "paper churches" (legal church organizations) for the purpose of carrying on union meetings. This tactic has generally been successfully defended in the courts thus far.

The union's organizing problems appear to differ from one institution to the next, depending on the nature of the inmate population. At the Ohio State Reformatory (Mansfield), for example, the inmates are overwhelmingly young, first-offenders doing "short time." Their incentives not to join the union are probably more powerful than those the union can offer. They perceive their freedom as being not too distant a goal and they are well aware that union activity could be interpreted as nonconformity to institutionally prescribed normative behavior (Ohio Connections, 1973: 6). Two other examples of pressures which create difficulty for the union effort may be seen at the Ohio Reformatory for Women (Marysville), where the women who met the parole board after participating in a strike all received thirty, sixty, and ninety day "flops"; and at London Correctional Institution, where there have been at least three different inmate groups which may have, despite their protestations to the contrary, competed for power (Ohio Connections, 1973: 6).

Currently, the O.P.L.U. is not a union, legally or technically speaking; it simply *calls* itself a union. It claims to have petition signatures for about sixty percent of the inmate population in the state. On May 1, 1973, the union presented representatives of the governor's office with about 1,500 inmate signatures requesting that the O.P.L.U. be recognized as their exclusive bargaining agent. The union is attempting to get each inmate who joins to pay one dollar per month in dues, but it is clear that this financing, along with a few private donations, will not suffice for very long. It would appear that affiliation would be necessary at some point. Such affiliation could be quite helpful in securing jobs for inmates and ex-convicts. However, significant interest of organized labor in such an affiliation has not been indicated, despite the interest of a few leaders (and ex-leaders), such as James R. Hoffa (Jackson, 1972:210).

GOALS OF THE O.P.L.U.

According to the official publication of the O.P.L.U. (Ohio Connections, 1973: 5), the goals of the union are as follows:

(1) Salaries: We believe that all workers should be paid at least the minimum wage set by law, and we should, ideally, be paid on the same basis as civilian employees. This is the goal of the O.P.L.U.: "to see prisoners treated as the civilians they were and will be again."

(2) Legislation: We support and encourage all legislation beneficial to prison labor.

(3) The O.P.L.U. wishes to develop apprenticeship programs that are meaningful to, and appealing to, the prison labor force.

(4) We support increases in institutions' (correctional institution) staff salaries so more qualified personnel can be hired.

(5) Establishment of self-help academies and vocational programs subsidized by the O.P.L.U.

(6) Workmen's Compensation for all Ohio prisoners.

(7) Rehabilitation programs for the handicapped.

(8) Protect human, civil, and legal rights of prisoners.

(9) Correct dangerous working conditions.

(10) Encourage private industry to come into institutions.

(11) Combat cruelty and injustice wherever found in the prison system.

(12) Affiliate with outside unions.

It appears, from reading the publications of the various prisoners' movements around the country, that the goals of the organizations are essentially the same, with some twists owing to local differences in laws, conditions, and so on. An analysis of some of these goals is, explicitly or implicitly, included elsewhere in this paper.

OTHER PRISONERS' UNIONS

As previously mentioned, the O.P.L.U. was not the first prisoners' union in the United States. To provide some perspective, a brief overview of the prisoners' union movement might be useful.

The first U.S. prisoners' union was formed in California in 1970 when the inmates at Folsom Prison submitted a list of 29 demands, including the right to form a labor union (Irwin and Holder, 1973: 1). These demands followed several disturbances and a nineteen-day strike, centering on inmate dissatisfaction with the indeterminate sentence, the "adjustment centers," and the shooting of three black inmates at Soledad. The Folsom strike and the ensuing demands reflected a new level of knowledge and sophistication on the part of the inmates. Support for a union developed from both inside and outside, and culminated in several meetings in various parts of the state to organize the union. The initial constitution and regulations of the organization were structured so that it would be controlled from the outside (largely by ex-convicts) rather than from within. Tactically, it was felt that this would facilitate negotiations.

The major goals of the California union, which now has locals in all fourteen "joints," can be listed as follows (Irwin and Holder, 1973:1):

(1) the abolition of the indeterminate sentence system and all its ramifications;
(2) the establishment of workers' rights for the prisoner, including the right to collectively organize and bargain;
(3) the restoration of civil and human rights for the prisoners.

In reality, a great deal of the impetus for the other prisoners' unions in the United States came from this first union. San Francisco Local 9 of the California Prisoners' Union has now been in operation for over two years, has a staff of at least twenty full and part-time employees, and is involved in many activities on behalf of inmates, including planning a national prisoners' union movement (Irwin and Holder, 1973:2).

The union in New York was officially established at Greenhaven Prison on February 7, 1972 (Comeau, 1972: 966). One unique aspect is that it requested affiliation with District 65, Distributive Workers of America. This request was granted by the labor union, and the prisoners then considered themselves "public employees" under the Taylor Law (Public Employees Fair Employment Act). However, the Public Employees Relations Board of New York turned down the inmates' request for recognition and for the right to collective bargaining. The union has appealed that ruling (The Outlaw, 1973a: 2).

The Prisoners' Union of Massachusetts is active at Walpole, where it claims to have ninety percent of the inmates as members. Negotiations with officials at the prison and in the capital apparently came very close to achieving formal recognition of the union, but also resulted in a guards' strike and may have been related to the ouster of

Commissioner Boone. Walpole has also recently experienced a major disturbance. Other local chapters in Massachusetts are forming at Framingham, Concord, and Norfolk (The Outlaw, 1973a:2).

In North Carolina, the prisoners' union claims to have 2,300 members and fully operative outside offices. It reportedly has the support of the state AFL-CIO and some ministers. Similarly, Michigan reports 2,100 members at Jackson and Marquette (The Outlaw, 1973a: 1-2).

The New England Prison Coalition, including Maine, Vermont, Rhode Island, Massachusetts, and New Hampshire was formed on May 15, 1973. This coalition is designed to unify prisoners' movements in that region, where the distances separating prisons are considerable (The Outlaw, 1973a: 2).

Other states where prisoners' unions are reportedly forming include Georgia (Atlanta Federal Prison); Washington, D.C. (Lorton); Kansas (Leavenworth); Minnesota (Sandstone and Stillwater); and Washington (Monroe and Steilacoom) (The Outlaw, 1973a; 2-3).

Internationally, the strongest inmate unions are probably to be found in the Scandinavian countries, along with some of the more progressive penal practices. In Sweden, for example, representatives of all 5,000 Swedish prisoners negotiated in 1971 with the National Correctional Administration after a hunger strike (Ward, 1972: 240). Despite the comparatively advanced conditions under which most Swedish prisoners live, they still believe that collective action is necessary to obtain those rights which they do not have, such as guaranteed minimum wage comparable to that of civilian labor (Ward, 1972: 240). The organizations known as KRUM (in Sweden) and KRIM (Denmark) help provide outside, as well as inside, pressure on the correctional administrations to make positive changes. However, indications are that, although the Swedish people, for example, are highly unionized and do not see unionization inside prisons as particularly threatening, the LO (Trade Unions Congress) controls much of the bargaining and has thus far refused to allow FFSU (a national confederation of prisoners' unions) to bargain collectively for wages (Choate, 1972: 112). So it would appear that even the Scandinavian unions are still struggling for a number of rights they believe are being denied prisoners.

REACTIONS OF CORRECTIONS ADMINISTRATORS

Directors of state corrections departments have opposed the formation of inmate unions. In Ohio, following an eleven-day strike at the Southern Ohio Correctional Facility, the state director was quoted as saying:

These men [the inmate strikers] are convicted felons—convicted of breaking the laws of society. Under no circumstances will I recognize their so-called union [WBNS-TV, 1973].

The official reaction of the administration has not changed from that statement. However, a policy memorandum written by the director's administrative assistant and dealing with inmate unions perhaps more thoroughly reflects the department's thinking on the matter (Weisenberg, 1973). This memo states, perhaps quite perceptively, that

a hasty entrance into this venture [inmate unions] could cause long-range detriment to the inmate body, as public opinion could react in a negative way to the trends of the correctional system, causing a backlash to the programs and changes of the last few years [Weisenberg, 1973: 5].

This argument is one which hinges on public opinion, as yet untested, but it is clearly a plausible one. The "programs and changes" referred to in the quotation have had a community-oriented focus and have attempted to develop alternatives to incarceration. As a result, the state's prison population had decreased significantly and continues to do so.

Elsewhere in the memo, suggestions are made that the security and custody needs of the institutions be used to "control the organization and formation of inmate unions" (Weisenberg, 1973: 2). Strategy also includes taking the case to the people of the state "instead of having some half-cocked pedestrianic attorney [presumably a reference to attorneys for the prisoners' union] doing it for you and misconstruing the facts to the public" (Weisenberg, 1973: 3). The implication that only one side is in possession of the "facts" is perhaps an indication of the amount of distance already separating the two camps.

With respect to the Ohio union's goal of a minimum wage, it appears that the department intends to rely on the Thirteenth Amendment to the U.S. Constitution ("Neither slavery nor involuntary servitude, except as punishment for crime whereof the party shall have been duly convicted, shall exist within the United States or any place subject to their jursidiction") and Article 1, Section 6 of the Ohio Constitution ("There shall be no slavery in this state, nor involuntary servitude, unless for the punishment of crime") to resist that goal (Weisenberg, 1973: 4).

As for concrete behavioral reactions to the union movement thus far, reports indicate that Ohio's administrators have reacted in the same manner reported to have occurred in California, where the first forty inmates to join the union were transferred to other institutions all over the state (Seidman, 1971: 6). In Ohio, the legal counsel for the prisoners' union reports that on June 9, 1973, a number of inmate union leaders were transferred from Chillicothe Correctional Institution to Southern Ohio Correctional Facility and placed in a security area. Later indications are that a number of other union leaders have undergone the same transfer from other institutions. At Lebanon Correctional Institution, several inmate leaders were placed in "administrative isolation" (a euphemism for "the hole") after "conspiring to organize against the institution." What they organized was a food boycott. They apparently violated the superintendent's policy statement (the first in Ohio regarding the union), which read, in part:

It is the policy of this administration to prohibit a prisoner union or its equivalent or activities within the institution to organize such a union and violators will be subject to disciplinary action or other appropriate action [The Outlaw, 1973b: 7]

Other reactions experienced in Ohio include the parole board "flops" mentioned earlier for the inmate strikers at the Ohio Reformatory for Women.

Although qualitatively somewhat different, it is clear that there are parallels between the reaction of corrections officials and administrators to prisoners' unions and the reactions, years ago, of management to labor union organizing efforts. To determine the extent of opposition to inmate unions and inmate bargaining, Comeau (1972) surveyed all the state corrections departments. Obtaining nearly a fifty percent response rate, Comeau reported the following results:

(1)   Would you oppose the formation of inmate labor unions to bargain with administrators concerning prison working conditions?
      (Yes: 20; No: 3)
(2)   If a labor union could be structured so that threats to security and order within the institution could be brought below current levels, would you oppose its formation?
      (Yes: 15; No: 8)
(3)   Are you opposed to all forms of "bargaining" between inmates and administrators?
      (Yes: 10; No: 13)

Comeau concluded that, although the responses indicated an unwillingness to accept inmate unions at present, they also seemed to reflect the belief that *some* form of bargaining would quite often be accepted. It was noted that, as perceived threat to institutional security diminishes, acceptability of the idea of inmate unions increases (Comeau, 1972: 967). He also stressed that, with respect to the general opposition of the correctional administrators, his research indicated that much of their fear about the unions was based on their belief that certain inmates would become and remain leaders through force and the coercion of others. They feared that problems of internal security and control might develop, and they cited the difficulty of "bargaining" with inmates who are often maladjusted and socially deviant (Comeau, 1972: 978-979). Many of them made references to the tragic use of the "trusty" guard in the Arkansas system.

It is clear from this evidence that if prisoners' unions hope to change the opinions of administrators, they will have to convince them that the unions do not threaten institutional security and that they will be able to control internal power struggles so that they do not end up with a union representing the views and interests of only the most powerful inmates. This will not be an easy task.

LEGAL CONSIDERATIONS

Do inmates have the legal right to form unions? Although no Constitutional or statutory provisions deal *directly* with this question, there are a number of pertinent rulings bearing on closely related matters. As Comeau (1972: 969) notes, "The right to unionize is itself a composite of . . . more fundamental freedoms."

Until 1944, it was widely held that prisoners were "slaves of the state" who had forfeited all personal rights (Ruffin v. Virginia, 1871). This view was based on the Thirteenth Amendment to the U.S. Constitution and on various state constitutional provisions, such as Ohio's (quoted earlier). But in 1944 (Coffin v. Reichard), the sixth circuit court held that "a prisoner retains all the rights of an ordinary citizen, except those expressly, or by necessary implication, taken from him by law." This ruling has often been cited by those advocating expanded rights for prisoners.

In 1948, however, a somewhat different view was advanced. In Price v. Johnston (1948), the Supreme Court of the United States held that "lawful incarceration brings about the necessary withdrawal or limitation of many privileges and rights, a reaction justified by the considerations underlying our penal system." This ruling, of course, has been cited by those seeking to justify restrictions on the rights of prisoners.

The Price decision places the burden of proof on the inmate to show why he should have a particular "right." The Coffin ruling clearly places the burden on the state to demonstrate a compelling need to restrict the "right."

Recently, however, a trend has developed which relies on the application of the "clear and present danger test" to such matters. In 1968, in Jackson v. Goodwin, the fifth circuit court held that

> the state must strongly show some substantial and controlling interest which requires the subordination or limitation of these important consti-

tutional rights, and which justifies their infringement; and in the absence of such compelling justification, the state restrictions are impermissable infringements of the fundamental and preferred First Amendment rights.

A review of the pertinent legal precedents indicates that the courts have "chipped away" at the restrictions of the Thirteenth Amendment in most of these cases and in others involving the following issues: the expression of dissatisfaction with prison administrations; expressing political beliefs; petitioning for the redress of grievances; exercising freedom of association; engaging in organizing activities; and other rights which, taken together, practically constitute the right of unionization. But probably the strongest single judicial statement on the subject came in 1972 from Judge Oakes (Goodwin v. Oswald) of the second circuit court. In that case, the prison warden had prevented the delivery of letters from attorneys giving legal advice to 980 inmates on organizing a union. The judge stated, in his opinion:

There is nothing in federal or state constitutional or statutory law of which I am aware that forbids prison inmates from seeking to form, or correctional officials from electing to deal with, an organization or agency or representative group of inmates concerned with prison conditions and inmates' grievances. Indeed, the tragic experience at Attica . . . would make correctional officials, an observer might think, seek more peaceful ways of resolving prison problems than the old, ironclad, solitary-confinement, mail-censoring, dehumanizing methods that have worked so poorly in the past. Promoting or at least permitting the formation of a representative agency might well be, in light of past experience, the wisest course for correctional officials to follow.

After a thorough review of the relevant judicial decisions and legal issues involved, the following conclusions seem apparent:

(1) If inmates have a right to unionize, this right is clearly secondary to the state's interest in maintaining a secure and orderly penal system.

(2) Where contests develop in this matter, the state must show clear and present undesirable effects on the institution, as a minimum, in order to win its case.

(3) With respect to the minimum wage goal of the inmates and their efforts to be recognized as public employees, it would appear that, under the National Labor Relations Act, inmates probably could *not* meet the definition of "employee" (Comeau, 1972: 968). However, there is nothing in Ohio law to *prevent* the state from recognizing inmates as employees, but only if the state *wishes* to do so (as it has with several labor groups representing staff in correctional institutions). The only law in Ohio specifically dealing with public employees is the Ferguson Act, prohibiting strikes.

(4) The right to unionize probably hinges on the ability of the inmates to demonstrate that the union would have substantial control over its

members and that it would pose no threat to the internal security and order of the institution.

SUMMARY AND CONCLUSIONS

The increasing militancy of Ohio's prisoners has recently evolved from rioting and requests for better conditions to an increasingly sophisticated organizational effort in the form of a prisoners' union with the political rhetoric of demands. This kind of movement is not indigenous to Ohio, but is reflected in a number of other states and appears to be strongest in the Scandinavian countries. The prisoners' union has been opposed by state corrections departments, largely on the basis of perceived threats to institutional order and security and (more latently) because of the pressure of the guards and unions representing guards. The tactics of the state departments seem calculated to destroy union organizing efforts by separating inmate leaders from the general inmate population.

Legally, it would appear that if inmates have the right to form a union, it is secondary to the state's need to maintain orderly and secure penal institutions. The state will be required to demonstrate a compelling need whenever it restricts inmate rights. Inmates will be required to show that their unions pose no threats to internal order and security. Minimum wage demands by inmates may be granted by states, but need not be at the present time.

In conclusion, it is widely known that inmates have probably always "bargained" with their keepers. That tacit agreements and tradeoffs occur inside prisons is no secret. So it should be clear that one of the main issues with respect to an inmate union is whether the bargaining should continue to be informal and individual (which clearly favors the more powerful or advantaged inmates), or whether it should be more participatory and open. This general question is clearly more important than the specific form an inmate union should take.

Even if inmates are successful in forming unions, however, and even if such unions are successful in helping to improve the conditions of the prisoners, we can still expect that the demands will continue. As Ward (1972: 241) notes, the relative deprivation concept is useful in understanding this process of escalating demands. Nevertheless, it seems that unless a threat to the security of our institutions can be demonstrated, other arguments against prisoners' unions usually can be reduced to the thesis that prisoners should be punished and that deprivation of rights is the best way to accomplish that goal. One would hope that Bentham's "less-eligibility" principle would not still be the deciding factor in modern penology.

CASES

COFFIN v. REICHARD (1944) 143 F. 2d 443, 445.
GOODWIN v. OSWALD (1972) 462 F. 2d 1237.
JACKSON v. GOODWIN (1968) 400 F. 2d 529.
PRICE v. JOHNSTON (1948) 334 U.S. 266, 285–286.
RUFFIN v. VIRGINIA (1871) 62 Va. (21 Gratt.) 790, 796.

REFERENCES

Choate, R.
    1972   "Liberating Sweden's prisons." Toronto Globe and Mail (September
            30): 112.
Comeau, P. R.
    1972   "Labor unions for prison inmates: an analysis of a recent proposal
            for the organization of inmate labor." Buffalo Law Rev. 21 (Spring):
            963–985.
Irwin, J. and W. Holder
    1973   "History of the prisoners' union." The Outlaw: J. of Prisoners'
            Union 2 (January/February): 1–3.
Jackson, B.
    1972   "Prisoners and the minimum wage: slavery is alive and well." Nation
            215 (September 18): 209–212.
Martinson, R.
    1972   "Collective Behavior at Attica." Federal Probation 36 (September:
            3–7.
Ohio Citizens' Task Force on Corrections
    1971   Final Report. Columbus: Ohio Department of Urban Affairs.
Ohio Connections: Journal of the Ohio Prisoners' Labor Union
    1973   "Around the state." 1 (March): 5–6.
The Outlaw: Journal of the Prisoners' Union.
    1973a "Nationwide unions coming together." 2 (May/June): 1–3.
    1973b "Policy statement." 2 (May/June): 7.
Seidman, D.
    1971   "The prisoner and the union." Nation 213 (July 5): 6–7.
Ward, D. A.
    1972   "Inmate rights and prison reform in Sweden and Denmark." J. of
            Criminal Law, Criminology, and Police Sci. 63 (June): 240–255.
WBNS–TV
    1973   "The noon report" (June 5).
Weisenberg, B.
    1973   Memorandum, May 14.

35

THE FUTURE OF INSTITUTIONS

NATIONAL ADVISORY COMMISSION ON
CRIMINAL JUSTICE STANDARDS AND GOALS

THE FUTURE OF INSTITUTIONS

For Adults

From the standpoint of rehabilitation and reintegration, the major adult institutions operated by the States represent the least promising component of corrections. This report takes the position that more offenders should be diverted from such adult institutions, that much of their present populations should be transferred to community-based programs, and that the construction of new major institutions should be postponed until such diversion and transfers have been achieved and the need for additional institutions is clearly established.

However, the need for some type of institution for adults cannot be denied. There will always be a hard core of intractable, possibly unsalvageable offenders who must be managed in secure facilities, of which there are already more than enough to meet the needs of the foreseeable future. These institutions have and will have a difficult task indeed. Nevertheless, the nature of imprisonment does not have to be as destructive in the future as it has been.

With growth of community-based corrections, emphasis on institutional programs should decline. However, the public has not yet fully supported the emerging community-oriented philosophy. An out-dated philosophy continues to dominate the adult institution, thus perpetuating a number of contradictory assumptions and beliefs concerning institutional effectiveness.

Source: From *Corrections*(Washington, D.C.: U.S. Government Printing Office, 1973), pp. 349–356 (editorial adaptations).

One assumption is that the committed offender needs to change to become a functioning member of the larger law-abiding society. But it seems doubtful that such a change really can take place in the institution as it now exists.

Another assumption is that the correctional system wants to change. Even though research results have demonstrated the need for new approaches, traditional approaches have created inbred and self-perpetuating systems. Reintegration as an objective has become entangled with the desire for institutional order, security, and personal prestige. As long as the system exists chiefly to serve its own needs, any impending change represents a threat.

Correctional personnel who are assigned responsibility for the "treatment" of the committed offender traditionally have taken the attitude that they know what is best for him and are best qualified to prescribe solutions to his problem. Descriptions of offender problems compiled by personnel also have been traditional—lack of vocational skills, educational deficiencies, bad attitudes, etc.

Aside from the contradictory assumptions prevailing in the correctional field, adult institutions are plagued by physical shortcomings described previously in this chapter. Adult facilities generally are architecturally antiquated, overcrowded, inflexible, too large for effective management, and geographically isolated from metropolitan areas where resources are most readily available.

A major problem in adult institutions is the long sentence, often related more directly to the type of crime committed than to the offender. How can vocational training and other skill-oriented programs be oriented to a job market 20 years hence? What should be done with a man who is capable of returning to society but must spend many more years in an institution?

Conversely, individuals sentenced to a minimum term often need a great deal of assistance. Little can be accomplished at the institutional level except to make the offender aware of his needs and to provide a link with community resources. For these offenders, the real assistance should be performed by community resource agencies.

Correctional administrators of the future will face a different institutional population from today's. As a result of diversion and community-based programs, the committed offender can be expected to be older, more experienced in criminal activity, and more difficult to work with. The staff will have to be more skilled, and smaller caseload ratios will have to be maintained. Personnel standards will change because of new needs.

If a new type of institution is to be substituted for the prison, the legitimate needs of society, the system, and the committed offender must be considered.

For Juveniles and Youths

Use of State institutions for juveniles and youths should be discouraged. The emerging trend in treatment of young offenders is diversion from the criminal justice system. When diversion is not possible, the focus should be on community programs.

This emphasis reverses assumptions as to how youthful offenders should be treated. Previously there was a heavy emphasis on the use of institutional settings. Now it is believed that young offenders should be sent to an institution only when it can be demonstrated clearly that retaining them in the community would be a threat to the safety of others.

The nature of social institutions is such, however, that there is considerable delay between a change in philosophy and a change in practice. Despite major redirection of manpower and money toward both diversion and community programs, progress is slow. Use of major State institutions for juvenile delinquents is declining, but it seems likely that these facilities will continue to be used for some offenders for some time. Therefore, standards for their improvement and operation are required.

Arguments for diversion and alternatives to incarceration largely are negative, stemming from overwhelming disenchantment with the institution as a setting for reducing criminal behavior. Many arguments for community-based programs meet the test of common sense on their own merits, but are strengthened greatly by the failing record of "correctional" institutions. As long as institutional "treatment" is a dispositional alternative for the courts, there must be a continuing effort to minimize the inherently negative aspects and to support and maximize the positive features that distinguish community programs from institutionalization.

The failure of major juvenile and youth institutions to reduce crime is incontestable. Recidivism rates, imprecise as they may be, are notoriously high. The younger the person when entering an institution, the longer he is institutionalized, and the farther he progresses into the criminal justice system, the greater his chance of failure. It is important to distinguish some basic reasons why institutional programs continuously have failed to reduce the commission of crime by those released.

Lack of clarity as to goals and objectives has had marked influence on institutional programs. Programs in youth institutions have reflected a variety of objectives, many of which are conflicting. Both society and the other components of the criminal justice system have contributed to this confusion.

A judge may order a juvenile committed as an example to others or because there are no effective alternatives. The police officer, whose function is to provide community protection, may demand incarceration for the temporary protection it provides for the public. The public may be fearful and incensed at the seriousness of an offense and react by seeking retribution and punishment. To the offender, commitment means he has been banished from society.

Institutions do succeed in punishing, but they do not deter. They protect the community temporarily, but that protection does not last. They relieve the community of responsibility by removing the young offender, but they make successful reintegration unlikely. They change the committed offender, but the change is more likely to be negative than positive.

While it is true that society's charges to the correctional institution have not always been clear or consistent, corrections cannot continue to try to be all things to all publics. Nor can the institution continue to deny responsibility for articulation of goals or objectives. The historical tendency of corrections to view itself as the passive arm of other state agents has resulted in almost total preoccupation with maintaining order and avoiding scandal.

Youth institutions have implicitly accepted the objectives of isolation, control, and punishment, as evidenced by their operations. policies, and programs. They must seek ways to become more attuned to their role of reducing criminal behavior. That the goal of youth institutions is reduction of criminal behavior and reintegration into society must be made explicit. This pronouncement is not sufficient to eliminate their negative aspects, but it is a necessary first step.

Another contributing factor to the failure of major youth institutions has been their closed nature. The geographic location of most institutions is incompatible with a mission of services delivery. Their remote locations make family visitation difficult and preclude the opportunity to utilize the variety of community services available in metropolitan areas. They have been staffed largely with local residents, who, unlike the young offenders, are predominantly white, provincial, and institutionally oriented.

Most existing institutions were built before the concept of community programming gained acceptance. They were built to last; and most have outlasted the need for which they were established. For economic reasons, they were constructed to hold large numbers of people securely. Their structure has restricted the ability to change and strongly influenced the overall direction of institutional programing.

Many administrative policies and procedures in youth institutions also have contributed to their closed nature. The emphasis on security and control of so many people resulted in heavy restrictions on visiting, mail, phone calls, and participation with community residents in various activities and programs. For reasons that are now archaic, most institutions have been totally segregated by sex for both residents and staff.

All these factors have worked together to create an environment within the institution totally unlike that from which the population comes or to which it will return. The youths, often alienated already, who find themselves in such institutions, experience feelings of abandonment, hostility, and despair. Because many residents come from delinquent backgrounds, a delinquent subculture flourishes in the closed institution. This in turn, reinforces administrative preoccupation with security and control.

Large institutions are dehumanizing. They foster an increased degree of dependency that is contrary to behavior expected in the community. They force youths to participate in activities of little interest or use to them. They foster resident-staff relationships that are superficial, transient, and meaningless. They try to change the young offender without knowing how to effect that change or how to determine whether it occurs.

With the shift in emphasis to changing behavior and reintegration, the major institution's role in the total criminal justice system must be reexamined. Changing that role from one of merely housing society's failures to one of sharing responsibility for their reintegration requires an attitude change by the corrections profession. The historical inclination to accept total responsibility for offenders and the resulting isolation clearly are counterproductive.

The public must be involved in the correctional process. Public officials, community groups, universities, and planning bodies must be involved in program development and execution. Such sharing of responsibility will be a new operational role for institutions. This refocus implies substantive changes in policy, program direction, and organization.

The institution should be operated as a resource to meet specific needs without removing responsibility for the offender from the community. Direct involvement of family, school, work, and other social institutions and organizations can have a marked positive impact on decreasing the flow of delinquents into corrections and on the correctional process.

Community responsibility for offenders implies more than institutional tours or occasional parties. It implies participation in programs with institutional residents both inside the institution and in the community. Education, recreational, religious, civic, counseling, and vocational programs, regardless of where they are held, should have both institutional and community participants. Public acceptance of community-based programs is necessary, especially when they operate next door.

The institution always has existed in a changing world, but it has been slow to reflect change. Correctional administrators require the impetus of community development to respond and adapt to changing conditions and needs.

As diversionary and community programs expand, major institutions for juvenile and youthful offenders face an increasingly difficult task. These programs remove from the institution the most stable individuals who previously had a moderating influence on others' behavior.

The most hardened or habitual offender will represent an increasing proportion of those committed to institutions where adequate services can be provided by a professional staff, trained paraprofessionals and volunteers. All staff and participants must be prepared to serve a "helping" role.

More committed offenders than ever before have drug abuse problems. The ability to cope with this phenomenon in an environment isolated from the community has not been demonstrated. The aid of community residents must be enlisted in innovating, experimenting, and finding workable solutions.

Few treatment opportunities have been offered for the intractable offender. Common practice is to move such individuals from the general population and house them in segregation or adjustment centers. The concept of an ongoing treatment program for this group is recent but will become increasingly important as institutional populations change. The understanding and tolerance of the community will be crucial in working with these individuals.

It is no surprise that institutions have not been successful in reducing crime. The mystery is that they have not contributed even more to increasing crime. Meaningful changes can take place only by attention to the factors discussed here. Concentrated effort should be devoted to long-range planning, based on research and evaluation. Correctional history has demonstrated clearly that tinkering with the system by changing individual program areas without attention to the larger problems can achieve only incidental and haphazard improvement.

THE CORRECTIONAL DILEMMA

A major obstacle to the operation of an effective correctional program is that today's practitioners are forced to use the means of an older time. Dissatisfaction with correctional programs is related to the permanence of yesterday's institutions—both physical and ideological. We are saddled with the physical remains of last century's prisons and with an ideological legacy that equates criminal offenses with either moral or psychological illness. This legacy leads inexorably to two conclusions: (1) the sick person must be given "treatment" and (2) "treatment" should be in an institution removed from the community.

It is time to question this ideological inheritance. If New York has 31 times as many armed robberies as London, if Philadelphia has 44 times as many criminal homicides as Vienna, if Chicago has more burglaries than all of Japan, if Los Angeles has more drug addiction than all of Western Europe, then we must concentrate on the social and economic ills of New York, Philadelphia, Chicago, Los Angeles, and America.

This has not been our approach. We concentrate on "correcting" and "treating" the offender. This is a poor version of the "medical" model. What is needed is a good version of the "public health" model, an attempt to treat causes rather than symptoms.

If the war against crime is to be won, it will be won ultimately by correcting the conditions in our society that produce such an inordinate amount of criminal activity. These conditions include high unemployment, irrelevant education, racism, poor housing, family disintegration, and government corruption. These, among others, form the freshets that make the streams that form the rivers that flood our criminal justice system and ultimately its correctional institutions.

Public policy during the coming decades should shift emphasis from the offender and concentrate on providing maximum protection to the public. A more just society, offering opportunity to all segments, would provide that protection. The prison, call it by any other name, will not. It is obsolete, cannot be reformed, should not be perpetuated through the false hope of forced "treatment," and should be repudiated as useless for any purpose other than locking away persons who are too dangerous to be allowed at large in free society.

For the latter purpose we already have more prison space than we need or will need in the foreseeable future. Except where unusual justification can be proved, there is no need to build additional major institutions—reform schools, reformatories, prisons, or whatever euphemisms may be used to designate them—for at least 10 years. Further, the use of major State institutions for confinement of juveniles should be totally discontinued in favor of local community-based programs and facilities.

In view of the dearth of valid data to substantiate the rehabilitative effectiveness of institutional programs, we have no basis for designing more effective physical facilities. Under these circumstances, new construction would represent merely a crystallization and perpetuation of the past with all its futility.

Under prevailing practices, institutional construction costs are excessive. They now run as high as $30,000 to $45,000 per inmate in some jurisdictions. Costs of operation vary widely, from $1,000 per year per inmate to more than $12,000.[84] Construction of new major institutions should be deferred until effective correctional programs to govern planning and design can be identified, and until the growth of a more selected inmate population dictates. The potentially tremendous savings should be expended more productively in improving probation, parole, and community-based programs and facilities.

PLANNING NEW INSTITUTIONS

It cannot be overemphasized that unusually convincing justification of need should be required as a logical precedent to planning a new institution. Yet there are many impediments to recognizing this rationality in planning. One of them is fragmentation of the criminal justice system.

The traditional division of the entire system into several parts—police, courts, institutions, and field services—and more fundamentally, the concept that the criminal justice system exists apart from society and unto itself, have created an administrative and organizational climate that allows the construction of new institutions with little or no real consideration of other possible solutions.

The most fundamental question to be addressed in the planning of institutions is the reason for their existence. They obviously represent the harshest, most drastic end of the spectrum of possible correctional response.

Different States have different philosophies. Some rely heavily on incarceration, others do not. (See Table 32.) Some concentrate on size and security; others build more varied facilities.

This absence of correctional consistency poses a serious handicap to the administration of an equitable criminal justice system.

If protection of society is seen as the purpose of the criminal justice system, and if it is felt that this protection requires sequestration of some offenders, then institutions must exist to carry out this purpose. Immediately the planner is confronted with the question, "What kind of institutions?"

Of fundamental importance to any planning are the values and assumptions dictating the policies. Programs and structural responses

TABLE 32

Comparative Use of State Correctional Institutions

Ratio of Prisoners in State Institutions to State Population	Number of States with Ratio
1 to 2,501 and over	1
1 to 2,001–2,500	4
1 to 1,501–2,000	8
1 to 1,001–1,500	21
1 to 501–1,000	16

Sources: Data from 1970 Census and ACA *1971 Directory*.

are fixed by those policies. Their underlying values affect all subsequent planning and implementation. For nearly two centuries this Nation has used the correctional institution as its primary response to illegal behavior. It is long past time for legislators, administrators, and planners to collect and examine the results of this vast institutional experience. Scholarly evaluation currently available suggests that our prisons have been deficient in at least three crucial areas—conception, design, and operation. These areas and two others—location and size—should be given serious consideration in all correctional planning.

Conception

The correctional institution has been poorly conceived, in that it is intended to hide rather than heal. It is the punitive, repressive arm whose function is to do the system's "dirty work."

Design

The designers of most correctional institutions generally have been preoccupied with security. The result is that they create demoralizing and dehumanizing environments. The facility design precludes any experience that could foster social growth or behavioral improvement. Indeed, institutions more often breed hostility and resentment and strip inmates of dignity, choice, and a sense of self-worth.

Operation

The punitive function and design of correctional institutions is reflected in their operation. Containment and control command a lion's share of resources. Activities aimed at modifying behavior and attitudes or at developing skills often are limited or absent altogether.

The daily routine is dominated by frustration, idleness, and resentment, punctuated by the aggressive behavior such conditions breed.

Correctional institutions often are designed and constructed with little consideration of their place in the overall corrections system. Some system needs are duplicated, while others go unmet. Many administrators of maximum and medium security centers state that only 20 to 25 percent of their inmates need that level of security. Yet centers offering community programs are extremely scarce or nonexistent.

Improper design may prevent an institution from fulfilling its assigned function. Use of dormitories in maximum security prisons, for example, permits physical violence and exploitation to become a way of life. Conversely, inmates who are not considered a threat to others may be housed in single inside cells, with fixed furniture, security-type plumbing, and grilled fronts and doors.

Institutions intended as "correction centers" may have no more than two or three classrooms and a small number of poorly equipped shops to serve as many as a thousand inmates. This is token rehabilitation. Programs and facilities provided by "centers" that hold persons 24 hours a day from one year to many years may be totally inadequate for occupying the inmate's time. Here idleness is a way of life.

Lack of funds, haphazard planning, faulty construction, and inadequate programing and staffing all may account for failure to design and build institutions to serve their assigned functions adequately. Fund allocations may be insufficient because costs are unknown. Space may be programed without knowledge of the actual needs for a particular activity. Planners and programers may develop schemes without consulting architects and engineers. Architects may be engaged without being given adequate guidelines.

The architect often is inexperienced in design and construction of correctional facilities. To overcome this lack he may visit an institution serving an entirely different purpose. Errors are replaced and compounded because few institutions are worthy of emulation. New mistakes and inconsistencies, therefore, are built on top of existing ones.

Location

Location has a strong influence on an institution's total operation. Most locations are chosen for reasons bearing no relationship to rationality or planning. Results of poor site selection include inaccessibility, staffing difficulty, and lack of community orientation.

In the early days of America's prison history, penitentiaries were built where the people were—Philadelphia, Pittsburgh, Columbus, Trenton, Baltimore, and Richmond. The urban location had nothing to do with the prevailing theory of penology. The idea was to isolate the prisoner—and he was isolated, even though his prison walls pressed tightly against the city streets.

During the last century, rural settings usually were chosen for new correctional institutions. This remoteness may have been relatively unimportant when America was predominantly a farm country. Lifestyles—rural and urban—had not yet hardened in their contrasting molds. At a time when the prison was viewed almost exclusively as a place of quarantine, where better than the remote reaches of a State?

These no longer are valid reasons, nor have they been for a quarter of a century. America has become increasingly urban. Lifestyles and values, born not only of population diversity but of ethnic differences, create gaps of understanding wider than the miles separating city dwellers from farmers.

The rhetoric, if not the purpose, of corrections also has changed. The ultimate objective now being expressed no longer is quarantine but reintegration—the adjustment of the offender in and to the real world.

But in 1972 correctional institutions still are being built in some of the most isolated parts of the States. Powerful political leaders may know little about "reintegration," but they know a pork barrel when they see one. Urbanites resist the location of prisons in the cities. They may agree on the need for "reintegration" of the ex-offender, but this objective is forgotten when city dwellers see a prison in their midst as increasing street crime and diminishing property values.

The serious disadvantages of continuing to construct correctional institutions in sparsely populated areas include:

1. The impossibility of using urban academic and social services or medical and psychiatric resources of the city.
2. The difficulty of recruiting professional staff members—teachers, psychologists, sociologists, social workers, researchers, nurses, dentists, and physicians—to work in rural areas.
3. The prolonged interruption of offenders' contacts with friends and relatives, which are important to the reintegration process.
4. The absence of meaningful work- and study-release programs.
5. Most importantly, the consignment of corrections to the status of a divided house dominated by rural white guards and administrators unable to understand or communicate with black, Chicano, Puerto Rican, and other urban minority inmates.

Other human services long since have moved away from dependence upon the congregate rural institution. Almshouses of old have been replaced with family assistance; workhouses, with employment insurance; orphanages, with foster homes and aid to dependent children; colonies for imbeciles, with day care and sheltered workshops. Durgs have made obsolete the dismal epileptic facilities and the tuberculosis sanitariums of yesteryear. Asylums are rapidly yielding to community mental health approaches.

All of these human services changed because isolated institutions proved to be unsuccessful, expensive, and even counterproductive as responses to specific human problems. They also changed because better treatment methods were developed, making the isolated institutions largely obsolete and treatment in the natural community setting feasible and advisable.

And so it should be with corrections.

Size

Traditionally, institutions have been very large, often accommodating up to two and three thousand inmates. The inevitable consequence has been development of an organizational and operational monstrosity. Separation of large numbers of people from society and mass confinement have produced a management problem of staggering dimensions. The tensions and frustrations inherent in inprisonment are magnified by the herding together of troubled people. Merely "keeping the lid on" has become the real operational goal. The ideal of reform or rehabilitation has succumbed to that of sheer containment, a goal of limited benefit to society.

The usual response to bigness has been regimentation and uniformity. Individuals become subjugated to the needs generated by the institution. Uniformity is translated into depersonalization. A human being ceases to be identified by the usual points of reference, such as his name, his job, or family role. He becomes a number, identified by the cellblock where he sleeps. Such practices reflect maladaptation resulting from size.

Almost every warden and superintendent states that his institution is too big. This hugeness has been the product of many factors, including economics, land availability, population of the jurisdiction, the influence of Parkinson's Law, and an American fetish that equates bigness with quality. (A half century ago, one State built the "world's biggest wall" only to bow to another jurisdiction that gleefully surpassed it two years later.)

Any attempt to establish an optimum size is a meaningless exercise unless size is related directly to the institution's operation. The institution should be small enough to enable the superintendent to know every inmate's name and to relate personally to each person in his charge. Unless the inmate has contact with the person who has policy responsibility and who can assist him with his personal difficulties and requests, he will feel that the facility's prime purpose is to serve the system and not him. The reverse also is true: if the superintendent does not have contact with the inmates, his decisions will be determined by demands of the system and not by inmate needs.

The size of the inmate housing unit is of critical importance because it must satisfy several conditions: security, counseling, inmate social and informal activities, and formal program requirements. Although security conditions traditionally have been met with hardware and electronic equipment, these means contradict the purposes of corrections and should be deemphasized. Security is maintained better by providing small housing units where personal supervision and inmate-staff contact are possible and disturbances can be contained easily.

Informal counseling is easier in the small housing unit because the inmate-counselor ratio is not as threatening as in the massive cellblock and negative group pressure on the inmate is minimized.

Many institutions are poorly cooled, heated, and ventilated. Lighting levels may be below acceptable limits. Bathroom facilities often are insanitary, too few, and too public. Privacy and personal space hardly ever are provided because of overriding preoccupation with security. Without privacy and personal space, inmates become tense and many begin to react with hostility. As tension and hostility grow, security requirements increase; and a negative cycle is put into play.

A REVIEW OF CORRECTIONAL STANDARDS

Correctional practice in the United States seems to defy standardization. Each State is virtually independent in its choice of correctional options. The U.S. Bureau of Prisons operates Federal prisons and has no mandate to regulate State institutions. The National Bureau of Standards has made studies for corrections but has no means of influencing change. The Law Enforcement Assistance Administration, under the providions of the Safe Streets Act, has provided the impetus for State and local governments to determine their own approaches to corrections and other criminal justice problems. Consequently, the efforts of LEAA in large part have been directed to monitoring the fiscal and not the programmatic aspects of its grants.

The Constitution of the United States reserves to the States the power to promote the health, safety, morals, and general welfare of its citizens—the so-called police power—and in large part because of this power and the implications of Federalism, the legislative and executive branches of the national government never have been authoritative in establishing or enforcing correctional standards. The judiciary is becoming so. The Federal Judiciary, however, is drawing upon the "due process" and "cruel and unusual punishment" amendments to the Constitution to define new standards for corrections and, more importantly, is enforcing them. Judges see the Constitution as the ultimate source of certain correctional standards articulated in various court decisions. Thus in *Holt* v. *Sarver,* 309 F. Supp. 362 (E.D. Ark. 1970), aff'd, 442 F. 2d. 304 (8th Cir. 1971), the District Court, with the ultimate concurrence of the Federal Court of Appeals, held that imprisonment in the Arkansas State Prison System constituted "cruel and unusual punishment" and gave the State two years to correct the situation or release all prisoners then incarcerated in the State facilities.

Some statutes also are a source of standards. Every jurisdiction has its own laws spelling out certain requirements for the correctional establishment. A few examples show they usually are explicit.

All prisoners who are suffering from any disease, shall be segregated from the prisoners who are in good physical condition.

All prisoners who are found or considered to be habitual criminals, evil-inclined, shall be segregated, and not allowed to be among or mingle with those of opposite inclination.

Every warden shall provide that such person shall have, at least two hours daily, physical exercise in the open.

No prisoner shall be confined in a cell occupied by more than one individual.[85]

These and other standard-setting statutes are honored most frequently in the breach. In April, 1972, for example, the Court of Common Pleas in Philadelphia found in that city's prison system 161 violations of State statutes. Together, said the court, these transgressions added up to the violation of those provisions of both State and Federal Constitutions dealing with cruel and unusual punishment.[86]

The United Nations also has developed policy statements that attempt to set standards for correctional practices. Usually they are broad, idealistic, and ignored.

Private groups have contributed richly to the articulation of correctional standards. The objectives of these groups vary. An association of correctional professionals will have a different orientation than a group of civil libertarians or a manufacturer of security equipment. Each promotes those standards most in accord with its own objectives. The presence of so many interest groups, coupled with the lack of specific enforceable legislation at the State level, has resulted in an unorganized profusion of standards that sometimes are helpful but often are confusing. None provides the comfort of unquestioned authority of substantiated research.

Currently existing standards seem to be more oriented to administration than to goals or to offenders. This is quite natural because neither inmates nor philosophers usually serve on principal standard-writing committees. Individuals who do serve have careers and professional fortunes tied up in the operation of institutions. Results are colored by the limits of vision individuals bring to the task. Fundamental, essential changes at the goal level likely will come from a body not restricted by an operational orientation. Change, for a variety of reasons, seldom comes from within and hardly ever without resistance.

SCIENTIFIC GUIDANCE
OF
INSTITUTIONAL POLICIES

INTRODUCTION

How can the scientific method help to solve the administrative problems of correctional agencies? The answer to this question depends on a clear understanding of the basic premise involved. If the function of prisons is to mete out *punishment*, the issues are different from those that might be raised if their purpose were to reform, rehabilitate or educate. The concept of *treatment* (based upon the general clinical medical approach) seems to have been abandoned by many authorities, although by no means all. In fact, the use of the scientific method in evaluating the effects of treatment was wholly or mainly responsible for the current disaffection with this philosophy.

Since considerable doubt has been cast on the medical model and its application to penal practice, what is the current status of the scientific method? Is the present climate of opinion more favorable to it? It must be acknowledged that more than a hint of cynicism can be detected in current debate about crime and criminals, and about the appropriate role of social scientists in this area.

The fate of offenders is deliberated at the interface between moral values and technology. It is to be expected that efficient methods for reforming offenders could be devised, but perhaps the main question is whether such methods would be ethical. To what extent must "treatment" intrude into an offender's life to be effective? What degree of intrusion is permissible on ethical grounds? What moral restraints should we seek to place on "experiments" or even on innovations? The interface between ethics and science is a largely uncharted terrain. In that lonely place prison administrators are now making grave ethical decisions with little help from moral philosophers or research workers.

Professor Donald Cressey, in the first reading in this section, points out the problems that arise from conflicting penal theories. There is slight evidence that any modifications of actions or procedures based on a given theory have produced the desired results. If theory can assist, then it would seem that we need better theories. As Professor Cressey traces the history of penal thought, the reader will note that questions

of values have often been enmeshed with theory and indeed with speculation. A system has been created, however, that is highly resistant to
change of any kind.

In the second selection Professor Daniel Glaser states that progress
has been made, in that we have learned in recent decades to ask better
questions. He points out that we have come to recognize different *kinds*
of offenders (types?) who need different *kinds* of treatments. An important question of values is raised at once by this "better" scientific
question: Should different *kinds of offenders* (who may have committed
exactly similar crimes) be treated differently because their *needs* are
different? In any event, what is meant by a "need" when we talk about
a person who is incarcerated *because* he has committed a crime? If a
person does not want to change, who has the right (or duty) to say that
he "needs" to be changed? These, and still subtler "scientific questions,"
may raise further and more difficult issues of ethics.

The use of actuarial prediction tables as a basis for determining certain actions to be taken in regard to various offenders has ethical implications. Should what is likely to happen as a consequence of the
application of law be of any concern to the law?

We may, of course, decide to deal with objective situations rather
than with persons in the hope of preventing or reducing the impact of
crime. And this approach may indeed cause less ethical malaise. This aspect of the crime problem is taken up briefly in the final selection. As
Professor Leslie T. Wilkins states, "It is necessary as a matter of considerable urgency, that we unscramble the technological, medical, scientific
and moral questions in relation to dysfunctional behavior." When we
define the *kinds of questions* more clearly, we may be able to identify
more readily the specific approach that might be most effective. We
cannot solve all problems of deviant behavior by law, nor can we resolve
all legal problems by scientific research; our main problems are related
to ethics and human values. On these crucial issues all modern thinking
seems lamentably confused.

36

SOURCES OF RESISTANCE TO INNOVATION IN CORRECTIONS

DONALD R. CRESSEY

There are four principal and interrelated sources of resistance to innovations in the field of corrections. These are: conflicting theories regarding efficiency of measures for maximizing the amount of conformity in the society; the social organization necessary to administering correctional programs; the characteristics and ideologies of correctional personnel; and the organization of correctional clients with respect to each other and to correctional personnel. In each case, the basis of the resistance to correctional change in general has special implications for resistance to change which would permit and encourage offenders and ex-offenders to serve as employees of correctional agencies, especially as rehabilitators.[1]

CONFLICTING PENAL THEORIES

The governing of persons who have some degree of freedom is no easy task, even in a small organization such as a family, a business firm, a university, a probation agency, or a prison. In a larger organization such as an army or a nation, it is even more difficult.

Two basic problems confront all persons who would insure that others follow rules. One is the problem of obtaining consent to be governed. Governors must somehow get the governed to agree, usually unwittingly, to the governors' definition of morality, deviance, and deficiency. In this context, at least, it is correct to say that whoever controls the definition of the situation controls the world.

The second problem is one of maintaining the consent of the governed once it has been obtained. Those who are attempting to

Source: From *Offenders as a Correctional Manpower Resource* (Washington, D.C.: Joint Commission on Correctional Manpower and Training, June 1968), pp. 31–49. Reprinted by permission of the author and publisher.

maximize conformity must be prepared to cope with nonconformity. This means that they must constantly be seeking appropriate measures to control those members whose conduct indicates that they have withdrawn, at least partially or temporarily, their consent to be governed. In utilizing these measures, governors must not inadvertently take actions which significantly diminish the degree of consent that has been given. In child-rearing, to take a simple example, parents must not punish their disobedient children so severely that the children rebel and become even more disobedient. In crime control, governments must not take actions which alienate solid citizens. All correctional devices must be administered in such a manner that the behavior of criminals is changed but the consent of the governed is not lost. Official punishment of criminals, especially, must be exercised with caution. If punishment of criminals is to be accepted by the recipients and by citizens generally, it must be imposed "justly," in measures suitable to correcting deviation without stimulating rebellion.

The rule-making bodies of social groups seldom have a unitary ideology regarding the procedures to be used for inspiring and maintaining conformity. A father, for example, may at one time spank his son for violating family rules and at another time overlook known violations, all the while believing that whatever action he takes is "for the good of the child" or "for the good of the family." In a nation, comparable inconsistencies in implementing a desire for a maximum amount of conformity are found in criminal law and in correctional agencies, owing to contradictions in the penal law theory which lies behind them. Since correctional agencies are, by and large, creatures of legislative processes, one who would understand resistances to correctional innovation must understand the theory on which legislatures operate in criminal matters.

One body of theory maintains that conformity to criminal laws is maximized by swift, certain, and uniform punishment of those who deviate. The "Classical School" of criminology which developed in England during the last half of the eighteenth century and spread to other European countries and to the United States, popularized this notion. The objective of the leaders of this school was to provide advance notice that crime would have punishment as its consequence and to make the imposition of punishments less severe and less capricious than it had been.[2]

According to the ideology popularized by these men, all persons who violate a specific law should receive identical punishments regardless of age, sanity, social position, or other conditions or circumstances. The underlying principle of behavioral and social control developed here is the idea of deterrence. By means of a rational, closely calculated system of justice, including uniform, swift, and certain imposition of the punishments set by legislatures for each offense, the undesirability and impropriety of certain behavior is emphasized to such a degree that it simply does not occur to people to engage in such behavior.

Although this set of theory is not now—and never was—used in its pure form, it is one of the pillars of our contemporary system of corrections. This becomes apparent whenever legislators demand a harsher penalty for some offense, whenever the very existence of probation and parole systems is attacked, and whenever correctional leaders are castigated for trying to introduce changes based on the view that offenders are in need of help. All developed societies maintain a powerful legal organization for corporate imposition of measured amounts of suffering on offenders. By acting collectively to take revenge on criminals, society is said to reinforce its anti-criminal values. In this setting, the notion that criminals themselves should be used as correctional agents is especially vulnerable because it implies that a criminal deserving of punishment will be utilized to mitigate the punishments deserved by other offenders.

A second body of theory is based on the belief that law violations and law violators must be handled individually so far as punishment is concerned. The extreme idea of equality promoted by the Classical School was almost immediately modified at two points. First, children and "lunatics" were exempted from punishment on the ground that they are unable to calculate pleasures and pains intelligently. Second, the penalties were fixed within narrow limits, rather than absolutely, so that a small amount of judicial discretion was possible. These modifications of the classical doctrine were the essence of what came to be called the "Neo-Classical School." The principle behind the modification remains as another of the pillars of our contemporary system for administering criminal justice. The basic idea was, and is, that the entire set of circumstances of the offense and the entire character of the offender are to be taken into account when deciding what the punishment, if any, shall be. "Individualization" of punishment has extended the principle of exemptions to persons other than children and the insane, and this means, of course, that judicial discretion is to be exercised officially.[3]

Our basic conceptions of justice are closely allied with these two contradictory sets of penal theory. These conceptions of justice, intermingled with the two sets of theory, have taken the form of ideologies regarding the "proper" measures to be used for securing and maintaining the consent of the people to be governed by the formulators and administrators of the criminal law. When implemented, the ideologies become directives for action on the part of correctional personnel. But since both the ideologies and the theories behind them are contradictory, we cannot logically expect correctional workers to be consistent in their methods of dealing with lawbreakers and potential lawbreakers. Correctional workers are called upon to play a game they cannot win. They are to ensure that punishments are uniformly imposed on those who violate the law. We are confident that this action will maximize the amount of conformity in the society. But they also are to adjust the punishments to individual cases, thus ensuring that punishments are neither so lenient nor so severe that the degree of conformity will diminish.

The first set of theory implies that, if the price of crime is low, everyone will buy it. Legislatures state, symbolically at least, that crime and criminals must be abhorred or the crime rates will rise. Attempts to handle criminals as if they have basic human rights are therefore resisted. Handling them as if they were capable of serving as correctional workers compounds the resistance. But correctional workers also are to ensure that the price of a crime is not so high that exacting it will result in loss of control of offenders and others. When punishments are too severe or otherwise unjust, citizens may not openly demonstrate their withdrawal of consent. But in a pattern of passive resistance they may well shield criminals from the law enforcement process. Even if they do not commit crimes, they may learn to overlook crimes, with the result that the law's effectiveness in maximizing conformity diminishes.

We assign to each correctional worker the difficult task of striking the delicate balance between leniency and severity of punishments, and between imposing punishments uniformly and imposing them irregularly. This delicate task, it may be argued, cannot be assigned to criminals or ex-criminals because their prior experiences have made them incapable of being disinterested. Traditionally, any grouping of criminals or ex-criminals has been viewed as undesirable, on both custodial and rehabilitative grounds. Association among prisoners meant, and still means, a banding together of dangerous men who could plot for some nefarious purposes. To avoid such association, prison workers have, by and large, substituted psychological solitary confinement for the physical solitary confinement characterizing the early Pennsylvania institutions.[4] In probation and parole, it has from the beginning been against the rules for offenders to associate with each other, partly because it was feared that any association would lead to criminal conspiracies, thereby decreasing the security of the society. It also was assumed that, if offenders were allowed to associate, the more criminalistic of them might contaminate the less criminalistic. The question of why the reverse would not be true has rarely been raised.[5]

In recent times we have, in addition, asked correctional personnel to "treat" criminals. To the degree that treatment is an alternative to punishment, not a supplement to it, its introduction into the correctional process is an attempt to mitigate penalties with a view to maximizing the degree of consent of the governed and thus the amount of conformity. Probation, prison, and parole workers are expected to execute the penalties "prescribed by law" so that offenders and others will learn that they cannot get away with law violation, thus increasing the amount of conformity. But correctional workers also are expected to modify those penalties so that offenders will be "treated" and the amount of conformity thereby increased. Introduction of treatment programs is resisted because they mitigate prescribed penalties. At the same time, correctional workers are accused of inefficiency if criminals are not rehabilitated.

SOCIAL ORGANIZATION OF CORRECTIONAL WORK

Because our society and its penal law theories have been ambivalent about what should be done with, to, and for criminals, it is not surprising to find that correctional work has been, almost from the beginning, characterized by ambivalent values, conflicting goals and norms, and contradictory ideologies. However, such a state of flux is not necessarily an impediment to correctional innovation. Viewed from one perspective, a state of disorganization or unorganization provides unusual opportunities for innovation. For example, an analysis of the Soviet industrial system concluded that conflicting standards and selective enforcement of an organization's rules permits supervisors to transmit changes in their objectives to subordinates without disrupting the operation of the system; permits subordinates to take initiative, be critical, make innovations, and suggest improvements; and permits workers who are closest to the problem field (usually subordinates) to adapt their decisions to the ever-changing details of circumstances. The following comment about the last point is especially relevant to corrections:

The very conflict among standards, which prevents the subordinate from meeting all standards at once, gives him a high degree of discretion in applying received standards to the situation with which he is faced. Maintenance of conflicting standards, in short, is a way of decentralizing decision-making.[6]

As conceptions of "the good society" have changed, conceptions of "good penology" and, more recently "good corrections" also have changed. This has meant, by and large, that new services have been added to correctional work and new roles have been assigned to both correctional workers and their clients. Moreover, these additions have been made without much regard for the services and roles already existing. The process seems different from that accompanying similar growth of manufacturing and sales corporations, for the new roles have been organized around purposes that are only remotely related to each other. This could mean, as in the case of Soviet industry, that anything goes.

But in correctional work change has been slow and sporadic despite conflicting principles which seem to make anything possible. Ambivalence and conflict in social values and penal theories have produced correctional organizations inadvertently designed to resist change.

In the first place, a shift in correctional objectives now requires changes in the organization, not merely in the attitudes or work habits of employees. In prisons, for example, there is a line organization of custodial ranks, ranging from warden to guard, and salary differentials and descriptive titles (usually of a military nature) indicate that a chain of command exists within this hierarchy. Any prison innovation whose goals cannot be achieved by means of this hierarchy must either modify or somehow evade the organization of custodial ranks.

Positions for prison school teachers, industrial foremen, and treatment personnel are not part of the chain of command. Neither do such sets of positions make up a "staff organization," in the sense that positions for experts and advisors of various kinds make up a staff organization in a factory or political unit. The persons occupying positions outside the hierarchy of ranks in correctional systems do not provide persons in the hierarchy with specialized knowledge which will help them with custodial and management tasks, as staff personnel in factories provide specialized knowledge which assists the line organization with its task of production. In corrections, the "staff organization" actually is a set of separate organizations which competes with the line organization for resources and power. Systems of non-line positions, such as those for treatment, training, and industrial personnel, are essentially separate organizations, each with its own salary differentials and titles.

The total structure of corrections consists of three principal hierarchies—devoted respectively to *keeping, using,* and *serving criminals.* But the total system is not organized for the integration of the divergent purposes of these three separate organizations. In this situation, innovation by members of any one of the three organizations is necessarily a threat to the balance of power between them and the members of the other organizations.

Resistance to using criminals as correctional workers is to be expected because this role, in fact, is part of *none* of the three separate organizations. Further, the role is a threat to the authority structures and the communication and decision-making patterns of all of them.

Secondly, most innovations in correctional work can be introduced and implemented only if the participation, or at least the cooperation, of all employees is secured. In factories, there are separate but integrated hierarchies of management personnel and of workers, and many kinds of orders for innovation can flow freely downward from management offices to factory floors. For example, if the manager of an aircraft factory decides to innovate by manufacturing boats instead of airplanes, a turret-lathe operator can readily accept the order to change the set-up of his machine in such a way that part of a boat is manufactured.

But in correctional work, management is an end, not a means. Accordingly, management hierarchies extend down to the lowest level of employee. The correctional worker, in other words, is both a manager and a worker. He is managed in a system of controls and regulations from above, but he also manages the inmates, probationers, or parolees in his charge. He is a low-status worker in interaction with his warden, chief, or director, but he is a manager in his relationships with inmates or other clients. Because he is a manager, he cannot be ordered to accept a proposed innovation, as a turret-lathe operator can be ordered. He can only be persuaded to do so.

Criminals or ex-criminals serving as correctional workers, even if unpaid, must be given the management responsibilities assigned to all correctional workers. Addition of this role to a correctional organization is subject to a kind of veto by any of the correctional workers in the organization, for each plays a management role.

But even though all correctional employees are managers as well as workers, the agencies and institutions which they manage are not owned by them. Each correctional agency has a number of absentee owners, and these owners have varying conceptions about policy, program, and management procedures. If they were questioned, it is probable that each would have a distinct opinion about using criminals and ex-criminals in correctional work. Because of differences in theoretical conceptions in the broader society, the contemporary environment of correctional agencies contains overlapping groups with interests in seeing that physical punishments are imposed, groups with interests in reducing physical punishments, and groups with varying ideas for implementing the notion that criminals can be re-formed only if they are provided with positive, non-punitive treat-ment services. The interests of such groups converge on any particular correctional agency, and the means used by correctional administra-tors for handling their contradictory directives gives correctional agencies their organizational character.[7]

We have seen that, to some degree, resistance to correctional in-novation resides in the internal order of the system, especially in the structure requiring that all employees and some clients share policy. But, to an even greater degree, resistance resides in the network of competing or cooperating interest groups, which vary from time to time. Caplow has pointed out that we should expect to find the strictest control of even *non*-occupational behavior attached to those occupations which have important role-setting obligations in the soci-ety, are identified with sacred symbols, and have relatively low sta-tus.[8] Correctional work qualifies on all three criteria. Factionalism among employees which develops whenever a significant change is made in the work of a correctional agency, is closely linked with changing interests of authorities external to the agency.

Correctional agencies are in a very real sense "owned" not by "the public" at large but by specific outside groups. Punitive, cus-todial, and surveillance activities are supported and maintained by a different convergence of interests than are production activities, edu-cational activities, religious activities, and counseling and therapeutic activities.

One type of interest group emerges when an existing group sees existing or possible activities of the correctional program as a means for achieving its own objectives.[9] For example, inmate leaders some-times operate as an interest group and press for control over routine decisions because such control gives them additional power to exact recognition and conformity from other inmates. Political leaders be-come an interest group when they see a parole agency as a resource for discharging political obligations, and they demand that the agency be so organized that the skills of political appointees, not experts, can be used. Church groups sometimes band together to support or oppose a correctional program on moral grounds. Because there is a strong belief in our society that "doing a good job" is a reward in it-self and that laziness and lack of "self-discipline" are sinful, such groups tend to support custody, work programs, and training rather than "treatment." Prison guards become an interest group when they perceive that prison discipline for inmates is becoming so relaxed that the guards might be in danger.

Another type of interest group is directly concerned with preventing innovations which threaten its existing activities or plans. Police often constitute an interest group of this kind. They, even more than correctional workers, are charged with keeping the crime rate low, and they tend to oppose any correctional change which might reduce the degree of custody and surveillance. Similarly, social welfare groups and educational groups oppose any correctional changes which threaten to upset treatment and training routines; industrial groups oppose any organization of employment or employment services which will compete with them; and labor groups oppose any innovation which might reduce the number of jobs for non-criminals.

Other interest groups exist as such because they are obligated to groups directly involved in correctional activities. A group interested in family welfare, for example, may side with prisoners' aid societies and put pressure on correctional administrators by means of speeches, newspaper publicity, and endorsements. In response, still other groups side with correctional interest groups organized around different values. The innovation or lack of innovation which is the issue in conflict may be lost in the political dispute between the various coalitions.

In this situation, effective action on the part of a correctional administrator depends upon realistic assessment of the power possessed by interest groups. When he makes a commitment to any given group or to any coalition of groups, his freedom of action is henceforth limited. If, at the same time, he decides not to commit himself to other groups or coalitions, his freedom to introduce innovations is limited even more. He is able to make some innovative moves because the mandates given by correctional interest groups ordinarily are stated in broad terms and consequently have broad tolerance limits. For example, the directives coming from interest groups usually specify objectives but ordinarily do not spell out in great detail the means to be used for achieving them. Accordingly, the correctional administrator can "compromise" by adjusting in minor ways the networks of interest groups which differ in significant respects from each other.

The conservatism of corrections is in part a reflection of the necessity for caution in making such compromises. As power and influence are redistributed in the network of interest groups, new forms of correctional activities emerge. These become routinized as a new compromise, a new balance of interests. Such routinized activities, then, are at any given moment what Ohlin has called "the crystalized solutions of the problematic or crisis situation from which they emerged.[10] Correctional personnel at all levels participate in routinized activities and in that way are allied with correctional interest groups, whether they know it or not. This is the situation in which all employees share policy-making functions with management, making innovation extremely difficult.

If he is skillful, and if his organization is big enough, the correctional administrator can segregate his audiences by giving one part of his organization to one interest group while giving another part to a group with conflicting interests. For example, an interest group made up of social workers might be maneuvered so that it concentrates its concern on the boys' school or on correctional work with children generally, while an interest group composed of law enforcement personnel might have its interests reflected in one prison. Even one entire unit of a correctional agency, such as a prison or a parole unit, may be given to interests supporting a welfare and treatment policy, while another unit is given to interests supporting a punitive and surveillance policy. But the specialization of correctional units should not be overemphasized. Every unit reflects the interests of many different groups, making change difficult.

It is significant, however, that no important interest group has been pressuring for the use of correctional clients as rehabilitation agents. On the contrary, the moral and almost sacred character of correctional work encourages existing interest groups to oppose such an innovation. Any innovations proposed by correctional workers are subject to veto by some of the influential owners of the agencies employing them.

CONSERVATISM OF CORRECTIONAL PERSONNEL

Perhaps it is ambivalence and conflict in penal theory, together with a complex structure of correctional organizations, that underlies the most striking attitude among correctional workers—an attitude of "standing by." The ambivalence in theory has permitted various interest groups collectively to establish organizational structures which are extraordinarily difficult to change. But interest groups often can be pacified by external appearances and a display of organizational charts, and perhaps it is for this reason that internal pressure for significant innovation rarely occurs.

There certainly is variation from state to state and from agency to agency, but if one looks at correctional workers as a whole he sees among them very little concern for the design of innovations which would put real rehabilitative processes into the "treatment" organizations of prisons and probation-parole agencies. These structures were created some years ago in response to pressures from interest groups.

As indicated, however, the mandates given correctional administrators by interest groups tend to be stated in broad terms. Consequently, the mere creation of "treatment" organizations within correctional institutions and agencies pacified some of the groups pushing treatment as a correctional objective. By and large, groups pressuring for "treatment" of criminals have left invention of the processes for administering "treatment" up to the correctional workers themselves, and correctional workers have not been innovative. Rather than experimenting with techniques based on rehabilitation or treatment principles specifically related to corrections, they have used processes vaguely based on general psychiatric theory. The resistance to innovation here has been more in the form of indifference than in the form of planned conservativism. There are two simple kinds of evidence that this kind of resistance is present in corrections.

First, the establishment of "treatment" organizations has permitted workers to engage in "treatment services" without ever defining them. It is extraordinarily difficult to define and identify "rehabilitation techniques" and even more difficult to measure the effectiveness of such techniques.[11] The objective of "treatment" programs in corrections is to change probationers, prisoners, and parolees so that they will no longer be law-breakers. Yet, so far as I know, no correctional worker has ever been fired because so few of his clients have reformed. Perhaps this indifference to employee efficiency arises because a scientific technique for modification of attitudes has yet to be stated and implemented. Instead of precise descriptions of techniques for changing attitudes, the correctional literature contains statements indicating that rehabilitation is to be induced "through friendly admonition and encouragement," "by relieving emotional tension," "by stimulating the probationer's self-respect and ambition," "by establishing a professional relationship with him," "by encouraging him to have insight into the basis of his maladjustment," etc. We need to know—but we do not know—how these things are accomplished and, more significantly, how, or whether, they work to rehabilitate criminals. Two practicing correctional workers who turned textbook writers have commented:

Stripped to their essentials, these "instructions" boil down to exhortations to treat, to befriend, and to encourage. In effect, our treatment personnel are often told little more than to *go out there and rehabilitate somehow*—precisely how is not indicated. A military commander who confined his strategic orders to the commands, "Be brave, be careful, and be victorious" would be laughed out of uniform. Often, however, the technical directions given to correctional workers are scarcely more specific.[12]

Because treatment structures have been introduced in defiance of interest groups demanding that corrections be organized for punishment, custody, and surveillance, there has been a tendency on the part of correctional workers to define "treatment" negatively. Rather than identifying what treatment is, they have been content to assert what it is not: Any method of dealing with offenders that involves purposive infliction of pain and suffering, including psychological restrictions, is not treatment. This premise obviously must create strain in a total correctional organization that is expected to be restrictive and punitive. In the processes designed to implement it, there seems to be a mixture of social work and psychiatric theory, humanitarianism, and ethics of the middle class.[13]

Second, because correctional administrators must justify all aspects of their total organization to one interest group or another, the research undertaken by research bureaus located in correctional agencies tends to be somewhat programmatic, rather than the kind that provides the basis for real change in the techniques used to change criminals. For example, research in California indicated that if parole caseloads are reduced to 15 and parolees are accorded "intensive supervision" during the first 90 days after release and then transferred to the normal 90-man caseloads for regular supervision, only slight reductions in parole violation rates occur.[14] But no one knows *why* this experiment, like others, turned out the way it did, principally because no one knows what, specifically, was involved in "intensive supervision" or "intensive treatment" that is not included when the procedure is not "intensive." The experiment seemingly was introduced as much to reduce caseloads as to determine whether a correctional innovation was effective.

Correctional workers should not be blamed or attacked for what appears to be a lack of progress in developing basic principles on which to build sound correctional practice. The condition seems to be rooted in the very nature of the occupation, so that it is not easily changed. At least an attitude of "standing by" seems to be rooted in correctional work in a way that experimental and innovative attitudes are not. Four principal conditions seem to be associated with this conservatism: humanitarianism, poor advertising, bureaucracy, and professionalization.

Humanitarianism as "Treatment"

One of the principal handicaps to developing and utilizing new rehabilitation techniques in modern corrections arises from the fact that we introduced and continued to justify humane handling of criminals on the ground that such humanitarianism is "treatment." One significant consequence is a confusion of humanitarianism and treatment. In speaking of prisons, for example, we now are likely to contrast the "barbaric" conditions of the eighteenth century with the enlightened "treatment methods" of our time, especially in California. Yet we do this knowing that an insignificant porportion of all persons employed in American prisons are directly concerned with administration of treatment or training. We do not know what percentage of probation and parole workers is engaged in treatment and training, and what percentage is engaged in mere surveillance. Neither do we know what percentage of an individual worker's time is devoted to each of these activities. We are inclined to say that *all* probation and parole workers are engaged in treatment and that *all* of a worker's time is devoted to this end.

On what do we base this notion that holds, essentially, that probation and parole are, by themselves, treatment? Perhaps we base it on a logic that goes something like this: Humanitarianism is treatment. Parole is humanitarian. Therefore, parole is treatment. Thus, when we say that criminals are being "treated," we mean something like "They are being treated well," *i.e.*, handled humanely. It has been shown that, in prisons, a pattern of indulgence among employees is itself considered "treatment" by professional personnel serving as administrators.[15]

Correctional workers are increasingly being asked to show the effects of "treatment," but they can produce little evidence of efficiency because much of what has been called "treatment" is merely humanitarianism. Budgets for "treatment" have been doubled in some states, but the recidivism rate has remained constant. Over the years, punitive measures, custodial routines, and surveillance measures were relaxed on the ground that such humanitarian relaxation is treatment. Now it is becoming necessary to try to show why this "treatment" has not been more effective. Occasionally someone argues, usually in connection with a budget request, that no treatment principles have been invented and that, therefore, treatment has never been tried. More often, it is indirectly argued that humanitarianism disguised as treatment has not worked because "inhumane" persons and policies in corrections and in society have opposed it. It would appear that correctional leaders have been so busy defending humanitarianism, on the ground that it is treatment, that they have not had time to develop treatment principles and practices. For that matter, they have little time to study the possibilities of applying principles developed by outside psychologists and sociologists.

Poor Advertising

The second condition associated with conservatism in correctional theory and practice, poor advertising, is closely related to the first.

Humanitarians have left to correctional agencies themselves both the problem of justifying humanitarianism on the ground that it is treatment, and the problem of implementing that humanitarianism. But correctional workers are by their very nature poor propagandists for the humanitarian view, even if it is called "treatment." Correctional agencies are political units whose budgets and activities are, in the last analysis, controlled by politicians. And most politicians who want to continue being politicians must be opposed to crime as well as to sin and man-eating sharks. It simply is not expedient for a government worker to advocate being "soft" on criminals, even if he thinks he can show that being "soft" is somehow more efficient than not being "soft."[16] Police and prosecuting attorneys are excellently organized for promotion of the view that criminals should be dealt with harshly, but correctional workers are not, and probably cannot be, as efficiently organized for the humanitarian point of view.

Bureaucracy and Housekeeping

The third condition associated with the conservatism about theory and practice in correctional work is the bureaucratic organization necessary to the continuation of correctional agencies themselves. In the "good old days" of corrections, the probation-parole worker, at least, was somewhat of an individualist who played it by ear. Some of these workers got a variety of wild ideas about rehabilitation from a variety of sources and then tried them out on specific probationers and parolees. Most of the ideas did not work, but some of them seemed to be effective, and a few of those that seemed effective changed the course of correctional work.

This style of individualism is rapidly disappearing, especially in large agencies located in urban areas. Instead of rather independent workers who are trying out wild ideas, we have men who are not allowed to go into the field until they have proved to a training officer their ability to recite and adhere to agency policy, who are given "professional supervision" so they will not deviate from that policy, who are the recipients of newsletters that tell them what the "team" is up to, and who are expected to be familiar with the standard operating procedure set forth in manuals written in the home office for the guidance of men in the field. Like prison guards in the olden days, probation-parole workers are becoming strapped down by bureaucracy.

There is no reason to believe that the bureaucratization of correctional work should involve processes different from the processes of bureaucratization elsewhere.[17] One effect of bureaucratization is conservatism and routinization. On a simple level, the work done by employees must be performed within the framework of an 8-hour day and a 40-hour week, and this means that it must, by and large, be performed at a special work station. On a more complex level, it may be observed that in a bureaucracy there are bureaucrats, and a bureaucrat is primarily concerned with housekeeping. It is for this reason that one keen observer of the American scene calls bureaucrats "women in men's clothing." The male principle, he argues, is that of wasteful and reckless experimentation, risk, and creation. The female principle is that of compromise, conservation, monopoly, complacency, and "results."[18] In correctional work, it appears, we have become housekeepers rather than reckless experimenters. Perhaps this is in part why outsiders are likely to view correctional workers as "weak sisters" and "old women."

Experimentation and innovation have traditionally involved individualistic processes quite different in nature from bureaucratic administrative processes. In fact, some of the most significant inventions made in the last two centuries were made by men who did not have the qualifications for making them. That is, these innovators were individualistic and creative, but not formally trained for or employed in the area of science or technology where their discoveries were made. The inventor of the cotton gin was an unemployed school teacher, the inventor of the steamship was a jeweler, the inventor of probation was a shoemaker, and the inventor of conditional release and parole was a sailor. Innovators and experimenters are not necessarily good "team men." A famous chemist, Cavendish, had an immense dislike of people, and he dismissed any maid working in his house if he so much as laid eyes on her. Darwin, who had no formal scientific training, withdrew to a country house and had very little association with professional colleagues or anyone else.

In correctional agencies that have grown to the point where professionalism and concordant bureaucracy have appeared, individual innovation, experimentation, and attempted implementation of wild ideas must necessarily be controlled. If this is not done, organizational routines might be embarrassingly upset. One control procedure is creation of a "research team," a "research division," or a "planning and development section," which is to contain the experimenters. This custom can block innovation, for the larger the team, the more difficult it is to get concurrence that racially new concepts are worth risking the team's reputation on. After all, if the new plan goes sour, is attacked, ridiculed, and deprecated, the time and energy of all the team members, not just one crackpot, are brought into question. In corrections, a research team is not necessarily conducive to development of radically new procedures, such as using offenders and ex-offenders as correctional workers. Someone has said that sociology has been characterized by a retreat into methodology, meaning that sociologists have refused to take stands on social issues and have instead increasingly been concerned with the methods by which they arrive at conclusions. By the same kind of reasoning, we can observe that correctional innovation might be starting to experience an analogous type of retreat—a retreat into research.

Profession vs. Occupation

The fourth condition associated with conservatism among correctional workers is professionalization. Because professional personnel such as social workers, psychologists, and psychiatrists have constituted an interest group pressuring for "treatment" in corrections, it is somewhat paradoxical to observe that strong resistance to further change is characteristic of this group. There is no doubt that professional personnel have been instrumental in diminishing the punishment-custody-surveillance aspects of corrections, largely in the name of "treatment." However, the same personnel tend to be conservative with reference to changes in professional practices themselves. "Professionalization" implies standardization of practice, with the result that the kind of bureaucratization just discussed is perhaps more characteristic of professional personnel than anyone else in corrections.

Among the characteristics of a profession is monopolization of specialized knowledge, including theory and skills.[19] When an occupation is professionalized, access to its specialized knowledge is restricted, definition of the content of the knowledge is uniform, and determination of whether a specific person possesses the knowledge is determinable by examination. Further, professional personnel ordinarily establish formal associations, with definite membership criteria based on possession of the specialized knowledge and specifically aimed at excluding "technically unqualified" personnel. The name selected by the association generally is unusual enough so that not just anyone can use it, again indicating a monopoly on a piece of theory and a set of skills. If the profession has developed a code of ethics, as professions eventually do, the code consists of a number of interrelated propositions which assert the occupation's devotion to public welfare and, more important to conservatism, stipulate standards of practice and standards for admission. Neither practitioners nor trainees can be allowed to "go it alone" in such a way that new or different standards are developed. They must learn the established code and behave according to the standards it implies. They must, in other words, accept the professional culture. In most instances, professions make their conservatism legal by gaining legislation which limits practice to those who have passed a state-administered examination or who are certified by the state upon completion of a specialized course of study, usually in a university. Often it is a crime for uncertified persons to perform the acts reserved to members of the profession. Concurrently, practices such as the privilege of confidentiality might be reserved for professionals.

In correctional work, these characteristics of professionalization are especially relevant to the proposition that correctional clients themselves should be used as workers and managers of the rehabilitation process. "Professionalization" of correctional work has stressed monopolization of knowledge of "treatment," "rehabilitation" or "reformation" processes, not of knowledge about custody, management, surveillance, and repression. Accordingly, "professionalization" has come to stand for the ideology of "professional personnel" such as psychologists, psychiatrists, and social workers.

The proposal that clients be used as correctional rehabilitators boldly asserts that persons characteruzed by professional correctional personnel as "laymen" or "subprofessional workers" can achieve what professionals say can be achieved only after years of specialized training. After having participated in a half-dozen or more years of pre-professional and professional training and after having worked his way up in a hierarchy of occupational and professional ranks, the professional in corrections is likely to take a dim view of any suggestion that what he is doing could be done as efficiently (or perhaps more efficiently) by a person without his training and experience.

Moreover, "professionalization" implies that personnel will *not* engage in certain practices, just as it implies that certain practices are reserved to an elite group of personnel. Status as a professional person implies a position of high rank involving little or no dirty work. An admiral does not expect to chip paint, and a doctor does not expect to carry bedpans. As nursing has become professionalized in recent years, nurses do not expect to carry bedpans either. And as social work has become professionalized, social workers do not expect to carry baskets of food to the poor. Such activities are "unprofessional." In correctional work, innovations which would require the professionals to perform the equivalent of chipping paint, carrying bedpans, and carrying baskets of food to the poor are bound to be resisted by the professionals. Yet since World War II almost everyone working in the field of rehabilitation has argued that involvement in this kind of work, especially in "milieu therapy," is essential to rehabilitation.

It also should be noted that correctional administrative positions are increasingly being assigned to professional personnel. When this is the case, an administrator's income and status often depend upon his ability to maintain professional practices which over the years have been defined as "standard" and "good." One who is the director of a correctional rehabilitation program or crime prevention program does more than try to rehabilitate criminals or prevent crime. He administers an organization that provides employment for its members, and he confers status on these members as well as on himself. In other words, personal and organizational needs supplement the societal needs met by administration and utilization of various correctional techniques. The personal and organizational needs are met by correctional institutions, agencies, and programs. By utilizing or advocating use of "professional methods" in correctional work, a person may secure employment and income, a good professional reputation, scholarly authority, prestige as an intellectual, the power stemming from being the champion of a popular cause, and many other personal rewards. An agency organized around administration of "professional methods" may fill such needs for dozens, even hundreds, of employees.

Because of personal and organizational investments, personnel dedicated to rehabilitating criminals are likely to maintain that criminality is reduced by whatever it is they are doing. Vague statistical measures of efficiency are valuable and useful because they decrease the range of points on which disagreements and direct challenges can occur.[20] Yet any suggestion for radical change is an implicit criticism, and it therefore is helpful if the efficiency question can be avoided by announcing that the proposed change would introduce procedures that are "substandard" or "unprofessional."

More specifically, acquisition and preservation of the knowledge and ethics of the social work profession is becoming an essential characteristic of what we are beginning to call "the corrections profession" and "the professional correctional worker." Education for the corrections profession has been considered the province of schools of social work. The assumption generally has been that students being educated for participation in the social work profession are, at the same time, being educated for the corrections profession. This means that students of social work cannot be given specialized knowledge and skills which are peculiar to correctional work but which are, at the same time, inconsistent with the ideology, theory, and standards of social work. Further, it is commonly but erroneously assumed that correctional work is so desirable that we can afford to require larger and larger proportions of all correctional personnel to have social work degrees, as we have been doing in recent years.

The individualistic theory of rehabilitation promulgated by social workers and other psychiatrically oriented personnel implies that until one has had at least six years of university training he is not qualified to try to rehabilitate a criminal. Since a highly educated staff has been considered a good staff, more highly educated personnel are sought. But this trend toward professionalization blinds professionals and non-professionals alike to innovations which would involve a lowering of educational standards for correctional workers. Use of offenders as correctional workers is resisted because, considered from the traditional viewpoint, such personnel do not possess indispensable social work skills.

OFFENDERS' RESISTANCE TO INNOVATION

Correctional clients are notoriously resistant to correctional innovations which would change them to significant degrees. In the first place, they usually have good reasons for not trusting the personnel paid to implement any rehabilitation program. It is a fact that some procedures used in administration of criminal justice are based on the theory that society must be hostile toward criminals in order to emphasize the undesirability of nonconformity. Criminals are committed to the care of correctional agencies against their will, and no amount of sugar-coating hides from them the fact that the first duty of correctional personnel is to protect society from criminals, not to rehabilitate individual criminals. Criminals often find it difficult to distinguish between correctional procedures designed to punish them and correctional procedures designed to help them.

Similarly, they are not at all confident that correctional personnel ostensibly engaged to help them are not actually engaged to assist in punishing them and keeping them under control. They note, for example, that in most prisons the treatment and rehabilitation specialists are subordinate to officials who emphasize the necessity for maintaining order, even if maintaining order interferes with treatment practices. They know that the prison psychiatrist or social worker might have the task of stopping "rumbles" and "cooling out" threatening inmates, rather than rehabilitating criminals. They know that revocation of probation or parole depends as much on the attitudes of the probation-parole officer as on the behavior of the client. Further, they know that the pressures put on them to reform or become rehabilitated have as much to do with the good of "society" or the good of middle-class property-owners as they have to do with the good of the individual criminal himself. Most criminals have very little confidence that the immense amount of data collected on them will be used for their benefit. As a sophisticated ex-convict has written, "The prisoner's need to live and the system's attempt to live for him (and off him) can never be reconciled."[21] In current correctional circumstances, clients have a minimal sense of obligation to the personnel controlling their fate. If, as McCorkle and Korn argued some years ago, criminals are intent on rejecting their rejector,[22] correctional programs will succeed only if the degree of rejection by society is diminished.

Second, neither criminals nor ex-criminals are convinced that they need either existing correctional programs or any program which might be invented in the future. They cooperate with correctional workers, not in order to facilitate their own reformation but in order to secure release from surveillance as quickly as possible and as unscathed as possible. Prisoners, for example, participate in group therapy, group counseling, and individual "intensive treatment" programs as much from a belief that doing so will impress the parole board as from a conviction that they, as individuals, need to change.

Once a criminal has gone through the impersonal procedures necessary to processing him as a law violator, about all he has left in the world is his "self." No matter what that self may be, he takes elaborate steps to protect it, to guard it, to maintain it. If it should be taken away from him, even in the name of rehabilitation or treatment, he will have lost everything. Old-fashioned punishment-custody-surveillance procedures were designed to exterminate each criminal's self. New-fangled correctional programs are designed to do the same thing. Although many criminals, especially inmates, favor "rehabilitation," strong resistance occurs when the rehabilitation technique hints at "brain-washing" or any other procedure which would change the essence of "what I am." A pill or an injection which would change a criminal into a non-criminal without changing the rest of him probably would be accepted with enthusiasm by most criminals. But attempts to change criminals into non-criminals by significantly changing their personalities or life styles threaten to take away all they have left in the world.

Third, probationers, parolees, and even ex-offenders are not likely to become very excited about any program which expects them to look upon the task of rehabilitating themselves as a full-time job. Taking a pill or an injection would be so much easier. Criminals, like others, have been taught that efforts at rehabilitation involve "technical," "professional," or even medical work on the part of a high-status employee, not hard work on the part of the person to be reformed. Moreover, for most criminals crime has been at most a moonlighting occupation or a brief, temporary engagement, and it follows that any personal involvement in their own rehabilitation also should be a part-time affair. Charles Slack demonstrated that it helps if delinquents are paid to perform duties believed by the experimenter to be reha-bilitative.[23] But some criminals would resist even if they were offered training for full-time paid employment as people-changers. The mar-ket for their skills is vague. Further, delinquents and criminals com-monly assume, perhaps correctly, that rehabilitators play a feminine, sissy role. Finally, many criminals and ex-criminals fear that even if they accepted employment as correctional workers they would find the work dull and boring, as some non-offenders do.

Fourth, a special kind of resistance to rehabilitation attempts is encountered in prisons, where inmates are in close interaction and have developed their own norms, rules, and belief systems. Wheeler has shown that inmate attitudes are not as opposed to staff norms as even inmates believe.[24] Nevertheless, for most prisoners, adjustment means attachment to, or at least acceptance by, the inmate group, Moreover, an inmate participating in a rehabilitation program, no matter what its character, is likely to be viewed as a nut, as a traitor, or as both. Strong resistance will be encountered when efforts to change individual criminals would, if successful, have the result of making them deviate from the norms of their membership groups and reference groups.[25] Even among probationers and parolees there is likely to be attachment to the values and beliefs of persons partici-pating in what Irwin and Cressy have described as the "thief subcul-ture," becuase this subculture stresses norms of "real men" and "right guys."[26]

It should be noted further that even when correctional programs are organized so as to make socially acceptable groups available to offenders, members of socially acceptable groups including some cor-rectional workers are not always ready to accept socially unacceptable offenders. When criminals and ex-criminals do band together to form anti-crime societies such as Synanon, they usually are shocked and then discouraged by finding that few persons, especially professional correctional workers, share their enthusiasm for their "cause."

Fifth, the special handling of some criminals is resisted by other criminals because the special handling is viewed as unfair. Criminals, perhaps more than other citizens, are concerned with justice, and one conception of justice views "special treatment" as unjust "special privilege" or "special favor." In prisons, especially, the punitive-cus-todial-administrative view is that all prisoners are equal and equally deserving of any "special privileges." They are not, of course. But when treatment criteria cannot be understood, handling inmates as special cases is likely to be interpreted to mean that the inmates in question are being given special privileges with reference to restrictive punishment. A prisoner who is released from prison because he has become "adjusted" or "rehabilitated" is not, from a treatment point of view, being granted a special privilege. But as he is being discharged for treatment reasons, he also is being released from the restrictions deliberately and punitively imposed on him. Accordingly, the discharge is likely to be viewed as a "reward" for good behavior. If, in the eyes of other inmates, the prisoner being discharged is no more deserving of release from punishment than they are, then the discharge is considered unjust special privilege. Similarly, an inmate who is a bad actor in prison might be assigned to what inmates regard as a "good job" as therapy for his misconduct. Because it is often assumed that an inmate will begin to behave responsibly if he is given a position of responsibility, he might even be given a job as a correctional worker. But this therapeutic manipulation of the individual's environment might be viewed by inmates as an unjust reward for misconduct.

If this attitude were held by many inmates it would be a serious threat to institutional security. Inmates might rebel in response to the "injustice" of "special privilege." Or, on the other hand, they might start misbehaving so as to win for themselves a similar "reward." Were "inmate need" the sole criterion used for distributing goods in short supply, then inmate cooperation in meeting institutinal needs would be minimal.

Treatment programs which would create such problems, or which threaten to create such problems, are roundly resisted by administrators and inmate leaders alike. The same thing is true in correctional work with probationers and parolees, but perception of special handling as unjust is limited because these clients are not in close association with each other. In prisons, the basic interpersonal relationship among inmates is one of dominance and subordination. This relationship is the foundation on which peace and order are maintained. But, as McCleery has shown, both the relationship of dominance and subordination and the social order supported by it depend upon an official policy of treating all inmates as equals.[27] If the dominant inmates' demands for equality among all inmates were not met, the whole inmate social structure might be upset every time a busload of new inmates arrived.

In other words, peace in prisons depends upon a system in which inmates, not officials, allocate status symbols and special privileges. Any rehabilitation program which would require officials to allocate these symbols and privileges is likely to be viewed as unjust and therefore to be resisted.

37

ACHIEVING BETTER QUESTIONS: PROGRESS IN CORRECTIONAL RESEARCH

DANIEL GLASER

A review of a half century's research in corrections reveals much that is useful. Yet a study of its influence suggests that the primary contribution of past research to correctional progress is not in its answers to the questions that were investigated, but in its guidance to more fruitful questions.

WHAT WORKS?

The highway of correctional history is paved with punctured panaceas such as the perennial prescriptions of smaller caseloads and more counseling. In the 1950's and early 1960's these were accepted as curealls, and prescribed for all offenders. Thanks to research, primarily controlled experiments in California, we now know better.[28] We know that no single policy or service rehabilitates all offenders, and we have saved millions by vetoing proposals from practitioners who still recommend these costly expenditures for everyone.

"What works?" was the usual question raised by early promoters of correctional evaluation research. The answer suggested in the provocative Martinson review is: "With few and isolated exceptions . . . rehabilitative efforts . . . have had no appreciable effect on recidivism."[29] This conclusion is applied to academic education, vocational training, individual counseling, group counseling, transforming the institutional environment, medical treatment, early release, intensive supervision, and community treatment. Martinson's persuasive interpretations of his findings are: (1) The impact of rehabilitation effort has usually been negligible by comparison with that of the crime-generating conditions in our society, or in our correctional

Source: From *Federal Probation*, XXXIX, 3(September 1975): 3-9. Reprinted by permission of the publisher.

institutions; (2) some rehabilitation efforts may actually have consequences opposite to those intended, for they seem to foster more crime than they prevent; (3) deterrence alone—from the punishment involved in arrest and confinement regardless of the correctional program—often has an important impact which researchers overlook.

Actually, in over 40 percent of the correctional evaluation studies that Martinson summarizes in his article, he indicates distinctly positive results for some programs for certain types of offenders or in some circumstances,[30] and often negative effects are evident from the same program for other types of offenders.[31] The differential impact revealed in so many studies dramatizes how unsound was the thinking of those who expected that a single service or procedure they were testing would reduce recidivism for almost all offenders.

Correctional researchers and their sponsors have often resembled the many medical adventurers who sought a single remedy for all human ailments, but were eventually discredited. Instead, medicine and all other complex applied science efforts that have been very fruitful—for example, making synthetic fibers, increasing crop yields, or finding oil—have advanced beyond the global "What works?" question. To some extent they moved, as many advocate for corrections, to the question of "What works best for what subjects or materials under what circumstances?" The greatest gains, however, have come from answering questions that begin with "Why."

Knowledge grows not just from objective evidence, but from an interaction between evidence and inference. In all well-established sciences, theory guides research and research tests theory. Therefore, that which is accepted as the scientific basis for practice in agriculture, engineering, medicine and other applied sciences more clearly successful than criminology, consists not so much of specific facts as of established explanatory principles that can guide practical decisions. Accordingly, the most important queries, if we are to gain useful knowledge from correctional research, are of the type: "Why does a program reduce recidivism in certain kinds of offenders under certain circumstances?" and "Why does this program not reduce recidivism in other kinds of offenders or in other circumstances?" But how are scientific answers to such questions procured?

WHY DO OFFENDERS CHANGE OR NOT CHANGE?

In any applied science, the answers to "why" questions—the explanations—come from established theory of the underlying "pure" sciences. Thus the answers in engineering come mainly from physics and the explanations in scientific agriculture come from chemistry, plant physiology, genetics and microbiology. In corrections we are concerned with the conduct of people, individually or collectively. Accordingly, our explanations must come from the behavioral or social sciences. They will be special applications to corrections of general principles that account for the patterning of human behavior in a large variety of circumstances. Psychology, sociology, anthropology, economics, and history can all be useful.

From modern psychology we draw the well-validated laws of learning, notably: Rewarded behavior tends to be repeated, while behavior that is not rewarded tends to be extinguished—to disappear; behavior that is punished in circumstances where it previously was rewarded tends to disappear only while it evokes punishment, and to recur thereafter unless alternative behavior has been rewarded in these circumstances; behavior that previously was rewarded intermittently is less readily extinguished by interruption of the rewards than behavior that previously had always been rewarded.

From social psychology, a field shared by psychology, and sociology, we gain an appreciation of the extent to which people find their primary rewards in a favorable conception of themselves, we recognize that this self-conception comes mainly from their view of the attitudes of others toward them, and we therefore understand why they seek the companionship of those whose approval they evoke. From sociology and anthropology we learn the basic law that social separation fosters cultural differentiation, so that forced or voluntary segregation of those whose behavior is deviant fosters deviant subcultures. From economics we learn the laws of supply and demand, and of reciprocity in exchange, which explains the continual emergence of channels for the marketing of stolen goods, narcotics and illegal services, as well as many correlates of property offenses.

In addition to these abstract principles applicable to humans in all times and places, there are historical trends pertinent to understanding and controlling contemporary crime in the United States. Technological changes have accelerated urbanization and have raised the demanded levels of educational attainment. Thus the median years of schooling of adults in our country rose between the 1940 and 1970 censuses from 8 to more than 12 years. The poor from the rural United States mainland—especially the South—and from adjacent Spanish-speaking areas have been crowded•into our slums since World War II. Their children and grandchildren were linguistically handicapped in our schools, and thus were more impeded in legitimate pursuits than were youth of previous eras, when educational deficiencies were not such a drawback. Therefore, it should not be surprising if today's youth with school problems are more predictably attracted to the alternative opportunities for distinction that theft, drugs or violence can provide, especially when with associates who have similar problems.[32] Furthermore, the decline of family businesses, the inventions that reduce chores in the home, the high rates of divorce and separation, and the growth of age-specific recreational facilities, have increased the separation of adolescents from adults in virtually all segments of our population and thus impeded traditional social control of delinquency by the family.

Unfortunately, little research of the past half century has directly focused on applying such behavioral and social science knowledge to corrections. Nevertheless, these explanatory perspectives can guide criminal justice policies and can give future investigations a more adequate grounding in both basic science and past criminological research than has been typical of correctional studies thus far.

WHAT WORKS FOR WHOM AND WHY?

It follows from the preceding comments that the focus of both policy and research in corrections should be on particular types of offenders, rather than on all of them collectively. Yet there is an infinite variety of ways of classifying criminals into types. Furthermore, no very elaborate and useful classification scheme can be applied with complete precision to a large cross section of correctional clientele, for most offenders have manifested some attributes distinctive of several categories in these schemes.

This difficulty in the use of any classification systems reflects several facts. First of all, many so-called types—for example, "novice" and "professional"—represent only extremes of a continuous dimension with all degrees of gradation, and with most offenders in our courts scattered somewhere between the extremes. Secondly, most criminal careers include some diversity of offenses and are describable by several different dimensions rather than a single one. Thirdly, people are somewhat inconsistent, so that a description of one period in their lives does not always fit another period.

Despite these problems in using typologies in corrections (and in most of the behavioral and social sciences), valid and practical explanatory and predictive generalizations can be made in terms of conceptually pure types, as long as it is recognized that there is frequent need to qualify or supplement them when dealing with actual cases. This procedure of starting with idealized types is analogous to a physician's use of medical principles formulated in terms of classic cases of a particular ailment, which must be modified in practice when the patient shows multiple ailments or other complications that require application of additional principles, rather than just those that would be considered if attention could be limited to the predominant ailment.[33]

This brief article cannot discuss all useful distinctions among correctional clientele, but research and theory indicate that three dimensions for classifying offenders are especially important in the guidance of criminal justice policy, and in anticipating the most fruitful new questions for researchers:

A. Commitment to a Career in Crime

Studies using anonymous questionnaires indicate that a majority of adults in the United States at one time or another, especially during adolescence, engage in shoplifting or other crimes for which serious penalties could be imposed, but that they do not persist in these activities. The high success rates of probation for adult first offenders,[34] and of community treatment rather than incarceration for so-called "neurotic" juvenile offenders,[35] suggest that those who get involved in crime but are not committed to it as a career are readily deterred by the threat of punishment and may be helped by counseling. Apparently, because such people have experienced enough rewards in pursuits and relationships that would be jeopardized by the stigma of crime, they have a stake in conformity with the law; if they forget this when they become involved in an offense, their arrest before they engage in much serious illegal activity makes crime unrewarding for them. The longer they are incarcerated, however, the less their stake in conformity is likely to become and the greater will be the prospect of their developing and accepting a conception of themselves as criminals.[36]

The other extreme of this dimension consists of people who have experienced much success in criminal pursuits and little in alternatives to crime. These include many juvenile recidivists who typically are unspecialized in their offenses, and adult professional criminals who tend to be specialists.[37]

Juveniles highly committed to criminal careers have usually had years of conflict with authorities and of enculturation in delinquent groups. Research indicates that they have lower recidivism rates following traditional institution confinement than after early release to their homes with intensive counseling by psychologists and social workers.[38] They also have lower recidivism rates as youthful inmates of penitentiaries if in typical programs than if in psychotherapy.[39] They benefit, however, from financial aid or graduated release through halfway houses rather than direct release,[40] and from intensive programmed education in correctional programs,[41] perhaps because most have previously had little successful experience in work or school when residing in homes of weak parental influence and in high delinquency neighborhoods.

The above findings support social science theory which suggests that to change such recidivistic youth one must foster their attaining rapport with adults whom they cannot readily manipulate, as well as their experiencing gratification in adult roles. Paraprofessionals, par-inversely with education and directly with extreme poverty. The reversal of this decline, from the mid-1950's to the mid-1970's, prob-large and necessarily regimented juvenile correctional institutions by small home facilities, custodially secure if necessary, should also be effective. Such experiments should be extended and their evaluation continued,[42] as well as programs directed to making education and work experiences more satisfying and successful for these youth.

Not enough is known of factors in recidivism reduction for professional criminals. The laws of learning imply that such long rewarding but often interrupted illegal pursuits are not readily changed. Case studies and the ages of known offenders, however, suggest that most eventually terminate their criminal careers, some in middle and some in old age. This usually occurs following extensive imprisonment, after which they either acquire legitimate trades or businesses, for a comfortable income, or more often, accept a very low standard of living.[43]

The preceding paragraphs describe the extremes of one dimension, commitment, although each paragraph could be considered descriptive of a distinct type. As suggested earlier, most offenders dealt with by a court or a correctional agency may be intermediate between these extremes. Furthermore, it is often difficult to assess commitment precisely; indeed, the official criminal record may not reveal it as accurately as indirect evidence, such as the discrepancy between an offender's standard of living in the community and his or her known legitimate income. Obviously, more research focused on the measurement, causes and consequences of commitment to criminality is much needed.

B. Violence of Offenders

Violence is a dimension of crime of special concern to the public. The rates of violent offenses known to the police, and of violent offenders among those confined in correctional institutions, have been increasing almost continuously for more than a decade. Meanwhile, the proportion of these crimes that are deadly has also increased markedly, reversing a 50 percent decline in our homicide rate from the early 1930's to the mid-1950's. In addition, the median age of persons arrested for homicide dropped sharply during the 1960's and 1970's.

Major factors in the decline of homicide for over 20 years after 1933 probably were the increasing urbanization and education of the population; homicide rates were higher in rural than in urban areas, then, especially in the Southern states, and they have always varied inversely with education and directly with extreme poverty. The reversal of this decline, from the mid-1950's to the mid-1970's, probably results from: (1) concentration in highly povertous urban slums of people from areas of the United States and Latin America with the highest homicide rates; (2) the already discussed increased isolation of youth from adults in our society; (3) especially, the fourfold increase in annual rates of manufacture and import of handguns in the United States between 1962 and 1968, and the continued high rates of handgun proliferation since then.[44]

Despite these trends and the public's concern, not much correctional research has focused on violence. Efforts to predict such offenses on parole yielded little of practical value,[45] apparently for three reasons: (1) the already indicated low specialization of juvenile recidivist offenders in any particular type of offense; (2) the relative rarity of recidivist offenders with careers purely in violent crime, despite the national publicity which some of them receive; (3) the apparent deterrent effect of penalties, and the consequent low recidivism rates of first offenders sentenced for such crimes.

What seems to be more promising is a focus of research on altering the behavior of those who have had repeated physical altercations, whether in crimes for which they were convicted or in fights that were not prosecuted but that nevertheless impeded their adjustment at school, at home, at work or in institutions. Studies thus far suggest at least three fruitful approaches to this task. The first is with experiments in crisis intervention and role-reversal training for the violence-prone, as pioneered by Bard and Toch.[46] Since rates of violence are directly correlated with associates who share a "subculture of violence," and inversely correlated with education, a second type of desirable experiment is with training of the violence-prone in verbal communication skills, whether through programs such as the Dale Carnegie course, active group therapy, inmate government, debating clubs, team sports, or any other formal groups stressing inhibition of violence and fostering verbal interaction in its place. Closely related is a third type of research, on facilitating and encouraging mixtures of offenders of diverse backgrounds and ages, and of both sexes, as well as increasing gratifying personal contacts with ex-offenders or with non-offenders (for example, through the Quaker or senior citizen visitor programs).

C. Alcohol and Drug Abuse

Throughout the known history of these statistics in the United States, a large majority of arrestees for misdemeanors, a smaller majority of arrestees for violent felonies, and an appreciable percentage of arrestees for other types of felony, were under the influence of alcohol at the time of their offense. Particularly extensive were small-scale forgeries and other petty property crimes committed by chronic alcoholics without funds when anxious to initiate or to continue drinking sprees. Added to these offenses in the past decades have been habitual property crimes perpetrated to pay the high costs of addiction to opiates. A large fraction of correctional clientele in the past quarter century have been sentenced for possession or sale of drugs, often discovered when they were arrested for other offenses.

It seems evident that we are moving to an ethic of letting people "do their own thing" to their bodies with any type of substance, provided they do not injure others; even if they impair their health and neglect their family obligations, the criminal law seems ineffective to correct their addiction. This ethic prevailed in the 1930's with the repeal of our alcohol prohibition laws; since then we only try to educate people on the risks they may be imposing on themselves by drinking too much, but alcoholic beverages are available for purchase if anyone wishes to use or abuse them. Decriminalization of public drunkenness by medical detoxification centers replacing jails for drunks, and the growth of methadone maintenance for heroin addicts, also suggest the shifting of responsibility for dealing with drug abuse from criminal justice to public health and education institutions. While these developments probably will reduce drug-related crimes, they may also reduce nondrug offenses and affect police and court decisions and efficiency; these hypotheses pose important questions for researchers in the coming decades.

Why Does Correctional Policy Change or Not Change?

The newest and perhaps the future's most important sources of theory for correctional studies may well be political science and its related sub-discipline, political sociology. Possibly the major reason correctional researchers are developing an interest in these perspectives has been the repeated frustration of efforts to change policy and practice by traditional types of scientific inquiry.

One method of explaining this past frustration is to study the differences between what was presumed to happen to correctional practice or offender experience and what actually occurred in various research projects that failed to reduce recidivism. Efforts to motivate inmate participation in counseling, education, or vocational training in prison, by propagating the belief that any or all of these will reduce their term of confinement before parole, may only increase their manipulative and insincere participation in these activities; it may impair rather than encourage the utilization of these services by offenders who sincerely seek such aid for self-improvement.[47] What is more, a little schooling or vocational training may be antirehabilitative in corrections, by increasing unrealistic expectations and subsequent frustration, as compared with sufficient quantity and quality of education to make a very definite increase in an offender's economic and social opportunities.

A second approach is to investigate the tactical moves, negotiations and bargaining of special interest groups in resisting or achieving correctional change. The pioneer and continuing leader in this field has been Harvard's Professor Lloyd E. Ohlin, both in his theoretical writing,[48] and in his already cited and prospective studies on the closing of juvenile correctional institutions in Massachusetts. Additional research of this type is beginning to emerge, but much more is needed.

CONCLUSION

The history of science, Thomas Kuhn points out, is marked not by continuous cumulative growth so much as by periodic incremental jumps or surges following the introduction of new perspectives for looking at problems.[49] Dramatic revolutions for correctional science are not suggested here, but a series of new perspectives are pointed out as the most important gains from the past half-century of correctional research.

38

DIRECTIONS
FOR CORRECTIONS

LESLIE T. WILKINS

BELIEFS VERSUS DATA

The subject matter of penology lies somewhere between religion, morals, and politics, and is buffeted by changing technology and the state of knowledge. Perhaps this is why, if you ask the average man-in-the-street (or on the Clapham omnibus for that matter!), what ought to be done about thieves and robbers, drug addicts and sexual deviants, it is expected that whatever views he may express will be asserted with considerable conviction and certitude. On the other hand, if you were to ask a person who has been associated with an academic study of these problems there will be far less conviction and certainty expressed. Furthermore, the layman will seldom differentiate between the two quite different questions; what ought to be done, and what kinds of treatment might be meted out to offenders such that they were least likely to commit any further crimes. Questions of values and questions of efficiency are all too often confused.[50]

PERSONS, THINGS, AND SITUATIONS

Acts which are defined as crimes are, of course, assumed to be undesirable to the majority of the population. There are also other kinds of events which have similarly undesirable consequences. However, the fact that an act is considered to be a crime focuses attention on the offender as the cause almost to the exclusion of other elements in the crime situation—the opportunities, the physical environment, the victim or, indeed, the law itself. The belief that crime can be solved by dealing only with one element in the complex of forces and situations is indicated in the language which is used. A crime is

Source: From *Proceedings of the American Philosophical Society,* 118, 3(June 1974): 235–247. Reprinted by permission of the publisher.

said to be solved when a person has been identified who performed the act. When somebody can be blamed, there is little else which seems to be regarded as necessary—all television dramas of the who-done-it variety end there. The idea of crime control through environmental planning; the study of victimless crimes; the analysis of opportunity and target hardening and all other methods which are not totally offender-related are quite new.[51] It is still a heresy to suggest that some crime problems can be generated and exacerbated by what is done (with the best of all possible intentions) to reduce the problem. The modification of economic theory to consider illegal transactions has not yet had much attention and it is not surprising that few successes can be quoted in the development of macro-control methods of crime prevention.

While I shall deal with certain aspects of penology (which is concerned with the ways in which offenders are dealt with), this should not be taken to indicate that it is my view that the major impact upon the dysfunctional behavior which we designate as crime, can be best controlled by inventing further forms of punishment, treatments, or conditionings. Rather than seek to deal with social ills because they are believed to be causes of crime, I would recommend that we should deal with them because they are social ills. Rather than expect that a more than marginal change in the incidence and prevalence of crime might be related to action concerning offenders, I would expect more profit to arise from research investment in the study of victims, the environment in which crimes take place, the decision processes of criminal justice personnel, and the economics of the illicit market place. In short, the excessive emphasis in the past upon the offender has not paid off and if we are to deal realistically with crime it is necessary to study less romantic and dramatic elements— to emphasize *things* and *situations* in relation to *decisions.*

If a different perspective is taken in regard to the balance of elements in crime control, the offender (who is usually poor and will always be with us) may fit into the picture in a somewhat different way. There are outstanding problems in relation to rational and ethical action with regard to offenders. Even if he ceases to be the chief focus of our attack upon crime, the offender has to be dealt with, if only because he is *there.*

SOCIAL CONTROL AND MORALS:
SOCIO-CULTURAL NORMS FOR PUNISHMENT

The problem of crime is larger than the problem of the offender. In order to establish a setting for the consideration of penology in contemporary society it seems necessary first to note some of the more general socio-cultural factors which may underlie differences in approach and give an indication of the background to some problems.

It is interesting to note that it is possible for persons from almost any country to be tourists in other countries throughout the world without running into difficulties with the criminal law; this despite that fact that, in law, a person who is visiting a different country is assumed to have agreed to abide by the laws of that country. We might, from this observation, assume that the moral values and norms supported by the law and for breach of which penalties will be incurred, are of considerable similarity in almost all countries of the world. This is indeed the case. The imposition of laws by colonial powers was complained of by many countries which have recently gained independence. National commissions, set up in these countries to work out a law more suited to the culture and new national identity have failed to produce criminal codes differing in any significant degree; and such differences have related to religious practices or victimless crimes. There are certainly few differences in the norms supported by the criminal law among the countries of the Western world.

Despite this similarity of the expected forms of behavior on the part of citizens and residents of the countries of, for example, the European Common Market, the extent of punishment seems to vary widely. There are no satisfactory international statistics which would enable comparisons in any degree of detail. However, there is one figure which seems to be highly comparable and which has a high degree of expected accuracy. Persons who are in prison in any country are counted; counted very frequently! Persons who have lost their liberty because of accusation of criminal behavior may represent various categories of persons, but all are clearly defined by the appropriate authorities in the country as being unworthy of being at liberty within that culture. The proportion of the populations of countries (a) at liberty and (b) incarcerated, would seem to provide one reasonable measure. The incarceration rate in the early 1970's in Holland is about twenty-five per hundred thousand; in England and Wales about one hundred per hundred thousand; while in Norway it is about fifty per hundred thousand.[52] Both Canada and the United States (national) have rates about 200 per hundred thousand. The range of difference in the incarceration rate between countries at the present time is far greater than the range of variation which can be found within any country for which data exist over the last hundred years. For England and Wales, for example, it is necessary to go back as far as 1852 to find an incarceration rate as high as that which now applies in that country. Between the two world wars the incarceration rate dropped to around the same figure as now characterizes Holland, namely, less than thirty per hundred thousand. Other countries show less variation over the last fifty years. Thus we may conclude that differences in incarceration (the proportion of the society which is defined as outcast) varies more between countries than within countries. As one crude measure of the effectiveness of the action taken to deal with criminals, it might be expected that the countries with high incarceration rates would show less crime—particularly as they have followed the same policy for many years. Exact tests cannot be made, but it is evident that there is no correlation in the expected direction. If a correlation exists, it indicates that the countries with lower incarceration rates over long periods of time have less crime today than those which have consistently practiced a more punitive policy.[53]

THE STAGE ARMY OF PRISONERS

The main component of the variation in the incarceration rates in different countries is the mean time for each offender, rather than the number of offenders. Lack of data regarding releases from prison on parole and by other procedures makes it impossible to determine precisely the average period of incarceration for similar crimes in different countries, since the length of sentence does not always provide a base. However, most countries seem to have developed a loose general tariff of penalties and to have established implicit conventions regarding the disposal of offenders for crimes of varying levels of seriousness and frequency. Within countries where analyses have been made of the increase in the incarceration rates, the major proportion of the increase has been found to be due to the increase in the going rate for certain offenses.[54]

It may be suggested that criminal sanctions possess some characteristics in common with money—they may become devalued. The application of this factor to the specific sanction of the fine is self-evident. Thus for the punishment to be constant in proportion to the deprivation of goods, the sum of money must be increased. Christie[55] (1968: p. 165) raises an analogous point. "When daily existence is characterized by greater security against need, more leisure, and fewer limitations on self-development, then a lesser deprivation of these benefits will compensate for the same crime." While this may be a reasonable inference regarding changing penal values within a society it is difficult to fit this explanation to the differences between countries, because according to this the United States, having the highest standard of living should show a lesser punitive index than other Western countries. A different form of devaluation might be a better analogue. Punitive values may be related to prior values in the same country or jurisdiction—there is a going rate for burglary of, say, (x). This value (x), because it does not seem to deter or correct offenders is subsequently raised to $(x + d)$; and gradually the $(x + d)$ value becomes the going rate for the same crime. This means that the same stage army of prisoners goes around and around, spending longer on the inside than before. Except for the members of this circulating brigade of outcasts the changing punitive values are of only symbolic importance.

The Prison Commissioners' Reports for England and Wales have shown for many decades the proportion of offenders who, once received into prison, were later again returned to prisons.[56] Although the data may be somewhat unreliable, an almost identical proportion has been shown for the last fifty years.

LEARNING ABOUT EFFECTIVENESS
OF PENAL MEASURES

Various authorities in societies have been punishing other members of society from time immemorial. It would seem reasonable to suppose that something was learned during that period. On consideration, however, it will be realized that learning can only take place if there is, in the system, some form of feedback. Could anybody ever learn to play darts if between them and the target was a screen over which the darts were lobbed? Yes, perhaps, if there was somebody on the other side who reported what each dart achieved. Decision-makers in the criminal justice procedures are, as it were, lobbing darts (offenders who are found guilty) over a screen where they are out of sight. Few, if any, decision-makers obtain information as to the outcome of their decisions to incarcerate, fine, place on probation, or discharge. Decisions are made as though rightness or wrongness has nothing to do with what happens as the result of the decision; indeed this view is often explicitly argued—the quality of the very process of coming to a decision provides sufficient justification for the belief that the decision is right.

It will be noted that I have spoken of punishment. This is not a fashionable word. It has become customary to speak of penal measures as "the treatment of offenders." Prisons, we are told, should be called "correctional institutions," and we even have special places called "medical facilities." In short, the public has been sold a medical model for the treatment of offenders.

It is difficult to see how an analogy with medical procedures could become so generally accepted within a framework of justification of decisions (whether implicit or explicit) which is independent of consideration of outcomes. The term "treatment of offenders" is usually taken to suggest far more than a euphemism for punishment. Indeed to make this suggestion would be found offensive to almost any official in the field.

The medical analogue[57] in the field of penology has many ramifications. Indeed the majority of the questions of procedures and moral implications derive from this model. It is certainly assumed, even on the part of most of the general public, that offenders are not sent to prison merely to be punished. It will be obvious that the questions which may be asked about punishment differ from those which might be asked about treatment. Punishment requires a moral justification; treatment, while not being without moral constraints, requires an assessment of effectiveness. Punishment may be justified with respect to past events alone, while treatment must take into account probable future states. (Will the patient live?)

At this point, let us take the present rhetoric about penology on its own merits. What can be said of the effectiveness of penal measures? For practitioners in the field, measures of effectiveness present difficulties. Methods which are seen as moral necessities are also, by that token alone, seen as effective. What is good, must be right. It is obviously better to give prison inmates trade training than to leave them idle or engaged on mundane tasks of no later value to them. This may be correct in a moral sense—it is more humanitarian, and hence, better, but it does not follow that fewer crimes will be committed later by those who have had the trade training. Logic is not enough to prove effectiveness; hard data are required.

In recent years there have been a number of research studies and attempts to assess the effectiveness of correctional procedures. A summary of these studies may be useful.[58]

THE PRESENT STATE OF KNOWLEDGE

It must first be noted that the low level of sophistication of research, the lack of rigor of the analysis and the imprecision of the language used in the field of penology are seldom equaled in any area of serious study. Bailey was able to show that the greater the degree of rigor in the research methods which were used in different studies to evaluate penal treatment, the less was the likelihood that the studies would claim successful outcomes.[59]

It is difficult to claim any degree of generality for the findings of research carried out in a specific geographic location or with respect to any particular class of offender. Some results do seem to be supported when the research is replicated in other jurisdictions, but other findings do not seem so robust. It is often difficult to decide whether the limitations of the findings are or are not due to the limitations of the data or the research models. It should also be noted that money for research investigations into penal matters usually comes from the same source as the money to support the programs to be assessed. In order to be persuaded to put up money for reforms or training programs in prisons, legislators must, it seems, be told that the new idea will work better than the old. The tendency to assume that enlightened treatment (group therapy, psychiatric counseling, trade training, work release, or any current fashion in social work) must necessarily result in fewer reconvictions for the offenders concenred, coupled perhaps with the fear that rigorous testing might prove this faith unfounded, has had serious impacts upon research designs and the publication of research results. There are problems arising from incompetence, unbridled enthusiasm, economy, misunderstanding, and many other factors, not excluding plain political suppression and distortion of results, which make the interpretation of the present state of knowledge in this field extremely hazardous.

In attempting a summary of the position at this time it is inevitable that personal prejudice will obtrude to some degree; some would accept results which I would regard as too uncertain to list, while others might include more among the unsatisfactory proof category. Nonetheless, with an intention to be fair, the following is my list of truth claims.

a)   Humanitarian methods of treatment (e.g. probation or fines) are *no less* effective in reducing the probability of an offender to recidivate. This statement seems to hold for developed countries of the Western world. (Note: no claim is made as to the deterrent effect upon others who are not offenders.)

b)   Because humanitarian methods usually involve less intervention in the personal life of the offender, they are usually cheaper than methods which require more stringent supervision. Until more is known about saving souls it would seem to be good policy to save money.

c)   In particular, money may be saved in the reduction of unnecessary expenditure on the provision of security devices. Very few incarcerated persons require maximum security.

d)   Harsh penalties are supported by the beliefs of many experienced persons, but there is, to date, no research which has shown any support for these forms of belief.

e)   Studies of deterrence to others seem to indicate that for trivial offenses there may be some relation to severity of the penalty. This is not an invariable result, as there have also been studies which have shown an increase in the crime (e.g. using slugs in parking meters), following upon publicity regarding some heavy exemplary penalties. For more serious crimes there is evidence that neither the penalties which actually exist in law, nor the beliefs about the penalties which would follow from a criminal act (and these differ), have any impact upon the probability of committing the act.

f) It is generally believed that when an object is defined (or labeled), this fact does not change the thing so defined. There is, however, strong evidence to show that the very fact of labeling people can influence their subsequent behavior. A large body of theory named, appropriately enough, "labeling theory" has been developed and the general findings are supported by research in many countries.

g) It is possible to predict with reasonable accuracy the non-specific recidivism of offenders who are found guilty on one or more occasions. Correlations between 0.40 and 0.50 are expected. Estimates of such probabilities by statistical methods exceed in efficiency clinical judgments of similar probabilities for similar groups.[60]

h) The case-load size of a probation officer is not associated with the probability of his cases to commit further crimes.

In summary and in one simple phrase, it is not unreasonable to say that research findings tend to show that the less it is found necessary to interfere with the personal autonomy of the offender, the better are his chances for going straight in the future. This is true after making all corrections possible for the different risks involved, by use of matching designs or mathematical modeling. Furthermore it is known that the levels of perceived necessity of interference with the personal autonomy of offenders varies within extremely wide limits. So far it has been impossible to carry out research into treatment of offenders where a control group was given only a placebo. Thus while there is evidence that very little is as good as much, there is no evidence as to what might happen if nothing at all were done. We might suppose, however, that the impact would be greater upon the general citizenry than upon the offender population!

CONSEQUENCES OF MEDICAL MODEL

At the present time, no known correctional methods support the use of the medical model. Differential treatment effects have not been isolated, despite apparently wide differences in the treatment actually given. Bloodletting and leeching were characteristic of medical practice in the past but today methods which do not improve the prognosis for recovery would not be acceptable to medical ethics. If correctional procedures cannot show treatment effects then the medical analogue seems to break down on this point.[61]

There are many other unsatisfactory elements in the medical model of treatment of offenders, not only in terms of inadequate representation (mapping) which the model affords, but in the concomitant perspectives on problems and policies. However, until quite recently, the most prevalent humanistic and modern view in penology was concerned with the medical model and hence sought to demonstrate the effectiveness of treatment through the establishment of diagnoses. Indeed reception and classification prisons came to be called "Diagnostic Centers"—again rather more than a mere euphemism.[62] Medical analogies are quite widely accepted by the courts and in institutions and among informed members of the general public. Of course, some cases which appear in court do represent medical problems, but these, rather than tending to add support to the model, actually stress the inappropriateness of legal concepts in relation to physical or mental dysfunction.

In the early days the offender was to be rehabilitated by inculcation of habits of industry, and trade training was the reformers' demand. Later came more concern for the psyche, and group therapy and related measures became the vogue. Most recently, of course, token economies and other such procedures which derive from theories of operant conditioning are the most fashionable. The psychiatric, conditionsing or other medical analogies have much in common with the nineteenth-century sin-and-wickedness model. Each of these conceptual frameworks denies that the offender is, by his act, commenting not only upon himself but also upon society. All we have to do to solve the problem of crime is to solve the problem of the offender—get him out of his laziness, help him solve his personality problems, cure him of his madness, help (or make) him adjust to our society because our society is obviously good!

BADNESS OR MADNESS, OR MERELY BEHAVIOR?

A small group of realists are now taking the view that crime cannot be simplified into either badness or madness; that the problem of crime is the problem of human behavior. Taking note of the research and evaluation of the treatment model they claim that, if this model was ever likely to work at all, this fact should have been evident before now. They claim, and I think correctly, that more punitive measures can be and are applied in the form of treatment than would be the case if we were more honest and discussed punishment in clear terms. Most of this group would claim that probation and parole supervision are not therapy but are intrusive and onerous restrictions on reasonable personal autonomy. Moreover, the terms on which parole is granted are such as to ensure that any person who, for any reason, is wanted for return to prison can be so dealt with without further access to the courts or counsel.

A tract which strongly represents these views, entitled *Struggle for Justice*,[63] was recently published by a group of Quakers. It is interesting that it is the Quakers who are again becoming heavily involved in the debate about penology.

QUANTIFICATION OF MORAL VALUES

The treatment concept or medical analogy provides an escape from important questions. It is difficult to say how much time in incarceration is sufficient on moral grounds to repay a crime of some specific level of seriousness. Such decisions invoke a kind of moral calculus and require also some basis in equity. When a judge could play the role of god or act without challenge on behalf of the king, this was not important. A personal view substituted for a more generally acceptable moral standard. With increased communications and a wider interest in the criminal outcasts, questions began to be asked. Furthermore, some people, even such as newspaper men, began making comparisons between the sentence lengths meted out in different jurisdictions and in different parts of the same jurisdiction; they also went so far as to suggest that there should, perhaps, be less variation.

But the claim for equity has no meaning if we can use the treatment argument. Treatment is not punishment and hence comparisons are invalid. Thus, by this model, the length of time of incarceration is not expected to be a function of the crime, but rather is to be determined by a need for treatment on the part of the individual offender. It would be wrong to release a person before he is cured; and how long this will take cannot be stated in advance. The kind of treatment indicated is not a matter for public debate, but for experts in private consultation with the patient and other experts.

To treat every person as a unique individual may seem a very pleasant and moral code of behavior. Indeed it is, but only under certain conditions. (I shall return to this as the issue of personal autonomy.) In making decisions which affect others, the treating of each person *decided about* as a unique individual, means that there can arise no question of equity, since equity implies some basis for comparison. Thus in the name of treatment, good works and attention to the needs of the offender, a jargon developed which sounded humanistic, modern, and scientific to some, and soft and pampering of criminals to others. In fact it was neither, becoming only an excuse for the exercise of individual judgment or professionalism on the part of those in a position to make the decisions. Many decisions had a profound effect upon the offender but could not be challenged in court nor subject to appeal, and many were made in closed chambers.

Moreover, the offender who might wish to modify his behavior so as to obtain an early release could not obtain any clear idea as to what action on his part might help or prejudice his case. If he was seen as sick, perhaps he should play sick at least at first, since to claim that he was not sick would perhaps be construed as a further symptom of his troubles![64]

DECISION ERRORS

a) Producer Versus Consumer Risk

In any decision there are always two ways of being wrong. A decision is incorrect if we reject the hypothesis when it is in fact true, and also (although not necessarily equally) wrong if we accept the hypothesis when it is in fact false. Since in almost every case of a decision there are some future consequences, a trade-off between types of error will almost always exist, although not always clearly in consumer-producer terms. If it is insisted that every guilty person must be punished (or treated), then it must follow that this involves a much higher risk that the innocent will also be incorrectly punished than would be the case where we were prepared to allow that some guilty might go free.

In the criminal justice procedures there seems to have developed a somewhat peculiar argument with a view to avoiding this issue. It seems to be held that errors in decisions are of no consequence so long as the individual concerned was honest and tried his best (intent) to make the right decision. The criterion of a decision seems to be determined, on this theory, by the quality of the processes involved in making it, and is in no way related to the possible kinds of outcomes. This, I would assert, is neither a moral nor a rational point of view; it tacitly implies a belief in perfection (or the pursuit of perfection) as a goal and as the ultimate criterion of moral value; it does not seek to come to terms with uncertainty and the probability of error; it is so obviously unrealistic that it is immoral.

It seems that we must behave as though, no matter what decisions are made, no matter how experienced the decision-makers, no matter how effective the methods upon which reliance is placed, some decisions will be made incorrectly. To start from the opposite postulate is to claim a form of divinity.

That error is an integral part of any decision or measurement appears to be a difficult concept for some persons to accept. Even if they give verbal accord with the concept of the generality of error, they do not usually accept the consequences which follow in terms of the strategies which should be employed. It has been claimed by one learned judge that, although some of his decisions might, at a later date, be proved to be wrong, they were nonetheless quite correct at the time they were made![65] The business world is more realistic. In quality control, for example, it is recognized that there is a consumer risk and a producer risk, and that these must be weighed in terms of inspection policy. No business could ignore the consumer risk, since to do so would soon result in bankruptcy; conversely, no business could seek to produce a perfect product at all times, reducing the consumer's risk to zero, since to do so it would need to spend far too much on inspection and in rejection of defective batches of the product, and would thus cease to be competitive.

In the field of crime there are many kinds of issues where the consumer-producer-risk model would be useful. It may be, for example, that in some areas fear of crime may lead to such heavy policing that it becomes replaced by the fear of the police. But this kind of consideration is beyond the range of the topic of today's paper. We are examining issues concerned with the disposition of offenders after the finding of guilt by a court.

b) Past and Future

If the disposition of the offender is made only in terms of his offense—a single event which has taken place in the past and which is known in some detail—the nature and qualities of errors in decisions are not closely analogous with the consumer-producer model. However, it is difficult to assume that decisions regarding disposition of offenders are made on any such simple terms. Indeed, if they were, the wisdom of such a basis for decision might be questioned.

The implications for the two classes of error in the disposition of offenders are most clearly seen in the application of the medical analogy, where the probable future criminality of the offender is given consideration. No matter how high the correlation between observations and the predicted outcome, some persons predicted as recidivists will not, in fact, be found guilty of further crimes, while others who will be predicted as successful, will in fact be subsequently found guilty of some further offenses.[66] These are two kinds of error. The problem is not how to eliminate these errors, although we may attempt to reduce them, but since we cannot expect ever to achieve a correlation of 1.0, we must consider the relative weight of the two kinds of error. Is a false positive as bad as a false negative? If not, what is the ratio which can be regarded as morally acceptable? It is surprising that despite the considerable concern in the legal and criminological literature for decisions such as sentencing or the granting of parole and the like, the emphasis is on getting the decision right, rather than upon moral aspects of the accommodation of error, uncertainty, and probability. The issue of uncertainty becomes the more apparent when use is made of actuarial tables to facilitate decisions.

As had been noted earlier, actuarial methods, applied to predictions of recidivism, are superior to subjective assessments.[67] Actuarial predictions are, of course, given in terms of probabilities and expressed numerically, and not in terms of "probable cause" or "beyond reasonable doubt." It is, for example, possible to identify a class of offenders who have a probability of 0.90 of committing another offense. Such tables of probabilities have been criticized by criminal justice practitioners as inaccurate—they point out that among the 90 per cent risk category, for every 100 offenders there will be ten who will be incorrectly classified as recidivists. The objection has some point if all the cases in the 90 per cent category are treated as failures, since this is treating a 90 per cent category as though it were a 100 per cent category, and, as we have noted, such a category cannot exist. The problem is not with the estimation of risk categories, but with the difficulty of accomodating the concept of risk at all in legal or moral decisions.

To some extent the dilemma may be avoided by failing to take note of any probable future states. A court may take the view that it should act with respect to the past and only to the past. If a person has committed a violent act, the court may be justified in punishing him accordingly. If, however, the court assumes that past violent acts provide information about future such acts, the position is changed. There is then the question of error to be resolved. There may be a small amount of information about the likelihood of future criminal acts encoded in the past acts, but it is a very small amount. It is difficult to say when a decision is, in fact, based only on past behavior. The average citizen (as well as the businessman and the courts) tend to make implicit predictions on the basis of observations of, and from knowledge about, past events. People tend to believe that persons who have committed violent acts *are* dangerous persons—a continuous state is inferred from discrete events. In this respect most people are mostly wrong. There are a few cases in which they may be right, and these are too often better remembered than are the others.

c) Proneness to Violence

A recently completed study utilized a very large variety of psychological tests which were expected to be predictive of violent acts and supplented these with a number of other items of data. A base sample of just over 4,000 young men was available from one of the major institutions in California. This represents the most comprehensive attempt to obtain prediction tables for violence-proneness carried out to date. The authors (Wenk and Emrich)[68] claim that their results "strongly suggest that a useful violence index could be constructed. ..." At some remote future date, perhaps, but the results would seem to require an adjustment of moral trade-off. Let their data speak for themselves.

Those individuals who have the top 260 scores were classified as violent-prone, and the remainder of the sample as not violent-prone. On the first step with variable one (history of violence), twenty-eight individuals were correctly classified as violent-prone as they were also found to be in the violent sub-sample (true positives). These hits stand against 256 individuals who were misclassified. According to the prediction index, twenty-four persons were classified as non-violent (false negatives); and 232 persons were classified by the index as violent-prone and turned out to be non-violent (false positives).

d) Moral Trade-off

Thus, in order to pick up about half of the persons who were violent, approximately nine out of every ten persons would be inappropriately treated as though they would also be violent offenders. It will be noted that the best predictor from the very large battery of items proved to be the previous incident of violence. The authors tried to improve on this by adding information but found that, "On the second step with variables one and two, twenty-one persons were correctly classified as violent-prone ..." and the prediction deteriorated at each further step.

The implications of the two kinds of error in decision-making are made very clear in these data. How many persons who are suspected (wrongly) of being dangerous is it reasonable to incarcerate (i.e. treat as dangerous), in order to be right about some others? Is it reasonable, for example, to incarcerate as probably dangerous, one hundred persons of whom ten may be correctly assigned to the dangerous category? (This represents the level possible with the present state of knowledge.) If ninety wrong for ten right is too high a price, then would fifty for ten be morally acceptable? If not fifty, then what other number? If we act at all, there has to be some number. The only way to ensure that we do not incarcerate any person incorrectly is to incarcerate none, and conversely, if we wish to incarcerate all potentially dangerous persons, we must incarcerate all persons, since everybody has some risk of committing a violent act. Immediately we invoke the future risk of crime, or as soon as we make inferences about the state of the person as the justification for our action, we must attend to the problem of the trade-off of errors.[69]

It may be suggested that a person who has once committed a violent act (or, perhaps, some other criminal act) has by that token forfeited his right to the same trade-off level as the person who has not committed such an act. However, the same constraints apply. The basic division is: (*a*) to deal with the person in terms of an idea of just deserts in respect of the past act or acts which we call criminal, or (*b*) to consider the moral aspects of the trade-off of false positives as against harms which might be saved to unknown victims. A mixed strategy would require a model of a form rather like that shown in table 33.

There is difficulty even in establishing a hierarchy in the first column. It is necessary to decide whether two non-violent crimes proven are equal to, greater or less than one violent crime in terms of the impact upon the tolerated ratio of false positives to true positives in the category concerned. Further, it might be considered that the seriousness of the crimes should be taken into account, and perhaps also the interval between any two crimes. Would a similar diminution of the *p*-value for false positives be acceptable as a moral basis if of two crimes one crime were more serious than another. Clearly whatever may be decided could be fitted to some kind of linear function which expresses moral acceptability in terms of the seriousness of the offense(s) and the probability of false positives. But judicial decisions are not usually discussed in such terms.

FROM TREATMENT—TOWARDS EQUITY

An Application of a Model

Much of the information with regard to the impact of prison upon offenders derives from research into parole decisions. Case history data are obtained on follow-up of parolees during supervision in the community and provide a basis from which to assess the effectiveness of treatment, training, and other penal measures.

Decisions by parole boards have many similarities with judicial decisions in sentencing.[70] However, it must be noted that parole decisions can apply only to persons who have been sentenced to prison, whereas the courts decide whether prison is, in their view, necessary in each case. Thus parole decisions represent a selected sample of decisions and may be considered to relate to the more serious cases.[71]

TABLE 33

Classification of Person	Level of False Positive Regarded as Morally Acceptable
(1) No proved offenses*	none tolerated
(2) One prior, non-violent proved offense	some slight reduction in the value of (p)*
(3) One prior violent proved offense**	p-value less than above? (by how much?)
(4) Two prior non-violent proved offenses**	lower p-value than line (2) or line (3) or both
(5) Two prior violent .... &c	? ? ? ? (see below)

*p = estimated probability.
**By "proved offenses" is meant cases which have been through the "due process of criminal justice"—not arrests.

Recently, the United States (Federal) Parole Board gave permission for, and indeed cooperated with research workers in, a study of their decision-making.[72] Files were made freely available, and these and other data were supplemented by frank discussions between the research workers and the Board chairman and members. Prior to the research the Board had insisted that it did not have a policy, except that each case was decided on its merits and that each petitioner was treated as a unique individual.[73] Certain critics had seen this as resulting in arbitrary and capricious decisions. Research revealed that the Board was not capricious, and that a policy did, in fact, exist. There was a strong tendency for the amount of time offenders were held in incarceration to be a function of two factors, namely, (a) the seriousness of the offense for which the person was found guilty;[74] (b) the probability (subjective and/or objective) that further offense(s) might be committed if the offender were released on parole.[75] (A "salient factor score" is obtained for each case.)

These factors are almost independent of each other; indeed some of the most serious crimes tend to be associated with a much lower than average probability to commit further crimes. Another consideration, not completely independent, was the behavior of the offender while in prison.[76] However, a two-dimensional model was considered to be adequate as a first approximation. The results of mapping the model (seriousness x risk) on to the Board's previous case decisions were communicated to the Board. A conclusion was reached that the model could be used to provide guidelines for future decisions. These guidelines are in the form of a matrix of time of imprisonment graduated in two-dimensions in a consistent pattern.

The least serious and lowest risk cases are to be detained the least time, and there are progressive increments in time detained in incarceration in each dimension.

The model expressed in guidelines enables the Board to review its policy as such, determining issues in terms of principles rather than on a case-by-case basis. The guidelines also enable deviations from the pattern to be identified and considered specifically. Every six months the Board is provided with data showing how decisions have been made in comparison with the model. Reasons given by decision-makers for departures from the guideline times are also considered. There is, thus, a review procedure and a form of quality control of the decision process. A base line is now determined and any changes can be consciously made and the impact of changes assessed. There is, of course, no intention that the guidelines should make change less easy or probable, but only that changes shall be recognized as such and assessed in terms of policy. If the pattern of decision-making is deviating from policy, either the policy can be changed or the decision can be brought more into line. It will be noted that there is a trade-off issue in the parole decision model which is similar to that posed in the more general case. The two-dimensional guidelines for decisions provide a gradient in terms of the time an offender is detained in prison. Should, it may be asked, the gradient be similar for each of the dimensions—or are increments in seriousness (least to most) more important than increments in risk category (least to most). There are also different possibilities for assessing the gradients. However, if the least serious set of cases (say, lowest tenth percentile) defines the low point for time detained, and the most serious set (say, ninetieth percentile) defines the high point, then there may be said to be an average time gradient over all risk groups. Similarly, the lowest risk group, summed over all levels of seriousness, and the highest risk group also summed over all levels of seriousness, may provide a basis for calculating the average time gradient for risk category. We may then ask whether seriousness is more important than risk, or whether both are regarded as equally significant—in this case the same average gradient should presumably apply to each factor.

On this model the Federal Parole Board tends to give more weight to the seriousness dimension than to that of risk. This does not seem unreasonable. Perhaps the most important consideration arising from the research and its application is that the gradients can now be identified, studied, compared over time (and eventually, perhaps between jurisdictions), and form the basis for informed criticism leading to further modifications of policy in the light of this and other kinds of information. The model, even with the analysis of gradients, does not give any indication of what is the right period for incarceration, nor, of course, whether any incarceration is right. Perhaps all times are too long, or too short. Perhaps the gradients in each direction should be steeper or less steep. The model does not define the boundaries, but can ensure that the variations between decisions are not erratic. The model can be claimed to help with questions of equity if not of jutice. It is, specifically, not concerned with treatment in terms of the medical analogue.

There may appear to be some inconsistency in the use of the second dimension of risk in a model which focuses upon equity. If a future perspective is taken, then the issue of false positives can surely arise. However, in this particular case the dimension of risk may be seen in two ways. It is true that items from the case files (additional to the information about the kind of crime accounted for by the seriousness dimension) do in actual fact prove to be predictive of future criminality.[77] But these items relate, in the main, to features of the past criminal career. It seems equally as reasonable to defend the additional penalty (more time to be served) for high risk persons (low salient factor score) as it is to seek to defend the decisions on predictive grounds. We have, then, at least at the moment and in this specific case, a situation where an unsatisfactory model and a more satisfactory one lead to similar courses of action. The seriousness of the commitment crime, plus prior criminal record and style of life of the offender are reasonable grounds for considering the penalty (for those who see imprisonment as a penalty), while at the same time those who believe in treatment tend to agree that it takes more time to treat a person who has committed a serious crime and who also had a long record of offenses. Perhaps agreement as to what is to be done, which derives from such basically different propositions, provides one further indication of our lack of knowledge in this field.

THE NEW DIRECTIONS?

It is necessary, as a matter of considerable urgency, that we unscramble the technological, medical, scientific, and moral questions in relation to dysfunctional behavior; when this is done we may find appropriate problem-solving methods for each kind of issue.

Something like prisons will be needed for a long time. They are needed for the separation from society of persons who cannot be expected to function safely in freedom. Prisons also provide the means of punishment which does not have the unpleasantness of other punishments like flogging and death. Society will continue to demand forms of punishment. It is not unreasonable for persons who have suffered from some crime to demand that the offender "get out of here." When "out of here" did not mean into some other similar society (such as the next state!), and when transport was slow, there were several variations of the general theme of "out of here." Few areas of the world can today employ such methods. The prison has to suffice.

According to any reasonable definition of treatment, no prison provides treatment.[78] If then treatment is indicated in any case which may first be discovered through the criminal justice process, the diversion of that case from the penal system is required. Not only have the correctional services failed to demonstrate that they provide treatment, it would, indeed be inappropriate for them to do so. The legal system is concerned with matters of guilt, human rights, and the concept of responsibility—in short, moral, not medical and not technological questions.

It would seem to follow that no offender should be detained in prison for one day longer than is justified in terms of his offense and his prior record of crimes merely because he is seen to be in need of, or to be under treatment. The prison exists to serve the community, not the prisoner.

The prison is there because society demands it, and because society pays for it. Prison is a kind of factory where the product is punishment, and we buy its products through taxation. We are also paying for offenders to be kept away from us and decent people like us, at least for a period of time. This purchase of relief may have some value in reduced risk, but again there is the question of the moral value of the trade-off to be resolved. If any taxpayer thinks that correctional services are helping offenders to rehabilitation or reintegration into society, the evidence is all against him.

It may be argued that we should continue to hide our heads in the treatment sands, because, if prisons come to be seen for what they are—places for isolation and punishment—then they might degenerate further and become even less acceptable on moral grounds. The opposite case can also be made with equal plausibility since the treatment perspective, as we have noted, provides an excuse for many inequitable measures and even abuses of power. Perhaps a more honest descriptive language would lead to more effective and more humanitarian procedures. Or, perhaps, an honest language is morally desirable in its own terms?

The methods whereby prisons are operated need not involve very different procedures from those currently in fashion. There is no reason why persons who are incarcerated (for purposes of isolation, punishment or both) should not be: (*a*) treated humanely; (*b*) taught trades; (c) provided with socially useful activities in their captivity; (d) adequately rewarded for work done; (e) given groups therapy or other treatments (medical or psychiatric) if they volunteer for it; (f) provided with similar protections as those given to persons on the outside in so far as is feasible; (g) permitted to spend their time in captivity in as dignified a manner as is possible. The prisoner is still to be seen as a person while the society within which he is permitted to move is constrained.

There are many things which can now be done to humanize prisons. All these should be done, not because it is good for the prisoners, but because it is good for society and the prison staffs. If prison officers are to keep a special kind of isolation-society in operation they need every incentive and means to maintain their dignity, humanity and sense of humor.

SUMMARY AND CONCLUSION

There is a similarity to my prescription for the outside society and the inside (prison) society. Outside the prison system I would argue for consideration of those elements in the crime which extend beyond the persons and actions of the offender (e.g. the victims, situations and environments, and the law itself), while within the prison and penal system I would similarly argue that we must take a broader perspective to include the institutional structure, the decision processes, the custodial personnel, and even the architecture as well as the inmate himself. To get the criminal's behavior into perspective we must see it in relation to the environment in which the act is embedded—whether this is the constrained society of the prison or the larger free society. This is the systems theoretic approach. The treatment model cannot do this, moreover, like other treatments penal treatments are liable to serious side-effects.

Emphasis upon the guilty offender, to the exclusion of other considerations can almost certainly lead us to underestimate the impact of crime-control measures upon the liberties of all. The most subtle form of emphasis upon the offender is that which persuades us that we are doing all this for his own good—because it is all treatment! To defend society, it is necessary to defend the criminal.

If we are going to deal with the social dysfunction which we call crime, we must deal with it as a social problem and not as sickness nor as separate unconnected events which are due to individual wickedness. We must seek to remove the field of crime from the level of political slogans where a "war on crime" can quickly become a "war on criminals," and, moreover where "criminals" may be none too clearly defined.

Is it possible to make the general public concerned about dangerous situations or criminogenic states without reduction of these to the form of the dangerous person? The prisons belong to the taxpayers. What is done in prisons and in the courts is done with taxpayers' money. Do those who pay for it have a clear idea of what they want from the penal system? Do they even know what they are getting? Is there adequate accountability by the penal system to the community? To ask the questions is to answer them.

I think, nonetheless, that we shall move rapidly towards a new approach to crime. My grounds for this are that expenditures on criminal justice have more than doubled in the last four years.[79] Anybody can see that, by following a policy of more-of-the-same (a linear trend projection will suffice), we shall soon be bankrupt; not because of crime, but because of what we are doing about it.

A projection of bankruptcy, it may be thought, is a great incentive to change the order of business. My fear, however, is that in criminal justice, the data are so bad, the philosophies so muddled, the symbolism so powerful, the language so dishonest and slogans so useful and easy, that rational projection does not apply. Perhaps the public will not buy a new model for criminal justice until they crash the present one. Unfortunately there are not many alternative models on the drawing boards. But even if there were, no simulation methods for testing them have been developed. Research has been directed towards patching up those holes in the system which have disturbed administrators, and in the course of this has often made still further holes. Radical analysis and propositions of alternatives, together with fundamental research, have not attracted supporting funds.

Only those who have made a serious study of the problem of crime acknowledge that they do not have sufficient information. Everybody else, and especially politicians, knows exactly what should be done. In criminal-justice matters, the degree of confidence with which views are expressed tends to be inversely proportional to the quality of knowledge.

NOTES

History and Current Status
SECTION I

1. Prisons are mentioned in the historical records of ancient Japan, China, Egypt and Greece, and in the latter Empire period are noted in the Roman law. In literature and folklore, as well, they are mentioned as existing during very early periods of civilization: The *Shu Ching,* a collection of Chinese Poetry, history and philosophy, edited by Confucius, notes the building of prisons by the Emperor Fuen VIII about 2000 B.C. (*Le Chou-King, un des livres sacrés des Chinois,* trans., by Joseph de Guignes, [Paris, 1770], p. 72.)

2. Ralph B. Pugh, *Imprisonment in Medieval England* (Cambridge, 1968), esp. Chap. 1. This work gives a very detailed picture of early imprisonment and conditions during the medieval period.

3. For a greater exposition of this view, see Thorsten Sellin, "Penal Servitude: Origin and Survival," *Proceedings of the American Philosophical Society,* Vol. 109, No. 5 (Oct., 1965).

4. Gotthold Bohne, *Die Freiheitsstrafe in den Italienischen Stadtrechten* des 12.-16. *Jahrhunderts* (Leipzig, 1922), I, p. 78.

5. "Mamertine Prison", *Builder* (London), XXXIII (July 3, 1875), p. 593.

6. A 14th century Carthusian house known as Mount Grace had a series of walled enclosures 27 feet square around a central cloister. Each contained a little two-story house for a monk providing a living room with fireplace, a small bedroom, a study and a workroom. There was a garden, a privy and piped water, and the monk might work and meditate with no contacts with the outside.

7. William Dugdale, *Monasticom Anglicanum* (London, 1817), I, p. 218.

8. F. A. Karl Krauss, *Im Kerker vor und nach Christus* (Freiburg, 1895), p. 331.

9. Thorsten Sellin, *Pioneering in Penology* (Philadelphia, 1944), pp. 102–110.

10. Very early in the game, architects began to use a castle-like Gothic style for prisons. This became nearly invariable in both the Auburn- and the Pennsylvania-inspired prisons and even in some of Hopkins' 20th century institutions, though by this time the style was lighter and less elaborate. The 20th century telephone-pole or Auburn prisons without a wall have been as devoid of a distinctive style as a warehouse. But with more normal living and working arrangements for inmates in contemporary minimum security institutions, the style became little different from that of a residential school. More ordinary building materials, greater use of glass, lively colors and more informal, smaller living units characterize these new facilities.

11. For a history of these developments, see David Rothman, *The Discovery of the Asylum: Social Order and Disorder in the New Republic* (Boston: Little, Brown, 1971), chs. 3 and 4.

12. Harry Elmer Barnes, *The Story of Punishment* (Montclair, N.J.: Patterson-Smith, 1972), ch. 6.

13. Data from American Correctional Association, *1971 Directory of Correctional Institutions and Agencies of the United States of America, Canada, and Great Britain* (College Park, Md.: ACA, 1971).

14. Gustave de Beaumont and Alexis de Tocqueville, *On the Penitentiary System in the United States and Its Application in France,* H. R. Lantz, ed. (Carbondale: Southern Illinois University Press, 1964), p. 48.

15. ACA, 1971 Directory.

16. All statements in this report are based on data from these 592 institutions. Excluded from the data base are all of Massachusetts' 14 correctional facilities, the majority of which failed to report, and 2 nonreporting facilities in Georgia.

17. Included in the category of classification or medical centers are facilities known as reception, classification, or diagnostic centers, as hospitals, and as psychiatric units.

18. Other State correctional facilities may exist in these jurisdictions, but they are not administratively separate from the closed prison.

19. The Scandinavian Research Council for Criminology has started a project in 1974 to compare incarceration rates. It will try to make the rates more meaningful by also researching the sanctioning process in mental hospitals, institutions for alcoholics, different sorts of juvenile institutions. Personal letter, Professor Antilla, Helsinki.

20. We are indebted to Professor Antilla for this point.

21. Even murder rates are only crude indicators. The Finnish Government emphasized to us that several countries have large numbers of deaths "statistically" unaccounted for by murder, illness, accident or natural causes.

22. For an account of this development, see David J. Rothman, *The Discovery of the Asylum: Social Order and Disorder in the New Republic* (Boston: Little, Brown, 1971).

23. Gustave de Beaumont and Alexis de Tocqueville. *On the Penitentiary System of the United States and Its Application in France,* H. R. Lantz, ed. (Carbondale: Southern Illinois University Press, 1964), p. 49.

24. Hans W. Mattick and Alexander Aikman, "The Cloacal Region of American Corrections." *Annals of the American Academy of Political and Social Science,* 381 (1969), p. 114.

25. Law Enforcement Assistance Administration. *National Jail Census, 1970: A Report on the Nation's Local Jails and Types of Inmates* (Washington, D.C.: U.S. Government Printing Office, 1970), pp. 6-7.

26. Hans W. Mattick, "Contemporary Jails in the United States, An Unknown and Neglected Area of Justice," in Daniel Glaser, ed., *Handbook of Corrections* (Skokie, Ill.: Rand McNally, forthcoming), draft page 144.

27. Stuart A. Queen, *The Passing of the County Jail* (Banta, 1920), p. 7.

28. Edwin Sutherland and Donald Cressey, *Principles of Criminology,* 6th ed. (Philadelphia: Lippincott, 1960), p. 364.

29. *National Jail Census,* 1970, pp. 10-11.

30. Nebraska Commission on Law Enforcement and Criminal Justice, *For Better or For Worse? Nebraska's Misdemeanant Correctional System* (Lincoln, 1970), pp. 97-105.

31. National Council on Crime and Delinquency, *A Regional Approach to Jail Improvement in South Mississippi: A Plan—Maybe a Dream* (New York: NCCD, 1971), p. 40.

32. Hans W. Mattick and Ronald Sweet, *Illinois Jails: Challenge and Opportunity for the 1970's* (Washington, D.C.: Law Enforcement Assistance Administration, 1970), p. 49.

33. Mattick, "Contemporary Jails," draft p. 47.

34. American Civil Liberties Union, *The Seeds of Anguish: An ACLU Study of the D.C. Jail* (Washington, D.C.: ACLU, 1972), pp. 3, 5.

35. *The Seeds of Anguish,* p. 1.

36. *National Jail Census,* 1970, p. 4.

37. *National Jail Census,* 1970, pp. 4-5.

38. Idaho Law Enforcement Planning Commission, *State of Idaho Jail Survey of City and County Law Enforcement Agencies* (Boise, 1969), pp. 12-13.

39. Daniel Glaser, "Some Notes on Urban Jails" in Daniel Glaser, ed., *Crime in the City* (New York: Harper and Row, 1971), p. 238.

40. Mattick, "Contemporary Jails," draft page 67.

41. Mattick and Sweet, *Illinois Jails,* p. 368.

42. California Board of Corrections, *A Study of California County Jails* (California Council on Criminal Justice, 1970), p. 102.

43. Mattick and Sweet, *Illinois Jails,* pp. 255–256.

44. *National Jail Census,* 1970, p. 9.

45. Mattick, "Contemporary Jails," draft p. 74.

46. Nebraska Commission on Law Enforcement and Criminal Justice, *For Better or For Worse?,* p. 27.

47. Idaho Law Enforcement Planning Commission, *Idaho Jail Survey,* p. 9.

48. President's Commission on Law Enforcement and Administration of Justice, *Task Force Report: Corrections* (Washington, D.C.: U.S. Government Printing Office, 1967), p. 164.

49. Mattick, "Contemporary Jails."

50. Glaser, "Some Notes on Urban Jails," p. 239.

51. John R. Kimberly and David B. Rottman, "Patterns of Behavior in Isolating Organizations: An Examination of Three County Jails," (Urbana: University of Illinois Department of Sociology, 1972).

52. *National Jail Census,* 1970, p. 191.

53. Allan J. Davis, "Sexual Assaults in the Philadelphia Prison Systems and Sheriff's Vans," *Trans-Action,* 6 (1968), p. 9.

54. Glaser, "Some Notes on Urban Jails," p. 241.

55. National Clearinghouse for Criminal Justice Planning, "Spring 1972 Survey of State Jail Standards," unpublished source documents, Urbana, Ill., 1972.

56. Mattick, "Contemporary Jails," draft p. 147.

57. National Council on Crime and Delinquency, *A Regional Approach: A Plan—Maybe a Dream* (New York: NCCD, 1971).

58. "Liberty County, Georgia's Regional Detention Center Lightens Burdens on Area Jails," *American County,* 36 (1971), 9–11.

59. Allan Ashman, *North Carolina Jails* (Chapel Hill: University of North Carolina Institute of Government, 1967), p. 17.

60. Frederic D. Moyer, et al., *Guidelines for the Planning and Design of Regional and Community Correctional Centers for Adults* (Urbana: University of Illinois Press, 1971).

61. See Court Employment Project, *Quarterly Report: December 1, 1970–February 28, 1971* (New York, 1971).

62. See Vermont Department of Corrections, *Biennial Report for the Two Years Ending June 30, 1970* (Montpelier, 1970), pp. 15–16.

63. California Board of Corrections, *Minimum Jail Standards* (Sacramento, 1971), pp. 18–20.

64. The term "dormitory" can often apply to an area containing cells.

65. Many jails, especially the smaller ones, operate with sworn police officers serving the jail on a rotating basis. Some of these officers may have been reported as full-time employees even though they worked only part time in the jail.

66. These reports, one for each State, were prepared by the Statistics Division, National Institute of Law Enforcement and Criminal Justice of the Law Enforcement Assistance Administration. For explanations of the limitations of the data and definitions see the Appendix of this report.

67. These figures are provided by the LEAA reports. Percentages and other interpretations were extrapolated from the original figures.

68. Advisory Commission on Intergovernmental Relations, *State-Local Relations in the Criminal Justice System* (Washington, D.C.: U.S. Government Printing Office, 1971), p. 15.

69. Examples of appropriate activities might be: development of regional Federal facilities for female offenders; and the development of special facilities for "mentally ill offenders," a group which has fallen between psychiatric and correctional institutions.

70. *State-Local Relations in the Criminal Justice System,* p. 17.

71. Warren G. Bennis, *Organization Development: Its Nature, Objectives, and Prospects* (Reading, Mass.: Addison-Wesley, 1969), p. 2.

72. Much of the following discussion is drawn from Arthur C. Beck and Ellis D. Hillman, eds., *A Practical Approach to Organization Development through Management by Objectives* (Reading, Mass.: Addison-Wesley, 1972).

73. Robert E. Blake, et al., "Breakthrough in Organization Development: Large-scale Pro-

gram that Implements Behavioral Science Concepts," *Harvard Business Review,* 42 (1964), 133–155; and Warner W. Burke, "A Comparison of Management Development and Organization Development," *Journal of Applied Behavioral Science,* 7 (1972), 569–579.

74. Hugh Estes, "Some Considerations in Designing an Organizational Structure," in Mason Haire, ed., *Organization Theory in Industrial Practice* (New York: John Wiley, 1962), p. 15.

75. Mason Haire, "Biological Models and Empirical Histories of the Growth of Organizations," in Mason Haire, ed., *Modern Organization Theory* (New York: John Wiley, 1959), pp. 272–276.

76. Rensis Likert, "A Motivational approach to a Modified Theory of Organization and Management," in Mason Haire, ed., *Modern Organization Theory* (New York; John Wiley, 1959), pp. 184–217.

77. Rensis Likert, *New Patterns of Management* (New York: McGraw-Hill, 1961).

78. Thomas Mathiesen, *Across the Boundaries of Organizations: An Exploratory Study of Communications Patterns in Two Penal Institutions* (Glendessary, 1971).

79. David Schreiber and Stanley Sloan, "Management by Objectives," *Personnel Administration,* 15 (1970), 20–26.

80. Robert Perlman and Arnold Gurin, *Community Organization and Social Planning* (New York: John Wiley, 1972), p. 238.

The Correctional Institution as a Community
SECTION II

1. Piri Thomas, *Down These Mean Streets* (New York: Alfred A. Knopf, Inc., 1967), p. 281.

2. "Gleaning" is one term which is not natural to the prison social world, and the category itself is not explicitly defined. Convicts have recognized and labeled subparts of it, such as "intellectuals," "programmers," and "dudes on a self-improvement kick," but not the broader category which I have labeled gleaners. However, whenever I have described this category to convicts, they immediately recognized it and the term becomes meaningful to them. I chose the term gleaning because it emphasizes one very important dimension of this style of adaptation, the tendency to pick through the prison world (which is mostly chaff) in search of the means of self-improvement.

3. David W. Maurer, *Whiz Mob* (Princeton, N.J.: Princeton University Press, 1964), p. 196.

4. Erving Goffman has described this mode of adaptation, which he calls "playing it cool" in *Asylums* (Garden City, N.Y.: Doubleday Anchor Books, 1961), pp. 64–65.

5. Thomas, *op. cit.,* p. 280.

6. John Irwin and Donald Cressey, "Thieves, Convicts, and the Inmate Culture," *Social Problems* (Fall 1962): 150.

7. Black, *You Can't Win,* pp. 104–105.

8. Donald Clemmer, *The Prison Community* (New York: Holt, Rinehart & Winston, 1966), pp. 123, 127.

9. Malcolm Braly, *On the Yard* (Boston: Little, Brown and Co., 1967), pp. 106–107.

10. Fifteen percent of the 116 ex-prisoners were classified as "jailers."

11. Irwin and Cressey, *op. cit.,* p. 149.

12. Claude Brown, *Manchild in the Promised Land* (New York: Macmillan Company, 1965), p. 412.

13. In the sample of 116 ex-prisoners, the records indicated that 19 percent had followed a gleaning course in prison.

14. Malcolm X and Alex Haley, *The Autobiography of Malcolm X* (New York: Grove Press, 1966), p. 171.

15. *Ibid.,* p. 173.

16. *Ibid.,* pp. 173–174.

17. This movement was foretold by Malcolm X (see *The Autobiography of Malcolm X,* p. 183).

18. The difficulties encountered by a white researcher attempting to carry on participant observation within the tense and racially charged atmosphere of a maximum security prison cannot be minimized. The fact that access to the prison had been arranged by Professor Nor-

val Morris, a strong advocate of prison reform whose liberal positions were well known to the inmate leadership, was a considerable advantage. From the outset the researcher maintained a position of complete honesty about the purposes of his research. Contacts with the security guards were cordial but kept to a minimum. Every effort was made to earn the confidence of the gang leadership. The legal background of the research proved to be a valuable asset in establishing an informal exchange relationship with key informants. In addition, several times during the research the writer was able to intercede with the administration on behalf of inmates, thereby enhancing his credibility.

19. Contrast this statement with Goffman's (1961:14) sober view of initiation into the total institution.

> The recruit comes into the establishment with a conception of himself made possible by certain stable social arrangements in his home world. Upon entrance, he is stripped of the support provided by these arrangements. In the accurate language of some of our oldest total institutions, he begins a series of abasements, degradations, humiliations and profanations of self. His self is systematically, if often unintentionally mortified. He begins some radical shifts in his moral career, a career composed of the progressive changes that occur in the beliefs that he has concerning himself and significant others.

20. Compare this with Goffman's (1960: 48–60) discussion of the privilege system which is said to structure the routine of the total institution.

21. Clemmer (1958) characterized leadership as unstable and as emerging only within the context of the primary group.

22. Alfred C. Kinsey, et al., *Sexual Behavior in the Human Female* (Philadelphia: W. B. Saunders Company, 1953), pp. 642–689.

23. Alfred C. Kinsey, *et al.*, *Sexual Behavior in the Human Male* (Philadelphia: W. B. Saunders Company, 1948), pp. 327–393.

24. Paul H. Gebbard, *et al.*, *Sex Offenders* (New York: Harper & Row, 1965).

25. From a preliminary analysis of the differences between the pre-institutional and the institutional sexual outlet of adult male prisoners interviewed by the Institute for Sex Research, the institutional rates are only one-tenth of one-fifth of noninstitutional rates. For some males, the institutional rates are nearly zero.

26. For a discussion of the necessity of socially facilitating cues for sexual arousal and performance, see John H. Gagnon and William Simon, "Pornography: Raging Menace or Paper Tiger," *Trans-Action* 4, 8 (July–August 1967): 41–48; and William Simon and John H. Gagnon, "Pornography: The Social Sources of Sexual Scripts," a paper presented at the 17th Annual Meeting of the Society for the Study of Social Problems, San Francisco, August 1967.

27. Alfred C. Kinsey, *et al.*, *Sexual Behavior in the Human Male*, pp. 497–509.

28. Estimates may be found in the following sources: Joseph Fishman, *Sex in Prison* (New York: National Library Press, 1934), pp. 30, 40 percent; Gresham Sykes, *Society of Captives*, 35 percent; Donald Clemmer, "Some Aspects of Sexual Behavior in the Prison Community," *Proceedings of the American Correctional Association* (1958), 40 percent. Preliminary estimates from the Institute for Sex Research data are 35–45 percent.

29. The notions of "active" and "passive" in homosexual relationships are more obscuring of the actual conditions of the behavior than they are enlightening. The psychiatrist, Irving Bieber has suggested the words "insertor" and "insertee" be substituted for active and passive, since these latter words assume that role behavior in sexual act has major meaning in psychological personality terms. (*Homosexuality* New York: Basic Books, 1962, pp. 238–254.) For an attempt at clarification of this confusion see William Simon and John H. Gagnon, "Homosexuality: The Formulation of a Sociological Perspective," *The Journal of Health and Social Behavior* 8, 3 (September 1967): 177–185.

30. Robert Lindner, "Sexual Behavior in Penal Institutions," in *Sex Habits of American Men*, Albert Deutsch, ed. (New York: Prentice Hall, 1948), pp. 201–215; Arthur Hoffman, "Sex Deviation in a Prison Community," *Journal of Social Therapy* 6, 3 (1955): 170–181; George Devereaux and M. C. Moss, "The Social Structure of Prisons and the Organic Tensions, *Journal of Criminal Psychopathology* 4, 2 (October 1942): 306–324.

31. See Seymour L. Halleck and Marvin Hersko, "Homosexual Behavior in a Correctional School for Adolescent Girls," *American Journal of Orthopsychiatry* 32, 5 (1962): 911–

917; Rose Giallombardo, *Society of Women: A Study of a Women's Prison* (New York: John Wiley & Sons, 1966); David Ward and Gene Kassebaum, *Women's Prison: Sex and Social Structure* (Chicago: Aldine, 1965); Sidney Kosofsky and Albert Ellis, "Illegal Communications Among Institutionalized Female Delinquents," *The Journal of Social Psychology* 48 (August 1958): 155–160.

32. The two volumes are Ward and Kassebaum, *Women's Prison,* and Giallombardo, *Society of Women.* For an excellent comparative discussion, see the joint review of these volumes by Sheldon Messinger, *The American Sociological Review* 32, 1 (February 1967): 143–146.

33. Robert Martinson, "Solidarity Under Close Confinement: A Study of the Freedom Riders in Parchman Penitentiary," *Psychiatry,* May 1967; and, *Treatment Ideology and Correctional Bureaucracy: A Study of Organizational Change,* unpublished Ph.D. dissertation, University of California (Berkeley), 1968.

34. Robert Martinson, "The Age of Treatment: Some Implications of the Custody-Treatment Dimension," *Issues in Criminology,* Fall 1966. (Reprinted in Ch. 7, *Crisis in American Institutions,* eds., Jerome H. Skolnick and Elliott Currie, Boston: Little, Brown and Company, 1970).

35. *Ibid.,* p. 480.

36. All quotes from the hostages are from: Warren H. Hanson, M.D., "Attica: The Hostages' Story," *The New York Times Magazine,* October 31, 1971.

37. Robert Martinson, "Attica: The Politics of Armageddon," *New America,* September 12, 1971.

38. *"The Age of Treatment," loc. cit.*

39. Richard H. McCleery, "Authoritarianism and the Belief System of Incorrigibles," pp. 260–306, in *The Prison,* edited by Donald R. Cressey, (New York: Holt, Rinehart and Winston, 1961).

40. "The Attica Revolt: Hour by Hour," *The New York Times,* October 4, 1971.

41. All quotes from: Clark Whelton, "Attica and the Alamo," *Village Voice,* September 23, 1971.

Specific Programs in Correctional Institutions
SECTION III

1. Note, *Beyond the Ken of the Courts: A Critique of Judicial Refusal to Review the Complaints of Convicts,* 72 Yale L. J. 506 (1963). The author notes that the phrase "hands-off doctrine" is taken from Fritch, "Civil Rights of Federal Prison Inmates," a document prepared in 1961 for the Federal Bureau of Prisons. The quotation from the court opinion is from Banning v. Looney, 213 F.2d 771 (10th Cir.), *cert. denied* 348 U.S. 859 (1954).

2. Coffin v. Reichard, 143 F.2d 443, 155 A.L.R. 143 (C.C.A. Ky. 1944).

3. Fortune Society v. McGinnis, 319 F. Supp. 901 (D.C. So. Dist. N.Y. 1970).

4. Palmigiano v. Travisono, 317 F. Supp. 776 (1970).

5. Rhem v. McGrath, U.S.D.C. So. Dist. N.Y., July 30, 1971, 70 Civ. 3962.

6. N.Y. Laws of 1970, ch. 479.

7. For a discussion of the development of remedies and the limitations still governing many courts, see Goldfarb and Singer, *Redressing Prisoners' Grievances,* 39 Geo. Wash. L. Rev. 175 (1970), particularly 243 *et seq.*

8. Holt v. Sarver, 309 F. Supp. 362 (1970), *aff'd* 442 F.2d (8th Cir. 1971).

9. Bryant v. Hendrick, Philadelphia Court of Common Pleas, Aug. 11, 1970.

10. Curley v. Gonzales, U.S. Dist. Ct. N. Mex., Feb. 12, 1970.

11. The ombudsman program is discussed in "Interim Hearing on Desirability of a Correctional Ombudsman," Assembly Interim Committee on Criminal Procedure, California Legislature (1970); Spector, *A Prison Librarian Looks at Writ-Writing,* 56 Calif. L. Rev. 365 (1968). The Maryland statute sets up an equivalent office in its act for an Inmate Grievance Commission (Session Laws of 1971, ch. 210, added as § 204F in art. 41, Md. Ann. Code).

The Center for Correctional Justice reports as follows on the ombudsman programs in Oregon and Alberta, Can.:

"These two programs appear to have given all citizens (in Alberta) and prisoners (in Oregon) a way to correct individual cases of injustice, inefficiency or oversight. The Ombudsmen have been successful in cutting through bureaucratic red tape and in assuring that prescribed regulations are followed in specific cases. Officials at the Oregon Penitentiary are convinced that the Ombudsman has contributed to a more stable atmosphere. On the other hand, the Ombudsmen seem to have made little progress in changing the general policies and procedures under which government agencies operate. (For example, Oregon prisoners now have some assurance that the written rules concerning disciplinary procedures will be followed: the rules, however, remain unchanged.) This is not surprising in Oregon, where the prison Ombudsman, after sixteen years' experience as a guard, continues to be responsible to the Superintendent and to share most of the basic assumptions of correctional personnel. Recently, the Ombudsman has become frustrated by the necessity of acting as a middleman between inmates and staff and by his lack of independent power to change practices that seem unfair. The inmates express faith in the Ombudsman's sincerity but doubt in his ability to do anything more than 'play politics.'

"The Alberta Ombudsman, a former Commissioner of the Canadian Mounted Police, has made a few steps in the direction of challenging accepted practices. Apparently, he has achieved a large public following and favorable press. However, in a recent case where he questioned the operation of powerful real estate cooperatives, he was subjected to questioning by a specially created committee of inquiry, contrary to statute. In addition, the Ombudsman is the only employee in the province of Alberta who has not received a raise in salary since 1967. We have discovered already that this inability to be completely free of political pressures may plague our project as well." First Quarterly Progress Report, 1971.

12. *New York Times*, Feb. 7, 1970.

13. "Officers of the American Bar Association's Young Lawyers Section and several members of the Junior Bar of Texas made a series of visits to Texas prisons last week. This visit was part of the Young Lawyers Section's nation-wide prison visitation program, which is intended to help improve correctional services and conditions by drawing public attention to both the positive and negative aspects of prisons.

"Since last November, section members have toured a dozen prisons. In Texas, they visited units of the Texas Department of Corrections as well as local jails and observed conditions and interviewed inmates, guards and prison officials. . . .

"Prison visits to observe conditions and interview inmates make up the first of three major phases in the program. The second phase consists of offering legal services to the inmates on both criminal and legal matters. Law schools at the University of Washington and the University of Kansas are already assisting prisoners in such programs. The final phase of the program is the development of prison reform legislation at the federal and state levels." 9 Cr. L. Reporter 2121, May 12, 1971.

14. NCDD, Standard Act for State Correctional Services, 1966.

15. United States v. Simpson, 436 F.2d 162 (D.C. Cir. 1970).

16. Singer, *Confining Solitary Confinement: Constitutional Arguments for a "New Penology,"* 56 Iowa L. Rev. 1251 (1971).

17. On petitions signed by next of friend, see Note, *Habeas Corpus vs. Prison Regulations, a Struggle in Constitutional Theory*, 54 Marq. L. Rev. 50, 54–59 (1971).

18. Edwin H. Sutherland and Donald R. Cressey, *Principles of Criminology*, 6th ed. (Philadelphia: J. B. Lippincott, 1960), p. 327.

19. John P. Conrad, *Crime and Its Correction* (Berkeley: University of California Press, 1965), p. 17.

20. United Nations Department of Economic and Social Affairs, *Standard Minimum Rules for the Treatment of Prisoners and Related Recommendations* (New York: UN, 1958).

21. *Struggle for Justice*, A Report on Crime and Punishment in America prepared for the American Friends Service Committee (Hill and Wang, 1971), pp. 36–37.

22. Carl F. Jesness, *Development of a Sequential 1-Level Classification* (Project SEQUIL) (Sacramento: California Youth Authority, 1970).

23. Allen F. Breed, "The Significance of Classification Procedures to the Field of Corrections," unpublished consultant's paper prepared for the President's Commission on Law Enforcement and Administration of Justice, 1967.

24. Breed, "The Significance of Classification Procedures."

25. Francis H. Simon, *Prediction Methods in Criminology, Including a Prediction Study of Young Men on Probation* (London: H.M. Stationery Office, 1971.)

26. H. Ashley Weeks, *Youthful Offenders at Highfields* (Ann Arbor: University of Michigan Press, 1963).

27. U.S. Bureau of Prisons, Policy Statement, Dec. 16, 1969.

28. Marguerite Q. Warren, *Interpersonal Maturity Level Classification: Juvenile Diagnosis and Treatment of Low, Middle, and High Maturity Delinquents* (Sacramento: California Youth Authority, 1966).

29. Martin A. Levin, "Crime and Punishment and Social Science," *The Public Interest,* 27 (Spring 1972).

30. Home Office Research and Statistics Department, *Summary of Research* (London: H.M. Stationery Office, 1969).

31. Described in Marguerite Q. Warren, *Correctional Treatment in Community Settings: A Report of Current Research,* paper prepared for the Sixth International Congress on Criminology, 1970.

32. William McCord, Joan McCord, and Irving K. Zola, *Origins of Crime* (New York: Columbia University Press, 1959).

33. Don C. Gibbons, *Changing the Lawbreaker: The Treatment of Delinquents and Criminals* (Englewood Cliffs, N.J.: Prentice-Hall, 1965), p. 39.

34. Freeman, et al., "A Classification System That Prescribes Treatment," *Social Casework,* 46 (1965): 423-429.

35. R. MacGregor, "Developmental Considerations in Psychotherapy with Children and Youth," paper presented at the annual conference of the American Psychological Association, 1962.

36. David E. Hunt and Robert H. Hardt, "Developmental Stage, Delinquency, and Differential Treatment," *Journal of Research in Crime and Delinquency,* 2 (1965): 20-31.

37. Warren, *Interpersonal Maturity Level Classification.*

38. Warren, *Correctional Treatment in Community Settings.*

39. American Prison Association, Committee on Classification Case and Case Work, *Handbook on Classification in Correctional Institutions* (New York: American Correctional Association, 1964.)

40. Elliot Studt, Sheldon Messinger, and Thomas P. Wilson, *C-Unit: Search for Community in Prison* (New York: Russell Sage Foundation, 1968).

41. William E. Amos and Raymond Manella, *Delinquent Children in Juvenile Correctional Institutions* (Springfield, Ill.: Charles C. Thomas, 1966).

42. Marguerite Q. Warren, "Classification of Offenders as an Aid to Efficient Management and Effective Treatment," *Journal of Criminal Law, Criminology and Police Science,* 62 (1971): 239.

43. On this general subject the New York State Special Commission on Attica (McKay Commission) took a forthright stand. Number 1 in its list of principles to serve as guidelines for restructuring of the prison system is the following: "If prisoners are to learn to bear the responsibilities of citizens, they must have all the rights of other citizens except those that have been specifically taken away by court order. In general, this means that prisoners should retain all rights except that of liberty of person. These include the right to be adequately compensated for work performed, the right to receive and send letters freely, the right to have and express political views, the right to practice a religion or to have none, and the right to be protected against summary punishment by state officials. When released from prison, they should not be saddled with legal disabilities which prevent them from exercising the rights of free men." (p.xvi).

44. Several of these studies are summarized in my book, *The Effectiveness of a Prison and Parole System* (Indianapolis: Bobbs-Merrill, 1964), Chapter 12.

45. See John Clark and Eugene Wenninger, "Social Class, Area, Sex and Age as Correlates of Illegal Behavior Among Juveniles," *American Sociological Review* 27 (December 1962): 826-834; Albert J. Reiss, Jr. and Albert L. Rhodes, "The Distribution of Juvenile Delinquency in the Class Structure," *ibid.,* 26 (October 1961): 720-32.

46. Published in 1961 by the Viking Press, and republished by them in 1964 in paperback as Compass Books No. C 168.

47. *Ibid.*, pp. 34–45.

48. *Ibid.*, pp. 89–95.

49. John M. McKee, "Reinforcement Theory and the 'Convict Culture,'" Proceedings, American Correctional Association, 1964, pp. 171–178.

50. *Manual of Correctional Standards,* (New York: The American Correctional Association, 1959), p. 232.

51. Daniel Glaser, "How Institution Discipline Can Best Serve Correctional Purposes," *American Journal of Correction* 27, 2 (March–April 1955): 3–6, 22.

52. O. F. Lewis, *The Development of American Prisons and Prison Customs, 1776–1845* (Albany: Prison Association of New York, 1922), pp. 169–170.

53. *Ibid.*

54. O. F. Lewis, "Inmate Self-Government a Century Ago," *The Delinquent* 8 (1918): 9.

55. Zebulon R. Brockway, *Brockway, Fifty Years of Prison Service: An Autobiography* (1912), p. 96.

56. Helfman, "Antecedents of Thomas Mott Osborne's 'Mutual Welfare League' in Michigan," *Journal of Criminal Law and Criminology* 40 (1950): 597.

57. *Ibid.*

58. Calvin Derick, "Self-Government," *Survey* (September 1, 1917): 473.

59. Reported in Enoch C. Wines, *Punishment and Reformation: A Study of the Penitentiary System* (Lane rev'n, 1923), p. 408.

60. Thomas Mott Osborne, *Society and Prisons* (1916), p. 164.

61. Frank Tannenbaum, *Crime and the Community* (1938), p. 416.

62. Wines, *op. cit.*, pp. 397–398.

63. *Ibid.*, pp. 407–408.

64. Howard B. Gill, "The Norfolk State Prison Colony at Massachusetts," *Journal of Criminal Law and Criminology* 22 (1931): 107.

65. *Ibid.*

66. Hermann Mannheim, *The Dilemma of Penal Reform* (London: George Allen & Unwin, Ltd., 1939), p. 56.

67. Max Grunhut, *Penal Reform* (Oxford: Clarendon Press, 1948), p. 209.

68. Frank T. Flynn, "The Federal Government and the Prison-Labor in the States, I: The Aftermath of Federal Restrictions," *Social Service Review* 24 (March 1950): 20–21.

69. Selig Perlman, *A Theory of the Labor Movement* (New York: Augustus M. Kelley, 1949), pp. 182–200.

70. O. F. Lewis, *The Development of American Prisons and Prison Customs,* p. 48.

71. Howard B. Gill, "The Prison Labor Problem," *Annals of the American Academy of Political and Social Science* 157 (September 1931): 84.

72. Attorney General's Survey of Release Procedures, Vol. 5, *Prisons* (Leavenworth, Kansas: Federal Prison Industries Press, 1940), pp. 29–30.

73. Blake McKelvey, *American Prisons* (Chicago: University of Chicago Press, 1936), pp. 103–104.

74. *Ibid.*, pp. 98, 105.

75. Flynn, *op. cit.*, pp. 20–21.

76. Manuel Lopez-Rey, "Some Considerations of the Character and Organization of Prison Labor," *Journal of Criminal Law, Criminology, and Police Science* 49 (May–June 1958): 10–28.

77. John C. Burke, "A Warden's View on Vocational Education in Correctional Treatment," *Proceedings of American Prison Association, 1946,* p. 137.

78. Wade K. Springsted, "Industries on the Treatment Team," *Progress Report* 10 (April–June 1962): 11.

79. "Policies Relating to Inmate Industrial Assignments," *Progress Report* 8 (April–June 1960): 10.

80. Wesley O. Ash and Walter L. Barkdull, "California's Trade and Advisory Councils," *American Journal of Correction* 23 (May –June 1961): 10.

81. F. Emory Lyon, "Prison Labor and Social Justice," *Annals of the American Academy of Political and Social Science* 46 (March 1913): 149-50.

82. Springsted, *op. cit.*, p. 12.

83. Lyon, *op. cit.*, p. 149.

84. Louis N. Robinson, *Penology in the United States* (Philadelphia: John C. Winston Co., 1923), p. 181.

85. Daniel Glaser, *The Effectiveness of a Prison and Parole System* (Indianapolis: Bobbs-Merrill Co., 1964), pp. 234-35.

86. Daniel Glaser, *The Effectiveness of a Prison and Parole System* (Indianapolis: Bobbs-Merrill Co., 1964), pp. 406-7.

87. Leon Jansyn, Jr., "Problems and Counseling in Pre-Release," *The Prison Journal* (Autumn-Winter 1966), p. 1.

88. Anthony Catalino, "A Prerelease Program for Juveniles in a Medium-Security Institution," *Federal Probation* (December 1967), p. 29; J. E. Clark, "The Texas Prerelease Program," *Federal Probation,* (December 1966), pp. 53-58; Paul J. Eubanks, "Pre-Release Instruction Program—Apalachee Correctional Institution," *Proceedings of the American Correctional Association,* 1963, pp. 327-332; Clarence Guienzi, "Federal Pre-Release Guidance Centers: A Half Decade Later," *Proceedings of the American Correctional Association,* 1966, pp. 314-321; Edward B. Murray, "The Role of the Probation Officer in Prerelease Preparation," *Federal Probation* (December 1967), pp. 29-35; Nathan S. Nackman, "A Transitional Service Between Incarceration and Release," *Federal Probation* (December 1963), p. 46; H. E. Kachieski, "An Approach to Parole Preparation," *Federal Probation,* (June 1956), p. 29; Ronald W. Vanderwiel, "Pre-Release Programs and Pennsylvania," *The Prison Journal* (Autumn-Winter 1966), pp. 14-20.

89. J. E. Baker, "Preparing Prisoners for Their Return to the Community," *Federal Probation* (June 1966), p. 46.

90. *Ibid.,* p. 49.

91. Ben Lohse, Parole Administrator, "Pre-Release Operations: Institutions," California Department of Corrections, May 1967 (dittoed report).

92. On 20 of the 120 questionnaires returned, all items were dutifully checked with no additional comments. After talking with several of the inmates, it was decided that this group should be treated separately and is not included in the table. This tends to underestimate the interest, but avoids the gross overestimation that would occur by their inclusion.

93. Suggested in conversation with Bob Doran, departmental training coordinator, California Department of Corrections.

94. Suggested in correspondence with J. E. Baker, Warden, Penitentiary of New Mexico.

95. The five department heads which comprise the Program Management Committee are: chief of case management, chief correctional supervisor, supervisor of education, superintendent of industries, and coordinator of mental health programs.

96. The department heads referred to are chief, case management (or chief, C&P); chief, correctional services; coordinator, mental health programs; superintendent, industries; supervisor, education and vocational training.

Fusion of Institutional and Community Programs

SECTION IV

1. A discussion of these principles is contained in Charles R. Henderson, *Prison Reform and Criminal Law* (New York, Russell Sage Foundation, 1910), pp. 39-63.

2. For a brief description of these systems and reference sources, see Edward H. Sutherland and Donald R. Cressey, *Principles of Criminology, 7th ed. (New York: J. B. Lippincott Co.,* 1966), pp. 506-510.

3. Blake McKelvey, *American Prisons* (Chicago: University of Chicago Press, 1936), pp. 25-26.

4. *Ibid.,* pp. 109-115.

5. One of the most perceptive and vigorous attacks on the indeterminate sentence and

parole system appears in a publication of the American Friends Service Committee, *Struggle for Justice*, 1971.

6. McKelvey, *op, cit.,* p. 71. Also cited in George G. Killinger and Paul F. Cromwell, Jr., eds., *Penology: The Evolution of Corrections in America* (St. Paul: West Publishing Co., 1973), p. 62.

7. Thorsten Sellin, "The Origin of the Pennsylvania System of Prison Discipline," *Prison Journal* 50, 2 (Spring–Summer 1970): 13–21. A detailed history of the Walnut Street Jail is presented by Negley K. Teeters, *The Cradle of the Penitentiary: The Walnut Street Jail at Philadelphia,* 1773–1835 (Pennsylvania Prison Society, 1955).

8. *The Attorney General's Survey of Release Procedures* (Washington, D.C.: U.S. Government Printing Office, 1940).

9. The President's Commission on Law Enforcement and Administration of Justice, *The Challenge of Crime in a Free Society* (Supt. of Documents, U.S. Government Printing Office. 1967), pp. 159–185. Also see the more detailed report of the *Task Force on Corrections* (Supt. of Documents, U. S. Government Printing Office, 1967). These findings and recommendations received further consideration from the Reports of the Violence Commission, *cf.,* National Commission on the Causes and Prevention of Violence, *Crimes of Violence* (Supt. of Documents, U.S. Government Printing Office, 1969) 12:523–599.

10. National Advisory Commission on Criminal Justice Standards and Goals, *Corrections* (Supt. of Documents, U.S. Government Printing Office, 1973).

11. Sheldon Krantz, *The Law of Corrections and Prisoners Rights* (St. Paul, Minn.: West Publishing Co., 1973).

12. A preliminary report was presented to the American Sociological Association in August, 1973, in New York City. Richard W. Wilsnack and Lloyd E. Ohlin, "Preconditions for Major Prison Disturbances" (unpublished paper, 1973).

13. Although these views are too well known to require detailed documentation, those seeking a recent and persuasive brief are referred to Hans W. Mattick, *The Prosaic of Prison Violence,* University of Chicago Law School Occasional Paper, 1972.

14. See, for example, Herman G. Stark, "Alternatives to Institutionalization," *Crime and Delinquency* 13 (1967): 323.

15. See Jewett T. Flagg, "A Businessman's Interest in Corrections," *Crime and Delinquency* 6 (1960): 351, for the employer's views.

16. See District of Columbia Department of Corrections, *In-Program and Post-Release Performance of Work-Release Inmates: A Preliminary Assessment* (Washington, D.C., 1969); and Gordon P. Waldo, Theordore G. Chiricos, and Leonard E. Dobrin, "Community Contact and Inmate Attitudes," unpublished study, Florida State University, Tallahassee, c. 1970. For a tentative assessment of community-oriented programs, see LaMar T. Empey, *Alternatives to Incarceration* (Washington, D.C.: U.S. Department of Health, Education, and Welfare, 1967).

17. See Franklin E. Zimring, *Perspectives on Deterrence* (Rockville, Md.: National Institute of Mental Health, Center for Studies of Crime and Delinquency, 1971), p. 89.

18. See Frank R. Scarpitti and Richard M. Stephenson, "A Study of Probation Effectiveness," *Journal of Criminal Law, Criminology, and Police Science* 59 (1968): 361–369; and California Criminal Statistics Bureau, *Superior Court Probation and/or Jail Sample: One Year Followup for Selected Counties* (Sacramento: 1969).

19. LaMar T. Empey, *Alternatives to Incarceration,* p. 2. See also Carol Crowther, "Crimes, Penalties, and Legislatures," *Annals of the American Academy of Political and Social Science* 381 (1969): 147–158.

20. This involvement has already begun on many fronts. For a typical report, see "Citizen Involvement," *Criminal Justice Newsletter,* March 13, 1972, p. 46.

21. Saul Pinick, Robert F. Allen, and Neale W. Clapp, "Adolescent Integrity from Highfields to Essexfields and Collegefields," paper presented to the National Conference on Social Work, 1966. See also LaMar T. Empey and Maynard L. Erickson, *The Provo Experiment* (Heath, 1972).

22. For a history of this function of the institution, see David J. Rothman, *The Discovery of the Asylum: Social Order and Disorder in the New Republic* (Boston: Little, Brown, 1972).

23. Described in Columbus B. Hopper, *Conjugal Visiting at the Mississippi State Penitentiary,* (privately printed), and Hopper, *Sex in Prison: The Mississippi Experiment with Conjugal Visiting* (Baton Rouge: Louisiana State University, 1969). See also *NCCD News,* April 1972, "Conjugal Visits: More to Them than Sex."

24. See, for example, "The Family Visiting Program at the California Correctional Institute, Tehachapi, July 1968," in *Annual Research Review,* 1970 (Sacramento: California Department of Corrections, 1970), p. 43.

25. See Richard E. Ericson and David O. Moberg, *The Rehabilitation of Parolees* (Minneapolis: Minnesota Department of Corrections, 1969), p. 42.

26. *Kriminalvarden,* 1968 (Stockholm: Swedish Correctional Administration, 1969). Has summary in English.

27. See William L. Claiborne, "Special Course at American University—Lorton Inmates Learn about Outside Life." *Washington Post,* February 19, 1972.

28. There remains some disagreement among professionals as to the most effective approaches to be adopted in the educational area. See *New York Times,* March 26, 1972, p. 54. "Prison Officials Back Reform of Education for Inmates but Differ on Details."

29. Connie Schoen, "Things Volunteers Do," *American Journal of Correction* (1969): 26-31.

30. Norman Holt, *California Prerelease Furlough Program for State Prisoners: An Evaluation* (Sacramento: California Department of Corrections, 1969).

31. California Department of Corrections, *Short-Term Return Unit Program* (Sacramento: 1968).

32. *Citizen* is defined here to mean, generally, persons other than correctional clients or those hired primarily to give a service in relation to them.

33. See, for example, International Prisoners' Aid Association, *International Directory of Prisoners' Aid Agencies,* 1968 (Milwaukee, Wisconsin: International Prisoners' Aid Association, 1968).

34. U.S., President's Commission on Law Enforcement and Administration of Justice (National Crime Commission), *The Challenge of Crime in a Free Society* (the General Report) (Washington, D.C.: U.S. Government Printing Office, 1967), p. 159.

35. Benedict S. Alper, *Community Residential Treatment Centers* (New York: National Council on Crime and Delinquency, 1966), pp. 6-10.

36. Gordon H. Barker, "Volunteers in Corrections," consultant paper prepared for the U.S. President's Commission on Law Enforcement and Administration of Justice (National Crime Commission) (Washington, D.C.: U.S. Government Printing Office, 1967), pp. 16-19.

37. Joe Alex Morris, "Royal Oak Aids Its Problem Youth," *Reader's Digest* 87 (October 1965): 163-167.

38. See Jack Otis, "Correctional Manpower Utilization," *Crime and Delinquency* 12 (July 1966): 261-271.

39. *Task Force Report: Corrections,* p. 104.

40. *Ibid.,* p. 103.

41. See Robert K. Merton, *Social Theory and Social Structure* (Glencoe, Ill.: Free Press, 1957), p. 199; and W. Richard Scott, "Theory of Organizations," in *Handbook of Modern Sociology,* Robert L. Faris, ed. (Chicago: Rand, McNally, 1964), p. 510.

42. *Task Force Report: Corrections,* p. 109.

43. U.S. Joint Commission on Correctional Manpower and Training, *The Public Looks at Crime and Correction,* Washington, D.C., February 1968.

44. Frank Remington, "The Jurist Frame of Reference in Parole" (New York: National Parole Institutes, 1963). (Mimeographed.)

45. George B. Leonard, "A New Liberal Manifesto," *Look* 32 (May 28, 1968: 29.

46. Clarence Schrag, "Towards a Correctional Model," an unpublished paper submitted to the National Crime Commission.

47. John M. Martin and Gerald M. Shattuck, "Community Interventions and the Correctional Mandate," consultant paper prepared for the U.S. President's Commission on Law Enforcement and Administration of Justice (National Crime Commission) (Washington, D.C.: U.S. Government Printing Office, 1967).

48. See Howard Becker and Blanche Geer, "Latent Culture: A Note on the Theory of Latent Social Roles," *Administrative Science Quarterly* 5 (September 1960): 304–313.

49. The Family, although an obvious focus of important interventions, is excluded from this discussion.

50. LaMar Empey, "Peer Group Influences in Correctional Programs," consultant paper prepared for the U.S. President's Commission on Law Enforcement and Administration of Justice, (National Crime Commission) (Washington, D.C.: U.S. Government Printing Office, 1967), p. 22.

51. McCorkel, *et al., The Highfields Story;* LaMar T. Empey and Jerome Rabow, "The Provo Experiment in Delinquency Rehabilitation," *American Sociological Review,* 26 (October 1961): 679–696.

52. See *Reaching the Fighting Gang* (New York: New York City Youth Board, 1960).

53. See "Proposal Submitted to Office of Economic Opportunity, 1968—Corrections," Joint Youth Development Committee, Chicago, 1968. (Mimeographed.)

54. Gus Tyler, "The Criminal and the Community," *Current History* 53 (August 1967): 104.

55. Martin and Shattuck, *op. cit.,* pp. 34–36.

56. "Case Management Project: A New Approach to the Management and Delivery of Court Services" (Winston-Salem, North Carolina: Forsyth County Domestic Relations Court, 1968), p. 8. (Mimeographed.)

57. See Judith G. Benjamin, Marcia K. Freedman, and Edith F. Lynton, *Pros and Cons: New Roles for Nonprofessionals in Corrections* (New York: National Committee on Employment of Youth, 1965).

58. Norman Holt and Rudy A. Renteria, "Prerelease Program Evaluation: Some Implications of Negative Findings," *Federal Probation* (June 1969): 40–45.

59. "1968 Legislative Changes," *The Penal Code of the State of California* (Los Angeles: Legal Book Corp., 1967), pp. 43–44.

60. In other states the usual practice is to limit participation severely. For example, eligibility for work furlough in Minneapolis is described as follows: "In the Criminal Division of our court appear law violators who generally do not qualify for confinement under the act (furlough) because they are jobless, are excessive drinkers of alcoholic beverages, are common prostitutes or 'skid row' characters, have no permanent place of abode, or are dangerous criminals." The writer goes on to note that traffice offenders make the best candidates. Elmer R. Anderson, "Work Release Sentencing," *Federal Probation* (December 1964): 7–11.

61. See, for example, the descriptions in "Part Time Prisoners," *Prison Journal* (Spring 1964).

62. Rudy A. Renteria, Parole Agent I and formerly prerelease coordinator at the Southern Conservation Center, was responsible for the program's development and spent considerable work on the forms and evaluation. See, for example, our previous paper, Norman Holt and Rudy A. Renteria, "The 72-Hour Furlough Program at the Southern Conservation Center: A Two Month Evaluation," Conservation Division Research Unit, California Department of Corrections, March 1969 (mimeo.).

63. Administrative Information and Statistics Section, "Median Time Served by *Male Felons* Released from Prison by Quarter," Research Division, California Department of Corrections. Human Relations Agency, January 1969 (mimeo.).

64. Holt and Renteria, *supra* note 1.

65. See Anonymous, "My First Workday on Parole," *Federal Probation* (December 1954): 15–17.

66. The questions were developed to parallel those asked of furloughees from two Norwegian prisons and thus provide some cross-cultural comparison. H. Toch, "Prison Inmates' Reactions to Furlough," *Journal of Research in Crime and Delinquency* (July 1967): 261.

67. Donald Clemmer, "The Prisoners' Pre-Release Expectations of the Free Community," *Proceedings of the 89th Annual Congress of the American Correctional Association 1959,* p. 284.

68. The importance to therapy of the client's plan, including specific goals for improvement,

was emphasized in an address by Dr. Glasser at a training conference for California parole agents, held at Exhibition Park, Los Angeles, in the summer of 1968.

69. Ruth S. Cavan, *Criminology*, 3rd ed. (New York: Thomas Y. Crowell, 1962), p. 485.

70. Robert Scott, "Passes and Furloughs," *American Journal of Correction* (January–February 1965): 30.

71. President's Commission on Law Enforcement and the Administration of Justice, The Challenge of Crime in a Free Society 348–49 (1968).

72. California State Assembly Office of Research, Crime and Penalties in California 25 (1968).

73. American Bar Association Advisory Committee on Sentencing and Review, American Bar Association Project on Minimum Standards for Criminal Justice, Standards Relating to Sentencing Alternatives and Procedures 49 (1967).

74. San Francisco Committee on Crime, A Report on San Francisco County Jails and City Prisons 7 (1969).

75. A. Bandura, *Aggression: A Social Learning Analysis* (1973); McCorkle & Korn, *Resocilization Within Walls*, 293 Annals 88 (1954).

76. G. Fairweather, *Social Psychology in Treating Mental Illness: An Experimental Approach* (1969).

77. California Department of Corrections, Work and Training Furlough Program (1970); District of Columbia Department of Corrections, In-Program and Post-Release Performance of Work Release Inmates, *Research Report No. 13* (1969); Harrison, *Two Year Follow-Up Study of the First 100 Inmates Admitted to the San Mateo County Work Furlough Facility,* San Mateo County Service League (1970); Newman & Bielen, Work-Release: An Alternative in Correctional Handling (1967) (unpublished thesis in Pennsylvania State University).

78. California Penal Code § 1208 (West 1966).

79. It should be noted that many control group failures were later involved in work furlough programs.

80. Within group analyses of recidivism as a function of criminal and social background were performed and are available on request from the authors.

81. Inmates with two prior convictions were included in this comparison because the number of inmates with zero or one prior convictions was too small for meaningful analysis.

82. Background variables were also combined into a composite "favorability rating." This analysis is available on request from the authors.

83. National Council on Crime and Delinquency, Report of Adult Correctional Facilities Consultation: San Mateo County, California (1970).

84. Data derived from a 2-year study of more than 100 institutions by the American Foundation Institute of Corrections.

85. Purdon's Penn. Stat. Ann., Title 61, ch. 1, secs. 2, 4, and 101.

86. Court of Common Pleas for the County of Philadelphia, Pennsylvania, February Term 1971 = 71-2437, Complaint in Equity (Class Action), filed April 7, 1972.

Scientific Guidance of Institutional Policies

SECTION V

1. The theory regarding the efficacy of using criminal groups as media of change and targets of change has been spelled out in a series of articles over a period of almost 15 years, and this theoretical discussion will not be repeated here. See the following articles by Donald R. Cressey: "Contradictory Theories in Correctional Group Therapy Programs," *Federal Probation* 18 (1954): 20–26; "Changing Criminals: The Application of the Theory of Differential Association," *American Journal of Sociology* 61 (1955): 116–120; "Social Psychological Theory for Using Deviants to Control Deviation" in *Experiment in Cultural Expansion: Proceedings of a Conference on the Use of Products of a Social Problem in Coping with the Problem* (Sacramento: California Department of Corrections, 1964), pp. 139–152; "Social Psychological Foundations for Using Criminals in the Rehabilitation of Criminals," *Journal of Research in Crime and Delinquency* 2 (1965): 49–59. See also Rita Volkman and Donald R. Cressey, "Differential Association and the Rehabilitation of Drug

Addicts," *American Journal of Sociology* 69 (1963): 129–142; and Donald R. Cressey and Edwin H. Sutherland, *Principles of Criminology*, 7th ed. (Philadelphia: J.B. Lippincott Company, 1966), pp. 378–380, 548–557, 675–680.

2. See Leon Radzinowicz, *A History of the English Criminal Law and Its Administration from 1750*, 1 (New York: Macmillan, 1948), pp. 268–449.

3. We cannot here discuss the arguments of the "Positive School" of criminology whose leaders in the nineteenth century popularized individualization by denying individual responsibility and advocating an essentially nonpunitive reaction to crime and criminality. See George B. Volk, *Theoretical Criminology* (New York: Oxford University Press, 1958), pp. 27–40; and Cressey and Sutherland, *Criminology*, pp. 56–58, 313, 354–355, 683–684. The idea of individualization had elements of novelty in its formulation, but Cohen has pointed out that to a considerable degree "it was but a reassertion of the old idea of equity (epieikia) as the correction of the undue rigor of the law, a corrective to the injustice which results from the fact that the abstract rule cannot take into account all the specific circumstances that are relevant to the case. It assumes its simplest and oldest form in the pardoning power. . . . Some religions, indeed, make God's forgiveness His most glorious attribute." Morris R. Cohen, *Reason and Law* (Glencoe, Ill.: Free Press, 1950), p. 53.

4. See Donald R. Cressey, "Prison Organization" in *Handbook of Organizations*, James G. March, ed. (New York: Rand-McNally, 1965), pp. 1023–1070.

5. See George H. Grosser, "External Setting and Internal Relations of the Prison," in Richard A. Cloward, et al., *Theoretical Studies in Social Organization of the Prison* (New York: Social Science Resources Council, 1960), pp. 130–144.

6. Andrew Gundar Frank, "Goal Ambiguity and Conflicting Standards: An Approach to the Study of Organizations," *Human Organization* 27 (1958): 8–13.

7. See Philip Selznick, *Leadership and Administration* (Evanston, Ill.: Row Peterson, 1957); and Mayer N. Zald, "The Correctional Institution for Juvenile Offenders: An Analysis of Organizational 'Character,'" *Social Problems* 8 (1960): 57–67.

8. Theodore Caplow, *The Sociology of Work* (Minneapolis: University of Minnesota Press, 1954), p. 129.

9. See Lloyd E. Ohlin, "Conflicting Interests in Correctional Objectives," in Cloward *et al.*, *op. cit.*, pp. 111–129.

10. *Ibid.*, p. 126.

11. See Donald R. Cressey, "The Nature and Effectiveness of Correctional Techniques," *Law and Contemporary Problems* 23 (1958): 754–771.

12. Richard R. Korn and Lloyd W. McCorkle, *Criminology and Penology* (New York: Henry Holt, 1959), p. 593.

13. See Donald R. Cressey, "Limitations on Organization of Treatment in the Modern Prison," in Cloward *et al.*, *op cit.*, pp. 78–110.

14. Ernest Reimer and Martin Warren, "Special Intensive Parole Unit: Relationship between Violation Rate and Initially Small Caseload," *National Probation and Parole Association Journal* 3 (1957): 1–8.

15. See Cressey, "Prison Organization," p. 1059.

16. See Donald R. Cressey, "Professional Correctional Work and Professional Work in Correction," *National Probation and Parole Association Journal* 5 (1959): 1–15.

17. See Robert K. Merton, *Social Theory and Social Structure*, 2nd ed. (Glencoe, Ill.: Free Press, 1957, pp. 198–199.

18. David Cort, *Is There an American in the House?* (New York: Macmillan, 1960), pp. 175–176.

19. See Caplow, *Society of Work*, pp. 139–140; and Cressey, "Professional Correctional Work and Professional Work in Correction," pp. 2–3.

20. See Donald R. Cressey, "The State of Criminal Statistics," *National Probation and Parole Association Journal* 3 (1957): 230–241.

21. W. H. Kuenning, "Letter to a Penologist" in Prison Etiquette, Holley Cantine and Dachine Rainer, eds. (Bearsville, N.Y.: Retort Press, 1959), p. 132.

22. Lloyd W. McCorkle and Richard Korn, "Resocialization within Walls," *Annals of the American Academy of Political and Social Science* 293 (1954): 88–98.

23. For a summary statement regarding this experiment, see Ralph Schwitzgebel, "A New Approach to Understanding Delinquency," *Federal Probation* 24 (1960): 31–35.

24. Stanton H. Wheeler, "Role Conflicts in Correctional Communities" in *The Prison: Studies in Institutional Organization and Change,* Donald R. Cressey, ed. (New York: Holt, Rinehart and Winston, 1961), pp. 229–259.
25. See Harold H. Kelley and Edmund H. Volkhart, "The Resistance to Change of Group-Anchored Attitudes," *American Sociological Review* 27 (1952): 453–465.
26. John Irwin and Donald R. Cressey, "Thieves, Convicts and the Inmate Culture," *Social Problems* 10 (1962): 142–155.
27. Richard McCleery, "Communication Patterns as Bases of Systems of Authority and Power" in Cloward, et al., *op cit.,* pp. 49–77.
28. The classic controlled experiments include: the SIPU (Special Intensive Parole Unit) series, described in Daniel Glaser, *The Effectiveness of a Prison and Parole System,* Abridged Edition (Indianapolis: Bobbs-Merrill, 1969), pp. 310–312; the PICO (Pilot Intensive Counseling Organization) Project, reported in Stuart Adams, "The PICO Project," in Norman Johnston, Leonard Savitz and Marvin E. Wolfgang (eds.), *The Sociology of Punishment and Correction,* Second Edition (New York: John Wiley, 1970), pp. 548–61; CTP (Community Treatment Project) reported in Ted Palmer, "The Youth Authority's Community Treatment Project," *Federal Probation* (March 1974); Group Counseling in Prison, reported in Gene Kassebaum, David A. Ward and Daniel M. Wilner, *Prison Treatment and Parole Survival* (New York: John Wiley, 1971).
29. Robert Martinson, "What Works?—Questions and Answers About Prison Reform," *The Public Interest* (Spring 1974).
30. For details, see Ted Palmer, "Martinson Revisited," *Journal of Research in Crime and Delinquency,* in press 1975.
31. For example, in the PICO and CTP experiments cited above, and in Francis J. Carney, "Correctional Research and Correctional Decision-Making," *Journal of Research in Crime and Delinquency* (July 1969).
32. Travis Hirschi, *Causes of Delinquency* (Berkeley: University of California Press, 1969), chapter 7, is one of the best of many sources of data on this.
33. For a fuller analysis of typing problems and solutions, see Daniel Glaser, "The Classification of Offenses and Offenders," in Daniel Glaser, ed., *Handbook of Criminology* (Chicago: Rand McNally, 1974).
34. Ralph England, "What is Responsible for Satisfactory Probation and Post-Probation Outcome?," *Journal of Criminal Law, Criminology and Police Science* (April 1957).
35. Ted Palmer, "The Youth Authority's Community Treatment Project," *Federal Probation* (March 1974).
36. Robert G. Culbertson, "The Effect of Institutionalization on the Delinquent Inmate's Self Concept," *Journal of Criminal Law and Criminology* (March 1975).
37. Marvin E. Wolfgang, Robert M. Figlio, and Thorsten Sellin, *Delinquency in a Birth Cohort* (Chicago: University of Chicago Press, 1972), pp. 188–90; James A. Inciardi, *Careers in Crime* (Chicago: Rand McNally, 1975).
38. Ted Palmer, "The Youth Authority's Community Treatment Project," *Federal Probation* (March 1974).
39. Francis J. Carney, "Correctional Research and Correctional Decision-Making," *Journal of Research in Crime and Delinquency* (July 1969).
40. Reis H. Hall, Mildred Milazzo, and Judy Posner, *A Descriptive and Comparative Study of Recidivism in Pre-Release Guidance Center Releasees* (Washington, D.C.: U.S. Department of Justice, Bureau of Prisons, 1966); Robert Jeffrey and Stephen Woolpert, "Work Furlough as an Alternative to Incarceration: An Assessment of its Effects on Recidivism and Social Cost," *Journal of Criminal Law and Criminology* (September 1974); and Craig Reinarman and Donald Miller, *Direct Financial Assistance to Parolees: A Promising Alternative in Correctional Programming* (Sacramento: California Department of Corrections, Research Report No. 55, May 1975).
41. Brian N. Odell, "Accelerating Entry Into the Opportunity Structure: A Sociologically Based Treatment for Delinquent Youth," *Sociology and Social Research* (April 1974); H. L. Cohen and J. Filipezak, *A New Learning Environment* (San Francisco: Jossey-Bass, 1971).

42. Lloyd E. Ohlin, Robert B. Coates, and Alden D. Miller, "Radical Correctional Reform: A Case Study of the Massachusetts Youth Correctional System," *Harvard Educational Review* (February 1974); Yitzhak Bakal, ed., *Closing Correctional Institutions* (Lexington, Mass.: D. C. Heath, 1973).

43. Daniel Glaser, *The Effectiveness of a Prison and Parole System,* Abridged Edition (Indianapolis: Bobbs-Merrill, 1969), pp. 32–34, 36, 40, 41; James A Inciardi, *Careers in Crime* (Chicago: Rand McNally, 1975), pp. 73–74.

44. George D. Newton, Jr., and Franklin E. Zimring, *Firearms and Violence in American Life,* a staff report submitted to the National Commission on the Causes and Prevention of Violence (Washington, D.C.: U.S. Government Printing Office, 1969), chapter 4; Colin Loftin and Robert H. Hill, "Regional Subculture and Homicide," *American Sociological Review* (October 1974).

45. Ernst A. Wenk, James A. Robison, and Gerald W. Smith, "Can Violence Be Predicted," *Crime and Delinquency* (October 1972).

46. Morton Bard, "Family Intervention Police Teams as a Community Mental Health Resource," *Journal of Criminal Law, Criminology and Police Science* (June 1969); Hans H. Toch, *Violent Men* (Chicago: Aldine Publishing Company, 1969).

47. Gene Kassebaum, David A. Ward, and Daniel M. Wilner, *Prison Treatment and Parole Survival* (New York: John Wiley, 1971), preface and chapters 5 and 6.

48. Lloyd E. Ohlin, "Conflicting Interests in Correctional Objectives," in Richard A. Cloward, et al.: *Theoretical Studies in Social Organization of the Prison* (New York: Social Science Research Council, 1960), pamphlet 15; Lloyd E. Ohlin, "Organizational Reform in Correctional Agencies," in Daniel Glaser, ed., *Handbook of Criminology* (Chicago: Rand McNally, 1974).

49. Thomas S. Kuhn, *The Structure of Scientific Revolutions* (Chicago: University of Chicago Press, 1962).

50. John Hogarth, *Sentencing as a Human Process* (Toronto, 1971); see also reviews in *Osgood Law Journal* 10, 1 (1972): pp. 269–272.

51. C. Ray Jeffery, *Crime Prevention through Environmental Planning* (Beverley Hills, 1971).

52. Nils Christie, *Changes in Penal Values* in *Scandinavian Studies in Criminology* (Oslo, 1968), pp. 161–172; see also Leslie T. Wilkins, *Social Deviance* (London, 1964), pp. 162–166.

53. No causal relationship is, of course, presumed. However, there is some ground for postulating that penal measures suffer from devaluation. It has also been suggested that the probability of detection, rather than the penalty if found guilty, has the major preventive impact.

54. Analyses have been presented from time to time demonstrating this fact in the annual publication *Criminal Statistics of England and Wales* (London: H.M.S.O.).

55. Nils christie, *op. cit.,* in 3, p. 165.

56. Commissioners of Prisons, *Annual Reports, England and Wales* (London: H.M.S.O.).

57. By medical model is meant the analogy with clinical medicine—preventive or social medicine and epidemiological research are different models and are not discussed.

58. Leslie T. Wilkins, *Evaluation of Penal Measures* (New York, Random House, 1969), pp. 109–113.

59. Walter C. Bailey, "Correctional Treatment: An Analysis of One Hundred Correctional Outcome Studies," *Journal of Criminal Law, Criminology and Police Science* 57, 2 (1966): pp. 153–160.

60. Paul E. Meehl, *Clinical vs. Statistical Prediction* (Minneapolis: University of Minnesota Press, 1954).

61. The medical analogue breaks down in other ways too, although there are some specific cases where it might seem to apply. For a more detailed discussion of the inadequacy of the medical model, see Leslie T. Wilkins, *Evaluation of Penal Measures* (New York: Random House, 1969), pp. 18–20.

62. Jessica Mitford, *Kind and Usual Punishment* (New York: Knopf, 1973).

63. American Friends Service Committee Report, *Struggle for Justice* (New York, 1971).
64. Gene Kassebaum *et al.*, *Prison Treatment and Parole Survival* (New York: John Wiley, 1971), p. 5.
65. Personal communication: speaker may be assumed to wish to remain anonymous.
66. Leslie T. Wilkins, *Evaluation of Penal Measures* (New York, Random House, 1969), p. 125-130.
67. See fn. 59.
68. Ernst A. Wenk and Robert L. Emrich, "Assaultive Youth: An Exploratory Study of the Assaultive Experience and Assaultive Potential of California Youth Authority Wards," *Journal of Research in Crime and Delinquency* 9, 2 (1972): pp. 171-196.
69. It will be noted that the concept of a state is central to the medical model. The justification of an inference that a state exists in relation to a crime must depend upon information about factors and situations *other than* the crime itself. A question then arises as to whether the legal process is qualified to make inferences in regard to matters which are not specifically within the ambit of law, but which relate to medicine or physical conditions.
70. The dichotomy between incarceration and liberty is beginning to be eroded by new correctional procedures such as weekend incarceration and halfway houses. However, the major decision in any individual case must be whether the offender be left in liberty (or nearly so), or must be placed in captivity (or nearly so). Such decisions are not available to the parole boards, who can consider for release only after incarceration. There are also legislative constraints upon the range of decisions which both parole boards and judges can make. No research study in any way parallel to the Federal Parole Board project has been made in respect of judicial sentencing and legislative intent in fixing ranges for penalties for crimes. One fact may be inferred with some safety—legislators in fixing minimum penalties are not concerned with the medical analogue for the treatment of offenders.
71. Department of Justice, Law Enforcement Assistance Administration, Parole Decision-making Project Reports (twelve reports in series). To be published shortly.
72. The research was funded by the Department of Justice, Law Enforcement Assistance Administration, and carried out by a research team under the auspices of the National Council on Crime and Delinquency and the School of Criminal Justice, State University of New York at Albany.
73. This is, of course, the medical model.
74. The assessment of the seriousness of the offense is subjective, but is still capable of being systematized. The Board ranked offenses and established a seven-point category scale for seriousness. Studies have shown that there is a very high degree of consensus between persons of quite different social, ethnic, and economic backgrounds in regard to the assessment of the ranking for seriousness of crimes.
75. The original prediction score was derived by the use of statistical analysis of prior case material. The probability was found to be associated with facts about the commitment offense, such as whether there were co-defendants and the type (not seriousness) of crime; previous criminal career; prior treatment; employment; education. Only one item was future oriented, namely whether the parolee would reside with his wife and/or children after release. The main weight was found to be required to be placed upon the prior criminal record—this was the most predictive datum. It must be stressed that the items which were given weight in the probability assessment *were not* subjective, identified, or assessed by the research workers, but were derived from analysis of partial data.
76. Behavior in prison is not found to be related to the probability of subsequent criminal activity. Nonetheless it is regarded as reasonable to give some weight to behavior which may have been particularly bad or particularly good. The identification of any such behaviors by the interviewing officer would be a valid reason for him to argue for a departure from the time set by the guidelines.
77. Those who would take the more optimistic view of the ability of those-who-would-do-good to make others better, tend to criticize prediction tables because they do not show any significant weight to factors which relate to the time in the institutions or to different situations when the offender is released. The failure of prediction methods to show any such weights is not due to the fact that such items have been left out of the analyses: many such items are put into the equations but the methods whereby the tables are obtained (multiple

regression and/or discriminant function analysis) clearly indicate that any weighting of these factors would be inappropriate and would reduce the predictive power. This is a further proof that treatment effects cannot be recognized by analyses of past records.

78. Many books have been published on this point. Among the more recent and more powerful is that by Jessica Mitford (fn. 62 above).

79. The National Advisory Commission suggests that the annual cost of an effective criminal justice system will reach between $20 and $30 billion in 1983. Even this estimate presumes that the rate of increase in expenditure which has characterized the last few years will diminish. In fact the expenditure doubled in four years from 1968 to 1972; there certainly was not any doubling in the efficiency nor a comparable reduction in recorded crime or the fear of crime.

INDEX

OF NAMES, ORGANIZATIONS, AND PROGRAMS

INDEX

OF SUBJECTS

First offenders, 464
Food pilferage, 135–138
Forest camps, 35
Foster homes, 405–406
Functional units, concept of, 365–381
  advantages, 367–368
  disadvantages, 368–369
  evaluation, 380
  role of management, 378–379
  staff activities, 373–378
  structure, 369–373
Furlough, activities of inmates during, 426–431
  difficulties encountered, 438–439
  family response to, 431, 437–438
  inmates' reactions, 431–434
Furlough programs, 422–441. *See also* Work furlough programs
  description, 423–425
  evaluation, 434–436
  inmate selection criteria, 425–426

Gangs, 186–203
  characteristics, 189–190
  functions, 191–193
  inter-gang relations, 196–197
  prison administration and, 197–200
  prison violence and, 255–256
  socialization, 190–191
  social roles, 193–195
Gleaning, 177–180
Grievances, of inmates, 269, 357–364
  of prison personnel, 360–361
Group homes, 405–406
Group therapy, 314–316
Gunsels, definition of, 205, 216

"Hard time," 223–224
Homicide rates, 519
Homosexuality, female, 234–237
  male, 230–234
Humanitarianism, concept of, 396, 502–504
"Hustle," the, definition of, 217–219

Imprisonment. *See also* Community-based correctional services; Prison
  adaptation, *see* Adaptation
  alternatives, 54, 62–63, 405–406, 442–459
  and early Christian Church, 4–6

Imprisonment (*cont'd.*)
  criminalizing effects, 310, 397–399
  history, 16–18
Incarceration, *see* Imprisonment
Inmates. *See also* Convicts; Offenders
  classification, *see* Classification
  discipline and, 306–313, 325–326
  furlough and, 426–434, 438–439
  gangs, *see* Gangs
  grievances, 269, 357–364
  leadership, 498
  militancy in, 460
  paranoia in, 315–316
  patterns of adaptation, *see* Adaptation
  peer groups, 419–420
  pretrial detainees, 42–43, 70, 86–87
  relationship with prison personnel, 73–74, 131–135, 152–154, 157–160, 306–313
  rights of, 261–270
  role in institution, 127–128
  self-government, 320–332
    advisory councils, 326–332
    discipline and, 325–326
    history, 321–325
  separation of, 94, 158–159, 272
  social organization, 122, 135–138, 154–157, 186–188, 204–219
  treatment, *see* Rehabilitation
  unionization, *see* Unions and unionization
  violence and, *see* Violence
  visiting of, 265, 269–270
Institutions, *see* Facilities
Interest groups, 498–499, 500–502, 506–509
Isolation cells, 305

Jailing, concept of, 174–177
Jails (local), administration, 73–74
  characteristics, 68–70, 91–92
  conditions, 70–74
  definition, 91, 149
  facilities, 71–72, 92–93
  history, 67–68
  inspection of, 75–77
  personnel, 72–74, 96–99
  planning for, 77–85
  purposes, 160–164
  rehabilitation and, 99–101
  services in, 94–96
  social organization, 149–166
Juvenile delinquents, 28–29, 412–413